P9-CFO-376

Inequality and Instability

Inequality and Instability

A Study of the World Economy Just Before the Great Crisis

JAMES K. GALBRAITH

OXFORD
UNIVERSITY PRESS

Oxford University Press, Inc., publishes works that further
Oxford University's objective of excellence
in research, scholarship, and education.

Oxford New York
Auckland Cape Town Dar es Salaam Hong Kong Karachi
Kuala Lumpur Madrid Melbourne Mexico City Nairobi
New Delhi Shanghai Taipei Toronto

With offices in
Argentina Austria Brazil Chile Czech Republic France Greece
Guatemala Hungary Italy Japan Poland Portugal Singapore
South Korea Switzerland Thailand Turkey Ukraine Vietnam

Published by Oxford University Press, Inc.
198 Madison Avenue, New York, New York 10016

www.oup.com

Library of Congress Cataloging-in-Publication Data
Galbraith, James K.
Inequality and instability : a study of the world economy just before the Great Crisis / James K. Galbraith.—1st ed.
p. cm.
Includes bibliographical references.
ISBN 978-0-19-985565-0
1. Income distribution. 2. Economic policy. 3. Globalization—Social aspects. 4. Power (Social sciences)
5. Economic development—Research. 6. Global Financial Crisis, 2008–2009. I. Title.
HC79.I5.G35 2012
339.2—dc23 2011026835

1 3 5 7 9 8 6 4 2

Printed in the United States of America
on acid-free paper

for Luigi Pasinetti
inspiration and friend

Kepler undertook to draw a curve through the places of Mars, and his greatest service to science was in impressing on men's minds that this was the thing to be done if they wished to improve astronomy; that they were not to content themselves with inquiring whether one system of epicycles was better than another, but that they were to sit down to the figures and find out what the curve in truth was.

—Charles Sanders Peirce (1877)

CONTENTS

ACKNOWLEDGMENTS

This book is a collective work, to which I claim the status of author only with the forbearance and agreement of my principal collaborators: Dr. José Enrique Garcilazo, Dr. Olivier Giovannoni, Dr. Joshua Travis Hale, Dr. Sara Hsu, Dr. Hyunsub Kum, Daniel Munevar Sastre, Sergio Pinto, Dr. Deepshikha RoyChowdhury, Dr. Laura Spagnolo, and soon-to-be-Dr. Wenjie Zhang. Each of them contributed to the research underlying the work that follows, as documented by the coauthored articles cited throughout.

A special further word of thanks goes to Laura for producing a consistent and accurate list of references and to Wenjie for converting the original figures and tables into a common format suitable for publication in black and white. Without their meticulous contributions, this book would not have been finished.

Our joint work has been organized for many years under the rubric of the University of Texas Inequality Project, and much corroborating detail, including full datasets, can be found at http://utip.gov.utexas.edu. I am grateful for the efforts over many years of others in the group, not directly represented herein but frequently cited, especially Hamid Ali, Maureen Berner, Amy Calistri, Paulo Calmon, Pedro Conceição, Vidal Garza-Cantú, Junmo Kim, Ludmila Krytynskaia, Jiaqing Lu, Corwin Priest, George Purcell, and Qifei Wang. I've had encouragement over many years from the following departed friends: Peter Albin, Robert Eisner, Elspeth and Walt Rostow, and Alexey Sheviakov. Recent discussions with Jing Chen, Ping Chen, Sandy Darity, Tom Ferguson, and David Kiefer have been most helpful. All my life, Luigi Pasinetti has been a model for clarity and rigor and in recent years a steadfast friend of this research, and so I dedicate this book to him.

Work on this book first got under way during my year in 2003–04 as a Carnegie Scholar, and I am deeply grateful especially to Pat Rosenfield of the Carnegie Corporation of New York for that support. Recent backing came from the endowment of the Lloyd M. Bentsen, Jr., Chair in Government/Business Relations at the LBJ School of Public Affairs. As noted in Galbraith and Berner (2001), the early work of the Inequality Project was supported by the Ford Foundation, for which I remain indebted to Becky Lentz and to Lance Lindblom, just retired from the Cummings Foundation.

I thank the editors and publishers of these journals for permission to adapt and extract from my articles in their pages: *América Latina Hoy*; *Banca Nazionale del Lavoro Quarterly Review*; *Business and Politics*; *Cambridge Journal of Regions, Economy and Society*; *CESifo Economic Studies*; *Claves de la Economía Mundial*; *Economists' Voice*; *European Journal of Comparative Economics*; *International Review of Applied Economics*; *Journal of Current Chinese Affairs*; *Journal of Economic Inequality*; *Journal of International Politics and Society*; *Journal of Policy Modeling*; *Review of Income and Wealth*; *Social Science Quarterly*; and *WIDER Angle*. Throughout, the Levy Economics Institute of Bard College has been a faithful ally and publisher of my research.

I thank my agent, Wendy Strothman; Joe Jackson and the team at Oxford University Press; the superb copyeditor Tom Finnegan; and numerous readers and referees on the original journal articles and on this manuscript.

The support of the LBJ School, our Dean Robert Hutchings, his predecessor Jim Steinberg, Associate Dean Bob Wilson, and the hard work of my assistant Felicia Johnson are warmly acknowledged.

I thank my children, especially Eve and Emma, and even more especially my wife, Ying Tang, for putting up with everything, including Monday morning research meetings with coffee and donuts around the dining room table for years and years.

However, in the end, someone must take responsibility, including for errors, and that's me.

Austin, Texas
September 12, 2011

Inequality and Instability

CHAPTER 1

The Physics and Ethics of Inequality

In theory, theory and practice are the same. In practice, they aren't.
—Attributed to Yogi Berra

In the late 1990s, standard measures of income inequality in the United States—and especially of the income shares held by the very top echelon[1]—rose to levels not seen since 1929. It is not strange that this should give rise (and not for the first time) to the suspicion that there might be a link, under capitalism, between radical inequality and financial crisis.

The link, of course, runs through debt. For those with a little money, it is said, the spur of invidious comparison produces a want for more, and what cannot be earned must be borrowed. For those with no money to spare, made numerous by inequality and faced with exigent needs, there is also the ancient remedy of a loan. The urges and the needs, for bad and for good, are abetted by the aggressive desire of those with money to lend to those with less. They produce a pattern of consumption that for a time appears broadly egalitarian; the rich and the poor alike own televisions and drive automobiles, and until recently in America members of both groups even owned their homes. But the terms are rarely favorable; indeed, the whole profit in making loans to the needy lies in getting a return up front. There will come a day, for many of them, when the promise to pay in full cannot be kept.

The stock boom of the 1920s was marked by the advent of the small investor. Then the day came, in late October 1929, when margin calls wiped them out, precipitating a run on the banks, from which followed industrial collapse and the Great Depression. The housing boom of the 2000s was marked by a run of aggressively fraudulent lending against houses, often cash-out refinancings to the small homeowner.[2] The evil day came again in September 2008, when Fannie Mae, Freddie Mac, Lehman Brothers, and the giant insurance company AIG all failed. Over the months and years that followed, home values collapsed, wiping out the wealth and financial security of the entire American middle class, accumulated for two-thirds of a century.[3] The associated collapse of the mortgage bond and derivatives markets precipitated a worldwide flight to safety, which in Europe developed into the crisis of sovereign debt for Greece, Ireland, Portugal, and Spain.

Thus in a deep sense inequality was the heart of the financial crisis. The crisis was about the terms of credit between the wealthy and everyone else, as mediated by mortgage companies, banks, ratings agencies, investment banks, government-sponsored enterprises, and the derivatives markets. Those terms of credit were what they were, because of the intrinsic instabilities involved in lending to those who cannot pay. Like any Ponzi scheme, or any bubble, it is a matter of timing: those who are in and out early do well and those who are not nimble always go bust. As Joseph P. Kennedy said in the summer of 1929, "Only a fool holds out for the last dollar."

Yet to those economists whose voices dominated academic discourse this was an invisible fact. Their models of "representative agents" with "rational expectations" treated all economic actors as if they were actually alike; even if all incomes were not equal, the assumption that consumption preferences were independent meant that relative position played no role in the theory.[4] Further, in their notions of "general equilibrium" financial institutions such as banks made no appearance. In the classification system of the *Journal of Economic Literature* there was (and is) no category for work relating inequality to the financial system. In other words, both inequality and financial instability were largely blank spots in dominant theory; neither concept was important to mainstream economics, and the relationship between them was not even thought of.

The economists in the tradition espoused, for example, by Professor Benjamin Bernanke at Princeton were devoted to the view that—except for occasional bouts of bad policy, caused by a central bank creating either too much money or too little—the economy always tends toward stability at full employment. Following the stabilizing prescriptions of Milton Friedman, bad policy could be avoided and crises of the sort we endured in the 1930s could not recur. Wise policy, inspired by wise principle, had given us a "Great Moderation"—a new world of stable output growth, high employment, and a low-and-stable inflation rate. This would not be disturbed in any serious way by credit markets. Until just a month before the crisis broke into public consciousness in August 2007, the official prognosis of the Federal

Reserve Board—by then chaired by the same Professor Bernanke—was that all problems in the housing sector were "manageable."

This was the pure product of something economists called the quest for "logically consistent microfoundations for macroeconomics": an economics completely disengaged from the sources of financial and economic instability. Not only was there no recognition of inequality, and not only was there no study of the link of inequality to financial instability; there was practically no study of credit and therefore no study of financial instability at all. In a discipline that many might suppose would concern itself with the problems of managing an advanced financial economy, the leading line of argument was that no such problems could exist. The leading argument was, in fact, that the system would manage itself, and the effort (by government, a human and therefore flawed institution) to "intervene" was practically certain to do more harm than good. In retrospect, it all seems almost unbelievably odd.

At the same time, there was (and is) a substantial group of economists who did (and do) study the problem of economic inequality. But they do so for other reasons, and they are not closely connected to the core of mainstream economic theory. This group is concerned primarily with poverty; with wage structures; with the conditions of family life; with the effects, efficiency, and adequacy of social policies, including education, training, child care and health care, and notably in comparative context between the United States and Europe. They do often-excellent work with large datasets, though usually only in cross-section. Given the limitations of their data, they have little capacity to explore the evolution of inequality over time; indeed, the making of a reliable comparison between countries may require factoring out the influences of the "stage of the business cycle." This group thus had no interest in the issue's macroeconomic dimensions and made practically no contribution to the study of inequality and credit relations. Their study of inequality was divorced, entirely, from the study of economic dynamics, and it therefore posed no challenge to the dominant doctrines.

Yet another group of economists had spent time and effort on the links between inequality and economic development in the wider world, in a way that might potentially have brought them into dialogue with the dominant theory. These economists were pursuing the lead provided back in 1955 by Simon Kuznets, whose work tied inequality to the level of income and stage of development, and they used the facilities of the World Bank and later of the United Nations to obtain greatly expanded data on inequality in countries around the world during the intervening decades. In recent years, this work concentrated on an attempt to discern how inequality influences the prospects for economic growth, so it did have a dynamic aspect. But the dynamics were, at best, primitive: the question under investigation was generally whether an equal or an unequal society would do a more efficient job of savings, capital investment, and expansion of productive capacity over time. No analysis of finance, credit relationships, or the instability of the growth process entered into this work, and it does not appear that those involved ever seriously considered raising the point. So the dialogue with mainstream theories of growth and equilibrium, which might have happened, never did.

Further, analyses in this vein of development economics were hampered by the poor quality of the underlying measures, an artifact of the sparse and often-primitive surveys used to gather the underlying information on economic inequality over half a century or longer. Faced with noisy data and many missing observations, researchers were obliged to rely heavily on a compensating sophistication of technique, and the studies were often a triumph of complex econometrics over clear information. Perhaps not surprisingly, as well, consistent findings stubbornly refused to appear. Whatever the merits of each individual research project, the results often contradicted one another: some studies concluded that greater equality fosters growth, while others came to the opposite view. Thus a (modestly liberal) vision stressing the importance of broad-based development (and education, especially) contested with a neo-Victorian vision stressing the importance of enhanced savings, even if it should require highly concentrated wealth. No general consensus emerged, beyond agreement that Kuznets's simple insights would no longer suffice. As we shall see later, even this verdict was highly premature.

Thus although there was interest in inequality among economists—and there has been all along—neither major group of active empirical inequality researchers made a link between the micro- or developmental issues that they were pursuing and macroeconomic conditions. And so, like the macroeconomists, they too were unprepared to examine the relationship between economic inequality and the global financial crisis.

Apart from data quality, the study of economic inequality has faced another substantial limitation, not often remarked on because we tend to take it for granted. It concerns the frame of reference from which the available data are drawn. In most cases, this is the nation-state. We almost always measure and record inequality by country. We do this because (for the most part) only countries engage in the practice of sampling the income of their citizens. Thus only countries compile the datasets required for the calculation of inequality measures. Studies of inequality by smaller geographic units, such as American states or Chinese provinces or European regions, are rare. Studies of inequality across multinational continental economies, such as Europe, are practically nonexistent, not for lack of interest but for apparent lack of information. This would not be a problem if all economies followed national lines, but they do not. In some cases (increasingly rare these days), a smaller unit is appropriate. In many more, economies now function smoothly across national lines, and the people in neighboring lands inhabit the same economic space. Thus as the economically relevant regions change—with the integration of Europe and North America or the breakup of the Soviet Union, for example—inequality studies tend to suffer an increasing mismatch between the questions one would like to answer and the information available to answer them with.

At the same time, a few researchers have taken on what is in some ways the biggest inequality data challenge, which is to measure economic inequality across the entire world. "Imagine there's no country" is the way one of these pioneers put it (Bhalla, 2002); let's try to determine just how unequal all the people of the world are when seen as a single group. The most distinguished efforts here belong to Branko Milanovic, who has carefully assembled the best information from a wide range of sources at the country level. But the limitation of this work lies in the fact that only a few years of comparable data are supported by the mass of underlying information. Most other studies purporting to assess inequality at the global level are actually based on a comparison of average income levels across countries (adjusted for purchasing power parity, PPP). This is useful work for some purposes, but it suffers from uncertainties associated with the comparative measurement of total income, and especially with PPP adjustments.[5] No one would take it as a substitute for the analysis of changing distributions within countries.

This book originated in dissatisfaction with an economics of inequality pushed to the backstage of comparative welfare analysis and development studies, and especially with the limitations of the evidence underlying these various lines of research. Without disparaging any of them—or even wishing to contradict their findings in most respects—it seemed to us more was required. And there was of course a greater dissatisfaction with the larger economics—with an economics that denied the possibility of financial instability, was unprepared for the Great Crisis, and takes no account of inequality at all.

Our premise has been that a new look at these topics requires new sources of evidence. One can talk about inequality as a moral or social or political problem, and one can philosophize about it, as many do, in the abstract. And there are inequalities affecting people by gender, race, and national origin that can be identified in purely qualitative terms. But you can't actually study economic inequality without measuring it.

For reasons explained in detail later, other researchers had already pushed the available data to the limits of their information content—indeed beyond those limits in many cases. Further progress, new insights, and the resolution of controversies would require broader, more consistent, and more reliable numbers. It would take, we thought, a considerable expansion of the measures of inequality by country and by year—or even by month—and also the capacity to calculate measures of inequality both at lower (provincial) and higher (international, continental, and global) levels of aggregation. This could not be done by conventional methods, which could not, by their nature, change the boundaries of their coverage or the inconsistencies of their method, nor escape the historical limitations on the times and places where surveys were actually conducted.

How, then, could we escape those limitations? New numbers were needed. Where might they be found? The answer rested on a simple insight: the major contours of inequality between people could be captured, substantially, by measures of inequality between *groups* to which those persons belong. Grouping is a very general idea. Individuals invariably belong to groups; they live in particular places, work in particular sectors or industries and can be classed by gender, race, age, education, and other personal attributes. And even though there is not much one can do to rectify a dearth of information about individuals, the archives are full of information about groups—publicly available and free for the taking.

Thus, for example, in China it is well known that a fair fraction of the economic inequality in that vast country reflects the difference in average income levels between city and countryside, and between the coastal regions and the interior. A simple ratio of the average incomes in the city to the countryside (say) would be an indicator—however crude—of the trends in inequality over the country as a whole. If this were all you had, it would still be better than nothing.[6] And one might be able to get a crude measure of this kind regularly—perhaps every year—permitting one to develop a portrait of movement over time. Therefore—so we thought—it would be much better to have ongoing (even if crude) measures of this kind than to insist on excellent measures that might be available for only a few years, if at all.

So much is true, but in fact we can do better than just taking crude ratios. To take China as an example: the country is divided into thirty-five provinces,[7] and the government routinely collects data on sixteen major economic sectors in each province, for a total of 560 distinct province/sector categories. Thus it is possible to know the average income and population size, every year, of all of these 560 categories. From this, it is easy to compute the dispersion of income between these groups, each weighted by the importance of the group. The movement of inequality across these categories will capture practically all of the major forces of change sweeping through China: interregional forces such as the rise of wealthy Guangdong, Shanghai, and Beijing, and intersectoral forces such as the rise of banking and transport and the relative decline of farming and (retail) trade.[8] It stands to reason these great forces, playing out across the Chinese landscape and among the great spheres of activity making up the Chinese economy, are the dominant sources of changing inequality in Chinese incomes.

That's the idea—but are measures of this kind any good? Since China also has some good income surveys, we can test this question directly. It turns out inequality measures computed from this grouped information are quite close substitutes for inequality measures of the ordinary kind. They show the same general trends over long periods of time. Yet the grouped measures are much easier to calculate, and they rely on information that is freely available from official sources, making the measurement of inequality a suitable pastime for graduate students. A further advantage is much greater specific detail—as to who was gaining and who losing and by how much, and exactly when. Thus the consequences of policies and external events come clearly into view.

These and similar sources of data are practically ubiquitous—anyway, they are very common—in economic statistics worldwide. They could therefore provide the foundation for a new generation of inequality studies, with a degree of detail, consistency, coverage, and also reliability not available to those using traditional methods. This is the work I present in the pages that follow.

The Simple Physics of Inequality Measurement

There is no computational secret. Our method was lifted straight from the work of a University of Chicago econometrician, Henri Theil, who published originally in 1972. Theil in turn developed his ideas on the measurement of inequality from the work in information theory of the pioneer computer scientist Claude Shannon of MIT. Shannon measured the information content of an event as a decreasing function of the probability that it would occur: the less likely an event, the more information it provides, if in fact it happens. (There is no information—no surprise—in the occurrence of an event foreseen with certainty.) Theil converted Shannon's formula into a measure of inequality, with value zero when all parties have the average income (and thus, given the value of one income, we know with certainty all the others). The formula is simple, and closely related to the measure of entropy in thermodynamics; given any dataset meeting minimal requirements, it can be implemented on a spreadsheet within a few minutes.[9]

This last observation is critical for economic analysis, because the historical records are full of tables detailing the total income (or payroll) of some category or other, together with the population (or total employment) in that category. This is all the information required to compute the between-groups component of a Theil statistic. Thus readily available archives available from practically any country and many multinational agencies can be mined to generate a large archive of inequality measures, each of which could be cross-checked against the others. In many cases, the measures could also be combined and aggregated so as to achieve measures of inequality *across* populations that had never been measured directly as a unit—such as the continent of Europe or the entire population of the globe.

Theil showed his measure is additive. That is, given the measured inequality *within* a set of groups (provinces, sectors, industries, occupations), and a measure of the inequality *between* those groups, the total inequality of the population is a weighted sum of the inequality between groups and the inequality within them. This is a valuable feature for many purposes, especially because it permits subsets and supersets of groups to be formed—depending on the research question. Instead of tailoring research questions to the available data (surveys can be almost obsessively interested in personal traits such as age, education, race, and gender), it becomes possible to pick and choose among (often) copious sources of data for the inequality measure best suited to the research question.

Further, many datasets are hierarchical; they provide information on the same population at higher grouping levels (such as the American states) as well as lower ones (such as counties, or precincts, or households, or industrial sectors, or even individuals) nested within those higher levels. Given a hierarchical dataset, the more refined the division of the population into groups, the more groups one will have, and the closer the measure of inequality between groups will approximate the measure of inequality across the full population. At the final and lowest level of disaggregation, of course, the "between-groups" and "full-population" measures converge to the same value, since every individual at this level is also a group. But the interesting question is, How far down the ladder is it really necessary to go in order to develop an accurate and adequate idea of what the data show?

As the work proceeded, we realized that quite crude levels of disaggregation, such as the division of countries into states or provinces and the division of the economy into major sectors, are usually sufficient to capture the major movements of inequality over time. Higher levels of disaggregation often add little to the picture one obtains from a distance. A good analogy is to a digital photograph, where even a grainy resolution captures the major features of the terrain. More detail is usually better, of course, but it comes with a cost, just as a finer photograph takes up more storage space on a digital drive.

Further, with the coarse-grained spatial information sets commonly available—say, at the country level—it is sometimes possible to develop information on a fine timescale—say, by month rather than by year. This is especially useful for extending the study of inequality into the sphere of macroeconomics and finance, since those subjects rely on repeated sampling of economic information over time. In digital photography, if you set a low resolution you can photograph faster and save the pictures more quickly.

Another fun fact we discovered by accident, fairly early in the research. In most country datasets, the category structures (particularly if they are geographic and political, such as states, provinces, counties, and so forth) are unique to that country. It is thus impossible to make a meaningful comparison between a Theil statistic measured across provinces (say) for one country and a Theil statistic measured across provinces for another. But if the category structures applied to *different* countries or regions are *the same*, then comparison becomes possible. Indeed, the measures of inequality for different countries computed from standardized international datasets are roughly proportional to the best comparative measures available from survey data. This means industrial datasets, which use the same classifications for different countries, have a terrific advantage: they can be used to measure the comparative level of inequality across countries. This technique permits very cheap replication and extension of comparative inequality measurement, which, when undertaken by conventional methods is slow, costly, and limited by the quality of the survey data.

The measures remain generally (though not always) valid even where the coverage of the categorical data is quite limited, as for instance when one has comparative data only on pay within manufacturing sectors and not for services, finance, or the gray economy. This may seem counterintuitive, and it doesn't always hold true—but in a fairly large share of cases, it does. The reason is that the inner workings of an economy are highly interdependent, and the various parts usually (though not always) bear a consistent relationship to one another. For example, manufacturing of all types is almost always better paid than farm labor, so an increase in inequality within manufacturing usually also means an increase in the differential between low-wage manufacturing and pay on the farm. Even though the datasets we have available are necessarily restricted in scope to those parts of the economy where income is most easily measured, the part of the economy one observes is (usually, though not always) a window from which the view gives a fair idea of the part one does not see directly.

Thus, we discovered something quite rare in economic analysis: an unplowed field, full of fresh information covering the economy practically of the entire world, which could be brought to bear on a controversial topic in new and original ways. And at very low cost—something quite important to a research effort conducted on a shoestring.

A research program as ambitious as this one demands a large dose of humility and caution; there are things that can go wrong, and some of them surely will. Here are a few of the major qualifications.

First, our data—especially those used for international comparison—almost invariably offer only partial coverage of the population and therefore only indirect evidence on the parts not observed. There is a bias toward the formal sector and toward larger enterprises; there are reasons some things are measured routinely and others are not. Often, the inequalities between groups that we measure are more volatile than inequalities that others find in the larger society beyond the scope of our measures; this is because change in manufacturing is more rapid than in other sectors. In some situations—and we find this especially true for complex (and financialized) economies like the United States and the United Kingdom—the evidence from structures of wages and pay runs counter to the larger picture we obtain when capital incomes are included in the observational frame. It is still true that the measures are generally reliable as indicators and generally comparable across countries; it's just that this is not always so. One must therefore be careful, and warnings will be repeated as specific measures are introduced in the pages ahead.

Nevertheless, over much of the world and most of the period under observation, the partial and indirect measures we have assembled are fairly reliable indicators of larger developments, and our crude measures correspond reasonably well to the more carefully developed but much sparser and more expensive measures that populate other studies. Especially because we are mainly concerned with statistics, in our judgment the gain obtained through assembling a more complete historical record far outweighs the risk associated with error in any particular data point.

The Ethical Implications of Inequality Measures

Most of those attracted to the study of inequality are motivated, at least in part, by concern that inequality is excessive. I share this perspective, and in my view the data bear it out: in most of the world, and in the world as a whole, inequality is too high. Human happiness and social progress would be served by bringing it down. Further, in much of the world we found that our measures of inequality were sensitive indicators of political events: rising after coups d'état and financial crises, occasionally falling in wars and revolutions, and otherwise behaving well in good times and poorly when times are bad. In general, increasing inequality is a warning sign that something is going wrong—and a pretty good indicator throughout history that untoward developments may be on the horizon.

But as our work progressed, it became increasingly detached from the common politics of the inequality debates. For the United States, for example, we do not find an inexorable rise in inequality suffusing the entire society. On the contrary, after the upheavals of the early 1980s pay *structures* remained largely stable, and inequalities of *pay*—that is, what working people earned for work—actually declined in the 1990s (as I had already documented in my 1998 book, *Created Unequal*). What drove rising inequalities of *incomes* in the United States in this period and through the 2000s was largely the behavior of the capital markets, and the incomes of people most closely associated with them. In other words, inequality went up mainly because of rising stock prices, asset valuations and the incomes drawn from stock option realizations and capital gains, as well as wages and salaries paid in sectors that were financed by new equity.

These incomes, at the very top, were highly concentrated in a tiny fraction of the United States. Basically, fifteen counties contributed all of the rise in inequality measured between counties from 1994 to 2000, meaning that if they had been removed from the dataset the rise in overall inequality would not have occurred. Of these, just five (New York; three counties in Northern California associated with Silicon Valley; and King County, Washington) contributed about half of the rise in total inequality, again measured between counties, in the late 1990s. An American resident in Ohio or Georgia saw very little of this directly.[10] For this reason I do not believe that rising inequality, in those prosperous years, could ever have been turned to the electoral advantage of an egalitarian Left. The problem was not that rising economic inequality was unpleasant; on the contrary, it led to better economic outcomes for most workers. The problem was that the mechanism could never be sustained. And you don't observe how things end, until they do.

In these and other ways, we learned to be cautious about imposing political interpretations on measures of inequality. Inequality is an unavoidable feature of economic life. The question of how much is too much is worth exploring—and so is the question of how little is too little. Most of all, what is interesting are the questions of cause and effect. What are we seeing? Why are we seeing it? What do the measures tell us about the uses of power in the world?

In short, we do not study inequality because it is shocking. We study inequality mainly because it is informative. We study it because it enables us to understand the economic world in which we live, in ways that were not accessible to us before. One of the most important of those ways is precisely the neglected linkage between inequality and instability, between finance and society, and between economic and social differences and the risks of financial crisis.

Plan of the Book

This book begins, in chapter 2, with a look at the datasets that have formed the foundation of work on inequality in the world economy since the mid-1990s. Though the inspection is necessarily critical, the limitations and defects of that information set are not those of the researchers who compiled it. Instead they reflect the inconsistent, sporadic, and intermittent character of the underlying surveys, as conducted around the world over the years by disparate official and nongovernmental organizations. Everyone who has worked with this data knows this to be true, but many who have only read the statistical summaries and research results do not.

Chapter 2 then goes on to explain how in principle an approach based on grouped data can be used as an alternative to the survey record. The approach has the immediate advantage of providing a relatively complete historical record. And it has the additional property that group structures can be exploited to give measures at different levels of geographic aggregation, including both subnational (provinces) and supernational (continental regions), for which separated surveys were never undertaken. In the limit, large bodies of grouped data can be mined to show the presence of common patterns in the world economy.

Chapters 3 through 5 take a global view, using the raw material of a common body of industrial statistics, compiled by the United Nations over the period from 1963 into the early 2000s. Direct measures of inequality in manufacturing pay, presented in chapter 3, offer the clearest test in modern data of Kuznets's original hypothesis in its essential form. This held that the fundamental forces behind changing inequality were, first, the changing structure of an economy in the course of development, and second, changes in the relative pay rates in the major sectors. Industrial data amount to an incomplete test of this idea, but they do establish that Kuznets was, and remains, broadly correct. The failure to find supportive evidence in survey data is therefore due to the incomplete and noisy character of those data, complicated by the fact that household income inequality, which most surveys attempt to measure, is an imperfect reflection of the pay rates with which Kuznets was principally concerned.

Our principal addition to Kuznets's insight lies in the discovery of a common global pattern to the movement of inequality—a pattern showing the existence, and power, of worldwide macroeconomic forces affecting the distribution of earnings within countries. This finding is subversive of work assuming that nation-states have a large degree of leeway in policy decisions affecting inequality. It turns out they don't; the large forces affecting inequality inside most countries, worldwide, originate outside national frontiers, and the evidence shows pretty strongly that most countries, especially smaller ones, lack the will and the wherewithal to resist.

In chapter 4, we further explore the relationship between measures of inequality based on industrial pay and those based on surveys of income or expenditure. The central theme is not how different these measures are, but how similar in critical respects. It turns out that our measure of disparity of pay across industrial sectors is a very good instrument for, or approximation of, survey-based measures of income or expenditure inequality. So it is possible to construct a simple statistical model with a formula for translating one set of measures into the other. In this way, we present a consistent global dataset of estimated measures of income inequality for households, calibrated to the standard and familiar format of the Gini coefficient. This body of work permits a further assessment of the existing body of global inequality measures, their dispersion across countries, and their movement through time.

Chapter 5 makes a first application of the global dataset to a current problem: the relationship between type of government and economic outcomes. Do certain regime types systematically generate more or less inequality than others? In particular, there is a body of literature in political science arguing that democracies tend to be egalitarian, as compared to authoritarian or dictatorial regimes. This argument is easily testable in our framework, and we find the result holds only for a subclass of democracy, namely social democracies that have been in stable existence for a long period of time. And it turns out, perhaps not surprisingly, that social democracy is not the only regime type to show a systematic relationship with lower inequality: the same was true for communist regimes in their heyday, and it is true for Islamic republics. Dictatorships of other ideological types—again not surprisingly—show higher levels of inequality than other regime types.

Chapters 6 and 7 turn attention to the United States. Chapter 6 surveys the incredibly rich data environment that is contemporary America. It's an applied economist's delight, permitting the calculation of inequality by almost any geographical or sectoral unit. We show in particular that the rise in inequality in the contemporary United States, to a peak that was reached in 2000, was very closely associated with the information-technology boom and the rise in stock market valuations for the technology sector. This is a story that I first developed in *Created Unequal*, a book that appeared two years before the top of the technology bubble. The full run of data through the bubble and bust bears it out: inequality measured across counties in the United States corresponds very closely to the proportional movement of the (technology-heavy) NASDAQ stock index. And it is also the case that a very large share of the rise in the topmost incomes, as reported in tax data, was concentrated in just a handful of counties closely associated with the technology boom, above all for workers in Silicon Valley and Seattle, and their bankers in Manhattan. After the boom crested in 2000, we show, the pattern changed; in the expansion of the Bush era the geographic gains were most noticeable in the counties surrounding Washington, D.C., and the main sectoral gainers were associated with the growth of government and of the national security sectors in those years.

American states are political units, and they have a special importance in the outcome of presidential elections in the United States, which are decided on a winner-take-all basis by state through the Electoral College. Chapter 7 applies inequality measurements calculated at the level of American states to two questions: the effect of inequality on voter turnout, and the relationship between economic inequality and election outcomes. There are two substantial findings. First, we report that states with higher inequality tend to have lower turnout of potentially eligible voters in presidential elections—a result consistent with the idea that in high-inequality states wealthier voters have a strong interest in restricting access to the ballot among the poor. The second finding is that even though the overall level of inequality is not associated with party choice, a measure of inequality that captures the geographic dispersion of rich and poor within a state is strongly associated with election outcomes. In particular, geographically stratified states tend to vote Democratic, while geographically homogeneous states, however equal or unequal, tend to vote

Republican. We offer the hypothesis of geographic stratification as a potential resolution of the paradox proposed by Andrew Gelman on the relationship between income level and voting in American politics, which holds that richer individuals vote Republican while richer states tend Democratic.

Chapters 8 and 9 turn attention to Europe, which has been in recent decades the scene of the world's greatest experiment in economic integration: the creation of the European economic union and the eurozone. Europe has also been plagued with chronic high unemployment, which has been attributed in the prevailing literature to the "rigidity" of the European labor markets. The work in these two chapters challenges this view by asking (and answering) two questions. First, is it true that "rigid" labor markets within Europe were associated with comparatively high unemployment—especially when one defines *rigidity* as being characterized by a relatively egalitarian distribution of wages? We show that in fact the opposite is the case: European countries with strongly compressed wage distributions actually enjoyed significantly lower unemployment rates, and they continue to do so. Second, is it true that European wage structures are "rigid" in the sense of showing little tendency to fluctuate over time? We show it is a mistake to carry out an analysis of this question at the level of the individual European nation-state, since the largest flux in relative wages within Europe lies in the movement of wages of some states against others, mainly due to exchange-rate changes in the pre-euro era and between euro and non-euro countries inside Europe. From the standpoint of a multinational investor, these fluctuations are just as important as "flexibility" inside countries—and if they are taken into account, the notion of Europe as a region of rigid wage structures simply dissolves. The only reasonable conclusion is that the "labor market rigidity" explanation of chronic European high unemployment is just wrong, in every imaginable way.

Chapters 10 through 12 afford a glimpse into the role an analysis of inequality can play in assessing contemporary developments in a wide range of countries around the world. For the purpose of these illustrations, we chose from among many national and regional studies that have been published on Russia, India, Mexico, Colombia, Turkey, and North Africa in addition to those presented here. We devote a chapter to China, the world's largest and fastest-growing country, a chapter showing in detail and graphically how incomes within China gravitated toward the large urban centers and toward sectors with economic power during the reform era. The next chapter is devoted to Brazil and Argentina, two countries that came to repudiate the Washington-consensus model of economic development and fashioned instead a model of evolution toward social democracy and a functioning welfare state, with a concomitant reduction of inequality after profound economic crises discredited the neoliberal model. The final chapter of the three takes up the case of Cuba, the one socialist country that managed to weather the collapse of Soviet communism without, so far, fundamentally transforming its economic system. Using data from Cuban government sources, we illustrate the very large and traumatic adjustments that Cuba nevertheless underwent in the changed circumstances of the post-Soviet era, adjustments without which it is unlikely the Cuban model would have survived at all.

The work in this book is unified by two things. The first is a common method, involving the calculation of fresh measures of economic inequality from disparate but structurally similar datasets, and so expanding the universe of empirical information on which analyses of economic inequality can be based. The second is a common set of observations, relating to the critical role played by the financial sector, and the international financial regime, in bringing on a vast increase in global inequality from 1980 to 2000. With the rare exception of Cuba—a country almost uniquely isolated from Western finance—it is clear that the story of inequality is a story of forces that buffet the economy of the entire world, and have their origin in the global markets for money and credit as well as in the terms on which global lending and borrowing has been conducted. Credit relationships, in other words, are the stuff of global politics and global economics—as they are of global financial crisis. The economics of inequality is, in large measure, an economics of instability; inequality is the barometer, in many ways, of the instabilities that global credit relationships create. The final chapter takes up the question of lessons, from this research, for global economic and financial governance.

Notes

1. As reported by Thomas Piketty and Emmanuel Saez (2003).
2. About 82 percent of mortgage originations in the boom were refinancings, and about 60 percent of those had a cash-out feature. See Bethany McLean and Joseph Nocera (2010).
3. To be underwater on one's mortgage is, in effect, to be insolvent, and in 2010 about a quarter of American mortgage holders were in this position.
4. James Duesenberry's relative income hypothesis (1949) was a significant exception in the theoretical and textbook literature of the 1950s and 1960s, but it was substantially forgotten by the 1980s.
5. Notably, PPP measurements for China are highly problematic. And since China is about a quarter of the world's population, mismeasurement of average income in China can have a significant effect on the measure of global inequality across persons.
6. The many researchers who rely on 90–10 or 90–50 quantile ratios from sample surveys in the United States realize the same thing: a crude indicator is usually good enough for many purposes in this line of work.

7. The number was increased from thirty-three by administrative reorganization in 1997.
8. It will in fact capture each of the intersectoral forces within each of the provinces—so that if you want to find out (for instance) the changing contribution of pay in the education sector in Beijing to overall inequality in China, you can do so.
9. The resulting measures are also consistent with the findings of the important subfield known as "econophysics," but this relationship will not be developed here.
10. This fact raised questions about sweeping claims made for the effects of technological change and of trade on inequality, work that dominated the discussions while never rising to a persuasive standard of evidence. In 1998, in *Created Unequal*, I offered one of the first critiques of the notion that inequality in the United States could be explained by "skill-biased technological change." Since then, many others reached the same conclusion, and the "skill-bias" hypothesis has largely faded from view, though it lingers (as bad ideas in economics often do) in textbooks and journalistic discussion. Coming to stronger and better-founded conclusions on these issues was a major motivation for this research.

CHAPTER 2

The Need for New Inequality Measures

If science consists in a search for patterns in data—and just as much, if it consists in applying formulae to facts—then the study of economic inequality suffers from an original sin. From the beginning, the job of measurement was badly done. In most countries, measures of economic inequality never became part of the official statistical routine, in the national income accounts or labor statistics. Among governments, the United States is one of just a handful that release an annual measure of income inequality based on a substantial household survey. Observations and measurements of inequality across countries and through time have for the most part relied on occasional and in many cases unofficial surveys, with results that are sparse, often conceptually inconsistent, affected by differences in top-coding practice and subject to the hazards of sampling.

The historical record of these efforts, once undertaken, is what it is. One cannot take a retrospective survey; there is no way to go back to a household and ask what its income was five, ten, or twenty years in the past. Thus the gaps can't be filled; the methods with which the original data were created cannot be used to repair the archives. And yet interest in inequality persists, the need for information persists, so economists and applied statisticians make do with the data at hand. For much of the postwar period, data were sparse, so the few researchers who worked in the area concentrated on developments within single countries, such as the United States, the United Kingdom, or India, extrapolating common patterns of economic development from a small number of historical cases. Everyone knew this was not a very satisfactory way to proceed.

The Data Problem in Inequality Studies

In 1996, Klaus Deininger and Lyn Squire of the World Bank (hereafter DS) published a collection of many disparate surveys of income and expenditure inequality and compiled those meeting certain criteria[1] into a single "high-quality" panel. In an early (and widely used) version, they were able to locate 693 country-year observations since 1947 that met their desired standards of quality. In a field parched for data, this work was a breakthrough. DS transformed comparative research on inequality, especially outside the narrow sphere of the developed world. Dozens of papers have since used the DS compilation or its close successors, of which the most notable is a large compilation by the World Institute for Development Economics Research (WIDER) of the United Nations University at Helsinki.

The WIDER dataset has more observations than DS, but otherwise it retains many of the same general characteristics. Like DS, it is a collection of historical surveys mainly from the published record, with the virtues, defects, and inconsistencies of that record. And although efforts to expand and improve the measures continue, mainly by identifying past studies that were originally overlooked, the numbers are destined to remain problematic in many ways. Despite the growing number of observations, the coverage remains sparse and unbalanced, with very few high-quality observations for many countries in the developing world. More particularly, the DS (and related) inequality data are based on various income definitions and reference units that measure different things and cannot easily be reconciled to each other. We shall return to this point below, but first we should look at what some of the numbers appear to say about cases and countries with which, in many instances, readers are directly familiar.

Within the OECD—the club of rich countries for which economic information ought in principle to be reliable—the original DS data provide comparative measures that often lack credibility on their face. For example, the Scandinavian countries appear to be in the middle range of OECD inequality, despite their small size, homogeneous populations, high union coverage, unified wage bargaining practices, and long traditions of egalitarian social democracy. Meanwhile Spain appears as a *low-inequality* country despite its relatively late emergence from fascism and relatively impoverished backcountry, while France appears at the very top of the OECD inequality tables. Of course, the data could be correct, and Spain might be more egalitarian than Sweden. But it would be hard to find a Spaniard or a Swede who thinks so, or a Frenchman who believes that average inequality in his country has historically been more than in the United States. Findings of this type appear to defy common sense, something that should at the least provoke some cautious checking of the numbers.

There is another, slightly subtler, problem with the DS inequality measures for the OECD. The trend of inequality over time differs between countries, going up in some cases and down in others. This would suggest an "each unto

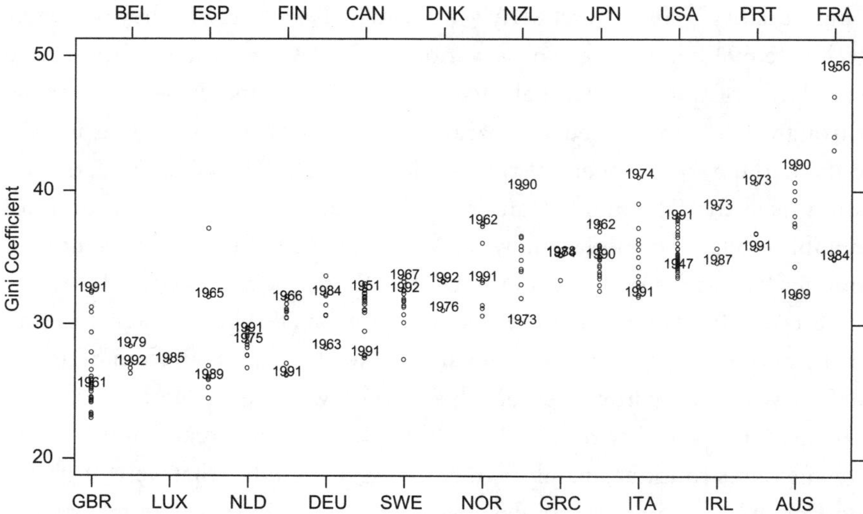

Figure 2.1. Measures of inequality in the OECD from Deininger and Squire.

itself" pattern of change, depending perhaps on the economic circumstances and policies of differing governments, so that some countries chose policies that reduced inequality while other chose policies that increased it. In a world of economic integration, common shocks, and policies that are increasingly shared, especially in Europe, this is improbable. As a matter of intuition if nothing more, like causes and integrated institutions should produce similar patterns of change in neighboring countries. This is contrary to what the DS data appear to show. Figure 2.1, which ranks the OECD countries from left to right by their average DS score and shows the first and last year of data for each country, illustrates both of these types of anomaly.

Moving outside the OECD, one enters the great world of the developing countries, in which many inequality researchers take a keen interest. But here we encounter another problem. DS and its successors offer only infrequent measures of inequality for much of Africa, Latin America, and Asia—in many cases fewer than five annual observations over fifty or more years.[2] The United States, Great Britain, Bulgaria, India, and Taiwan are among the few countries for which DS provide annual or nearly annual observations over long periods of time. Studies attempting to assess the time trend of inequality worldwide must worry about the bias that may be associated with a history of irregular surveys, especially since surveys are more likely to be taken in quiet times than in turbulent ones. To deal with this, researchers may either restrict their attention to a subset of the data in order to achieve a better semblance of balance, or else attempt to fill in the gaps by extrapolation. The first approach is taken by Forbes

(2000), who uses five-year intervals, and by Alderson and Nielsen (2002), who deal with only sixteen OECD countries. Sala-i-Martin (2002a, 2002b, 2006) takes the second approach, in some instances taking it to extremes, in order to generate a worldwide dataset. But this involves heroic guesswork. Among other things, where only a single observation is available Sala-i-Martin assumes that no change occurred over the whole period under study.[3]

The reservations expressed here are not new. Atkinson and Brandolini (2001) present a critique of DS (and related datasets) that focuses, in part, on the many different types of data that are mixed up in the dataset. These include measures of expenditure inequality and of income inequality, measures of inequality of gross and of net income, and measures of inequality of both personal and household income.[4] The comparability of these various measures is questionable, but what can one do? Expenditure surveys are prevalent in some parts of the world, and income surveys in others; there is no way to go back to the source interviews and convert one into the other. DS (1996) and (1998) suggest adding 6.6 Gini points to measures of inequality in expenditure data, in order to make the figures comparable to measures of income inequality. But Atkinson and Brandolini (2001, p. 790) are skeptical: "We doubt whether a simple additional or multiplicative adjustment is a satisfactory solution to the heterogeneity of the available statistics. Our preference is for the alternative approach of using a data-set where the observations are as fully consistent as possible."

All in all, Atkinson and Brandolini urge reliance only on studies from which the underlying micro information can be recovered. This is the approach taken by Milanovic (2002b, 2007) in his efforts to measure the "true" dimension of household income inequality at the level of the entire planet. Milanovic's work, so far as it goes, is highly persuasive. However, this approach is limited by its own cost and complexity and the limited availability of surveys. Milanovic has been at this for many years, and despite heroic efforts the time dimension remains substantially inaccessible to his method.

There are yet other problems. Within individual countries, the range of fluctuation in the DS data is occasionally far too wide to be plausible. For instance, the measure of inequality in Sri Lanka plummets by 16 Gini points during the three years from 1987 to 1990. There is an increase of almost 10 Gini points in Venezuela in just one year, 1989–90, and there are nine cases where changes of more than 5 Gini points happened over a single year. That would be a massive redistribution, in one direction or the other—if in fact it occurred. Changes of such speed and magnitude are unlikely, except when they coincide with moments of major social upheaval—and at such moments household income surveys are rarely undertaken.

It's helpful to take a closer look at the comparability issues. Here a principal concern is the different types of source data. The "high-quality" DS data includes inequality measures of three distinguishable types. Some are expenditure-based and some are income-based. Some are per capita and some relate to households. Among the income measures, some are gross and others are net of tax. Bias from different data types may well be systematic, not random, since certain countries tend to conduct one type of survey and not the other. In general, Latin America and the OECD have favored income surveys, but expenditure surveys predominate in Asia. Expenditure surveys tend to give more egalitarian results, but by how much? Without overlapping observations, it is difficult to tell, and the appropriate adjustment may vary from one country to the next. For a closer examination of this point, see the source characteristics of the DS data in table 2.1.

If household gross income (HGI) is assumed to be the preferred reference category, only 39 percent of DS observations worldwide fit precisely into this category. If household net income (HNI) is added, the combined share increases to 52 percent.[5] In other words, at least 48 percent of the DS data cannot be classified as measures of household income. They are instead measures of expenditure, which excludes saving, or of personal income, which would have to be aggregated into households to achieve comparability with the household measures.

Table 2.2 shows that the simple mean differences between expenditure-based and income-based inequality, and between household and per capita inequality, are significant and substantial. The distribution of sources across regions is also notably unbalanced. Most South Asian, African, and Middle Eastern countries use expenditure surveys, most Eastern European countries use per capita income, and only half of inequality measures from Latin American countries are household income. Even among OECD members, only half (52 percent) of observations are based on household gross income.

Table 2.1. **Reference Units and Data Types in the Deininger-Squire Dataset**

	Reference Unit								*Total*	
	Household		*Household Equivalent*		*Person*		*Person Equivalent*			
Source	Gross*	Net	Gross	Net	Gross	Net	Gross	Net	Gross	Net
Expenditure**		23				104		1		128
Income	254	72		12	108	46		34	362	164

Notes: * Indicates whether the measure of income is gross or net of taxes. ** Indicates whether the survey measure is of expenditure or income.

Table 2.2. **Data Types by Region in the Deininger-Squire Dataset**

		Non-OECD Countries						*OECD Countries*					
Region		HGI	HNI	HNE	PGI	PNI	PNE	HGI	HNI	HNE	PGI	PNI	PNE
East Asia and Pacific	N	36			14	26	8	44					
	mean	42.53			34.73	29.62	34.47	35.32					
Eastern Europe and Central Asia	N	5	5		61	19							
	mean	41.4	27.48		25.76	22.91							
Latin America	N	57		2	32		12						
	mean	50.07		49.93	51.48		42.43						
Middle East and North Africa	N			3			16						
	mean			40			41.33						
North America	N							68					
	mean							33.92					
South Asia	N	22		8		1	33						
	mean	39.73		31.55		30.06	32.44						

continued

Table 2.2 (continued)

Region		***Non-OECD Countries***						***OECD Countries***					
		HGI	HNI	HNE	PGI	PNI	PNE	HGI	HNI	HNE	PGI	PNI	PNE
Sub-Saharan Africa	N	5	3	1			36						
	mean	50.7	57.82	54.21			43.86						
Western Europe	N							17	76	9		33	
	mean							36.77	32.06	28.63		26.19	
Total	N	125	8	14	107	46	105	129	76	9		33	
	mean	45.75	38.86	37.6	34.63	26.86	39	34.78	32.06	28.63		26.19	

Notes: HGI = household gross income, HNI = household net income, HNE = household net expenditure, PGI = per capita gross income, PNI = per capita net income, PNE = per capita net expenditure.

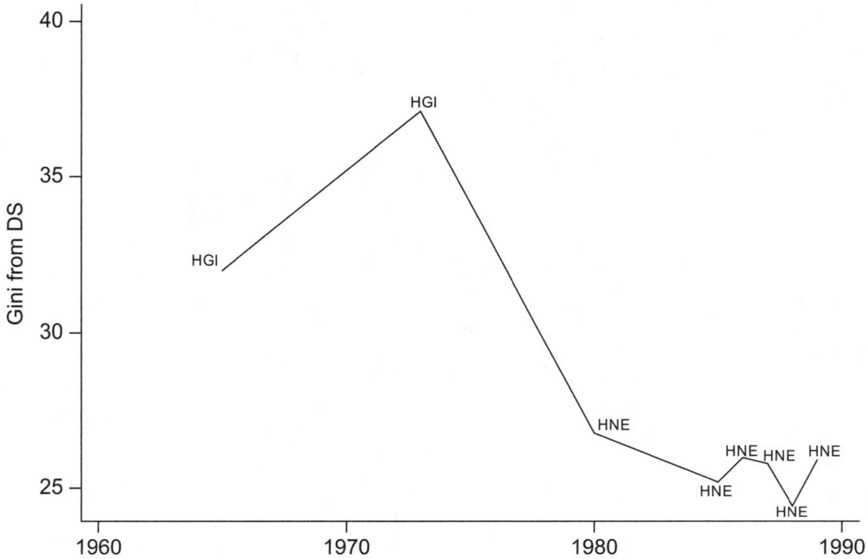

Figure 2.2. Inequality in Spain, as reported by Deininger and Squire.
* HGI: Household Gross Income HNE: Household Net Expenditure.

To complicate things further, measures of inequality sometimes vary within the same country. For instance, inequality measures for Spain are based on two sources: household gross income (HGI) and household net expenditure (HNE). The shift from one type of measure to the other no doubt partly explains the decline in measured inequality for Spain, as illustrated in figure 2.2, and why the average level of inequality for Spain appears low in the DS data, as seen in figure 2.1. In other words, it's the type, and not the quality, of the measure reported by DS that gives the implausible result. There need be no actual error in any of the measurements for this sort of thing to happen. Similar situations affect 30 out of 104 countries (4 from the OECD[6] and 26 from outside the OECD,[7] including 14 Latin American countries) where the information is available.

Regression analysis using dummy variables is an easy way to assess how important the differences in data type may be. Table 2.3 shows the results when the DS inequality measures are regressed on dummies indicating the different types, along with additional dummies reflecting the regional origins of the data. In the first row, only dummies for source characteristics are included; these estimates indicate that, on average, net income and per capita–based measures of inequality are lower than gross and household-based measures.[8] In the next row, controls for region reveal that, on average, Eastern Europe shows the lowest level of inequality, while Latin America, Africa, and the Middle East show much higher inequality than Western Europe. Once we control for regions, the type of data

Table 2.3. **Effect of Data Type and Region in the Deininger-Squire Data**

	Expenditure	*Person*	*Net*	*Constant*	*EAP*	*ECA*	*LAC*	*MENA*	*NA*	*SAS*	*SSA*
Coefficient	0.296	−0.15	−0.21	3.661							
	(10.97)**	(7.7)**	(10.1)**	(282.14) **							
Coefficient	0.010	−0.11	−0.119	3.551	0.09	−0.18	0.41	0.37	−0.03	0.12	0.44
	(0.42)	(7.7)**	(6.5) **	(191.7)**	(4.5)**	(7.45)**	(17.4)**	(9.33)**	(1.20)	(4.6)**	(14.9)**

Notes: Income = 0, expenditure = 1; household = 0, person = 1; gross = 0, net = 1; EAP = East Asia and Pacific; ECA = Eastern Europe and Central Asia; LAC = Latin America; MENA = Middle East and North Africa; NA = North America; SAS = South Asia; SSA = sub-Saharan Africa; WE = Western Europe (base dummy, omitted).* Significant at 5%, ** significant at 1%.

remains a significant determinant of the measure, with one exception: the mean difference between income and expenditure measures of inequality disappears.

It thus appears that income-expenditure differences are highly correlated with regional differences that are now controlled explicitly. This finding leaves us in a state of doubt: are the differences we observe—between, say, India and Brazil—true differences in inequality between these countries, or merely an artifact of the practice of measuring incomes in Brazil but expenditures in India? To sort this out, we'd need something new and independent: a standard measure of comparison across the regions that employ different approaches to the measurement of inequality.

For those seeking an alternative to the DS and WIDER approaches, the Luxembourg Income Studies (LIS) are an attractive option, in the form of a harmonized transnational dataset carefully built up from the underlying microsurveys. LIS also presents a much more plausible picture of the cross-sectional pattern of variations in income inequality within the OECD: Scandinavia comes in low, while Spain and the rest of southern Europe come in high. But there is a price to be paid for the care taken: although the LIS coverage is gradually expanding, it is even sparser than DS and not well suited to panel or time-series analysis of inequality measures. LIS is therefore mainly a tool for detailed analysis of differences in income, benefits, and living standards—the traditional area of interest of social welfare economists. It is not designed for larger purposes, among them a broad study of the movement of inequality over time or its relationship to larger macroeconomic and financial forces.[9] It can't be used to help standardize the disparate data types available in DS and WIDER, especially outside the OECD. Nor can either LIS or DS be used to probe the evolution of inequality at the subnational level, for instance within and between states, provinces, and regions of large countries such as the United States, Russia, China, and Brazil.

The question thus arises: Can anything be done? More and better data are definitely needed. Is there any way to get them?

Obtaining Dense and Consistent Inequality Measures

Around 1996, researchers associated with the University of Texas Inequality Project (UTIP) began exploring the use of semi-aggregated economic datasets—that is, data organized and presented by industry or economic sector or by geographic region—as a source of information on levels and changes in inequality. The work is far advanced and the methods, which are very simple, are now well established, with many articles and two books published on various specialized topics.[10]

This work is based on a simple insight. The distribution of economic earnings is built up in any given national economy out of deeply interlaced institutional entities: firms, occupations, industries, and geographic regions. That being so, consistent observation of the movement of these entities, taken at their average values and compared to each other, is often sufficient to reveal the main movements of the distribution as a whole. This is true even if the coverage of the economy is not comprehensive or wholly representative, so long as the grouping structures are kept consistent from one observation to the next. The reason is that institutional relationships throughout an economy tend to persist, so that the relative positions of parts of the economy that can be observed easily (the formal sector) and those that are not easily observed (the informal sector) do not usually change rapidly over time.

Further, the movement over time of inequality is often determined by forces that work from the top down. These forces broadly differentiate the income paths of people working in different industries or parts of the country. Therefore, datasets that capture the average incomes of major groups of people, such as by industry or sector or region, may contain a sufficiently large share of information on the evolution of economic inequality to serve as good approximations for the movement of the distribution as a whole. These semi-aggregated, categorical datasets, in other words, are an important data resource, with strong potential for improving our knowledge of the level and change in economic inequality, and for comparing one entity to the next. But—possibly because economists tend to be trained to the virtues of the survey and the primacy of the individual—they have been largely overlooked, and except by UTIP they have not been used much in work of this kind.

Datasets of this type are, from a computational point of view, extremely simple. One needs a dataset divided into groups, with the only restriction being that the groups are "mutually exclusive and collectively exhaustive" (MECE). This means that groups cannot share members, and you can calculate an inequality measure only for the populations covered by the groups. We need just two facts about each group: its total income (or payroll) and its total population (or employment). From this, one can easily calculate two ratios: the share of each group in the whole population under study, and the ratio of each group's average income to the average of the population as a whole. The "Theil element," as we'll call it, is just the product of these two terms, multiplied by the log of the second term.

What we'll call the "between-groups component" of Theil's T is equal to the sum of the Theil elements across all groups. Thus, for m groups:

$$T^B = \sum_{i=1}^{m} \left\{ \left(\frac{p_i}{p} \right) * \left(\frac{y_i}{\mu} \right) * In \left(\frac{y_i}{\mu} \right) \right\}$$

where $\frac{p_i}{p}$ is a group population weight and $\frac{y_i}{\mu}$ is the ratio of average income in group i to the average income of the whole population. Because of the logarithmic term, Theil elements are positive for groups with above-average income and negative for groups with below-average income. The sum across groups is, however, always positive (thanks to the asymmetry, above and below one, of the middle term in the Theil element). This equation is the full extent of the mathematics required for the computation of inequality measures in this book.

Theil (1972) showed that this measure is a consistent lower-bound estimate of total inequality, meaning that actual inequality will always be equal to or higher than the observed between-groups component.[11] But actually the measure contains much more information than what this very modest statement indicates, particularly if you calculate it repeatedly, always in the same way, over time. Thus a coarse disaggregation of the data (say, a two-digit standard industrial classification) typically yields the same general picture of movement through time as a fine disaggregation (say, a four-digit SIC[12]). Coarse disaggregations capture less inequality than finer ones, so the Theil measure increases as one moves to finer classification grids.

Up to very fine disaggregations, the method will almost always leave a larger share of total inequality *within* groups (and therefore unobserved) than *between* them. So it is almost always true that group-based inequality measures greatly understate the total amount of inequality. But even though this may seem at first glance to be a serious limitation, it is actually just a detail. In studies of inequality, we are usually interested in two types of questions. First: How has inequality in a given place changed over time? Is it rising or is it falling? By how much, in relation to what it was before? Second: Is inequality in place A greater or less than inequality in place B? By how much? Neither question type requires that one measure total inequality for the entire population of A or B. It is not even necessary that one's measures be proportionate to total inequality. For the measures to be comparable across time, it is only necessary that the *changes* in the measures be proportionate to the *changes* in total inequality.[13]

For any given geographic region—such as a continent, country, or province—once a reasonable degree of segmentation is achieved[14] the fact of proportionality in changes is easily established even though the constant of proportionality remains unknown. That is, the main patterns of change in inequality are going to be reflected in changes between the groups into which that region is divided. Thereafter, further refining the classification scheme increases the measure of inequality, but it does not greatly alter the pattern of change. The principle is again similar to digital photography: everything is in the frame, and the relevant trade-off is between resolution and file size. Putting it in mathematical terms, Conceição et al. (2001) demonstrated that the T statistic is a *statistical fractal*, meaning it is approximately self-similar at different scales. This can be shown in principle and demonstrated in practice, using datasets arranged to permit multiple levels of disaggregation.[15]

Extended mathematical treatments of the Theil statistic are readily available (for instance, Conceição and Ferreira 2000), and we shall not be concerned to repeat them here. The basic point is that it would be hard to conceive of a simpler, more flexible, or more generally reliable way to measure inequality or to track changes in inequality over time.

A first advantage of this approach is that economic data suitable to calculations of this type are very common. Within the OECD coverage is universal, detailed, and available in consistent formats over long periods with short sampling intervals, annually back to the early 1960s, and even monthly in many cases. In the United States, historical data series have so far permitted construction of continuous series back to the late 1940s and of linked series going back to 1920 (Galbraith and Garza-Cantú 1999 is an example.) Outside the OECD coverage is very broad; for example, in Africa one can develop more than 700 country-year observations through 1999. The corresponding number in DS is 63.

Second, sector and regional data yield richly detailed information concerning the precise pattern of relative gains and losses as inequality changes. One can see at a glance exactly which provinces (and sometimes which cities) gain, and at whose expense, and which precise sectors were advantaged and which were hurt.[16] These cross-cutting categorical structures can often be used together, so that the unit of observation is a sector within a region or province; in this way, a very fine grid can be laid over the patterns of economic change in the region under study.

Third, there are international datasets with harmonized category schemes.[17] They have the interesting property of imposing the same number and type of group structure—industries or sectors—on different countries. It turns out that this works to normalize the measures of pay or earnings inequality drawn from these sources. Such measures are therefore comparable between countries and are excellent instruments for the (unavailable) survey-based measures of income (or expenditure) inequality that one might (ideally or habitually) like to have.[18] The resulting measures correspond closely to the rank orderings obtained by benchmark studies such as the LIS, and although one has to be careful when working with data from some parts of the larger world, it seems that the property of intercountry comparability holds very widely.

This was a surprising finding, and it retains (even for us) a touch of mystery after many years of working with the data. But it checks out repeatedly, and perhaps most dramatically in the simple fact that neighboring countries with closely linked economies tend to report similar inequality measures, while the differences between countries grow as the geographic and economic ties between them weaken. No similar consistency appears in maps using the DS data.

The calculations made in this way can be compared to the measures in existing datasets, such as DS. It turns out they tend to confirm that the quality of the latter, taken as individual data points and allowing for differences of data type, is usually quite high. Where sample surveys exist, the pattern of matching is close. For a sample of 485 observations matched by country and year, inequality in manufacturing pay drawn from United Nations Industrial Development Organization (UNIDO) Industrial Statistics is a highly significant predictor of DS inequality, after controlling for survey type and for the share of manufacturing employment in population. The coefficients are very stable across specifications, and the regression framework captures up to 60 percent of the variance in DS data. We shall pursue this line of work in chapter 4.

The international dataset just mentioned, UNIDO's Industrial Statistics, forms the basis of a global inequality dataset, developed in the mid-2000s by Hyunsub Kum, that we call UTIP-UNIDO, with more than thirty-two hundred observations. This is our most important resource for the development of analysis at the level of the globe as a whole, since it puts most countries into the same measuring frame, and on an annual basis going back to the early 1960s. But in addition, rich datasets are available for the United States, for the European Union, and for many individual countries,[19] made up of sectoral information nested within subnational geographic regions, or of smaller geographic regions within larger ones.

Thus, for the United States, it is possible to obtain detailed sectoral and also county decompositions for each state, so that the changing patterns of contribution to inequality by region and sector can be examined in fine detail. For Europe, it is possible to obtain measures of income by sector within provincial-level (known as NUTS-1 in European statistical jargon) regions. For many countries, it is possible to obtain information by sectors, provinces, and sectors within provinces, so that one has, from year to year or even month to month, a great deal of fine detail on the changing distribution of economic rewards.

This information can be displayed very conveniently in a stacked bar graph, of which figure 2.3 gives an example for income by county within the state of New York.[20] Notice that the graph is made up of a sequence of bars. Each bar has information for a particular year. In this case, each bar represents the contribution of the counties within the whole state to income inequality in the United States as a whole. Counties with average incomes above the national average are represented above the zero line; low-income counties lie below it. Since New York is a rich state, a large number of its counties have incomes above the national average. New York State's contribution to national inequality, in a given year, is the sum of the distances above and below the zero line—one of them being positive, the other negative. Thus one can get an idea of whether the state's contribution is rising or falling by looking at the total height of the bar in that year.

The contributions of every county are represented by the segments into which each bar is divided. They are ranked in the legend from largest to smallest on the positive side, and then from smallest to largest on the negative side. Each county's contribution depends on two things: how big the county is in terms of population, and how far its income departs from the national average. By organizing the chart so that the counties are ranked every year according to their contributions to inequality in the final year, we obtain a visually intuitive result: the sweep of the eye from left to right shows the evolution of the composition of income in the state over time.

In this case, the prominent role of wealthy Manhattan (New York County, home of Wall Street), New York State, in increasing U.S. inequality in the 1980s is plainly visible in the data: Manhattan is the large block rising above the zero line. After Manhattan, Westchester and Nassau make the largest positive contributions. The Bronx and Kings make the largest negative contributions. A similar chart for California, not surprisingly, would show the important roles of the Silicon Valley counties of Santa Clara, San Francisco, and San Mateo in rising U.S. inequality during the information technology boom in the late 1990s.

Compared to sample surveys, where the information about individuals is typically limited to a small number of (highly repetitive) personal characteristics such as age, race, gender and education that were deemed to be of interest a priori and included on the survey form, the information content of inequality measures done in this way is very high. And the approach opens many avenues for detailed case studies of modern economies, in all their actual geographic diversity and technical complexity. But two points are especially important.

First, since collection of data by region and sector is usually a bureaucratic function carried out regularly by most governments, data of this type permit

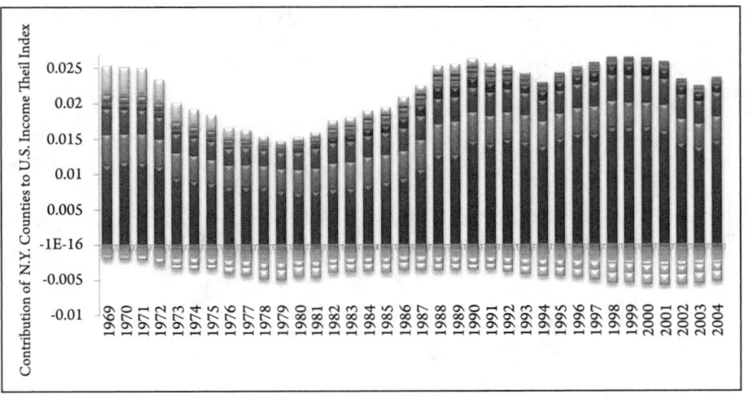

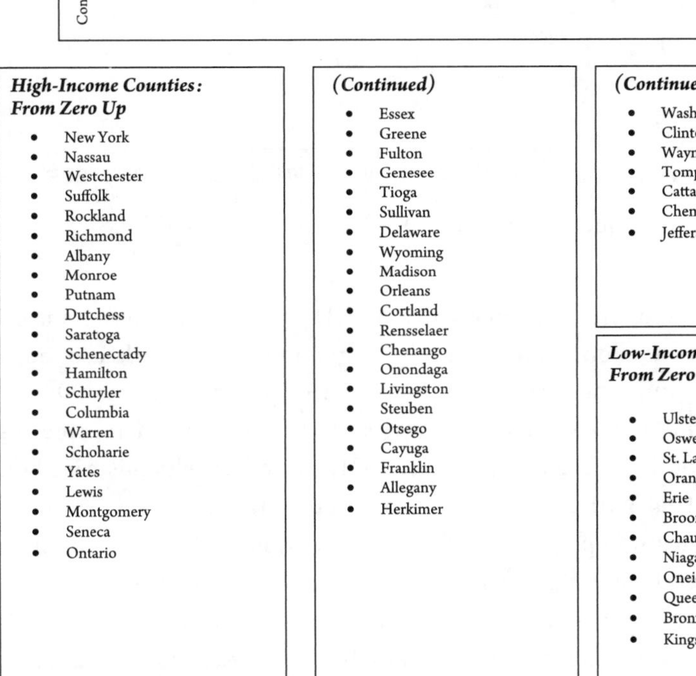

Figure 2.3. Contribution of New York counties to U.S. inequality, 1969–2004.

creation of very long, dense, and complete time series of the movement of inequality.[21] Second, if the category structures are consistent across countries, the measures of inequality derived from those categories will broadly reflect the relative degree of inequality in the whole populations.

These properties taken together mean that—if one has a harmonized dataset with a common categorical structure—it is possible to convert measures of industrial wage inequality computed using the Theil statistic into measures of *estimated* household income inequality, and so to generate dense, consistent datasets of estimated *income inequality* measures in Gini format.[22] The UTIP

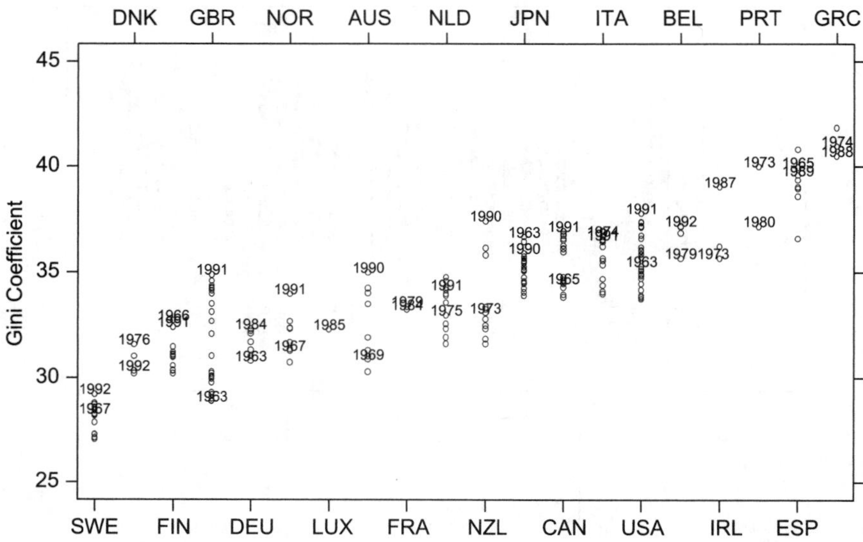

Figure 2.4. Income inequality in the OECD, UTIP-EHII measures.

Estimated Household Income Inequality (EHII) dataset—another Hyunsub Kum creation—has about three thousand observations for the world economy, or roughly four times the coverage of DS, from 1963 into the early 2000s. All are estimated on a single conceptual basis, namely household income inequality gross of tax.[23] Calculation of the EHII estimates, which is based on UNIDO Industrial Statistics, is presented in chapter 4.

To pull a conclusion prematurely from that work, figure 2.4 presents EHII measures of gross household income inequality for the OECD countries, again ranked from left to right by average value, and again with first and last years indicated. Note that common sense now prevails: by these measures the Scandinavian countries are low, while Spain, Portugal, Greece, and the United States are high. Note also that the prevalent trend is toward increasing inequality in almost all of the countries, Denmark being a lonely exception. A similar trend toward increasing inequality will be found in this data for non-OECD countries, as we shall see. A general principle of our work is that where two datasets conflict, some degree of preference should go to the one that tends to confirm the obvious.

Grouping Up and Grouping Down

For valid economic inference, inequality should be measured at the appropriate geographic and economic scale. However, researchers using survey data are limited by the (usually national) scope of the available surveys, and although the national scale is generally the appropriate one, this is not always so. Sometimes one needs a multinational or continental measure; sometimes one would like to measure matters at the level of the state or province. Combining surveys is difficult; dividing them up may be impossible. However, many practical questions depend on aggregating or disaggregating the observational unit to the correct level, which may be something less than the world but more than a country—say a continent or a trading region, as with the European Union or the North American Free Trade Agreement (NAFTA).

Sector and regional data can be used for the purpose of assessing inequality at other-than-national levels. Indeed, measures can be computed readily, taking advantage of the aggregation and disaggregation properties of the Theil statistic. Thus it is possible to measure inequality (say, between regions) across the whole of continental Europe (say, for the purpose of U.S.-Europe comparisons), or to measure within-geographical-unit inequality (between sectors) at the level of European regions or American states. This is especially useful for analysis of labor markets or for voting analysis, where the data need to be matched precisely to the political unit.

A particularly urgent need for such data is apparent in modern Europe. Europe has become a single, complete, unified economy. It has no internal borders, no trade barriers, perfect capital mobility, and no formal barriers to migration. It has a common currency, in large part. In taking this step, the eurozone abolished international-but-intra-European exchange rate fluctuation, giving every European an income measured in the same currency unit.

Yet if you wanted to know, say, the degree of inequality or the poverty rate in "Europe," where would you turn? Ideas are stuck where statistics are: at the national level. And so long as statistics drawn at the continental level are lacking, one cannot correctly model poverty, inequality, labor markets, or the effects of macroeconomic policy in "Europe." For instance, each European country maintains its own assessment of who is poor, but under a system of unified European data everything would change. There would, for instance, be virtually no poor in Germany and only a handful of "middle class" people in Poland or the Baltic states.[24]

Frequent comparison is also made between the inequality of pay in the United States and in Europe, for the purpose of explaining (what was until recently) the chronically higher rate of European unemployment. Such comparisons (as in figures 2.1 and 2.4) generally show the United States to be more unequal than most (though not all) countries of Europe. This finding tends to buttress the conventional conclusion that (before the Great Crisis) the United States enjoyed fuller employment because its labor markets are more "flexible," meaning they are more willing to reward high skills and price low skills at rates that justify employment of low-skilled labor.

Using the Theil method to assess the inequality of Europe *as a whole* overturns this argument simply but decisively. Although inequality is low within many European countries, the inequalities *between* countries are quite large. This does not matter if one assumes Europe to consist of many isolated labor markets—but this is something the European Union has ensured that Europe is not. Adding in the between-countries component of inequality, one finds that inequality in industrial pay—to take an example easily computed from harmonized data—across Europe taken as a single entity is substantially *higher* than in the United States. This finding was first reported in Galbraith, Conceição, and Ferreira (1999), where we used the OECD Structural Analysis dataset to show that pay inequality measured across sectors in European manufacturing, taken as a whole, exceeded that in the United States by around 30 percent. Even if workers are not fully mobile between countries, capital is; from the standpoint of an international investor or a transnational corporation, wage differentials between Germany and Spain, after adjusting for productivity, should matter a lot.

Galbraith (2007b) directly compared income inequality between the (subnational) regions of Europe with similar measures taken across the American states, both computed, in this case, as *between-regions* Gini coefficients.[25] These inequality measures confirm the 1999 findings: for the EU-15 the measures were 40 percent higher than in the United States; for the EU-25 interregional inequality proved to be more than twice that in the United States.[26] These calculations suggest a different conclusion from the standard intercontinental comparison of inequalities: that the United States is more unequal *at close range*, while Europe is much more unequal *over long distances*. Again, there is a vast amount of corroborating data, as well as commonsense observation, to buttress this conclusion.

Clarifying the inequality picture now forces us to look again at the supposed relationship between inequality (which we can also call "labor market flexibility") and unemployment. The standard story—that flexibility is rewarded by high employment—collapses under this revision of the evidence. But a quite different, and relatively straightforward, alternative story emerges from the rubble. Inequality in pay structures, it turns out, is highly and positively correlated with unemployment, across space and over time. The more inequality, the more unemployment. This may seem surprising at first, but in fact the reasons are not very complicated. In part, the simple fact that some jobs offer much higher pay provokes people to leave their present job and accept unemployment, for a time, as the price of obtaining a chance for a better one. In part, inequality may reflect the same depressed labor market conditions that prevail among lower-paid workers and produce unemployment. But it is clear that inequality is no cure for unemployment, and that if inequality is seen to rise, the likely consequence must be higher, not lower, unemployment.

This is borne out by the evidence within Europe as well. In Europe, countries with lower inequality—in Scandinavia, notably—have almost always enjoyed lower unemployment, and Europe as a whole had very low unemployment during the postwar, social-democratic era, when economies were isolated from each other by capital controls and egalitarianism was enforced by powerful unions. Those days came to an end in the early 1970s.

Unfortunately for the Europeans, the inequalities at long distance that appear with the emergence of an integrated Europe appear highly significant for determination of chronic unemployment, since they motivate displacement, migration, and undermining of previously coherent national labor standards. The European Union means that these inequalities matter more and more. Thus as Europe becomes more integrated, both the relevant measure of inequality and the chronic rate of unemployment have gone up. We will return to this story later; for now it's sufficient to note it as an illustration of the usefulness of comprehensive and reliable inequality measures, taken at an appropriate observational scale.

Equally useful, the ubiquity of regional and sector data permits analyses of the relationship between inequality and other variables—such as unemployment—to be pursued at the subnational level. In Europe, for example, there is a large variation in unemployment rates between regions within countries; this variation is often larger than the variation of unemployment rates between countries. Yet the standard analysis of European unemployment in terms of differing *national* labor market institutions can take no account of the variations arising inside countries. Regional measures of inequality, developed for Europe by Enrique Garcilazo, are well adapted to this analysis. Models based on these measures show that inequality is also a significant determinant of unemployment at the regional level, again in precisely the opposite sense to that suggested by the conventional theory: more inequality is associated with more, not less, unemployment.[27]

Regional data are useful also for political analysis. The American states are political entities, an important fact given the state basis of the Electoral College. Travis Hale has developed panel measures of inequality within American states on principles similar to EHII; these can be correlated to measures of voting turnout and voter preference. The results show that inequality suppresses turnout. It is also possible to create a measure of economic polarization across space—we'll call it geo-economic polarization[28] within states—which

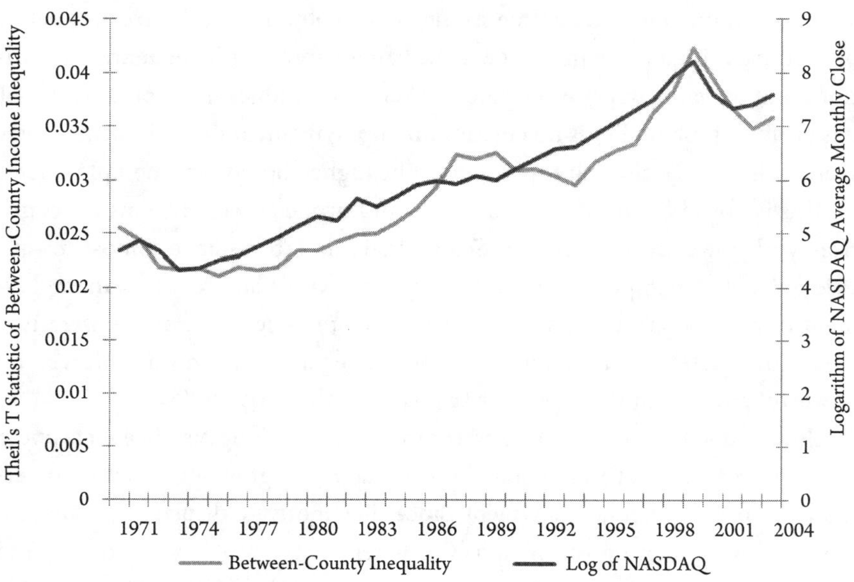

Figure 2.5. Inequality between Counties in the US and the (log) NASDAQ stock index, 1971–2004.

as it turns out is highly correlated with recent presidential election outcomes. American states that are highly polarized along spatial lines (generally, with a strong divide between urban on the one hand and suburban-rural on the other) tend to vote Democratic; those that are predominantly rural or suburban tend to vote Republican. Intriguingly, as states change along this dimension (California and Connecticut are longstanding examples, Colorado and Virginia more recent ones) they have also evolved politically in the direction indicated by the model—that is, greater geo-economic polarization has in recent years inclined an American state toward the Democratic Party.

Finally, measures of inequality at the subnational level can be used to explain the regional and sectoral basis of movements in the overall income distribution, as captured by sample surveys. For instance, standard census measures of income inequality in the United States show a peak in 2000, followed by a decline. Galbraith and Hale (2006) first showed that this measure is closely tracked by a measure of income inequality calculated from tax data tabulated at the county level. Thus variations observed between American counties are, for this period at least, a good instrument for variations occurring in the whole population.

A measure based on counties can offer quite precise insight into the sectoral causes of rising income inequality—a topic that brings us back to the relationship between inequality and financial instability. The Theil measure of inequality across counties over thirty-three years (1971–2004) is highly correlated to the (log) of the NASDAQ stock price index, with the principal contributions to rising inequality coming from the counties of Silicon Valley and similar technology centers. Moreover, if the income growth of just five counties[29] were removed from the data, about half of the increase in between-county income inequality in the late 1990s United States would disappear; removing fifteen counties takes care of all of it. The decline in inequality that followed the end of the boom is entirely explained by the stock market crash, which was centered on technology stocks. Figure 2.5 presents the two series.

Overall, this research underlines the importance of distinguishing carefully between sources of income in the United States. As the "econophysics" literature has recognized, the distribution of what is called income is an amalgam of two very different things: the distribution of earnings or pay, which tends to be quite stable except for the influence of variations in hours worked; and the distribution of property income,[30] which dominates the top of the scale and tends to follow a power law (Chatterjee, Yarlagadda, and Chakrabarti 2005). Since ownership of stocks is skewed to the top of the distribution, the parameters of the power law vary with valuations in the stock market. This, along with the comparative stability of pay-based incomes, accounts for the high degree of correlation between stock market prices and the income distribution. It also demonstrates that the distribution of taxable income is a poor proxy for inequality in wages, making data from this source largely ill suited for investigation of issues related to pay for work. Finally, it shows that the issue of rising income inequality in the United States is not, by and large, a phenomenon that has run from the top to the bottom of the structure. It is, rather, a phenomenon that reflects, in the main, an extreme increase in incomes of a tiny group at the very top.

The distribution of earnings reflects an institutional structure of wage rates governed by structured relativities within organizations. This is generally very stable (Galbraith 1998; Kitov 2005, 2007). Despite the focus of economic theory on the effects of technology, trade, immigration, and other forces on hourly wage rates, such hourly wage rates are not observed directly; almost all of the empirical work on changing wage distributions relies on measures of weekly or monthly earnings. The variation in earnings is largely a matter of fluctuations in hours worked (which may trigger overtime payments, affecting the *average hourly wage* but not the notional *wage rate*). Inequality in earnings is therefore closely related to open unemployment, as figure 2.6 illustrates using monthly data for American manufacturing from 1953 to 2005 (with shaded periods indicating recessions). Significant effects of labor-force participation and of the exchange rate on this measure have also been found (Giovannoni

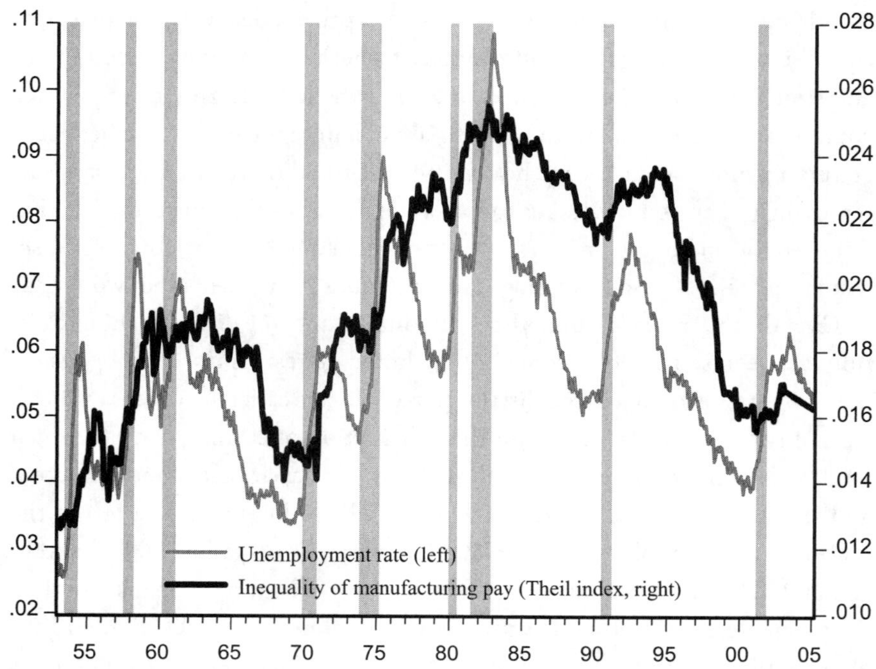

Figure 2.6. Pay inequality in manufacturing and unemployment in the US, 1953–2005, monthly data. (Recessions marked in vertical grey bars.)

2007), and Galbraith, Giovannoni, and Russo (2007) show that it is Granger-caused by the movement of the term structure of interest rates, a measure of the stance of monetary policy.

This last finding has interest in part because Federal Reserve officials have regularly been at pains to deny the proposition that monetary policy can affect inequality. But the evidence for pay inequality strongly indicates that it has. Indeed, to the considerable extent that monetary policy influences the stock market, one can also argue that the pattern of overall income inequality is substantially affected as well by the stance of monetary policy—something Federal Reserve officials have also been at pains, over the years, to deny.

Similar results hold for Europe, where inequality as a whole declined with declining unemployment from 1995 to 2000 (Galbraith and Garcilazo 2005). Moreover, analysis of unemployment by regions in Europe reveals a common time pattern, which strongly associates the rise in unemployment across the continent with implementation of the Maastricht Treaty in 1993. This pattern lends support to those who argue that European unemployment has an important macroeconomic component, determined by the policy stance of European authorities taken together and as a whole. Chapter 8 returns to this issue.

Conclusion

Given the problems and defects of the previously available datasets, much published work in international comparison of inequality measures and their movement over time has to be regarded with suspicion. However, we now know that the individual studies behind those datasets are not generally bad; the problem is the scarcity of measures and the differences in method between them. Therefore, industrial, sectoral, and regional data can be deployed effectively to fill gaps and repair inconsistencies in standard measures of economic inequality. The resulting datasets permit annual time series and balanced panel regression analyses of inequality, practically for the first time, especially outside the OECD. Use of the Theil statistic also permits calculations of inequality measures at scales other than national, permitting for the first time the choice of scale—regional, national, continental or even global—to be tailored to the research question. All of this opens up rich territory for exploration.

As we've seen, the calculations have a disconcerting effect on conventional views. Among other things, they show that the movement of overall *income* inequality in the United States over time is largely governed by the stock market, an artifact of financial boom and bust. Meanwhile *pay* inequality in both the United States and Europe largely rises and falls with unemployment over time, although other factors (among them exchange rate movements and political regime changes) play a role. Thus the financial and the macroeconomic, which have been practically neglected in conventional studies of economic inequality, start to emerge in central roles.

Within Europe, countries with less pay inequality systematically enjoy less unemployment, other things equal. This result contradicts the standard model that places blame for chronic unemployment on labor market rigidity, though it is consistent with well-established models of search and migration and of induced productivity change. Further, evaluation of inequality at the continental level demonstrates that pay inequality in the United States is *less*, not greater, than in Europe. Again this tends to refute the view that the superior employment performance of the United States is due to high inequality in pay structures. It calls attention instead to the neglected international dimension of European inequality—a dimension of increasing relevance as the continental economy becomes more integrated.

We turn next to exploring the movement of inequality at the level of the global economy, a subject that has drawn considerable academic interest in recent years. It will turn out that this, too, has an unmistakable macroeconomic and financial component.

Notes

1. According to DS (1996), a data point is deemed "high-quality" if the underlying survey meets three criteria: (1) coverage of all types of income, including in-kind income, (2) coverage of urban and rural households, and (3) focus on households rather than individuals. In our work with DS data, we restrict attention to data points deemed high in quality and providing national coverage.
2. The original DS data are apparently no longer posted at the World Bank, but an updated dataset with fifteen hundred observations is available at http://go.worldbank.org/9VCQW66LA0. This dataset includes measures from DS, LIS, WIDER, and other sources. Increasing the number of observations in this way is useful but does not address the consistency issue; for this reason the general critique of DS presented here remains relevant.
3. Obviously, this procedure will be without bias only if it happens that there is no systematic pattern in the global evolution of inequality. See Milanovic (2002a) for a detailed critique of Sala-i-Martin's interpolations.
4. There are four types of household-size adjustments applied in the DS data: household, household equivalent (weighted by the number of persons), person, and person equivalent (wherein the effective number of household members is assumed to be the square root of the actual number).
5. This table is based on the 652 observations whose categorical information is available in the DS data.
6. They are Spain, Germany, Denmark, and Finland.
7. They are Brazil, Chile, Columbia, Costa Rica, Guatemala, Guyana, Honduras, Jamaica, Mexico, Panama, Peru, Venezuela, Sri Lanka, Pakistan, Mauritius, Zambia, Seychelles, Malaysia, Philippines, Bulgaria, Czech Republic, Hungary, Poland, Romania, Russia, and Yugoslavia.
8. Grün and Klasen (2003) and Dollar and Kraay (2002) also found that household-based and gross income–based measures are typically higher than expenditure measures. These various findings are all derived from differing data and model specifications. Dollar and Kraay use the expanded DS data (n = 814) with fixed effects, and Grün and Klasen use the World Income Inequality Database (WIID, n = 2,033) with more detailed reference units (World Institute for Development Economics Research, 2000). We use a subset of the original DS data (n = 652) with the three dummies specified in table 2.3. We experimented with a fixed-effects model with similar results. One inconsistency between our analysis and other studies is that in a simple OLS specification expenditure-based measures are higher than income-based measures in our study. But as discussed later in the main text, this estimate loses its significance when other control variables enter into the model. We use the estimates from table 4.1, model 3 in our EHII (estimated household income inequality; see chapter text at note 22) estimation.
9. Similarly, WIDER's Data Set Version 1.0 has 221 data points for sixty-seven countries over twenty-six years, from 1970 to 1996. In a recent paper Biancotti (2006, p. 3) writes, "We exclusively considered data above a certain level of comparability, resulting in 217 observations selected for our panel out of a total of 5067."
10. Published papers and books include Conceição and Galbraith (2000); Conceição, Galbraith, and Bradford (2001); Ferguson and Galbraith (1999); Galbraith (1998, 1999, 2002a, 2002b, 2006a, 2007a, 2007b, 2007c); Galbraith and Berner (2001); Galbraith and Garcilazo (2004, 2005); Galbraith and Garza-Cantú (1999); Galbraith and Hale (2006, 2008); Galbraith, Krytynskaia, and Wang (2004); Galbraith and Kum (2003); Galbraith, Priest, and Purcell (2007), Galbraith, RoyChowdhury, and Shrivastava (2004); Galbraith, Spagnolo, and Munevar (2008); Galbraith, Spagnolo, and Pinto (2007); Garcilazo-Corredera 2007; and Kim (2002, 2005).

11. The within-groups component is, of course, simply unobserved. But the consistency of category structures across time implies that changes in the between-groups component track changes in the entire distribution, and this is the key point for time-series comparison.
12. Similarly, disaggregation to the county level (in the United States, 3,150 counties) yields a precise picture, whereas disaggregation to the state level (fifty states plus the District of Columbia) yields a coarse image of the same picture.
13. Since inequality between group averages is often more volatile than inequality across the whole population, this amounts to saying (for instance) that it is sufficient that a 10 percent change in the between-groups measure consistently reflects a 3 percent change in total inequality.
14. Usually a two-digit industrial classification or a high-level geographic classification, such as state or province, is adequate.
15. Industrial classification schemes are arranged in this hierarchical way, with the number of digits in the code permitting categories to be fully nested within higher-level categories. Geographic information also usually has this feature: precincts within census blocks within counties within states, to give an American example.
16. A further advantage of this data is that they can be displayed very attractively with geographic information systems mapping, although for the purposes of a book this is problematic, since a clear GIS representation requires color.
17. As in the cases of UNIDO's Industrial Statistics or the European Commission's REGIO regional dataset.
18. A further detail is that these measures can be obtained at very low cost. Source data are often available at no charge, and the computation time is measured in hours.
19. In addition to OECD member countries (including Mexico and South Korea), UTIP papers are available on Russia, China, India, Argentina, Brazil, Costa Rica, and Cuba. For example, Krytynskaia divided the Russian economy into some twelve hundred region-sector cells for each of eleven years, 1990 through 2000; Wang divided the Chinese economy into more than six hundred region-sector cells over the years 1979–1997.
20. The figure displays the contribution of counties within New York State to overall U.S. inequality, measured across all counties. They are drawn from local area personal income statistics; the computation was by Travis Hale.
21. Where such time series can be compared to high-quality, continuous sample surveys of income, as for the United States and Canada, the measures generally correspond well.
22. The Gini coefficient, first developed by the statistician Corrado Gini in 1912, is the most common and most widely understood measurement of inequality. In a box showing the cumulative incidence of income, it represents the proportionate area, between a Lorenz curve and a hypothetical line representing perfect equality, and takes a value between 0 and 1, where 0 would represent perfect equality and 1 would represent concentration of all income in the wealthiest person. The Gini has the advantage of being easily compared from one distribution to the next, but the disadvantage that it cannot be decomposed straightforwardly into the inequalities of subpopulations (Pyatt, 1976).
23. Estimates on any other basis—net household income, gross or net expenditure, personal as against household inequality—can be computed readily from the information generated by the EHII estimation procedure.
24. In the Americas, it is similarly clear that the concept of "national labor supply" has lost meaning to a degree. The United States has a large reserve in Mexico and points south, and an even larger virtual reserve in China, India, and elsewhere. However, the integration of capital and other markets between the United States and its trading partners is not nearly so complete as is the case in Europe.
25. Gini coefficients were appropriate here because the number of European regions is much larger than the number of U.S. states, and a Theil-to-Theil measure would show even higher European inequality on that account.

26. Galbraith (2007b) argues that modern Europe resembles the United States of the 1930s, when a vast income differential dating to the Civil War separated the deep South from the rest of the country. This is comparable to the post–Cold War differentials between Eastern and Western Europe. A relentless politics of regional income convergence, beginning with the New Deal, has largely erased the erstwhile regional differentials in the United States.
27. Standard models of equilibrium unemployment under conditions of inequality, such as Harris and Todaro (1970), predict that a high level of inequality generates incentives to migrate and to search for employment, hence higher unemployment on a sustained basis. This pattern is clearly observed in European data. Further, the Swedish economists Meidner and Rehn (1951, exposited in Turvey 1952) argued that wage compression would generate more rapid productivity growth, higher average income, and a greater capacity to absorb, retrain, and reemploy those displaced by technical change. In modern Europe, the Scandinavian countries have set the pace over the decades by running open economies with strongly compressed wage structures. The problem with the conventional view, emphasizing "labor market flexibility" as a cure, is twofold: it overlooks both migration incentives and endogenous productivity growth. It is not surprising that the data do not fit.
28. The measure in Galbraith and Hale (2008) is the ratio of income inequality between census blocks to the overall estimate of income inequality in the state.
29. The five counties are Santa Clara, San Francisco, and San Mateo in California; King County, Washington (home to Microsoft); and New York, New York, the financial capital. Galbraith and Hale (2006) first report this calculation.
30. Property income in this context needs to be considered broadly, including salaries paid from funds raised on the capital markets, which became a significant source of personal income during the technology boom.

CHAPTER 3

Pay Inequality and World Development

In his 1955 presidential address to the American Economic Association, Simon Kuznets offered a simple, elegant argument relating inequality to the process of industrialization. Before industry, say in late-feudal Great Britain or the early northern United States, agriculture consisted largely of small freeholds, tenantry, and family farms. Income from work was limited by the natural scope of family labor and the talents and efforts of the village craftsman. Factories and city life introduced division of labor, leading to higher living standards for a rising urban working class, including factory workers and eventually professionals, engineers, and machinists. Since this group enjoyed more income than their country cousins, economic inequality rose.

Later on, migration and ultimately the industrialization of agriculture displaced the farmers from their land. As the agricultural population declined in proportion to the total, so too did the significance of the urban-rural income gap. Therefore, inequality would decline as incomes continued to rise, simply because the population transitioned from being primarily rural to primarily urban. Cities, with all their economic diversity, are naturally more unequal than the countryside, so matters would not again return to an egalitarian starting point. But Kuznets did expect that as industrialization matured, unionization and social democracy would reduce the initially high inequalities of the townsfolk, so that overall inequality would continue to decline as industrial development deepened.

What Kuznets Meant

The basic mechanism of Kuznets's argument was thus the transition from country to town and from farm to factory as average incomes rose. The consequence was a definite relationship between inequality and income: inequality would first increase and later decline as cities swallowed the rural population. This was the inverted U that later economists would call the "Kuznets curve."[1] Given the sectoral transition that lies behind it, this is something that can happen just once in the history of any particular country. It is also a relationship limited strictly to the distribution of pay for work. Under feudalism and colonialism as well as in the American South, great estates, plantations, and slavery were the norm, and the distribution of total income could not have been more equal on the farm than in the town. Kuznets was aware of this, and he explicitly excluded nonlabor incomes—such as the rents due to landlords, or monopoly profits or (later on) technological "quasi-rents"—from his argument.

The essential point in Kuznets's analysis was, therefore, not the discovery of some universal pattern in the relationship between inequality and income. It was the statement of a principle: that change in (pay) inequality is largely guided by intersectoral transitions in economic activity. Such transitions are a characteristic phenomenon of economic development and change. The key determinant of economic inequality is the structural composition of the economy itself—as among agriculture, industry, mining, services, finance, and government, for example. This is obviously very slow-moving. There is a second key, which can move more quickly, namely, the differential between average incomes earned in each of these areas.[2] Change in the proportions (long run) and in the differentials (short run) is the key to change in inequality; this is the enduring lesson of Kuznets's 1955 argument.

In recent years, this message has been blurred to the point where it can no longer be read. The element of structural transition, which was foundational for Kuznets, has largely been lost. Nothing much has replaced it, except for opportunistic empiricism. In this vein, some studies go looking willy-nilly for inverted U-curves in time-series data, whether or not they reflect any sort of intersectoral transition and whether or not they restrict their coverage to pay for work. Unsurprisingly, the results are weak. Cross-sectional analysis (comparison between countries) has also been inconclusive, but this too should be no surprise: even with good data a sampling from an actual inverted U can yield a positive, negative, or zero slope, depending on which places and times fall within the sample.[3]

Other papers have changed the question. Instead of asking (as Kuznets did) whether there is a characteristic pattern to inequality in the development process, they ask whether high or low inequality better serves to foster rapid economic growth, meaning a rapid rise in income level. This work presumes that the initial level of inequality is *not* primarily a structural outcome but instead a policy choice, capable of being made by public authority, such as through policies supporting universal education or investments in infrastructure.[4] The empirical question then becomes whether a high or a low level of inequality is likely to be followed by a higher or a lower rate of economic growth, for some period into the future.[5] Without saying so, this work presumes that Kuznets was simply wrong about the key role of differences in industrial structure and the stage of economic development in determining what inequality is likely to be at any given time.

This recent line of work complicates the issue, perhaps most of all by speculating that a relationship exists between a *level* of inequality, measured at some *point* of time, and a *rate of change* of income, measured over a later *interval* of time. How a level of any variable can consistently affect a subsequent rate of change in another variable is difficult to understand. Pushing the argument to its absurd limits, if a relationship of this kind holds in the short run, then it should be possible to accelerate the growth rate *permanently* by maintaining the inequality variable permanently in the favored position. This would be a perpetual motion machine, which is forbidden by the laws of physics. And in empirical studies there is also the question of exactly what the starting point and the lag structure for such an analysis should be. Presumably—and in practice—different moments of time, with different "initial" levels of inequality, and different time intervals will yield different answers to the research question. Which of the answers would be the correct one? There is not any clear theoretical guidance on this point. Kuznets's view that the key relationship was between the level of income and the level of inequality (and therefore between changes and changes, conditional on the starting point) avoids tricky questions of time intervals; either the relationship exists at one moment in time, or it does not.

Still others have taken evidence of rising inequality alongside rising incomes, in high-income countries such as the United States, as a sign that the Kuznets hypothesis is no longer valid even though it might have been valid at some earlier time.[6] This interpretation accepts that structural change drives inequality in the long run but rejects the simple inverted U. The argument becomes that the United States and other wealthy countries are in a later form of intersectoral transition, away from manufacturing industry and toward technology, finance, and services, and that this must imply a different, more complicated relationship between the rise of income and change in inequality.

Part of this argument rests on the fact that as an economy grows more complex, it also becomes impossible to make the clear and clean separation that Kuznets relied on between pay for work and pay arising from profit, rent, and market and financial power. In some sectors (especially in technology and finance), what is reported to the tax authorities as wages or by firms as payroll derives from funds raised on capital markets or the realization of capital gains. This in turn introduces the possibility of very short-term changes in inequality due to changing short-term circumstances—including some related to public policy, but others that may be driven by bubbles, speculation, or sharp practice—that are reflected in rapidly changing asset prices. Thus the element of average-pay differentials between sectors takes on greater importance, while the slow-moving process of changing economic structure recedes into the background.

Further still, as economic regions integrate it becomes necessary to consider the relationship of each to all the others. Patterns of trade, movements of labor, and interdependencies of the financial system may all cause the distributional characteristics of one system to influence those of another. In the limit, a global economy may have global forces that affect intersectoral differentials and the movement of inequality.

We take the view here that this layered vision is almost obviously correct. At the foundation, economic inequality must depend primarily on economic structure and the stage of development: all agrarian feudal societies, all countries in the early stages of industrialization, all advanced technological economies, and all oil fiefs will resemble each other more than they resemble other countries. In a second layer, and especially in complex systems with strong financial sectors and asset markets, short-term movements of the intersectoral differentials take on an important role. And there must be a transnational element, reflecting the integration of economies and the influence of the large and strong over the small and weak.

But we also think that all this is in no contradiction to Simon Kuznets. He combined theory, history, and common sense, and he was very well aware that the world continues to change. He would not have been surprised or disturbed to see his original historical description modified in this way by events. The question to ask next is, Was it?

New Data for a New Look at Kuznets's Hypothesis

So, in the sense just given, was Kuznets basically right after all? Is there a systematic relationship between economic structure—taking into account also the differentials between structural elements of an economy—and economic inequality? Is there a relationship, in particular, between the level of income and the level of inequality, allowing the relationship to be elaborately nonlinear and to shift from time to time? Having restated the argument, the question requires another look.

Apart from the theoretical questions of what exactly to expect, as an empirical project the issue of a consistent relationship between inequality and the level of development is obscured by the gaps, inconsistencies, difficulties of clear interpretation, and general noisiness of the datasets that have been deployed to analyze this question. It is easy to grow discouraged when the data do not cooperate and such a consistent relationship between income and inequality cannot be found. But the failure to find a relationship in bad data is a nonresult, which establishes nothing. It remains always possible that a cleaner, clearer look at the data will reveal patterns that cannot be found in sparse, noisy, and inconsistent data.[7] Another look therefore requires new evidence. As Holmes said to Watson in "The Case of the Copper Beeches": "Data! Data! Data! I cannot make bricks without clay!"

This section provides the bricks with which a coherent evaluation of the Kuznets hypothesis—conceived broadly as a consistent relationship between the level of economic development and the level of economic inequality,[8] on a global scale and in the context of economic developments in the late twentieth century—can be made.

The UTIP-UNIDO global dataset, described in the previous chapter, has a number of virtues as an arbiter of the Kuznets relationship. In the first place, it is a dataset that at least nominally covers only pay; as Kuznets preferred, the complications of profit and rental income are excluded from the source information. (Not entirely so, since in advanced economies some income that a theoretical economist would recognize as profit and some rent are recorded as pay. However, the restriction to manufacturing here does mean that, for the most part, the variations directly associated with the flux of the financial sector and its major clients are not directly covered.) Second, the structure of the data has been harmonized over many countries and years, so that the Theil inequality measures can be compared. This means that in comparison with survey-based datasets, the numbers are unusually free of selection bias and noise.

The UTIP-UNIDO data can be used to demonstrate that reasonable specification of the relationship between pay inequality and development is, as Kuznets also believed, of a curve relating *levels* of inequality to *levels* of income. As it turns out, there is a relationship of this type in the data. It is broadly downward sloping in most countries; strong growth reduces inequality, most of the time. However, there are exceptions at both tails of the distribution. China is a low-income country still in the canonical transition of agriculture to industry; hence inequality rises with more rapid growth there, and this connection shows up even in a dataset restricted only to inequality inside manufacturing. This is Kuznets's classic vision for early development, prolonged in the Chinese case by the vast reserve of peasantry even as the country builds the world's largest cities. However—outside of sub-Saharan Africa where in most cases industrialization never seriously got under way—most of the world is past the early stages of urbanization.

As expected from our discussion above, the United States and a few other rich countries, notably the UK and Japan, are on upward-sloping income-inequality surfaces. These countries supply capital goods and financial services to world markets, and so their highest incomes vary positively with the business and trade cycle (Galbraith 1998; Conceição and Galbraith 2002). In booms associated with rapidly growing investment or rising exports, income in the high-income sectors, especially technology and finance, tends to rise rapidly—in part because (as discussed above and below) these incomes derive partly from activities in the capital markets. Thus rising income is associated with rising inequality of incomes. And the phenomenon shows up in manufacturing *wages*, because some of the affected industries—notably the advanced electronics sectors that formed the core of the information-technology boom—are conventionally classed as manufacturing activities. They stand in for the whole of the advanced-technology sector as drivers of increasing inequality.

The "augmented Kuznets curve" that takes all of this into account appears to have the form of a sideways inverted S. Figure 3.1 presents a stylized illustration.

As noted, for the purposes of evaluating his hypothesis Kuznets himself narrowed the focus to measures of inequality of pay.[9] Many studies reflect or restate this; for example, Williamson (1982, p. 2) argues that "trends in the distribution of wage and salary income by occupation and skill have been shown to be far better correlates of trends in the size distribution" of income than are conventional measures of shares going to wages, profits, and rent. Acemoglu (1997) identifies increased earnings and wage inequality as the main components of rising income inequality in the United States. And in Brenner, Kaelble, and Thomas (1991), a number of studies that test the Kuznets hypothesis from measures of wage inequality are collected and reported. So the use of pay in measuring inequality for this purpose, though not simple, can be taken as largely noncontroversial.

The further step that we take, which is to narrow things further to measures of inequality in *manufacturing* pay, is harder to justify. The data do not contain explicit measures of agricultural, service, or other informal incomes. They thus cannot directly identify the canonical Kuznets movement out of agriculture

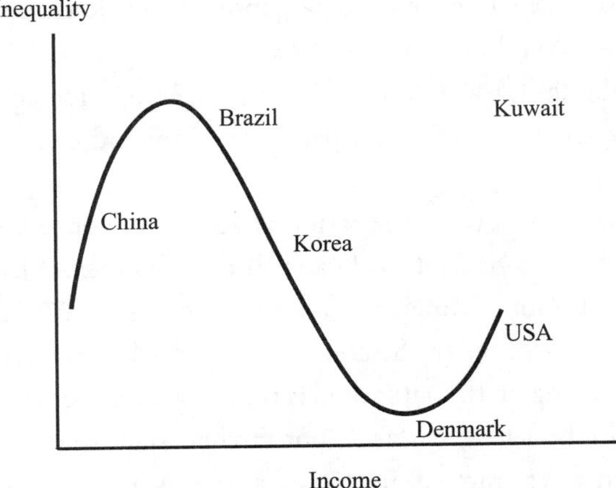

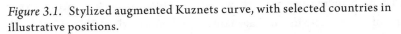

Figure 3.1. Stylized augmented Kuznets curve, with selected countries in illustrative positions.

and into industry. I shall argue, however, that in modern data this limitation is not crippling; in fact it is not usually even very serious.

The use of data restricted to manufacturing pay is of course motivated foremost by practicality; the dataset exists and nothing comparable with broader coverage exists on a worldwide basis. But even though the use of inequality measured only within manufacturing may seem at first glance out of character with Kuznets's effort, it is empirically solid and justified by several considerations.

The basic reason it works is that in most circumstances manufacturing pay inequality is likely to be closely related to the broader inequality of all forms of pay. This particularly includes the differentials between manufacturing and agriculture. Thus, even though we may have no direct observation of pay scales on the farm, we can infer from what is going on within manufacturing what is likely to be going on between factory and farm rates of pay.

To see the relationship, consider the basic fact that in the course of economic development people are drawn from agriculture into manufacturing in the first place by a wage differential. This differential need not be large, but it has to exist; otherwise people will not leave the farm.

Now, when wage inequality increases within manufacturing (something that almost always happens during economic slumps), what does this mean? Almost always, it will mean the *relative* wage of the lowest-paid sectors (garment trades, for instance, an entry point for many rural workers and especially women into the manufacturing sector) is falling. That is, everyone in manufacturing may be losing, but those at the bottom are losing more. If this had no implications for agriculture, it would follow that the wage at the low end of the manufacturing spectrum would dip toward, or even below, the competing agricultural wage. And if this happened, then of course people would abandon manufacturing and go back to farming.

But this pattern of reverse migration is very rarely observed. Only in the most extreme conditions (in fact, I can't think of any, apart from the forcible evacuation by the Khmer Rouge of Cambodian cities in 1976) do people actually retreat from the cities to the countryside. So what must have happened? The most likely thing, in this situation, is that wages on the farm also got hit by the slump and fell at least as far, if not farther, such that the garment jobs remained roughly as attractive (relatively) as they were before. And so inequalities must have increased, not just within manufacturing but in the larger economy of manufacturing and agriculture, taken together. This is, after all, plain common sense.

Next, consider wage differentials *inside* manufacturing. If there were no systematic relation between agricultural wages and wages in manufacturing, then logically there could be no systematic relationship between categories inside manufacturing either. There is no particular reason to hold the boundary between manufacturing and (say) agriculture as sacrosanct, reflecting some fundamental divide within an economy, and to suppose that the boundary between (say) sewing shirts and forging steel is somehow less fundamental. In fact, there are pretty good reasons for thinking that some of the divides inside manufacturing are more difficult to bridge, as with some jobs held for men or for people with particular training, whereas it is relatively easy to move from the farm to the sewing table.

If categories inside manufacturing were really distinct in this way, we ought to observe rank orderings of manufacturing wage categories that differ across countries and change through time, as absolute wages rise in one area but not in some other, due for example to changing patterns of demand for the final product. In fact, we don't have many such observations; such differences and rank-order changes are rare.

Two examples are shown in figure 3.2, which plots the ratio to the median wage for twenty-eight manufacturing industry categories in the United States against those of two countries at different times (Great Britain in 1968 and Korea in 1988). The figure illustrates a general truth, namely, that although inequality within manufacturing may go up and down, or be higher or lower in one country than in another, this has little effect on the rank order of average wages across different industries. There is every reason to believe the same is

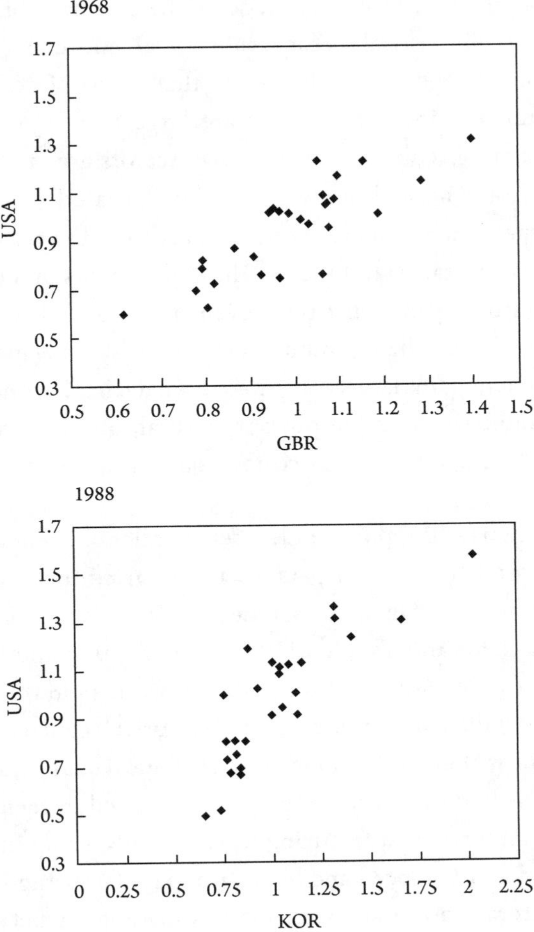

Figure 3.2. Interindustry wage rank order across countries, selected years.

true of the rank order between branches of manufacturing and those other activities that are called services or agriculture. The latter are just as much part of the economy as manufacturing is; the only reason they are not in the datasets is that they are often paid informally or in kind or by very small business units, and they are not so easily captured by established economic records.

It follows, therefore, that changing inequality within manufacturing is likely to be a good proxy for changing inequality within the larger structures of pay.

Two more arguments support use of a measure of manufacturing pay inequality as a representation of inequality in the larger structures of pay. Kuznets's hypothesis was based mainly on between-sector pay inequalities in a two-sector (agriculture-industry) model of the economy, but the role of inequality within the industrial sector is substantial in its own right. In *Created Unequal* (Galbraith 1998), I demonstrated that in the United States the inequalities within the industrial sector are large compared to inequalities within services or agriculture; the latter two sectors are (as Kuznets indeed argued in the case of agriculture) relatively egalitarian. Pay is low and flat in farming, and the same is true of services, apart from the very distinct FIRE (finance, insurance, real estate) sector. Thus movements of inequality within manufacturing strongly influence the movement of inequality as a whole. This is even truer for industrializing countries where the share of manufacturing in total employment remains large, compared to what it has become in the United States. Such countries are often postagricultural, but preservice; therefore, they should be found, if Kuznets is correct, on a declining income-inequality surface.

Finally, as Barro (2000) points out, recent studies on inequality and development go beyond the shift of persons from agriculture to industry as a source of the evolution of inequality. One such focus is the role of technological change. In Galor and Tsiddon (1997a) and Aghion and Howitt (1998), technology raises the concentration of skilled workers in the advanced sectors as against unskilled workers in backward sectors. Of course, manufacturing is the activity most affected by modern technological change, and some parts of it are more affected than others. Inequality induced by technology should therefore have an intramanufacturing feature, showing up in changing pay differentials between advanced and backward manufacturing industries, and also an intersectoral feature, showing up as a widening gap between manufacturing and other activities. Again, *Created Unequal* showed this was true (before Barro), documenting the role of high-technology industries in rising pay inequality for the United States.

Of course, practical issues remain important here. If we had good comparative data routinely covering every aspect of economic life, we would use it. But we don't. Manufacturing payrolls, however, have been measured with reasonable accuracy as a matter of official routine and in a mutually consistent way in most countries around the world for nearly fifty years. The UNIDO Industrial Statistics are the repository of this data, which is based on the International Standard Industrial Classification (ISIC), a single systematic accounting framework of recognized quality.[10]

The UNIDO source permits calculation of inequality measures for nearly 3,200 country-year observations, covering more than 150 countries during the period 1963 to 1999 (and a considerably larger number through the early

Table 3.1. **UTIP-UNIDO Inequality Measures: Distribution of Observations by Region and Time**

Continent	*Before 1965*	*1966–1970*	*1971–1975*	*1976–1980*	*1981–1985*	*1986–1990*	*1991–1995*	*1996–1999*
Africa	28	91	111	122	116	87	97	40
Asia	36	78	92	104	109	102	82	33
Europe	55	104	110	115	120	122	103	47
South America	11	21	27	35	41	46	43	17
Central and North America	24	48	62	58	67	55	49	20
Oceania	6	12	15	15	19	20	16	5

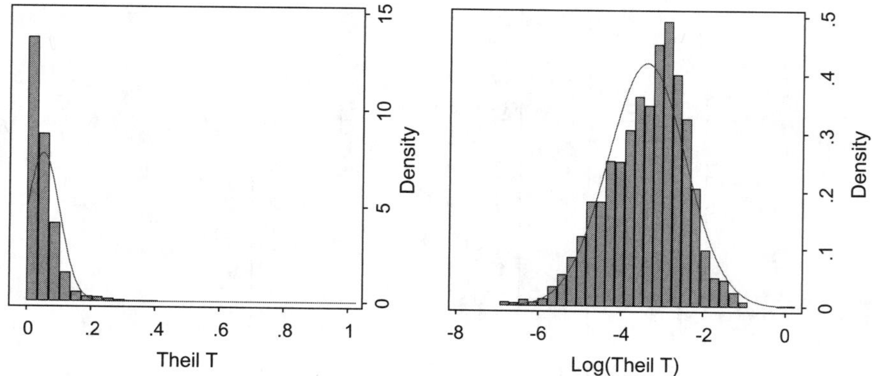

Figure 3.3. Distribution of the UTIP-UNIDO Theil inequality measures.

2000s, which are not part of the analysis presented here). The University of Texas Inequality Project has computed these measures (Theil statistics between industrial groups) and refers to them, as noted earlier, as the UTIP-UNIDO dataset.[11] Matching this data to real gross domestic product (GDP) per capita, from the Penn World Tables version 5.6,[12] and including only countries with four or more observations on both variables, reduces the data to 2,836 country-year observations. The coverage of observations in region and time is found in table 3.1.

Observations are annual for virtually all of the Americas, Europe, and Asia; only in Africa and for small island countries are there significant gaps in coverage. The regularity of the results is also notable: it appears that a distribution of measures of distribution is approximately log-normal. Figure 3.3 presents distributions of the UTIP-UNIDO Theil measures before and after log transformation.[13]

Looking at a few familiar countries can help establish whether the data are credible. They show, for instance, that the United States experienced rising inequality in industrial pay from the early 1970s, as did Great Britain though with more fluctuations, as shown in the bottom part of figure 3.4.[14] This finding is exactly matched in many other studies using survey data, for instance in Levy and Murnane (1992); Juhn, Murphy, and Pierce (1993); and Acemoglu (1997). Since it is reasonable to assume that the United States and UK both have highly reliable annual measurements of income inequality,[15] it is useful to compare our measures of manufacturing pay inequality with their income inequality measures for the years where both datasets report observations. Figure 3.4 lays out this comparison, with British data on the left, American on the right, Gini coefficients for income inequality on the top, and Theil

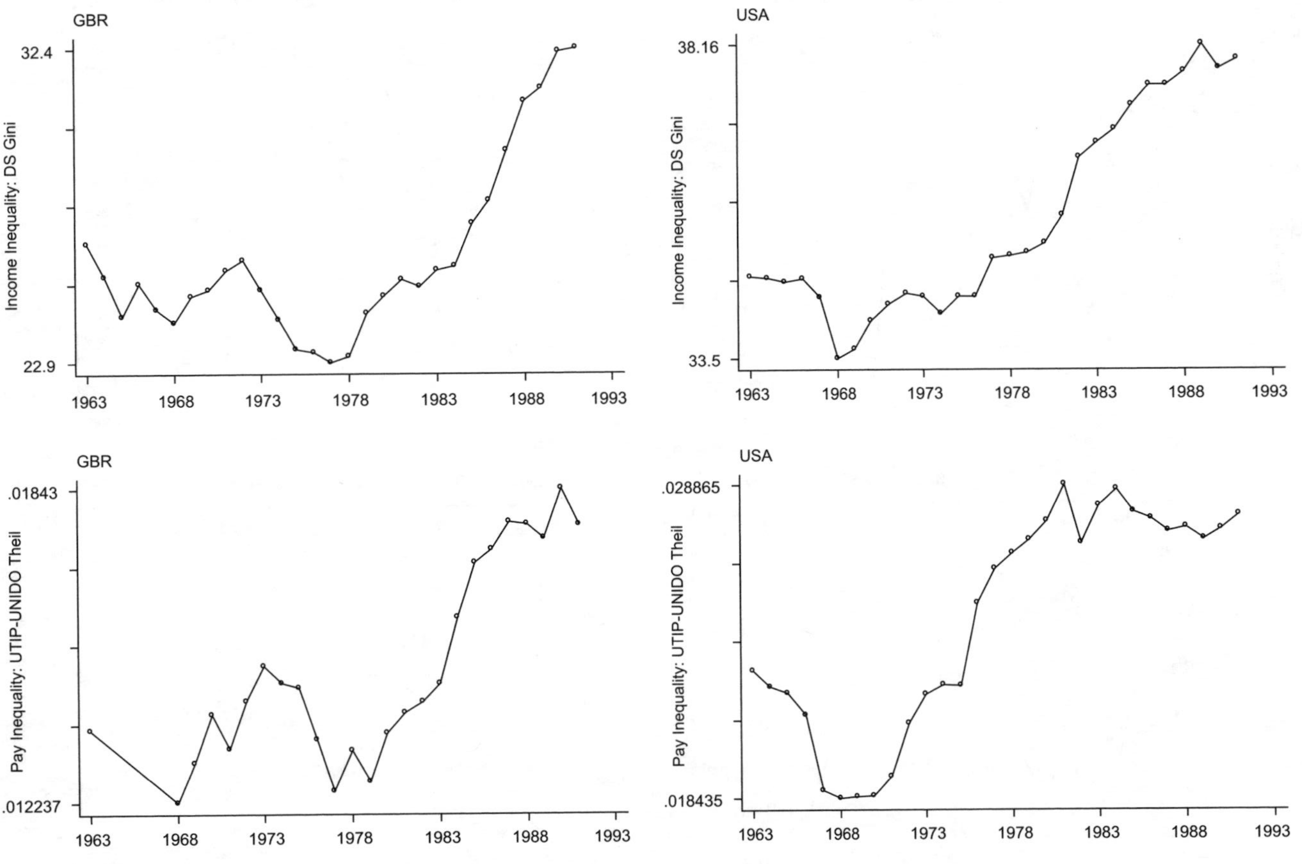

Figure 3.4. Inequality in income and in manufacturing pay for the US and Great Britain, 1963–1993.

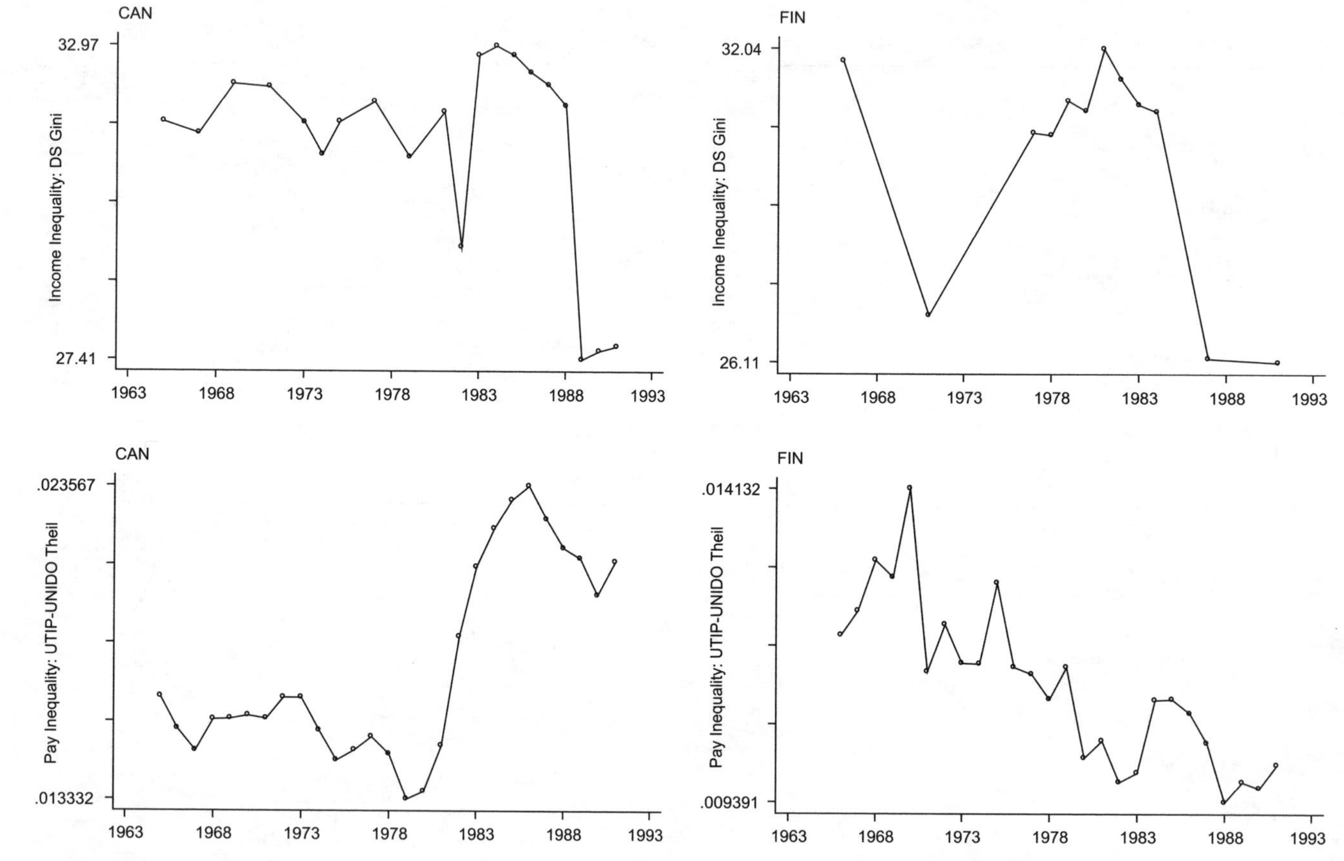

Figure 3.5. Inequality in income and in manufacturing pay for Canada and Finland, 1963–1993.

statistics on manufacturing pay inequality on the bottom. It is easy to see that, in these cases where both measures are reliable, the series are similar.

Alas, this happy correspondence between measurements is not generally the case. Figure 3.5 shows Canada and Finland, two cases where the DS and UTIP-UNIDO measures diverge.[16] The question then, of course, is, Which of these measures is likely the better indicator of overall inequality and its movement through time? There is no unambiguous answer to this question; where there are differences it is necessary to look at the numbers and make a judgment.

Looking at the dispersion of measures over the entire dataset can help render a judgment. The left panel of figure 3.6 presents a simple series of unweighted means of log (Theil) UTIP-UNIDO pay inequality measures, annually for developed (OECD) and less developed (non-OECD) countries, together with bands indicating the standard error of the series. From this, one can see that (1) in general, within-country inequality measures are higher for developing countries, (2) both OECD and non-OECD countries experienced increasing pay inequality since the early 1980s, and (3) the gap in pay inequality between developed and developing countries remains nearly steady over four decades. Atkinson and colleagues (1995) use data from the Luxembourg Income Study (LIS) to show there has been a significant rise in inequality in OECD countries since 1980. These pay inequality measures show the same picture at the same time for the same countries. In addition, UTIP-UNIDO data show evidence of rising inequality outside the OECD, in countries that lie largely beyond the coverage of the LIS.

When the same procedure is applied to the DS data, great fluctuations both within and between groups appear from year to year, as shown in the right panel of figure 3.6. In 1964 and 1966, but not in other years, non-OECD countries appear to enjoy *less* income inequality *on average* than OECD countries. This is a result that can occur in an erratic and nonrepresentative dataset,[17] but it is very unlikely to represent the real-life facts. And since the early 1980s, although non-OECD countries appear to have experienced increased income inequality, OECD countries in DS appear to have not—despite the fact that pay inequalities increased in both groups of countries, and that the industrial sector is generally much larger in the OECD countries. In many other comparisons of summary measures across time and space, the DS data yield equally doubtful results. The UTIP-UNIDO measures, on the other hand and despite their questionable origins in a partial measure of payrolls and incomes, nevertheless appear to enjoy a consistency in results and a correspondence to common sense that lend confidence to their use. We therefore

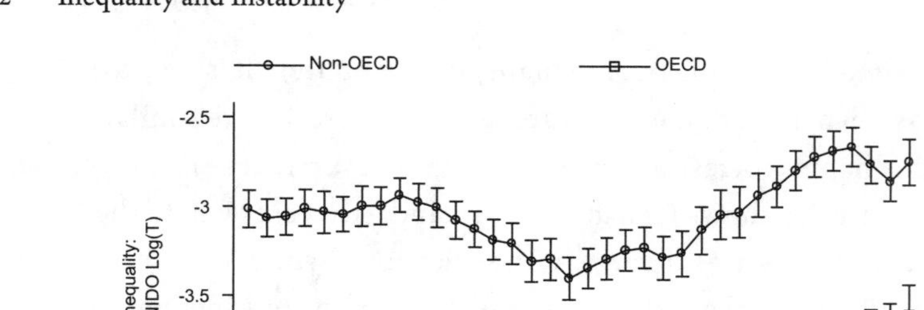

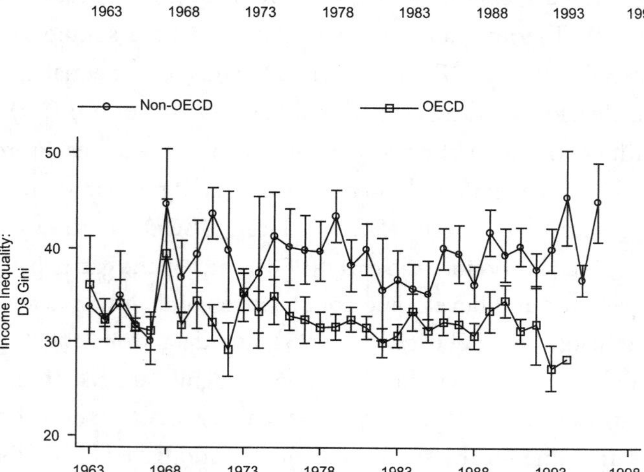

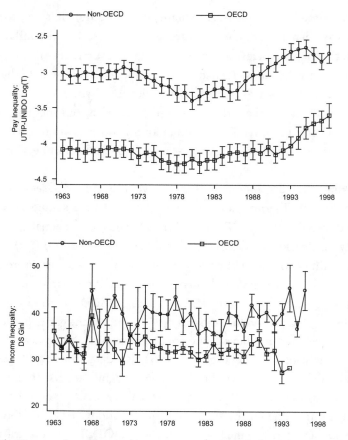

Figure 3.6. Time-series of inequality measures (means and standard errors).

turn to attempting to discover whether they can cast light on the Kuznets hypothesis in broad terms.

Pay Inequality and National Income: What's the Shape of the Curve?

Having established a credible body of measurement, we can now examine the relationship that interested Kuznets, between inequality and economic development, with the latter expressed as per capita national income. Empirical work need not be restricted to a test of the inverted U per se; as we have argued this particular shape is only an instance of the broader phenomenon of intersectoral transitions that Kuznets perceived. The more general question is, Is there a reasonable, stable, detectable relationship between inequality and per capita income? If there is, we can then ask whether that relationship would have satisfied Kuznets, or surprised him.

This approach differs from many studies that have tried to test the original inverted-U shape of the Kuznets hypothesis. Even if the inverted-U curve were a reasonable depiction of the inequality-income relationship in a certain characteristic phase of economic development, there is no reason the (complete or symmetric) inverted-U curve should be found in data regardless of source, coverage in time and region, and underlying state of development. The UTIP-UNIDO data come mostly from after the 1960s. We are therefore in a world of advancing industrialization, and most countries should be over the peak of the transition out of agrarian life. It would therefore be unsurprising if the inverted U, which was based in part on nineteenth-century experience, were no longer present. Williamson and Lindert (1980) also emphasize this point.[18]

The questions before us are, Can new data cast light on this by-now ancient question? In the modern world, if a Kuznets relationship exists in the broad sense, how precisely will it depart from the original version focused on industry and agriculture? How will it incorporate the effects of technology and finance? How will it reflect the position of those countries that are specialized in very narrow economic niches, such as oil and minerals, and whose income-inequality trajectories Kuznets did not attempt to discuss at all? For this, we need to resort to an exercise in econometrics, which some readers may find daunting.[19] An exposition in plain English will resume shortly.

Whereas many additional control variables are discussed in the literature, for simplicity it is useful to focus on a simple, unconditional relationship. Two equations illustrate. The first is a simple linear expression, and the second is a quadratic that permits the expression to capture a curvature in the income-inequality relationship.

Here, Y indicates GDP per capita measured in 1985 international dollars (GDPPC), and I represents an inequality measure, in this case the UTIP-UNIDO Theil index. Both variables are in log form.[20] The error term ϵ_{it} is assumed to satisfy white noise assumptions; subscripts $_i$ and $_t$ indicate country and year respectively. The α_i refers to country-specific effects in panel estimation; these effects will capture country-specific differences in excluded control variables.

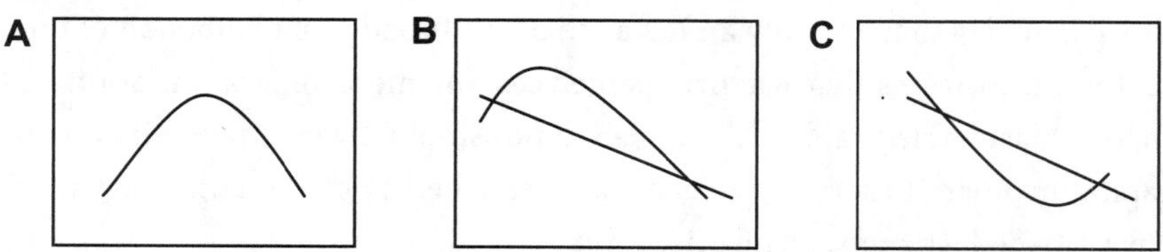

Figure 3.7. Turning points in a Kuznets relation.

Broadly, in a linear relationship the Kuznets-consistent relationship between wage inequality and real income should be negative, insofar as (1) poor countries are more unequal than richer countries as a rule, and (2) most countries are

$$\mathbf{Ln(I_{it})} = \beta_1 * \mathbf{LnY_{it}} + \alpha_\iota + \varepsilon_{\iota\tau} \tag{3.1}$$

$$\mathbf{Ln(I_{it})} = \beta_2 * \mathbf{LnY_{it}} + \beta_3 * (\mathbf{LnY_{it}})^2 + \alpha_\iota + \varepsilon_{\iota\tau} \tag{3.2}$$

to be found on a downward-sloping Kuznets relationship, having already passed the peak of the agriculture-industry transition. Meanwhile the trough associated with a position of advanced supplier to the world economy (as in figure 3.1) will forever remain accessible only to a few. Thus, we expect that $\beta_1<0$.

Equation 3.2, which permits curvature, offers another way to test this reasoning. In this equation, we expect $\beta_2>0$ and $\beta_3<0$; $(|b_2|>|b_3|)$ is usually expected in testing for the Kuznets inverted-U curve. In this case, the expected turning point would be in the middle of observations, as shown in figure 3.7 (A). However, if the data are collected mostly from the downward portion of an inverted-U shaped curve, then $\beta_2<0$ and $b_3<0$ $(|b_2|>|b_3|)$ are possible. In this case, the inverted-U curve is asymmetric, with an elongated right tail. Thus the expected turning point would be on the left of the income scale, as sketched in figure 3.7 (B). A third possibility is based on the (Conceição and Galbraith 2001) findings of rising inequality at the very top of the distribution. If the argument is valid, then a new upward turn could be added to the original Kuznets inverted-U curve. In this case, a downward slope could be assumed over most of the range, which means $b_2<0$ and $b_3>0$ $(|b_2|>|b_3|)$. The turning point would then be found on the right of the income range, as depicted in figure 3.7 (C).

To begin a process of estimation with prevalent and traditional methods, we apply standard OLS with robust standard errors to pooled cross-section data. In this case, $\alpha_i = \alpha$ and the time subscripts are ignored in equations 3.1

Table 3.2. **Inequality and GDP: Pooled Cross-Section OLS Regressions**

Dependent Variable	*Log (UTIP-UNIDO)*		*DS Gini*	
Log (GDPPC)	−0.444	0.463	−1.952	32.128
	(6.21)**	(0.37)	(−1.91)	(1.39)
Square of Log (GDPPC)		−0.056		−2.075
		(−0.69)		(−1.47)
Constant	0.221	−3.376	52.679	−85.408
	(0.4)	(−0.69)	(5.90)	(−0.92)
Observations	2836	2836	567	567
R-squared	0.214	0.217	.004	0.072

Notes: Relevant t-statistics in parentheses. * Significant at 5%. ** Significant at 1%.

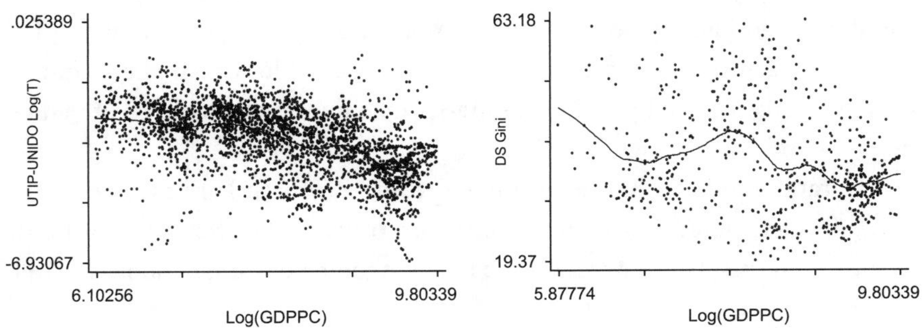

Figure 3.8. GDP and inequality: Nonparametric regressions.

and 3.2. The results are given in table 3.2. For comparison, we also present the results if the DS income inequality measures are used as the dependent variable. As table 3.2 shows, the estimate of β_1 in linear equation 3.1 is negative and significant, and the estimates of β_2 and β_3 appear to support an inverted-U curve as depicted in figure 3.7 (B), with an elongated right tail—but only very weakly at best, since the coefficient estimates are not significant and the model fit is almost negligible.

A nonparametric approach yields similar evidence from another angle. When the running mean smoother is applied to pooled data, a downward quadratic curve emerges. Figure 3.8 is a graphical presentation of these nonparametric regressions using Cleveland's Running Mean Smoother; the corresponding result from DS data is also reported.

Several considerations render this cross-sectional approach undesirable. First, the Kuznets curve is concerned mainly with the within-country *evolution* of inequality during the course of economic development, whereas a cross-sectional approach relies mainly on between-country variations over a limited time span. Second, country-specific factors that may be unobservable or excluded from the model are not controlled for in this framework. Third, a pure cross-section approach is valid only if the relationship of inequality to economic development is similar across countries, that is, if countries tend to follow identical development paths separated only by differences in time. Since this is an implausible assumption, it is not safe to rely on estimates from cross-sectional analysis exclusively.

Panel estimation, usually referred to as fixed-effects and random-effects modeling, offers a way forward. Panel regressions control for unobservable country-specific effects, which could result in omitted variable bias in cross-sectional regressions. In the fixed-effects model, these effects can be handled by adding country-specific dummy variables to the equation.[21] The same logic can be applied to control for unobservable time-related omitted variables; this is done by adding a time-specific dummy variable (v_t) to equations 3.1 and 3.2.

In a random-effects model, country-specific effects (α_i) are assumed to be normally distributed and uncorrelated to any other explanatory variable in the equation. In this data, since only the log of income per capita and its squared

Table 3.3. **Inequality and GDP: Panel (Fixed-Effects) Model Estimates**

Estimator	***Fixed Effects***	***Fixed Effects***
Log (GDPPC)	–0.068	–0.932
	(2.06)**	(2.74)**
Square of Log (GDPPC)		0.052
		(2.55)**
Constant	–2.830	0.706
	(10.64)**	(0.50)
Observations	2836	2836
R-squared	0.214	0.136
Countries	116	116

Notes: Dependent variable is Log (UTIP-UNIDO); relevant t-statistics are in parentheses.
* Significant at 5%. ** Significant at 1%.

term are included as explanatory variables, the likelihood of correlation between country-specific effects and log (GDPPC) would be high. Thus, a fixed-effects model that does not require these assumptions seems more reasonable, despite some loss of efficiency.[22] Table 3.3 presents the estimates from fixed-effects models[23] using equations 3.1 and 3.2.

The estimates of β_1 in equation 3.1 by fixed-effects models are consistently negative and significant, as expected. However equation 3.2 suggests another aspect of the evolution of inequality. When country-specific effects are controlled, an ordinary U shape emerges, instead of the inverted U ($b_2 < 0$ and $b_3 > 0$) as Fields and Jakubson (1994) and Ram (1997) suggest.[24] The fixed-effects model suggests \$7,797 in real GDP per capita as the predicted turning point, around the 80th percentile of the income scale.

A closer look suggests that yet more work is needed. In equations 3.1 and 3.2 the error term (ϵ_{it}) is naïvely supposed to be white noise, satisfying the standard IID~$(0,\sigma^2)$ assumption. However, this is not reasonable in longitudinal data. If the assumption of zero serial correlation is not correct, then standard errors of the estimates are biased, leading to biased test statistics. Autoregressive specification, usually AR(1), is recommended to cope with this problem. Applying the AR(1) procedure to fixed-effects and random-effects models following Baltagi and Wu's method (1999) can deal with the unbalanced panel structure of this data. Then equation 3.1 is modified as:

$$\mathbf{Ln(I_{it})} = \beta_1 * \mathbf{LnY_{it}} + \alpha_\iota + \varepsilon_{\iota\tau} \tag{3.3}$$

Equation 3.2 is modified as:

$$\mathbf{Ln(I_{it})} = \mathbf{b_2} * \mathbf{lnY_{it}} + \beta_3 * (\mathbf{LnY_{it}})^2 + \alpha_i + \varepsilon_{it} \tag{3.4}$$

$$\text{where } \mathbf{e_{it}} = \rho * \mathbf{e_{it-1}} + \eta_{it}.$$

and where ρ is a correlation coefficient among (ϵ_{it}, ϵ_{it-1}) and η_{it} is again conventional white noise satisfying the IID~$(0,s^2)$ assumption.

The estimation of equations 3.3 and 3.4 is presented in table 3.4. As can be seen, the estimates of β_1 exactly correspond to expectation. Compared with table 3.3, the magnitude of the coefficient estimate and its significance level both increase sharply. As the autocorrelation coefficient (ρ) indicates, the serial correlation problem in the error term is serious enough to hamper reliable inference in the earlier specification.

The estimates from equation 3.4 consistently indicate an ordinary U curve with high significance. However, if this result is examined carefully,

Table 3.4. **Inequality and GDP: Panel Estimates with Autoregressive Error**

Estimator	***Fixed Effects***	***Fixed Effects***
Log (GDPPC)	−0.348	−0.586
	(16.71)**	(7.79)**
Square of Log (GDPPC)		0.029
		(3.29)**
Constant	−0.479	−0.495
	(13.77)**	(14.24)**
Rho	0.804	0.803
Observations	2,720	2,720
Countries	116	116

Notes: Dependent variable is Log (UTIP-UNIDO); relevant t-statistics are in parentheses. * Significant at 5%. ** Significant at 1%.

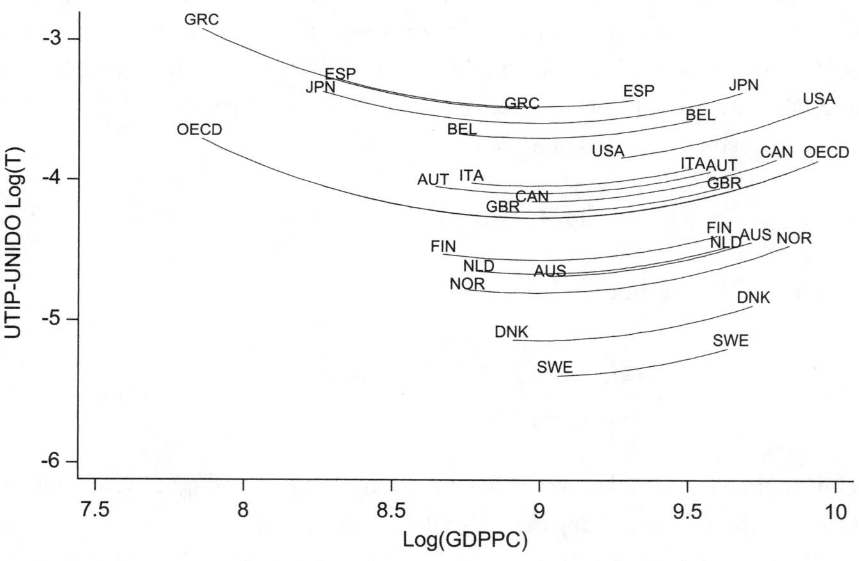

Figure 3.9. Predicted values based on fixed-effects model for OECD countries.

it is apparent that most of the observations are placed on the downward part of this U curve. An upward slope is observed only at the right end of the income scale. Thus at the end of the day we have evidence in support of Conceição and Galbraith's 2001 conjecture of an "augmented Kuznets hypothesis."[25] As noted above, this conjecture relates rising inequality in rich countries to the procyclical behavior of advanced technology and services, and it also takes account of the highly unequal character of certain wealthy monoculture economies, notably the oil principalities of the Persian Gulf. Figure 3.9 presents predicted values from the panel regression, especially for several OECD countries, that seem to lead to a Kuznets curve sloping down over most of its range but rising again at the right end of the income scale.

Thus the relationship between pay inequalities and income, for most countries in the period since 1963, remains essentially downward-sloping. Increases in income are associated with declining inequality, and poor countries have higher inequality, in general, than rich ones. There are some recent exceptions to this rule, but in our postindustrial age they mainly lie at the top, rather than at the bottom, of the income scale. The upward turn makes the pattern of inequality look like an ordinary U, but with a very short right tail. This pattern is consistent and significant across differing estimators, especially when various econometric problems are taken into account, all of which suggests that something more than chance is at work.

We conclude that even after fifty-five years, the insights of Simon Kuznets are, in broad terms, hard to improve on. Yes, the world does change, and having left their agrarian roots behind countries do not return to them. But the levels of inequality across countries appear largely determined by their place in the hierarchy of incomes, and the movement of inequality over time is still, to a substantial extent, a consequence of the intersectoral transitions that continue to occur, modified by fluctuations in the relative pay between major sectors.

And yet, this is not the whole story either. Kuznets largely restricted himself, as development economists are wont to do, to the trajectories of individual countries. It is, however, not only necessary but also possible to use these data to inquire into the relationship between countries. We are no longer in the age of empires, it is true. Still, the fact that there exist over two hundred countries in the world does not make it reasonable to assume that each goes its own way, independently of the others.

Global Rising Inequality: The Soros Superbubble as a Pattern in the Data

As noted in our theoretical discussion, virtually all recent work either assumes or concludes that national characteristics alone govern the evolution of inequality and economic growth. If this were true, it would follow that national policy choices are the key to lower inequality, either in the short run (through intersectoral wage compression) or the long (through structural change).

But the presence of a Kuznets relation in transnational data already tells us that the evolution of inequality must have a global (or at least an interconnected) dimension. We know that growth rates are not independent. Entire regions, and sometimes the entire world, can go into booms and busts together. Thus in the commodities boom of the 1970s we should expect inequalities to have declined, as poorer countries improved their living standards. Likewise, the deep slump that occurred in 1982 and continued for many years thereafter should have pushed up inequality in countries that were, structurally, on a downward-sloping Kuznets plane. As growth (in many cases) reversed, countries in this position should have moved backward in income and upward in inequality, losing gains they had previously achieved through industrialization and economic development.

With a fixed-effects model, we can judge this global element in changing inequality directly. The model estimates not only country effects, showing the importance of persisting national institutions and industrial structures to (industrial earnings) inequality, but also a full set of yearly time effects. These show the changes in inequality that are common to the world economy, whether caused by common worldwide patterns in economic growth or by other factors. In short, they separate out the common dimension, given by the global time effects, from the effects of merely national variations in growth rates, which remain to be captured by the GDP variable.

Table 3.5 presents fixed-effects models comparing the coefficient on log of GDP per capita for a one-way (country only) and a two-way (time and country) fixed-effects model. The effect is to strengthen the model results substantially. Note by how much the slope of the coefficient on (national) GDP increases when (global) time effects are taken explicitly into account.

Figure 3.10 illustrates the time effects in this model. The figure presents powerful evidence of a *global* pattern in the movement of inequalities measured (as here) within countries, and this pattern is marked most strongly by a trend toward higher industrial earnings inequality after 1980. These events were not autonomous, not separate events in different countries; they were synchronized. Contrary national efforts—if there were any—were largely overwhelmed by the global forces. Thus the model suggests that national policy choices respecting inequality were secondary; any approach to reducing inequality must address changes in global economic conditions as a dominant force.

The pattern of the time effects has several distinct turning points, whose timing strongly suggests what was behind them. The first turning point, from

Table 3.5. **Inequality, Time, and Country: One-Way and Two-Way Fixed Effects**

Estimator	*Fixed Effects (Country)*	*Fixed Effects (Country and Time)*
Log (GDPPC)	−0.068	−0.423
	(2.06)**	(9.94)**
Constant	−2.830	−0.122
	(10.64)**	(0.37)
Observations	2836	2836
R-squared	0.214	0.260
Countries	116	116

Notes: Dependent variable is Log (UTIP-UNIDO); relevant t-statistics are in parentheses. * Significant at 5%. ** Significant at 1%.

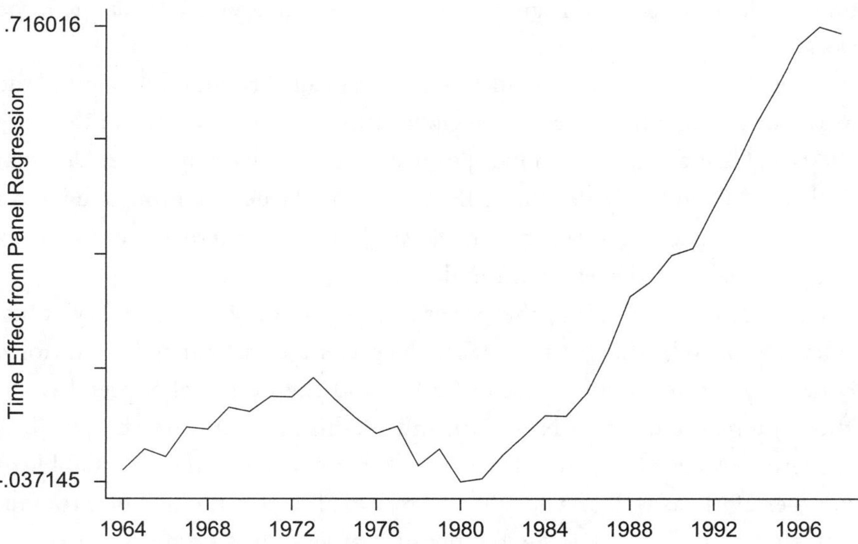

Figure 3.10. Global time-effects from the fixed-effects model.

modest increase to a period of declining inequality, occurs around 1973. If one asks whether there was any economic event of global reach that coincided with this date, the answer is not very far to seek: the final end of the Bretton Woods fixed exchange rate system occurred that year. A general pattern of declining inequality then continues through the 1970s, years of global inflation, negative real

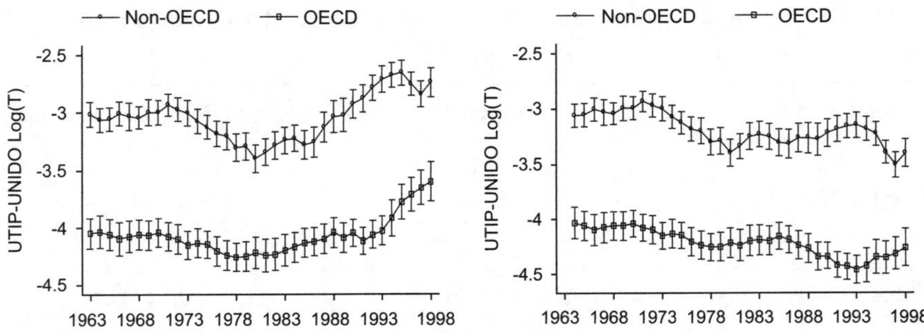

Figure 3.11. Actual and simulated pay inequality: A comparison with and without the global component of rising inequality after 1981.

interest rates, booming commodity markets, and rapidly accumulating debts. It ends in a sudden reversal of the global trend in 1980–81. This is the onset of the debt crisis, marked by high real interest rates and commodity price deflation, a collapse of economic growth, and mass unemployment throughout the world.

After the great reversal around 1981, rising inequality continues around the world for twenty years. There are regional crests in Latin America in the early 1980s, in Central and Eastern Europe, including the collapsing Soviet Union in the late 1980s and early 1990s, and then in Asia in the period through the Asian crisis of 1997. But with these ebbs and flows, the overall pattern is one of strongly rising inequality all the way to the millennium.

And then around 2001, the pattern of globally rising inequality stops. What happened? There was another deep change in financial conditions. Following the technology crash of 2000 and the events of September 11, 2001, interest rates set in New York and Washington fell very sharply. This triggered a revival in commodity markets that peaked with the oil bubble of summer 2008, as well as a vast boom in home financing, much of it fraudulent, that collapsed in late September of that year. It is pretty much as one would expect from a basic knowledge of world financial history and common sense. World conditions appear overlaid on the Kuznets curve, vitiating among other things national policy autonomy in the determination of inequality levels.

A simple simulation exercise can illustrate the significance of the global component in rising inequality overall. Suppose the global component of inequality had, for whatever reasons, remained after 1981 at the average value that pertained before 1980. Figure 3.11 shows the effect on average inequality in the OECD and non-OECD countries separately. The left panel replicates figure 3.5, showing mean values and the standard error, or variation of the individual country values about the mean. The right panel shows the corresponding simulated values. As the figure indicates (and the arithmetic would lead one to suspect), the global component of rising inequality was sufficiently large that, had it not happened, the rise in pay inequalities in manufacturing after 1981 would not have occurred.

The investor George Soros has identified the period after 1980 as a "superbubble" in world financial markets. By this, he means it was a time when economic growth became dependent on unstable financial relations. This work demonstrates that the superbubble was also a supercrisis for the world's poorer people—a prolonged period of worsening pay gaps in most countries around the world. This pattern strongly suggests that the proper conceptual domain for the study of global inequality is *macroeconomic,* and that macroeconomic forces common to the entire global economy can be identified in the data. Indeed the evidence strongly suggests that global finance is a *principal* source of changing global patterns of pay inequality.

Conclusion

The UTIP-UNIDO data constitute a new source of information about cross-country differences and annual trends in inequality, computed from measures of industrial pay in a standard international dataset. The advantage of this approach is consistent, accurate, reliable annual measurement for many countries of a variable that, even though not representing the whole of income inequality, nevertheless has an undoubted influence on income inequality and is also interesting in its own right for theoretical and practical reasons. These measures are particularly important for an assessment of the Kuznets hypothesis relating inequality and economic development, especially insofar as that hypothesis is formulated as a relationship mainly relating national income to inequalities of pay.

There is a clear downward-sloping relationship between inequality and national income in these data for most countries, vindicating a core premise of the Kuznets hypothesis, namely, that inequality tends to decline with economic progress in the process of successful industrialization. Most of the observations lie clearly on this downward-sloping surface. However, at least one major country, China, remains on an upward-sloping trajectory, and there is evidence that for the richest countries the relationship may reverse, yielding rising inequality as incomes increase. This leads to an upright augmented Kuznets curve with a turning point at a high income level. As argued earlier in the chapter, this finding is fully consistent with the spirit of Kuznets's argument.

There is also strong evidence that this (mainly) downward-sloping Kuznets relationship shifted relentlessly outward in the years between 1982 and 2000 for developing and developed countries alike. This evidence points to changes in the global economy, largely independent of national policies, generating higher inequalities almost everywhere. The outward shift reversed, to a small degree, from 2001 to 2004, when global credit conditions finally eased.

The personal or household distribution of income has traditionally been considered as a problem largely in applied microeconomics, specifically labor economics, and therefore a function of supply and demand in markets. This has permitted analysts to focus on policy choices at the national level, where they have often been preoccupied with such issues as education, training, and the structure of labor markets. The new data suggest, instead, that macroeconomics—*global macroeconomics,* with an emphasis on financial governance and financial instability—is the correct framework for coherently explaining the relationship between inequality, unemployment, and growth. The data show clearly that Kuznets was right about an organic relationship between inequality and intersectoral change at the national level, although the precise character of the relationship evolves with economic change. The missing ingredient, now supplied, is the influence of Keynesian and Minskyan forces at the global level—that is to say, of financial forces operating on the world's economy as a whole.

Appendix

ON A PRESUMED LINK FROM INEQUALITY TO GROWTH

This appendix presents a brief discussion of the recent literature that seeks a prior inequality and later growth rates. This literature is at sharp odds with itself over lines of causation. Thus Forbes (2000) argued that increases in inequality are followed in the short run by increased rates of economic growth. She refers to several theoretical models prefiguring her result, including those of Bénabou (1996), who emphasizes complementarities between individuals' human capital in local as opposed to global interactions, and of Galor and Tsiddon (1997b), who stress the role of technological change in raising the concentration of skilled workers in the advanced sectors. Forbes's argument and finding challenged a popular view that *decreasing* inequality should lead to improved conditions for growth. Models positing a negative relationship were rooted in the apparent experience of East Asia following land reforms and the spread of universal primary education (Birdsall, Ross, and Sabot 1995).

In both of these models, the relevant increases in inequality would certainly have an interindustrial character—not exclusively perhaps, but prominently so. That is, they would show up in an increasing differential of pay between advanced and backward industries within the manufacturing sector. This fact permits an evaluation of Forbes's hypothesis using the UTIP-UNIDO data. Forbes's model takes the general form

$$\mathbf{Growth}_{it} = \beta_1 \mathbf{Inequality}_{i,t-1} + \beta_2 \mathbf{Income}_{i,t-1} + \gamma \mathbf{X}_{i,t-1} + \mathbf{v}_i + \mathbf{u}_t + \mathbf{e}_{it}.$$

Growth stands for growth rate measured over a five-year interval, and the **X** is a matrix of conditioning variables on education and market distortions drawn from the Barro-Lee (1994) and Penn World Tables datasets, respectively. Income is per capita real GDP measured in 1985 international dollars. Data limitations restrict Forbes to 180 observations across forty-five countries, nearly half in the OECD. The 180 observations are five-year intervals that are not overlapping within countries, but that of course do overlap across countries. Country (v_i) and period (u_t) dummies control for country and time effects respectively.

This evaluation follows Forbes's general model, except insofar as the UTIP-UNIDO dataset has many more observations than the Barro-Lee dataset of conditioning variables, so we omit the $\mathbf{X}_{i,\,t-1}$ and rely on country and time effects alone.

Reestimating the Forbes equation, using the Gini coefficients she reports but without the conditioning variables or the lag, gives model 1, with 193 observations. In all cases, we control for log per capita GDP. As table 3.A1 illustrates, this model does not yield a significant coefficient for the DS Gini inequality variable. The same regression using the UTIP-UNIDO Theil data does show the Forbes result: a positive coefficient on the inequality measure as a determinant of the current (five-year) period rate of growth (model 2). However, the significance of the estimate is marginal. The inconsistency of the estimates is also a problem, as discussed below.

Models 3 and 4 of table 3.A1 repeat this exercise for a one-period (five-year) lag in the growth rate (122 observations). In these models, significance disappears entirely; neither the DS nor the UTIP-UNIDO measures show any relationship to subsequent growth rates for this sample. We conclude that Forbes's finding of such a relationship must depend on introduction of the control variables; it apparently cannot be replicated without them. Moreover, as model 5 illustrates, running the same five-year exercise on the full UTIP-UNIDO sample (1,571 overlapping observations) reverses the Forbes result and supports Birdsall. Now inequality has a negative effect on growth over the following five years, and the coefficient is ostensibly significant.

A disadvantage of this procedure, discussed by Forbes, lies in the presence of a lagged endogenous variable on the right-hand side. Moreover, with a near certainty of serial correlation in the error terms (due to time overlap, especially in model 5) and an absence of independent instruments, the Chamberlain B-matrix or the Arellano-Bond (1991) procedures cannot be used to overcome these difficulties. The upshot is that one cannot be confident of the statistical significance on the coefficient on inequality in model 5—the only significant result in this table—and the comfort these estimates lend to the equality-is-good-for-growth hypothesis should be counted as modest.

Models 6 and 7 of table 3.A2 show panel estimates for a one-year lag, first using data from the full DS dataset (209 observations) and then a matched set of UTIP-UNIDO Theil measures. Here annual values instead of five-year average values of each variable in the data are used. Neither shows a significant effect of inequality on growth in the following year. Finally, model 8 shows panel estimates for the full UTIP-UNIDO dataset with a one-year lag (2,267 observations). Again, there is no significant relationship between inequality and subsequent growth in the estimates.[26]

Still, the sign of the coefficient on inequality does contradict the proposition that increases in pay inequality are likely to produce improvements in subsequent growth rates as a general rule. If this relationship cannot be found in pay data, it is almost surely not valid for income data either. Thus the evidence shows that Forbes's results cannot be replicated in a more comprehensive dataset based on a more relevant measure of the inequality of pay. This would appear to weigh against accepting either the Bénabou or the

Table 3.A1. **Inequality, Income, and Growth: Five-Year Average Growth Rates**

	Model 1	*Model 2*	*Model 3*	*Model 4*	*Model 5*
	No Time Lag			*Five-Year Lag*	
Dependent variable	Growth	Growth	Growth (+5)	Growth (+5)	Growth (+5)
Intercept	–29.936	–36.002	16.967	18.158	44.76
	(–2.37)*	(–2.83)*	(0.9)	(0.32)	(16.59)**
DS	0.056		0.108		
	(0.9)		(1.22)		
UTIP-UNIDO		26.134		21.981	–4.973
		(2.04)*		(0.14)	(–2.64)*
Log (GDPPC)	2.951	3.876	–2.364	–2.014	–13.654
	(2.0)	(2.53)*	(–1.23)	(0.3)	(–16.59)**
R-squared	0.79	0.8	0.76	0.77	0.65
N	193	193	122	122	1571
No. of countries	50	50	33	33	81
No. of years	32	32	26	26	28

Notes: Growth = growth rate of per capita GDP, one-period lag (5-year average). DS = high-quality Gini coefficient from Deininger and Squire dataset. UTIP-UNIDO = interindustry Theil coefficient from UTIP, based on UNIDO Industrial Statistics. Log (GDPPC) = log of per capital real GDP, in 1985 international dollars. Relevant t-statistics are in parentheses. * Significant at 5%. ** Significant at 1%.

Galor and Tsiddon theoretical arguments for a link between higher inequality and subsequently increasing growth.

Notes

1. Robinson (1976) gave a simple formal model of the inverted U. In classic studies, Ahluwalia (1976) and Papanek and Kyn (1986) supported the Kuznets hypothesis with curves estimated from empirical data. Fields (1980) is an early exploration of the relationship of poverty and inequality to growth.
2. Kuznets did not emphasize this second factor, understandably insofar as it was not likely to be important in the broad sweep of the agriculture-industry transition, and

Table 3.A2. **Inequality, Income and Growth: Annual Measures**

	Model 6	*Model 7*	*Model 8*
		One-Year Lag	
Dependent variable	Growth (+1)	Growth (+1)	Growth (+1)
Intercept	33.683	40.324	22.861
	(1.79)	(2.39)*	(5.32)**
DS	0.054		
	(0.56)		
UTIP-UNIDO		–6.356	0.465
		(–0.23)	(–0.18)
Log (GDPPC)	–3.823	–4.234	–3.083
	(–2.13)*	(–2.38)*	(–5.59)**
R-squared	0.66	0.66	0.24
N	209	209	2267
No. of countries	22	22	105
No. of years	33	33	35

Notes: Growth = growth rate of per capita GDP; lagged 1 year. DS = high-quality Gini coefficient from Deininger and Squire dataset. UTIP-UNIDO + interindustry Theil coefficient from UTIP, based on UNIDO Industrial Statistics. Log (GDPPC) = log of per capital real GDP, in 1985 international dollars. Relevant t-statistics are in parentheses. * Significant at 5%. ** Significant at 1%.

perhaps also because he did not have access to short-term data. But it is reasonable to treat it as implicit in his line of argument.

3. Tsakloglou (1988) defends the inverted-U hypothesis, with institutional qualifications. Anand and Kanbur (1993) and List and Gallet (1999) offer early critiques of the standard form of the inequality-development relationship. Randolph and Lott (1993) argue that the income-inequality relation slopes downward but that the effects of development on equalization are weak and slow. Thorbecke and Charamulind (2002) provide a review of many papers in this area.
4. How the initial period is chosen, except by happenstance of the data, is often not clearly explained.
5. Levine and Renelt (1992); Caselli, Esquivel, and Lefort (1996); and Chang and Ram (2000) are examples. The underlying ideas are roughly that the increased saving associated with high inequality supports growth, or alternatively that the wide distribution of opportunity associated with low inequality promotes incentives to work, to the same effect.

6. This was the position taken with me by the late Paul Samuelson, in private correspondence.
7. The famous phrase of U.S. Defense Secretary Donald Rumsfeld—that the absence of evidence is not evidence of absence—is relevant here. If a noisy dataset shows no evidence, that is absence of evidence, not conclusive proof that a relationship does not exist. On the other hand, if an imperfect dataset shows a relationship, that is strong evidence that a relationship does in fact exist.
8. Or equivalently, change in income can be related to change in inequality, consistent on position in the structural relationship. The remainder of this chapter is adapted with major revisions from James K. Galbraith and Hyunsub Kum, "Inequality and Economic Growth: A Global View Based on Measures of Pay," *CESifo Economic Studies* 49(4), 2003, 527–56.
9. We use "pay" to refer to what is reported as "payroll" in manufacturing surveys. It will include wages and salaries, and it may also include a measure of the value of fringe benefits.
10. Among mainstream economists, Rodrik (1999) and Berman (2000) have endorsed the comparability and accuracy of the UNIDO dataset. However, the category schemes have changed from time to time, introducing complications with inequality measures, which have to be overcome by careful adjustment of the data. Unfortunately, this slows the production of updates whenever the underlying dataset is improved.
11. To clarify, responsibility for the inequality calculations rests entirely with UTIP; UNIDO is the supplier of the underlying dataset on payrolls and employment. The most recent version of the UTIP-UNIDO dataset can be downloaded from the UTIP at http://utip.gov.utexas.edu.
12. The Penn World Tables (Heston, Summers, and Aten, 2002) are available at http://pwt.econ.upenn.edu/.
13. Because of the skewness of the Theil statistic, we prefer the log transformation in econometric work.
14. There is a sharp increase in measured interindustrial pay inequality in the United States after 1997, due almost entirely to rising earnings in the computer sector.
15. In the DS dataset, the Gini for the United States is based on household income, but that for Great Britain is based on per capita income.
16. There are many possible reasons for this divergence, among them measurement error, missing observations, and conceptual differences.
17. Here the sparseness of the DS dataset is largely at fault: country coverage shifts radically from one year to the next, lending instability to global averages calculated yearly.
18. Kuznets also faced this limitation. As Lindert (1991, p. 213) observes, despite "his fairly certain argument on decreasing inequality with economic growth, he was much less certain about earlier trends, voicing only the hunch that there may have been a slight movement toward wider gaps between rich and poor in the earlier phases of modern economic growth."
19. In presenting it, I am again grateful for the work of my collaborator, Hyunsub Kum.
20. We employ a log transformation of GDPPC for two reasons: (1) its distribution is much more like the normal than that of GDPPC, and (2) it is superior in a J-test for a nonnested model (Davidson and MacKinnon 1981). Additional support comes from the test result for linearity and log-linearity, also proposed by Davidson and MacKinnon (1981) and Greene (2000), which favors Log (Theil) as the dependent variable and Log (GDPPC) as the independent variable.
21. Greene (2000) also notes that this can alleviate potential heteroscedasticity across countries.
22. Related to this, we perform two formal specification tests. One is Breusch and Pagan's LM test (1980), to see the relevance of random-effects specification. If the test statistic rejects the null hypothesis (which it does in this case), then a random-effects model would be preferred. The other test is a Hausman test for specification (1978). The null

hypothesis in this test is that country-specific effects are not correlated with any regressors in the model equation, implying that the estimates are efficient. If this null is rejected, the random effects model estimates are inconsistent and fixed-effects model specification would be preferred. Our test results show that a random-effects model yields inconsistent estimates in equations 3.1 and 3.2. Based on these test results, the estimates from a fixed-effects model appear more robust in present circumstances.

23. Before assaying the interpretation of estimates, I will note that it is clear that the fixed-effect model suffers from heteroscedasticity. Modified Wald test statistics are all significant at any conventional level. However, this is not surprising considering the data: more than 75 percent of variations in inequality stem from cross-country differences rather than from variation through time within country. As far as goodness of fit goes, only 0.8 percent of total variation in inequality is explained by the time variable in DS data, and it is significant only at a 5 percent level. In our data, this magnitude is 3 percent, which is still small, but statistically significant at any conventional level.
24. Especially Ram (1997) uses DS data.
25. See also Galbraith (1998) and Conceição and Galbraith (2001). Milanovic earlier made use of this phrase in an unrelated context; we appropriate it with due apologies.
26. It is interesting that there is evidence here of unconditional convergence: countries with lower GDP per capita tended to have higher growth rates, all things taken into account, in the sample period.

CHAPTER 4

Estimating the Inequality of Household Incomes

As described in chapter 2, the University of Texas Inequality Project (UTIP) has produced a global inequality dataset, based on the Industrial Statistics database published annually by the United Nations Industrial Development Organization (UNIDO). This dataset has approximately 3,200 observations over thirty-six years (1963–1999), in the original version, with updates into the early 2000s so far.[1] It is based on source data that are likely to be accurate and consistent, both through time and across countries. It offers a direct way to measure the change in inequality in manufacturing earnings over time, and we have argued that these measures are good instruments (or approximations) for the overall change in earnings inequality in most countries and a good basis for making international comparisons of inequality levels. The density of coverage permits detailed checking for consistency through time and between countries, and despite their quick-and-dirty nature these measures hold up under this scrutiny very well.[2]

However, the calculations do not measure household income inequality. UTIP-UNIDO is a set of measures of the dispersion of pay using the between-groups component of a Theil index, measured across industrial categories in the manufacturing sector. Though there is evidence that the UTIP-UNIDO measures provide a sensitive index of changes in distribution generally, the exact nature of the correlation between an establishment-based measure of manufacturing pay inequality and a survey-based measure of household income inequality is not clear, particularly in comparisons across countries.

This chapter offers a way to combine the information in the DS data with the information in UTIP-UNIDO, along with a certain amount of additional information, in order to accomplish two objectives. The first is to separate the useful information from the doubtful in the DS dataset itself. The second is to permit a more informed filling in of missing information about household income inequality. In effect, we replicate the coverage of the UTIP-UNIDO dataset with *estimated* measures of household income inequality, based on the relationship between inequality of household incomes, inequality of industrial pay, and other variables. The result is a dataset for estimated household income inequality that is calibrated to the DS values where they exist, yet much more comprehensive than DS and consistently adjusted to reflect a household income inequality basis.

Estimating the Relationship between Inequalities of Pay and Income

Pay inequality and income inequality are different economic concepts. But they are not unrelated. In most countries, manufacturing pay[3] is a significant component of all pay. And pay is everywhere the largest single element in income. Moreover, the manufacturing sector is not sealed off from the economy at large. Largely unskilled (and low-wage) workers in manufacturing are substitutes for unskilled (and low-wage) workers in services and agriculture, and vice versa. For this reason, as argued in chapter 2, it is likely (though *not* certain) that changes in inequality inside manufacturing will tend to mirror changes in inequality in the structure of pay overall.[4]

A second issue of comparability concerns the difference in measurement methods. The between-groups component of a Theil statistic is a relatively volatile measure, compared to inequality measures based on the full population.[5] Survey-based approaches to inequality usually calculate and report a Gini coefficient. The Gini coefficient, which measures the area between the Lorenz curve[6] and the diagonal of equal shares, is a well-known measure with a simple interpretation: a measure of zero reflects absolute equality while a measure of one reflects complete concentration in a single person. Typical national Gini coefficients range from around .25 at the low end up to .60 or so for the very-highest-inequality countries,[7] and these measures have an increasingly intuitive acceptance for many observers, especially since they can be compared directly. In contrast, the absolute value of the Theil statistic is not intrinsically meaningful; Theil statistics are useful only when compared to other Theil statistics—either comparably calculated measures for other geographic entities or their own past values.[8]

Suppose, then, that one has two datasets. The DS (or its later enhancements) attempts to measure household income inequality but does so imperfectly, owing to inconsistencies in the underlying measurements and other problems. The UTIP-UNIDO measures the dispersion of manufacturing pay across industrial sectors, a much narrower economic concept, but it does so with precision.[9] Let's assume that (apart from biases associated with data types, which we have discussed) measurement errors in DS are random for practical purposes. Though patterns of measurement error may exist, there is no reason to suspect they were designed into the construction of the dataset.

In that case, this model applies:

$$\mathbf{DS} = \alpha + \beta * \mathbf{T} + \gamma * \mathbf{X} + \varepsilon \tag{4.1}$$

where *DS* represents the DS measure of inequality (in Gini coefficients), *T* represents the measured dispersion of manufacturing pay[10] and **X** is a matrix of conditioning variables including dummies for the three types of data source (G, H, I)[11] and other relevant economic variables.

Three economic variables could be found for which coverage was sufficient and for which a good theoretical rationale exists for considering them as determinants of income inequality: (1) the ratio of manufacturing employment to population (MFGPOP), (2) the share of urban population (URBAN), and (3) population growth rate (POPGROWTH).[12] These independent variables may be matched to just under 500 observations in the DS "high-quality" dataset.[13]

A word of theoretical justification is appropriate in each case. First, it is obvious that the importance of the manufacturing sector in total economic activity varies widely from place to place (and in some places also over time). The ratio of manufacturing employment to population affords a crude-but-effective measure of the relative size and importance of manufacturing in the economy, and conversely of the relative size and importance of services, agriculture, natural resource extraction, and government taken together. In general, since manufacturing tends to be more heavily unionized than the other sectors, and since industrialization is associated historically with the development of the middle class, we expect higher shares of manufacturing employment in population to be associated with lower inequality.

To justify inclusion of urbanization, note that Kuznets (1955) observed that urban centers tend to encompass more diverse and complex forms of economic activity than rural areas—which are, virtually by construction, the domain of agriculture.[14] Wealthy people live in cities. Thus urbanization should be associated with greater inequality, other things equal, at least so long as there remains a significant rural population against which the wealth of the cities can be compared. Note that as incomes rise two phenomena occur together: urbanization (associated with rising inequality of incomes) and industrial deepening (associated with declining inequality in manufacturing pay). The effect of urbanization on inequality thus offsets, to a degree, that of industrialization per se on household incomes, and it is appropriate to include it in a regression relating pay inequalities to income inequality.

The population growth rate is best thought of as merely an available proxy for the age structure of the underlying population. A population that is growing rapidly will include a larger number of children and young people, necessarily. Households will accordingly be larger on average and of greater variability in size. Households with lower income are likely to have more children than their wealthier counterparts. This may work to increase per capita income inequality, and it could have an effect on inequality measured across households.

Table 4.1 presents linear regression results. The first model includes only the three dummies for the types of source (Income/Expenditure, Household/Per capita, Gross/Net) in the DS data (model 1). The result indicates that inequality measures based on income and expenditure are significantly different. Whether income inequality is measured on a gross or net basis also makes a considerable difference. However, these patterns become less clear when other conditioning variables are added; the gross-net variable loses significance while the income-expenditure remains significant only at the 10 percent level in models 3 and 5. On the other hand, the household–per capita difference is significant at the 10 percent level through all the models and at the 5 percent level in two of them.

The UTIP-UNIDO pay inequality measure (*T*) is strongly associated with the DS income inequality measure (*DS*). *T* alone accounts for almost 25 percent of variation in *DS*; adding in dummies for the types of data raises the R^2 to around 49 percent (model 2). Running the model in log-log form generates elasticity estimates between 0.106 (model 5) and 0.165 (model 2). Thus a rise in the Theil measure of manufacturing pay dispersion between 6.06 and 9.43 percent is estimated to correspond to a 1 percent increase in a Gini coefficient for household income inequality. Given the much greater volatility of the Theil measure and also the greater volatility of manufacturing pay compared with household income,[15] this appears to be a reasonable value.

The ratio of manufacturing employment to population (MFGPOP) has the expected negative sign with significance at the 1 percent level consistently. This indicates that an economy with a larger manufacturing sector

Table 4.1. **Deininger-Squire Inequality as a Function of Data Type and Economic Variables**

	Model 1	*Model 2*	*Model 3*	*Model 4*	*Model 5*
Expenditure	0.272	−0.015	−0.139	−0.124	−0.146
	(3.89)***	(0.19)	(1.64)	(1.45)	(1.96)*
Person	−0.145	−0.121	-0.081	−0.072	−0.081
	(1.92)*	(2.49)**	(1.88)*	(1.71)*	(2.16)**
Net	−0.179	−0.086	−0.042	−0.048	−0.025
	(2.84)***	(1.60)	(0.83)	(0.95)	(0.58)
Ln(UTIP-UNIDO)		0.165	0.118	0.117	0.106
		(5.47)***	(4.99)***	(5.02)***	(4.82)***
MFGPOP			−0.002	−0.002	−0.002
			(3.88)***	(3.80)***	(3.31)***
URBAN				0.001	0.001
				(0.89)	(1.23)
POPGROWTH					5.687
					(2.98)***
Constant	3.611	4.249	4.205	4.156	3.984
	(98.47)***	(37.40)***	(46.91)***	(39.56)***	(35.44)***
Observations	484	484	484	481	481
R-squared	0.24	0.49	0.59	0.59	0.63

Notes: Dependent variable is natural logarithm of Gini from Deininger and Squire. Income = 0, expenditure = 1, household = 0, per capita = 1, gross = 0, net = 1. * Significant at 10%; ** significant at 5%, *** significant at 1%.

shows lower income inequality, other things being equal. By adding this to manufacturing pay inequality and the types of data (model 3), we can account for almost 60 percent of all the variation in the DS dataset.[16]

Adding the variables of urbanization and population growth (model 5) raises the proportion of variation explained by another 3 percentage points. Population growth enters positively at the 1 percent significance level. The urbanization ratio is estimated as a positive factor, but the coefficient is not significant.

Table 4.2 gives the results of fixed-effects and random-effects estimations, in which we control separately for the particular characteristics of each country in the dataset. It is well known that the variation of income inequality is much larger

Table 4.2. **Deininger-Squire Inequality and UTIP-UNIDO: Fixed and Random Effects**

	Model 1F	*Model 1R*	*Model 2F*	*Model 2R*	*Model 3F*	*Model 3R*
Expenditure	−0.151	−0.011	−0.160	−0.059	−0.175	−0.059
	(3.09)***	(0.29)	(3.36)***	(1.57)	(3.62)***	(1.54)
Person	−0.049	−0.061	−0.045	−0.052	−0.048	−0.051
	(2.86)***	(3.64)***	(2.66)***	(3.20)***	(2.81)***	(3.15)***
Net	−0.034	−0.084	−0.021	−0.057	−0.016	−0.057
	(1.19)	(3.26)***	(0.74)	(2.26)**	(0.59)	(2.24)**
Ln (UTIP-UNIDO)	0.099	0.119	0.084	0.094	0.079	0.094
	(8.63)***	(11.47)***	(7.18)***	(8.75)***	(6.60)***	(8.73)***
MFGPOP			−0.001	−0.002	−0.001	−0.002
			(4.29)***	(6.72)***	(4.50)***	(6.50)***
URBAN					0.001	0.000
					(1.57)	(0.30)
POP-GROWTH					−0.578	0.491
					(0.81)	(0.74)
Constant	3.961	4.136	3.985	4.129	3.893	4.112
	(84.61)***	(92.58)***	(86.32)***	(97.79)***	(51.38)***	(71.76)***
N	484	484	484	484	481	481
Country	81	81	81	81	81	81

Notes: F and R represent fixed- and random-effects models, respectively. Dependent variable is natural logarithm of Gini from the Deininger-Squire dataset. Income = 0, expenditure = 1, household = 0, per capita = 1, gross = 0, net = 1.; ** significant at 5%, *** significant at 1%.

across countries than through time. Thus an explicit control for country may better capture the evolutionary relationship among variables.[17] Here is the equation:

$$I_{it} = \alpha + \beta * T_{it} + \gamma * X_{it} + u_i + e_{it} \qquad (4.2)$$

As the table shows, pay inequality continues to have a very significant relationship with income inequality in all cases. The estimated coefficients are between 0.079 and 0.119 in both random- and fixed-effects models, and they are reasonably consistent with the previous results from OLS. The fact that the elasticities are lower than in the pooled regression does suggest that country fixed effects appear to account for part—but by no means all—of the relationship between manufacturing pay and overall income inequality.

The share of manufacturing employment to total population (MFGPOP) retains its separate significance at the 1 percent level, and the coefficients in all cases are positive and stable as expected. Interestingly, the magnitudes of both coefficients (T and MFGPOP) do not change much in different specifications, which means their effects are relatively independent from those of the additional variables. On the other hand, addition of controls for country obliterates the significance of the latter two conditioning variables, urbanization and population growth, showing that these variables influence inequality only to the extent that they differ across countries. Accordingly, even though this exercise does not discredit use of urbanization and population growth in the regression, it inclines us to regard pay inequality and manufacturing employment share as key independent determinants of income inequality.

Overall, the regression exercise confirms for us that there is a predictable relationship between inequality measures based on manufacturing pay and those based on surveys of income or expenditure, where the two datasets have overlapping observations, and so long as one controls for the many types of income and expenditure survey that the DS dataset (and its successors) consists of. This is reassuring on two counts. First, it tells us that the problem with DS is not arbitrary and fatal flaws in measurement, but the simple and irreducible fact that there are not enough good and consistent measurements to carry out the research we would like. Second, it tells us that the UTIP-UNIDO measures do a good job of mimicking the DS measures where the latter are available; it is therefore likely that they constitute a good source of information about inequality for years and countries where a corresponding survey does not exist.

Finding the Problem Cases: A Study of Residuals

A good job is not the same, of course, as a perfect job. The fact that UTIP-UNIDO is a useful instrument for a measure of household income inequality in general does not mean that the correspondence between measures is equally close in all cases. It is therefore worthwhile to examine whether there are patterns in the differences between one set of measures and the other.

The residuals from the ordinary least squares regressions reported in the previous section can usefully indicate those countries in the DS dataset where Gini coefficients may be too high or too low.

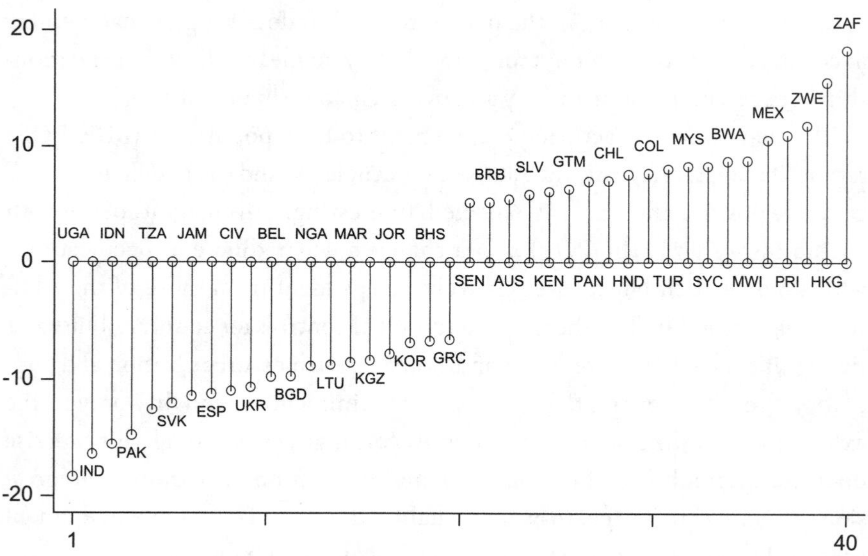

Figure 4.1. Selected residuals: DS Gini compared with EHII values.

The model implicitly assumes there is no *systematic* bias in the DS data. There would be no way to correct for a systematic tendency of the DS data to be too high or too low, and this is a good thing, because the regression could not detect it, if it were so. The deeper concern is with cases where the DS household income inequality measures have yielded results simply out of character with pay dispersions and related factors after controlling for the differences in data sources (H, G, I). There may be instances when the DS measures are implausibly low (undervalued) or implausibly high (overvalued), compared to the model prediction. In those cases, we need to judge whether we may be looking at a deficiency (such as an important omitted variable) in the model.

Figure 4.1 presents selected countries whose average Gini values are out of line with the predicted Gini values of our model 3, using OLS estimation with 484 observations.[18] The y-axis in this figure indicates the difference in Gini values between the predicted and the observed.

This figure includes some very important cases. Four major South Asian countries—India (IND), Indonesia (IDN), Pakistan (PAK) and Bangladesh (BGD)—exhibit reported Gini coefficients considerably lower than what their manufacturing employment shares and pay dispersions would appear to justify. The prevalence of expenditure-based surveys is known to play an important role in this region, and their manufacturing shares are all low by advanced-country standards. But these factors are taken into account in the regression, and even beyond this the estimates are low. The same, not surprisingly, appears true for Spain (ESP), which remains an incongruous choice, by any intuition, to be Europe's most egalitarian country.

On the other side, South Africa (ZAF) stands out with a Gini measure 18.2 points higher than would be justified by manufacturing pay differentials and manufacturing's share in the economy. Is this real or not? Independent studies of South Africa (Milanovic 2007) do find very high inequality—along with Brazil, among the highest in the world. Perhaps most of this is in fact due to South Africa's unique combination of first-world development and racial repression. However, this explanation would not apply to the very high Gini coefficients recorded in some other sub-Saharan countries lacking both South Africa's wealth and development and its recent apartheid past. Moreover, since part of the South African manufacturing labor force is made up of nonwhites, and they are no doubt more heavily represented in low-wage industrial sectors, it would seem that some of the effects of apartheid on pay should have been captured in the observed manufacturing pay dispersion, rather than in the residual. The South African inequality numbers are a puzzle, and resolution of the discrepancy remains open to further research.

As noted, the DS values for six other sub-Saharan African countries, farther removed from colonialism and apartheid, are also quite high in relation to predictions. Manufacturing pay dispersions may be barely relevant to economic structure in most of them. However, given that we can match only nineteen inequality observations for fifteen sub-Saharan countries—in most cases, only one observation per country—comparisons in this region should be treated with great caution.

Other high measures in the DS dataset are for Latin American countries: Mexico (MEX), Puerto Rico (PRI), Honduras (HND), Panama (PAN), Chile (CHL), and Colombia (COL). Mexico is an interesting case, since notably the *manufacturing* pay dispersion across industries there is not very different from that found in the United States. For most of the period under study, moreover, Mexico maintained effective protection for staple agriculture, with a high price for home-grown maize, which surely worked to reduce urban-rural differentials below what one often observes in the Third World. Yet surveys report Mexican income inequality on a par with that in Brazil, a larger country, split by the Amazon, where racial and agricultural patterns are very different. This seems implausible, especially for the period of Mexican history before NAFTA, which greatly increased economic inequality between northern Mexico and the rest of the country.

Finally, we note the case of Hong Kong, where DS Gini coefficients are over 15.5 Gini points higher than our model would predict. This is a telling case, since Hong Kong is a city-state with no agriculture to speak of, and therefore

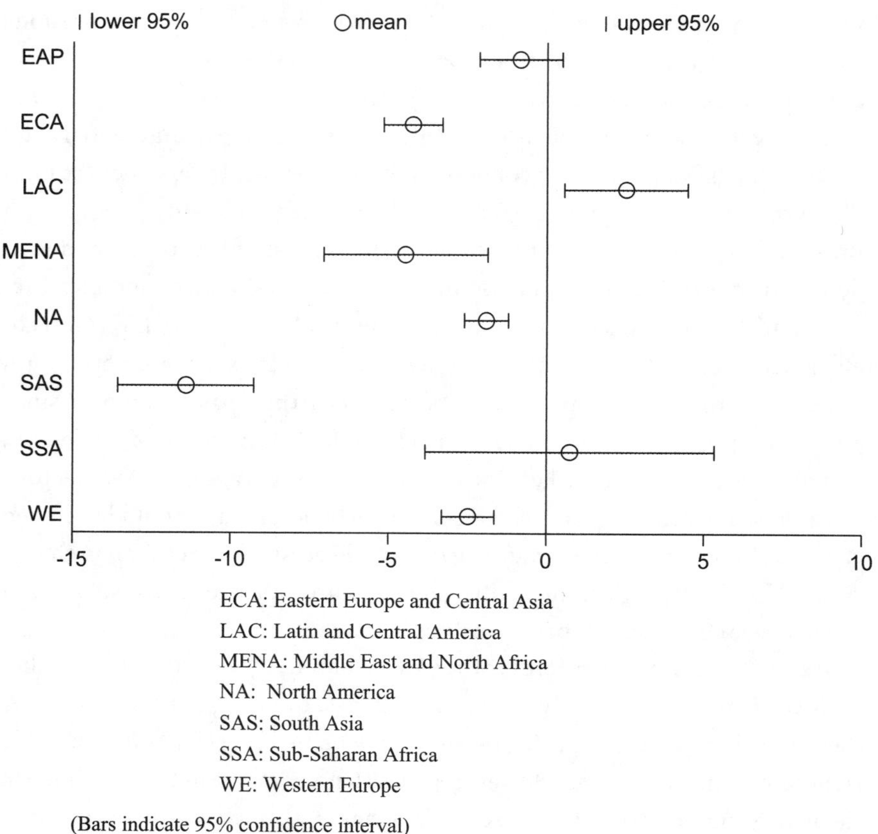

Figure 4.2. Mean value and confidence interval for the difference of DS and EHII.

no urban-rural differential. It is true that cities have high inequality and Hong Kong has rich people, but this seems to be an extreme measure. If true, it may reflect Hong Kong's rather special status as a financial center for the PRC.

Figure 4.2 assesses regional patterns in the residuals, averaging them across the major regions. Several major regions have roughly offsetting high and low estimates, but others have a systematic tendency to come in high or low. The largest consistent apparent underestimates of inequality are in South Asia, as already noted, where DS typically report Gini values comparable to those given for northern Europe and Scandinavia. Parts of East Asia and the Pacific region are also apparently underestimated, but very high values for Malaysia (a heavily industrialized country with a 30 percent manufacturing share) and Hong Kong bring the average up. As noted, the largest *apparent* overestimates of income inequality are in Latin America and sub-Saharan Africa—one of the most urbanized developing regions, and one of the most rural.

Resolving these discrepancies is a task beyond the scope of this work, and it is unlikely they will be resolved. The leading possibilities are (1) missing variables in our model, which could account for the high Gini values in places such as South Africa and Hong Kong, and (2) discrepancies in how surveys are taken in different places, which seems to us the more likely explanation for the very low inequality measures in India or Indonesia. Idiosyncratic differences in income measurement across regions with different cultural and political characteristics, in how surveys are administered, and in how they are responded to should not be surprising, and those differences may be difficult to detect from the reports on the surveys. However, in some cases—notably in sub-Saharan Africa outside South Africa—we simply have too few surveys to judge whether the numbers are plausible or not. Prudence suggests mainly working on comparisons in other regions, where the grounds for confidence in measurement are stronger.[19]

Building a Deep and Balanced Income Inequality Dataset

As noted, the original "high-quality" subset of the DS dataset had fewer than seven hundred observations, with later versions eventually doubling that number. The UTIP-UNIDO dataset has around thirty-two hundred observations. On the assumption that the relationship between the UTIP-UNIDO Theil and the DS household income inequality has been estimated accurately, it is possible to calculate an estimated household income inequality (EHII) measure to match each UTIP-UNIDO pay dispersion measure. As we calculated it, EHII is based on just two exogenous variables: pay inequality and manufacturing share, plus dummies for data type. The variables for urbanization and population growth are dropped, as they add little to the explanatory power of the regression while imposing some restrictions on the coverage. EHII is calculated from OLS estimates with conditioning variables in model 3 as described above.[20] In its log form the "EHII Gini" is simply

$$\mathbf{EHII} = \alpha + \beta * \mathbf{T} + \gamma * \mathbf{X} \tag{4.3}$$

where *EHII* stands for estimated household income inequality, *T* for UTIP-UNIDO pay inequality, and **X** a matrix of conditioning variables, including the three types of data source (H, G, and I) and manufacturing employment share to population (MFGPOP). The intercept (α) and coefficients (β and γ) are deterministic parts extracted from OLS estimation of model 3 in table 4.1.[21]

This dataset has, we believe, three distinct advantages over DS. First, with roughly three thousand estimates, the coverage basically matches that of UTIP-UNIDO, providing substantially annual estimates of household income inequality for most countries, including developing countries that are badly underrepresented in DS. Second, this dataset borrows accuracy from the UTIP-UNIDO pay dispersion measures. Thus changes over time and differences across countries in pay dispersion are reflected in income inequality, in proportion to their historical importance with due adjustment for the employment weight of manufacturing in different economies. Third, all estimates are adjusted to household gross income as a reference,[22] and unexplained variations in the DS income inequality measures (previously *e*) are treated for what they probably are: inexplicable. They are therefore disregarded in the calculations of the EHII Gini coefficients.[23]

This procedure will lead to differences, which may in some instances be best resolved in favor of the DS measures. We call attention particularly to those cases where the EHII estimates are much lower than the DS Gini coefficients. In fact, 11.1 percent of the DS data are higher than 50 Gini points, whereas EHII data suggest that pay inequality and manufacturing employment share could produce such values in only a few cases. If the DS values are accurately measured, they must be reflecting phenomena occurring in other parts of the economy,[24] or perhaps nonlinearity of the relationship between predictor and predicted variables in the extreme cases.

How good are the EHII estimates for those countries that are not extreme cases? Figure 2.3 already offered estimates for household income inequality in the OECD countries, corresponding to the compilation in figure 2.1 of measures from the DS data. It is worth noting that the EHII Gini coefficients are more narrowly spaced over time than those reported by DS, which indicates that changes of inequality in the OECD countries are much smaller than those reported by DS. They are more consistent in increasing from the start to the finish of the dataset; in most cases, later inequality is higher. Also the rank order places the Scandinavian countries at the low end of OECD countries, with the Mediterranean countries ranking consistently high. No surprising phenomena, like Spain and France in figure 2.1, turn up. We consider this to be a good beginning.

As noted, figure 4.2 presents mean differences between the EHII estimates of income inequality and those of DS by regions, alongside 95 percent confidence

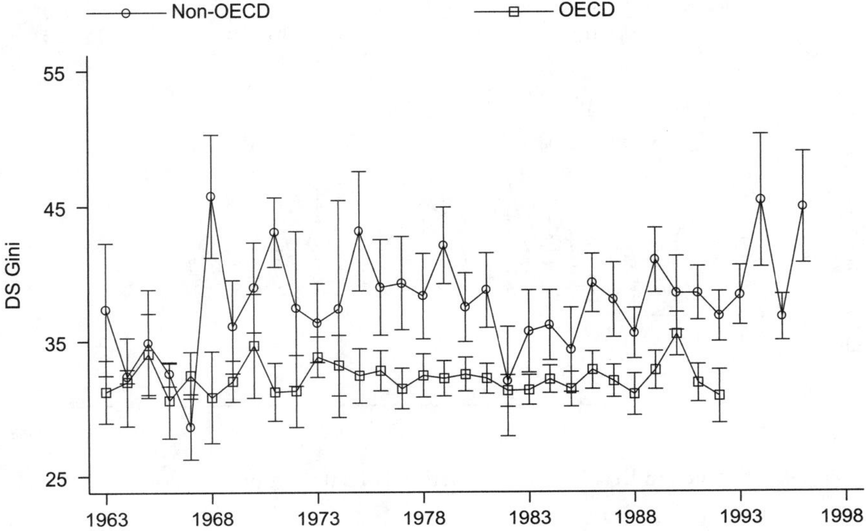

Figure 4.3. Trends of inequality in DS for OECD and non-OECD countries.

intervals. The figure illustrates the discrepancies between the two datasets, especially for South Asia (SAS), Latin America (LAC), and Middle East and North Africa (MENA), and the fact that for other regions discrepancies are far less. For the OECD countries (Western Europe and North America) where direct measurement of household income inequality is likely to be most advanced and most consistent, there is not much *systematic* divergence between average values for the two datasets. It's just that the individual values, the comparative values, and the directions of movement do differ, in ways that do not seem to favor the DS measures.

The question of perhaps greatest interest and controversy in the field is this: Is household income inequality rising or not? Figure 4.3 presents unweighted average values of income inequality for each year from DS, grouped into two large categories: OECD and non-OECD member countries. For each group and year, a bar indicates the standard error of the observations for that year.

The answer given by the DS data is confusing. Overall there is actually no trend in the data for OECD member countries. There does appear to be a rising trend outside the OECD after 1982, but the average values do not rise above their values in the mid-1960s. And the extent of the upward trend depends very much on the degree to which one accepts that a sharp downward trend in average inequality in the developing world from 1979 to 1982—more than 10 Gini points in only three years—actually did occur. Of course, it is easier to

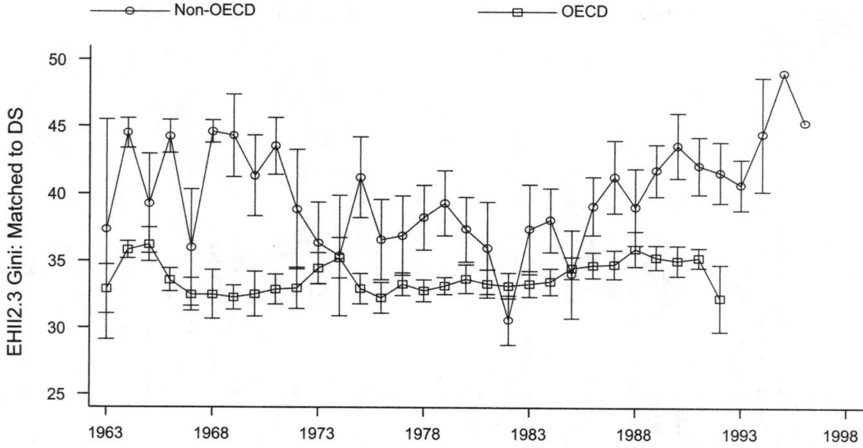

Figure 4.4. Trends in EHII when matched to DS data sample.

believe this than that inequality in the entire developing world jumped nearly 20 Gini points in 1968 alone, or that it bounced down some 8 Gini points in 1995, only to bounce back the same amount in 1996.

There is not really much of a puzzle in these matters. The main reason for the instability is simply the very sparse and unbalanced character of the DS dataset. The sample selection changes so radically from one year to the next that no very meaningful generalizations can be drawn from movements in the mean or the standard deviation from year to year.

Figure 4.4 gives the answer that would be presented by the EHII dataset, were the observations restricted to the same countries and years included in DS. The EHII dataset has some clear advantages. The big bump of 1968 is now merely the rebound from a (still-implausible) down blip in 1967. And it does appear that outside the OECD inequality has reached new highs lately, no doubt partly due to the rise of inequality in the postcommunist states. Still, the implausible downdraft of 1982 remains visible in these data. The reason turns out to be simple: the DS dataset for 1982 reports observations for only a handful of non-OECD countries, and all of them (Bulgaria, China, Korea, Hungary, Poland, and Taiwan) happen to be low-inequality countries in everybody's measures. Similar changes in sample also account for much of the other year-to-year volatility, especially in 1994–1996. This again points out the key pitfall of the DS dataset: no matter how accurate the individual data points may be, if coverage is so sparse, variable, and erratic then observations about averages are inevitably at risk for a high degree of selection bias.

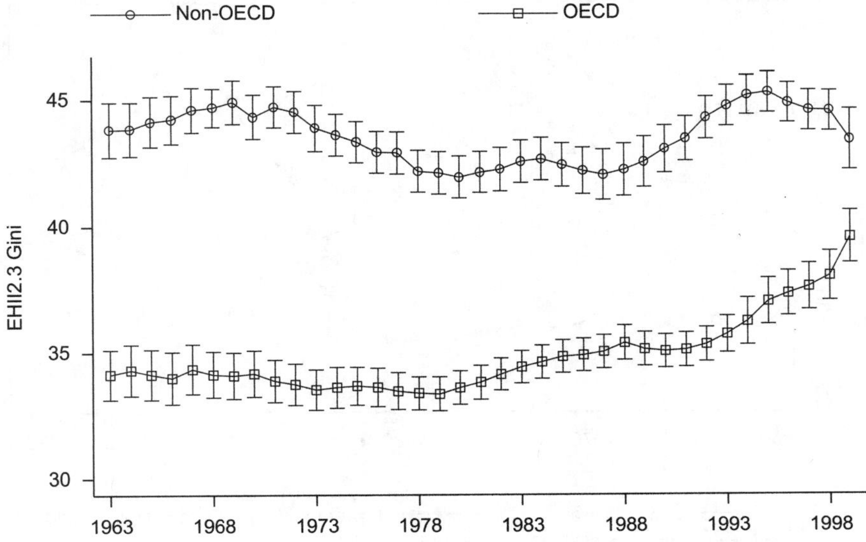

Figure 4.5. Trends of inequality in EHII (N=3,179).

The corresponding advantage of the EHII dataset is highly extensive coverage. Figure 4.5, which is based on all of the observations, illustrates this. What is instantly visible is the fact that average values stabilize, and standard errors narrow dramatically, when compared to the particular sample of countries and years used by DS. The EHII dataset gives fairly unambiguous testimony as to the direction of movement of inequality in the global economy. It is strongly and steadily upward for the OECD countries beginning in 1979, which coincides with the advent of Thatcherism and monetarism, and eventually of Reaganism and supply-side economics. This is the period of high real interest rates, debt crisis, and enforced liberalization, of steady attack on the welfare state—and it shows.

Among non-OECD countries, the relationship between the UTIP-UNIDO and the DS data is likely to be weaker, since pay (and especially manufacturing sector pay) is a smaller part of a complex structure of formal and informal incomes. It is interesting that a secular downward trend ends in 1982 but a sharp rising pattern, in these measures, begins only around 1987. This finding is in some contrast to findings based on measures of pay dispersion alone (see chapter 2), which find the clear upturn in those measures beginning in 1982 for both OECD and non-OECD countries. The period of rising inequality after 1989 appears to peak around 1995, though we suspect that the lower average for 1999 is spurious, owing to lags and missing observations[25] in the reporting of underlying data, mainly to UNIDO.

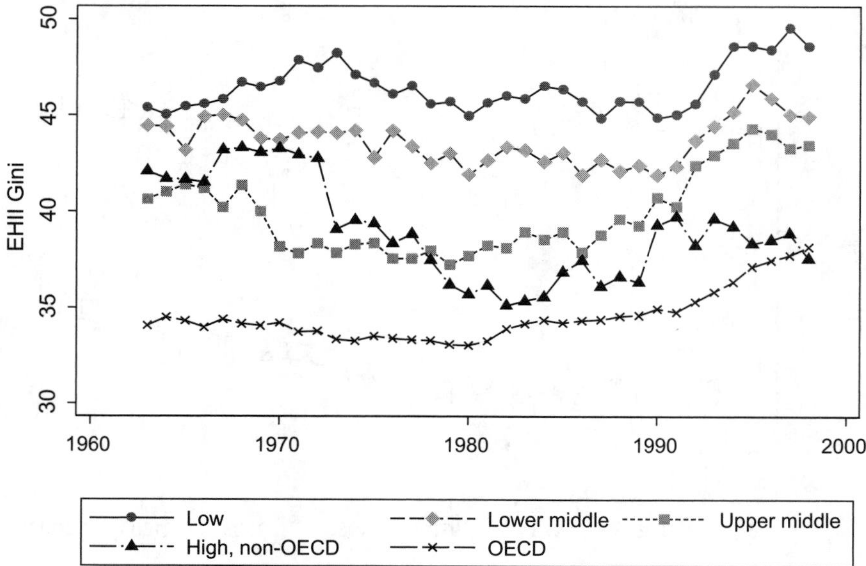

Figure 4.6. Trends of inequality in EHII by income level.

Figure 4.6 shows that rising inequality outside the OECD after 1987 or 1989 is not mainly a phenomenon of the transition countries. Rather, it occurs in all income categories,[26] except that of high-income non-OECD countries—a mixed lot including the small oil sheikhdoms. There is a general pattern of rising inequality in the non-OECD world in the age of globalization, consistent with the pattern found in chapter 2 but starting somewhat later. Also, the long downtrend through 1989 in non-OECD countries is more striking, given (once again) that the EHII data are constructed in part from manufacturing pay inequality data that are clearly rising dramatically after 1982. There may be selection effects here as the composition of the sample changes.

A plausible conjecture not involving bias is that increasing manufacturing activity outside the OECD worked to offset the effect of rising inequalities in the pay structure on household income. This would certainly be an interesting twist to the globalization debate. However, these data do show that eventually the tendency toward rising household income inequality became practically universal.

Conclusion

The evidence of manufacturing pay dispersions, alongside other broad demographic and developmental indicators, can be brought to bear on the issue of global household income inequality. This approach draws on the systematic information contained in the World Bank's income inequality datasets. In so doing, it makes possible extraction of the more useful measures from the DS dataset, while pinpointing and calling attention to the wide range of measures that remain problematic.

The results suggest several conclusions. First, there is good reason to believe that household income inequality is much more consistently distributed across space than the DS dataset would have one believe. Countries similarly situated and economically open to each other (in northern Europe, for instance) usually do not display widely differing income dispersions. Second, income inequality measures do not, in real life, change over time with the high speed and amplitude found in the DS numbers, within either countries or cross-country averages. Third, where Gini coefficients above 50 may well exist on the planet, outside the Middle East they would have to be accounted for by factors entirely separate from manufacturing pay dispersions, urbanization, and population growth. The literature on high inequality in Africa and Latin America especially should take account of this finding; it is necessary to find the omitted variables (if they exist) that explain the high measures. Fourth, there is evidence that inequality in the major countries of South Asia (and also in Indonesia) is much higher than a casual reading of the DS data would suggest. Some of this is clearly due to reliance on expenditure surveys, and the EHII method is a reasonable way to correct for the differences in measurement so introduced.

Finally, there is strong evidence that inequality did in fact rise, through most of the world (but not everywhere) in the age of globalization. These increases are consistently visible in our measures for OECD countries beginning in the early 1980s. The strong correspondence of this trend to previously observed trends in manufacturing pay may reflect the importance of manufacturing pay to income shifts in industrial countries. Outside the OECD, where manufacturing is a smaller and more variable component of economic activity, it appears that the largest increases in household income inequality generally started later (even though rising pay dispersions in manufacturing began, as shown previously, with the debt crisis). However, by the late 1980s inequality was rising almost everywhere, by almost all measures, whether of pay or income.

Notes

1. Because of changes in UNIDO's category structure, the dataset has not yet been updated past 2003, but in principle it could be.
2. This chapter is adapted from James K. Galbraith and Hyunsub Kum, "Estimating the Inequality of Household Incomes: Toward a Dense and Consistent Global Data Set," *Review of Income and Wealth*, Series 51, Number 1, March 2005, 115–43.

3. This refers to what is reported as payroll in manufacturing surveys, including wages, salaries, and fringe benefits.
4. Wade (2002) concurs with this conclusion.
5. This appears to be the case because inequality for a full population is relatively large but reflects differentials (such as occupational differentials within companies, seniority differentials, and gender differentials) that are generally very stable. By contrast, the inequality between the means of fairly large groups (such as two-digit industries in the standard industrial classification) tends to be quite small but variable in response to changing economic conditions affecting the employment and profitability of the component industries.
6. The Lorenz curve plots the cumulative share of income (on the vertical axis) against the cumulative share of the population (on the horizontal axis). It therefore usually requires an underlying survey of individual or household incomes. It can be estimated from quantile shares, but these are built from microlevel survey data. Estimating an approximate Lorenz curve from overlapping grouped datasets is possible, but generally not a preferred way to proceed.
7. The Gini coefficient is often multiplied by a factor of one hundred so as to give units in integers; we will refer to "Gini points" when using that convention.
8. There are also subtle differences in how these two measures capture the inequality of a distribution, with the Theil statistic tending to emphasize the effect of the highest incomes on inequality. But this need not concern us here since it will be fully accounted for in a regression coefficient relating the two measures.
9. The UNIDO Industrial Statistics from which the UTIP measures are calculated report just two measurements for each industrial category: total employment and payroll in nominal domestic currency units. Calculating this inequality measure requires no adjustment for inflation, or purchasing power parity, and poses no other issues of method. The major difficulty in extracting comparable Theil coefficients from the dataset lies in the occasional discontinuities in the number of industrial categories UNIDO reports for different countries and years. In most cases, we have overcome this difficulty by reconstructing the original categories from the published data. On rare occasions, missing measurements of payroll or employment were filled in by interpolation. A fuller discussion of the issues involved in measuring dispersions of manufacturing pay by these means appears in Galbraith and Kum (2003).
10. To improve the efficiency of the estimates, particularly since the UTIP-UNIDO measures are strongly log-normal in their distribution, we take the log of both inequality measures. Thus the coefficient will be a measure of the elasticity of income inequality with respect to a Theil measure of manufacturing pay dispersion.
11. G = 0 if measure is based on gross, otherwise 1; H = 0 if measure is based on household, otherwise 1; I = 0 if measure is based on income, otherwise 1. The information is extracted from the DS data.
12. The population variable is derived from World Development Indicators (World Bank 2007) and the Penn World Tables (Heston, Summers, and Aten 2002).
13. We have often been advised to include a measure of government transfer payments in this exercise, but there are two problems. First, paucity of data cuts down the degrees of freedom drastically. Second, when we ran the regression on the reduced dataset, the coefficient on transfers as a share of GDP was not significant. An evident explanation is that the equality of the pay structure is a good predictor of the generosity of social security systems.
14. Kuznets (1955, p. 8) noted that "other conditions being equal, the increasing weight of urban population means an increasing share for the more unequal of the two component [rural and urban] distributions." We thank Branko Milanovic for calling this remark to our attention.

15. Household income includes incomes from other sources such as nonlabor wage, land, and capital.
16. We further check the estimated coefficients for Theil and MFGPOP by separating the data into groups by type of source (income, expenditure, gross, net, household, per capita). Estimates of Theil are all significant at the 1 percent level, and those of MFG-POP are also significant except in one case (expenditure only). Signs of estimates are all expected, and not much change in the magnitude of estimates is found.
17. The properties of fixed- and random-effects models are discussed in Greene (2000) and Baltagi (1995). In our analysis, the fixed-effects model is preferred to the random-effects model in all cases. Hausman-test statistics are all significant at a less than the 1 percent level.
18. Residuals from model 5 produce similar results.
19. Readers of the original article on which this chapter is based may notice that my judgment has evolved with reflection and evidence. In that paper, we were considerably more inclined to doubt the reasonableness of DS measures that diverged strongly from our model predictions. The important point, though, is that the value of supplementary data does not depend on nailing down the superiority of one dataset over another in every single case.
20. Whether to include or exclude the coefficient estimates on the dummy variables is a judgment call, which we make in favor of inclusion for a number of reasons, especially (1) our priors; (2) the evidence from selected countries such as Spain, where both types of survey are available; and (3) the fact that these variables are significant in the fixed- and random-effects models. On the other hand, after reflection we decided against including regional dummies or calculating the EHII data from models that included country fixed effects. Such an approach, in our judgment, would have amounted to assuming the correctness of the DS data, when one purpose of the exercise is to identify those countries and regions where discrepancies exist and further study is needed.
21. It is possible there are some instances of selection bias. For instance, inequality will be understated where the unemployment rate is high since industrial job losses affect mainly low-income workers. Also, in very rich countries trends in capital income can lead to large differences between the trends of pay inequality and of income inequality, as we discuss later for the case of the United States.
22. It would be a small matter to recompute the estimates to any basis desired: expenditure, gross income, net income, household, or per capita.
23. We remain open to persuasive reasons to transfer additional information from the DS dataset to the estimation of our own measures, but our philosophical position is to approach this issue conservatively. We will add new information to the underpinnings of our estimates when there is strong reason to believe that the resulting estimates would be markedly improved, and only when the sacrifice in terms of coverage is not great. We rejected suggestions to include measures of union coverage or social security systems on the grounds that to do so would reduce coverage to a few hundred cases.
24. EHII has a higher sample mean than DS: 41.4 Gini points compared to 36.3. This reflects the larger proportion of values for non-OECD countries. The standard deviation is smaller for EHII: 7.5 against 9.4 Gini points. The minimum EHII value is 19.7 compared with 17.8 for DS; the maximum is 64.7 compared to 63.2. We are skeptical of the higher values, insofar as the assumption of linearity is less likely to hold for extreme values.
25. The number of countries for the year 1999 is reduced from more than fifty to seventeen.
26. This categorization is based on national income level adopted from the World Development Indicators (World Bank 2007).

CHAPTER 5

Economic Inequality and Political Regimes

One of the temptations of a new data source is that it can be used to reexamine familiar questions. This chapter takes up one of them, namely, the relationship between political democracy and economic equality. In general, we ask whether political systems matter: Does the degree of economic inequality depend on the type of government? In particular, we examine the widely discussed proposition that democracy is an egalitarian form of government. When the people choose, can they (and do they) choose to be more equal, one to another, than is the case under other forms of government?

Our work casts new light on this question; better data do produce a clearer answer.[1] It appears that long-standing "social democracies" do reduce inequality, but most political democracies are not of this type or have not been around long enough. But this exercise also illustrates a difficulty associated with large-scale *qualitative* classification schemes, such as those used to distinguish between types of government. To compare inequality to something else, you need both the inequality measures and data of acceptable quality on the other thing. The business of measuring inequality in a pay structure is (in principle) fairly clear-cut, because we have a single consistent data source and a single method of calculation; anyone else working with our method and data would get the same answers that we do. But the task of developing a category scheme for all of the world's governments is truly daunting; it involves many subjective choices, all of them open to question. There is a diversity of classification schemes in use, and practically any decision one makes might be made differently by another.

Democracy and Inequality in Political Science

Work on inequality and democracy began long ago, and the long view has been that democracy must be broadly egalitarian. This intuition is tied to American history ("All men are created equal"), to Benthamite utilitarianism ("the greatest good of the greatest number"), and to the veil of ignorance in the justice theories of John Rawls. As we have seen, Simon Kuznets also touched on the relationship; the rise of egalitarian social democracy was part of the order of economic development as seen by many economists in the postwar years, including by some—Joseph A. Schumpeter and also Friedrich von Hayek—who decidedly did not approve.

In line with Kuznets, Lenski (1966) developed a theory of distribution stating that industrialization and modernization, along with democracy, work to reduce inequality over time. Cutright (1963, 1967) contributed an early empirical effort, using a calculation of inequality between sectors as a dependent variable, and finding that a more equal distribution of power is related to a more equal distribution of earnings.[2] Since then scholars have sought to refine the definition of democracy, examine more closely its relationship to power, and distinguish between stable democracies and those that come and go.[3] They have only occasionally reconsidered or challenged the fundamental proposition that democracy and equality go together.

Recently, political scientists have developed more precise conceptual schemes, to provide a formal mechanism that would connect democracy to economic equality. Timmons (2008) divided this work on the relationship into three categories: a median-voter mechanism, political competition for public support, and democratically imposed labor market regulation. For example, Acemoglu and Robinson (2000) proposed a median-voter mechanism, according to which democratic governments intervene to redistribute income under electoral pressure. The median voter always has less than the mean income, so the pressure from below should always be for redistribution from rich to poor. Saint-Paul and Verdier (1993) proposed that political competition for public support in a democracy induces an increase in consumption-equalizing public services, increasing equality. And Katz and Autor (1998) viewed democracy through the lens of labor market regulation, under which inequality may be reduced by a policy of wage-rate compression, imposed on a less-egalitarian market. In all of these models, though the mechanisms vary, democratic institutions generate egalitarian results.

Some authors argue that the causal relationship runs the other way, from a prior state of equality to democracy and from inequality to authoritarian rule. Arguing now in this vein, Acemoglu and Robinson (2001) asserted that elites in unequal societies prevent redistributive democracy from emerging. In Acemoglu and Robinson (2006), they take the case further, to assert that *only* countries with a middling level of equality democratize; those with too much equality feel no need to become democratic,[4] while those with too little are blocked as before. Bourguignon and Verdier (2000) examined the relationship between democracy, inequality, and economic development in a model where political participation is determined by the level of education. They argued that higher incomes per capita support democracy and growth, while a higher level of inequality impairs both growth and democracy.[5]

Numerous empirical studies examine the alleged effect of democracy on inequality. Perotti (1996) used data predating Deininger and Squire. Li, Squire, and Zou (1998) invoked DS to claim that expansion of political liberties reduces economic inequality. Tavares and Wacziarg (2001) used DS to examine the relationship between democracy and economic growth and found that democracy is linked to greater equality. Again using DS and controlling for economic and location variables, Sylwester (2002) also found that democratization reduces inequality. Boix (2003), using DS as well, argued that democracy is associated with greater equality, whereas authoritarian regimes are associated with inequality. Reuveny and Li (2003) argued that democracy *and* trade reduce inequality. Lee (2005) examined the interaction between democracy, public sector size, and inequality, concluding once again that the larger public sector in democracies reduces inequality.

Over time, repetition of this result made a difference, and the notion that democracy promotes equality had by the early 2000s achieved the status of conventional wisdom. Yet some skeptics remain. Gradstein and Milanovic (2004, p. 21) conducted an extensive review, covering fifty years. They state:

> While the earlier research failed to detect any significant correlation between democracy and inequality, more recent studies based on improved data sets and bigger data samples typically cautiously suggest existence of a negative relationship between the two. Two hypotheses seem to be especially promising in the light of this recent research: one that defines democracy in terms of the length of democratic experience, and another that specifies a curvilinear relationship between democracy and inequality.

However, in a later paper that examined 126 countries from 1960 to 1998, Gradstein, Milanovic, and Ying (2001) found that the effects of democratization on inequality are actually quite weak. And Gradstein and Milanovic are skeptics for a more immediate reason: they looked at Eastern Europe after 1989, finding strong evidence of *rising* inequality in the democratic transition. Apparently, the strength of the effect depends on the starting point, and there may be starting points more egalitarian than democracy. Further, stability and persistence matter; countries that have only recently acquired the trappings of democracy—let's say just enough to fool a political scientist or the U.S. State Department—should probably not be expected to enjoy the egalitarian fruits of democratic government (if there are any) for a while.[6] Practice makes perfect.

In all cases, the core idea is that *over time* political democracies create an environment within which "economic democracy" can arise in the form of powerful trade unions, social democratic parties, responsive legislatures, and other equalizing institutions. It follows also that in "transitions to democracy" egalitarian outcomes should not be expected until sufficient time has elapsed for those strong equalizing institutions to develop.[7] And they may not develop at all; in unstable democracies—those that are threatened say by coup d'état, or are hostage to external creditors—equalizing institutions will remain weak. Although democratic formalities may be observed, the policy outcomes that might otherwise come with time do not arrive.

A major empirical issue, as always, is the nature and reliability of the measures. The problems of prior measurements of economic inequality we have already discussed in detail.[8] The standard political science datasets on democracy and authoritarianism also are open to skepticism as to what it is, exactly, they capture. Especially, the meaning of the term *democracy* has changed over time. Observers attempting to distinguish democracies from nondemocracies generally draw on concepts of participation (voting rights and civil liberties), competition (presence of other parties), and free and fair elections. In contrast to an inequality measure, some of the scoring (and weighting) of characteristics such as civil liberty is inevitably subjective. But efforts to reduce subjectivity, by focusing on rituals such as holding elections, do not necessarily move things in the right direction. There are plenty of ways to subvert an election, from vote suppression to lopsided deployment of campaign cash to actual fraud in counting the ballots. Alternatively, there may be a free and fair choice, but only between candidates who do not present substantive differences on the most critical issues. Countries holding elections that don't matter may—and often will—be classed formally as democracies, but without actually having popular self-government in a meaningful sense of the term.

Getting down to practical questions, there is the issue of how best to code and classify complex institutions and governing traditions. Some indices score the presence or absence of democracy as a simple (1-0) binary variable. This is a problem, since obviously some places are "more democratic" while others are less so. Recognizing this, other measures assess a "degree of democracy" on a continuum.[9] But a continuum of what? The established indices typically run from "democratic" to "authoritarian" or "totalitarian," suggesting that democracy is mainly about the presence or absence of political and civil freedom. But in relation to inequality, continua of this type are highly problematic. They tend to treat authoritarian regimes of all types as though their most important characteristic is simply how far removed they may be from democracy on the dimensions of political freedom and formal self-government. No distinction is drawn, for instance, between fascism and communism, two authoritarian regime types that, despite their diametric ideological opposition, reflected the mortally opposed class bases of their respective appeal. In an argument about political systems and inequality, this distinction might seem fairly important.

Empirical classification of regime types began with examinations of democracy and modernization by Lipset (1959) and Cutright (1963). This work was furthered by Dahl (1971) and Gurr (1974). It was made more usable by Gurr, Jaggers, and Moore (1990) with the creation of the Polity II database, now a major source for comparative political science (Marshall and Jaggers 2002). Gastil (1991) followed with the creation of the Freedom House database. Since then, additional work has been done to refine or respecify regime classification systems. Munck (1996) produced a rich review of regime classification, summarizing the methods used to construct typologies in the political science literature. One of the most popular methods is to base classification on the attributes that define procedural rules, such as the number and type of actors who are allowed to gain access to power, the methods of access to power, and the rules for making binding decisions. On this procedural basis, regime types can be roughly classified as democratic, authoritarian, or totalitarian. Then there are subtypes (presidential democracy or parliamentary democracy) and hybrids (formal democracy, clientelistic democracy, full democracy, restricted democracy), derived by adding subsidiary attributes to the core categories.

Today the most widely used political regime databases are those of Freedom House (2004), Polity, and Vanhanen (2000). They all grade political regimes on continua between democracy and dictatorship, which is to say that all of them conflate communism and fascism into a single category. Freedom House looks at political and civil rights, using a subjective scale to rank degree of democracy, partly in terms of election outcomes, partly in terms of balance of power. The Polity measure of democracy is based on the degree of competitiveness of political participation and government recruitment and the degree of democratic constraint on the chief executive. Vanhanen also looks at competition and participation, measuring percentage votes for smaller parties and the percentage of adults voting in elections.

Cheibub, and Gandhi (2004) took the binary approach, dividing regime types between democracy and dictatorship, on the basis of data from Przeworski, Alvarez, Cheibub, and Limongi (2000), updated and extended. A secondary variable distinguishes among parliamentary, mixed, and presidential democracies. Hadenius and Teorell (2007) examined authoritarian regimes (as identified by Polity and Freedom House) and subclassified them in terms of hereditary succession, use of military force, and the presence or absence of popular elections. Separate categories are used for democracy as a whole, as well as military regimes, monarchies, theocracies, transitional regimes, civil war, and foreign occupation, for a total of twenty classification types.[10] In short, it's a complicated business.

In an article examining classification of democratic regime types, Elgie (1998) distinguished "dispositional" and "relational" properties. Dispositional properties refer to such questions as whether there is a president or a prime minister, whether they are popularly elected and whether or not they serve for a fixed term. Relational properties refer to the actual patterns of political action. Elgie argued that the best way to classify the regime types is on the basis of dispositional properties alone. Finally, the World Bank Database (Beck, Clarke, Groff, Keefer, and Walsh 2001) included descriptive information about elected executive and legislative officials and their parties, as well as indices of electoral competitiveness and government stability.

That the debate over regime classification has centered on using a democracy-dictatorship binary variable or a continuum reveals the extent to which scholars have overlooked important regime characteristics, notably self-declared ideology (or religion) as with communism or Islam, external rule as in the case of colonies, and political chaos under civil war. There is also a tendency to downplay the time factor required for institutional development; countries are classed as democracies from the moment they adopt democratic institutions. Since these factors would seem on the face of it important for relating political systems to economic outcomes, we felt the need for a modified approach taking characteristics of this type into account.

A Different Approach to Political Regime Types

A first step toward an improved look at the effect of political regimes on inequality requires creating a more flexible *typology* of political regimes. The question we're interested in is very general: After taking into account the effects of income level, stage of development, and other nonpolitical variables, does political regime type affect economic inequality? There is no special need to pose this question in terms of democracy per se; democracy is just one regime type among many—and democracies may well differ among themselves, depending on their longevity, stability, and ideological histories. The point is to compare democracy to other regime types, having sorted and classified as carefully as we can.

There is also no need to impose a prior hypothesis on the direction of effect, even though we may well have some expectations about how regime type affects inequality. A simple analysis may just ask whether regime types differ—yes or no—and only if the answer is yes is it helpful to ask about direction. Nor is it necessary to place regimes on a scale, as indices or continuous classification schemes do. Creating continua in this way implicitly *imposes* an ordering of effect, which is unnecessary for our purpose and may confuse the results. All we need is a simple listing of attributes associated with political regime types at a given time.

We thus depart from the "degree of democracy" method of classification used in the Freedom House and Polity databases in that we do not impose any ordering on our categories. We depart from the binary classifications by not necessarily restricting our classifications to a single characteristic. (It is possible, for instance, to be a dictatorship and in civil war at the same time.[11]) Our maintained hypothesis is simply that regime types may differ systematically in the amount of inequality present in the societies they govern. We say nothing a priori about the significance, direction, or magnitude of these differences, although we are obviously interested in whether it will turn out that democracies—or some types of democracy—have systematically lower economic inequality than other regime types.

The simplest way, and one of the most flexible, to organize the evidence is to construct an array of dummy variables. These are binary choices in every case, but they classify every country, every year, on multiple dimensions. Thus a country may be a democracy or not. If a democracy, it may be recently established or not.[12] It may be a dictatorship or not. It may be a communist state or not. It may be at war or at peace. It may be a colony or not. It may be an Islamic state or not. And so forth.

As in Alvarez, Cheibub, Limongi, and Przeworski (1996), we classify as democratic those governments that hold fair elections for the chief executive office and for the legislative body. We define *recent democracies* to be those that emerged from some other form of government—military dictatorship, communism, or colonialism, say—sometime during the period under study (1960 to 2005). And we allow an extra dummy variable for "social" democracies, to distinguish long-standing welfare states (especially in northern Europe) from other democratic forms. Finally, unlike Alvarez and colleagues, we reserve a separate category for "pseudo-democracy," a condition of democratic formalism but in which opposition parties are effectively prohibited from winning elections. This is a way of dealing with Mexico in the years before 1995, among just a few similar cases, where the term *dictatorship*—though occasionally used—did not seem to us to be exactly right.

Whereas Freedom House and Polity treat all "authoritarian" regimes as being essentially alike, differing only in degree, our approach allows distinctions according to type of government, recognizing that communist regimes and Islamic Republics engage in economic policies quite different from those pursued by other authoritarian regimes. Communist and Islamic states are self-classified; they are labels applied by the regimes themselves, bespeaking in both cases a certain egalitarian spirit, especially pronounced in the communist case. Dictatorship is a catch-all category for one-person rule with no similar connotation. We do not distinguish between military and civilian dictators, since the latter could rarely survive without military support.

European colonies lack a fully sovereign government, since they are by definition ruled from outside. In the past, many colonies were governed in practice according to the creeds of laissez-faire that prevailed in nineteenth-century Europe; in modern times the few that remain (mostly small islands, for instance in the Caribbean) tend to partake of the social welfare systems present in the mother country. They also tend to be largely self-governing despite their continuing affiliation with the "home country." But we lacked sufficient inequality measures on the modern European colonies, so this variable also was not estimated separately. We maintain a category as well for states in the highest state of political chaos, namely civil war, which impairs the ability of the state to impose its rule; this too proved empirically nonviable because of a shortage of inequality measures. A full description of our political regime classification is given in the first appendix to this chapter.

Analysis and Results

Our regression analysis is quite simple and proceeds in two steps. First we regress the UTIP-UNIDO inequality measures on our categorical measures of regime type, a simple dummy-variable analysis with minimal controls intended to establish whether significant differences between regime types exist. We then add a raft of conditioning variables to the regression, following Galbraith and Kum (2005) and other sources. For comparison, we later extend the analysis using the DS inequality dataset as the source of dependent variables. For further comparison, we also regress the UTIP-UNIDO dataset on the leading political regime classification datasets, notably those of Polity/Freedom House, the World Bank, Hadenius, and Cheibub and Gandhi.

The conditioning variables in the second phase were of three types: economic variables, regional indicators, and time-fixed effects. The economic variables are just two: the log of gross domestic product per capita and a standard measure of openness to international trade.[13] Regional indicators assess whether broad differences of location in the world matter; are the countries of Latin America systematically different from (say) the countries of Europe or Asia? Regional categorical variables consisted of indicators for location in North America, Central and Eastern Europe, sub-Saharan Africa, Latin America and the Caribbean, East Asia, the Middle East and North Africa, Oceania, Western Europe, the former USSR, and South Asia. Time-fixed effects assess whether there is a common trend in the inequality data, as discussed in chapter 3, after controlling for all other factors.

The baseline regression used our political regime classification and the two economic variables. Table 5.1 shows the results. Substantial and plausible results emerge: communist states, social democracies, and Islamic republics have lower inequality than other regime types, in that order of effect. Recent democracies have *higher* inequality than would otherwise be expected, and it is very much higher inequality than with long-established social democracies, other things equal. There is no significant effect for ordinary dictatorships or pseudo-democracies. In this regression, GDP per capita lacks a significant independent effect on inequality, but trade openness appears to increase it.

Table 5.2 presents a model with the regional controls added in. Thus the model is now able to distinguish between the effects of changing regime types within regions, relative to the inequality norms of that region. Seven of eight regions show significant regional effects, and the ordering (from low to high: Western Europe, Central and Eastern Europe, North America, Oceania, East Asia, Latin America, sub-Saharan Africa) contains no surprises. When regions are controlled for, regime type remains strongly significant and several further findings emerge. Communist states continue to have the lowest inequality scores, now followed by Islamic republics and then social democracies. Dictatorships now show significantly higher inequality, and recent democracies even more, than would be expected without knowledge of regime type. Overall, the slope of the income-inequality surface is now positive and significant,[14] suggesting that after normalizing for regions there is an income-inequality

Table 5.1. **UTIP-UNIDO and Regime Type with Minimal Controls**

	Parameter Estimate	*T Value*	*P Value*
Intercept	-1.49842	−35.34	<.0001
Dictatorship	0.14886	5.98	0.8006
Communist regime	-0.60612	−17.05	<.0001
Islamic republic	−0.12384	−2.08	0.0381
Social democracies	−0.41899	−15.73	<.0001
Pseudo-democracies	0.05886	1.50	0.1337
Recent democracies	0.10108	3.97	<.0001
Log of GDP per capita	0.01739	1.47	0.1425
Degree of openness (exports + imports)/GDP	0.00035541	2.09	0.0369
N	2,204		
R^2	36.20%		
Adjusted R^2	35.97%		
F value	155.70		
Pr > F	<.0001		

Note: Dependent variable is the log of the UTIP-UNIDO Theil statistic.

relationship. The control variable for openness is not significant, suggesting (very reasonably) that countries tend to have degrees of openness similar to their neighbors and trading partners.

The degree of explanation—almost 46 percent of the variation in inequality measures between countries, covering 2,204 country-year observations, seems to us to be quite impressive.

One final thing stands out from this model: a dog that didn't bark. When we introduced time-fixed effects into the model, on top of the regime type, and regional and economic controls, none of the dummies for years is significant and the fit of the model does not improve. In other words, the key feature of the model that emerges from chapter 3 is no longer there.

What happened? Various experiments with alternative specifications suggest that the key lies in the special category of recent democracies. Because of the way we've defined the term, there is no graduation, in our data, from this status. But of course some democracies are more recent than others. And there was a proliferation of recent democracies with the collapse of the Soviet Union and its Eastern European dependencies—a proliferation that, because of the particular

Table 5.2. **UTIP-UNIDO and Regime Type with Controls and Time-Fixed Effects**

	Parameter Estimate	*T Value*	*P Value*
Intercept	−1.41622	−32.10	<.0001
Dictatorship	0.08940	3.68	0.0002
Communist regime	−0.47373	−13.16	<.0001
Islamic republic	−0.23395	−3.97	<.0001
Social democracies	−0.09594	−2.98	0.0029
Pseudo-democracies	0.04754	−1.25	0.2133
Recent democracies	0.18025	7.05	<.0001
East Asia	−0.20630	−7.04	<.0001
Commonwealth of Independent States	−0.01653	−0.35	0.7256
Western Europe	−0.47117	−14.27	<.0001
Oceania	−0.27200	−6.81	<.0001
Central and Eastern Europe	−0.29935	−8.94	<.0001
North America	−0.28563	−5.88	<.0001
Sub-Saharan Africa	0.07487	3.00	0.0027
Latin America	−0.08152	−3.09	0.0020
Log of GDP per capita	0.02351	2.13	0.0335
Degree of openness (exports + imports)/GDP	0.00009740	0.61	0.5396
N	2,204		
R^2	45.71%		
Adjusted R^2	45.29%		
F value	108.17		
Pr > F	<.0001		

Note: Dependent variable is the log of the UTIP-UNIDO Theil statistic.

form it took, involved large increases in observed inequality. There was also an earlier revival of democracy in Latin America, which involved much higher rates of inequality than previously owing to the lingering effects of military rule and neoliberal globalization. Similar developments can be observed in sub-Saharan Africa, especially South Africa after 1992.

Thus the recent-democracies variable is capturing the time trend observed in the earlier model. In the end, this simply reflects the fact that political institutions, social norms, and international pressures coevolve, and there are limits to our ability to sort out which is the causal factor and which the caused.

As a test of data quality, we next we ran the same model against the Deininger and Squire Gini coefficients. This is a much smaller data universe, with just 431 country-year observations.

The results are disappointing. The explanation of variance drops to just 11 percent of this much smaller dataset. Practically nothing is significant, and of the few variables that are, those for communist states and social democracies have signs counter to expectation. The GDP per capita variable is significant, but now with a negative sign. Only the dummy for recent democracies and the regional control for Western Europe behave as they do in the UTIP-UNIDO models.

Table 5.3 reports the results. Adding in the controls used in chapter 3 to account for the various data types in the DS dataset does not improve matters.[15] Although those controls do boost the proportion of variance explained by the equation, the variables for political regime type and for economic characteristics remain unstable and insignificant. Only the regional controls correlate consistently with the DS data. We suspect that the results reflect primarily the sparse and erratic coverage of the DS dataset—the fundamental limitation of this raw material. On the other hand, the fact that consistent and stable relationships between regime type and inequality measures do appear in the UTIP-UNIDO data is reasonably persuasive evidence, in our view, that those relationships actually do exist.

When other political classification schemes are introduced in lieu of our own, the results are mixed and contradictory. Only the Cheibub-Gandhi index shows democracy associated with lower inequality. When the Polity/Freedom House and World Bank indices are used, the relationship is significant but it goes the other way; democracy is associated with higher inequality. The same is true using the Hadenius qualitative classification scheme; the coefficient for the class of democracies is positive and significant.[16] The mostly likely explanation is, in our view, the failure of this dataset to distinguish between long-standing social democracies and postdictatorship parvenus. In all of these regressions save one, the available sample size is smaller, and in all of them the degree of explanation is substantially less than in our model.

The results demonstrate that the approach of measuring democracy along a confected scale of values, and especially on the basis of the current-moment characteristics of the country, is prone to generate inconsistent relationships.

Table 5.3. **The Deininger-Squire Gini and Regime Type with Full Controls**

	Parameter Estimate	*T Value*	*P Value*
Intercept	43.59121	16.05	<.0001
Dictatorship	0.93645	0.73	0.4629
Communist regime	6.95565	2.44	0.0153
Islamic republic	−2.88274	−0.78	0.4347
Social democracies	3.86958	1.84	0.0658
Pseudo-democracies	−1.05265	−0.53	0.5936
Recent democracies	3.58294	2.58	<.0001
East Asia	3.93426	1.88	0.0610
Commonwealth of Independent States	−0.01653	−0.35	0.7256
Western Europe	−5.68375	−2.66	0.0082
Oceania	−2.91700	−1.11	0.2693
Central and Eastern Europe	0.59735	0.17	0.8682
North America	1.91972	0.61	0.5437
Sub-Saharan Africa	1.17605	0.83	0.4088
Latin America	1.81002	1.22	0.2224
Log of GDP per capita	−2.25738	−3.34	0.0009
Degree of openness (exports + imports)/GDP	−0.00044019	−0.03	0.9746
N	431		
R^2	11.40%		
Adjusted R^2	7.76%		
F value	3.13		
Pr > F	<.0001		

Note: Dependent variable is the "high quality" Gini coefficient from Deininger and Squire.

We have more sympathy with the categorical approach deployed by Hadenius and Teorell, but not with their classification choices. Apart from the failure to separate out recent democratic converts, they missed important opportunities by not distinguishing between communist states and other dictatorships, and perhaps also by not distinguishing Islamic theocracies from those (if any) associated with other religions.

Conclusion

In general, we find that political regime types have had important effects on economic inequality when they meant to. In particular, communist and Islamic regimes experienced lower inequality than economics and geography would otherwise have predicted. And this is true both before and after controlling for regional variables. It seems clear—for better or worse—that the egalitarian ideology of these systems was not a matter of empty words.

Social democracies are also associated with lower inequality, but this is the only type of democracy for which the relationship holds. The defining feature of social democracies is their stability and endurance: those countries classified as social democracies had all become so in the midtwentieth century, before the start of our data. New democracies elsewhere in the world show no particular ability to reduce inequality in this data; on the contrary, they have higher inequality than would be "normal" for their region and income levels—although this picture may be changing, to some degree, with new evidence from Brazil and Argentina, which we will take up in a later chapter. The communist transition to democracy produced higher, not lower, inequality, as everyone knows.

As a policy rule, this analysis suggests that reduction of inequality is generally and at best a slow affair. It is the consequence, in general, of steady institutional progress over a long period of time. Dramatic reductions in inequality are rare, and they may not be especially desirable.[17] Politically driven *increases* in inequality, on the other hand, are often quite sudden; at any given moment, they may be just a coup, a civil war, or a collapse in regime type away.

Appendix I

POLITICAL REGIME DATA DESCRIPTION

We classified political regimes between 1960 and 2005, annually for each country. Regime types were social democracies, recent democracies, pseudo-democracies, Communist states, Islamic republics, dictatorships, civil war, and European colonies.

Countries that did not exist prior to a certain date were not classified before that date. Countries that were of a particular regime type as of 1960 use 1960 as the start date. For example, we note that Sweden was a social democracy between 1960 and 2005, even though democracy extended beyond this period, both prior to and after this time.

Countries that experienced fair, multiparty elections over the entire 1960–2005 period, uninterrupted by other types of regimes, were classified as stable democracies, though this classification was not used in the regressions. The classification held even if one party won repeatedly in multiparty elections. Countries with this distinction were Australia, Austria, Belgium, Canada, Costa Rica, Denmark, Finland, France, Germany, Iceland, India, Ireland, Israel, Italy, Japan, Luxembourg, Netherlands, Netherlands Antilles, New Zealand, Norway, Puerto Rico, Sweden, Switzerland, United Kingdom, United States, and Venezuela. All of these except for Costa Rica, India, Israel, Puerto Rico, the United States, and Venezuela also qualified as social democracies in our scheme.[18] Countries that were "stable" but not "social" democracies have no specific dummy variable attributed to them; they form part of the backdrop or baseline comparison in the regression.

Countries that adopted free, multiparty elections for some period after the data begin in 1963 were classified, over the period of free multiparty electoral rule, as recent democracies: Albania (1992–2005), Algeria (2004–2005), Angola (2003–2005), Argentina (1960–1961, 1963–1965, 1973–1975, 1983–2005), Armenia (1992–2005), Bahamas (1974–2005), Bangladesh (1972–1974, 1991–2005), Barbados (1967–2005), Belize (1982–2005), Benin (1960–1962, 1991–2005), Bolivia (1960–1963, 1982–2005), Bosnia and Herzegovina (1996–2005), Botswana (1967–2005), Brazil (1960–1963, 1985–2005), Bulgaria (1991–2005), Burkina Faso (1960–1965), Cape Verde (1991–2005), Central African Republic (1993–2002), Chile (1960–1972, 1989–2005), Colombia (1960–1969, 1975–2005), Republic of Congo (1992–1996), Cote d'Ivoire (1990–1998), Croatia (1996–2005), Cyprus (1960–1962, 1965–2005), Czech Republic (1993–2005), Czechoslovakia (1990–1992), Dominican Republic (1962–1963, 1967–1969, 1978–2005), Ecuador (1960–1962, 1968–1969, 1979–2005), El Salvador (1993–2005), Ethiopia (1992–2005), Fiji (1971–2005), Gambia (1970–1993, 2001–2005), Ghana (1992–2005), Greece (1960–1966, 1975–2005), Guatemala (1997–2005), Haiti (1990, 1994–1996, 2005), Honduras (1960–1962, 1981–2005), Hong Kong (1997–2005), Hungary (1990–2005), Indonesia (1999–2005), Jamaica (1962–2005), Kenya (1992–2005), South Korea (1980–2005), Latvia (1992–2005), Lesotho (1967–1969, 1993–1997, 2000–2005), Liberia (2004–2005), Lithuania (1992–2005), Macao (2000–2005), Macedonia (1991–2005), Madagascar (1960–1972, 1991–2005), Malawi (1994–2005), Malaysia (1963–2005), Malta (1964–2005), Mauritius (1969–2005), Mexico (2000–2005), Moldova (1993–2005), Mongolia (1990–2005), Mozambique

(1994–2005), Myanmar (1960–1961), Namibia (1991–2005), Nepal (1991–2001), Nicaragua (1984–2005), Nigeria (1960–1965, 1980–1983, 2000–2005), Panama (1960–1967, 1989–2005), Papua New Guinea (1976–2005), Paraguay (1989–2005), Peru (1980–1989, 2001–2005), Philippines (1960–1971, 1987–2005), Poland (1990–2005), Portugal (1974–2005), Romania (1990–2005), Russian Federation (1992–2005), Samoa (1962–2005), Senegal (1960–1962, 1981–2005), Seychelles (1991–2005), Sierra Leone (1961–1966, 2002–2005), Singapore (1965–2005), Slovakia (1993–2005), Slovenia (1991–2005), Somalia (1960–1968), South Africa (1993–2005), Spain (1976–2005), Sri Lanka (1960–1982, 2002–2005), St. Vincent and the Grenadines (1980–2005), Suriname (1976–1979, 1987–1989, 1991–2005), Taiwan (1992–2005), Thailand (1974–1975, 1988–1990, 1992–2005), Togo (1960–1962), Tonga (1971–2005), Trinidad and Tobago (1962–2005), Turkey (1961–1979, 1983–2005), Uganda (1962–1965), Ukraine (1992–2005), Uruguay (1960–1972, 1985–2005), Yemen (1995–2005), and Zambia (1964–1971, 1991–2005).

We call "pseudo-democracies" those regimes that held elections for candidates of one party alone. This includes countries that, at one extreme, have outlawed other parties (as in, for example, Zambia) and countries that have held elections under the guise of multiparty elections but have set up the election so that only one party was actually eligible to win (e.g., the election was not fair, as in Azerbaijan). Pseudo-democracies were Azerbaijan (1992–2005), Burkina Faso (1991–2005), Cape Verde (1976–1990), Colombia (1970–1974), Dominican Republic (1970–1977), Gabon (1960–1962), Liberia (1960–1979), Mexico (1960–1999), Rwanda (1963–1972, 1979–1989), Seychelles (1980–1990), South Africa (1960–1992), Tunisia (1987–2005), Uganda (1996–2005), and Zambia (1972–1990). They are distinct from dictatorships, but only nominally so.

All countries that did not hold free and fair multiparty elections and were authoritarian in rule may be classified as dictatorships. For example, we classified monarchies in which multiparty elections do not take place as dictatorships, since classifying monarchies on the existence of a monarch alone would throw into question cases such as the United Kingdom and Canada, which are stable democracies that clearly differ from countries such as Afghanistan (1960–1977), Burundi (1962–1992), and others. Further, we separated dictatorships that self-classified as communist regimes or Islamic republics into the latter groups.

Dictatorships (other than communist or Islamic) were Afghanistan (1960–1977), Algeria (1963–1990, 2000–2003), Argentina (1962, 1966–1972,

1976–1982), Bahrain (1972–2005), Bangladesh (1975–1990), Benin (1963–1974), Bhutan (1960–2005), Bolivia (1964–1981), Brazil (1964–1984), Burkina Faso (1966–1990), Burundi (1962–1992), Cameroon (1960–2005), Central African Republic (1960–1992, 2003–2005), Chile (1973–1988), Democratic Republic of Congo (1960–1969, 1992–1995, 2003–2005), Republic of Congo (1960–1991, 1998–2005), Cote d'Ivoire (1960–1989, 1999–2001), Cuba (1960), Dominican Republic (1960–61), Ecuador (1963–1967, 1970–1978), Egypt (1960–2005), El Salvador (1960–1979), Eritrea (1993–2005), Ethiopia (1960–1973), Gabon (1963–2005), Gambia (1965–1969, 1994–2000), Ghana (1960–1991), Greece (1967–1974), Guinea (1960–2005), Haiti (1960–1989, 1991–1993, 1997–2004), Honduras (1963–1980), Indonesia (1960–1998), Iran (1960–1978), Iraq (1960–1993, 1998–2003), Jordan (1960–1969, 1972–2005), Kazakhstan (1992–2005), Kenya (1964–1991), South Korea (1960–1979), Kuwait (1961–2005), Kyrgyzstan (1992–2005), Lesotho (1970–1992, 1998–1999), Liberia (1980–1988, 1997–1998), Libya (1960–1968), Madagascar (1973–1990), Malawi (1964–1993), Mauritania (1960–1990), Morocco (1960–2005), Mozambique (1975–1976), Myanmar (1962–2005), Nepal (1960–1990, 2002–2005), Nicaragua (1960–1983), Nigeria (1971–1979, 1984–1999), Oman (1960–2005), Panama (1968–1988), Paraguay (1960–1988), Peru (1960–1979, 1990–2000), Philippines (1972–1986), Portugal (1960–1973), Qatar (1972–2005), Rwanda (1973–1978, 1995–2005), Saudi Arabia (1960–2005), Senegal (1963–1980), Seychelles (1977–1979), Sierra Leone (1967–1990), Spain (1960–1975), Sudan (1973–1982), Suriname (1980–1986, 1990), Swaziland (1968–2005), Syria (1961–2005), Taiwan (1960–1991), Tanzania (1964–2005), Thailand (1960–1973, 1976–1987, 1991), Togo (1963–2005), Tunisia (1960–1986), Turkey (1960, 1980–1982), Uganda (1966–1979, 1990–1995), United Arab Emirates (1971–2005), Uruguay (1973–1984), Yemen (1990–1993), North Yemen (1960–1961, 1971–1989), South Yemen (1967–68), and Zimbabwe (1980–2005).

Communist regimes and Islamic republics are classified according to the countries' own self-classification as such. Communist regimes were Albania (1960–1991), Benin (1975–1990), Bulgaria (1960–1990), China (1960–2005), Democratic Republic of Congo (1970–1991), Cuba (1961–2005), Czechoslovakia (1960–1989), East Germany (1960–1989), Mongolia (1960–1989), Poland (1960–1989), USSR (1960–1991), South Yemen (1969–1985) and Yugoslavia (1960–1990). Islamic republics were Afghanistan (2002–2005), Iran (1979–2005), Libya (1969–2005), Mauritania (1991–2005), and Pakistan (1972–2005).

Virtually all of the European colonies in 1960 have since been transferred to sovereign hands. Colonies listed were Algeria (1960–1962), Angola (1960–1974), Bahamas (1960–1973), Bahrain (1960–1971), Barbados (1960–1966), Belize (1960–1981), Botswana (1960–1966), Cape Verde (1960–1975), Fiji (1960–1970), Gambia (1960–1964), Hong Kong (1960–1996), Jamaica (1960–1961), Kenya (1960–1963), Kuwait (1960), Lesotho (1960–1966), Macao (1960–1999), Malawi (1960–1963), Malta (1960–1963), Mauritius (1960–1968), Mozambique (1960–1974), Namibia (1960–1990), Papua New Guinea (1960–1975), Qatar (1960–1971), Rwanda (1960–1962), Samoa (1960–1961), Seychelles (1960–1976), Sierra Leone (1960), St. Vincent and the Grenadines (1960–1979), Suriname (1960–1975), Swaziland (1960–1967), Tanzania (1960–1963), Tonga (1960–1970), Uganda (1960–1961), and Zimbabwe (1960–1979). However, there was not enough overlap with the inequality data to justify including this variable in the model.

Periods of civil war were also classified separately, since the chaos brought by civil war is often a more powerful economic and political signal than the type of imperiled regime per se. Civil war periods were Afghanistan (1978–2001), Algeria (1991–1999), Angola (1975–2002), Bangladesh (1971), Bosnia and Herzegovina (1991–1995), Burundi (1993–2005), Democratic Republic of Congo (1996–2002), Republic of Congo (1997), Cote d'Ivoire (2002–2005), Croatia (1991–1995), Cyprus (1963–2005), Dominican Republic (1965–1966), El Salvador (1980–1992), Ethiopia (1974–1991), Guatemala (1960–1996), Iraq (1994–1997, 2004–05), Jordan (1970–1971), Liberia (1989–1996, 1999–2003), Moldova (1992), Mozambique (1977–1993), Nigeria (1966–1970), Pakistan (1971), Rwanda (1990–1994), Sierra Leone (1991–2001), Somalia (1991–2005), Sri Lanka (1983–2001), Sudan (1960–1972, 1983–2005), Uganda (1980–1989), Yemen (1994), North Yemen (1962–1970), and South Yemen (1986). As with European colonies, we did not have the inequality data sufficient to justify inclusion of this variable.

Control variables used included world regional categories (North America, Central and Eastern Europe, sub-Saharan Africa, Latin America and the Caribbean, East Asia, the Middle East, North Africa, Oceania, Western Europe, CIS, and South Asia) and World Bank data on GDP per capita and openness to international trade. Time-fixed effects were also tested as part of sensitivity analysis, but (thanks to construction of the recent democracies variable) they were not significant in these regressions.

Appendix II

RESULTS USING OTHER POLITICAL CLASSIFICATION SCHEMES

When the Cheibub and Gandhi index of democracy is used to explain the UTIP-UNIDO inequality measures, dictatorships appear to be more unequal than democracies. Table 5.A1 shows this result alongside the regional controls, which are broadly similar in all of the regressions, and the economic controls, which vary from one to the next.

Table 5.A1. **UTIP-UNIDO Inequality and the Cheibub and Gandhi Democracy-Dictatorship Index with Controls and Time-Fixed Effects**

	Parameter Estimate	*T Value*	*P Value*
Intercept	–1.41318	–28.27	<.0001
Cheibub Index (0 democracy, 1 dictatorship)	0.14564	6.91	<.0001
East Asia	–0.18817	–4.46	<.0001
Commonwealth of Independent States	–0.00905	–0.17	0.8643
Western Europe	–0.71993	–20.96	<.0001
Oceania	–0.45633	–10.42	<.0001
Central and Eastern Europe	–0.53817	–14.62	<.0001
North America	–0.54581	–10.11	<.0001
Sub-Saharan Africa	0.05230	1.69	0.0910
Latin America	–0.12929	–4.00	0.0020
Log of GDP per capita	0.04912	3.64	0.0003
Degree of openness (exports + imports)/GDP	–0.00020258	–1.07	0.2862
N	1,680		
R^2	37.00%		
Adjusted R^2	36.65%		
F value	81.60		
Pr > F	<.0001		

Note: Dependent variable is the log of the UTIP-UNIDO Theil statistic.

Again using UTIP-UNIDO as the measure of inequality, the Polity/Freedom House regime classification points toward the opposite conclusion: that (other things equal) democracies are *more* unequal than dictatorships (table 5.A2).

Substituting the World Bank democracy index, as with Polity/Freedom House, also generates the result that more-democratic nations are more unequal.

Again using UTIP-UNIDO to measure inequality, but now substituting the Hadenius categorical regime classification scheme, the regression again finds that inequality increases with democracy, as it does with "theocracy,"

Table 5.A2. **UTIP-UNIDO Inequality and the Polity/Freedom House Democracy Index with Full Controls**

	Parameter Estimate	*T Value*	*P Value*
Intercept	−1.48851	−25.39	<.0001
Polity FH (0–10, 10 most democratic)	0.02322	6.63	0.0002
East Asia	−0.20923	−4.13	<.0001
Commonwealth of Independent States	−0.02279	−0.40	0.6867
Western Europe	−0.77353	−18.60	<.0001
Oceania	−0.45828	−8.74	<.0001
Central and Eastern Europe	−0.55583	−12.81	<.0001
North America	−0.56536	−8.64	<.0001
Sub-Saharan Africa	0.02294	0.64	0.5253
Latin America	−0.15110	−4.01	<.0001
Log of GDP per capita	0.05833	3.67	0.0003
Degree of openness (exports + imports)/GDP	−0.00017078	−0.80	0.4260
N	1,328		
R^2	36.20%		
Adjusted R^2	35.61%		
F value	62.17		
Pr > F	<.0001		

Note: Dependent variable is the log of the UTIP-UNIDO Theil statistic.

Table 5.A3. **UTIP-UNIDO Inequality and the World Bank Democracy Index with Controls and Time-Fixed Effects**

	Parameter Estimate	*T Value*	*P Value*
Intercept	–1.34254	–21.91	<.0001
World Bank Index (1–10, 10 most democratic)	0.00009788	2.49	0.0128
East Asia	–0.10231	–2.19	0.0291
Commonwealth of Independent States	0.07524	1.25	0.2103
Western Europe	–0.50321	–13.68	<.0001
Oceania	–0.32066	–6.58	<.0001
Central and Eastern Europe	–0.42085	–9.94	<.0001
North America	–0.40485	–6.32	<.0001
Sub-Saharan Africa	0.07389	1.98	0.0480
Latin America	–0.00563	–0.15	0.8791
Log of GDP per capita	0.02566	1.60	0.1095
Degree of openness (exports + imports)/GDP	–0.00025427	–1.2	0.2263
N	2,204		
R^2	31.25%		
Adjusted R^2	30.57%		
F value	45.68		
Pr > F	<.0001		

Note: Dependent variable is the log of the UTIP-UNIDO Theil statistic.

while decreasing with "one-party military regimes" and with monarchy. These results lack both theoretical rationale and intuitive plausibility (Table 5.A4).

Table 5.A4. **UTIP-UNIDO Inequality and the Hadenius Regime Classification with Controls and Time-Fixed Effects**

	Parameter Estimate	*T Value*	*P Value*
Intercept	−1.30044	−21.14	<.0001
Democracy	0.05305	2.08	0.0374
Multiparty monarchy	0.11767	1.24	0.2143
No party monarchy	0.02724	0.47	0.6391
Theocracy	0.30816	2.75	0.0060
Monarchy	−0.09786	−1.67	0.0942
One party	−0.05182	−1.47	0.1408
Military one party	−0.34422	−6.11	<.0001
Military multiparty	−0.04242	−0.83	0.4089
East Asia	−0.11996	−2.68	0.0074
Commonwealth of Independent States	0.07403	1.31	0.1902
Western Europe	−0.55212	− 15.91	<.0001
Oceania	−0.31843	−6.80	<.0001
Central and Eastern Europe	−0.45462	−11.31	<.0001
North America	−0.38864	−6.89	<.0001
Sub-Saharan Africa	0.05648	1.63	0.1038
Latin America	−0.04920	−1.39	0.1655
Log of GDP per capita	0.00622	0.35	0.7284
Degree of openness (exports + imports)/GDP	0.00008826	0.39	0.6945
N	1,421		
R^2	35.86%		
Adjusted R^2	34.98%		
F value	41.21		
Pr > F	<.0001		

Note: Dependent variable is the log of the UTIP-UNIDO Theil Statistic.

Notes

1. This chapter builds on original data work by Sara Hsu (2008), revised and extended by Hsu and by Wenjie Zhang. The datasets are available at the UTIP site.
2. "Distribution of worker participation income among industry sectors" is Cutright's phrase. During this early period, Jackman (1974) and Bollen and Grandjean (1981) argued that the effects of democracy on inequality were inconclusive.
3. Regime stability is discussed extensively in Cutright (1963), Bollen and Jackman (1989), and Gurr, Jaggers, and Moore (1990).
4. The experience of the communist regimes of Eastern Europe at the end of the 1980s raises a question about the validity of this proposition, but it is also possible that inequality rose (from "too little" to "just right") in those countries before democratization.
5. In an empirical evaluation of these ideas, based on a multilevel analysis of World Values Survey data in thirty-five countries, Wells (2006) states that income inequality reduces support for democracy. Houle (2009) finds that inequality does not have a systematic effect on democratization, so the evidence of a causal effect running from economic conditions to democratization remains indecisive.
6. Relevant work includes Cutright's stable democracy index (1963), Bollen and Jackman's examination of measures of democracy and stability (1989), and Gurr, Jaggers, and Moore's measure of regime persistence (1990). See also Desai, Olofsgard, and Yousef (2003) and Erikkson and Persson (2003). Gradstein and Milanovic (2004) also discuss the importance of regime persistence. Bollen and Jackman (1989) emphasize the importance of separating measures of political regime, particularly democracy, from measures of regime stability, while Gurr and colleagues (1990), in their construction of the widely used POLITY II dataset, separately examine elite instability.
7. The case of a strong equalizing but nondemocratic institution—the communist party—that collapses in the run-up to transition would seem to be a natural extension of this literature.
8. In the political science literature, the problems have been noted by Chong (2004).
9. See Elkins (2000) for further discussion of this issue.
10. Specifically, the Hadenius and Teorell categories are limited multiparty, partyless, no-party, military, military no-party, military multiparty, military one-party, one-party, other, one-party monarchy, monarchy, rebel regime, civil war, occupation, theocracy, transitional regime, no-party monarchy, multiparty monarchy, multiparty occupied, and democracy.
11. In practice, we found that the overlapping cases were not sufficiently numerous to matter, so for practical purposes we used mutually exclusive categories.
12. Esping-Andersen (1990) proposed three categories: the liberal state, in which modest social-insurance plans dominate; the conservative state, in which status differentials are preserved; and social democratic states, in which universal social rights are expanded. In our earlier work, we used Esping-Andersen's social democratic category for particular nations and classified the remaining democracies (both conservative and liberal states) as conservative democracies. Gough and Wood (2004) extend Esping-Andersen's work to developing countries that lack welfare states in the Western sense of the term.
13. Measured as the sum of exports and imports, divided by GDP, expressed in percentage terms.
14. This is not necessarily inconsistent with a nonlinear relationship containing a downward-sloping part, as described in chapter 2. For reasons of simplicity, we omitted the quadratic term in these regressions.

15. As noted in chapter 3, these are income versus expenditure measures, measures based on households versus measures based on personal incomes, and measures based on gross income (or expenditure) versus those calculated net of tax.
16. The Vanhanen index of regime classification showed insignificant results, and we do not report those regressions.
17. One example is a dramatic and violent drop in inequality that shows up for Iran in 1979.
18. Germany was classified as a social democracy even though a part of its current population lived under communism until 1989. Some might argue that social democracy ended in the UK with the arrival of the Thatcher government in 1979, or in New Zealand with the neoliberal reforms of the early 1990s.

CHAPTER 6

The Geography of Inequality in America, 1969 to 2007

Strange though it may now seem, for the first forty years after World War II the topic of economic inequality in America was a backwater, attracting little interest and very little research. Among economists, a broad consensus held that inequality was stable or declining, that the American middle class was dominant in both economics and politics and would remain so, and also that it was destined to absorb rich and poor alike into a single common social net. The general American self-image was not of "capitalism" or "free enterprise" but of the mixed economy, strongly stabilized by the New Deal, by a progressive income and estate tax, a high minimum wage, and later on by the impact of Lyndon Johnson's Great Society, especially Medicare and Medicaid but also parts of the War on Poverty. In 1969, when measured inequality reached its low point, there is no evidence that anyone anticipated the turnaround to come.

Wage and earnings (or pay) inequality—inequality measured across jobs—began to rise with the recessions of 1970 and 1973–1974 and then sharply in the back-to-back recessions of 1980 and 1981–1982, peaking initially around 1984. Pay inequality then stabilized, but household earnings inequality continued to rise, in part because the recessions and economic dislocation set off major changes in family life, increasing the number of low-income single parent households that would fall to the bottom of the income scales and also the number of double-income families without children that would move to the top.[1] Thus the shocks to jobs and pay had both direct and secondary effects, recreating income and living-standard differentials and class differences that had been muted, especially among white Americans, since the Great Depression and the Second World War.

Economists were perhaps the last group to realize this. Practically no professional attention was called to rising inequality before the mid-1980s, when Barry Bluestone and Bennett Harrison published *The Great U-Turn*.[2] Working with thin information but good instincts, they laid the blame squarely on deindustrialization and on the decline of unions that was then plainly under way, due in part to severe industrial recessions and in part to transnational production and offshore relocation of manufacturing jobs. Bluestone and Harrison were, however, left-labor–oriented economists, and it would not be for them to define how the profession as a whole would react to these events.

The response from within mainstream economics appeared in 1992, when John Bound and George Johnson published in the *American Economic Review* an article fingering a quite different culprit, which they called "skill-biased technological change." According to them, the deep cause of rising inequality was change in production methods, which were said to require a workforce with ever larger amounts of skill and training. This created a mismatch between skills and the demand for skill, an increasing return to education and a rise in inequality as those who were well positioned to take advantage of the demand for their specialized skills reaped the rewards at the expense of the dim and the slow. Since this was a market-based explanation, strongly rooted in microfoundations and leading to microsolutions, it quickly became the orthodox view. Yet there was no direct evidence for it, of any kind, and how it might apply to all of the low-skilled, small-shop service jobs that had become the overwhelming majority of American employment was never made clear. Criticism, as early as 1994 from Adrian Wood (who favored the trade-did-it theory), was given a briefly respectful hearing and brushed off.

The skill-bias view entrenched itself over the 1990s. For the mainstream, in addition to its supply-demand microfoundations, it had two comforting political features: it subsumed rising inequality into inevitable and desirable technical progress, and it placed the onus on individual workers to improve their lot through education and training. It thus deflected those who might be tempted to call for public action.

My engagement with this field began around 1995 on the request of Richard Leone at the Twentieth Century Fund (now the Century Foundation), who proposed that I write a monograph evaluating the role of trade as against technology. A review of the research to that point revealed that the actual evidence for the skill-bias thesis was almost unbelievably thin. There were no suitable datasets showing the rise of pay (as distinct from income) inequality in the United States on an annual basis, so one could not even tell exactly when increases that had been observed from separate surveys in (say) 1976 and 1988 had actually occurred.[3] Studies alleging direct links between particular technologies (computerization, notably) and changes in pay were very scarce and casually argued. And there was still less (in those days before DS) to support claims about what was happening in the rest of the world.

This led to the start of my work on the measurement of inequality, to the idea of applying the Theil statistic to employment and earnings data, and eventually to publication of *Created Unequal*, which presented new measures of pay inequality and used them to develop an early critique of the skill-bias hypothesis. Using annual data on pay inequality permitted events to be timed precisely, and so *Created Unequal* could show the clear link between inequality and unemployment within the manufacturing sector; it made the first sustained argument that the true causes of rising inequality in the United States were macroeconomic. The book was widely reviewed and well received—though not, especially, by mainstream economists. However, over the course of the early 2000s evidence from the 1990s gradually sank in, and several notable empirical economists dissented from the skill-bias argument, among them David Card of Berkeley (Card and DiNardo 2002) and Robert Z. Lawrence at Harvard (Lawrence 2000).

As everyone knows, *household income inequality*, a much broader construct than pay and especially than pay within manufacturing, increased in the late 1990s. Indeed, the rise in household income inequality was extreme, driving the most widely used and publicized measures, notably the annual calculations of the Census Bureau (Jones and Weinberg 2000), to record heights. These increases were associated not with remuneration for work—that is, with what we normally call "wages"—but with the asset price boom, especially in the information technology sector. One of the things I showed in *Created Unequal* was how the technology-producing sector had structured itself, almost uniquely within the American economy, to take advantage of venture capital and use those funds to bid up pay, especially in the higher ranks of the technology firms. The late 1990s gave ample proof that this was indeed the driving force behind the rise in income inequality as a whole in those years.

In income tax data, this appeared as stock options realizations, as capital gains, and as salaries and cash bonuses paid not from sales revenues but from funds that had been raised from investors.[4] Thus even though the pay distribution inside manufacturing—payments to hourly workers and salaried managers—benefited from compression thanks to overtime and strong demand for low-end workers, the taxable income share of the top 0.1 percent of tax filers rose sharply, as documented by Thomas Piketty and Emmanuel Saez from tax records. Piketty and Saez (2003) showed that the share of the very wealthiest in taxable income reached levels at least comparable to the late 1920s.[5] Meanwhile polemicists picked up on the outsized gap between chief executive officer compensation and average-worker pay—a stark ratio, even though it tends to overlook the fact that there are only five hundred Fortune 500 CEOs at a given time,[6] and that compared to hedge fund managers many of them are pikers.

Although economic orthodoxies die hard, the evidence against the notion that "skill bias" drives economic inequality becomes clearer with every passing year, and it can be reduced to a pair of major propositions. The first is that inequality in the structures of pay in America—the inequality that appears between jobs when one focuses on the working population alone, on people actually subject to the labor market—varies mainly with the rate of unemployment. Figure 2.6 has already illustrated this, using monthly data going back to 1953, though restricted to the manufacturing sector. The most likely reason for this close relationship is simply that the actual data are drawn from weekly earnings, not from hourly pay rates (which no dataset observes directly); and that unemployment varies closely with involuntary part-time work and with the availability of overtime, which apply more to the lower part of the wage scale (and not at all to people on salary). Thus inequality in manufacturing pay and unemployment in the larger economy reflect forces that are essentially the same. Apart from this, wage structures in America are surprisingly stable, reflecting settled differentials within companies and slow-moving changes in the major sectors that offer employment. The big changes in the overall distribution of pay for work are due to the changing composition of jobs, including the decline of manufacturing in total, and the enormous rise in jobs in the low-wage services sector.

The second key finding is that *income inequality*, which the Census reports from its Current Population Survey but which we can measure in many other ways, often moves in a different direction from inequalities that are restricted to pay for work. As noted above, in the late 1990s as manufacturing pay inequalities were falling income inequality surged to record highs. The reason once again is wholly clear: inequality in the structure of incomes largely follows the stock market. People at the very top of the income structure hold a large share of corporate stocks, pay themselves with stock options, and finance their companies with venture capital in a rising equities market. Small movements in the value of their asset holdings as measured on the stock exchange can and do dominate their income statements, their tax filings, and the movement of inequality in household incomes as a whole. In the late 1990s, it was the boom in technology markets that drove the capital wealth and the incomes of these individuals up, which also drove the inequality in (manufacturing) wage structures down.

As we have already seen, in figure 2.5, one interesting way to present income inequality in America is to measure it across the 3,150 counties that make up the

United States, using the income tax data presented in the Local Area Personal Income Statistics of the Bureau of Economic Analysis (BEA) at the Department of Commerce. A between-counties Theil statistic is easily computed from this data, and it tracks the Census Bureau's survey-based measure of household income inequality well. Figure 2.5 illustrated the close relationship between this measure and the proportional change (log) of the NASDAQ stock exchange index, whose stocks supply the financial wealth of America's technology billionaires and multimillionaires. This relationship holds until around 2003, after which a different set of forces appears to take over.

By now the evidence behind these basic propositions—bearing in mind that they refer to distinct economic constructs (pay, income)—is dispositive; there is little left to say about the particular debate over skill bias and no reason to dwell on it here. The question is, What do more recent data show, and what is there to add?

The standard approach to summary measures of inequality leaves a great deal of information either uncollected or on the cutting-room floor. To know that the share of the top 0.1 or 0.01 percent is rising or falling is perhaps interesting, but it doesn't answer the question, *Who are these people*? What do they do? How did their fortunes arise? And, especially, *Are they the same people from one business cycle to the next*? Or does the identity of America's biggest economic winners change, and is that change traceable to anything interesting? Such as, for example, the ebb and flow of credit conditions, or the rise and decline of political power?

Information on the precise patterns of gain and loss, by geography and by industry, can yield clues to these questions, and therefore a guide to the political economy of inequality in America. This chapter reports on an effort to furnish some of that information, using measures of interindustrial pay inequality and of between-area income inequality. The approach distinguishes clearly and in fine detail the winners and losers in specific periods. Thus the measurements open up new ways to investigate sources of change in the economy, and particularly the influence of changing power relationships and public policies on distribution.[7]

Between-Industry Earnings Inequality in the United States

In Kuznets's simplest model, there are two sources of inequality: the difference in average wages between farms and factories, and the distribution of the population across these two large sectors. Either a reduction of one of these sectors, leading to the economy being predominantly one or the other, or a diminution of the differential between them will decrease the inequality measured between them.[8] U.S. economic data are more complex, but we can still measure between-industry earnings inequality using the same principles; this is in effect what the Theil index does. Overall inequality between sectors depends on the differentials between average wages and their comparative size. Economic sectors are a particularly sensitive fault line, since the relative fortunes of sectors capture many important economic changes, but geographic information may in some respects be equally important. Sometimes economic change varies across activities. Sometimes it varies across places.

The BEA publishes annual earnings and employment data for industrial sectors of the nation as the whole and for individual states. Earnings are defined as "the sum of Wage and Salary Disbursements, supplements to wages and salaries and proprietors' income" and derive from a virtual census of employers' tax records (BEA 2008). As such, there is almost complete coverage of the (formal) working population with minimal reporting error.

From 1969 until 2000, data were organized according to the Standard Industrial Classification (SIC) coding system. Beginning in 2001, the BEA dropped the SIC schema in favor of the North American Industry Classification System (NAICS). To ease comparisons between the two taxonomies, the BEA released recoded data for the 1990 to 2000 period using the NAICS categories. Thus, there are two annual datasets with a decade of overlap, one from 1969 to 2000 and the other from 1990 to 2007.

In addition to measuring inequality between sectors (or places), Theil's T statistic allows us to identify winners and losers and those sectors most responsible for changing inequality. By examining the Theil elements, described in chapter 2, we can isolate the contribution of each sector to total inequality between sectors. The Theil element will be positive or negative, depending on whether the sector's average earnings are greater or less than the national average, with the contribution weighted by sector size.[9]

Figure 6.1 displays earnings inequality calculated with an SIC basis from 1969 to 2000 and a NAICS basis from 1990 to 2007 and Census Bureau measures of household income inequality over the same period (DeNavas-Walt, Proctor, and Smith 2008). Note that the Gini measure suffers from a break in series, which is due to a change in the top coding[10] and survey methods between 1992 and 1993; when you improve the quality of an income survey, measured inequality rises. The earnings inequality measures do not suffer from this problem. They are based on a relatively fine disaggregation of sectors-within-states—that is, oil drilling in Texas compared to farming in Utah compared to retail in Rhode Island

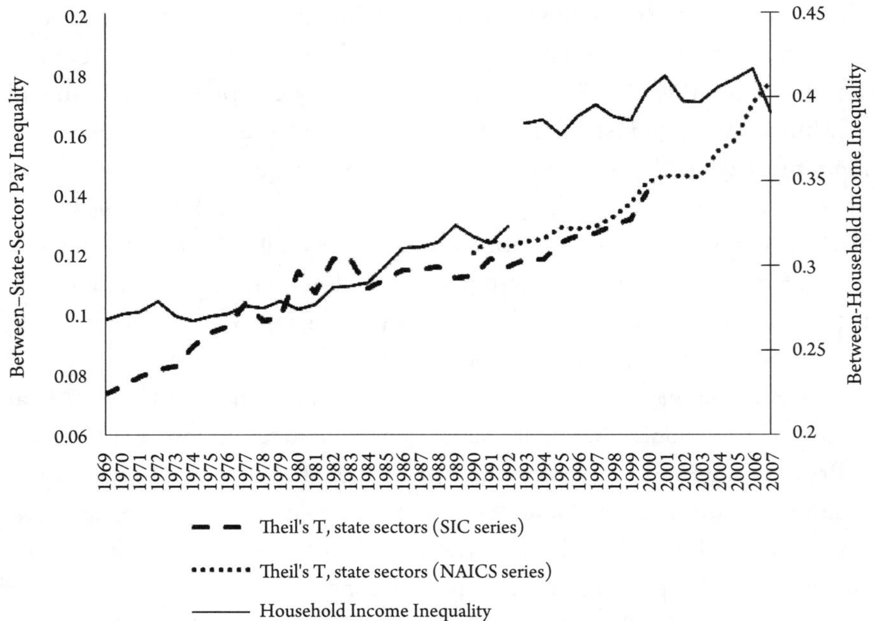

Figure 6.1. Between–state-sector earnings inequality and household income inequality 1969–2007.[5]

compared to all the other combinations of states and sectors—consistently measured over the time frame. Apart from the data break, the correspondence between this broad-based earnings measure and income inequality is very close.

Earnings inequality rose substantially over the last four decades, but the rate of change varied over the period. From 1969 to 1982, the between–state-sector measure of Theil's T increased 61 percent, but then earnings inequality remained flat until 1994—the pattern previously identified in *Created Unequal*. A renewed run-up from 1995 to 2007 was interrupted only by a pause from 2000 to 2003. The shift in coding regimens from SIC to NAICS has little effect on the pay inequality metric. Over the eleven data points where both coding schemes are available, the two series move in lock step. The correlation coefficient of the two series across the overlapping years of 1990 to 2000 is .98, and the year-over-year changes have a correlation of .88.

The richness of the BEA data allows us to explore earnings inequality through myriad lenses—broader or narrower sectors at the state or national level. It is useful at this point to compare measures of inequality at different levels of aggregation and disaggregation, and for this we can borrow the Lorenz curve momentarily from its normal use as underpinning for the Gini coefficient. Lorenz curves can be plotted piecewise from grouped data using

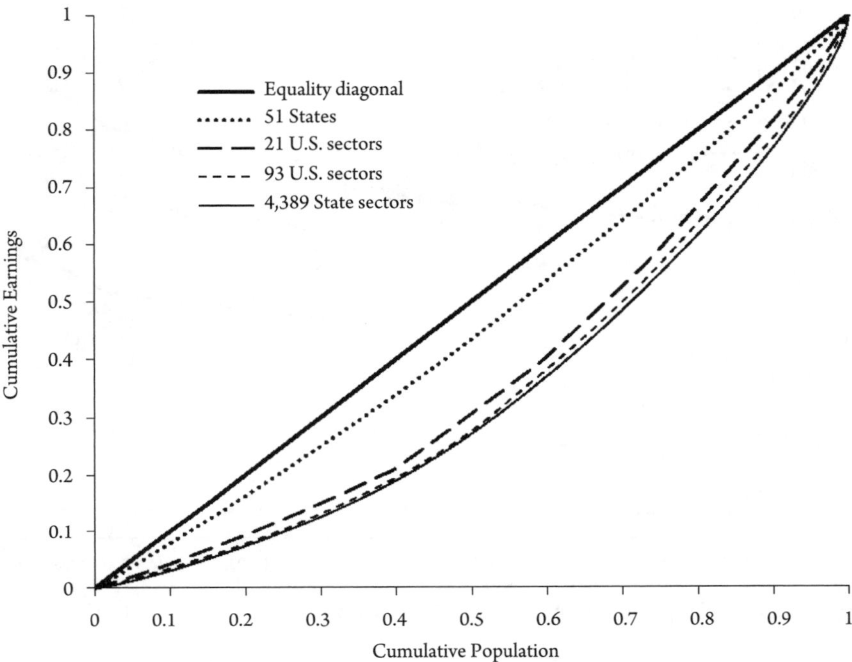

Figure 6.2. Lorenz curves for the U.S. distribution of pay in 2007 using various group structures.

the average income for each group, and this exercise helps to tell us by how much measured inequality increases when we move from a coarse to a fine level of aggregation.

Figure 6.2 displays Lorenz curves for four group structures in 2007: the fifty-one states[11] (all economic sectors included), twenty-one broad economic sectors at the national level, ninety-three narrowly defined economic sectors at the national level, and 4,389 narrowly defined economic sectors at the state level. (Some states lack a full deck of economic sectors.)

Each Lorenz curve has an associated Gini coefficient; they rise in order from 0.089 to 0.259 to 0.301 to 0.320. The figure and coefficients reveal two key facts. First, in the United States, sector matters more than geography, broadly drawn; inequality between states is now very low, and there is much greater variance in pay across sectors than across large distances. This corresponds to a basic reality of American life: it is fairly easy to move from one place to another while maintaining similar pay and the same line of work. Movement across industries, on the other hand, is difficult and can involve large gains or losses, even for relatively low-paid work but especially for high-paid work. This

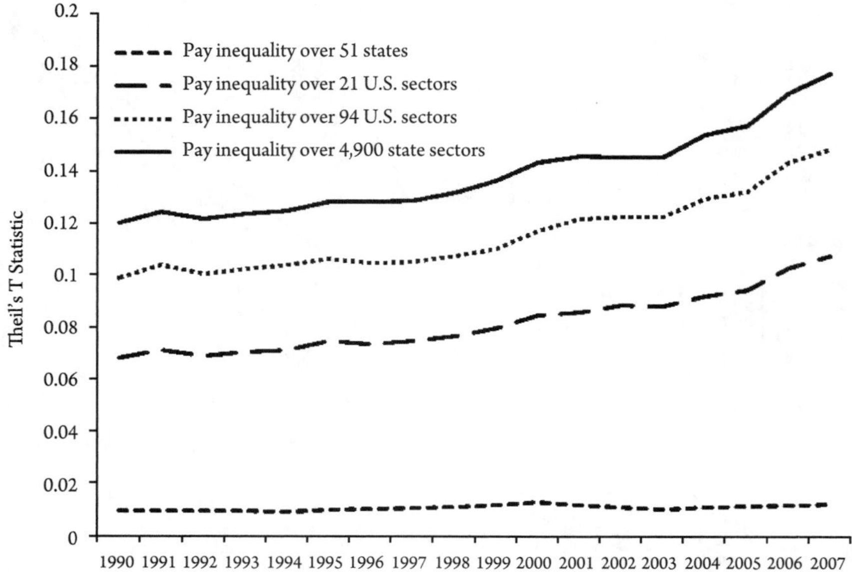

Figure 6.3. U.S. pay inequality, 1990 to 2007, calculated using alternative category structures.

may be why (as a casual observation) Americans tend to identify themselves by the industry they work in, and not so much by the place where they live.

Second, adding sector detail generates little additional information, and it increases the measure of inequality only by small amounts. The very coarse set of twenty-one broad national sectors actually captures the bulk of between–state-sector pay differences. Moving to the finer grid of ninety-three sectors adds only a bit more than four Gini points[12] to the measure. Breaking up the ninety-three into fifty-one separate state-level sectors adds less than two Gini points to the measure. Although for some purposes one would, of course, like to go all the way and obtain a "true Gini" based on the entire population, at the individual level, in practice there is no such measure; even the Census Bureau's measure, which is based on the Current Population Survey, is drawn from a sample of sixty thousand households, and for reasons explained in a note, sampling for the purposes of measuring an income distribution is a very hazardous procedure.[13]

Returning to the Theil statistic, we can make an easy calculation, at every level, of the evolution of inequality over time. Figure 6.3 displays this evolution of pay inequality from 1990 to 2007 using the same four category structures.

The measures generally move together over time, suggesting again that improvements in the classification structure may be more trouble than they are

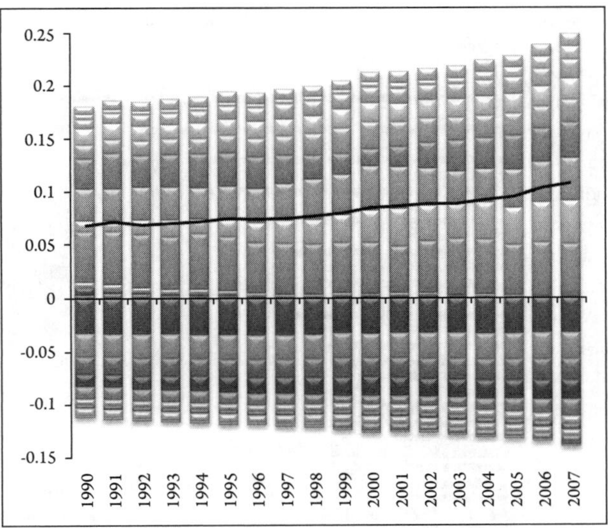

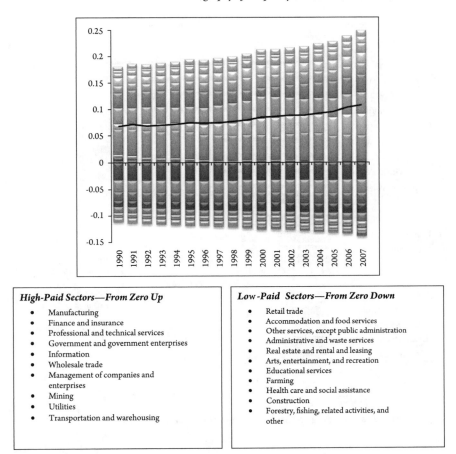

High-Paid Sectors—From Zero Up

- Manufacturing
- Finance and insurance
- Professional and technical services
- Government and government enterprises
- Information
- Wholesale trade
- Management of companies and enterprises
- Mining
- Utilities
- Transportation and warehousing

Low-Paid Sectors—From Zero Down

- Retail trade
- Accommodation and food services
- Other services, except public administration
- Administrative and waste services
- Real estate and rental and leasing
- Arts, entertainment, and recreation
- Educational services
- Farming
- Health care and social assistance
- Construction
- Forestry, fishing, related activities, and other

Figure 6.4. Theil elements of between-sector pay inequality in the U.S.,1990–2007.

worth. Yet each between-sector metric is useful in its own way. The twenty-one-sector national-level measure is the easiest to visualize, while the measures that use a larger number of sectors identify those narrow groups most responsible for inequality changes. The underlying Theil elements are a way to identify the culprits descriptively; there is no need to resort to econometrics.

Figure 6.4 breaks down the annual measures of pay inequality among the twenty-one broad national-level economic sectors into their constituent Theil elements. The black line tracks the overall Theil's T (the sum of all the elements),[14] while the stacked portions of the bar graphs show the individual components, one for each sector. The legend is organized such that all of the sectors above the horizontal axis in 2007—those with above-average earnings—are in the upper box, starting with the sector that contributed "most" to inequality: manufacturing. Likewise the lower box lists all the sectors contributing to

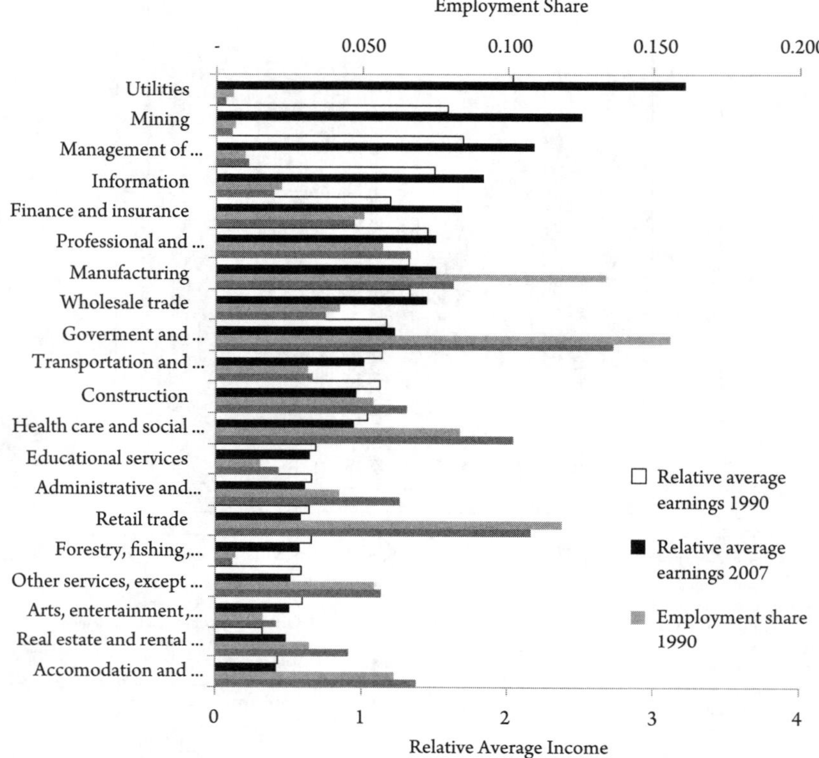

Figure 6.5. Relative earnings and employment in 21 U.S. sectors, 1990 and 2007.

inequality "from below" in 2007, that is to say, all those whose average pay was less than the national average. Not surprisingly, the list begins with the largest contributor to inequality having below-average earnings: retail trade.

Two trends that emerge clearly from figure 6.4 are the waning and waxing of the public sector since 1990 and, even more, the rising importance of finance and insurance, especially from 1990 until 2001. It is notable that the 1990s under President Clinton were not banner years for government and government enterprises; the public sector fared markedly better, in relation to the rest of the economy, under George W. Bush.

Taken as a whole, the period from 1990 to 2007 was one of rising earnings inequality. As Kuznets taught, the source of this increase could be either changes in relative wages or changes in sector employment shares, or both. Figure 6.5 shows the relative average wages and employment levels of the twenty-one sectors in 1990 and 2007. The sectors are ordered according to relative average income in 2007.

The largest contributors to inequality from above during this period were professional and technical services, and finance and insurance. Finance and insurance saw a slight decline in jobs over this period but still contributed to rising inequality with immense growth in relative earnings. Professional and technical services, spurred by the information technology revolution, gained employment share and experienced a small increase in relative earnings. Administrative and waste services, and real estate rental and leasing, which both boasted significant employment gains, added the most to inequality from below. Relative average earnings in real estate actually improved, but not enough to offset the flood of new jobs into what remains a low-paid sector. Overall the figure displays for us the complexity of rising inequality in America during these years, which nevertheless reduces to two core facts: rapidly growing pay in a few small high-paid sectors, and growing employment in a few large but low-paid sectors. However, the small number of sectors examined at this level still obscures some important facts. We do not know, from this information, just how concentrated income gains actually were.

When we increase the number of sectors, what do we find? We find that the increases in inequality are due mainly to changes in the relative pay of a very small number of subsectors, in a very small number of places, involving a very small number of people. Income inequality, in other words, is a matter of the "fat tail" of the income distribution. It has very little to do with changes affecting the broad middle of the working population, and very much to do with the incomes of a small number at the very top. (In this way, the analysis is fully consistent with the view from econophysics, which describes income distributions as being derived from two statistical distributions, the first a "most probable" Boltzmann distribution affecting most income earners and the second a "power law" affecting those at the very top.)

Common sense can guide the search for high-leverage sectors. The emergence of personal computing and information technology as major forces in the mid-to-late 1990s and the housing boom before the Great Crisis were hallmark economic phenomena of the last two decades. From 1996 to 2000, nominal earnings per job in computer and electronic manufacturing rose from $57,268 to $83,848. Likewise, from 2001 to 2006 earnings per job for construction of buildings grew from $53,140 to $66,112, and the sector added more than three hundred thousand jobs. Indeed, computer manufacturing and construction were two significant contributors to the increase in earnings inequality during these episodes.

Other sectors also saw wide swings in their fortunes, but they account for just a tiny part of the workforce. Thus the pay increases in sectors listed in table 6.1, which contained only 3.8 percent of all workers in 2001, accounted

Table 6.1. **U.S. Average Pay in 1996 and 2001 in 12 High-Growth Sectors**

Sector	*Average Wage*	
	1996	*2001*
Computer and electronic product manufacturing	$57,268	$78,198
ISPs, search portals, and data processing	$44,426	$68,175
International organizations, foreign embassies, consulates	$83,632	$107,550
Internet publishing and broadcasting	$54,116	$82,080
Funds, trusts, and other financial vehicles	$50,132	$79,931
Utilities	$82,384	$113,605
Oil and gas extraction	$49,765	$90,958
Broadcasting, except Internet	$91,831	$133,576
Securities, commodity contracts, investments	$46,249	$88,604
Petroleum and coal products manufacturing	$124,821	$200,367
Lessors of nonfinancial intangible assets	$91,556	$192,836
Pipeline transportation	$ 93,285	$299,978
All other sectors	$31,276	$38,099

for the entire rise in pay inequality during the information technology boom. The other 96.2 percent of the working population was, simply, unaffected, except by comparison with those 3.8 percent.

The boom sectors experienced a 58 percent climb in nominal average earnings in the five-year period from 1996 to 2001. All other sectors gained 22 percent. The employment growth rate in the highfliers, on the other hand, was roughly half that for the rest of the economy. This separation of the boom sectors from the rest of the economy explains *all* of the increase in between-sector inequality from 1991 to 2001. This is evident in figure 6.6, which parses Theil's T for between-sector earnings inequality into three components: inequality among the information technology boom sectors, inequality among the sectors in the rest of the economy, and inequality between the high-growth sectors and the rest of the economy from 1991 to 2001.

Inequality measured between the twelve high-leverage sectors in table 6.1 was essentially unchanged from 1991 to 2001. Inequality between the other eighty-two national-level sectors actually declined slightly, no doubt reflecting the effect of high employment and strong demand on hours and overtime in

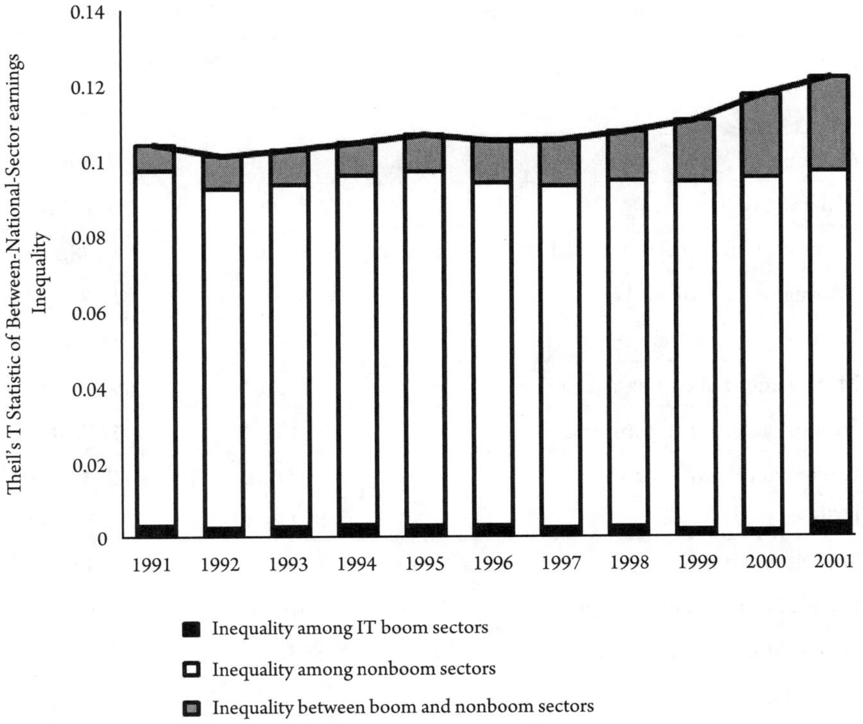

Figure 6.6. Between-sector inequality in the U.S., 1991–2001.

the lower-wage sectors. But inequality between the haves and have-nots rose sharply. It alone accounts for the entire 17.2 percent increase in between-sector earnings inequality during this period.

In the slump of 2000–2001, which signaled the end of the information technology boom, income inequality fell quite sharply. This again reflected the bust of the highfliers, and very little else, which is why that slump was perceived as mild by most Americans—even though it marked the end of an era.

In 2003, the economy began again to grow, and pay inequalities measured between sectors also increased. Our method quickly points to an often-overlooked fact. Except for finance, the big winners from rising income inequality after 2003 *were not exactly the same* as they had been in the information technology boom. They were different people, in different activities, and as we shall see they lived in different parts of the country. The recovery of the Bush years was, actually, more broadly based than had been true in the 1990s; it reflected wage gains in a wider array of sectors that contain a higher percentage of employment. But the pattern is similar. Table 6.2 shows average wages in fifteen high-growth sectors in 2003 to 2007.[15]

Table 6.2. **U.S. Average Pay in 2003 and 2007 in 15 High-Growth Sectors**

Sector	*Average Wage*	
	2003	*2007*
Military	$53,178	$71,616
Federal, civilian	$79,153	$98,844
Computer and electronic product manufacturing	$88,365	$108,125
Mining (except oil and gas)	$66,671	$89,371
Water transportation	$70,634	$93,452
Management of companies and enterprises	$83,618	$106,587
Support activities for mining	$61,650	$87,241
Chemical manufacturing	$97,062	$124,020
Utilities	$127,487	$157,138
Securities, commodity contracts, investments	$83,053	$113,907
Broadcasting, except Internet	$149,362	$197,862
Other information services	$34,490	$86,726
Oil and gas extraction	$ 98,979	$167,418
Pipeline transportation	$181,197	$263,350
Petroleum and coal products manufacturing	$185,070	$363,962
All other sectors	$38,989	$43,949

These sectors accounted for 7.4 percent of total jobs in 2007. From 2003 to 2007, average earnings in these "Bush boom" sectors increased 32 percent, while earnings in the rest of the economy averaged 13 percent, barely keeping pace with inflation. Yet (as in the 1990s) the rate of job growth in the highfliers was half of that for the other sectors over this period. After experiencing brief stagnation in earnings growth during the information technology bust, computer and electronic product manufacturing and securities, commodity contracts, and investing experienced strong rebounds in earnings from 2002 to 2007. However, none of these sectors regained the employment levels of 2000. To the contrary: computer and electronic product manufacturing shed 29 percent of its workforce from 2000 to 2007.

Figure 6.7 shows the contributions of inequality among the Bush boom sectors, inequality among all other sectors, and inequality between the high-growth sectors and lower-growth sectors from 2000 to 2007.

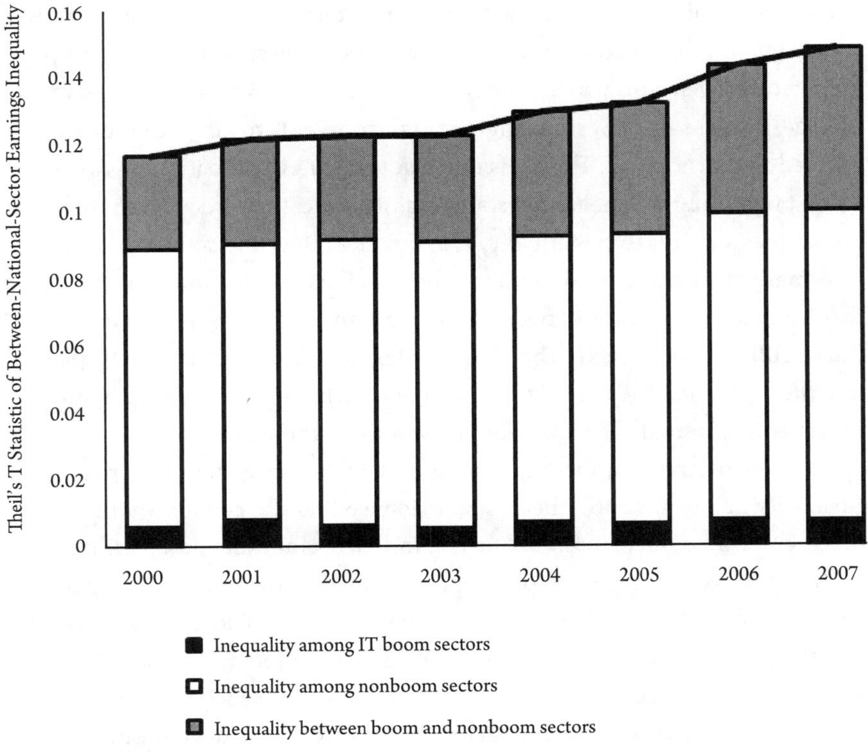

Figure 6.7. Between-sector inequality in the U.S., 2000–2007.

Unlike the information technology boom, during which inequality within the high-growth and low-growth sectors was relatively stable, the Bush boom saw rising inequality *among* the sectors in table 6.2, *among* the sectors in the rest of the economy, and *between* those sectors that surged ahead and those that stayed behind. Nonetheless, in this period, as before, the disparity between the haves and have-nots explains the majority of the total increase in between-sector earnings inequality.

By coincidence or design, sector performance seems to have a political dimension. Technologists and financiers were key supporters of President Clinton, and these sectors thrived under his leadership. Under President Bush, workers in extraction industries, the military, and, ironically, government did very well. This no doubt reflects the administration's policies of deregulation, including opening federal lands to mining and drilling. It reflects the commodities boom, which owed something to far lower interest rates after September 11, 2001. The oil business was consistently lucrative during the Bush years. And there was war.

The lagging sectors are also informative. Declining fortunes in the domestic auto industry in the 2000s, leading to the bankruptcy of General Motors in the

Great Crisis, mitigated the impact on total inequality of expansion and earnings gains in other sectors. The motor vehicles, bodies, and trailers and parts manufacturing sector, which consistently pays wages well above the national average, lost jobs and saw stagnant earnings from 2002 to 2007; thus inequality *declined* on that account. This is of course not good news, and it sounds a caution against regarding any inequality statistic as an indicator of social welfare per se. Sometimes a decrease in inequality is to be celebrated, and sometimes it is not.

A mere inspection of this evidence has obvious implications for the notion that inequality is a "race between education and technology," as Goldin and Katz (2008) have argued. The simple intersectoral dynamic shows, plainly, that *there are practically no jobs to be had in the winning sectors*. Employment in those sectors is small. It grows slowly, even when the sectors are booming.

So even if large numbers of young people "acquire the skills needed to advance" (Paulson, 2006), there is no evidence that the economy will provide them with employment in the hot fields. And there is another problem. To invest in education as a strategy is to presuppose that one knows, in advance, what the education should be for. Education is specialized. It does little good to train for jobs that, in the short space of four or five years, may (and do) fall out of fashion. Those who entered computer science in the late 1990s learned this the hard way.

The experience of the transition from information economy to war economy clearly indicates that we cannot know what to train for. Rather, education and training have become a kind of lottery, whose winners and losers are determined, *ex post*, by the behavior of the economy. Thus students who studied information technology in the mid-1990s were lucky; those completing similar degrees in 2000 faced unemployment. And who predicted that the *public sector* would fare so well, relatively speaking, under President George W. Bush? At present writing, with budget cutting all the rage, that moment too is over.

The Changing Geography of American Income Inequality

Figure 6.2 shows that variation in earnings across sectors, even when crudely aggregated, far surpasses the variation in earnings across states. But there is substantial geographic variation in the earnings and incomes as well. At the state level, per capita income ranged from $27,028 in Mississippi to $57,746 in Washington, D.C., in 2006, a ratio of better than 2:1 in favor of the capital. Measured across counties, the range is higher than 12:1, from a per capita income of just $9,140 per person in Loup County, Nebraska, to $110,292 in New York, New York.

The BEA definition of income includes wages and salaries but also incorporates rent, interest and dividends, government transfer payments, and other sources.[16] As such, income affords a broader picture of economic well-being than earnings. The ideal dataset for studying income inequality would include regular measurements of income for all individuals or households along with geographical and demographic identifiers. Such data exist in the form of income tax returns, but researchers do not have access to individual records.

However, as noted above, the BEA produces income and population estimates for every county in the United States annually.[17] These data are supplied through Local Area Personal Income Statistics in the Regional Economics Accounts (BEA 2008). Given this annual series, we calculate Theil's T for income inequality measured between counties.[18]

As with sector-based measures, changes in between-county income inequality have two components: changes in relative population and changes in relative incomes. Inequality declines when poor counties add income faster than rich counties or middle income counties add population faster than counties at either tail of the distribution. When rich counties get relatively richer, poor counties get relatively poorer, or middle income counties lose population share, inequality rises.

From 1969 to 2006, between-county income inequality in the United States increased, but the path was not smooth. In the first years of the period, from 1969 to 1976, cross-county inequality declined. Then a steady rise in inequality occurred until the mid-1980s, from which point it accelerated through the end of the decade. 1990 to 1994 saw another decline. There was then another increase, pushing this measure of inequality to a new peak in 2000, just as with the survey-based measure of income inequality and with the sector-based earnings measure. A steep decline followed through 2003. Figure 6.8 plots two series of U.S. income inequality, the Census Bureau between-household measure and the between-county measure. The two have similar trends, but the data break in the Census measure makes it incomparable before and after 1992, and difficult to compare with the single continuous between-counties measure. The between-counties measure also shows more variability from year to year, consistent with the normal behavior of a group-based Theil when compared to a sample-based Gini.

Figure 6.9 plots the between-state component of income inequality and the sum of the various within-state components of county income inequality from 1969 to 2006. The height of the bar represents total between-county inequality,

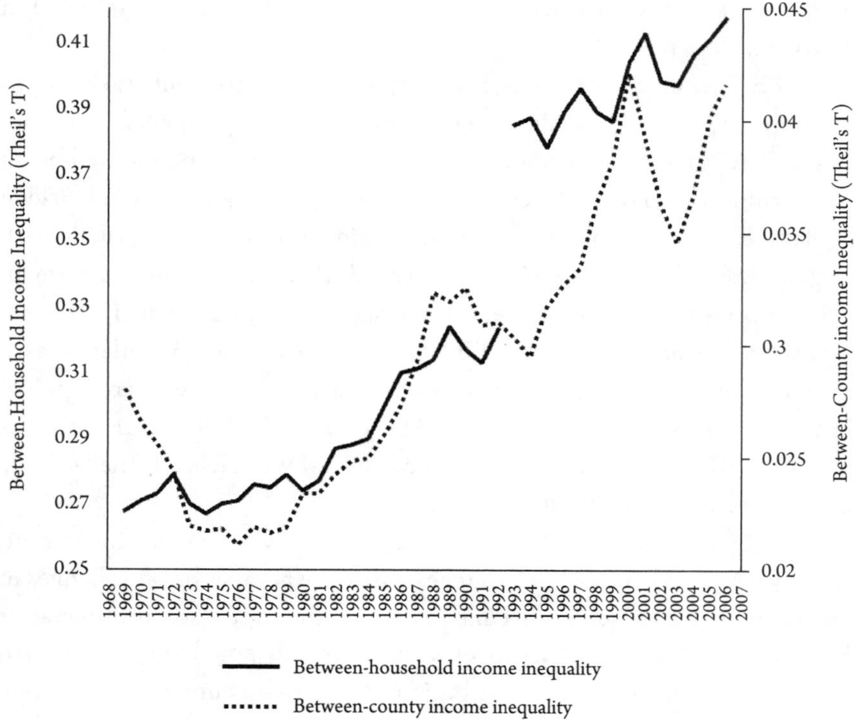

Figure 6.8. U.S. income inequality, 1969–2006: Households and counties.

and the white portion represents the between-state component. Thus this figure takes full advantage of the additive decomposability of the Theil statistic.

Despite a fairly high correlation in year-to-year movements, the between-states and between-counties components of inequality actually have different trends. Inequality between states *declined* over the entire period from 1969 to 2006, advancing the historic project of interregional convergence that has raised relative incomes in the Deep South since the New Deal. For example, although still the lowest in the nation, per capita income in Mississippi grew from 62 percent of national per capita income in 1969 to 74 percent in 2006. Alabama, Arkansas, Georgia, South Carolina, North Carolina, and Tennessee made similar gains. On the other hand, inequality within states but between counties rose, with a strong updraft in booms and downdraft in slumps. Of course, the biggest updraft came with the information technology explosion of the late 1990s.

In those years, the information technology boom and rising income inequality were both widely noted features of the American economy. One was celebrated, the other deplored. From January 1994 to February 2000, the

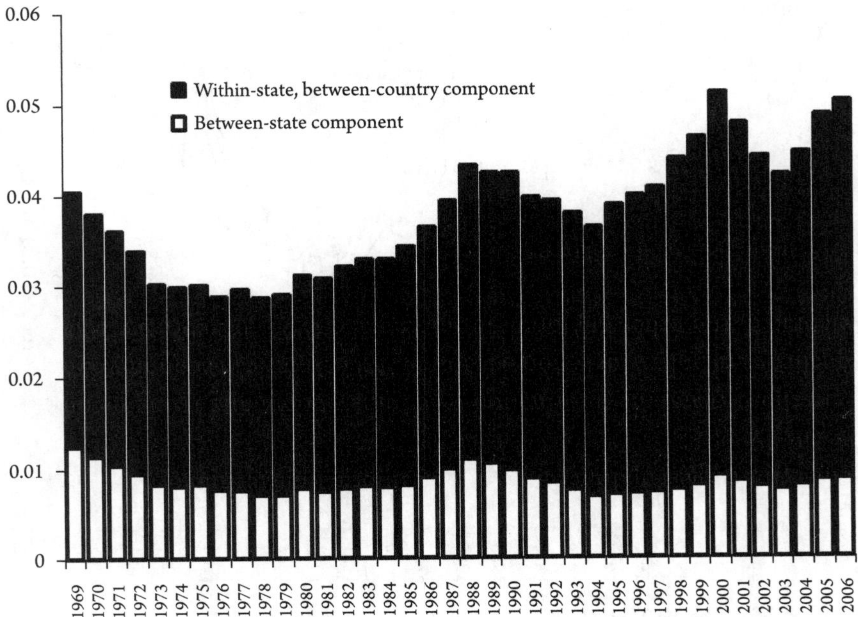

Figure 6.9. Components of Theil's T statistic of between-county U.S. income inequality, 1969–2006.

tech-heavy NASDAQ Composite index rose by 605 percent, from 776.80 to 4,696.69. Inequality as measured in the tax data likewise soared. Few noted that the two phenomena were, in fact, identical. As we have already seen, figure 2.5 matches the level of between-county income inequality against the natural logarithm of the NASDAQ Composite. The two series move together seamlessly from 1992 to 2004.

The concentration of increases in geographic inequality within states, but between counties, raises a question similar to that addressed in the previous section: How widely dispersed were the income gains? It's clear that they must have been concentrated, for otherwise many counties would have shared the income gains, and the between-counties component of income inequality would not have increased. But how concentrated, exactly, were they?

The answer to this question is easily found from the Theil elements. It is well known that technology firms are not distributed uniformly; they are concentrated in centers such as San Francisco and San Jose, Seattle, Raleigh-Durham, Austin, and Boston. Their financiers are concentrated in New York County, New York—otherwise known as Manhattan. Income growth in the counties surrounding these areas accounted for the bulk of the inequality increase in the late 1990s, and when the information technology bubble burst in 2000,

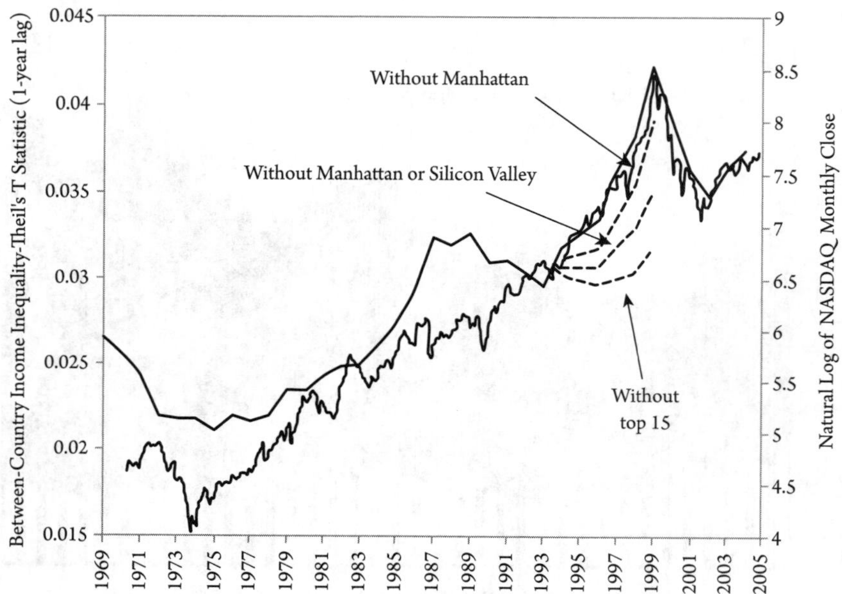

Figure 6.10. Theil's T Statistic of U.S. between-county income inequality, 1969–2006, plotted against the (log) NASDAQ composite index, with three counterfactual scenarios for income growth from 1994 to 2000, each omitting certain groups of counties.

falling relative incomes in these same areas reduced aggregate between-county inequality. In particular, the same four counties that contributed most to the increase in between-county income inequality from 1994 to 2000 contributed most to the inequality decline from 2000 to 2003: New York, Santa Clara, San Mateo, and San Francisco.

A little experiment can illustrate just how much the rise in inequality in the United States in the late 1990s owed to these places. Suppose we alter the dataset, selecting certain counties whose contributions to the overall increase in inequality was the largest. Suppose that for these counties we substitute a counterfactual income growth at just the national average for the period from 1994 to the end of the technology boom. What do we find? We find that doing this for just one county—New York—makes a substantial difference. Doing it for five counties—New York, Santa Clara, San Francisco, San Mateo, and King (Washington)—reduces the growth of between-counties inequality by half. Removing the top fifteen counties from the dataset in this way eliminates the increase in inequality altogether. Of these, almost all have distinctive presence in the technology sector. Figure 6.10 reproduces figure 2.5, but with the three counterfactual scenarios sketched in.

Table 6.3. **Population and Per Capita Income for Selected U.S. Counties and Years**

Population	*1994*	*2000*	*2003*	*2006*
San Francisco, CA	742,316	777,669	759,056	756,376
San Mateo, CA	674,871	708,584	$698,132	700,898
Santa Clara, CA	1,561,366	1,686,621	1,678,189	1,720,839
New York, NY	1,503,909	1,540,934	1,577,267	1,612,630
Per Capita Income	***1994***	***2000***	***2003***	***2006***
San Francisco, CA	$33,164	$55,658	$53,864	$69,942
San Mateo, CA	$33,628	$58,893	$52,235	$66,839
Santa Clara, CA	$29,255	$54,183	$46,569	$55,735
New York, NY	$56,905	$85,752	$82,904	$110,292
U.S.	$22,172	$29,845	$31,504	$36,714

Of course, the slump in 2000 took the bloom off the technology rose, and the NASDAQ never recovered its peak valuations. Yet inequality did start growing again, beginning in 2003, and from that point the inequality measure and the NASDAQ diverged. The rebound in inequality from 2003 to 2006 (the end of this run of data) was of three pieces. First, New York, New York recovered, as Wall Street tends to do when the economy picks up. Second, there was a concentration of increasing income around Washington, D.C., as the government grew massively in response to September 11 and the wars in Afghanistan and Iraq. This was a Beltway Boom. Third, there was growth of incomes in Southern California, New Orleans, Las Vegas, and Southern Florida, areas central to the housing bubble. The series ends before the housing bust, but the consequences of that event for these regions are easy to surmise.

Thus rising geographic income inequality from 1994 to 2000 was largely an artifact of the information technology boom. The bust undid the immediate income gains and reversed some of the rise in inequality. With the bust came large, arbitrary, and unnecessary losses on many who were not prepared to shoulder them. And yet it is difficult to be too harsh about a period that generated full employment, a compressed wage structure in parts of the economy, and technological transformation. As Robert Shapiro, former undersecretary of commerce for economic affairs, has written (Shapiro 2002):

> The . . . bubble represented an excess of something that in itself has real value for the economy—information technologies. The bubble began in overinvestment in IT and spread to much of the stock market; but at its core, much of the IT was economically sound and efficient. Further, these dynamics also played a role in the capital spending boom of the 1990s, and much of that capital spending translated into permanently higher productivity.

To this, we note again that the full employment achieved in the late 1990s raised living standards very broadly and engendered lasting productivity gains, as well as demonstrating that full employment can be achieved without inflation—something much of the economics profession had not believed possible before that time.

The 2003 to 2006 pattern is less benign. The national capital and the counties around it, in Northern Virginia and Southern Maryland, thrived amid a vast growth in war spending, as well as in other government spending, and no doubt also increased spending by private lobbies. The growth in Southern California, South Florida, and other areas was a precursor to the financial crisis.

The ultimate economic consequences should, as with the late 1990s, be judged in part by the worth of the activities undertaken. Three years into the financial crisis and the housing bust, ten years after the start of the Afghanistan war, and eight years into Iraq, it is very difficult to see what the long-term benefits of the income growth generated in the 2000s actually may be.

Interpreting Inequality in the United States

Long before the financial crisis, distributional issues in the United States were a bipartisan concern, bordering on obsession in some quarters but achieving at least respectful discussion even from conservative leaders. Thus Treasury Secretary Henry Paulson spoke out in 2006:

> Amid this country's strong economic expansion, many Americans simply aren't feeling the benefits. Many aren't seeing significant increases in their take-home pay.[19]

President George W. Bush, who early in his term famously addressed a group of "have-mores" as "my base," gave a conventional conservative's nod to the inequality issue in early 2007:

> The fact is that income inequality is real; it's been rising for more than 25 years. The reason is clear: We have an economy that increasingly rewards education, and skills because of that education.[20]

And Federal Reserve chairman Ben Bernanke, a veteran economist, gave himself over to reflections on the same topic a month later:

> Three principles seem to be broadly accepted in our society: that economic opportunity should be as widely distributed and as equal as possible; that economic outcomes need not be equal but should be linked to the contributions each person makes . . . and that people should receive some insurance against the most adverse economic outcomes.[21]

In an appearance on the *Charlie Rose Show* on September 20, 2007, former Federal Reserve chairman Alan Greenspan said it flatly: "You cannot have a market capitalist system if there is a significant mood in the population that its rewards are unjustly distributed." Thus the prevailing view on the political right.

What is striking about these concerns, though, is how little they reflect the actual phenomena of rising inequality in America from the mid-1970s to the present. Though it is true that American jobs shifted out of unionized manufacturing and into services, that phenomenon is not primarily one of large numbers being left behind. On the contrary: the labor force expanded, adding women, minorities, and younger workers at a high rate. Historic regional differences declined, as the South converged to the national average. And in the late 1990s, with full employment, wages for low-wage workers rose and poverty rates for minority populations hit all-time lows. In addition, measures such as the expanded Earned Income Tax Credit and a higher minimum wage kicked in, helping further to make work pay and to stabilize incomes at the bottom of the pay structure. Yet this was exactly the moment when income inequality hit its all-time high.

Clearly—and however uncomfortable it may be for some of the prevailing narratives on the American Left—it is necessary to take a different view.

Is income inequality bad for employment? Obviously not. Consider the increasingly close relationship between changes in employment and changes in U.S. between-county income inequality, as shown in figure 6.11.

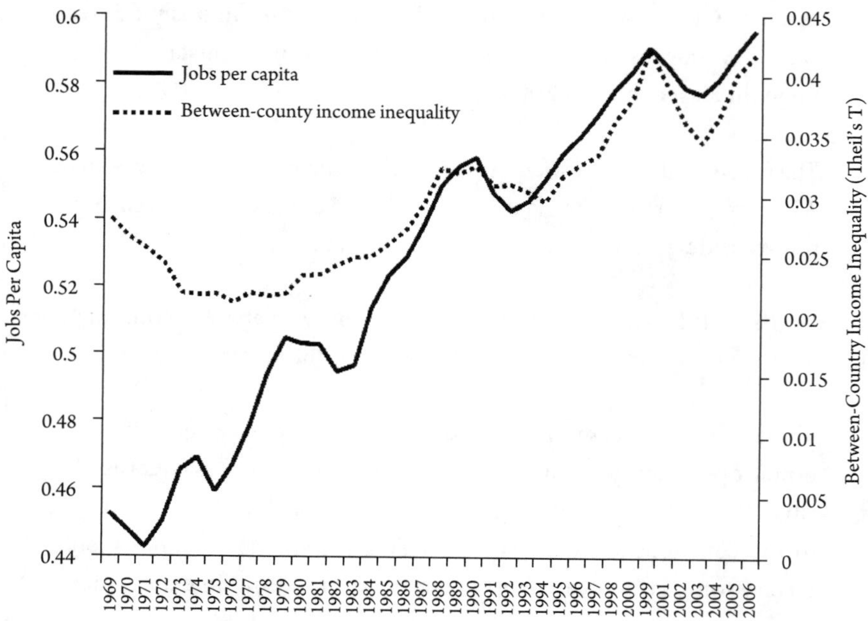

Figure 6.11. U.S. between-county income inequality and jobs per capita, 1969–2006.

From 1969 to 1989 the series measuring inequality and jobs per capita are only loosely linked. Over this period, the levels have a correlation of .47, and year-to-year changes are almost totally uncorrelated. However, since 1990 employment and inequality have moved together. The levels have a correlation of .95 and the year-to-year changes have a correlation of .79. What does this mean?

Very plainly, it means that since the 1980s the American business cycle has been based on financial and credit bubbles, and therefore on the enrichment, through the capital markets, of a very small number of people in a very few places. Truly we have become a "trickle-down economy"—as we were not before. A rising tide may lift all boats, but recent business cycles have been more like waves, whereby certain sectors and areas ride the peaks before crashing to the shore. This is a sign, surely, not of the social evil of inequality per se but of the instability of bubble economies, closely associated with inequality of income, wealth, and power, for which we now pay a fearsome price.

Conclusion

In recent decades in America, economic inequality increased. This was, however, not some general social process, widely spread across the structures of pay and income. It was, rather, mainly due to extravagant gains by those in finance and in the leading sectors of the day: information technology in the 1990s, and the military and mortgage booms of the 2000s. What is astonishing, however, is how few people actually enjoyed the income gains.[22] At their peak of expansion, the winning sectors did not generate many jobs; at best their success facilitated job creation in the many sectors that did not, themselves, experience rising wages.

What we can see, plainly, is that the American economy became leveraged, in such a way that its performance as a whole came to depend on the possibility of a very small number of people becoming very rich in very limited lines of work. In the first wave, information technology in the 1990s, the process could be justified, perhaps, by the potential gains affecting us all. In the 2000s, where growth was driven first by war and then for a few brief years by abusive mortgage lending, the saving grace is harder to see.

The deeper issue with inequality of this type is surely instability. That which rises like a rocket above the plain also eventually falls back to earth. And the problem with the trick of generating prosperity through inequality is simply that it cannot be continually repeated. The false starts to economic expansion since the Great Crisis in 2008—so quickly depleted by rising oil and food prices—are a sign that bubbles are no longer a plausible way to generate economic growth.

Notes

1. All of this is documented in *Created Unequal*.
2. In the early 1980s, I organized hearings on the topic for the Joint Economic Committee; witnesses were hard to find and the subject did not attract much attention. Indeed, as a young economist not distant from my professional training, I recall wondering why my boss, Rep. Henry S. Reuss, the chairman of the Joint Economic Committee at the time, was interested in the topic.
3. Thus one could not say whether the increases in inequality preceded or followed such major technological developments as widespread introduction of desktop computers. It turned out that increases in pay inequality were largely before 1984, while the spread of computers accelerated only afterward. (The first IBM PC was introduced in 1981, but major diffusion began with the economic recovery of 1983–1984.)
4. The use of those funds was knows as the "burn rate," prompting Michael Wolff's entertaining book of that title (1998).
5. This dramatic finding should, I believe, have been qualified in one respect. Piketty and Saez show a major increase in the share of taxable (adjusted gross income) going to the very top echelon in 1986–87, at a time that was otherwise generally tranquil and when there is very little observed change in the taxable incomes of the other 99 percent. The most reasonable explanation for this, in my view, is that the 1986 Tax Reform Act greatly expanded the definition of taxable income for top earners, while also taxing them at a lower rate. (This was the clear intention of the Act's designers, who were Capitol Hill allies of mine at the time.) Thus the income that appears in this data after 1986

was most probably present beforehand, but excluded from AGI owing to tax references that were removed in the 1986 law. The effect on the Piketty-Saez data would be to create a break in data; adjusting for it would therefore reduce the measured increase in the take of the topmost group.

6. The movement in this ratio is also an unreliable gauge of social trends. It was 525:1 in 2000 before plunging to 281:1 in 2002 (United for a Fair Economy 2007). No socialist revolution had occurred; the decline merely reflected the impact of the information technology bust on the earnings of people like Bill Gates.
7. The remainder of this chapter is adapted in part from James K. Galbraith and J. Travis Hale, "American Inequality: From IT Bust to Big Government Boom," *Economists' Voice*, 2006, vol. 3, issue 8, article 6.
8. Kuznets was not interested in inequalities stemming from nonlabor sources of income, such as capital gains, and deliberately excluded them from the analysis to avoid undue complications.
9. By construction, the sum of the positive elements must be greater than the sum of the negative elements.
10. Top coding refers to open-ended reporting of the highest incomes, which changed from "$250,000 and above" to "$1 million and above" in this instance. Improving the coverage of the top incomes has the unintended consequence of increasing measured inequality, with the ironic result that countries working harder to measure inequality report more of it, other things equal. (This may be, in part, why so many researchers and others in the 1990s came to deplore the supposedly higher inequality of the United States compared to major countries in Europe.) In the Theil approach, all cash payrolls are collected at their actual values and merged into the average for that region/sector. Each method has virtues and each has disadvantages.
11. We variously treat Washington, D.C., as a state and a county equivalent, depending on the context.
12. A Gini point is a 1 percent rise in the Gini coefficient.
13. Although it is practically instinctive for economists to believe that a large sample such as the CPS must be "representative," thought should be given to the peculiar nature of income distributions and therefore of the Gini coefficient. Income distributions have "fat tails": there are more extreme cases than one would expect from a normal distribution. Increasing the coverage therefore has the effect of adding to the proportion of extreme cases that are measured, and increasing the value of the reported Gini. For this reason, even though the Gini coefficient itself is standardized between 0 and 1 and therefore comparable across samples, it is comparable across populations only if sample sizes, top coding, and other methods are the same. Unfortunately, this is never the case in samples taken in different countries and often not the case for samples taken in the same country at different times. This, more than actual error in the measures, may account for the poor comparability of most, if not all, Gini-based inequality datasets across countries and over time.
14. Note, however, that the contribution of manufacturing to inequality, though large, remains stable over this period.
15. The increase in earnings for the other information services sector is an artifact of a change to the taxonomy. Internet publishing and broadcasting became part of other information services in 2007.
16. "Personal Income is the income that is received by all persons from all sources. It is calculated as the sum of wage and salary disbursements, supplements to wages and salaries, proprietors' income with inventory valuation and capital consumption adjustments, rental income of persons with capital consumption adjustment, personal dividend income, personal interest income, and personal current transfer receipts, less contributions for government social insurance. The personal income of an area is the income that is received by, or

on behalf of, all the individuals who live in the area; therefore, the estimates of personal income are presented by the place of residence of the income recipients" (BEA 2008).

17. Source data for BEA income estimates are from a host of government sources, including "the state unemployment insurance programs of the Bureau of Labor Statistics, U.S. Department of Labor; the social insurance programs of the Centers for Medicare and Medicaid Services (CMS, formerly the Health Care Financing Administration), U.S. Department of Health and Human Services, and the Social Security Administration; the Federal income tax program of the Internal Revenue Service, U.S. Department of the Treasury; the veterans benefit programs of the U.S. Department of Veterans Affairs; and the military payroll systems of the U.S. Department of Defense" (BEA 2008).
18. "Counties are considered to be the 'first-order subdivisions' of each State and statistically equivalent entity, regardless of their local designations (county, parish, borough, etc.). Thus, the following entities are considered to be equivalent to counties for legal and/or statistical purposes: The parishes of Louisiana; the boroughs and census areas of Alaska; the District of Columbia; the independent cities of Maryland, Missouri, Nevada, and Virginia; that part of Yellowstone National Park in Montana; and various entities in the possessions and associated areas" (National Institute of Standards and Technology 1990).
19. Remarks at Columbia University, August 1, 2006. Whether Secretary Paulson actually qualifies as a conservative is debatable, particularly following the publication in 2010 of his memoir of the financial crisis, *On the Brink*. But he worked for a conservative president and seemed to be one at the time.
20. State of the Economy Address at Federal Hall, New York, January 31, 2007.
21. Remarks before the Greater Omaha Chamber of Commerce, February 6, 2007.
22. Five percent of the workforce would be an extravagant estimate, counting very generously all the participants in the leading sectors, and micro tax data suggest at least an order of magnitude less. That is, major gains were restricted to a handful of people *within* the leading sectors, especially in technology and in finance.

CHAPTER 7

State-Level Income Inequality and American Elections

From the late 1960s onward, the United States *as a whole* has experienced rising wage and income inequality. But the relevant political unit in America is not the nation; it is the state. To search for effects of economic inequality on political behavior in a federal system, we need to examine developments below the national level—to assess relative changes in inequality in the different states. Rising inequality *within* states reflects the national trend, but variation occurs from state to state and year to year (Langer 1999; Bernard and Jensen 1998; Bernstein, McNichol, and Lyons 2006). If inequality has political consequences, it may be possible to detect those consequences in election outcomes.

Election outcomes, in turn, depend on two factors: who votes, and who they vote for. So in this chapter[1] we examine whether differences in income inequality at the state level are related to differences in voter turnout and in voter choice.

Why might inequality affect voter turnout? Brady (2004, p. 668) presents a speculative vote-mobilizing argument:

> An increase in inequality will not only reduce the incomes of lower-class families but also change that group's political circumstances. With the distressing change in social facts, lower-income people might decide to increase their political activity to redress the situation. They might decide that government should be used to adjust the degree of inequality by adjusting people's capacities, opportunities, luck or decision-making. It seems possible that lower-class activity might increase in these circumstances. It also seems possible that upper-class participation might increase in response.

This is a plausible argument, but reality could cut the other way. For instance, increasing inequality could lead to disengagement from political activity. The rich might lose interest and the poor might lose faith in government's ability to deal effectively with social problems. Poverty, unemployment, and economic hardship disrupt social relationships and cause psychological stress; thus when inequality rises so does the opportunity cost of civic participation (Rosenstone 1982). For all members of an unequal society, there are fewer "incentives for civic engagement" and reduced capacity to build social capital (Putnam 2000, p. 21). In this vein, Widestrom argues that "as economic inequality becomes increasingly concentrated and segregated, work disappears, voluntary organizations disappear, community networks fall apart, leaders stop mobilizing, and therefore voter participation declines" (2006, p. 6). More directly, inequality could affect turnout through vote repression. Faced with inequality-induced class conflict, the rich could simply move to restrict voting access for the poor, who are necessarily more numerous (Piven and Cloward 1988).

That there is a rich and ongoing history of turnout suppression as a political strategy in the United States is of course not exactly a secret. Voter registration requirements, voter identification requirements, location of polling stations, distribution of voting machines, restrictions on absentee balloting—all are part of the warp and woof of American politics in the recent past, and in battles to the present day. The question to pose, then, is whether there is a systematic relationship between economic inequality and election turnout.

Next, how might income inequality affect voter choice? This is a subtler issue. Inequality is an abstraction, a statistician's reality. It is not something voters observe directly; still less do they make consistent comparative judgments about it. It is, rather, a condition of the electorate itself. So we should perhaps look at inequality as an indicator of the condition of the population, as a feature of the kind of electorate we have, in relation to the political parties that exist. In the two-party United States, since the New Deal, the Republican Party has broadly represented business interests, while the Democrats have enjoyed a base among minorities and in organized labor. These patterns may be changing—with Reagan Democrats and Wall Street Democrats being cases in point—but they surely represent the postwar normal situation.

Several analysts argue that the Democratic Party, compared to the Republicans, is a diverse alliance with dissonant economic interests (Edsall 1984). If there is force behind these arguments, it could lead to greater Democratic strength in states that are more unequal, and therefore more diverse. But there is a simpler argument. More inequality means, arithmetically, a larger proportion of low-income voters. Presumably they have a class interest in Social Security,

Medicare, Medicaid, and other redistributive and otherwise interventionist public programs. Higher inequality also means a smaller middle class, which may already benefit from the welfare state but which, by the same token, has less interest in expanding it, and much less in bearing the burden of the associated taxes. These considerations suggest a slightly counterintuitive result: that the more egalitarian party benefits from a less-egalitarian starting point. On reflection though, this would not be surprising at all. It would simply reflect social processes in a largely stable society, where one party pushes for more equality, the other for less, with each stronger in those political units where conditions are more favorable to its case.

If this general line of analysis is correct, then a high-inequality state has two contrary forces at work. On the one side, the rich fear the poor and impose every difficulty in the path of the vote. (If the rich are white and the poor are black or brown, these matters are especially easy to see, as the entire history of the Voting Rights Act shows.) On the other side, the numerous poor, if they can gain access to the vote and representation from the parties—and if they can overcome the divisive forces to which they are likely to be subjected (Frank 2007)—then they are likely to vote to improve their economic position. If they succeed, the state has every prospect of becoming more egalitarian over time. It will therefore become less interested in further redistributive programs, and the party opposed to redistribution will gain strength.

But what determines the balance of power between a change-oriented majority and a vote-suppressing overclass in the first place? A simple possibility lies in the degree of autonomy accorded to poorer people *within* the political structure of the state. Voting, after all, is *local*. If a poor community is substantially self-governing, free (to the extent possible) of control by a local oligarch, it stands to reason that it will not suppress the vote. The key to rule from below, in other words, would appear to be an unequal state, but one in which the rich and the poor live apart from each other, so that the rich do not interfere directly in the voting behavior of the poor. This will more likely be true in bigger states, and in states where the rich and the poor are separated by accidents of political history or economic geography into different political units.

We will call this phenomenon the geographic stratification of incomes. This is a phenomenon related to (but distinct from) income inequality. Where dissonant communities live substantially apart, immediate conflicts are less likely to arise. Each can govern its own neighborhoods, with less interference or concern about the other. It may therefore be easier to maintain the uneasy coalition between working-class voters and elite contributors and candidates (Jacobs and Skocpol 2005) that characterizes the Democratic Party. Thus we argue that, independently of the effect of income inequality per se, geographic income stratification should favor Democratic candidates.

These thoughts lead to three empirical suppositions. First, more inequality should normally lead to lower voter turnout. Second, the effect of inequality on election outcomes is complex: higher inequality means, in principle, a left-leaning electorate, but this effect may be offset by lower turnout. Third, in states with higher geographic income stratification, the inequality effect should dominate the turnout effect, producing left-leaning election outcomes.

Some Initial Models Using Off-the-Shelf Data for the 2000 Election

We begin by restricting attention to a single election: the 2000 Bush-Gore contest. Using off-the-shelf data, we test whether inequality affects voter turnout and choice at the state level after accounting for other relevant factors. The explanatory variables are (1) income inequality, measured by state, using the U.S. Census Bureau's Housing and Household Economic Statistics Division Gini ratios of household income inequality (U.S. Census Bureau 2005b); (2) per capita income (BEA 2007); (3) the level of urbanization, quantified as the number of residents in Census Bureau urban clusters and urban areas divided by state population (U.S. Census Bureau 2005c); and (4) the proportion of white, non-Hispanic individuals in a state (U.S. Census Bureau 2006).

For the voter-choice models, the dependent variable is the Democratic Party's percentage of the two-party vote (Leip 2007). In the turnout analysis, the dependent variable is the participation rate of a state's voting-eligible population (McDonald 2007).

Table 7.1 displays descriptive statistics and table 7.2 expresses the population-weighted correlations among the variables just described for the 2000 election. A large voter turnout correlates with a richer, whiter—and more egalitarian—electorate. A high percentage of the population living in urban areas, higher minority populations, greater per capita incomes, and high inequality are all associated with a larger Democratic vote.

Model 7.1 is a straightforward cross-section regression that uses per capita income, the percentage of white non-Hispanic residents, the percentage of urban residents, and the inequality of household income to explain voter turnout (weighted by state population) at the state level for the 2000 presidential election.

Table 7.1. **U.S. State Incomes, Selected Characteristics, and Political Outcomes, 2000**

	U.S. Average	*State Minimum*	*State Maximum*
Per capita income	$29,847	$21,005	$41,489
Percentage white non-Hispanic	69.5	23.3	96.6
Percentage urban	79.0	38.2	94.5
Household Gini coefficient	.463	.402	.499
Percentage Gore (two-party)	50.3	28.3	65.6
Turnout percentage	54.2	44.2	69.5

Table 7.2. **Table of Correlations of Selected State Variables, 2000**

	Income	*White*	*Urban*	*Inequality*	*Gore*	*Turnout*
Income	1					
White	−0.209	1				
Urban	0.699	−0.577	1			
Inequality	0.248	−0.625	0.366	1		
Gore	0.755	−0.181	0.556	0.378	1	
Turnout	0.395	0.405	0.09	−0.332	0.381	1

Voter Turnout Cross-Sectional Model

$$\begin{aligned}\textbf{Turnout} = \beta_0 + \beta_1 * \textbf{Income} + \beta_2 * \textbf{White} + \beta_3 * \\ \textbf{Urban} + \beta_4 * \textbf{Inequality} + \varepsilon\end{aligned} \tag{7.1}$$

Table 7.3 displays the results for model 7.1. States with smaller minority populations and higher incomes had higher voter turnout, other variables held constant. The coefficient for the inequality variable is negative, as expected, but it is not statistically significant, once the minority variable is controlled for. This suggests, with some plausibility so far, that turnout is about poverty and race, not so much inequality per se.

Model 7.2 uses the same covariates to explain state-level outcomes in the 2000 presidential election.

Table 7.3. **The Voter Turnout Cross-Sectional Model, 2000**

Parameter	*Coefficient Estimate*	*Standard Error*	*T Value*	*Pr > |t|*
Intercept	0.495	0.203	2.44	0.0187
Income*	0.634	0.218	2.91	0.0056
White	0.149	0.066	2.27	0.0282
Urban	0.024	0.083	0.29	0.7694
Inequality	−0.564	0.367	−1.54	0.1313
$R^2 = .438$				

Note: * Expressed in hundreds of thousands of dollars.

Table 7.4. **The Voter Choice Cross-Sectional Model, 2000**

Parameter	*Coeff. Estimate*	*Standard Error*	*T Value*	*Pr > |t|*
Intercept	−0.539	0.248	−2.17	0.0351
Income*	1.226	0.266	4.6	<.0001
White	0.12	0.08	1.5	0.1418
Urban	0.075	0.101	0.75	0.4594
Inequality	1.161	0.448	2.59	0.0129
$R^2 = .627$				

Note: * Expressed in hundreds of thousands of dollars.

State-Level Presidential Choice Cross-Sectional Model

$$\textbf{Gore} = \beta_0 + \beta_1 * \textbf{Income} + \beta_2 * \textbf{White} + \beta_3 * \textbf{Urban} + \beta_4 * \textbf{Inequality} + \varepsilon \quad (7.2)$$

Table 7.4 displays the results for model 7.2. States with higher inequality tended to support Gore in 2000, even after controlling for the level of income, racial composition and urbanization. The race and urban variables do not appear to have significant independent effects after income and income inequality are considered. High average income is associated with a higher percentage of Democratic voting at the state level, opposite of the relationship at the individual level (McCarty, Poole and Rosenthal 2006; Bartels 2006; Gelman, Shor, Bafumi, and Park 2007).

In 2000 and 2004, the battleground states of Florida, Pennsylvania, and Ohio received a great deal of extra attention from the candidates (although Gore did pull out of Ohio well before the vote). The residuals in table 7.5 report

Table 7.5. **Residuals in Key Battleground States from the Voter-Choice Model, 2000**

State	*Actual Gore Vote*	*Predicted Gore Vote*	*Residual*
Florida	0.5	0.503	−0.003
Ohio	0.482	0.478	0.004
Pennsylvania	0.521	0.509	0.012

that model 7.2 predicts quite accurately for these three states. In particular, Florida was too close for the model to call—just like the actual election result. The result is nifty, but not necessarily dispositive.

New Estimates of State-Level Inequality and an Analysis of the Inequality-Elections Relationship over Time

Was 2000 an anomaly, or part of a broader and more general relationship between inequality, voter turnout, and electoral choice? In this section, we develop annual inequality measures for the states and explore fixed-effects models of voter turnout and electoral choice.

The decision to begin the analysis in 2000 was driven by the availability of Census Bureau inequality estimates in this year. At ten-year intervals, the U.S. Census Bureau (2005b) produces income inequality measures at the state level using data from long-form census samples. To move beyond linear interpolation of intercensal values, we need an annual dataset that measures earnings within states, from which we can create an inequality metric. Then we can anchor these new measures to the Census Bureau values, to estimate appropriate Gini coefficients.

The ideal dataset for constructing state inequality measures would contain household-level income data for every American, by state, in every year. Such data do not exist; or, rather, the IRS will not release them. The Census Bureau's Current Population Survey (CPS) furnishes individual-level sample data on a yearly basis. Langer (1999) estimates state Gini coefficients of household income annually from 1976 to 1995 using CPS data. Measures based on the CPS are subject to small sample sizes in smaller states, expression of income within ranges, and top codes that truncate large reported incomes.

Given these limitations, a *group*-based dataset with broad coverage that is consistent across time and space may be superior to sample data at the individual level. As discussed in chapter 6, the BEA in the U.S. Department of Commerce compiles data on wages and employment across dozens of industrial classifications for every state. The BEA source data include information from states' unemployment insurance programs, IRS records, and other official sources (BEA 2000). The main source for underlying data is the Covered Employees and Wages Program (ES-202) in the Bureau of Labor Statistics (BLS 2007).

Given yearly data on payroll and employment for a set of sectors within states, we calculate the between-group component of Theil's T statistic, a measure that yields a consistent lower bound for within-state pay inequality. Although the value of the between-group inequality will be much smaller than the unmeasured populationwide inequality, if the group structure (e.g., economic sectors in this case) is consistent and meaningful, then the two series tend to move together over time, and also in proportion across states, so that the Theil statistic is a good instrument for the unobserved Gini coefficient (Conceição, Galbraith, and Bradford 2001).

Trends in both the state and national series of pay inequality from 1969 to 2004 correlate highly to the decennial income inequality measures for states. The average correlation between the within-state intersectoral Theil statistics and the Census Bureau Gini coefficients of family income in 1969, 1979, 1989, and 1999 is .710.

The nationwide secular trend is so great that the average correlation between the *national*-level interindustrial Theil statistic of pay inequality and the census-based Gini coefficients of family income at the *state* level for the overlapping years is .936, stronger than the correlation of the two within-state measures. The close connection of the national values and the individual state series has two related explanations. First, because the national economy is highly integrated, many of the same factors that contribute to interindustrial pay inequality at the national level will filter down to the states. Second, national-level interindustrial pay inequality picks up broad macroeconomic factors that will affect sources of nonwage income. Interest and dividend incomes, rents, capital gains, and transfer payments are related to regional and national political, social, and economic forces, and these will be better captured by a national pay inequality measure than a state-specific metric.

To maintain the heterogeneity of the within-state variation yet also incorporate the common national factors, we create a synthetic measure of within-state income inequality that incorporates influences from both state and national pay inequality. For each state, we add pay inequality within states to pay inequality measured nationally, multiplied by a state-specific weighting factor that makes the average of the two Theil statistics equal in magnitude over the thirty-five years for each state. These linear combinations of the state and national interindustrial pay inequality measures correlate better to states' census-based Gini coefficients than either the state or the national series alone. The average correlation between the synthetic measure and the state Census Bureau Gini coefficients of family income for the overlapping years is .946.

Armed now with a full panel of pay inequality measures, OLS regressions relate these values to the Census Gini coefficient values for the overlapping years: 1969, 1979, 1989, and 1999. Given the regression coefficients (with separate estimates for all states), interpolations of the intercensal years generate income inequality measures in the familiar form of the Gini coefficient.[2] These estimates may then be deployed to study a range of causes and consequences of economic inequality, topics of rising scholarly and popular interest (Neckerman 2004).

Cross-sectional models relating the estimated Gini coefficients to voter turnout and electoral choice over the last several election cycles are quite noisy. The coefficient for inequality maintains the predicted sign—positive for Democratic share and negative for turnout—but is statistically significant only in some years (turnout in 1988, 1992, and 2004; choice in 2000).

Two-way fixed-effects models shift the focus from cross-sections to changes occurring within states. The control variables are relative income (measured as the proportion of state per capita income to national per capita income), the percentage of white non-Hispanic residents linearly interpolated from decennial values with official estimates for 2004 (Gibson and Jung 2002, U.S. Census Bureau 2006), and the proportion of states' populations living in metropolitan areas (BEA 2007). The explanatory variable of interest is state-level income inequality, as described above.

Turnout Fixed-Effects Model, 1980–2004

$$\begin{aligned}\mathbf{Turnout}_{it} &= \mathbf{Year}_t + \mathbf{State}_i + \beta_1 * \mathbf{Inequality} + \beta_2 * \\ &\mathbf{White} + \beta_3 * \mathbf{Income} + \beta_4 * \mathbf{Urban} + \varepsilon\end{aligned} \tag{7.3}$$

The results of the fixed-effects model are much stronger and more consistent; they indicate that rising inequality is a significant determinant of declines in electoral activity. Indeed, of the included predictors inequality is the only statistically significant explanatory variable, once fixed effects are taken into account.

Voter-Choice Fixed-Effects Model, 1992–2004

$$\begin{aligned}\mathbf{Dem}_{it} &= \mathbf{Year}_t + \mathbf{State}_i + \beta_1 * \mathbf{Inequality} + \beta_2 * \\ &\mathbf{White} + \beta_3 * \mathbf{Income} + \beta_4 * \mathbf{Urban} + \varepsilon\end{aligned} \tag{7.4}$$

Table 7.6. **A Turnout Model with Fixed Effects for Multiple Elections**

Parameter	*Estimate*	*Standard Error*	*T Value*	*Pr > |t|*
Inequality	−0.431	0.14	−3.09	0.0022
White	−0.072	0.077	−0.93	0.3537
Income*	0.019	0.037	0.51	0.611
Metro	−0.229	0.151	−1.52	0.1305
$R^2 = .9034$				

*Per capita income expressed as a proportion of national per capita income.

Table 7.7. **An Outcome Model with Fixed Effects for Multiple Elections**

Parameter	*Estimate*	*Standard Error*	*T Value*	*Pr > |t|*
Inequality	0.73	0.194	3.76	0.0002
White	−0.194	0.148	−1.31	0.1916
Income*	−0.075	0.083	−0.9	0.3704
Metro	−1.294	0.348	−3.72	0.0003
$R^2 = .9481$				

*Per capita income expressed as a proportion of national per capita income.

The voter-choice fixed-effects model covers the four election cycles through 2004; all postdate the Republican realignment in the South. These four elections show a great deal of stasis; three included a Bush on the Republican ticket, and three included a Southern New Democrat. Table 7.7 gives the results from model 7.4. Again, inequality is a significant determinant of the Democratic result, after accounting for fixed effects. Cycle-to-cycle changes in inequality help predict changes in voter choice, controlling for other factors often linked to inequality.

Model 7.4 focuses on the evolution of party affinity within states, rather than on cross-sectional differences between them. Income helps explain how states differ from one another in Democratic voting, but *changes* in state income levels from 1992 to 2004 do not offer much insight into whether a state is becoming more or less inclined to vote Democratic. The metropolitan variable presents a puzzle; the model indicates that growth in metropolitan population results in a more Republican electorate. This variable's inability to differentiate between suburbs and inner cities may account for this result.[3]

Again, the significance of the inequality variable does not directly imply that individuals consider income inequality when they decide to go to the polls and whom to vote for. At the ecological level, the inequality effect could be a mere artifact, reflecting the underlying relationship between income and voting. Low-income voters are less likely to vote, but they are more likely to vote Democratic; moreover, states with a large number of low-income voters will have a higher level of inequality. Nonetheless, because the Electoral College operates at the state level, the statistical effect of state-level inequality on voter turnout and electoral choice suggests that such inequality is a powerful force in determining the outcome of presidential elections.

Inequality and the Income Paradox in Voting

Multilevel analysis allows researchers to include individual-level characteristics, such as household income, and contextual attributes, such as income inequality, in a single model (Raudenbush and Bryk 2002). This approach addresses the concerns about aggregation bias expressed earlier and permits direct estimation of the impact of inequality on voter turnout and electoral choice. We are particularly interested in the effect of inequality, but the multilevel approach opens up other lines of inquiry. For instance, Gelman et al. (2007) use a multilevel model to explain the income paradox in voting: the fact that rich voters favor Republicans, but rich states tend to vote Democratic. The paradox causes confusion among those who have come to generalize Democrats as wealthy professionals and Republicans as blue collar "values voters"; Gelman shows that in *every* state there is a nonnegative correlation between income and Republican voting at the individual level. The question is why this does not translate to Democratic victories in poor states and Republican victories in rich ones, rather than the other way around.

As Gelman and colleagues (2007) show, the income paradox unravels when one considers the differences in strength of the relationship between individual income and Republican voting across the states. In rich states, such as Connecticut, the income-voting relationship is flat: rich people are only slightly more Republican than the poor. In poor states, such as Mississippi, the slope is very steep. The relatively weak association between income and party preference in the rich states helps to explain why, in the aggregate, high per capita income is associated with Democratic voting.

But why are Mississippians so apparently economistic, while Connecticut's citizens show less income bias in their voting behavior? "What's the matter with Connecticut?" as Gelman asks? More generally, why do the states differ in their income-party affinity slopes?

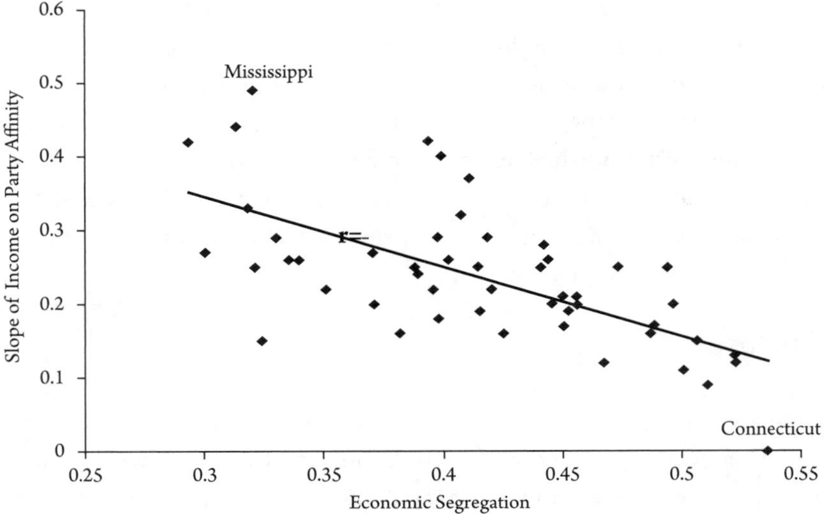

Figure 7.1. Economic segregation and the income/party line.

State-level income inequality measured across individuals plays a minor role at best. The cross-sectional Pearson correlation of the fifty state slopes (from Gelman et al. 2007) with the Census Bureau Gini coefficients of household income in 2000 is only .17. But *geographic income stratification* provides a more promising explanation.

Geographic income stratification measures the degree to which households of like income live near each other. A potential measure of such stratification is a Gini coefficient of between-census tract income inequality divided by the Gini coefficient of between-household inequality; this measures the proportion of income inequality attributable to neighborhood differences (Kim and Jargowsky 2005). Using data from the 2000 Census (U.S. Census Bureau 2005a), it is straightforward to build such a measure for each state. West Virginia shows the least segregation with a value of 0.293, and Connecticut has the most with a measure of 0.536. The average, weighted by state population, is .456.

As the scatterplot in figure 7.1 shows, income segregation is strongly associated with the income-Republican preference slopes in 2000; the correlation coefficient is -.65. This finding leads to a potential answer to the Gelman question, "What's the matter with Connecticut?" In states with a high level of economic segregation, the rich and the poor are spatially separated. Therefore, it would appear, they interfere less in each other's political lives, and the rich are less well placed to reduce the voting turnout of the poor. (Perhaps too, they dislike each other less than they normally would.) They are therefore more likely to form the kind of political coalition that gives life to the Democratic Party. States with low segregation are not inherently less unequal and may even be more so; but the rich and poor live in closer proximity. In these states, class conflict is more palpable, and a unified overclass tends to prevail. Like the other arguments presented at the top of this chapter, this one is speculative, to be sure. But we submit that it carries the awful ring of truth.

Conclusion

Our analysis suggests that high inequality levels are weakly associated with a larger Democratic vote and also with diminished turnout. These results are strengthened when fixed effects are introduced; rising inequality correlates to deepening Democratic preference and reduced turnout. When the spatial location of voting groups is considered, our results suggest that it is not so much the raw inequality of incomes that is decisive, but the existence of inequalities across populations that do not confront each other aggressively in daily and political life.

Notes

1. This chapter is adapted from James K. Galbraith and J. Travis Hale, "State Income Inequality and Presidential Election Turnout and Outcomes," *Social Science Quarterly* 89(4), 887–901.
2. These Gini estimates for the fifty United States and the District of Columbia annually from 1969 to 2004 are available at http://utip.gov.utexas.edu/.
3. An additional task for future research is to examine whether realignment of party strength changed the dynamic between inequality and party preference. Ferguson (2005) explores the role of religion in the states, a factor helping to explain the Republican takeover of the South. In his cross-sectional analysis of the 2004 presidential election, he finds that the link between state inequality and Democratic voting remains, after controlling for religiosity.

CHAPTER 8

Inequality and Unemployment in Europe

A QUESTION OF LEVELS

From 1974 to the present day, the specter of chronic mass unemployment has haunted the continent of Europe.[1] Paradise—the jobless rates of 2 percent or so that were common in the 1950s and 1960s—was lost. In particular, paradise had been lost in comparison to the United States, which enjoyed lower unemployment on average, a much higher employment-to-population ratio, and moments of undisputed full employment. Some observers worried that Americans worked too much (Schor 2002); others view European social protections as worth the price in joblessness (Rifkin 2004, Minc 2011). Clearly something had gone wrong. Before 1970, Europeans had enjoyed full employment alongside their vaunted social model. After the oil shocks and the recession, they seemed to have faced, and made, an ugly choice. To economists, reducing the matter to the most elementary terms, Europe chose equality over efficiency, while America made the opposite choice.[2]

Within Europe, there were differences in unemployment rates, and this too needed explanation. The 1970s and early 1980s had been shocks to a previously successful system. But some countries had managed the shocks and adapted better than others. Why? Soon a line of theory developed, unifying the experience within Europe with the comparison to America. The United States, it was said, enjoyed labor-market or "real-wage" flexibility. In the United States, wage rates would adjust to match the demands of the new economy to the skills of the labor force, raising wages for the educated while lowering them for those who did not adapt. Increased inequality was one consequence, but fuller employment was another.[3]

Inside Europe, those countries that liberalized their labor markets—jettisoning job protections, cutting unemployment insurance, and weakening unions, thus emulating the United States and freeing wages to adjust to the new patterns of supply and demand—would benefit from more jobs and higher incomes. In time this became a practically universal view, and a European policy orthodoxy. Movements to reform national labor markets were promoted, notably by the OECD (1994). Though qualifications can be found in empirical work such as that by Nickell (1997) and Blanchard and Wolfers (1999), these were largely swept aside, and for years greater wage flexibility has been the established official cure for European unemployment. It is being implemented as I write, following the Great Crisis, in adjustment programs imposed on Greece, Spain, Portugal, and Ireland, among other countries.

To be precise, the doctrine holds that greater wage flexibility—the supposed American model—is the cure for high unemployment affecting not Europe as a whole but each European nation-state taken as a separate labor market. The culprits must lie in national labor-market institutions. Reform and liberalize them, and joblessness should fall. Thus the unified theory has a (practically) unstated assumption, which is that the national borders within Europe are also economic borders. Neither local conditions nor the influence of economic policy at the continental level plays an important role in the policy debate.

Now, unemployment happens to individuals. But the unemployment *rate* is a matter of *place*. And places are nested inside larger places. The local has properties the nation may not share. The nation has characteristics that may not apply to the continent where it resides. In an integrated economy, the forces that operate on unemployment rates may extend over many horizons, from the near neighborhood to the entire world. This is just plain common sense. But it is neglected common sense, and the literature on unemployment in Europe ignores it, concentrating without reflection on *national* characteristics and *national* unemployment rates.[4]

Baker, Glyn, Howell, and Schmitt (2005) present a comprehensive review of the national-institutions approach to explaining European unemployment. It turns out that the actual evidence is weak. They find only one solid result, namely, that coordinated collective bargaining and (perhaps) union density are associated with *less* unemployment in Europe. Of course, this interesting finding is inconsistent with the predictions of the rigidities model. It is typically explained away, in European policy assertions, with the argument that the egalitarian, highly unionized, low-unemployment Scandinavians are different; they have their own model, and somehow the rules that apply within their model do not apply elsewhere.[5] This rationalization is a flagrant case of fitting form to fact.

There is also a dissenting position, which holds that restrictive macroeconomic policy rather than bad institutions is the European problem. Palley (2004) is among a handful of Keynesian voices arguing that interest rates and growth rates dominate determination of unemployment in Europe, but like the others he, too, roots relevant decision making at the national level. The higher policy discussion accepts that European policy—especially monetary policy, concentrated in the one pan-European economic institution, the European Central Bank—mainly influences the price level and not the levels of total output or employment. In this way, the European Charter decrees (and most European economists accept) that chronically high unemployment rates in post-oil-shock Europe result mainly from a clash between dynamic market forces and rigid, misguidedly socialist, dogmatically egalitarian national institutions.

In this chapter, we try a different approach. It begins with an effort to reconsider the character of unemployment from a theoretical point of view.

An Inequality-Based Theory of Unemployment

More than a half century ago, as noted at the start of this book, Simon Kuznets (1955) argued that inequality would rise in the early stages of economic development and transition to industrial growth. New urban centers were places of concentrated income and wealth. It was the *differential* between incomes in these places and those in the countryside that would become significant as cities grew, and decline only later as the proportion of the population remaining in the countryside shrank. This was, as we have seen, the most significant single factor behind Kuznets's inverted-U curve.

In 1970, John Harris and Michael Todaro offered a model capturing Kuznets's insight in a paper aimed mainly at development economists. In their model, workers migrate from a low-marginal-product rural sector to cities where minimum wages are imposed, and they accept a high probability of sustained unemployment in exchange for a low probability of getting one of those jobs and enjoying the resulting rise in income. The equilibrium condition is that the expected value of the gain is just equal to the cost incurred in leaving rural employment, and this condition entails substantial equilibrium unemployment—the work lost during the period of search. From this, a positive relationship between urban-rural pay inequality and equilibrium unemployment emerges. The greater the differential, the more migration, and the more milling around at the factory gates, hoping for a lucky break.

Although Harris and Todaro focused on East Africa (an impoverished and agrarian region), consider how their argument might apply in modern Europe. Modern advanced societies have an elite group of knowledge and finance workers, a core of manufacturing workers, and a large reservoir of workers in mundane services (Galbraith 1998). Access to knowledge and finance jobs is restricted by cartels and credentialing. The same is not true for manufacturing workers, who may be unskilled when hired but nevertheless enjoy wage premiums due to industry-specific labor rents. In manufacturing, workers' leverage over pay is governed by the advantages of design and process built into the machines, to which the workers learn quickly to adapt. Services workers with few skills enjoy few such possibilities. The pay in the services sector is therefore low and strongly influenced by social minima, which are decided substantially by politics. Services workers are like the earlier generation of farm workers in many relevant economic respects: they are numerous, they lack any form of market power, and they may be considered a reserve army of the *underemployed*.

So long as the differential between service wages and manufacturing wages is fairly small, *or* if it is possible to search for better jobs while working, most services workers will not abandon current employment to seek better. But on the other hand, if there are large differentials and obstacles to an on-the-job search, they will readily quit their present job in the hope of landing a new one. (In the event of failure, there is always another bad services job to return to.) As that happens, measured unemployment will rise. It has to; unemployment is defined, after all, as the condition of active search for a new job. As in Harris and Todaro, equilibrium local unemployment is a *positive* function of local pay inequalities.

The general concept that inequality creates an incentive to search, which then yields unemployment, has not been applied to Europe or to any developed-country setting so far as we know. But there is no compelling reason it should not be.

Why, then, should the experience of Europe be different after 1974 from what it was before? Two reasons come immediately to mind. The first is that inequality was driven up immediately by the oil shocks and recessions, including the loss of manufacturing jobs. It's not just that jobs are lost in recessions; the differentials among those that remain, and especially between the low-wage services and the better-paid and more advanced sectors that survive the blow, is larger than it was before. And second, there is the process of European integration. This generates rising inequality by the simple expansion of search horizons. In the 1950s, very few low-wage, rural or service-sector Europeans looked past their own national frontiers for work, unless pushed by political forces. By the 1990s, this was commonplace, as Poles flocked to London and Paris became the second-largest Portuguese city. The greater the distance over which one must search, the more necessary it is actually to quit, pack up, and go. Employers in a remote location rightly think that those at their door are needier, more motivated, and more dependent than those writing (or emailing) from afar.

The unhappy implication of this argument is simply that European integration itself, by forcing workers from countries with very different average income levels into the same labor pool, was inevitably destined to raise European unemployment. But both the prevailing economic theory and the prevailing notion of where labor markets begin and end—a notion that is entirely habitual and has nothing to do with any economic doctrine—would prevent this from being seen clearly by economists and policy makers alike.

Then there is a second argument, which adds a dynamic and longer-term element to the discussion.

Long ago, the work of the Swedish trade union economists Rudolph Meidner and Gösta Rehn (1951) underpinned what became the conceptualization of a distinctively Swedish or Scandinavian model. In fact, the Meidner-Rehn argument is general; it is not restricted in application to the special conditions of Scandinavia. Among other things, they pointed to a consequence of large inequalities in the structure of pay, which permit technologically backward firms to stay competitive, despite higher unit costs, by paying their workers less than more progressive firms. Thus a high degree of inequality in the wage structure would be associated with weak technological dynamism, a lower rate of investment in best-practice technique, and, over time, a lower average productivity and standard of living than would otherwise be the case.

Deliberate compression of wage differentials, on the other hand, puts the technological laggards out of business. It therefore releases labor, especially since backward businesses tend to be labor-intensive. But with active labor-market policies (providing retraining for displaced workers), a large investment-goods sector (replacing the lost capacity), and a policy of strong aggregate demand (assuring market growth sufficient to absorb the greater production), the end result can be rapid expansion by the technologically progressive firms. And to this is added a policy of international *openness*—rigorous rejection of trade protections—encouraging the advanced firms to find an ever-larger share of their markets in the wider world. In this way, over time a policy of social-democratic wage compression increases average productivity and average living standards; this is what actually happened steadily in Scandinavia from the 1940s through the 1990s. (What made the Meidner-Rehn model "Scandinavian" was only that it was invented and applied there—and ignored everywhere else.)

Some of the displaced and unemployed can then be absorbed in the expanding, advanced industries. Some can be retired; after all, in comparison with the lifetime of industries, individual working lives are fairly short. And many more can be maintained in subsidized, low-productivity employment—either public or nominally private-sector—essentially paid for by the surplus created in the high-productivity firms. In this way, egalitarian societies enjoy efficient use of all their labor resources, high absolute living standards and competitive advantages over societies that allow markets to adjust wages to an existing structure of relative productivities.

Region-Based Evidence on Inequality and Unemployment

Instead of the nation, our smallest unit of analysis is the region. In Europe, regions are a standard subnational geographic unit, for which a consistent data-collection framework is in place at Eurostat. There is, moreover, a great deal of variation in unemployment rates across regions, which is suppressed when the analysis is restricted to the national level. Thus it makes sense to begin to explain regional unemployment with regional factors, and then to build up the model, taking account of the national and then of the supranational (continental, or even global) forces that may be at work. Only in this way can we actually test for the origin of the forces affecting unemployment rates in any particular place.

We argue that unemployment at the local level is governed principally by four factors, two each on the demand and on the supply sides. On the demand side, obviously the growth rate of effective demand strongly conditions the availability of jobs; in periods of strong growth construction and investment jobs are notably abundant.

But so does relative average income. Richer places offer more employment of all kinds than poor places. The jobs may be in the public sector (because they have more tax revenue) or in the private services sectors (because the richer people have more discretionary private income). In poorer regions—assuming we are past the stage of subsistence agriculture—surplus labor is more likely to work, if at all, in the cash economy while reporting itself as unemployed.

On the supply side, labor force demography clearly matters. Young people are hard to employ and to keep employed. The more young people, the more people are just leaving school, and the larger the unemployment as this cohort looks for its first steady work.

The final argument is the controversial one. Contrary to the "flexibility" view, we hypothesize that regions with *more equal* pay structures will, other things held constant, experience *less* unemployment.[6] We have already given a basic explanation: in local areas where the differentials between low-paid jobs and better-paid jobs are not great, people do not usually take desperate action to improve their lot. The costs are too large, and the potential gains are too small. Further, for the Meidner-Rehn reasons also given above, regions with a long history of egalitarian pay are likely to be technologically progressive and relatively prosperous, so that even in the larger framework of national or international comparison people will tend to be content with their lot. Better to be a farmer in Norway than a technician in Greece.

Regional variables do not exhaust the possible sources of variation in unemployment. There are, of course, institutions and policies that are set at the national level, and they should be taken into account.[7] But this is easily done, since each country's special characteristics, all taken together, will show up in a panel regression as a fixed effect.[8]

Finally, the factors that work on the continental (or global) level need to be considered. Where a rise or decline in unemployment is common across the full spectrum of regions of Europe, it is reasonable to attribute it to policies and institutional changes emanating at least at the European level as a whole. Time-fixed effects capture these movements. Since Europe for the past twenty years has been a laboratory for economic integration and rule-bound policy making, it will be very interesting to see what pattern emerges in relation to three specific events: the Single European Act (1987), the Maastricht Treaty on European Union (1993), and the introduction of the euro (1999). All of these events fall within the frame of readily available data.

In this model, several significant factors are subject to policy control and hence the resulting unemployment is involuntary in Keynes's meaning (1936). They are, particularly, the growth rate, the degree of pay inequality at the regional level, and the contribution of European-level economic policy and institutional change to European unemployment. Other factors, among them population structure and national institutional characteristics, would have to be considered as sources of frictional or even of voluntary unemployment. So the analysis actually permits these competing theories to be weighed against each other; neither is excluded by the specification.

Finally, the framework may be applied to subsets of the population, which can be expected to have differing degrees of responsiveness to the forces at work. Women move in and out of work more than men. Young people face an inevitable transition from school to work. The choice for these groups is, What job to aim for? A worker who once accepts a low-wage job may be typed as low-productivity and cannot make the transition to higher pay as easily as a worker who has never been employed at all. For this reason, young people especially have an incentive to resist taking bad employment. Youth unemployment in unequal regions should therefore be expected to be an especially serious problem.

Migration is a reinforcing consideration. Certain countries have larger emigrant populations than others. Within a given population, older male workers tend to be more mobile than women or the very young. If acceptable jobs are not available in their immediate surroundings, they can be expected to search elsewhere, disappearing from the regional unemployment statistics. For this reason, the unemployment of less mobile subpopulations should show higher sensitivity to regional conditions, and less mobile subpopulations should generally experience higher unemployment rates than more mobile subpopulations.

Data are generally available for up to 159 regional entities across Europe, embedded within thirteen countries. Use of the region rather than the nation as the unit of geographic analysis actually has two distinct advantages. The first is that regions are more numerous and vary greatly from one to another. The second is that regions are also more homogeneous internally, as geographic units, than countries are. The standard deviation of population size for regions is merely a tenth of what it is for countries. Table 8.1 gives this information.

We thus propose a model in which regional unemployment rates depend on four regional factors: pay inequality (+), the youth proportion in the population (+), economic growth rate (-), and relative wages (-). The first two of these factors influence the supply of unemployed labor; the second two affect the demand for labor (or supply of jobs). In addition, we expect to find national differences in average unemployment rates and variations in unemployment common to all regions in Europe. These may be measured by country-fixed effects and time-fixed effects, respectively.

Placement of regional pay inequalities on the supply side of the labor market is an innovation. It is more conventional to treat local wage rates as the product of supply and demand, begging the question of whether these forces operate at the regional, national, or higher levels. In this analysis, we take the regional wage structure as a datum facing individual workers. We consider that this datum affects

Table 8.1. **Population Differentials for Nations and Regions in Europe**

Variable	*Observations*	*Mean*	*Std. Dev.*	*Min*	*Max*
Nations					
Population (000s)	169	28,128	25,164	355.9	80,759.6
Regions					
Population (000s)	1,853	2,306	2,556	22.5	17,663.2

how long they choose to search for employment. The greater the differential between high- and low-paid jobs in the local setting, the longer a rational person will hold out for one of the better jobs, accepting unemployment if necessary.

The main empirical innovation here lies in nearly comprehensive statistics of pay inequality measured across broad economic sectors at the level of European regions—the 159 entities over seventeen years (1984–2000). These were calculated by Enrique Garcilazo.

This calculation provides a new source of information on the relative inequality of the pay structures in the regions of Europe, and because the sector categories are standardized the measures are comparable across national boundaries as well as through time. The data sources are from Eurostat's REGIO database. We use compensation of employees and employment for 159 regional entities among sixteen major economic sectors. Regions are classified by NUTS level 2 except for the regions of Germany and United Kingdom, where data are available only at NUTS level 1. A list of economic sectors and regions are included in the appendix to this chapter.

The regional variable—average pay relative to the European average—is the ratio of each region's average wage relative to the average wage of Europe as a whole. Average pay is derived by dividing compensation of employees by employment for each year. The value should vary above and below 1, equaling 1 if the region has the same average wage as Europe.

The remaining regional variables—growth of GDP, and proportion of the population under twenty-four years of age—are constructed conventionally from REGIO.

The regression takes this reduced form, a two-way fixed-effects model:

$$\mathbf{UN} = \alpha + \beta_1 \mathbf{Theil} + \beta_2\ \mathbf{Relwage} + \beta_3\ \mathbf{GDPG} + \beta_4\ \mathbf{PopUn24} + \gamma_i\ \mathbf{Country} + \gamma_j\ \mathbf{Time}$$

where:

UN = Regional unemployment rate

Theil = Pay inequality across sectors for each region

Relwage = Average regional wages relative to the European average

GDPG = Growth rate of GDP at the regional level

Un24 = proportion of the regional population under twenty-four year of age

Country = Dummy to capture fixed-country effects

Time = Dummy to capture fixed-time effects

The model can be fitted for all of Europe using annual data from 1984 to 2000, with full information for a total of 1,465 region-year observations. The coefficients on the regional variables are reported in table 8.2. Different models reflect estimates for the whole population and its component parts: men, women, older and younger workers (age greater or less than twenty-five years).[9]

All the variables have the correct sign, and all but three are significant at conventional levels. Coefficients are systematically higher for less-mobile populations, except that GDP growth rates matter less for women—no surprise. R^2 is in the range of 60 percent for all models.

Higher growth at the local level reduces unemployment. Larger numbers of young people are associated with higher unemployment. The data on unemployment and inequality at the level of European regions support our hypothesis of a positive relationship between these two variables, though at a moderate significance level. In areas with high levels of pay inequality or a high number of young people, unemployment is bound to remain a chronic problem until those two issues specifically are addressed. None of this is surprising.

Relative income across Europe (measured as the relative pay at the regional level) also affects local unemployment rates. As expected, richer regions have less unemployment, other things equal. If the regression is taken literally, it implies that reduction in inequality of incomes across Europe (holding the average constant) would reduce unemployment in the poor countries. But at the same time it would increase it in the rich countries. Therefore this result is ambiguous in policy terms.

The regional variables taken together play a considerable role in explaining variance, but each level of analysis—regional, national, European—has a role to play. Table 8.3 lays out measures of the variance explained (for unemployment of all workers) when the model is specified without fixed effects, with one-way fixed effects, and with two-way fixed effects.

Coefficient estimates on the regional variables are also shown; these are notably stable except that the effect of GDP growth is to some extent absorbed by the introduction of time effects, indicating that macroeconomic forces tend to be common across the European regions.

It turns out that country-fixed effects are relatively unimportant for the large countries. Contrary to all the presumptions of the mainstream theory, the large countries do not appear to have major national-institutional differences after all. There are two exceptions. Taking France (with the closest to average unemployment for the period) as the base case and plus or minus 3 percent as the threshold, only Spain has much higher unemployment ceteris paribus than one would otherwise expect. In the UK, on the other

Table 8.2. **Unemployment and Inequality in Europe: 1984–2000**

	Total		*Male*		*Female*		*< 25 Years*		*> 25 Years*	
	Beta	***P Value***	***Beta***	***P Value***	***Beta***	***P Value***	***Beta***	***P Value***	***Beta***	***P Value***
Theil	4.97	0.04	3.22	0.13	6.80	0.04	11.97	0.03	4.08	0.04
PopUn24	57.02	0.00	50.58	0.00	76.46	0.00	112.32	0.00	38.04	0.00
RelWage	–7.08	0.00	–4.95	0.00	–9.91	0.00	–6.37	0.00	–7.43	0.00
G-GDP	–4.48	0.02	–5.67	0.00	–2.35	0.39	–6.30	0.17	–4.69	0.00
R^2	0.61		0.59		0.65		0.62		0.58	
N	1,465		1,465		1,465		1,465		1,465	

Notes: Dependent variable is the unemployment rate by region. Theil is an inequality measure calculated across sectors from Eurostat's REGIO. PopUn24 is the fraction of the population under the age of twenty-four. RelWage is the average wage in the region divided by the European average. G-GDP is the growth rate of the regional gross product.

Table 8.3. **Unemployment in Europe: Variance Explained Under Different Specifications**

	Regional		*Regional and Country*		*Regional and Time*		*All Variables*	
	Beta	***P Value***	***Beta***	***P Value***	***Beta***	***P Value***	***Beta***	***P Value***
Theil	4.03	0.18	4.81	0.04	5.39	0.09	4.97	0.04
PopUn24	50.20	0.00	48.64	0.00	54.23	0.00	57.02	0.00
RelWage	−2.82	0.00	−6.81	0.00	−2.21	0.00	−7.08	0.00
G-GDP	−11.83	0.00	−8.56	0.00	−9.49	0.00	−4.48	0.02
Regional	X		X		X		X	
Country			X				X	
Time					X		X	
R^2	0.16		0.57		0.21		0.61	

Note: Dependent variable is the unemployment rate for the whole population.

hand, unemployment is substantially lower than otherwise expected. Germany, with a positive fixed effect just over 3 percent, is a borderline case, but most of the German fixed effect is surely due to the special circumstances following reunification.[10]

Apart from this, neither the large countries nor Scandinavia have major differences in unemployment rates apart from those captured by the local variables. Relatively equality and high incomes account for low Scandinavian unemployment! They are, in other words, the Scandinavian model. Whether the Spanish and UK cases can be traced to particular causes is a matter for later research; we would want to investigate closely the effect of the cash economy in Spain and that of credit institutions in the UK.[11] But neither value can be attributed to Spanish wage rigidity or British flexibility, since the inequality of pay structures is already taken directly into account at the regional level.

There are however large *negative* fixed effects for small countries (Austria, Ireland, Portugal, Greece, and to a lesser extent the Netherlands). Figure 8.1 shows a map of the country-fixed effects.[12] This effect may be explained in some cases by the existence of large emigrant populations absent from the local labor force; the Portuguese in France are a well-known example. Austria is more difficult to explain. The Austrian result may be due to strategic wage setting, with Austrian workers close substitutes for Germans in competing

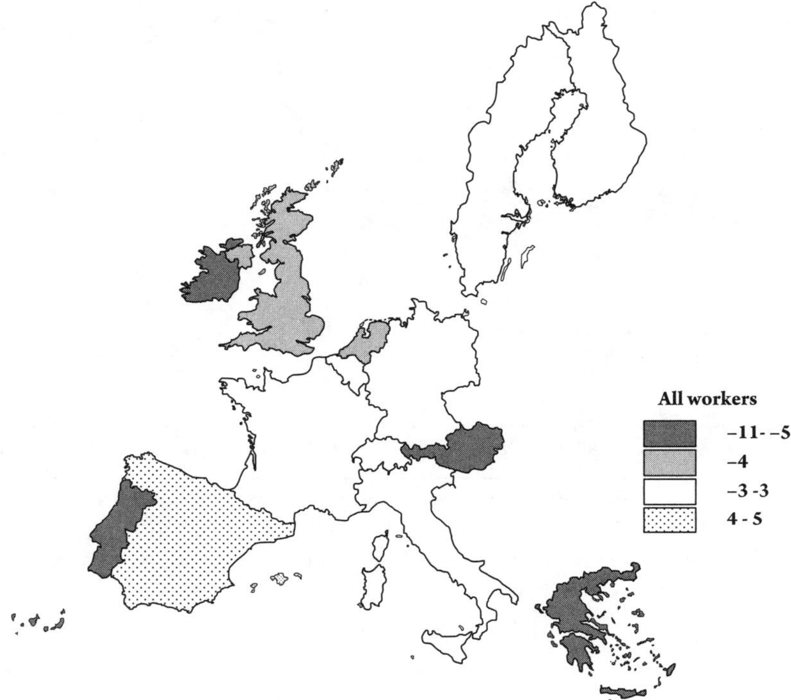

Figure 8.1. European unemployment: country-fixed effects, or differences between predicted and observed values that can be accounted for by national characteristics.

sectors, but cheaper. In an exploration reported in the appendix, we find that Austrian wages are indeed systematically lower than German on average in manufacturing, but actually higher than German in nontraded sectors.[13] The Irish credit bubble is by now a well-known (and tragic) story; however, one factor in attracting some jobs to Ireland during the boom may have been the fact that Irish wages in traded goods were persistently lower than British. Ireland, like Austria, had a centralized wage bargain for a time.

In Figure 8.2 we present the time effects associated with the two-way panel. These estimates show a striking increase in pan-European unemployment rates from 1993 to the end of the decade, which rise to a peak value of 4.6 points above the 1985 baseline in 1994 and settle above 2 full percentage points for most of the rest of the decade. This is a very succinct measure of the employment penalty associated, in general, with the Maastricht Treaty and its implementation. On a brighter note, introduction of the euro in 1999 had a good effect for a while; excess youth unemployment in Europe was reduced

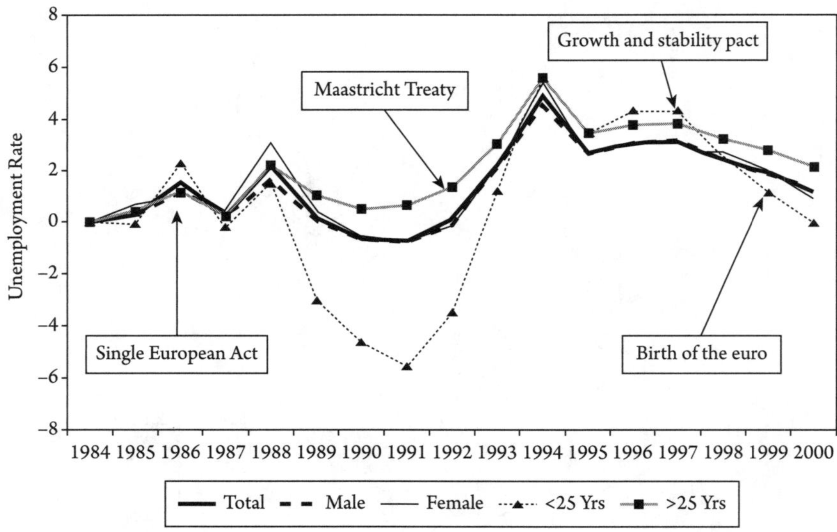

Figure 8.2. European unemployment—time effects or common trends across all European regions.

especially sharply after 1997, if these measures are correct.[14] However, we again now know that this was temporary, a result of the credit boom that followed elimination of exchange rate risks and introduction of low long-term interest rates, for the first time, in much of the European periphery, especially in Spain.

Finally, we replicate the estimates for subpopulations, including men, women, and very young workers. Not surprisingly, there are differences between these groups. As a broad rule, it appears that the less migratory a population, the higher its unemployment rate and the larger the effect of local labor market conditions on unemployment. The time effects are striking for all population groups. They show a sharp rise in unemployment common to all regions (and groups) beginning in 1993. This is an interesting break point in view of the introduction of the Maastricht Treaty on European Union at the start of that year. The effect continues through the 1990s and suggests that a substantial part of European excess unemployment—generally between 2 and 3 percentage points—reflects the influence of policy conducted *at the European level* since the Union. The monetary policy of the European Central Bank and the convergence criteria for the euro are leading suspects in this regard.

Inequality and Unemployment in Europe and America

Even after the Great Crisis, with the myth of a "naturally" low and stable U.S. unemployment rate shattered, many Europeans continue to believe in the "American model" of the flexible labor market. Therefore, "flexibilization" remains on the European agenda, with the idea that moving Europe toward American (precrisis) levels of inequality will move Europe toward American (precrisis) levels of employment. And indeed there is some logic to this: if a general economic relationship between inequality and unemployment exists, there is no immediately obvious reason it should differ between the United States and Europe. The question is, What is that relationship? And how might it square with the findings just reported, which show that within Europe the more unequal ("flexible") labor markets generally have *higher* unemployment?

It should be clear that making a correct analysis of the relationship between two place-based variables—unemployment and inequality—depends critically on drawing the correct *economic* boundaries around the places. Economic boundaries are not necessarily the same as the political ones.[15] This problem is complicated by the fact that economic boundaries change over time—a process called globalization.[16] In the United States, the implicit assumption for many years has been that Americans define themselves over the entire nation—sea to sea—even though very large numbers stay put, for at least their entire working lives, within the confines of a single state. In Europe, a different habit prevails. Historically, Europeans see themselves, and measure themselves, within the confines of countries that are in some cases very small. Europe is a broader, fuzzier horizon. However, in important ways—economically if not psychologically—all of this has changed.

The most dramatic and obvious of these changes are in the East. Thus, even though (say) Poland in the 1970s was a communist state, isolated from the West, today it is a province of greater Europe. The unemployed there are not the unemployed merely of Poland, but of all Europe. Some of them no longer see themselves as workers seeking to escape the low-wage countryside for Warsaw or Krakow, but as workers seeking jobs across the vast differentials separating Romania from Germany. Physically they may be in Germany (or Britain, or Sweden), knocking on doors. Or they may continue to live in Poland because they have not yet located jobs in Hamburg or Düsseldorf, because they don't qualify for German welfare, or simply because they prefer it. But the fact of their unemployment is no longer a problem entirely within Polish control. It depends partly on European demand and on European pay differentials.

That being so, a comparison between unemployment and inequality in Europe as against America should arguably treat Europe as a single economic union. A problem here is that there are no standard measures of inequality for Europe taken as a single, whole economy. All previous studies, save those cited here, compare the United States to individual European countries, ignoring the inequalities between European countries. In many parts of Europe, local or national inequality is low. In most big European countries, national levels of inequality are lower than in the United States; by most measures (including EHII) only Spain and Italy are close to the inequality levels observed in the United States. But wage and income differentials between European countries are quite high. No other studies have attempted to add inequality within European countries to the between-country component.

When they first tackled this question, using OECD data for manufacturing pay, Galbraith, Conceição, and Ferreira (1999) found that even though pay inequalities in manufacturing within-countries in Europe were usually lower than in the United States, the verdict is reversed once one takes account of between-country differentials, and the European measure comes out about 30 percent higher than in the United States. For Galbraith (2007b), Garcilazo calculated a direct and updated comparison of between-regions pay inequalities using measures of total payroll and total employment for 215 European regions and all fifty U.S. states, plus the District of Columbia.[17] This is not a full comparison of inequalities within the United States or across Europe. But it measures, quite directly, the incentive for long-distance economic migration and therefore the incentive to expose oneself to the risk of unemployment in order to gain the possibility of a high-income job. By comparison, inequalities within close geographic quarters may represent nothing more for employment than the incentive to commute (whether by train between the suburbs and downtown Paris, or by subway to Manhattan from the Bronx).

The results are striking. An EU-25 interregional Gini coefficient is about 0.235, or more than twice the value across the American states (0.101). Across continental distances, average European incomes are dramatically more unequal than are those in the United States. It is true that in Europe cost-of-living differences between regions are likely to be large, so that real-wage inequalities are smaller than the nominal earnings differentials. Nevertheless, for the purposes of a theory of unemployment, it is nominal earnings differentials that matter. Typically, migrants are willing to endure cramped and deprived conditions in their place of work, precisely in order to maximize the incomes sent back home, where purchasing power is magnified by low living costs. Hence nominal inequalities—for example, between Andalucia and Madrid, the Algarve and

Paris, or Poland and Frankfurt—drive both the competition for low-skilled jobs in the rich regions and, to a substantial extent, the unemployment rates.[18]

Thus the belief that European convergence toward American structures of pay inequality would help reduce European unemployment appears to be correct. But the usual implication—that Europeans must learn to tolerate higher inequality—is not. Rather, to achieve the employment goal, interregional pay inequalities within Europe must be *reduced*. This is because the relevant pay inequalities are actually *lower* in the United States than in Europe, once one takes into account the international and long-distance interregional differentials inside Europe.

The American interregional convergence is not something that merely happened. It was created, quite deliberately, by policy pursued over many decades, beginning in the 1930s, to bring about economic resurrection of the Deep South (and later of Appalachia, another impoverished region)—where poverty had festered for seven decades since the Civil War. Of course, there is no way to bring about a similar convergence in Europe, unless there is a unified policy to achieve it, with resource flows through European policy institutions. As the crisis unfolds, the hope for such a conceptual and policy breakthrough recedes; at the present writing it is perhaps farther away than at any time since the last European civil war ended, now also seven decades back.

Implications for Unemployment Policy in Europe

European data at the regional level permit thorough dissection of the sources of unemployment at the regional, national, and continental levels, and examination of the effects across different parts of the working population. The results show that the economists have been looking for the key to this particular car under the wrong lamppost. National institutions, quite clearly, do not matter much, in most of the big countries; the large countries of Europe for the most part resemble each other, in the net effect of their institutions on unemployment. What does matter are regional differences on one side—the structure of local economies and of their populations—and the forces affecting European economic conditions as a whole on the other. The latter are a powerful common effect, as is obvious from the common time trend. The analysis thus tends to pull away the curtain behind which European policy makers have been hiding.

On the demand side, raising the growth rate of GDP certainly reduces unemployment.[19] Moreover, income convergence would certainly help the poorer regions, and this suggests that policies explicitly targeted to achieve regional income convergence would also reduce the *divergence* in unemployment rates, if not necessarily their average level. This could be done by targeting income transfers to people and households in the poorer regions of Europe, by way of a common and unified pension scheme (European Pension Union), for instance. If the model is correct, the current policies of austerity imposed on Greece, Portugal, Spain, and Ireland will move everything in the opposite direction, increasing the divergence of incomes and the relative unemployment rates all along the European periphery.

Targeted measures that foster *prelabor* market opportunities for European youths would clearly help on the supply side. Such opportunities would enable young people to time their entry into paid employment so as to escape being tarred as relatively unproductive or as having started working life with a long stretch of unemployment. It should be noted that the United States does this very effectively, with high levels of university enrollment and military enlistment working to keep youths off the streets. As a result, youth unemployment in the United States is not (except for certain relatively small populations) nearly as serious a social problem as it is in Europe.[20]

Our most interesting implication is that measures to *reduce* the inequality of European wages at the regional level—for example, industrial development policies in poor regions, but also simple compression of the existing wage structures—would help reduce chronic unemployment on average among Europeans. This is quite the opposite of the common view that Europe needs *more* pay inequality ("flexibility") rather than less. There is no support in our data for the idea that European unemployment is due to excessive solidarity in the European wage structure.[21]

Our analysis of country-fixed effects lends no support to the search for a magic bullet in the form of national labor market institutional reforms. Perhaps the other large European countries should investigate the UK case very closely. Perhaps they should investigate Spain to learn what to avoid (except for the fact that, not being Spain, they have already avoided it). Perhaps there is something modest to be learned from Dutch active labor market policies; Holland (with low emigration) has somewhat lower-than-expected unemployment. Apart from that, there is little evidence that institutional differences between France, Germany, Italy, and the Nordic countries make a big difference to their unemployment rates; most of the differences between these countries' experiences seem fully accounted for by the local variables, which capture differences in pay structure, income level, and the age composition of the population.

Finally, the evidence reflects badly on the institutions and policy makers of the European Union. In a word, the Maastricht Treaty opened a half decade that can be qualified as disastrous, and from which recovery was still incomplete when the Great Crisis hit. Of course, the crisis then unleashed a wave of disasters in Europe, threatening the eurozone and bringing on vast pressures for deflationary policies on the poorer countries, who are being driven straight back to the destitution from which Europe was supposed to help them emerge. Convergence is no longer the order of the day; austerity, job cuts, recession, and rapidly rising unemployment are the new normal. Whether Europe will survive—whether it deserves to survive—may turn on whether Europeans and their policy makers come to grips with the catastrophic approach they have taken to the unemployment problem for most of the past thirty years.

Appendix

DETAILED RESULTS AND SENSITIVITY ANALYSES

The REGIO dataset permits us to extract annual datasets from 1984 to 2000 for the major countries of Europe. However, for a number of the small countries, among them Greece, Austria, Ireland, and Portugal, full data are available only for the second half of the 1990s. This raises two questions: whether those years are representative of the whole period for these countries, and whether the panel analysis as a whole would be different if they were excluded.

Table 8.A1. **Unemployment in Europe: National Fixed Effects for 1984–2000**

	Model 1		*Model 2*		*Model 3*		*Model 4*		*Model 5*	
	Total	*P Value*	*Male*	*P Value*	*Female*	*P Value*	*<25 Years*	*P Value*	*>25 Years*	*P Value*
BE	1.54	0.02	−0.35	0.53	5.16	0.00	−2.44	0.10	2.30	0.00
DE	3.32	0.00	4.12	0.00	2.97	0.00	−7.59	0.00	3.93	0.00
GR	−5.20	0.00	−5.12	0.00	−3.64	0.00	1.45	0.42	−6.82	0.00
ES	5.04	0.00	3.70	0.00	8.96	0.00	9.71	0.00	2.86	0.00
IE	−9.70	0.00	−6.48	0.00	−14.57	0.00	−24.12	0.00	−7.47	0.00
IT	0.53	0.17	−0.24	0.48	3.46	0.00	9.28	0.00	−1.69	0.00
NL	−3.69	0.00	−3.16	0.00	−4.03	0.00	−13.00	0.00	−2.79	0.00
AT	−6.03	0.00	−4.90	0.00	−7.05	0.00	−17.09	0.00	−5.12	0.00
PT	−10.79	0.00	−8.25	0.00	−13.86	0.00	−16.81	0.00	−10.43	0.00
FI	0.90	0.24	3.26	0.00	−1.97	0.06	3.30	0.06	0.42	0.51
SE	−1.06	0.11	1.88	0.00	−4.41	0.00	−3.70	0.02	−0.95	0.08
UK	−4.10	0.00	−0.28	0.60	−9.09	0.00	−12.64	0.00	−3.50	0.00

Table 8.A2. **Unemployment in Europe: Time-Fixed Effects for 1984–2000**

	Model 1		*Model 2*		*Model 3*		*Model 4*		*Model 5*	
	Total	*P Value*	*Male*	*P Value*	*Female*	*P Value*	*<25 Years*	*P Value*	*>25 Years*	*P Value*
1984	−0.36	0.70	−0.17	0.83	−0.70	0.58	0.06	0.98	−0.50	0.51
1986	1.11	0.18	1.60	0.03	0.36	0.75	2.35	0.22	0.75	0.28
1987	−0.10	0.91	0.08	0.91	−0.30	0.79	−0.14	0.94	−0.22	0.74
1988	1.76	0.03	1.38	0.06	2.38	0.04	1.70	0.37	1.72	0.01
1989	−0.17	0.83	−0.14	0.84	−0.27	0.80	−2.90	0.12	0.56	0.40
1990	−0.99	0.21	−0.83	0.23	−1.31	0.23	−4.59	0.01	0.04	0.96
1991	−1.11	0.17	−0.98	0.17	−1.45	0.19	−5.51	0.00	0.19	0.78
1992	−0.28	0.73	−0.09	0.90	−0.81	0.47	−3.44	0.07	0.84	0.22
1993	1.86	0.04	1.96	0.01	1.53	0.21	1.28	0.54	2.53	0.00
1994	4.57	0.00	4.31	0.00	4.70	0.00	5.72	0.01	5.09	0.00
1995	2.32	0.00	2.46	0.00	1.95	0.07	3.33	0.06	2.95	0.00
1996	2.74	0.00	2.88	0.00	2.45	0.02	4.39	0.01	3.30	0.00
1997	2.76	0.00	3.04	0.00	2.23	0.04	4.37	0.02	3.34	0.00
1998	2.06	0.01	2.03	0.00	1.97	0.07	2.63	0.14	2.74	0.00
1999	1.55	0.05	1.65	0.02	1.31	0.23	1.22	0.51	2.36	0.00
2000	0.83	0.33	1.25	0.10	0.21	0.86	0.05	0.98	1.64	0.02

Table 8.A3. **List of Regions: NUTS Level 1 for DE and UK, NUTS Level 2 for All Other Countries**

1	be1	Région Bruxelles—hoofdstad gewest
2	be21	Antwerpen
3	be22	Limburg (B)
4	be23	Oost-Vlaanderen
5	be24	Vlaams Brabant
6	be25	West-Vlaanderen
7	be31	Brabant Wallon
8	be32	Hainaut
9	be33	Liège
10	be34	Luxembourg (B)
11	be35	Namur
12	de1	Baden-Württemberg
13	de2	Bayern
14	de3	Berlin
15	de4	Brandenburg
16	de5	Bremen
17	de6	Hamburg
18	de7	Hessen
19	de8	Mecklenburg-Vorpommern
20	de9	Niedersachsen
21	dea	Nordrhein-Westfalen
22	deb	Rheinland-Pfalz
23	dec	Saarland
24	ded	Sachsen
25	dee	Sachsen-Anhalt
26	def	Schleswig-Holstein
27	deg	Thüringen
28	def	Schleswig-Holstein
29	deg	Thüringen
30	gr11	Anatoliki Makedonia, Thraki
31	gr12	Kentriki Makedonia

continued

Table 8.A3. (continued)

32	gr13	Dytiki Makedonia
33	gr14	Thessalia
34	gr21	Ipeiros
35	gr22	Ionia Nisia
36	gr23	Dytiki Ellada
37	gr24	Sterea Ellada
38	gr25	Peloponnisos
39	gr3	Attiki
40	gr41	Voreio Aigaio
41	gr42	Notio Aigaio
42	gr43	Kriti
43	es11	Galicia
44	es12	Principado de Asturias
45	es13	Cantabria
46	es21	Pais Vasco
47	es22	Comunidad Foral de Navarra
48	es23	La Rioja
49	es24	Aragón
50	es3	Comunidad de Madrid
51	es41	Castilla y León
52	es42	Castilla-la Mancha
53	es43	Extremadura
54	es51	Cataluña
55	es52	Comunidad Valenciana
56	es53	Illes Balears
57	es61	Andalucia
58	es62	Murcia
59	es63	Ceuta y Melilla (ES)
60	es7	Canarias (ES)
61	fr1	Île de France
62	fr21	Champagne-Ardenne
63	fr22	Picardie
64	fr23	Haute-Normandie

Table 8.A3. (continued)

65	fr24	Centre
66	fr25	Basse-Normandie
67	fr26	Bourgogne
68	fr3	Nord Pas-de-Calais
69	fr41	Lorraine
70	fr42	Alsace
71	fr43	Franche-Comté
72	fr51	Pays de la Loire
73	fr52	Bretagne
74	fr53	Poitou-Charentes
75	fr61	Aquitaine
76	fr62	Midi-Pyrénées
77	fr63	Limousin
78	fr71	Rhône-Alpes
79	fr72	Auvergne
80	fr81	Languedoc-Roussillon
81	fr82	Provence-Alpes-Côte d'Azur
82	fr83	Corse
83	ie01	Border, Midlands, and Western
84	ie02	Southern and Eastern
85	it11	Piemonte
86	it12	Valle d'Aosta
87	it13	Liguria
88	it2	Lombardia
89	it31	Trentino-Alto Adige
90	it32	Veneto
91	it33	Friuli-Venezia Giulia
92	it4	Emilia-Romagna
93	it51	Toscana
94	it52	Umbria
95	it53	Marche
96	it6	Lazio

continued

Table 8.A3. (continued)

97	it71	Abruzzo
98	it72	Molise
99	it8	Campania
100	it91	Puglia
101	it92	Basilicata
102	it93	Calabria
103	ita	Sicilia
104	itb	Sardegna
105	lu	Luxembourg
106	nl11	Groningen
107	nl12	Friesland
108	nl13	Drenthe
109	nl21	Overijssel
110	nl22	Gelderland
111	nl23	Flevoland
112	nl31	Utrecht
113	nl32	Noord-Holland
114	nl33	Zuid-Holland
115	nl34	Zeeland
116	nl41	Noord-Brabant
117	nl42	Limburg (NL)
118	at11	Burgenland
119	at12	Niederösterreich
120	at13	Wien
121	at21	Kärnten
122	at22	Steiermark
123	at31	Oberösterreich
124	at32	Salzburg
125	at33	Tirol
126	at34	Vorarlberg
127	pt11	Norte
128	pt12	Centro (PT)
129	pt13	Lisboa e Vale do Tejo

Table 8.A3. (continued)

130	pt14	Alentejo
131	pt15	Algarve
132	pt2	Açores (PT)
133	pt3	Madeira (PT)
134	fi13	Itä-Suomi
135	fi14	Väli-Suomi
136	fi15	Pohjois-Suomi
137	fi16	Uusimaa (suuralue)
138	fi17	Etelä-Suomi
139	fi2	Åland
140	se01	Stockholm
141	se02	Östra Mellansverige
142	se04	Sydsverige
143	se06	Norra Mellansverige
144	se07	Mellersta Norrland
145	se08	Övre Norrland
146	se09	Småland med öarna
147	se0a	Västsverige
148	ukc	North East
149	ukd	North West (including Merseyside)
150	uke	Yorkshire and the Humber
151	ukf	East Midlands
152	ukg	West Midlands
153	ukh	Eastern
154	uki	London
155	ukj	South East
156	ukk	South West
157	ukl	Wales
158	ukm	Scotland
159	ukn	Northern Ireland

Table 8.A4. **Sectorization Used to Calculate Regional Inequality**

Sectors by NACE-CLIO (1984–1994)	*Sectors by NACE (1995–2000)*
Fuel and power products	Agriculture, hunting, and forestry
Ferrous and nonferrous ores and metals, other than radioactive	Fishing
Nonmetallic minerals and mineral products	Mining and quarrying
Chemical products	Manufacturing
Metal products, machinery, equipment, and electrical goods	Electricity, gas, and water supply
Transport equipment	Construction
Food, beverages, tobacco	Wholesale and retail trade; repair of motor vehicles
Textiles and clothing; leather and footwear	Hotels and restaurants
Paper and printing products	Transport, storage, and communication
Products of various industries	Financial intermediation
Building and construction	Real estate, renting, and business activities
Recovery, repair, trade, lodging, and catering services	Public administration and defense; compulsory social security
Transport and communication services	Education
Services of credit and insurance institutions	Health and social work
Other market services	Other community, social, personal service activities
Nonmarket services	Private households with employed persons

Examination of the unemployment rates for the four countries suggests that the relatively low unemployment seen in Austria, Greece, and Portugal in the late 1990s is not wildly unrepresentative of their experience over the whole period, even though the absolute levels of unemployment do vary over time. The Irish case is very different, as Ireland passed from a high- to a

Table 8.A5. **Sensitivity Analysis: Total Unemployment Excluding AU, IE, GR, PT**

	Model 1	
	Total	***P Value***
Theil	31.75	0.00
PopUn24	71.48	0.00
RelWage	−6.15	0.00
G-GDP	−6.92	0.00
BE	1.29	0.05
DE	4.54	0.00
ES	4.21	0.00
IT	0.32	0.43
NL	−3.47	0.00
FI	1.38	0.07
SE	−0.52	0.43
UK	−4.69	0.00
1984	−0.36	0.70
1986	1.11	0.18
1987	−0.10	0.91
1988	1.76	0.03
1989	−0.17	0.83
1990	−0.99	0.21
1991	−1.11	0.17
1992	−0.28	0.73
1993	1.86	0.04
1994	4.57	0.00
1995	2.32	0.00
1996	2.74	0.00
1997	2.76	0.00
1998	2.06	0.01
1999	1.55	0.05
2000	0.83	0.33
R^2	0.63	
N	1240	

Table 8.A6. **Europe: Summary Statistics for Average Wages Across 16 Sectors, 1995–2000**

Extremadura

Variable	mean	min	max	N	p50
Average wage	21.49	5.4	65.5	72	16.35

Andalucia

Variable	mean	min	max	N	p50
Average wage	22.65	5.1	79.7	82	19.55

Navarra

Variable	mean	min	max	N	p50
Average wage	25.93	7.5	52.1	72	26

Stockholm

Variable	mean	min	max	N	p50
Average wage	35.59	16.7	64	88	36.15

Extremadura (unemployment rate for 2000 = 24.4 percent),
Andalucia (unemployment rate for 2000 = 25 percent),
Navarra (unemployment rate for 2000 = 4.8 percent),
Stockholm (unemployment rate for 2000 = 3.7 percent).

low-unemployment country in the mid-1990s. It would thus be inappropriate to regard the low country-fixed effect found for Ireland as representative of institutions producing low unemployment throughout the period. It represents, rather, the exceptional experience of the late 1990s, when Ireland experienced a powerful (and alas temporary) economic boom.

To test the second question, we ran the full panel regression, with two-way fixed effects, on a panel excluding Greece, Austria, Ireland, and Portugal. The results for the whole population are given in table 8.A5. Results for the male, female, young, and older subpopulations tell a similar story and are available from the author.

Table 8.A7. **Ratio of Austrian to German Average Wages by Major Sectors**

	1995	*1996*	*1997*	*1998*	*1999*	*2000*
Mining and quarrying	1.04	1.01	1.01	1.06	1.09	0.98
Manufacturing	0.88	0.88	0.88	0.89	0.92	0.86
Electricity, gas, and water supply	1.22	1.19	1.21	1.26	1.22	1.14
Construction	1.04	1.03	1.06	1.11	1.27	1.20
Transport, storage, and communication	1.03	1.00	1.03	1.07	1.18	1.14
Financial intermediation	1.06	1.07	1.08	1.09	1.23	1.18
Real estate, renting, and business activities	0.99	0.96	0.94	0.90	1.09	0.95
Public administration and defense; compulsory social security	1.16	1.15	1.13	1.10	1.12	1.12

The model is substantially unaffected by exclusion of the four small countries. All coefficients have the same sign, and all remain significant. One difference is that the relationship between inequality and unemployment is stronger, and the significance of the coefficient estimate on the inequality variable rises eightfold, when the four small countries are not included. We take this as confirmation that the inequality-unemployment relation is strong, and not an artifact of inclusion of the small countries in the late 1990s.

The between-groups component of Theil's T statistic is a compound measure influenced by both the relative wage rates between groups and the relative size of each group. A region with high inequality may have a large differential between the best-paid and worst-paid, or a marked bimodalism in the structure of employment or some combination of both factors. It is worth noting that the line of causality traditionally argued to hold in economics, which runs from unemployment rates to the pay structure, does not imply anything in particular about the structure of employment. If there exists an excess of unskilled workers, this should reduce the relative pay of unskilled workers, increasing inequality, but it would not necessarily change the technology employed in particular processes of production.

To offer an illustration of the roles of these two factors, we examine the structure of pay and employment in four European regions, two with high and two with low unemployment in the year 2000. The regions included in the

Table 8.A8. **Ratio of Irish to British Average Wages by Major Sectors**

	1995	*1996*	*1997*	*1998*
Mining and quarrying	0.71	1.05	0.86	0.87
Manufacturing	0.81	0.84	0.75	0.71
Electricity, gas, and water supply	0.74	0.65	0.70	0.63
Construction	1.32	1.27	1.17	1.11
Wholesale and retail trade*	1.35	1.39	1.32	1.29
Hotels and restaurants	1.15	1.05	0.97	0.90
Transport, storage, and communication	0.79	0.87	0.76	0.70
Financial intermediation	1.51	1.49	1.20	1.11
Real estate, renting, and business activities	1.19	1.13	1.07	1.02
Public administration and defense**	1.08	1.17	1.11	1.18
Education	1.27	1.30	1.17	1.10
Health and social work	1.52	1.48	1.39	1.22
Other community, social, personal service activities	0.97	0.90	0.66	0.57

* Repair of motor vehicles, motorcycles, and personal and household goods.
** Compulsory social security.

Table 8.A9. **European Unemployment and Inequality: Data Availability by Region and Year**

Year	*No. of Observations*												
1984	35	be (8)	it(20)	uk(7)									
1985	35	be (8)	it(20)	uk(7)									
1986	56	be (8)	es (17)	it(20)	pt(4)	uk(7)							
1987	69	be (8)	es (17)	fr(20)	it(20)	pt(4)							
1988	63	be (8)	es (18)	it(20)	nl(12)	pt(5)							
1989	84	be (8)	es (18)	fr(21)	it(20)	nl(12)							
1990	86	be (8)	es (18)	fr(21)	it(20)	nl(12)							
1991	78	es(18)	fr(21)	it(20)	nl(12)	pt(7)							
1992	78	es(18)	fr(21)	it(20)	nl(12)	pt(7)							
1993	57	es(18)	it(20)	nl(12)	pt(7)								
1994	45	es(18)	it(20)	pt(7)									
1995	133	de(16)	gr(13)	es(18)	fr(21)	it(20)	nl(12)	at(9)	pt(7)	fi(4)	se(6)	uk(7)	
1996	139	de(16)	gr(13)	es(18)	fr(21)	it(20)	nl(12)	at(9)	pt(7)	fi(6)	se(6)	uk(11)	
1997	136	de(16)	gr(12)	es(18)	fr(21)	it(20)	nl(12)	at(9)	pt(7)	fi(4)	se(6)	uk(11)	
1998	144	de(16)	gr(12)	es(18)	fr(21)	ie(2)	it(20)	nl(12)	at(9)	pt(7)	fi(6)	se(8)	uk(12)
1999	131	de(16)	gr(12)	es(18)	fr(21)	ie(2)	it(20)	nl(12)	at(9)	pt(7)	fi(5)	se(8)	
2000	96	de(16)	gr(13)	fr(21)	ie(2)	it(20)	at(9)	fi(6)	se(8)				
	1,465												

analysis are Andalucia and Extremadura, with high unemployment rates, and Navarra and Stockholm, with low unemployment rates:

Ranges for low-unemployment regions are much lower than for high-unemployment regions. We also find that low-unemployment regions have a substantially larger share of their employment near the mean, and less associated with the extremes of the distribution.

The conjecture that certain small countries with strong collective wage bargaining might generate domestic full employment at the expense of a larger neighbor can be evaluated directly for the case of Austria and Germany. The evidence is suggestive. As table 8.A7 shows, average wages in Austria are systematically higher than in Germany except in two sectors: manufacturing and real estate. Manufacturing is, of course, by far the larger of these sectors. Is this the secret of Austrian unemployment rates consistently half those of Germany?

Table 8.A8 gives a similar analysis of relative wages in Ireland and the UK in the late 1990s; if the data are accurate, a similar story may apply. Indeed, it is striking how much higher average pay in such sectors as finance, health, and education appears to be in Ireland than in England. But manufacturing pay is lower, and this could well have given Ireland the edge in location of new industry during the technology boom.

Table 8.A9 summarizes the data used in this chapter.

Notes

1. This chapter is adapted from James K. Galbraith and Jose Enrique Garcilazo, "Unemployment, Inequality and the Policy of Europe, 1984–2000," *Banca Nazionale del Lavoro Quarterly Review* 57(228), March 2004, 3–28. Reprinted in Richard P. F. Holt and Steven Pressman, editors, *Empirical Post Keynesian Economics: Looking at the Real World*. Armonk, NY: Sharpe, 2007, 44–69.
2. This simplification sits uncomfortably with certain facts, such as that French and German workers enjoy higher average productivity than their American counterparts. This chapter will not, however, attempt to follow the literature into every nook, cranny, and inconsistency. The point of constructing a fable is to give people something they can believe in, sparing them the obligation of closely examining the facts.
3. We have seen already that the actual relationship between pay inequality in American manufacturing and unemployment contradicts this view, but the view was developed largely without any felt need for supporting evidence, beyond superficial comparison of (household income–based) Gini coefficients and average unemployment rates.
4. There are two likely explanations for this focus. One is simply the convenience of data, which are collected and reported by national governments. The other is the economist's ingrained preference for individual-level data. But it is a fallacy, of course, to treat nation-states as though they were individuals, randomly sampled from some larger population.
5. My authority for this assertion stems from a conversation at a lunch at Bloomberg headquarters in New York with Jean-Claude Trichet, then the director of the European Central

Bank. That the Scandinavians were different and could not be emulated was his response to my question about their comparative success with low inequality and low unemployment.

6. One might suppose the causation to run the other way: that regional pay inequality would be simply a positive function of local unemployment rates. But although this is possible, two considerations suggest that it is not predominantly the case. First, unemployment rates vary much more than inequality measures over time. The effect of inequality on unemployment is therefore mainly cross-sectional (places with higher inequality experience higher unemployment chronically). Second, part of the greater inequality observed in a regional pay structure is due to the scarcity of decently paid middle-range jobs, and not exclusively to larger pay differentials per se, though in practice both may contribute. There is no compelling reason in neoclassical theory that higher unemployment rates should produce a gap in employment in the middle of the pay scale, as opposed to the bottom of it.
7. There have also been, in history, differences in how the unemployed are counted, which would show up at the national level. However, recent data are based on standardized measures.
8. Our analysis does not attempt to sort out the particular institutional factors behind differences in national unemployment rates, once local conditions have been controlled for. Rather, we seek to establish *how much* of the observed differences in unemployment can be attributed to national differences, and *for which countries* these differences are important. Introducing country-fixed effects permits this measurement to be carried out easily.
9. We report a linear version of the model; a log-log version gave similar results and is not reported.
10. There is also an interesting negative effect for youth unemployment in Germany, which could be picking up the effects of the apprentice system.
11. A good test prediction would be that the UK would experience sharply higher unemployment in the crisis than, say, Germany.
12 Table A1 (in the appendix to this chapter) presents the coefficient estimates.
13. We thank Richard Freeman and David Howell for jointly making the suggestion that we compare Austrian wages to German.
14. Appendix Table A2 reports the time effects and their significance level. Freeman suggests a link to large increases in university enrollment, especially in Spain.
15. To see this in the small, consider that there is obviously no such thing as a "Luxembourg labor market"—even though Luxembourg reports labor market statistics like any other OECD country.
16. Further, at a given moment in time, groups may experience different geographic horizons.
17. The measures are made comparable by presenting them in the form of Gini coefficients, which are calculated on the artificial assumption that every person within a state or region enjoys the same average income.
18. Furthermore, one can reasonably expect that cost-of-living differentials across Europe will decline over time. As markets continue to integrate, the traded-goods components of living costs will tend to equalize, leaving only the nontraded goods components (whose price levels depend on local wage levels, including rents, and the intangible elements of the living standard) as separating the costs of living in richer and poorer regions of Europe. Absent convergence of nominal wages, convergence of living costs will produce further divergence of real living standards. Convergence policy must therefore deal with nominal differentials, as expressed in the common currency unit.
19. That regional income convergence would do so is also possible, but this cannot be readily determined from our information, since our variable measures *relative* wages.
20. The high level of incarceration in the United States is an uglier side of this same story.
21. It is, however, possible that some small countries—Austria and perhaps Ireland—have for a time gamed the system at the expense of their larger neighbors.

CHAPTER 9

European Wages and the Flexibility Thesis

In the last chapter, we examined the relationship between wage inequality—a proxy for "flexibility"—and unemployment, to discover that, contrary to the theoretical argument and insistent policy prescription of the European mainstream, the actual evidence shows wage equality is good for employment. This is true at every level of analysis: regional, national, and continental. That is, egalitarian regions within Europe have less unemployment than highly unequal regions. Egalitarian countries within Europe have less unemployment than highly unequal countries. And—over the period under study—the United States had less pay inequality than Europe *taken as a continental whole*, and also less unemployment. Moreover, the analysis suggests that as Europe expanded and integrated, the continental inequalities became more relevant, adding upward pressure to unemployment.

This chapter takes up the issue of wage flexibility and rigidity in Europe from another angle and with a different technique.[1] The question asked here is, When we consider Europe as a whole, how much wage flexibility do we observe in fact? The shift here is from a static mode of observation to a dynamic one: in this chapter, we will be concerned with assessing the degree to which relative wages inside Europe are actually capable of changing over time. This is important because although part of the "rigidities" argument focuses on the allegedly egalitarian structure of European wages, another part of it focuses on the problem of "sclerosis," the ability or inability to change in response to change in technology and associated patterns of labor demand.

As discussed earlier, unemployment in Europe was practically nonexistent until the oil crises of the 1970s; since that time it has risen episodically but persistently and has become an intractable problem and a leading policy concern. A small group of Keynesians (Palley 2001, 2004; Arestis and Sawyer 2006) continue to insist that the blame lies with the tight fiscal and monetary policies, but the dominant view places responsibility on a rigid structure of

European wages, both excessively egalitarian and unable to adjust approximately to macroeconomic and supply-side shocks (Blanchard 2005). The widely accepted remedy in mainstream policy circles is *flexibilization* of European labor markets, by which is meant, for the most part, allowing wages at the bottom to fall and those at the top to rise.

Curiously, both competing perspectives agree on the core proposition that European wage structures are inflexible. Keynesians tend to see egalitarian wage structures as desirable per se; hence their admiration for the "European social model" and their preference for demand expansion as the policy of choice against unemployment, whereas for the mainstream school flexibility trumps equity and the fear of expansionary policy is that it might generate inflation. Intermediate positions also exist: moderate members of the mainstream sometimes favor expansionary demand policies, especially in deep crises, and moderate Keynesians, particularly if they were trained in the American tradition of the "neoclassical synthesis," do not always oppose "labor market reform."

One basis of the shared belief that European labor markets are (relatively) inflexible is to be found in a shared a priori commitment to viewing European labor markets as if they were separate and autonomous *and national*—one country, one labor market. In reality, though, it has been decades since it was reasonable to view the European economy in this way. And in fact, very few actors on the European economic scene would take this point of view.

Financial investors and multinational corporations have long viewed the countries of Europe as close substitutes and competitors for their investment; in recent years all barriers to economic interchange within Europe, including the nominal one of currency exchange, have been removed. European transnationals are increasingly *multinational*, on the model of Airbus; they distribute production across countries and seek, presumably, the optimum mix of integrated operations and low costs. Eliminating the uncertainties facing such corporations from arbitrary and unpredicted exchange rate movements was one of the major arguments in favor of fixing exchange rates irrevocably under the euro.

However, the fact remains that nominal exchange rate flexibility persisted inside Europe until 1999. And it persists today between the British pound, Swiss franc, and several Scandinavian currencies that remain outside the euro, as well as those of several accession countries that have not yet joined the euro. From the standpoint of a pan-European investor, this flexibility is the same as any type of relative wage flexibility: currency depreciation lowers wage costs in the country that depreciates. This presents us with an interesting natural experiment, a way of observing just how much relative wages have fluctuated in modern European history, and a way of assessing whether this form of wage cutting actually did lead to higher employment. So far as we know, no recent study[2] has linked this older tradition of analysis of currency adjustments, which was very common in the days of "fixed-but-adjustable exchange rates" under the Bretton Woods system, to the "modern" doctrine of labor market flexibility. It is as though economists who are focused on Europe have forgotten that there were once alternative ways—apart from breaking up unions and repealing job protections—to lower the relative wage.

This chapter thus studies the recent evolution of the European wage structure from a pan-European perspective. We measure the variability of relative wages for the region considered as a whole, in order to assess the relationship of relative wage change to changes in employment. We find considerable variability in relative wages seen this way. The next step is to ask, Can we determine why wages varied? In other words, can we link the movements of relative wages observed in the data to other patterns of economic change, also observable in the data at the same time? The idea behind trying to do this is to see whether there are any cases where relative wage *reduction* might have worked, in the sense of being associated with a successful recovery of employment. The relevance of the exercise to present policies of austerity, and the possibility of a sustained "expansionary fiscal consolidation," should be clear.

The difficulty of tackling this problem lies in the complexity of the data. Europe is a mass of countries, each of which records employment and payroll information on a plethora of economic sectors. There are thus hundreds of "dependent variables," and an even larger number of potentially important causal factors behind relative wage change. The traditional approach, parametric hypothesis testing, requires that one specify a theoretical relationship in advance. The test, carried out with regression analysis, then tells whether the hypothesis is reasonable or not. But in this situation one could run hundreds of regressions along those lines and not come to a persuasive conclusion; there are always more variables that one might have used.

So we'll take a quite different approach, following a method presented in *Created Unequal* (Galbraith 1998) and developed in Calistri and Galbraith (2001), which has the advantage of allowing us to sort through masses of information for common patterns, reducing matters to a manageable number of observational groups before attempting to analyze them. As noted, this work was carried out by Deepshikha RoyChowdhury under my supervision.

The next section of this chapter presents a brief literature review and theoretical foundations of the unemployment situation in Europe. The third section presents the analysis, and a final section presents the conclusion.

The Problem of Unemployment in Europe: A Reprise

Unemployment in Europe was very low from the end of the Second World War to the end of the 1960s. Since then it has increased through shocks and recessions, while falling little in years of growth. European unemployment before the Great Crisis averaged three times its 1960s values and roughly twice the level prevailing in the United States. Since the two regions had similar labor force participation rates and experienced the same shocks in the 1970s, explanations that rely on shocks alone are problematic. In 1985, Bruno and Sachs blamed European unemployment on declining total factor productivity growth, but this hypothesis later ran afoul of the fact that American employment recovered when the total factor productivity slowdown ended, but European employment did not. Reasoning along these lines led Blanchard (2005) and others to conclude that the differences must lie in the institutional capacity to adjust to shocks; hence the alleged relative rigidity of European wages emerges logically as the prime suspect in the rise and persistence of European unemployment.

Thus the dominant explanation for the problem of unemployment in Europe has become "rigid and sclerotic labor markets," supposedly blocking desirable adjustments to rapidly changing demand conditions. This explanation is called the *labor market flexibility (LMF) hypothesis*. It holds that such institutional factors as union coverage, union density, centralized wage bargaining, employment protection laws, taxes, unemployment benefits, and benefit duration render wages downwardly rigid. European unemployment is therefore a price of the European welfare state. In the previous chapter, we proxied all of these forces with measures of wage equality, and with national dummy variables to capture distinctive country characteristics, or "fixed effects."

The theoretical basis of the LMF hypothesis resides in neoclassical economics, according to which the labor market comprises supply and demand schedules that are functions of the real wage. The labor market clears at the intersection point of the two schedules; unemployment exists when the real wage fails to fall to its equilibrium level. To restore full employment, therefore, labor market reforms are required: weaker unions, less job protection, reduced unemployment benefits, cuts in the minimum wage. In recent years, such "reforms" have been promoted by the OECD's *Jobs Study* (OECD 1994) and by Layard and Nickell (1999), Phelps (1994), Nickell (1997), Siebert (1997), Haveman (1997), Blanchard and Wolfers (2000), Layard, Nickell, and Jackman (2005) and others. Rare dissenting critiques come from Baker et al. (2005), and from Howell (2005). Garcilazo (2005) offers an extensive review and critique of studies based on the LMF hypothesis.

A competing argument, the Macroeconomic Policy (MP) hypothesis, holds that European unemployment stems from bad macroeconomic choices, as argued by Baker and Schmitt (1998), Palley (1998, 1999), and Solow (1994). This hypothesis focuses on the anti-inflation monomania of the European Central Bank (and of the Bundesbank before it), and on the strict austerity imposed by the Maastricht criteria. Palley (2001, 2004) presents an empirical model incorporating both macroeconomic policy variables (interest rates, inflation rate, growth rate) and institutional variables (unemployment benefits, tax wedge, union coverage). He found that the institutional effects are not stable: when macroeconomic variables are included the coefficients of the institutional variables change sign and lose statistical significance.

Advocates of the LMF hypothesis and those of the MP hypothesis supply opposing explanations for unemployment and differing recommendations for dealing with it. Yet they agree, without having explicitly considered the matter, that European labor markets are in fact both national and rigid. We think this is a weakness of both viewpoints, subject to investigation that may enable us to test the LMF hypothesis persuasively. For if labor market reform works, then reducing relative wages should produce higher employment. No one expects this will be the only source of higher employment, of course. But in the entire history of Europe after the early 1960s, there should be, at the least, a few cases where this process can be shown to have worked.

We treat Europe just as a pan-European investor or a multinational corporation (MNC), intending to invest and create jobs in Europe, would do. For an MNC (or a bank), Europe is a highly integrated economy. Investing in one country instead of another is a *location* decision, which depends on *competitiveness* (Porter 1990). The flow of investment affects growth, employment, and wages. Relative wages can rise (or fall) particularly rapidly if exchange rates are flexible, and it is this source of relative wage variability inside Europe that we especially wish to investigate. It has been omitted entirely from the study of European labor markets up to now, at least in the period since the creation of the eurozone caused economists to forget, apparently, that Europe existed before the euro.

Assessing Wage Flexibility across Europe

We study the behavior of European wages over twenty-five years, using a dataset[3] covering fifteen countries of the European Union (EU)[4] and Switzerland and Norway. The dataset includes country-level data for total remuneration (measured in millions euro) and employment for each economic sector within each country from 1980 to 2005. The data are available for fifteen economic sectors[5] of each country. The dataset thus comprises 6,630 cells including 255 rows (seventeen countries times fifteen economic sectors) and twenty-six columns (years from 1980 to 2005). Using total remuneration and employment, we calculate the average remuneration (here called average wage) for each sector of each country, each year. We then compute the annual rate of change in average wages for each cell, yielding 6,375 cells arranged in 255 rows and twenty-five columns (years from 1980–1981 to 2004–2005). This is the degree of complexity we have to deal with.

To this second dataset, we apply cluster analysis to discover meaningful structures among the 255 cases. Cluster analysis is a technique in numerical taxonomy whose function is to combine observations in a dataset according to their degree of similarity to one another. In our case, the similarity we are interested in is the degree of co-movement of wage changes over time. The underlying principle is that two sectors having a high degree of co-movement can reasonably be treated as if they were the same—in particular, as if they were being influenced by the same economic forces as time passes. Thus little information is lost by combining them. The advantage is that a judicious process of combination simplifies the data enormously, often turning an inchoate mass of numbers into a relatively small number of clearly distinct groups with easily distinguishable histories.

We use a hierarchical clustering method known as Ward's method,[6] with the results displayed as a tree plot. The tree diagram shows the similarity and differences between the histories through time of our criterion variable (annual rate of change in average wages) of all pairs of cases under observation. Step by step, it reduces a large and cumbersome list of cases into a small number of meaningful clusters, while minimizing loss of information through aggregation.

Cluster analysis helps to discover meaningful structures in data, but it does not explain why they exist.[7] To help determine why clusters form, we employ a second tool, called discriminant function analysis. It generates coefficients called canonical scores, which may be associated with other time-series data that measure the historical forces driving the differences between clusters

(Ferguson and Galbraith 1999; Calistri and Galbraith 2001). In this way, we combine two nonparametric techniques to yield evidence on fundamental sources of variation in a complex dataset, again without significance testing. Galbraith and Lu (2001) give a compact technical summary of the mathematics behind this procedure. Both techniques are well established and easily implemented with standard statistical software packages, though the combination of them using time-series data appears to be an innovation.

The discriminant function is also known as a *canonical root* or a latent variable. It is a linear combination of independent variables, also called discriminating variables, expressed as

$$L = c + a_1 * x_1 + a_2 * x_2 + \ldots\ldots. + a_n * x_n. \tag{9.1}$$

Here the discriminating variable x_i is the annual rate of change in average wages of ith year (i = 1,2,. . . . . .25 for the time series 1980 to 2005). The a_is are unstandardized discriminant coefficients (or partial coefficients), which show the unique contribution of each variable (each year, in this analysis) to the classification of the discriminant function. In terms of standardized coefficients (b_is), the discriminant function is expressed as

$$L = b_1 * x_1 + b_2 * x_2 + \ldots\ldots. + b_n * x_n. \tag{9.2}$$

In the case of k clusters, discriminant function analysis yields (k-1) sets of b_is. For each set, discriminant function analysis permits us to compute a corresponding canonical score for each of the clusters. Using the b_is corresponding to the first discriminant function and substituting the x_i for each cluster into the equation, one gets a first set of canonical scores for all cluster cases. Similarly, the b_is corresponding to the second discriminant function yield a second set of canonical scores for all the cases, and so forth. The discriminant functions are orthogonal to each other, so that the first function maximizes the differences between the clusters, the second function maximizes the differences between the clusters after controlling for the first function, and so on.

The discriminant function analysis yields an eigenvalue corresponding to each discriminant function, which shows the importance of its corresponding function (eigenvector) in classifying a case into a cluster. The relative importance is represented in terms of percentage of variance explained by that discriminant function.

In this analysis the b_is are by construction sets of year-to-year coefficients, a constructed time series. Following Calistri and Galbraith (2001), we contend that the b_is correspond to some known or discoverable historical forces, which affect cases differently and work to separate the cases into clusters. So it is of interest to discover what these forces might actually be. To discover them, we can (simply) replace the b_is by some known economic time series and calculate a pseudoscore, which is analogous to the canonical score. The pseudoscore is expressed as

$$P = p_1 * x_1 + p_2 * x_2 + \dots\dots + p_n * x_n. \tag{9.3}$$

Here P is the pseudoscore and the p_is represent an economic time series that runs through period 1 to n (= 25).

Once pseudoscores for all the cases are obtained for a particular candidate historical force, we can calculate the correlation coefficient between the pseudoscores and the corresponding canonical scores. If the correlation is high and significant, we may argue that the b_is (corresponding to say, kth discriminant function) that separate clusters at the kth dimension represent such-and-such an economic force. If the historical record yields multiple possibilities, it is easy to choose; the one with the highest correlation between pseudoscore and canonical score is the most probable. This is to say, it is the economic time series that most likely leads to the pattern of variation in the behavior of average wages and that produces the observed cluster pattern. This is a very compact way to sort through potential causal factors, without running hundreds of regressions.

The final complication is simply that our dataset is very messy. Having clustered, we will find that few small groups are initially separated out, reflecting the exceptional variations of certain cases on the borders of the European Economic Community. But the rest will look like an undifferentiated mass, with no discernible internal structure. The solution to this problem, innovated by RoyChowdhury (2008), is simply to exclude the outlier groups and repeat the analysis. In this way structures that were not visible before begin to emerge. The process can be repeated, until one is satisfied that most of the meaningful variations in relative wage rates have, in fact, been accounted for. The procedure is thus iterative, and the intuition behind it may be evident to aficionados of fractal structure.

We perform the analysis at four levels, corresponding to smaller-scale variations and finer disaggregation of the underlying data. At each level, a cluster analysis is performed to obtain the cluster structure. After that, discriminant function analysis is performed using the cluster structure. For the first two dimensions, which separate the clusters maximally, canonical scores are obtained; corresponding to them, pseudoscores are obtained from candidate economic time series data. After that, the correlation coefficients between the pseudoscores and canonical scores are calculated. Details and findings are presented in the next section.

Clustering and Discriminating to Simplify the Picture

We first perform cluster analysis on all the 255 cases (economic sectors within countries) using the data for annual rate of change in average wages of each case from 1980 to 2005. Cluster analysis yields three well-defined clusters, indicating the most sharply differentiated patterns of wage change. Cluster 2 consists of seven sectors of Greece. Cluster 3 comprises seven sectors of Portugal. Cluster 1 consists of the remaining cases.

To determine why the 255 cases resolve into a group structure comprising three well-defined clusters, we perform a discriminant function analysis. As there are three clusters, the analysis yields two discriminant functions; the first and second functions account for 73.24 percent and 26.76 percent of the variability between the clusters respectively.

Figure 9.1 shows how the two discriminant functions discriminate between the three clusters. Along the x-axis the canonical scores corresponding to the first discriminant function (DF1-1)[8] are plotted. Along the y-axis the canonical scores corresponding to the second discriminant function (DF2-1) are plotted. The figure shows that DF1-1 separates cluster 2 from the rest of the cases, while DF2-1 separates cluster 3 from the rest of the cases.

We contend that the discriminant functions may represent economic time series that lead these particular groups of sectors in Greece and Portugal to behave differently over time relative to wages in sectors elsewhere in Europe. To discover what those economic forces might be, we compute pseudoscores as previously described, using various macroeconomic variables; the choice is opportunistic. We find that the correlations between the pseudoscores for the rate of change in investment in cluster 2's sectors relative to investment in all the sectors of other countries of Europe and the first canonical score are high; the correlation coefficients[9] vary from 0.64 for Belgium to 0.71 for Portugal. All are highly significant at the 0.01 level.

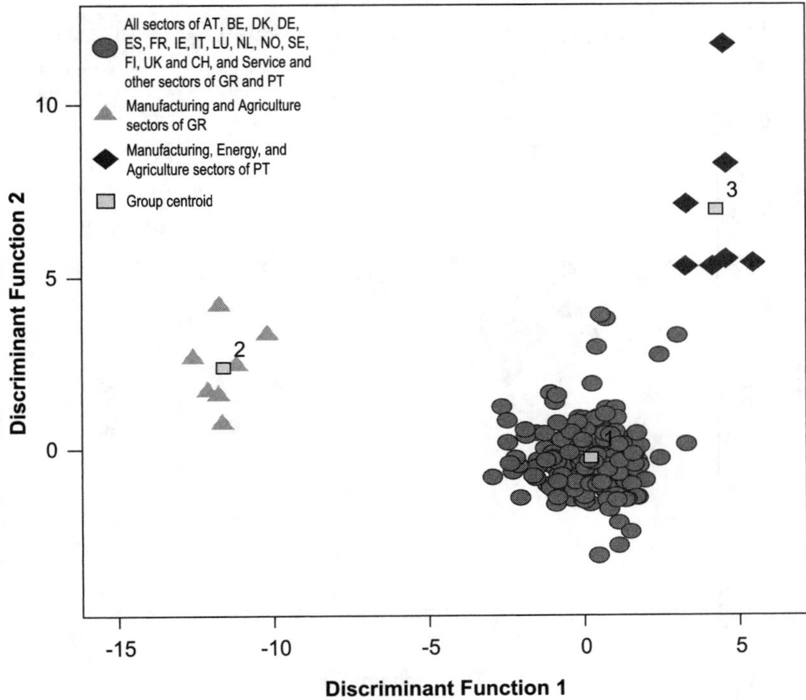

Figure 9.1. Canonical scores for level 1, 255 cases.

For DF2-1, we find that the correlations are highest between the second canonical score and the pseudoscores for rate of change in household expenditure (consumption) of Portugal relative to the household expenditure of other countries of Europe. All are significant at the 0.01 level except for Norway (significant at 0.05) and Luxembourg.

At this level of analysis, cluster 1 remains a huge cluster comprising 241 cases out of 255. It is possible that the two discriminant functions, depicting economic forces, may have dominated the forces that can discriminate between the cases inside cluster 1. If so, we may find further cluster structure by discarding clusters 2 and 3 as outliers. Hence, using the 241 cases of cluster 1 we perform a second level of analysis.

Cluster analysis on the 241 cases of cluster 1 in level 1 yields four clusters. In level 2, cluster 2 comprises predominantly the manufacturing sectors of Austria, while cluster 4 consists of all the sectors of the UK. Clusters 1 and 2 remain as big clusters each with 108 cases.

Next we perform discriminant function analysis again, which yields three discriminant functions that discriminate among the four clusters. The first, second,

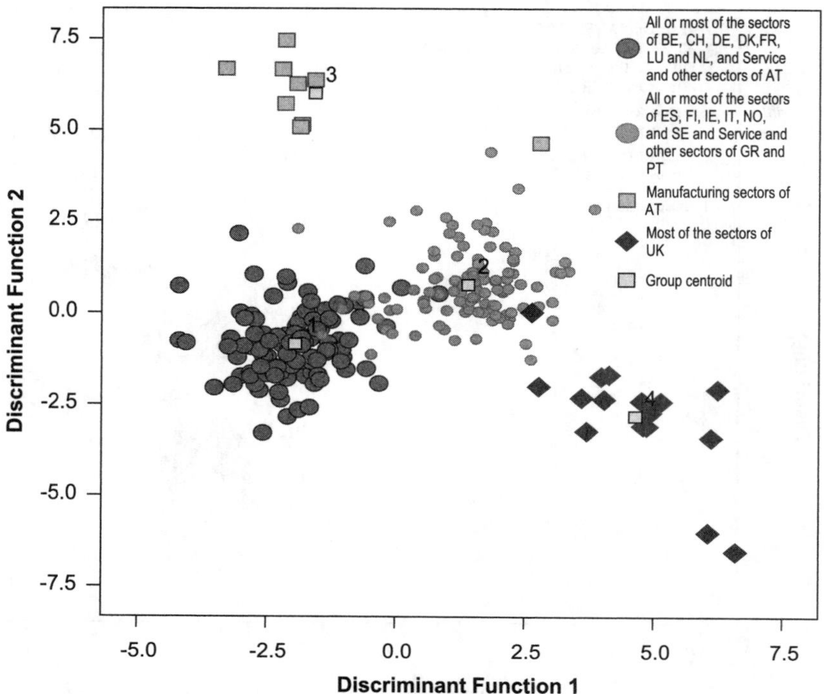

Figure 9.2. Canonical scores for level 2, 244 cases.

and third functions account for 51 percent, 30.5 percent, and 18.38 percent of the variation between clusters, respectively.

Figure 9.2 shows that DF1-2 mainly separates the UK from the rest of the cases, while DF2-2 mainly separates Austria from the rest. To find the economic forces behind this clustering, once again we use economic time series to calculate pseudoscores. The correlations between the pseudoscore for rate of change in the exchange rate of sterling relative to the exchange rates of other countries and the first canonical score are high, varying from 0.48 in the case of Spain to 0.81 for France. All correlations are highly significant at the 0.01 level. The analysis thus shows that the sterling exchange rate is a key determinant of the relative wage in the UK compared to the rest of Europe; when sterling rises, British wages go up. This happened massively in the 1980s, under the monetarist program of the Thatcher government, which took power in 1979.

For DF2-2 the correlations between the pseudoscore for the rate of change in GDP of Austria relative to that of other countries and the second canonical score are high. All are significant at the 0.01 level. Only the correlation coefficient in the case of Switzerland is not high; its absolute value is just 0.20, but it is nevertheless significant at the 0.01 level.

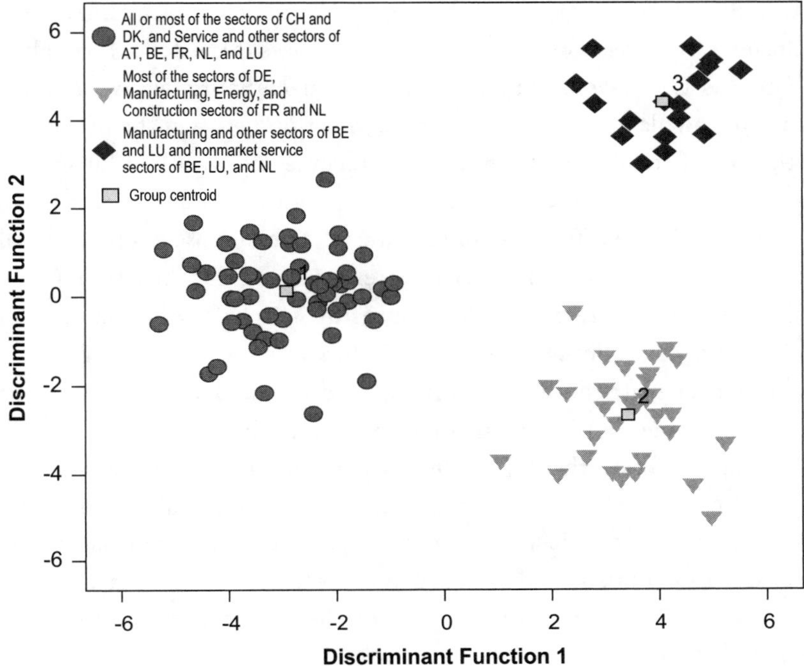

Figure 9.3A. Canonical scores for level 3-1, 108 cases.

At the second level of analysis, clusters 2 and 3 remain huge. We use each cluster to run two separate third-level analyses and discover further group structures within each of the two clusters.

The first level 3 analysis is on 108 cases of cluster 1 of level 2; clustering these cases yields three well-defined clusters. Cluster 3 consists predominantly of the manufacturing sectors of Belgium and Luxembourg and a few others. Cluster 2 consists of sectors of Germany, manufacturing sectors of France and the Netherlands, and some others. Cluster 1 consists of 60 cases including the service sectors of Austria, Belgium, France, and the Netherlands, all the sectors of Switzerland, sectors of Denmark, and a few others.

On the basis of this clustering, we again apply discriminant analysis. Figure 9.3(i) shows that DF1-3(i) separates cluster 1 from the rest of the cases. DF2-3(i) separates the cases of cluster 2 from the rest of the cases. The first and second functions account for 67.69 percent and 32.3 percent, respectively, of the discrimination between the clusters.

To find the economic forces that lead clusters 1 and 2 to behave differentially from the rest of the cases, pseudoscores are again calculated by using economic time series of Austria, France, Denmark, and other countries. The pseudoscores that we find here (figure 9.3A) are once again (changes in) investment and consumption.

DF2-3(i) separates the manufacturing sectors of Belgium and Luxembourg in cluster 3 from the cases in cluster 2 and the cases in cluster 1. Luxembourg is known as a tax haven, and we use taxes of Luxembourg relative to those of France to calculate pseudoscores. The correlation between the pseudoscore for the rate of change in current taxes on income and wealth of Luxembourg relative to those for France and the second canonical score is 0.55; it is significant at the 0.01 level. The taxes of Belgium relative to those of France are also used to calculate pseudoscores. Each correlation is significant at the 0.01 level.

We use as well the rate of change in investment in Belgium's sectors in cluster 3 relative to the investment in the sectors of other countries as pseudoscores and calculate the correlations with the second discriminant function. In some cases the correlations are high and significant.

Moving on to the other big cluster, we perform the second analysis at level 3 on 108 cases of cluster 2 of level 2 analysis. Cluster analysis yields three well-defined clusters. Cluster 2 consists of sectors of Greece; cluster 3 comprises sectors of Finland and some sectors of Norway and Sweden; and cluster 1 consists of 69 cases including sectors of Norway, Sweden, Portugal, Italy, Spain, Ireland, and some others.

From the clustering obtained from the cluster analysis, we perform DFA. Figure 3(ii) shows that DF1-3(ii) discriminates cluster 2 from rest of the clusters, while DF2-3(ii) discriminates cluster 3 from rest. The first and second functions account for 53.3 percent and 46.69 percent of the discrimination between the clusters respectively.

To find the economic forces that lead the wages of sectors in cluster 2 and those of cluster 3 to behave differently from the rest of the cases, we once again calculate pseudoscores. The correlations between the pseudoscore for rate of change in investment in Greece's sectors in cluster 2 relative to the investment in the sectors of Italy, Portugal, and Norway and the first canonical score are 0.40, 0.42, and 0.33, respectively. All are significant at the 0.01 level. (See figure 9.3B.)

In the case of DF2-3(ii), we use several economic time series of Finland, Norway, and Sweden to calculate pseudoscores. For both Norway and Finland, the correlation between the pseudoscores for the rate of change in the exchange rate of their national currencies relative to exchange rates of Greece, Spain, Ireland, Italy, and Portugal and the second canonical score are all high and highly significant.

In the case of Sweden, the correlations between the pseudoscore for the rate of change in investment relative to investment in sectors of Italy, Portugal,

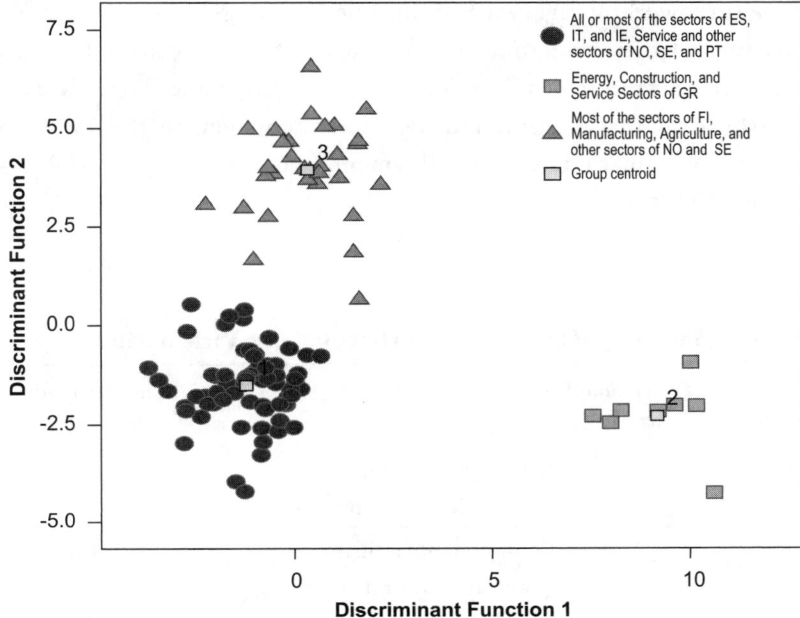

Figure 9.3B. Canonical scores for level 3-2, 108 cases.

Ireland, Spain, and Norway in cluster 1 and the second canonical score are high and significant.

Cluster 1 of the first analysis at level 3 comprises 60 cases and that of the second analysis at level 3 consists of 69 cases. We further perform two separate analyses to discover structures within these two clusters at a fourth level. To save space, these analyses are omitted here; broadly, they distinguish forces separating wage patterns in a number of smaller countries, in particular Austria, the Low Countries, and Scandinavia. Of particular interest, we find the evidence of an effect of oil prices on relative wages in Norway. Otherwise, differing rates of investment are the main apparent driver of relative wage change between these countries.

A summary of findings from all the levels of analyses is given in table 9.1.

The table shows that with just one exception (the UK) relative wage changes in Europe have been most closely associated with changes in spending, either consumption or investment. These are factors that operate on the demand side, and their direction of influence over wages and employment is not seriously in doubt; increases in either consumption or investment spending will raise *both* employment and the relative wage rate. It would appear therefore that the data do two things: they show it is possible to raise (or lower) relative wages in Europe by changing sectoral spending flows, and yet they lend almost no support to the proposition that lower relative wages can effectively raise relative employment. The UK exception—sterling overvaluation and high unemployment in the 1980s, followed by devaluation and employment recovery in the 1990s—is admittedly a big one.

Table 9.1. **Summary of the Main Forces Behind Wage Variation in Europe**

Level of Analysis	*Discriminant Function*	*Cluster*	*Macroeconomic Variable(s)*
Level 1	1	Manufacturing and agricultural sectors of GR	Investment
	2	Energy, manufacturing, and agricultural sectors of PT	Consumption
Level 2	1	14 sectors of UK	Exchange Rate
	2	Manufacturing sectors of AT	GDP
Level 3(1)	1	CH, some sectors of AT, DK, service sectors of BE, NL, and FR	Investment/ Consumption/ GDP
	2	Manufacturing sectors of BE and LU	Investment/Taxes
Level 3(2)	1	Service sectors of GR	Investment
	2	Sectors of FI, manufacturing sectors of NO and SE	Investment/ Exchange Rate
Level 4(1)	1	Service sectors of AT and NL	Investment
	2	Service sectors of DK	Investment/ Consumption
Level 4(2)	1	Service sectors of SE	Oil Price/Investment
	2	Service sectors of NO and IE	Oil Price/Investment

Conclusion

This chapter performs a systematic decomposition of wage variations across sectors and countries of Europe, taking the continent as a whole and treating wage variations as any multinational investor or corporation would be expected to do. The result challenges the notion of wage inflexibility in Europe. We find there is substantial systematic adjustment in European relative wages over time. This variability is primarily between nations, and it is associated with changing national economic fortunes, though not invariably so.

Given that variations exist, what is their relationship to employment changes? If the LMF hypothesis were correct, we should expect to find employment rising in countries that successfully reduce their relative wage rates, or at least sometimes. We did not test this proposition directly here; instead we asked what forces most effectively determined the changing relative wage rates that we observed. We found that differences in the movement of macroeconomic variables account for most of the variation in relative wage rates, one observes. Most notably investment, consumption, effective tax rates, and (in the case of Norway) oil prices are highly correlated with differential wage movements.

It is obvious that rising relative investment, or consumption, is associated with both rising wages and rising employment, and vice versa.[10] This suggests that, contrary to the LMF hypothesis, wages in Europe tend to rise and fall with, and not against, movements of employment. The UK appears as a major exception, having effectively deployed the tool of devaluation in the early 1990s on the way back toward high employment after years of depression-level unemployment. But it is the only such exception, and it is worth noting that the UK's boom in the 1990s, like that in the United States, owed at least as much to easy credit conditions as it did to a lower exchange rate. The employment gains of the 1990s were, for the most part, not in the traded goods sectors that should be most affected by depreciation.

The exercise thus casts grave doubt over the idea that unemployment in European countries can be explained by a failure of their wages to fall, or that unemployment can be remedied in general by policies aimed at cutting relative wages. For if this were true, cases would be observed. And we find (almost) none.

Appendix I

CLUSTER DETAILS

Table 9.A1. **Country Codes**

Code	Country
BE	Belgium
DK	Denmark
DE	Germany
GR	Greece
ES	Spain
FR	France
IE	Ireland
IT	Italy
LU	Luxembourg
NL	Netherlands
AT	Austria
PT	Portugal
FI	Finland
SE	Sweden
UK	United Kingdom
NO	Norway
CH	Switzerland

Table 9.A2. **Sector Codes**

Code	*Sectors*
ag	Agriculture, forestry, and fishing
ce	Mining and energy supply
da	Food, beverages, and tobacco
dbc	Textiles and clothing
dfgh	Fuels, chemicals, and rubber and plastic products
dl	Electronics
dm	Transport equipment
do	Other manufacturing
f	Construction
g	Wholesale and retail
h	Hotels and restaurants
i	Transport and communications
j	Financial services
k	Other market services
ns	Nonmarket services

Table 9.A3. **Cluster Analysis: Level 1**

Cluster 1						*Cluster 2*	*Cluster 3*
ATce	DEce	FIce	IEce	NLce	SEce	GRda	PTce
ATda	DEda	FIda	IEda	NLda	SEda	GRdbc	PTda
ATdbc	DEdbc	FIdbc	IEdbc	NLdbc	SEdbc	GRdfgh	PTdfgh
ATdfgh	DEdfgh	FIdfgh	IEdfgh	NLdfgh	SEdfgh	GRdl	PTdl
ATdl	DEdl	FIdl	IEdl	NLdl	SEdl	GRdm	PTdm
ATdm	DEdm	FIdm	IEdm	NLdm	SEdm	GRdo	PTdo
ATdo	DEdo	FIdo	IEdo	NLdo	SEdo	GRag	PTag
ATf	DEf	FIf	IEf	NLf	SEf		
ATg	DEg	FIg	IEg	NLg	SEg		
ATh	DEh	FIh	IEh	NLh	She		

continued

Table 9.A3. (continued)

Cluster 1						**Cluster 2**	**Cluster 3**
ATi	DEi	FIi	IEi	NLi	SEi		
ATj	DEj	FIj	IEj	NLj	SEj		
ATk	DEk	FIk	IEk	NLk	SEk		
ATns	DEns	FIns	IEns	NLns	SEns		
ATag	DEag	FIag	IEag	NLag	SEag		
BEce	DKce	FRce	ITce	NOce	UKce		
BEda	DKda	FRda	ITda	NOda	UKda		
BEdbc	DKdbc	FRdbc	ITdbc	NOdbc	UKdbc		
BEdfgh	DKdfgh	FRdfgh	ITdfgh	NOdfgh	UKdfgh		
BEdl	DKdl	FRdl	ITdl	NOdl	UKdl		
BEdm	DKdm	FRdm	ITdm	NOdm	UKdm		
BEdo	DKdo	FRdo	ITdo	NOdo	UKdo		
BEf	DKf	FRf	ITf	NOf	UKf		
BEg	DKg	FRg	ITg	NOg	UKg		
BEh	DKh	FRh	ITh	NOh	UKh		
BEi	DKi	FRi	ITi	NOi	UKi		
BEj	DKj	FRj	ITj	NOj	UKj		
BEk	DKk	FRk	ITk	NOk	UKk		
BEns	DKns	FRns	ITns	NOns	UKns		
BEag	DKag	FRag	ITag	NOag	UKag		
CHce	ESce	GRce	LUce	PTdbc			
CHda	ESda	GRf	LUda	PTf			
CHdbc	ESdbc	GRg	LUdbc	PTg			
CHdfgh	ESdfgh	GRh	LUdfgh	PTh			
CHdl	ESdl	GRi	LUdl	PTi			
CHdm	ESdm	GRj	LUdm	PTj			
CHdo	ESdo	GRk	LUdo	PTk			
CHf	ESf	GRns	LUf	PTns			
CHg	ESg		LUg				
CHh	ESh		LUh				

Table 9.A3. (continued)

Cluster 1			***Cluster 2***	***Cluster 3***
CHi	ESi	LUi		
CHj	ESj	LUj		
CHk	ESk	LUk		
CHns	ESns	LUns		
CHag	ESag	LUag		

Table 9.A4. **Cluster Analysis: Level 2**

Cluster 1				Cluster 2			Cluster 3	Cluster 4
ATce	DEce	FRce	NLce	ATag	GRce	LUce	ATda	BEag
ATf	DEda	FRda	NLda	BEk	GRf	LUh	ATdbc	FIns
ATg	DEdbc	FRdbc	NLdbc	DKdbc	GRg	LUk	ATdfgh	UKce
ATh	DEdfgh	FRdfgh	NLdfgh	DKdl	GRh	NOce	ATdl	UKda
ATi	DEdl	FRdl	NLdl	DKag	GRi	NOda	ATdm	UKdbc
ATj	DEdm	FRdm	NLdm	ESce	GRj	NOdbc	ATdo	UKdfgh
ATk	DEdo	FRdo	NLdo	ESda	GRk	NOdfgh	DEag	UKdl
ATns	DEf	FRf	NLf	ESdbc	GRns	NOdl	LUag	UKdm
BEce	DEg	FRg	NLg	ESdfgh	IEce	NOdm	UKk	UKdo
BEda	DEh	FRh	NLh	ESdl	IEda	NOdo		UKf
BEdbc	DEi	FRi	NLi	ESdm	IEdbc	NOg		UKg
BEdfgh	DEj	FRj	NLj	ESdo	IEdfgh	NOh		UKh
BEdl	DEk	FRk	NLk	ESf	IEdl	NOi		UKi
BEdm	DEns	FRns	NLns	ESg	IEdm	NOj		UKj
BEdo	DKce	IEag	NLag	ESh	IEdo	NOk		UKns
BEf	DKda	LUda	NOf	ESi	IEf	NOns		UKag
BEg	DKdfgh	LUdbc	PTf	ESk	IEg	NOag		
BEh	DKdm	LUdfgh	SEce	ESns	IEh	PTdbc		
BEi	DKdo	LUdl		ESag	IEi	PTg		

BEj	DKf	LUdm	FIda	IEj	PTh
BEns	DKg	LUdo	FIdbc	IEk	PTi
CHce	DKh	LUf	FIdfgh	IEns	PTj
CHda	DKi	LUg	FIdl	ITce	PTk
CHdbc	DKj	LUi	FIdm	ITda	PTns
CHdfgh	DKk	LUj	FIdo	ITdbc	SEda
CHdl	DKns	LUns	FIf	ITdfgh	SEdbc
CHdm	ESj		FIg	ITdl	SEdfgh
CHdo	FIce		FIh	ITdm	SEdl
CHf			FIi	ITdo	SEdm
CHg			FIj	ITf	SEdo
CHh			FIk	ITg	SEf
CHi			FIag	ITh	SEg
CHj			FRag	ITi	SEh
CHk				ITj	SEi
CHns				ITk	SEj
CHag				ITns	SEk
				ITag	SEns
					SEag

Table 9.A5. **Cluster Analysis: Level 3-1**

Cluster 1		*Cluster 2*	*Cluster 3*
ATce	Def	DEce	BEce
ATf	DEns	DEda	BEda
ATg	DKce	DEdbc	BEdbc
ATh	DKda	DEdfgh	BEdfgh
ATi	DKdfgh	DEdl	BEdl
ATj	DKdo	DEdm	BEdm
ATk	DKf	DEdo	BEdo
ATns	DKg	DEg	Bens
BEf	DKh	DEh	LUda
BEg	DKi	DEi	LUdbc
BEh	DKj	DEj	LUdfgh
BEi	DKk	DEk	LUdl
BEj	DKns	DKdm	LUdm
CHce	ESj	FRce	LUdo
CHda	FIce	FRda	LUf
CHdbc	FRg	FRdbc	LUns
CHdfgh	FRh	FRdfgh	NLns
CHdl	FRi	FRdl	
CHdm	FRj	FRdm	
CHdo	FRk	FRdo	
CHf	FRns	FRf	
CHg	LUg	IEag	
CHh	LUi	NLce	
CHi	LUj	NLda	
CHj	NLdm	NLdbc	
CHk	NLg	NLdfgh	
CHns	NLh	NLdl	
CHag	NLi	NLdo	
	NLj	NLf	
	NLk	NOf	
	NLag	PTf	
	SEce		

Table 9.A6. **Cluster Analysis: Level 3-2**

Cluster 1		*Cluster 2*	*Cluster 3*
BEk	ITce	GRce	ATag
DKdbc	ITda	GRf	DKag
DKdl	ITdbc	GRg	FIda
ESce	ITdfgh	GRh	FIdbc
ESda	ITdl	GRi	FIdfgh
ESdbc	ITdm	GRj	FIdl
ESdfgh	ITdo	GRk	FIdm
ESdl	ITf	GRns	Fido
ESdm	ITg		Fig
ESdo	ITh		FIh
ESf	ITi		FIi
ESg	ITj		FIj
ESh	ITk		FIk
ESi	ITns		FIag
ESk	ITag		IEdm
ESns	LUce		NOce
ESag	LUh		NOda
FIf	LUk		NOdbc
FRag	NOg		NOdfgh
IEce	NOh		NOdl
IEda	NOi		NOdm
IEdbc	NOj		NOdo
IEdfgh	NOk		NOag
IEdl	NOns		SEda
IEdo	PTdbc		SEdbc
IEf	PTg		SEdfgh
IEg	PTh		SEdl
IEh	PTi		SEdm
IEi	PTj		SEdo
IEj	PTk		SEf
IEk	PTns		SEag

continued

Table 9.A6 (continued)

Cluster 1		**Cluster 2**	**Cluster 3**
IEns	SEg		
	SEh		
	SEi		
	SEj		
	SEk		
	SEns		

Table 9.A7. **Cluster Analysis: Level 4-1**

Cluster 1	**Cluster 2**	**Cluster 3**	**Cluster 4**
Atf	ATce	BEf	CHce
ATg	ATns	BEg	CHda
ATh	BEh	BEi	CHdfgh
ATi	BEj	DKf	CHdl
ATj	CHdbc	DKg	CHdm
ATk	DEns	DKh	CHdo
Def	DKce	DKi	CHf
NLg	DKda	DKj	CHg
NLh	DKdfgh	DKk	CHh
NLi	DKdo	ESj	CHi
NLj	DKns	NLag	CHj
NLk	FRg		CHk
	FRh		CHns
	FRi		CHag
	FRj		FIce
	FRk		SEce
	FRns		
	LUg		
	LUi		
	LUj		
	NLdm		

Table 9.A8. **Cluster Analysis: Level 4-2**

Cluster 1		*Cluster 2*	*Cluster 3*	*Cluster 4*	*Cluster 5*
ESce	ITce	SEg	IEf	IEce	BEk
ESda	ITda	SEh	IEh	IEda	DKdbc
ESdbc	ITdbc	SEi	IEi	IEdbc	DKdl
ESdfgh	ITdfgh	SEj	IEk	IEdfgh	FRag
ESdl	ITdl	SEk	NOg	IEdl	IEg
ESdm	ITdm	SEns	Noh	IEdo	IEns
ESdo	ITdo		NOi	IEj	LUh
ESf	ITf		NOj		LUk
ESg	ITg		NOk		PTdbc
ESh	ITh		NOns		PTg
ESi	ITi				PTh
ESk	ITj				PTi
ESns	ITk				PTj
ESag	ITns				PTk
FIf	ITag				PTns
	LUce				

Appendix II

EIGENVALUES AND CANONICAL CORRELATIONS

Table 9.B1. **Eigenvalues and Canonical Correlations for Discriminant Functions at the Different Levels of Analysis**

Level	*Analysis*	*Discriminant Function*	*Eigenvalue*	*% of Variance*	*Cumulative %*	*Canonical Correlation*
1		1	4.29	73.237	73.236	0.901
		2	1.57	26.763	100	0.781
2		1	4.18	51.07	51.07	0.898
		2	2.49	30.54	81.61	0.845
		3	1.5	18.39	100	0.775
3	1	1	11.03	67.69	67.69	0.957
		2	5.26	32.31	100	0.917
3	2	1	7.42	53.3	53.3	0.939
		2	6.49	46.7	100	0.93
4	1	1	20.4	57.4	57.4	0.976
		2	11.26	31.68	89.07	0.958
		3	3.88	10.92	100	0.892
4	2	1	22.89	50.17	50.17	0.979
		2	14.04	30.76	80.92	0.966
		3	5.64	12.36	93.28	0.922
		4	3.07	6.72	100	0.868

Appendix III

CORRELATIONS BETWEEN CANONICAL SCORES AND PSEUDOSCORES

Table 9.C1. **Canonical Scores and Pseudoscores: Level 1**

Level	*Canonical Score (A)*	*Pseudoscore (B)*	*Country*	*Correlation between (A) and (B)*
1	1	Rate of change in investment of GR's manufacturing, agriculture, forestry, and fishing sectors relative to investment of all the sectors of:	BE	−0.639**
			DK	−0.589**
			DE	−0.655**
			ES	−0.612**
			FR	−0.604**
			IE	−0.508**
			IT	−0.651**
			LU	−0.710**
			NL	−0.616**
			AT	−0.666**
			PT	−0.717**
			FI	−0.515**
			SE	−0.571**
			UK	−0.395**
			NO	−0.362**
			CH	−0.541**
			Eurozone	−0.652**
			EU25	−0.644**
			All countries	−0.640**

continued

Table 9.C1. (continued)

Level	*Canonical Score (A)*	*Pseudoscore (B)*	*Country*	*Correlation between (A) and (B)*
1	2	Rate of change in household expenditure of PT relative to the household expenditure of:	BE	0.448**
			DK	−0.211**
			DE	−0.233**
			GR	0.403**
			ES	0.368**
			FR	0.480**
			IE	0.300**
			IT	0.425**
			LU	0.035
			NL	0.297**
			AT	0.395**
			FI	0.452**
			SE	0.586**
			UK	0.377**
			NO	0.171*
			CH	0.627**
			Eurozone	0.222**
			EU25	0.261**
			All countries	0.288**

* significant at 10 percent level.
** significant at 5 percent level.
*** significant at 1 percent level.

Table 9.C2. **Canonical Scores and Pseudoscores: Level 2**

Level	*Canonical Score (A)*	*Pseudoscore (B)*	*Country*	*Correlation between (A) and (B)*
2	1	Rate of change in exchange rate of UK's national currency per U.S. dollar relative to exchange rate of national currency per U.S. dollar of:	BE	−0.79**
			DK	−0.79**
			DE	−0.71**
			GR	−0.47**
			ES	−0.48**
			FR	−0.81**
			IE	−0.76**
			IT	−0.61**
			LU	−0.79**
			NL	−0.72**
			AT	−0.70**
			PT	−0.47**
			FI	−0.46**
			SE	−0.33**
			NO	−0.63**
			CH	−0.63**

continued

Table 9.C2. (continued)

Level	*Canonical Score (A)*	*Pseudoscore (B)*	*Country*	*Correlation between (A) and (B)*
2	2	Rate of change in GDP of AT relative to the GDP of:	BE	−0.691**
			DK	−0.638**
			DE	−0.501**
			GR	−0.549**
			ES	−0.699**
			FR	−0.682**
			IE	−0.673**
			IT	−0.635**
			LU	−0.618**
			NL	−0.702**
			PT	−0.691**
			FI	−0.569**
			SE	−0.638**
			UK	−0.592**
			NO	−0.469**
			CH	−0.197**
			Eurozone	−0.681**
			EU25	−0.723**
			All countries	−0.716**

Table 9.C3. **Canonical Scores and Pseudoscores: Level 3-1**

Level	*Canonical Score (A)*	*Pseudoscore (B)*	*Country*	*Correlation between (A) and (B)*
3(1)	1	Rate of change in investment of AT's sectors in cluster 1 relative to investment in the sectors of:	DE	−0.543**
			FR in cluster 2	0.638**
			NL in cluster 2	−0.525**
			BE in cluster 3	0.186
			LU in cluster 3	−0.210*
3(1)	1	Rate of change in investment of FR's sectors in cluster 1 relative to investment in the sectors of:	DE	−0.299**
			FR in cluster 2	0.681**
			NL in cluster 2	−0.299**
			BE in cluster 3	0.461**
			LU in cluster 3	0.1
3(1)	1	Rate of change in investment of NL's sectors in cluster 1 relative to investment in the sectors of:	DE	−0.184
			FR in cluster 2	0.634**
			NL in cluster 2	−0.401**
			BE in cluster 3	0.424**
			LU in cluster 3	0.144
3(1)	1	Rate of change in investment of DK relative to investment in the sectors of:	FR in cluster 2	0.614**
			NL in cluster 2	−0.249**
			BE in cluster 3	0.471**
			LU in cluster 3	0.209*
3(1)	1	Rate of change in consumption of DK relative to investment in the sectors of:	DE	−0.308**
3(1)	1	Rate of change in investment of CH relative to investment in the sectors of:	FR in cluster 2	0.492**
			NL in cluster 2	−0.152
			BE in cluster 3	0.326**
			LU in cluster 3	0.129
3(1)	1	Rate of change in consumption of CH relative to investment in the sectors of:	DE	−0.542**

continued

Table 9.C3. (continued)

Level	*Canonical Score (A)*	*Pseudoscore (B)*	*Country*	*Correlation between (A) and (B)*
3(1)	2	Rate of change in current taxes on income and wealth of BE relative to that of:	FR	0.516**
	2	Rate of change in current taxes on income and wealth of LU relative to that of:	FR	0.550**
3(1)	2	Rate of change in taxes on production and imports of BE relative to that of:	FR	0.576**
3(1)	2	Rate of change in taxes on production and imports of LU relative to that of:	FR	−0.210*
3(1)	2	Rate of change in total receipts from taxes and social contributions BE relative to that of:	FR	0.672**
	2	Rate of change in total receipts from taxes and social contributions of LU relative to that of:	FR	0.321**
3(1)	2	Rate of change in investment of BE's sectors in Cluster 3 relative to the investment in the sectors of:	BE in Cluster 1	−0.222*
			NL	−0.509**
			FR	−0.014
			DK	−0.079
			DE	−0.18
			CH	0.159
			AT in Cluster 1	−0.410**

Table 9.C4. **Canonical Scores and Pseudoscores: Level 3-2**

Level	*Canonical Score (A)*	*Pseudoscore (B)*	*Country*	*Correlation between (A) and (B)*
3(2)	1	Rate of change in investment of GR's sectors in Cluster 2 relative to the investment in the sectors of:	ES	0.267**
			FI	0.226*
			IE	0.149
			IT	0.393**
			PT	0.416**
			NO	0.325**
			SE	0.189
3(2)	2	Rate of change in exchange rate of FI's national currency per U.S. dollar relative to exchange rate of national currencies per U.S. dollar of:	GR	−0.672**
			ES	−0.765**
			IE	−0.757**
			IT	−0.763**
			NO	−0.505**
			PT	−0.76**
3(2)	2	Rate of change in exchange rate of NO's national currency per U.S. dollar relative to exchange rate of national currencies per U.S. dollar of:	GR	−0.59**
			ES	−0.574**
			IE	−0.655**
			IT	−0.61**
			PT	−0.694**
3(2)	2	Rate of change in investment of SE sectors in Cluster 3 relative to the investment in sectors of:	ES	0.533**
			IE	0.595**
			IT	0.665**
			PT	0.714**
			NO in Cluster 1	−0.242*

Table 9.C5. **Canonical Scores and Pseudoscores: Level 4-1**

Level	*Canonical Score (A)*	*Pseudoscore (B)*	*Country*	*Correlation between (A) and (B)*
4(1)	1	Rate of change in investment of CH relative to the investment in sectors of:	AT	0.732**
			NL	0.813**
	2	Rate of change in investment of DK relative to the investment in sectors of:	CH	−0.399**
			AT	0.423**
			NL	−0.277*
	2	Rate of change in household expenditure of DK relative to that in sectors of:	CH	0.509**
			AT	0.195
			NL	0.333**
	2	Rate of change in GDP of DK relative to the GDP in sectors of:	CH	0.388**
			AT	0.378**
			NL	−0.051

Table 9.C6. **Canonical Scores and Pseudoscores: Level 4-2**

Level	*Canonical Score (A)*	*Pseudoscore (B)*	*Country*	*Correlation between (A) and (B)*
4(2)	1	Rate of change in nominal oil price		0.601**
		Rate of change in real oil price		0.657**
	1	Rate of change in investment of SE's sectors in Cluster 2 relative to the investment in sectors of:	ES	0.451**
			IE	−0.456**
			IT	−0.552**
			PT	0.552**
			NO in Cluster 3	−0.114
	1	Rate of change in household expenditure of SE's sectors in Cluster 2 relative to the household expenditure in sectors of:	ES	0.453**
			IE	−0.236**
			IT	0.558**
			PT	0.389**
	1	Rate of change in GDP of SE's sectors in Cluster 2 relative to the GDP in sectors of:	ES	0.455**
			IE	0.113
			IT	0.296*
			PT	0.259*
	2	Rate of change in nominal oil price		0.446**
		Rate of change in real oil price		0.469**
	2	Rate of change in investment of NO's sectors in Cluster 3 relative to the investment in sectors of:	ES	0.573**
			PT in Cluster 5	0.562**

Notes

1. This chapter is adapted from James K. Galbraith and Deepshikha RoyChowdhury, "The European Wage Structure, 1980–2005: How Much Flexibility Do We Have?" UTIP Working Paper No. 41, May 15, 2007.
2. Except Galbraith and Garcilazo (2004), Garcilazo (2005), Galbraith (2006).
3. Source of data: Cambridge Econometrics.
4. The list of fifteen EU nations is given in table 9.A1 of appendix I.
5. The list of sectors is given in table 9.A2 of appendix I.
6. Ward's method minimizes the sum of squared Euclidean distance between any two (hypothetical) clusters that are formed at each step.
7. The technique is mostly used at the exploratory phase of research; there are no a priori hypotheses and there is no role for statistical significance testing.
8. DFi-j represents ith discriminant function of jth level analysis.
9. The correlation coefficients presented in the data analysis section are absolute values of the correlation coefficients. Their actual values are reported in appendix C.
10. The same would be true of a rising oil price in an oil producer such as Norway.

CHAPTER 10

Globalization and Inequality in China

As a matter of public rhetoric, few governments lay as much stress on the issue of rising economic inequality as that of China. The People's Republic may be the world's only major nation to have the goal of a "harmonious society" as a formal policy objective.[1] Chinese leaders regularly state their concern that the high inequalities that have emerged during China's reform period stand in conflict with that objective. This posture contrasts with that of political leaders in Europe, where policy discourse emphasizes the motifs of "fiscal consolidation" and "labor market reform," and also with the United States, where stated official concerns about inequality are submerged in an anodyne rhetoric of educational opportunity and skill development.

In China, the "actual issue" is fairly clear to everyone: the rise of a wealthy coastal zone, deeply integrated with the world economy, in contrast to an interior that, even though growing rapidly by its own past standards, remains quite far behind. To this one may add the effects of public and private investment in the biggest cities—especially Beijing, Shanghai, and Guangzhou—in raising these citadels to heights of prosperity never before seen in China. And to that one should also add the effect of market structures on the use of market power, increasing occupational differentials inside every region and city, and permitting accumulation of large private fortunes for the first time since the revolution. All of this has a vast, distorting effect on the Chinese population, pulling them to the cities despite a draconian system of internal migration control, and creating an extreme form of inequality-induced unemployment as the floating population looks for work.

Seen from the West, discussion of the "rise of China" often reflects preoccupation with the role of manufactured exports in Chinese economic growth, a sector conspicuous in Western markets and allegedly advantaged by China's policy of pegging the renminbi (RMB) to the U.S. dollar at a fixed (or at best slowly appreciating) rate. Seen from within China, however, the picture is different: in the "export-oriented" provinces of the Chinese coast, manufacturing is a low-wage, low-prestige activity, a point of entry to urban life from the hinterland, attractive in the main to young women with village schooling and few alternatives. Nor is manufacturing a dominant form of employment, even though it grew very rapidly in the years from 2002 to 2006. Low wages in Chinese manufacturing are therefore not a sign of low wages generally in Chinese cities, nor of a low living standard, especially for established and legal residents.

This chapter explores the forces behind the movements of inequality within China since the early 1990s, including the concurrent rise of export earnings and real estate prices and measures of trade and capital inflow.[2] Using data disaggregated by region and economic sector, we show that the rise in inequality in China since 2000 has more to do directly with the speculative activities associated with China's stock market and building boom, notably in Beijing, than with the growth in manufacturing employment and in Chinese exports since China joined the WTO in 2001. However, it seems evident that the two phenomena are connected; the flow of profits from the export boom has helped to feed the speculative fires in the capital and elsewhere, and it is not therefore surprising that the fall of one, in the crisis of 2008, should be linked to the fall of the other. This phenomenon raises questions relevant to a discussion of capital account regulation in China, as well as larger issues of economic management and resource allocation.

The Evolution of Inequality in China through 2007

By all measures, inequality rose rapidly in China beginning in the early 1990s (Riskin, Renwei, and Li 2001). Measurements by Galbraith, Krytynskaia, and Wang (2004) showed that much of the rise in that decade could be attributed to the relative gains of just one province and two municipalities (Guangdong, Shanghai, and Beijing), and to the relative earnings gains of just three sectors (transportation, utilities, and banking). Major regional laggards included the Northeast (Manchuria) and the Southwest (Sichuan); across sectors the major laggards included manufacturing, farming, and (retail and wholesale) trade.[3] As noted above, the position of manufacturing as a growing, low-wage sector illustrates the social position of the factory job in reform-era China, as an entry point to the cities for migrants from the (even-lower-wage) countryside and interior of the country.

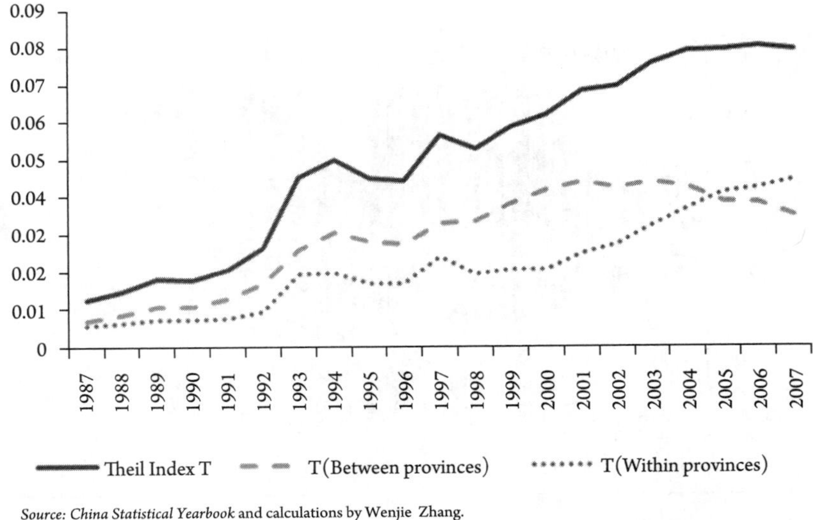

Source: China Statistical Yearbook and calculations by Wenjie Zhang.

Figure 10.1. Inequality between and within provinces in China, 1987–2007.

Figure 10.1 presents a broad overview of the evolution of pay inequality in China, overall and by region and sector, updated through 2007. The method consists of calculating the contribution of each sector within each province to the between-groups component of Theil's T statistic for the whole country, and then aggregating the components by sectors and provinces to achieve measures of inequality between provinces and within provinces. The figure shows that whereas during the 1990s inequality between provinces and inequality within provinces both rose, in the 2000s the behavior of these two dimensions of inequality diverged. Inequality between provinces peaked early in the 1990s and declined after 2001. In contrast, inequality within provinces (equivalently, inequality between sectors) continued to rise.

Figure 10.2 breaks out the changing interregional dimensions of Chinese inequality in a stacked bar graph. Each bar represents a year and each segment represents the contribution of a province to overall inequality in that year. The segments reflect both the population weight of the province (measured by observed employment) and the ratio between average provincial income and national average income. Contributions greater than zero indicate provinces with mean incomes above the national average; contributions below zero indicate those with incomes below. Overall interprovincial inequality is measured by the sum of all the elements in a given year. The legend is read across, from largest to smallest (largest positive to largest negative) contributions in 2007. The largest positive contribution (Beijing) is placed next to the zero line, while

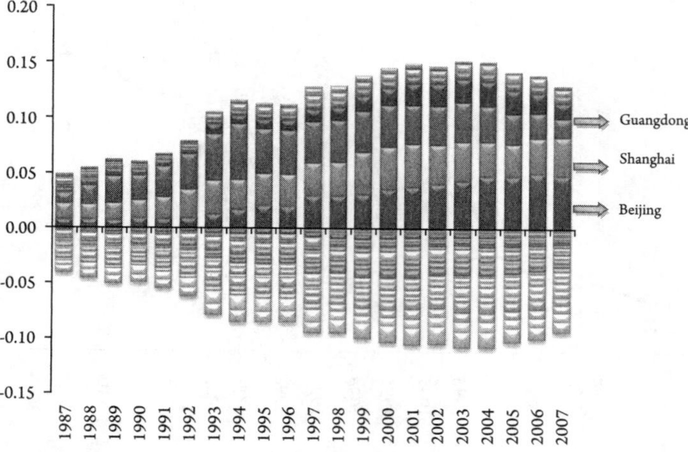

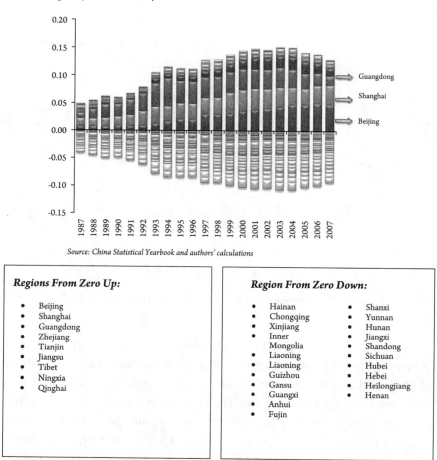

Source: China Statistical Yearbook and authors' calculations

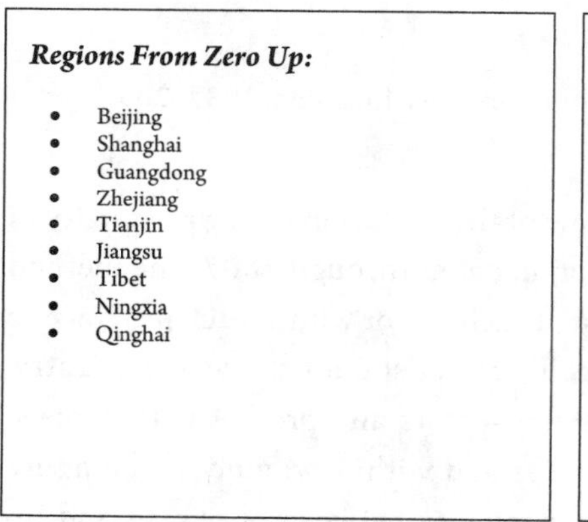

Regions From Zero Up:
Beijing
Shanghai
Guangdong
Zhejiang
Tianjin
Jiangsu
Tibet
Ningxia
Qinghai

Region From Zero Down:

- Hainan
- Chongqing
- Xinjiang
- Inner Mongolia
- Liaoning
- Liaoning
- Guizhou
- Gansu
- Guangxi
- Anhui
- Fujin
- Shanxi
- Yunnan
- Hunan
- Jiangxi
- Shandong
- Sichuan
- Hubei
- Hebei
- Heilongjiang
- Henan

Figure 10.2. Contribution of provinces to interprovincial inequality in China, 1987–2007.

the largest negative (Henan) is placed at the bottom of the bar. In this way, the eye easily tracks the evolution of relative contributions to inequality over time.

The figure shows that the enormous *relative* contribution of Guangdong province to overall inequality in China actually peaked as far back as 1994, while that of Shanghai reached its zenith around 2000 or 2001. Despite their positions as the seat of Chinese export trade and the financial center, respectively, both were regressing moderately toward mean income by 2005. This happened because Chinese development was diversifying, and incomes elsewhere were rising. Uniquely among the big three, the relative contribution of Beijing continued to rise. The recent rise of a fourth contender, Zhejiang province, rounds out the contrasting picture of convergence and divergence among the rich provinces, as the great Chinese coastal development boom matured.

Table 10.1 shows how trends in manufacturing employment across China during the early years of the new century played into this picture. It shows that in most Chinese provinces manufacturing employment declined from 2002 through 2006. But there were five great exceptions—Guangdong, Zhejiang, Fujian, Jiangsu, and Shandong—where manufacturing employment rose by a cumulative total of 4.9 million jobs during these four years. All are deeply involved in China's integration into world markets following accession to the WTO. Their expansion offset a net decline in manufacturing employment of 1.5 million jobs spread across the rest of the country, giving China as a whole a net gain in manufacturing employment exceeding 10 percent in that period. In four years, these five provinces added manufacturing jobs equal to 36 percent of the remaining manufacturing employment in the United States as of April 2008.[4] However, in relation to the Chinese population and even to officially recorded employment in other sectors, what is striking is how small these numbers actually appear to be. Even in China, manufacturing does not employ all that many people.

Obviously, the gains in manufacturing employment were closely tied to exports. After rising at just over 10 percent per year on average from 1999 through 2001 (two years of boom and one of recession in the United States), China's exports started to surge in 2002. They rose 21 percent that year, and then 35 percent in each of the two following years, before settling back to reported growth rates of 28 percent in 2005 and 27 percent in 2006. Overall the reported increase in exports in dollar terms from 2002 to 2006 amounts to an impressive 264 percent.[5]

As figure 10.2 illustrates, apart from the rise of Zhejiang the post-2001 export boom in China had little apparent direct effect on inequality as measured between provinces. This may seem strange on the surface, but the explanation

Table 10.1. **China: Number of Manufacturing Workers by Provinces**

Year and Region	*Jiangsu*	*Fujian*	*Shandong*	*Guangdong*	*Zhejiang*	*Rest of Country*
2002	216	134	272	255	97	1,933
2003	217	152	270	282	109	1,869
2004	223	181	280	315	152	1,810
2005	245	198	334	357	201	1,762
2006	281	215	342	387	240	1,786

Source: China Statistical Yearbook; in tens of thousands of persons.

is not complicated. Though manufacturing in China is a low-wage sector, within the high-wage southern provinces average pay in manufacturing is close to, or even slightly above, national average pay rates. (This is what makes jobs in those sectors attractive to long-distance migrants.) Thus an increase in the manufacturing share of employment would not necessarily increase overall pay inequality in China; the contribution to overall inequality of a sector whose average pay is close to the national average is necessarily small. This is sufficient to explain why strong growth in export-oriented manufacturing employment need not have had a dramatic impact, one way or the other, on the *inequalities* of Chinese society, or at least of its structures of pay.

So what caused the increase in inequality? Clearly the much higher incomes in banking, finance, and information technologies in Beijing, Shanghai, and Guangdong had a powerful effect; there is little else in the country quite like them. Figure 10.3 illustrates the contribution of the financial sector to inequality in the case of Beijing, alongside that of other sectors inside the municipality. As before, the legend is read from top to bottom (largest positive to largest negative contribution) while the contributions themselves are stacked in descending order above and then below the zero line for year 2007, with data for earlier years following the same order. Thus the chart shows clearly the remarkable increase in the relative importance of high finance in the capital of the People's Republic of China.

Finance and the Export Boom, 2002 to 2006

What, then, is the relationship—if any—of the rise of finance to the rise of trade? Table 10.2 presents the Chinese current account, as officially reported. It shows the remarkable growth in the official trade surplus in the period since China joined the WTO. Before the accession China generally reported small trade surpluses; after the turn of the century exports exploded. China's imports also rose sharply during this period, but exports measured in dollars grew even more, nearly quadrupling from 2000 to 2006—a rise of nearly three-quarters of a trillion dollars.

Thus China reported a trade surplus of $103 billion in 2006 in goods and services taken together; the figure for goods alone was $178 billion. Given a dollar value of Chinese GDP at the prevailing exchange rate on the order of $3 trillion in 2006, exports amounted to nearly a third of GDP by that time and trade openness (exports plus imports) to more than half.[6]

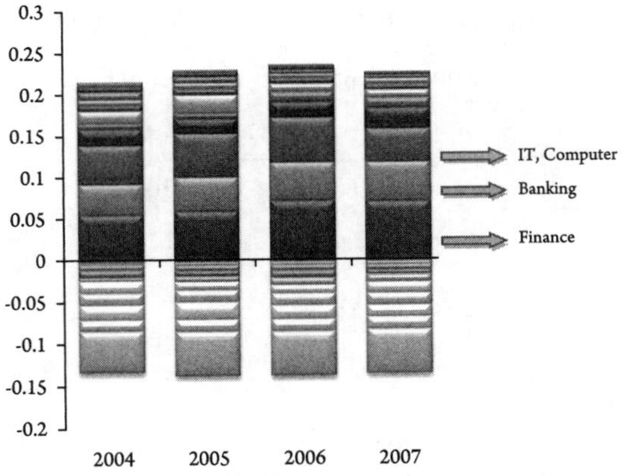

Source: China Statistical Yearbook and authors' calculations

Sectors From Zero Up:

- Finance
- Banking
- Information Transmission, Computer Service, and Software
- Scientific Studies, Technical Services, and Geological Prospecting
- Negotiable Securities
- Public Management and Social Organization
- Insurance
- Culture, Art, Sports, and Recreation
- Health Care, Social Security, and Social Welfare
- Electricity, Gas, Water Production and Supply
- Education

Sectors From Zero Down:

- Mining
- Farming, Forestry, Animal Husbandry, and Fishery
- Water, Environment, and Municipal Engineering Conservancy
- Resident Services and Other Services
- Wholesale Trade and Retail Trade
- Tenancy and Commercial Services
- Hotels and Catering Services
- Construction
- Transportation, Storage, and Postmanufacturing

Figure 10.3. Contribution to inequality between sectors, 22 Beijing sectors, 2004–2007.

This record may be considered in light of one of the most basic principles of international macroeconomics: the growth of imports depends on the domestic growth rate, while that of exports depends on growth in external markets. Thus when a developing country experiences a prolonged period of high internal growth, it is normal for a trade *deficit* to emerge. This is especially likely if the country in question is an importer of food and fuel, if commodity prices are rising, and if growth in the foreign markets is relatively slow. Many cases can be cited; exceptions are rare, and in the modern record they are largely confined to countries that maintain rigorously undervalued exchange rates and repressed domestic consumption, while rapidly improving

Table 10.2. **China: Balance of Trade, 1998–2006**

	Exports of Goods	*Imports of Goods*	*Balance of Trade*
1998	184	140	44
1999	195	166	29
2000	250	225	25
2001	266	244	22
2002	323	295	28
2003	438	413	25
2004	593	561	32
2005	762	660	102
2006	969	791	178
2007	1,218	956	262

Source: China Customs (trade data, http://english.customs.gov.cn/publish/portal191); billions of U.S. dollars.

the composition and quality of their exports. China's record of gain in its current account surplus in the face of rapid domestic economic growth is, we submit, strange.

The increasing value of Chinese exports is so large, and the share of exports in GDP has risen to such a high value, that one is tempted to distrust the figures. How can this be? Is China repressing domestic consumption to the point of starvation? If so, the suffering was very carefully concealed, for the large southern cities that were most tied up in the boom seemed, in those years, remarkably prosperous. Alternatively, one may look for radical changes in the composition of Chinese exports, or in their price, to account for the enormous rise in revenues attributed to this sector.

Information on the unit prices of imports from China are maintained by European authorities, while the United States reports price indices of imports in general. Little of consequence seems to have happened in either dataset. Nor does it seem that the composition of exports shifted dramatically toward higher-valued goods. In fact such shifts have been occurring, notably an increase of about three percentage points per year in the export share of the machinery and transport equipment sector. But this increase had been going on for a long time, and the gains after 2002 are not out of line with past experience. So even though China is always in the process of upgrading its manufactured exports, the major push behind the post-2001 boom has been expansion in reported shipments (quantities) rather than in the value-added associated with particular units (price or quality change).

Another piece of the picture concerns the processing trade, a large share of China's manufactured exports. China could be importing increasingly high-value goods (from, say, Japan) in order to finish them and export them again. But if this were the case, then reported unit values of Chinese *imports* in manufacturing would also be increasing, and so would the share of the processing trade in total trade. Neither appears to have occurred. Processing trade accounts for about 55 percent of Chinese exports, and this figure remained stable after 2001.[7] Although there is a slight progression in import prices in manufacturing from 2001 onward, no dramatic increase is observed.

There is no question that the boom was "real," in the sense that quantities surged, alongside manufacturing employment in the key exporting provinces. From the remarkable boom in manufacturing employment, coupled to the increase in unit sales, it appears plain that after 2001 China's exporters took full advantage of their position as a WTO-compliant country and multiplied their efforts and their results. The question then becomes: How might a simple increase in the quantities of the major commodities in the Chinese export basket yield not only an increase in export revenues but also a dramatic profits boom, contributing to an increase in the share of investment in the economy as a whole?

In a paper written before the magnitude of the export boom was clearly visible in the data (Galbraith 2006b), I offered a discussion of the environment facing Chinese light industry, and particularly of the hypercompetitive climate facing township, village, and cooperative enterprises whose losses are routinely financed by the banking sector. This environment—the Chinese call it "market socialism"—makes it difficult for Chinese manufacturers to earn large profits in the home market, which is perpetually glutted with consumer goods. I then asked: "Is there any way for the Chinese manufacturing firm to turn a profit? Yes: the obvious alternative to selling on the domestic market is to export. And export prices, even those paid at wholesale, must be many times those obtained at home."

The simple point is that prices earned by Chinese firms on their exports of consumer goods are much higher than on the same goods when sold in the domestic market. This is because light-industrial firms selling into the domestic market could not (or chose not to) adjust production to sales. That would imply imposing inventory controls—a costly process to introduce if none previously existed—and also accepting disruptions of production and therefore of the learning processes associated with quality improvement. Being unable or unwilling to do this, they took losses on unsold output, and (under market socialism) these are (or were) absorbed by lending from the banking sector, acting (in those years) to avoid the social repercussions of mass layoffs and factory closings.

A shift in the mix of Chinese production from the home to the external market would result, automatically, in higher average prices paid for goods, with no significant increase in costs, and therefore in much higher profits for the producers. It would not then be surprising that an export boom should lead to a profits boom. The speculative concentration of profit incomes in, for example, the stock market and in real estate, notably in Beijing, would be a predictable consequence. And indeed, this would appear to have been a key mechanism of rising inequality in China under the WTO.

It is worth noting that under the conditions just sketched there is a major difference between the role of export earnings in China's financial economy and the share of physical exports in the country's physical production. The former may be very large, because the sector represents a sphere of high profitability and is large in relation to the flow of funds in Chinese financial markets. But the latter is much smaller. The very great physical production sold in domestic markets is priced much lower, and *therefore it weighs far less in GDP than it does as a share of physical production.* The net result is that Chinese consumer markets are flooded with quality goods at very low prices—something anyone who shops there can observe directly. As a result, real wages in China are higher than a comparison of dollar wages to Western values would have one believe, and the weight of trade in the real economy is much lower than the national income accounts suggest.[8]

Trade and Capital Inflow

The channel from export profits to speculative investments would appear sufficient to explain the contribution of China's trade boom to its asset boom. But it may not be the only channel in operation. Since China still maintains capital controls, the question arises whether perhaps Chinese exporters have been overreporting exports to the Chinese authorities, for the purpose of bringing foreign capital into the country. Perhaps they have been overinvoicing the exports they actually made. Or perhaps they have been, even more simply, reporting exports to the authorities that were never made at all. This section considers this possibility, which has been discussed at least to some extent by Chinese officials.

There are straightforward reasons for it to be in the interest of Chinese firms to behave this way, if they could get away with it. The incentive stems from China's property and stock market booms, and from two regulatory facts: continued enforcement of controls over capital inflows per se in China, and legalization, in late 2002, of unlimited foreign currency accounts held in China by Chinese firms. The simple solution from the firm's point of view in this situation would be regulatory arbitrage: to launder the capital inflow through the current account.

Some economists have been watching investment conditions in China and analyzing the environment in terms of "hot money" inflows. Guonan Ma and Robert McCauley (2008) argue that interest rate differentials between 1997 and 2006 can tell us whether capital controls are effective.[9] They point out that hot money may be evidenced in the current account by rising inward remittances (rather than by fictitious exports).[10]

McCauley (2008) looks at capital inflows into Asia from 2002 onward, finding that capital inflows into Asian nations are responsive to volatility in global equity markets. Although China is not extensively discussed, McCauley describes patterns of hot money flows into Asia since 2002 as portfolio inflows, return of bank inflows, indirect foreign investment in local currency bonds, and the carry trade.

In 2003, there were several changes in China's financial sector making the environment more favorable to capital inflows. The interest rate began to look more attractive vis-à-vis the dollar, while the nondeliverable forward (NDF) premium began to decrease, indicating expectations of RMB appreciation against the dollar (Ma and McCauley 2008).

Further, in October 2002 the central government gave permission for all companies to hold foreign exchange accounts. Controls over foreign exchange purchases were relaxed for many businesses, including exporters, while the ability to open foreign exchange accounts was extended to firms outside bonded zones (Lehmanbrown 2002). The goal of this measure was to liberalize the current account, facilitating trade and reducing the state presence in credit markets. Table 10.3 shows that foreign exchange transactions within China increased tremendously beginning in 2003.

Thus the regulatory and investment environment was ripe for injecting capital inflows into China. Exporting companies with a willing partner simply had to overstate or overbill exports, and foreign exchange could be transferred into their bank accounts, from which it could be converted into RMB and used in domestic capital markets.

Table 10.3. **Foreign Exchange Transactions within China**

	Overall Turnover (in USD)	*USD Trading Volume*	*HKD Trading Volume*	*JPY Trading Volume*	*EURO Trading Volume*
2001	750.3	741.3	30.6	613.9	N/A
2002	971.9	951.1	108.8	730.8	1.1
2003	1,511.3	1,478.2	186.3	761.6	3.0
2004	2,090.4	2,044.1	244.9	1,349.6	1.9
2005	1,511.7	N/A	--	--	--
2006	3,445.1	N/A	--	--	--
2007	13,405.8	N/A	--	--	--
2008	29,828.9	N/A	--	--	--

Source: People's Bank of China (statistics portal, http://www.pbc.gov.cn/english/diaochatongji/); 100 million units.

Did they do so? The 2008 crackdown on short-term foreign exchange accounts, and the punishment of both foreign and domestic banks for violations of exchanging currency outside of controls, revealed how loose controls over foreign exchange accounts had become.

Further evidence comes from the exposure and punishment of a large underground bank headquartered in Shenzhen, which exchanged foreign currency and maintained foreign exchange accounts. All of these measures are attempts by the central government to curb hot money inflows and illegal foreign exchange transactions, in order to maintain better control over the current account.[11]

Part of the flow, too, may stem from overbilling exports to receive additional value-added tax[12] (VAT) rebates after the January 2002 legislation loosened restrictions over VAT rebates. However, in our calculation we do not see a large unit price increase for the year 2002, which would indicate that VAT abuses due to the legislation probably were not large.

Our conclusion on the hot money issue is that the trade data do not permit us to add much to the concern over this question already expressed by Chinese authorities on the basis of other evidence. The possibility existed. However, the broad (and no doubt the much larger) mechanism of capital inflow into China is hidden in plain view; it consists of the vast price differentials between China's internal and external markets, and the opportunities for profitability that opened up as China took export markets away from other countries, mainly in the Third World.

Profit and Capital Flows into Speculative Sectors

We now examine the extent to which these funds, both licit and otherwise, may have contributed to China's stock market and building booms and particularly to the "Beijing Bubble."[13] A clue to the phenomenon may be found in the percentage change in gross capital formation. This figure increases sharply in the post-2002 years, while the share of capital formation in GDP rises by seven percentage points between 2001 and 2004. This is the result of an enormous increase in construction of fixed assets such as plant and equipment, offices and housing. The increase in gross capital formation reflects the construction boom that is everywhere visible in urban China. Table 10.4 gives the basic information.

An inflow of export profits, an increase in the profit share in total income and any foreign capital would need to show up as reported profits in Chinese industry, not only directly but in the sectors ultimately targeted by investment and speculation. This too we observe. To take a specific instance, the Beijing

Table 10.4. **China: Gross Capital Formation**

	GDP (Billions of Current US$)	*Gross Capital Formation (Billions of Current US$)*	*Change in Gross Capital Formation (%)*	*Share of Gross Capital Formation in GDP (%)*
1996	856.1	346.2		40
1997	952.7	361.5	4	38
1998	1,019.5	378.2	5	37
1999	1,083.3	398.0	5	37
2000	1,198.5	420.9	6	35
2001	1,324.8	480.5	14	36
2002	1,453.8	550.5	15	38
2003	1,641.0	676.1	23	41
2004	1,931.7	835.7	24	43
2005	2,243.9	971.0	16	43
2006	2,668.1	1,085.8	12	41
2007	3,280.1	1,237.8	14	38

Note: Current U.S. dollars or percentage where indicated.

Source: World Bank (WDI Online, http://data.worldbank.org/data-catalog/world-development-indicators) and calculations by Sara Hsu.

Table 10.5. **Beijing Real Estate Statistics**

(Million Yuan)	*Real Estate Industry Operating Income*	*Real Estate Industry Total Profits*	*Investment in Office Buildings*	*Commercial Buildings Sold*
2000	-1,862.0	-1,303.0	4,521.9	424.8
2001	-1,046.0	-215.3	7,199.3	1,245.8
2002	-1,026.0	-587.1	9,732.6	2,595.3
2003	895.9	1,743.3	14,275.0	5,177.9
2004	8,661.1	10,701.0	18,789.0	5,883.4
2005	6,184.4	8,131.0	19,617.0	12,085.0
2006	11,053	14,959.0	21,674.0	16,256.0

Source: China Statistical Yearbook 2007.

real estate industry operating income and profit moves sharply from negative to positive numbers in 2003, a dramatic increase. Table 10.5 gives the data. Information on sales prices, staff working in real estate and construction, and the scale of construction in Beijing complete the picture; the coincidence in timing with the export boom is complete.[14]

Correlation is not causation, and obviously construction for the Beijing Olympics was not financed solely or even primarily from export revenues. Moreover, it's clear that the Olympics must have been a major reason (if not *the* major one) that speculative capital chose the capital, rather than (say) extending the building booms in the South. But it seems a reasonable inference that, in the event, export profits did flow disproportionately into the capital's banks and real estate developments. After all, the profits had to go somewhere, and they do not appear to show up elsewhere—at least not dramatically—in the Chinese economy at this time.

We note several further qualifications, arising from Chinese economic statistics as noted in other literature. First of all, there are well-known problems with Chinese GDP, particularly with overstatement of GDP growth rates for political purposes, and also with the notorious stability of reported Chinese GDP growth rates. There are familiar criticisms of the trade statistics, due to the treatment of reexports from Hong Kong.[15] There are also problems with achieving continuous measures of trade activity over recent years, due to shifts in statistical classifications, for example, as several export categories were broken into subcategories while others were discontinued. On the whole, however, we feel the evidence we have assembled presents a reasonably coherent and persuasive picture, one that makes sense as an account of the relationship between trade, profitability, speculation, and inequality in modern China.

Conclusion

The rise in Chinese inequality seems to have slowed in the middle of the first decade of the twenty-first century, mainly because growth began to be more evenly distributed across a second tier of coastal and southern provinces, perhaps along with policy efforts to foster somewhat faster relative growth in the north and west. Yet a significant force for continued increases in inequality remained, associated with the property boom and other speculative activities that concentrated on the national capital, Beijing, during the period immediately before the 2008 Olympics. One powerful mechanism behind the flow of funds into these sectors was a boom in profits associated with the increase in Chinese exports that followed WTO accession in 2001. There is reason to suspect that some additional speculative flows occurred by the device of laundering capital inflow through the current account.

The phenomenon of an exports boom leading to a profits boom leading to a speculative bubble has some disturbing implications in a country as concerned as modern China is with stability and sustainability. Equally, there are implications for China's concern with excessive inequality and associated developmental imbalances and migration incentives. Clearly, the unchecked flow of capital wealth into the leading cities—especially into Beijing—runs counter to development of a "harmonious society." It also raises questions about whether Chinese government policy can any longer dictate the broad spatial and sectoral patterns of economic development in the country—unless and until the flows of profit income are brought under effective regulatory control.

The world crisis that began in 2008 brought a double shock to China: one to export employment, notably in the southern coastal provinces, and the other to high-end real estate prices, most notably in Shanghai and Beijing. This, and the surge in commodity prices following the stabilization efforts in the West, no doubt reshaped the picture of relative incomes inside China importantly and uncomfortably. As the country settles into a broad slump in world trade and the inevitable post-Olympics real estate bust, the question to be considered is whether it is still within the government's power to deliver the bold promises for continued growth and effective redistribution.

Notes

1. Unless perhaps one counts the concept of "Gross National Happiness," as employed in the Kingdom of Bhutan.
2. This chapter is adapted and condensed from James K. Galbraith, Sara Hsu, and Wenjie Zhang, "Beijing Bubble, Beijing Bust: Inequality Trade and Capital Flow into China," *Journal of Current Chinese Affairs/China Aktuell* 2, 2009, 3–26.
3. These results are drawn from data on pay and employment in the *China Statistical Yearbook*. They are consistent with, but considerably more revealing than, surveys that have tended to characterize the growing gap in Chinese incomes as "urban-rural" or "coast-interior."
4. At the time of writing, we did not have complete data on the ensuing collapse, but it seems evident from press reports that a substantial part of this growth in employment and export production has since been reversed.
5. Again, clearly the subsequent crisis of export manufacturing greatly reduced, if not reversed, those gains.
6. The IMF's world economic outlook pegs nominal GDP for China in 2006 at $2 trillion, in comparison to which the official trade statistics look even larger (http://www.econstats.com/weo/index_glweo.htm).
7. http://www.mofcom.gov.cn/tongjiziliao/tongjiziliao.html.
8. Purchasing power parity measures, which are based on prices of internationally comparable goods in the richest cities, tend to yield a distorted view of Chinese real wages on two counts: they overstate the prices actually paid for wage goods inside China, and they count many goods and services that ordinary Chinese households never consume. For this reason Chinese households seem much poorer to statisticians than they do to themselves.
9. In this, Ma and McCauley support the view of Cheung, Chinn, and Fujii (2006) and Cheung, Tam, and Yiu (2006) that short-run arbitrage taking advantage of higher interest rates is difficult in China because of capital controls.
10. Yue Ma and Sun (2007) take as a given the hot money inflows cited in other sources, and they build a monetary model to show that exchange rate instability occurs when revaluations are anticipated; they also discuss policies that can strengthen a pegged exchange rate regime. Those authors find that the market-oriented interest rate mechanism can alleviate pressure on the exchange rate somewhat, but not fully. Additional policy measures such as relaxing or tightening capital movements and increasing autonomous domestic expenditure can help maintain the pegged exchange rate, while looking toward fully marketizing interest rates in the long run. Bouvatier (2007) also takes as a given the occurrence of hot money inflows into China and uses a Vector Error Correction Model to show that the central bank was successful in dampening domestic credit as international reserves increased.
11. In addition, real appreciation of the RMB in terms of the dollar beginning in December 2006 signaled a change in the desirability of purchasing RMB with dollars.
12. VAT rates range from 5 to 17 percent. The standard VAT rate is 17 percent.
13. We use the word "bubble" here in the ordinary-language sense of a strong and temporary boom. We cannot state that the Beijing real estate boom led to a bubble phenomenon in the technical sense, since lease price indices show little variation from sales price indices. See China Monthly Macro-Economics Statistics, National Bureau of Statistics, for price indices. In any event, as Gurkaynak (2008) argues, formal tests for asset price bubbles tend to be inconclusive.
14. Full details are in Galbraith, Hsu, and Zhang (2009).

15. Green (2000) writes that the United States exaggerates value-added in Hong Kong as around 25 percent of China's goods value, while China tends to understate these values. He believes the U.S.-China deficit may be the average of the two records. In any case, China's understatement of Hong Kong reexports has not changed over time, so it does not affect the general unit value trend.

CHAPTER 11

Finance and Power in Argentina and Brazil

The shift from China to South America is a move from a vast but idiosyncratic postcommunist case to something much more familiar: middle-income countries in the throes of financial globalization. This chapter compares the evolution of pay inequalities in Argentina and Brazil from the early 1990s through 2007.[1] The data cover the period of high neoliberalism in world policy, the crisis in each country, and their aftermath. In both countries, it turns out that the financial sector was the biggest single contributor to inequality and also to change in inequality. In both, the years leading up to crisis saw a big increase in the economic weight, power, and income of the banks. And then there was a decline in that weight as the crisis passed, economic growth was restored, and a more normal situation returned. In both countries, but especially in Brazil, the retreat of finance created economic space that was taken up by an expanding public sector alongside a truly dramatic reduction in deep poverty that marks Brazil as one of the success stories of the early twenty-first century.

What is different between the two cases is the timing. In Brazil, the return to a normal path of growth and development, associated with a decline in measured inequality as well as major progress against poverty, began to happen in the mid-1990s. In Argentina, it occurred only after the crisis in December 2001. By monitoring these developments soon after they occurred, Galbraith, Spagnolo, and Pinto (2007d, originally published 2006) were able to establish that inequality in these two major Latin American countries was in fact declining four years before this fact won wide notice in the larger literature on inequality in Latin America (López-Calva and Lustig, 2010).

The Modern Political Economy of Argentina and Brazil

Argentina and Brazil are the largest and most populous countries in South America, covering between them 63.3 percent of the continental area, 60.2 percent of the population and almost 70 percent of the GDP. Both experienced dire periods of military rule and dirty wars, beginning in 1964 in Brazil and 1976 in Argentina; democracy was regained in 1983 in Argentina and in 1984 in Brazil and consolidated with difficulty in the following years. Economically, over the twentieth century both countries moved in parallel from heavy reliance on agro-exports through a phase of import substitution, and toward an opening along neoliberal lines. Both have seen privatization of public utilities, trade and financial deregulation, equal treatment of local and foreign capital, deregulation of domestic markets, tax reforms, labor-market "reforms," and the creation of Mercosur, the Southern Common Market. In other words, both were for a time charter members of the neoliberal vanguard, though Argentina always more so than Brazil.

In the 1990s, following the failure of heterodox strategies for inflation control,[2] new economic strategies included aggressive measures to control inflation, necessary because both countries had ended the 1980s with hyperinflation. Under Carlos Menem, Argentina adopted the "Convertibility Plan." The Argentine peso was fixed to the dollar and a new legal framework governing money creation was put in place (De la Torre, Yeyati, and Schmukler 2002). Brazil implemented the "Plan Real" starting in 1994, under the government of Itamar Franco, with future president Fernando Henrique Cardoso as minister of finance. The Plan Real also pegged the real to the dollar, but with some room to float; this was accompanied by introduction of further market reforms.

In the late 1990s, the rigidity of the Convertibility Plan made Argentina more vulnerable to shocks, which duly arrived with the Asian crisis of 1997 and the Russian crisis of 1998. Brazil responded flexibly to the reduced inflow of foreign capital provoked by the Russian crisis, devalued the real and survived the shock. Argentina chose not to devalue, maintaining convertibility in the face of capital flight. This strategy failed in 2001, leading the Argentine economy and currency to collapse. There followed a period of political tumult culminating in the presidency of Nestor Kirchner, who stabilized the Argentine economy by defaulting on the debt and built a recovery based partly on repudiation of neoliberal doctrine. Argentina grew quite rapidly for half a decade following its crisis, and by the late 2000s the country had repaid debts to the IMF and exited from its tutelage.

Brazil, on the other hand, experienced a smooth transition from Cardoso to the presidency of Luiz Inácio (Lula) da Silva, of the Workers' Party, and Lula's government departed little from the mild-but-persistent reformism and outward orthodoxy of Cardoso. Internationally, Brazil also developed as a global power rather than a regional one, a member of the G-20, and (alongside China, India, and Russia) one of the four most prominent "emerging economies" of the world. By middecade, the two countries thus occupied differing positions along the political spectrum of Latin American democracies. The legacy of chaos placed Argentina among the new radicals, close to the antineoliberal governments of Venezuela, Uruguay, Ecuador, and Nicaragua. Meanwhile, despite the left-wing roots of its highly popular government, Brazil remained closer to the centrist camp, which includes Chile and Costa Rica.

Despite these differences, the recent evolution of inequality in both countries departs in similar fashion from the sorry experience of the 1980s and 1990s, reflecting the common change in external conditions and the similarities, more than the differences, in how they responded. In both places, economic inequality declined after the crisis. In both, the distributive patterns underlying this decline involve a sharp drop in the share of income passing through the hands of the banks, a modest recovery in the share passing through the state, and a moderate gain in the relative wealth of the hinterlands as compared to the major cities. In other words, declining inequality in this part of Latin America appears directly linked to a weakening of the political forces that supported neoliberal globalization in the first place.

Measuring Inequality

The experience of economic inequality in the two countries is marked by differences rooted in their divergent social histories and economic structure. Brazil—multiracial, divided by the Amazon, and having a legacy of plantation agriculture and slavery—has long been one of the most unequal countries in the world. Argentina, with a population of mostly European origin concentrated in Buenos Aires and a powerful urban labor movement, used to be one of the most egalitarian countries in Latin America. However, this status deteriorated significantly over the 1990s, with economic inequality increasing at a higher rate in Argentina than anywhere else in the region (Gasparini 1999). In the crisis years, Argentina was flecked with shantytowns, and the city nights in Buenos Aires were filled with the sounds of the cartoñeros, camp dwellers who would come in after dark to scavenge for recyclable cardboard and other materials.

Several studies have reported on trends in income inequality in Argentina and Brazil. Most rely on data derived from household surveys, with inequality measured using the familiar Gini coefficient. These data present many problems, among them a dearth of rural observations, nonresponse and invalid answers, misreporting, and periodic changes in survey design (Gasparini 2004), which make it difficult to compare results from one year to the next. Argentina was for some time a country with no inequality observations considered "high-quality" in the Deininger-Squire dataset of the World Bank.

Here we rely on datasets drawn from each country's employment and pension records. They have the strengths and weaknesses of official records: regular collection and consistent methods on the one hand, partial and biased coverage on the other. Still, for reasons given at length earlier in this book, inequality measures constructed from this data do add to an otherwise sketchy base of information. And this argument is best tested not in the abstract but by examining the results in some detail, in order to judge whether they are, in fact, useful and plausible.

Employment data for Argentina and Brazil are organized by sectors and presented within regions, so that the elementary unit of observation is the "region-sector cell." These datasets and our now-familiar Theil method permit us to measure the contribution of each major economic sector and of each geographic region to increases or decreases in overall pay inequality.[3] The data are not flawless, and they do not permit direct comparison of inequality in Argentina with that of Brazil. But they are likely to be consistent over time, and therefore changes in the measure of inequality from one period to the next are likely to reflect the bona fide influence of underlying events, whether parallel in the two countries or otherwise.

The method therefore permits us to make low-cost, accurate measures of trends in inequality and to do so quite quickly after events occur. This is especially true since in both Argentina and Brazil some of the underlying data are released monthly, which enables "high-frequency" calculation of inequality measures. It is also possible, as always, to illustrate the movement of the "Theil elements" over time using the device of a stacked bar graph. The contribution of each element—which may be a sector, region, or a sector within a region—to overall inequality can be read easily (from side to side) to determine which sectors and regions gained and lost relative position from year to year.

Sources of Data

Data for Argentina come from the monthly tax filings of private entities at the Federal Administration of Public Revenues (AFIP).[4] In these filings, each employer declares his or her employees in order to commit payment of contributions to social security within the Integrated Retirement and Pension System (SIJP).[5] The SIJP processed data on approximately five million salaried jobs from the entire country and covered almost every economic sector. These salary and employment data allow calculation of a Theil's T monthly across twenty-two economic sectors and by twenty-three provinces plus the city of Buenos Aires.

Data are available beginning in 1994; that was the year in which the reform of the Argentine pension system went into effect. Affiliation with the SIJP is mandatory for all workers over age eighteen who have as employment status (1) self-employed, (2) employed in the private sector, or (3) employed in the public sector, including by the national government or the provinces that participate in the SIJP. Military personnel, security forces, police staff, and workers under eighteen are excluded from the system (Law 24.241: Creation of the Integrated System of Retirement and Pension Benefits, 1993). Of course, the data do not cover those who work informally in the gray economy, which in Argentina is a large and unstable part of economic activity. We think, however, that the central characteristic of the informal sector is that observable pay within it (except for criminal activity, which is unobserved everywhere) is comparatively and uniformly low. People who have access to formal-sector jobs will, for the most part, take them. Therefore most of the inequality and most of the changes in inequality that can be observed in the economy will be in sectors covered by the SIJP.

Data for Brazil are published by the Brazilian Institute of Geography and Statistics (IBGE).[6] The data are obtained from the Central Register of Enterprises,[7] which is based on the economic surveys of IBGE. This database contains information about persons employed and wages earned by economic sectors, disaggregated according to the Brazilian Industry Classification (CNAE)[8] by region, state and municipality. Considerations respecting the informal economy are similar to those for Argentina.

Pay Inequality in Argentina, 1994–2007

The new millennium found Argentina with a transformed social and economic structure. In contrast to the privileged position it had enjoyed until the mid-1970s as one of Latin America's most advanced and successful economies, this

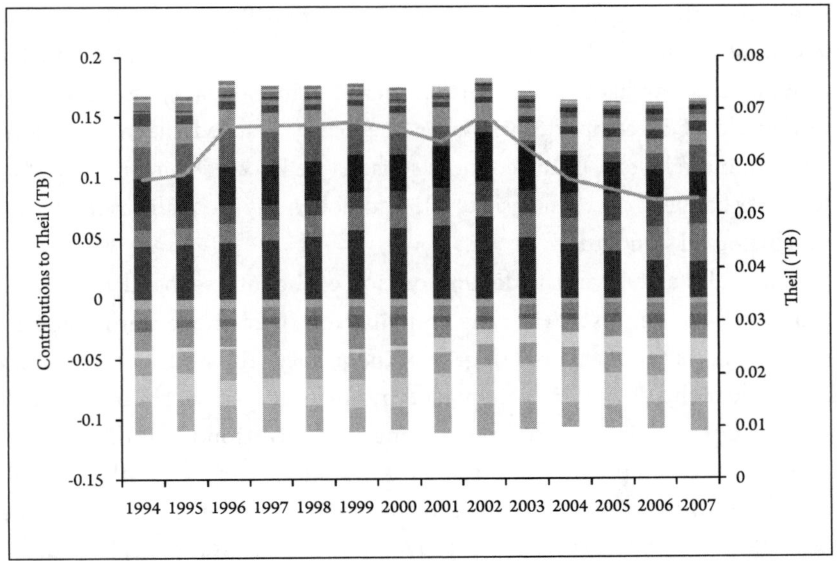

From Zero Up

- Financial Intermediation
- Mining and Quarrying
- Transport, Storage, and Communications
- Petroleum Derivatives and Chemicals
- Public Administration, Defense, and Extraterritorial Organizations and Bodies
- Supply of Electricity, Gas, and Water
- Transport Material
- Food, Beverage, and Tobacco
- Fishing and Related Services
- Basic Metals, except Machinery and Equipment

From Zero Down

- Manufacture of Textiles and Leather
- Hotels and Restaurants
- Other Community, Social, and Personal Services
- Construction
- Real Estate, Business Services, and Rentals
- Agriculture, Livestock, Hunting, and Forestry
- Social Services, Private Education, and Health
- Wholesale and Retail Trade and Workshops

Figure 11.1. Contribution to inequality by economic sector in Argentina, 1994–2007.
Source: Spagnolo, 2011.

was a paradigmatic case of economic failure, due largely to ineffective or misguided market reforms in the 1990s. These "reforms" show in our data as dramatically higher inequality, which suggests that Argentina's rising inequality in this period is a symptom of the causes of crisis—of the policies that led to crisis—rather than a result of the crisis itself.

The line embedded in figure 11.1 shows the overall pattern of the movement of inequality across economic sectors through 2007. We can divide the period into four stages. During the first, from 1994 to mid-1997, the inequality indicators increased. In the second stage, from mid-1997 to mid-1998, inequality remained almost stable. The third stage, from mid-1998 to 2002, was dominated by a deep economic crisis and substantial further increases in inequality, culminating in the debacle of December 2001, when inequality reached the highest levels recorded in the history of the country, so far as we know. During the last stage, inequality has been decreasing since 2002, although pay inequality remains high by all historical standards.

Figure 11.1 also gives the decomposition of the intersectoral Theil statistic by Theil element, showing the contribution of each economic sector to the sum that is the measured degree of inequality. The figure makes immediately clear the dominant role played by the financial sector in the evolution of inequality in Argentina over time. The intuition behind this is very simple: though employment in the banking sector is very small, per capita payrolls in the sector greatly exceed those paid anywhere else. And when the banks were in a position to improve their relative standing, they did so, expanding both employment and relative pay (presumably especially at the top of their internal scales). When conditions turned against them, relative pay in this sector and therefore the larger structure of inequality in Argentina declined.

Figure 11.2 presents the same information, but in a simpler format. The figure divides the Argentine economy into just two sectors, which we call "boom" and "nonboom," with finance playing the leading role in the boom sectors. These tend to be very small, but very rich. The figure shows how, in fact, inequality within the boom sectors (measured across provinces) is negligibly small. Inequality across the nonboom sectors is quite large, accounting for up to three-quarters of the inequality measured by the procedure. But this form of inequality is relatively stable, and in fact *it declines* in the period before the crisis, owing no doubt to the impact of credit inflows on employment and pay in the lower-wage reaches of the Argentine economy. Thus, more than 100 percent of the increase in inequality observed on this measure is due to the rising relative pay of the boom sectors, taken as a whole and on average, in comparison with everything else. This is the classic pattern of a credit bubble, as previously observed in the United States (see chapter 6).

Figure 11.3 shows the same information about overall inequality measured between sectors but this time with monthly data, which permit us to verify more precisely when things happened. The December 2001 financial crisis and the January 2002 devaluation stand out as having brought about decisive change in intersectoral relativities, with the overall effect of setting into motion a marked decline in the structure of pay inequality in the covered data. Argentina then

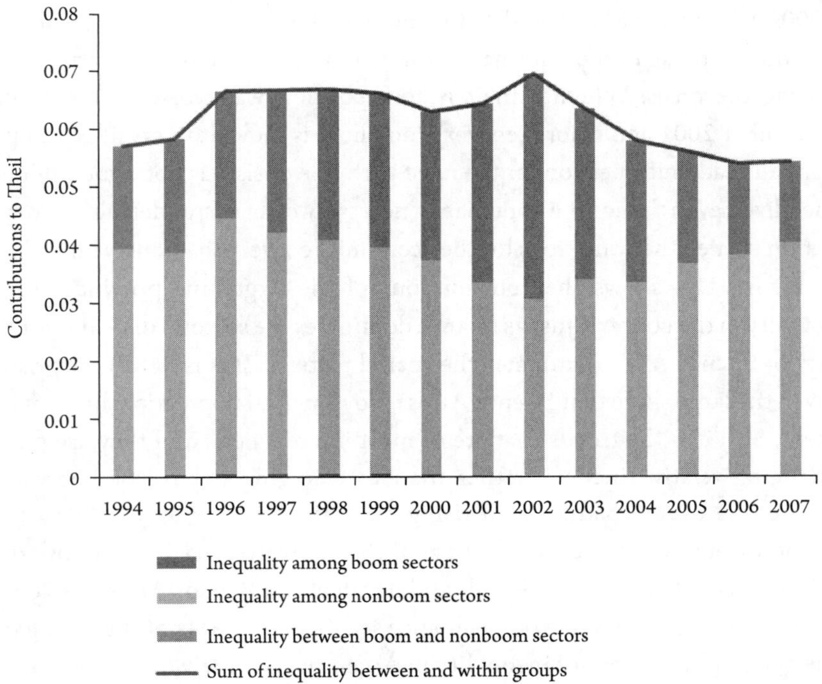

Figure 11.2. Simplified contribution of sectors to pay inequality in Argentina. Source: Spagnolo, 2011.

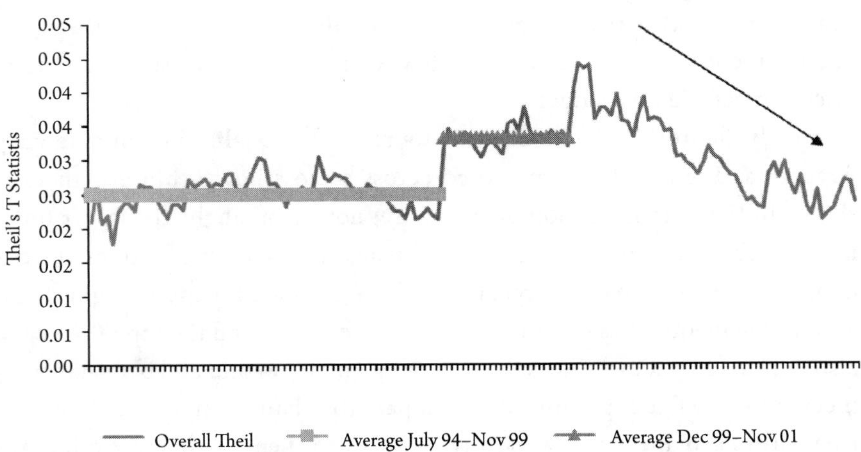

Figure 11.3. Pay inequality across sectors in Argentina, monthly data. Source: Authors' calculations based on SIJP data.

entered a period of strong economic recovery, which persisted through the 2000s. We caution again, though, that our data here do not include the relative position of those in the informal sector, who were certainly impoverished following the crisis. Whether their *relative* position was worse or better after December 2001 and before recovery took hold is difficult to say. It is also perhaps an academic question for the most part. The crisis was not a good thing in their lives, even though it was perhaps a necessary catharsis, as default and devaluation created the conditions for the economic recovery that followed.

Figure 11.4 shows the contributions of the Argentine provinces to inequality in the country. Just as finance dominates the sectoral distribution, the city of Buenos Aires dominates the spatial pattern. This is hardly surprising, given the large share that Buenos Aires enjoys in total population and employment. Still it is the trends that are of most interest here, and they are due to changing relative income, rather than to changing population shares. As before, the overall pattern is of rising inequality from 1999 to 2002 as the economy entered the terminal phase of the Convertibility Plan, followed by falling inequality after the default and devaluation. Buenos Aires has 78 percent of the aggregate value of the finance sector, and so it is not surprising that the geographic pattern of inequality in Argentina is mostly dominated by the intersectoral shifts in relative income. During 2002, the activity level in finance decreased by 18.2 percent in Buenos Aires City (Dirección General de Estadística y Censos 2003). One other geographic detail bears noting, which is that after November 2002 the economic situation of the provinces of Chubut, Tierra del Fuego, Santa Cruz, and Neuquén improved. These provinces rely heavily on export of petroleum. After the devaluation, the value of their production increased in peso terms, which was due mainly to the rise in domestic prices for petroleum products.

Finally, figure 11.5 combines two sources of inequality in contemporary Argentina. The inequality measured across sectors but within provinces is shown in the bottom section of the figure; not surprisingly, the larger provinces (such as Buenos Aires City and Buenos Aires Province) are more economically diverse and have larger internal inequalities. The topmost gray band adds in the inequalities measured between provinces, and the top of the bars, also indicated by a line, shows the sum of inequality within and between provinces. Thus the figure permits us to compare the changes in inequality occurring within provinces to that occurring between them. Although both move (as one should expect) along similar paths, it is striking how much larger the movement between provincial mean incomes is than in the intersectoral movements within provinces, particularly in the immediate run-up to and

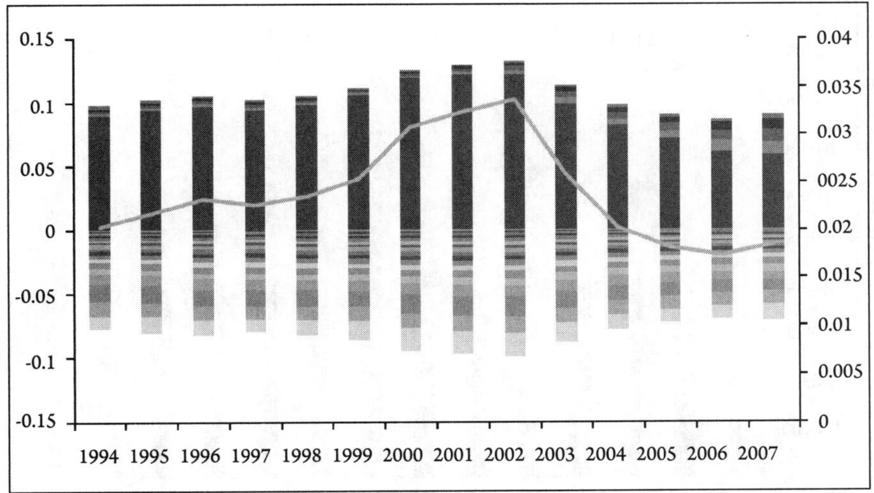

From Zero Up

- Buenos Aires City
- Chubut
- Neuquén
- Santa Cruz
- Tierra del Fuego

From Zero Down

- Catamarca
- San Luis
- Formosa
- La Rioja
- La Pampa
- Río Negro
- Jujuy
- Santiago del Estero
- San Juan
- Chaco
- Salta
- Corrientes
- Misiones
- Entre Ríos

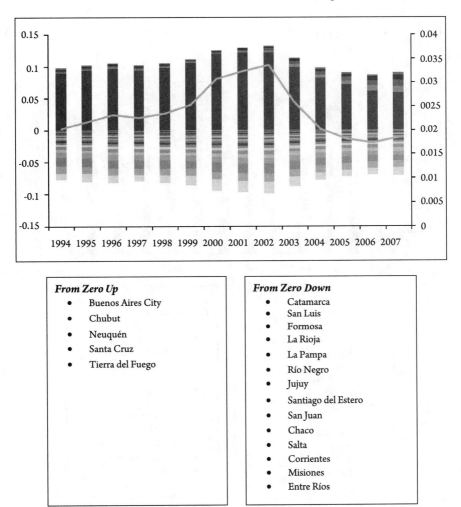

Figure 11.4. Contribution to inequality by region in Argentina, 1994–2007.
Source: Spagnolo 2011.

run-out from the economic crisis of 2001. These events were to a large extent a boom and bust of the capital city.

Pay Inequality in Brazil, 1996–2007

Crisis came to Brazil much earlier than to Argentina, culminating with the introduction of the real in 1994. In 1995, Fernando Henrique Cardoso took office as president, to be followed by Luis Ignacio (Lula) da Silva in 2003. Figure 11.6 presents the basic information on the contribution of all major

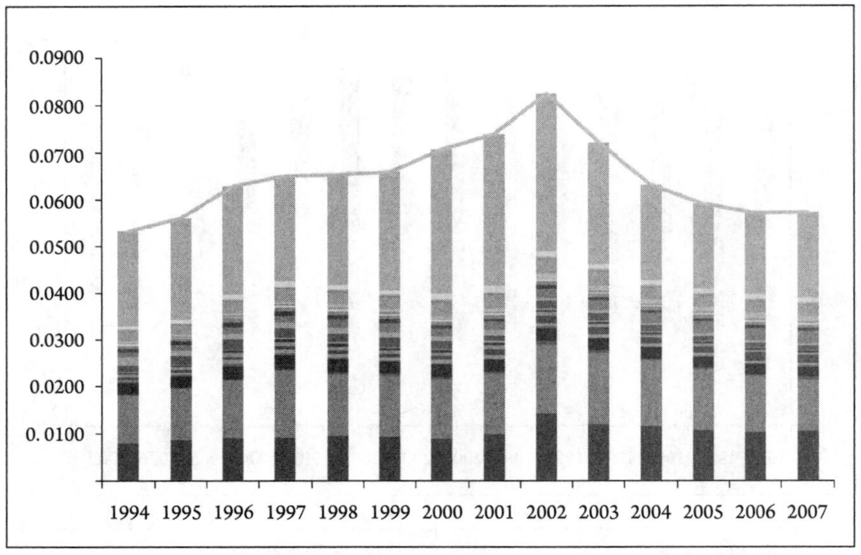

From Zero Up

- Buenos Aires City
- Buenos Aires Province
- Catamarca
- Córdoba
- Corrientes
- Chaco
- Chubut
- Entre Ríos
- Formosa
- Jujuy
- La Pampa
- La Rioja

(Continued)

- Mendoza
- Misiones
- Neuquén
- Río Negro
- Salta
- San Juan
- San Luis
- Santa Cruz
- Santa Fe
- Santiago del Estero
- Tierra del Fuego
- Tucumán
- Inequality between provinces

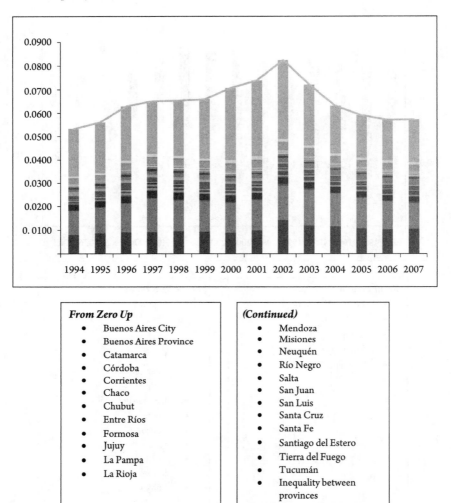

Figure 11.5. Inequality within and between provinces in Argentina, 1994–2007.
Source: Spagnolo, 2011.

sectors to pay inequality in Brazil, alongside a line showing the sum of the contributions, which is, of course, the between-sectors measure of the Theil index. (The topmost bar is the contribution of inequality between provinces.)

As figure 11.6 shows, after 1998 Cardoso's presidency was marked by steadily declining inequality in Brazil, a decline that continued throughout the Lula presidency and coincided with marked reduction in poverty in Brazil. Surprisingly for a country that entered the 1980s in the grip of a massive debt crisis and industrial recession, by 2005 extreme poverty in Brazil had fallen from 12.4 to just 5.9 percent of the population. The national poverty headcount ratio began falling

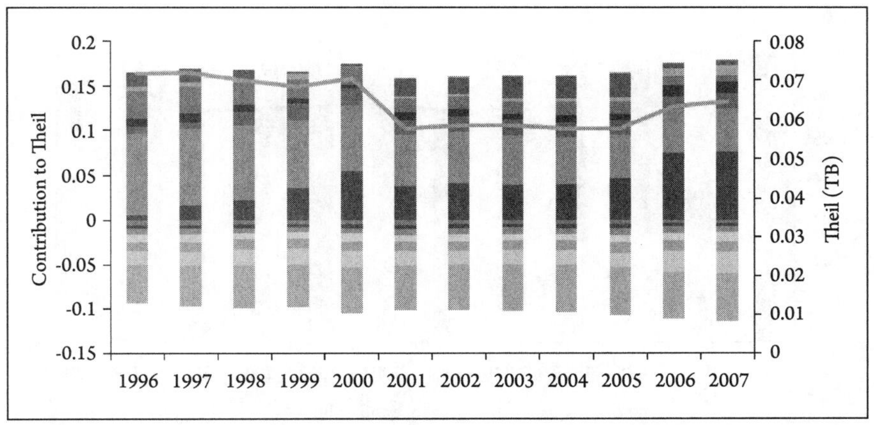

From Zero Up:

- Civil Service, Defense, and Social Security
- Financial Intermediation, Insurance, and Related Services
- Education
- Transport, Storage, and Communications
- Supply of Electricity, Gas and Water
- Mining and Quarrying
- Manufacturing Industries
- International and Extraterritorial Organizations

From Zero Down:

- Health and Social Services
- Agriculture, Livestock, Hunting, Forestry, and Fishing
- Other Collective, Social, and Personal Services
- Construction
- Hotels and Restaurants
- Real Estate, Rentals, and Business Services
- Wholesale and Retail Trade and Repair Workshops

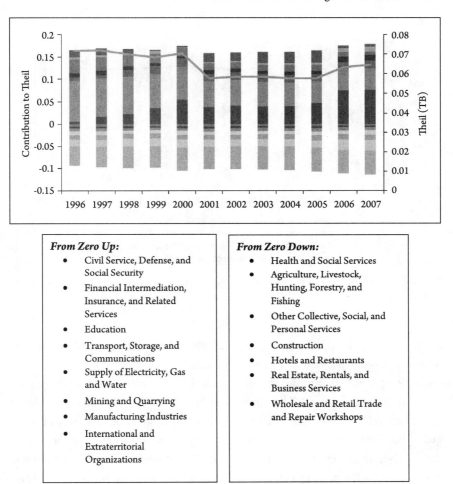

Figure 11.6. Inequality across sectors in Brazil, 1996–2007.

from around 35 percent in 2004, to reach just 21.4 percent in 2009, according to the World Bank.

What it is most remarkable in figure 11.6 is the downward trend in inequality following devaluation of the Brazilian currency, which occurred in January 1999. This downward trend is a combination of three principal factors: reduction in the relative income of the financial sector, by far the biggest contributor to inequality until 1999; improvement in the primary sector; and then an increase in the relative size and income of the public sector. By the mid-2000s the public service—with far more employees but lower average incomes—had replaced the financial sector as the largest contributor to overall inequality in Brazil, something that may portend future political problems

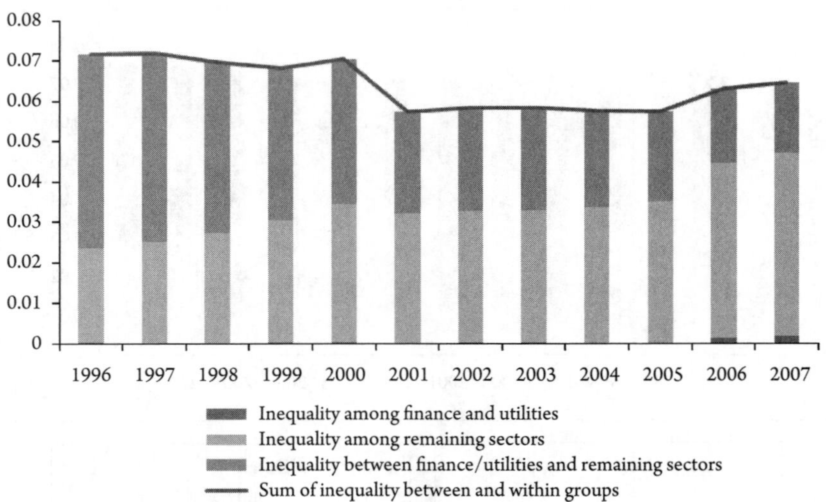

Figure 11.7. Simplified presentation of inequality by sectors in Brazil, 1996–2007.
Source: Spagnolo, 2011.

but for the moment appears to reflect a successful internal redistribution of resources toward provision of public services.

Once again it is helpful to present the same information in a simplified way, which is done in figure 11.7 by combining finance and utilities into one sector and considering all the other sectors together as a single unit. This way of organizing the data—again taking advantage of the easy aggregation properties of the Theil statistic—shows that inequality in all of the other sectors (that is, over the vast majority of Brazilian economic activity) actually increases steadily through 2007. This reflects the growing allocation of resources to the public sector, which is well paid in comparison with most private-sector activity. There is practically no inequality between finance and utilities on average, both being small and well-paid sectors. The entire decline in inequality that is observed, therefore, reflects the decline in the relative income of these two small but highly paid sectors, in comparison to everything else. Truly this appears to be a form of "taming the economic shrew."

Looking at the same data across regions rather than sectors, we find that inequality by region was generally increasing from 1996 until 2001, after which regional inequality returned to 1999 levels. Changes in regional inequality in Brazil are closely tied to changes in the relative position of São Paulo; when its contribution increases, overall inequality rises, and vice versa. São Paulo is, of course, the richest and most populous state in Brazil. In 2003, about 30 percent of workers employed in Brazil held jobs there. São Paulo accounts for 40 percent of the jobs in the financial sector, 37 percent of jobs in the real estate sector, 36 percent of manufacturing jobs, and 33 percent of jobs in health and social services.

Brasilia also makes a large positive contribution to regional inequality because it is the country's political center, and as such it employs a large percentage of the civil service. Finally, Rio de Janeiro contributes positively as well, thanks to its oil production and to the presence there of a large part of the civil service. Thus the rise of the civil service and decline of the banks has diffused incomes more evenly across the Brazilian landscape, though still with major concentrations in particular regions and large interregional differentials. Figure 11.8 illustrates these trends in the now-familiar format.

Figure 11.9, finally, shows one more way to cut the data. By dividing Brazil into its major geographic regions, and showing the sectoral inequality within each region, the figure illustrates an interesting point: practically all of the reduction of inequality inside the major regions occurred outside the South, Brazil's most prosperous and most unequal major region.

Conclusion

Argentina and Brazil made similar transitions, under similar conditions, from import substitution economic models to open market economies, and both experienced the instability and stress associated with the neoliberal economic climate. In both cases, following large increases inequality has been made to decline in recent years, as the countries retreated—to a degree—from neoliberal globalization.

In particular, inequality fell in both countries as the share of income passing through the financial sector and the richest urban centers declined; in both cases these phenomena between them explain most of the decline in economic inequality. It is fair to say that in both cases the capacity to make this happen arose in part from the favorable economic conditions of the years after 2001, when global interest rates fell to near zero and commodity prices recovered; in substantial part this was due to the pull of a growing Chinese market.

However, the two countries experienced these changes differently. In Argentina, the neoliberal model kept the country in a strong grip through the end of the 1990s, and inequality rose sharply alongside the relative position of the banks (and of Buenos Aires City) compared to the rest of the country. Only after the crisis in 2001 did Argentina begin to reverse these trends, amid a radical reshaping of the government and change in the ideological climate. In Brazil, the largest increases in inequality had already occurred,

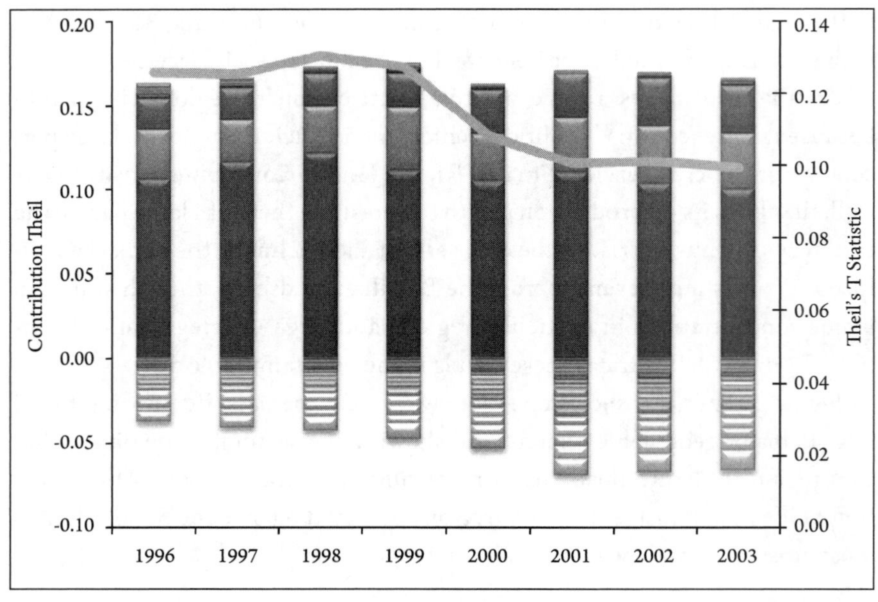

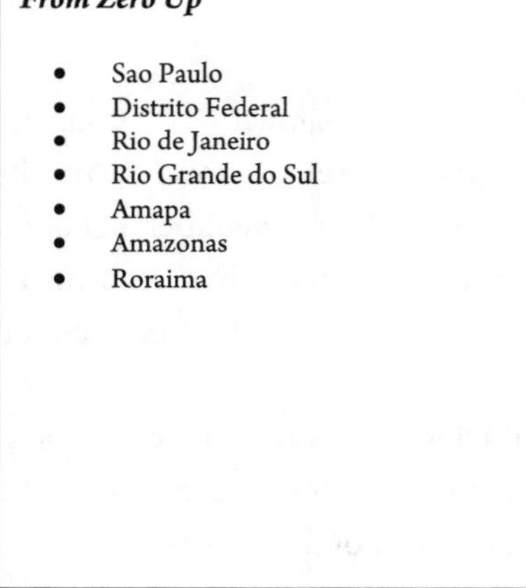

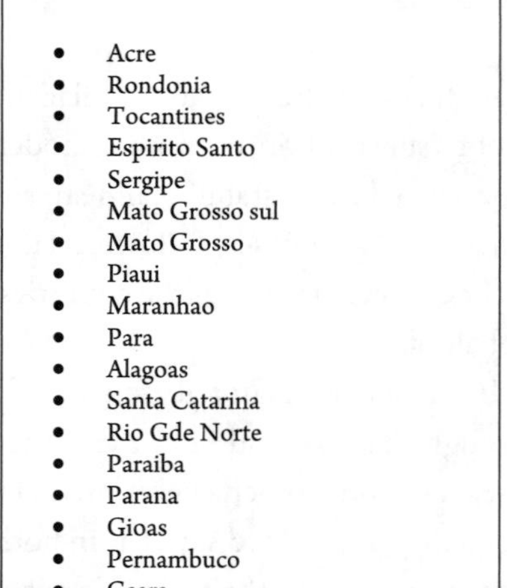

Figure 11.8. Contribution to inequality by region in Brazil, 1996–2003. Source: Authors' calculations based on IBGE data.

beginning in 1982 with the debt crisis. Brazil was able substantially to stabilize its macroeconomic environment beginning in 1993, with the result that the hypertrophy of the financial sector peaked and inequality fell in the following years; a major element of this was a growing role for the public sector.

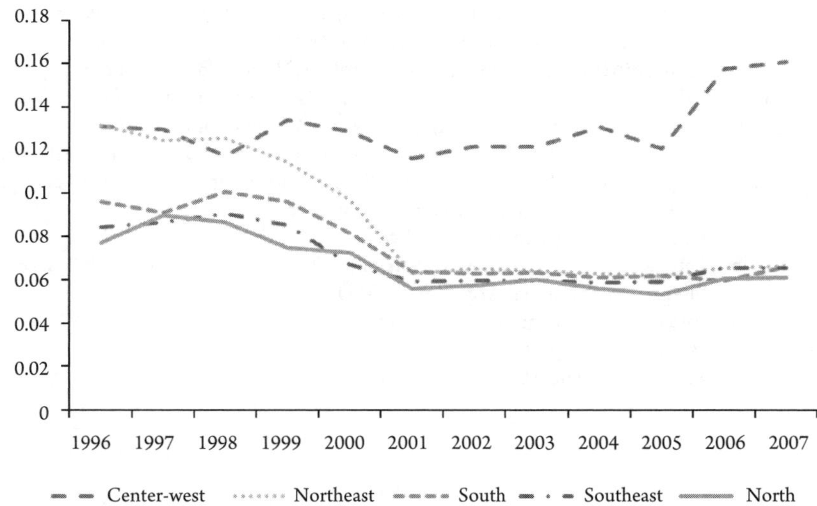

Figure 11.9. Inequality across sectors, within major regions of Brazil, 1996–2007. Source: Spagnolo 2011.

This pattern was established under the Cardoso government and continued under Lula, despite the change in party control and ideology. However, it was under Lula—operating under the vastly more favorable commodity and credit conditions of the 2000s—that poverty in Brazil moved dramatically downward.

To the extent that a bilateral comparison can lead to valid generalization, we suggest that major political changes are triggered not so much by the direction of economic change but by its speed and abruptness. Changes that Brazil began early and pursued steadily—an adjustable currency and an increasing orientation toward social needs—were resisted in Argentina until crisis and rebellion imposed them. The result was an ideological overshoot in Argentina, compared to Brazil.

Notes

1. This chapter is adapted from James K. Galbraith, Laura Spagnolo, and Sergio Pinto, "Economic Inequality and Political Power: A Comparative Analysis of Argentina and Brazil," *Business and Politics*, Berkeley Electronic Press, 2007 (9) 1. It draws also on Spagnolo (2011) with appreciation.
2. The relationship between policies in the heterodox period and inequality has been treated in earlier work; see Calmon, Conceição, Galbraith, Garza Cantú, and Hibert (2000).

3. We use sectors within regions and regions within sectors as the basis for making these calculations. Conceição, Galbraith, and Bradford (2001) showed that under general conditions these measures, taken together, closely track the evolution of the larger but unobserved T-statistic for the whole population. This is for two reasons: first, between-group measures across any reasonably fine division of the population into groups are likely to mimic change in the distribution across persons; and second, in any real-world situation large parts of the variation in overall inequality are invariably due to changes occurring between regions and between economic sectors.
4. Administración Federal de Ingresos Públicos.
5. Sistema Integrado de Jubilaciones y Pensiones. This system was recently renamed Sistema Integrado Provisional Argentino (SIPA).
6. Instituto Brasileiro de Geografia e Estatistica.
7. Cadastro Central de Empresas.
8. Classificação Nacional de Atividades Econômicas.

CHAPTER 12

Inequality in Cuba after the Soviet Collapse

The case of Cuba is practically unique: a country whose government remained not only nominally but in fact communist all the way through the first decade of the twenty-first century, and with possibly (until his retirement in 2008) the longest-serving head of government in the world. It is also a country whose internal workings remain obscure to most American economists, thanks to the long-standing embargo, the difficulty of travel even for academic purposes, and the resulting low level of contact.[1] Nevertheless, like other countries Cuba maintains economic statistics, and as elsewhere they can be mined for information.

Cuba followed a path unlike practically all other socialist countries after the fall of the Soviet Union. Two differences are especially noteworthy. First, there was no economic transition from a socialist model to one based on market principles. Although the political and social project that the Cuban revolution embraced was severely affected by the demise of the USSR, Cuba's government did not abandon the declared goal of an egalitarian society under state socialism. Second, there was no political collapse; the authority of the Castro brothers and of the Communist Party remained intact. These facts were entirely remarkable given the severity of the economic crisis, which may have been deeper than anywhere else in the post-Soviet world except possibly within the former Soviet Union itself. Unlike the countries of Eastern Europe, Cuba had nowhere to turn in 1991; it would not begin to replace the lost Soviet aid—especially subsidized oil—until after Hugo Chavez came to power in Venezuela in 1999.

This chapter analyzes the evolution of pay inequality in Cuba from the early 1990s through 2004, covering what was called the "Special Period in Times of Peace"—the difficult years following the collapse of the USSR.[2] The data are from Cuba's official accounts, which were obtained by Daniel Munevar Sastre while he was a student at the University of Pinar del Rio. They are used here as they have been used in the previous chapters: to compute inequality measures over time and to analyze the changing mix of incomes across regions and sectors.

The data underpin calculations that probably cannot be replicated meaningfully for more recent years, because as Cuba now opens up, the "official economy" in which transactions are recorded in local currency will come to represent a rapidly declining share of actual activity, and the power of the dollar, the euro, and the Canadian dollar are creating new inequalities in income and consumption. (Cuba is unlike other developing countries in that the informal sector is not the low-income sector; quite the reverse.) To a degree, this was already going on in the 1990s and early 2000s, and this qualification should be noted as we proceed. Still, even though there was money to be made for a considerable few in interaction with foreign tourists, until recently most ordinary Cubans did actually work for the state.

To analyze the evolution of pay inequality, we again use the between-groups component of Theil's T statistic, taking advantage once more of the stacked bar graph to show the relative changes in the contributions to inequality of economic sectors and regions over time. This method allows us to see quickly the intersectoral dynamics as the shock of the Soviet collapse played out. Among the curiosities, the method shows that in the Cuban case it was the services sector, first of all, that began the movement toward economic recovery, followed by the manufacturing sector. We further observe the transition of the Cuban economy from one based fundamentally on export of sugar (to the no-longer-extant Soviet market) to one based on services. Growth in tourism, along with expansion of social services, accounts for the large and growing contribution of the service sector to the Cuban economy during these years.

For four years leading up to 1999, the average wage in the social services sector was less than the average wage in the overall economy, and so the "Theil element" for that sector was a negative number. National policy during the Special Period was to maintain or increase salaries in the social services sector; meanwhile other sectors took the burden of the decline. After 1999, the fiscal crisis facing the Cuban state eased somewhat, and since that time wages in social services have on average exceeded the national average wage. This reflects no doubt in part political commitment to effective provision especially of health care and education, long the cornerstones of Cuban development strategy. This emphasis, of course, generally serves to decrease overall inequality in ways that are not captured by income statistics, and notwithstanding increases in the measured inequality of pay.

The manufacturing sector was greatly affected by the fall of the Soviet Union, because of the lack of value-added chains within the Cuban productive system. Fifteen years after the crisis, the country's industrial production had fallen by half. This decrease in production is associated with the disappearance of entire subsectors of Cuba's manufacturing economy; only the most competitive sectors, such as tobacco, metals (nickel), and chemicals, survived. These sectors have accordingly increased their share in total production.

During the worst part of the crisis period (1990–1993), average manufacturing wages fell below national average wages. However, in 1994 this trend reversed, and manufacturing enjoyed above-average wages thereafter. It is the relative prosperity of the surviving subsectors that largely explains the return of manufacturing to an above-average position in the structure of wages in general. In other words, although the number of people employed in manufacturing decreased and never recovered, the relative compensation of the whole sector rose, because of the fairly favored position of those who remained.

A regional analysis illustrates that Cuba's prosperous regions lie to its west. Almost all eastern provinces had (and have) average incomes below the national average. With the exception of Santiago de Cuba, the region does not have important tourist attractions and was underdeveloped throughout Cuban history, as well as being heavily reliant on sugar production. Conversely, those provinces that have important tourist attractions tend to have enjoyed above-average wages and continue to do so.

Finally, the data permit us to make some inferences—informed guesses, in any event—as to the effect of the observed structural changes on the position of women in the workforce. To the extent that Cuba's economy has shifted from agricultural-based to service-based, we observe a greater role played by women in two of the main pillars of Cuban social services: education and public health. In the other sectors, the impact of structural change on women is not as clear. It does not appear that women workers in Cuba were initially hit as hard as their counterparts in other post-Soviet states, where budget cutbacks took a heavy toll on state-supported services.

Data on Pay in Cuba

Economic data for Cuba are published annually by the National Statistical Institute (ONE[3]). The series reports the payrolls and employment rolls of state employees by economic sector and region. The data are of high quality, but limited; lack of information about those who are not employed by the state precludes capturing changes in wage inequality in their totality. In this, the Cuban payroll data pose a different problem from employment-and-earnings datasets in other developing countries, which exclude those working in the informal sector. In Cuba, for practical purposes the entire private sector qualifies as "informal." However, especially in the early part of this period, private employment of all types was fairly rigorously discouraged. According to official statistics, the state accounted for about 90 percent of all jobs in 1990.

Nevertheless, the state's monopoly on jobs was weakening, even before the massive reductions in state payrolls announced in 2010. The state share in total employment had fallen to 73 percent already by 2000. As Togores (2002) points out, one main reason for these changes is that the new (nonstate) sectors yield higher incomes. This is why the exclusion of these workers here tends to underestimate overall inequality, and to understate the magnitude of increasing inequality. Nevertheless, the data we are able to observe give, we believe, a credible picture of the direction (and also of the general structural character) of the changes; even the state sector is responsive, to a degree, to changing patterns of activity and marketplace demands, especially when they come from people—foreigners and tourists—with money. And, as noted, given the still-largely socialist character of the Cuban economy, the limitations on these data are not on the face of it more severe than in other developing countries, where we are left to speculate on the role of large informal sectors.

Evolution of the Cuban Economy, 1991–2005

Throughout the twentieth century, Cuba was hit by periodic economic and institutional crises and transforming events, notably the Great Depression, the Second World War, and the revolution, followed by a U.S. embargo on trade. After the revolution, Cuba became tied to the USSR, as a supplier of sugar and a recipient of cash and oil. As the Soviet Union declined throughout the eighties, so did Cuba, and when it collapsed, Cuba entered an acute crisis.

The fall of the Soviet Union brought an end to the Council of Mutual Economic Aid (CMEA), which until then had provided an institutional framework for international economic relations among the socialist countries. Disintegration of the CMEA was almost a death blow to the socialist accumulation model then existing in Cuba, which had been outward-oriented and subsidy-dependent. Even through the end-stage stagnation of European socialism in the late 1980s, the particular commercial agreements in effect with CMEA member

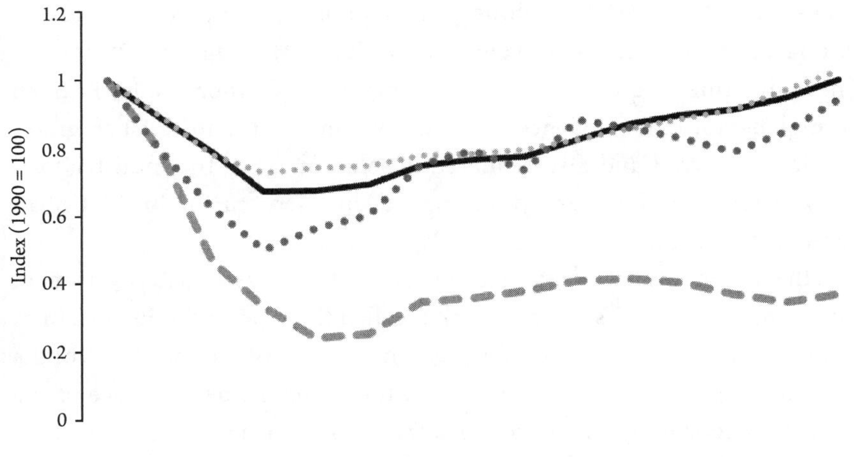

Figure 12.1. External shock effects over the Cuban economy, 1990–2005.
Source: ONE (1996); ONE (2000); ONE (2004)

countries allowed Cuba to mask the severity of its economic situation. This crisis brought to light the structural problems in the productive system of the country, such as specialization of exports in a few primary commodities, underutilization of economic resources, low levels of productivity and efficiency, and impractical institutions of enterprise management and labor relations (U-Echevarría Vallejo 2002). This list shows the effects of the shock on the Cuban economy in the early 1990s:

- Eighty-five percent of the external markets of the country disappeared.
- In 1993, exports fell to 21 percent of the level present in 1990.
- In 1993, imports were reduced to 27 percent of the level present in 1990.
- The terms of trade worsened by 50 percent.
- Access to external financing was nil [*Source*: ONE 2004].

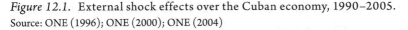

Within three years the GDP contracted by 35 percent, gross capital formation decreased by 70 percent, and total consumption was reduced by about 25 percent. And yet Cuba's government and institutions withstood the blow. By 2004, all the indices in figure 12.1 returned to the levels present at the end of the 1980s, with the exception of gross capital formation, which remained extremely depressed. This phenomenon is related to Cuba's high degree of dependence on the CMEA for supplies and capital. As an example, by 1989 three-quarters of the country's imports were concentrated in three groups: fuel (34 percent), machinery and equipment (32 percent), and raw materials and commodities (10 percent; ONE 2004); and nearly 75 percent of new investment equipment was being imported (Quiñones 2002). Given this high degree of dependence, the disappearance of the socialist commercial bloc paralyzed and also rendered obsolete most of the industrial capacity installed in the country, forcing a deep restructuring in the Cuban productive system.

In the face of this harsh external environment, in 1991 Cuba's government implemented a survival strategy, which it called the "Special Period in Times of Peace." The core objective of this program was to cushion the effects of the crisis on the population, so as to reorient the economic performance of the country to a course appropriate to the new environment, in such a way that the country could insert itself into the newly global capitalist market without abandoning the achievements of the Cuban social model.

Table 12.1 lists the main reform measures implemented in Cuba in these years. The reforms had two principal objectives, the first being to cope with the external shock through reorientation of international economic relations. The main measures taken to achieve this goal were (1) a new openness to foreign capital, (2) creation of mixed enterprises, and (3) legalization of possession of foreign currency. The second reform objective was to reduce the deep fiscal gap that emerged during the crisis, in which revenue declined 23 percent in 1993 compared to 1990, raising the fiscal deficit to an unsustainable 33 percent of GDP in that same year. This growth of the deficit was a direct consequence of the measures taken by the government to face the crisis; it maintained stable levels of expenditures and wages in the face of the paralysis of the productive system of the country. This policy generated strong internal imbalances because the rapid increase in the monetary base did not have as a counterbalance an increase in production; supply was inadequate to the available aggregate demand (Pérez 2000).

The main measure taken to cut the fiscal deficit was reduction in subsidies for losses granted to state enterprises. In the worst moment of the crisis, these had accounted for nearly 35 percent of GDP and almost 50 percent of the fiscal expenditures at the beginning of the nineties (ONE 2004). The reforms managed to stop the decline of GDP and set the stage for a long recovery, during which the country saw radical changes in its economic structure, particularly a direct transition from agriculture to services, and increasing reliance on earnings from the West and on capital inflow. These, however, set up new vulnerabilities that are being felt as a consequence of the financial crisis in the United States and Europe.

Table 12.1. **Summary of the Main Measures of the Process of Reform in Cuba**

Demonopolization	1992	Constitutional reform:
		Demonopolization of the institutional and state monopoly over foreign trade
Deregulation	1992	Constitutional reform:
		Recognition of mixed and other forms of property
	1993	Legalization of possession of foreign currency
		Creation of a retail trade chain in foreign currency
		Self-employment law
	1994	Laws pertaining to agricultural markets
		Law on creation of industrial and craftsmanship products
	1995	Foreign investment laws
		Opening of currency exchange houses
	1996	Laws to create duty-free zones
		Modification of law on custom duties
	1997	Reordering and revival of the internal consumption markets
Decentralization	1993	Creation of basic units of cooperative production in agriculture
		Creation of new business forms
	1994	Reorganization of the organs of central administration
	1995	Changes in the process of territorial and enterprise planning

continued

Table 12.1. (continued)

	1997	Law on organization of the banking system
Other measures	1994	Rise in prices of nonessential products
		Elimination of free services not relevant to the existing social policy in the country
		Tax reform
		Introduction of the Cuban convertible peso (CUC)

Source: Estructura Económica de Cuba, Tomo I (2002).

Implementation of reforms to deal with the harsh situation at the beginning of the nineties produced a fundamental change in the economic structure of Cuba. The service sector grew while the agricultural sector and some subsectors of manufacturing declined to the point of disappearance. On the agricultural side, in 1990 sugar represented 80 percent of the country's exports; by 2004 this was down to 13 percent. Meanwhile, the volume of physical production in manufacturing was in 1993 only 60 percent of that at the end of the eighties. Finally, positive changes in the service sector resulted from rapid growth of tourism, a sector relatively neglected in the Soviet era. During this period, tourism became the main source of foreign currency in Cuba, and by 1996 it generated almost 50 percent of the foreign currency the country earned that year (ONE 2004). Figure 12.2 summarizes the restructuring by showing the physical decline in sugar and other sectors, and the rise of the energy industry as Cuba's new leading industrial sector.

The general index of physical volume shows that only a few manufacturing subsectors have been able to return to levels of production similar to those before the crisis.[4] Within this group, a number stand out as having benefited from the participation of foreign capital: petroleum extraction, with a fivefold increase; manufacturing of raw metals; and manufacturing of chemical products.[5] This trend demonstrates the effects of the openness policy undertaken in the early 1990s, which encouraged increasing foreign capital investment and transfer of know-how to Cuba's productive system.[6] On the other hand, most of the remaining subsectors disappeared, owing to high dependence on supplies and technology from the now-vanished socialist countries of Europe.

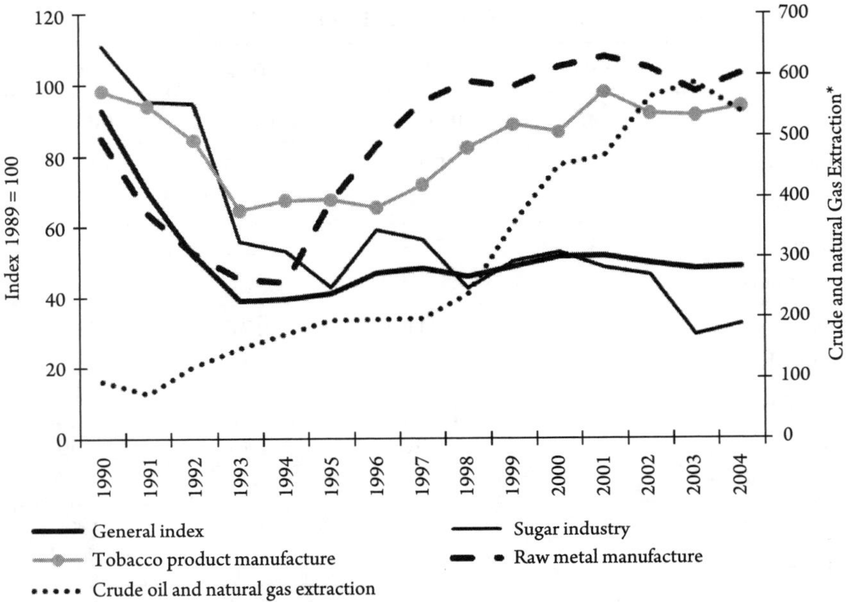

Figure 12.2. Cuba: Physical volume index by selected industry, 1990–2005.
Source: ONE (2004). *Right Scale: Only for crude oil and natural gas extraction

Table 12.2 highlights a key distinction between the sectors that survived and those that did not: the ability to produce efficiently and competitively for international markets, and perhaps even more, the ability to find outlets for commodity exports in a world market hostile and highly protective of farm output. Here sugar, which had dominated Cuban history for more than three hundred years, is again the paradigmatic case. The Cuban government was forced to close more than one hundred sugar mills in 2002,[7] on the basis of efficiency and cost-benefit criteria stemming from low prices in the international markets. Having abruptly lost its protected and privileged markets in the East, Cuba was blocked—by U.S. quota policies, the trade embargo, and massive subsidies to beet sugar in the European Union—from shifting its production capacity toward those potential markets.

Other subsectors of the manufacturing sector that bear witness to the importance of links with international markets, illustrated in table 12.2, are the mining and tobacco industries, which increased their share in the country's exports by 31 percent and 7 percent, respectively. Both sectors have returned to levels of production similar to those before the crisis with a greater value-added, as can be inferred from the rise in the value of exports.

Table 12.2. **Exports by Group of Products, 1990–2004**

	1990	%	*2004*	%
Total	5,414.9	100	2,180.5	100
Sugar industry products	4,337.5	80.10	271.5	12.45
Mining products	398.2	7.35	1,062.1	48.71
Tobacco industry products	114.4	2.11	217.0	9.95
Fishing industry	101.9	1.88	89.1	4.09
Agricultural products	183.9	3.40	32.8	1.50
Other products	279.0	5.15	508.0	23.30

Note: Pesos in millions.

Source: ONE (2004).

Within the service sector, the tourism subsector is remarkable because its contribution of income is based on foreign currency receipts, increasing by 400 percent over the period and reaching $2 billion per year by 2003. Cuba experienced a spectacular rise in tourism from two hundred thousand visitors per year in 1990 to two million in 2004 (ONE 2004), notwithstanding continued (and even strengthened) restrictions on visitors from the United States. In this sector, the participation of foreign capital made it possible for the country to meet increased demand, both through investment to raise the number of rooms available and also with transfer of management skills through hotel management contracts and creation of mixed enterprises in hotels and nonhotelier installations (Pérez 2000). As in all socialist countries, these talents had lagged (to say the least) in Cuba under the revolution. Other subsectors that have high value-added potential, including biotechnology, pharmaceutical and medical services,[8] and information technologies, have also risen in importance. On the other hand, behind this also lies the state: large investments made to the educational system and provision of health services that accounted for 26 percent of the country's public spending in 2004 may be partly responsible for the climate under which these gains were possible.[9]

Pay Inequality by Sector

This section evaluates the changes in wage structure and pay inequality in Cuba after the fall of the Soviet Union. We obtain a complete representation of the wages and employment by sectors and by regions, highlighting the (relative) winners and losers during the Special Period and the recovery that followed. During this period, the average pay in several sectors switches from being above to below the national average, and vice versa; these changes result in reversal of their "contribution to inequality" from positive to negative values (and vice versa). These fluctuations were brought about partly by the crisis and partly by reforms implemented during the Special Period.[10]

Our analysis confirms existing measurements showing that inequality in Cuba did increase during the 1990s. More important, our method allows us to study the factors behind those increases. We observe, for instance, that the rise in inequality is explained by differences in rate of wage growth in the sectors, not by decreasing wages in specific sectors; it is a function of an apparent decentralization in the structures of control. Clearly, the collapse of the Soviet Union did in fact force internal change on Cuban economic management; faced with the new economic realities, those sectors oriented toward international economy were able to detach themselves, to a degree, from the strict egalitarianism that had been possible when centralized power was combined with centralized control over the subsidies available to run the Cuban economy. However, the government still retained some discretion, and used it; even some sectors not directly involved in this international environment (such as social services) experienced growth in money wages.

As noted earlier, there was an upward trend in inequality during the Special Period starting in 1993 (figure 12.3). Until then, wages were paid within a very narrow range: from 1991 to 1993, in eight out of nine sectors average wages ranged between 180 and 200 Cuban pesos per month. The only exception to this generalization was in the commerce, hotels, and restaurants sector, which had (and still has) the lowest average official wage in the economy.

As seen in figure 12.3, there is a jump in inequality between 1993 and 1994, which is explained by a growing difference between the sector with the highest average wage (mining) and the lowest one (commerce, hotels, and restaurants). In the case of the mining sector, the average wage increased (in nominal terms, of course) 13 percent between 1993 and 1994. Meanwhile the average wage of the commerce, hotels, and restaurants sector decreased by 9 percent. In 1994, the average wage of the mining sector was 60 percent higher than the average

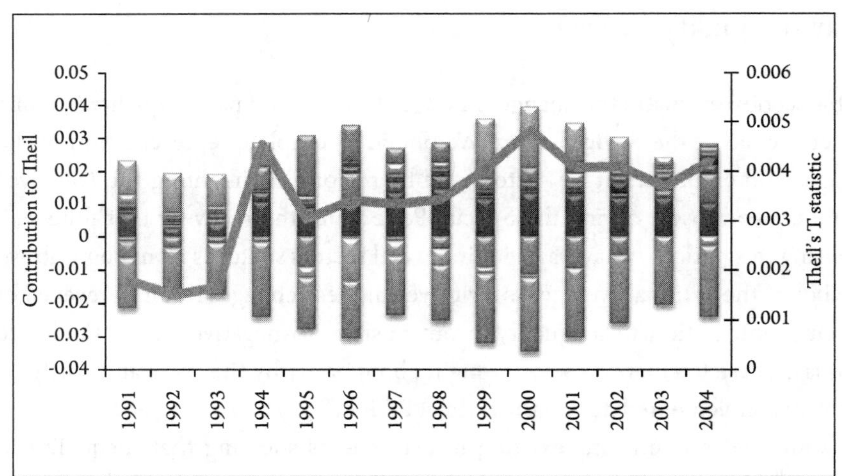

From Zero Up:

- Construction
- Agriculture, Livestock, Hunting, and Forestry
- Mining and quarrying
- Supply of electricity, gas, and water
- Financial Sector
- Transport, Storage, and Communications
- Manufacturing

From Zero Down:

- Social, communal, and personal services
- Commerce, Hotels, and Restaurants

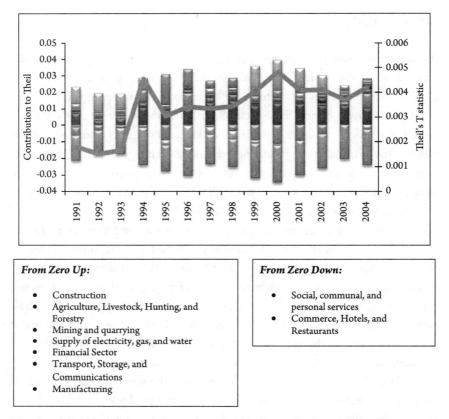

Figure 12.3. Contribution to Pay Inequality by Economic Sector in Cuba, 1991–2004. Source: Authors' calculations based on ONE data

wage in the commerce, hotels, and restaurants sector. The following year, there was an abrupt fall in inequality levels because of a recovery of wages in the commerce, hotels, and restaurants sector, which increased by 14 percent between 1994 and 1995. In contrast, the average wage in the mining sector increased by only 1 percent during this second period.

Between 1995 and 2000, inequalities again grew. During this time, average wages rose in all the sectors (in nominal terms), but at rates now free to differ by more than they ever had before. The sectors with the highest average wage gains were construction, mining, and finance. The commerce, hotels and restaurants sector also experienced a large increase in its nominal average wage in these years, a 16 percent change between 1995 and 2000 as activity in the sector continued to grow. In 2000, the inequality index reached its highest level for the years under study. The difference between this increase and the situation in 1994 is that by 2000 the construction sector had become the highest average wage sector, instead of mining. Since the construction sector is substantially larger than mining, this change implied a noteworthy increase in inequality overall.

In the fourth stage, between 2000 and 2003, there is a downward trend in Theil levels. During this period, nominal average wages in all sectors continued rising, maintaining the gap between the highest and lowest average wages. Reduction in Theil levels is explained by a decrease in employment levels in the manufacturing and construction sectors, being two with relatively high wages. The number of people employed decreased by 14 percent in the manufacturing sector and by 18 percent in construction, as the Cuban economy underwent its own version of an economic recession.

Finally, in the last years of the data, from 2003 to 2004, inequality measures again rise. Once again, the average wage in the mining sector exceeds that of the construction sector. There was a general upward trend because five of the eight sectors that were already relatively high-wage increased their contributions (mining; agriculture; manufacturing; transportation, storage and communication; and electricity, gas and water). In absolute terms, the social services sector's contribution remained the same, but the direction of the contribution changed from positive to negative. The change is explained by increases in the nominal average wage of some sectors (including manufacturing, agriculture, and transportation, storage, and communications) exceeding the average wage of the social services sectors. By 2004, the social services sector had the lowest average wage with the exception of the commerce, hotels, and restaurants sector.

During the Special Period, the government implemented policies to sustain provision of social services such as education and health care through the time of economic crisis (Barberia, de Souza Briggs, and Uriarte 2004). Table 12.3 shows that in 2004 the share of the social services sector within total public spending was 27 percent, in comparison to 20 percent in 1990. This is very high by Latin American standards. Indeed, in 2004 the social services sector was the largest in terms of employment, and except for 1994 the number employed in this sector increased throughout the entire period of study.

Policies to maintain and increase wages (in nominal terms) in time of crisis had wide-ranging effects on Cuba's economy. The most obvious effect was the increase in fiscal deficit during the Special Period. At a time when the government did not have the necessary financial resources, the deficit was financed with an increase in the money supply, without the sale of bonds or tax increases to counteract effects of this policy in the liquidity levels at the beginning of the nineties. The resulting inflationary tendencies

Table 12.3. **Social, Communal, and Personal Services as a Percentage of Public Spending in Cuba**

	1990	*1993*	*1996*	*1999*	*2002*	*2003*	*2004*
Social, communal, and personal services	3,815.7 (20%)	3,747.8 (29%)	3,610.6 (25%)	3,789.5 (24%)	4,266.8 (25%)	4,558.7 (25%)	5,072.7 (27%)

Note: Millions of pesos and percentage of GDP.

Source: Calculations by Daniel Munevar based on ONE data.

were not felt in the formal economy thanks to control and regulation of prices. But they were reflected in the informal economy, where basic goods were traded; prices increased dramatically relative to income. Real wages therefore fell—as could only be expected—during this period of exceptional hardship.

The mining sector (specifically nickel extraction) was harmed by the crisis just as other sectors were, but in 1994 it began a remarkable recovery. This sector's contribution to GDP increased from 91.6 to 223.9 million pesos, a growth of 144 percent from 1991 to 2004. Nickel production, the most important component of this sector, grew from 34,000 tons in 1991 to 76,000 tons in 2004. As figure 12.4 shows, the value of nickel exports had come to exceed the value of exports in the sugar industry.

The manufacturing sector is the second largest sectoral contributor to GDP, after the social services sector. In 2004, this sector contributed 25.2 percent of GDP, similar to what it contributed at the beginning of the 1990s, as table 12.4 shows.

It is evident that the main criterion differentiating the winning and losing manufacturing subsectors was the ability to adapt to a new economic environment, benefiting from Cuba's competitive advantage. In general, tradable goods performed better than nontradable goods.

Among the losing subsectors is the sugar industry, because of the reduction in demand and low prices in the international market. On the other hand, the influx of investment permitted the recovery of industries such as tobacco, mining (nickel), steel, and light manufacturing for the tourist sector. This change in the structure of the manufacturing sector is also observed in the composition of exports. Although there was a reduction in the value of

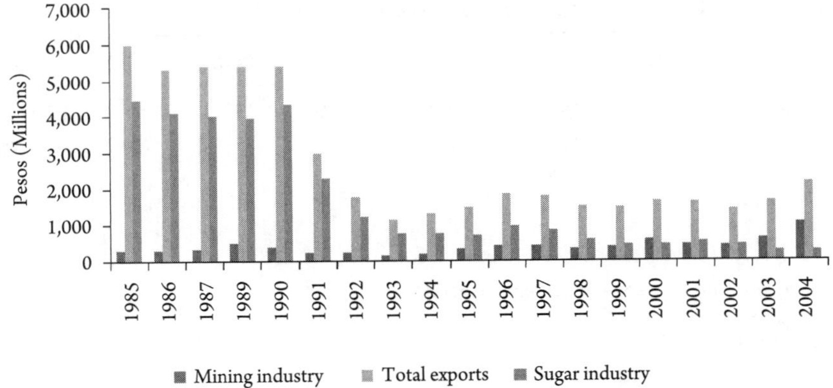

Figure 12.4. Cuban exports by groups of products, 1985–2004. Source: Authors' calculations based on ONE data

Table 12.4. **Cuban Manufacturing as a Percentage of GDP**

	1990	*1993*	*1996*	*1999*	*2002*	*2003*	*2004*
Manufacturing Sector	4,640.2 (24.4%)	3,103.6 (24.3%)	3,835.4 (27%)	4,594.9 (29.3%)	4,772.4 (27.5%)	4,677.8 (26%)	4,793.9 (25.2%)

Note: Millions of pesos and percentage of GDP.

Source: ONE (2004).

sugar exports, the value of nickel and tobacco exports rose. Furthermore, the value of pharmaceutical and biotechnological exports increased thanks to governmental investment (Economist Intelligence Unit 2005). As table 12.5 shows, from 1990 to 2004 there was a reduction in the agricultural sector's contribution to GDP from 9.2 percent to 6.67 percent.

Unlike other sectors that recovered after the crisis and in 2004 were back to their previous output levels, the agricultural sector did not enjoy any such recovery.

From 1972, the year in which Cuba became part of the CMEA, until the CMEA's collapse in 1991, CMEA countries paid a preferential price for sugar that allowed Cuba to import oil and other inputs for the productive system. The disintegration of the CMEA resulted in a decrease in the demand for Cuban products. This provoked a sharp decline in the availability of foreign currency, which in turn decreased Cuba's purchasing power to buy oil, fertilizers, pesticides, and agricultural machinery. The immediate

Table 12.5. **Cuban Agriculture as a Percentage of GDP**

	1990	*1993*	*1996*	*1999*	*2002*	*2003*	*2004*
Agriculture	1,756.3 (9.2%)	924.9 (7.2%)	1,075.4 (7.6%)	1,122.9 (7.17%)	1,232.3 (7.1%)	1,261.8 (7%)	1,264.4 (6.67%)

Note: Millions of pesos and percentage of GDP.

Source: ONE (2004).

effect of this situation was a fall in the productivity and production of the agricultural sector due to the shrinking of land area harvested and diminished crop yield due to a lack of fertilizers and pesticides.

After the immediate crisis passed in the mid-nineties, there were some improvements in Cuban agriculture due to the implementation of government reforms and an increase in foreign investments. This situation was reversed in 1997 and 1998 because the harvest was damaged by natural disasters (CEPAL 2000). The two main reforms were a restructuring of labor organization, namely a change from big state enterprises to two types of small cooperative, called Basic Cooperative Production Units (UBPC) and Agricultural Production Cooperatives (CPA), and the creation of free agricultural markets. These measures improved the sector's productivity and also altered the wage structure, because wage levels varied depending on the type of employer (state, cooperatives, or private producers), main agricultural activity (sugar, tobacco, citrus), and the destination of production (export, subsidized distribution, or sale in free market) (CEPAL 2000).

Two sectors that are inextricably linked to the well-being of the tourist sector are the commerce, hotels, and restaurants sector and the construction sector. The commerce, hotels, and restaurants sector began its expansion in 1998, with an increase in the number of people employed by the sector. The recorded Theil contribution was negative, because the average wage received in this sector was below the average wage of the whole economy. Yet workers in this sector held a privileged position because their wages were complemented by perks (such as tips) they received from the tourists they served. The positive contribution of the construction sector to pay inequality during the entire period of study is related to the economic boom of the tourism sector.

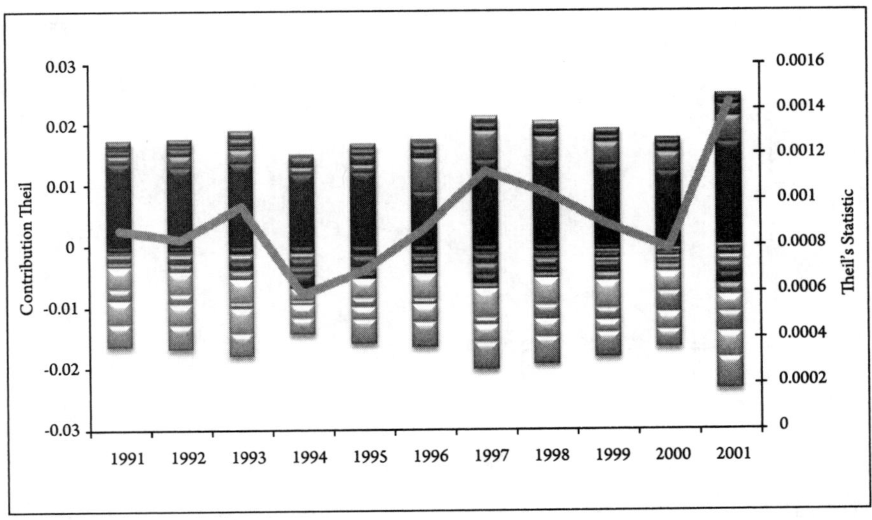

From Zero Up:

- Ciudad de la Habana
- Matanzas
- Ciego de Avila
- Las Tunas
- Cienfuegos

From Zero Down:

- Sancti Spiritus
- Isla de la Juventud
- Camaguey
- La Habana
- Villa Clara
- Holgin
- Granma
- Pinar del Rio
- Guantanamo
- Santiago de Cuba

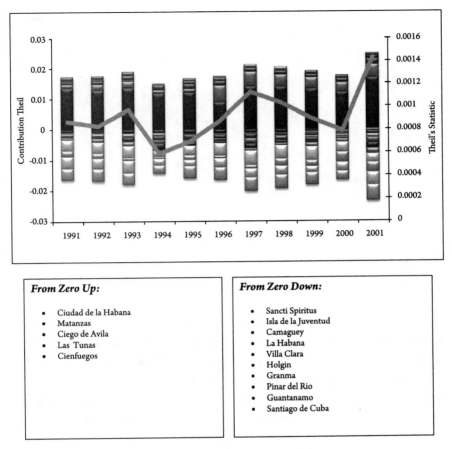

Figure 12.5. Pay inequality by region in Cuba, 1991–2001. Source: Authors' calculations based on ONE data

Pay Inequality by Region

Cuba is made up 15 regions, 13 provinces, the city of Havana, and the Island of Youth. Figure 12.6 shows an irregular upward trend in pay inequality levels among these regions. These interregional movements of pay inequality were largely associated with changes in two regions: the city of Havana and the province of Matanzas. The figure shows how the general trend was marked by fluctuations in the contributions of these two regions. The figure also shows the high- and low-income regions clearly. The former, with positive contributions to inequality, included the city of Havana, the provinces of Matanzas, Ciego de Avila, and Cienfuegos. The latter included Santiago de Cuba, Guantanamo, Pinar del Rio, and Granma. The regional analysis broadly confirms the pattern

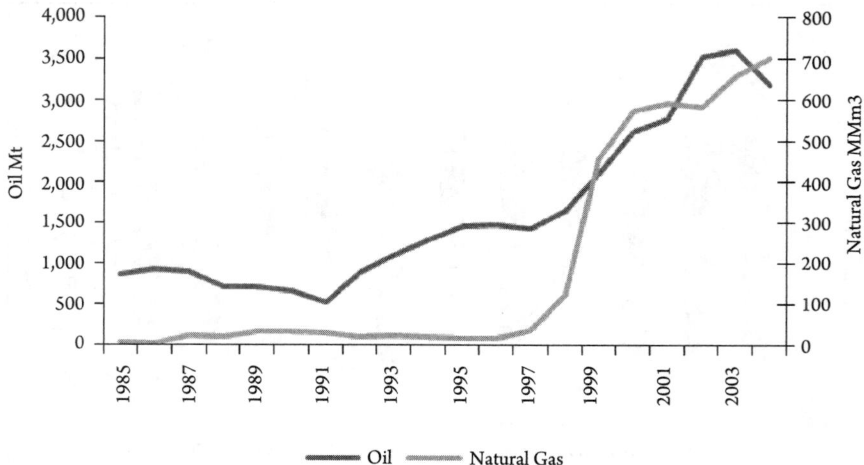

Figure 12.6. Cuban Oil and Gas Extraction, 1985–2004. Source: Authors' calculations based on ONE data

observed at the sector level. And the analysis reveals the country's division between east and west in terms of economic development and also shows how this division affected employment and wages in these two areas of the country.

The provinces with the highest average wages are also, of course, the most dynamic in economic terms. All have important tourist attractions such as the city of Havana, Varadero (Matanzas), Cayo Coco, and Cayo Guillermo (Ciego de Ávila) and Cienfuegos. Furthermore, since 1996 the province of Matanzas had the highest average wage in all of Cuba. Why? In addition to tourism, this province has oil wells. Until 1990, Cuba imported 12-13 million tons of oil per year from the Soviet Union. With the collapse, oil imports decreased by 60 percent in 4 years, from 13.1 million tons in 1989 to 5.5 million tons in 1993. However, as figure 12.6 shows, Cuba was able to make up some of this loss with domestic discoveries, facilitated by foreign capital investment.

Conclusion

The 1990s saw both the collapse of communism and a rising trend in inequality at a global scale. Cuba, as this chapter shows, was not unaffected. Nevertheless, given the special characteristics of the Cuban model it is important to highlight the particular features of the situation.

First, in Cuba the state was until the most recent reforms the main source of employment and determiner of wages. Thus, the evolution and changes in pay inequality are the direct and clear consequences of changes in economic policy that the country has implemented during the period of study, in which the process of opening to the entry of foreign investment stands out. This is in direct contrast with the experiences of other countries with market-based economies, in which the state sometimes plays an important but usually not central role in determining wages and employment. In this sense, the efforts made by the Cuban authorities to slow down the rising trend in wage inequality in the nineties are remarkable, especially considering the narrow range of policy alternatives available during the economic crisis.

Second, the existence of strong social security networks guarantees basic levels of equity within the country. Cubans benefit from a wide range of public services, including but not limited to universal and free access to medical and health services and education up to and through higher education. Because of the existence of this strong network, Cubans who have been hurt by changes in the economic structure, mainly workers related to the production of nontradable goods and services,[11] have had some cushion against the reductions in their income. Cuba's social security network has benefited women not only because they are receivers of services but also because women have increased their participation in the provision of these services. And the exchange of medical services for oil with Venezuela has, of course, played a role in stabilizing the Cuban economy.

Nevertheless, it appears clear at present writing that the Special Period unleashed forces of decentralization and therefore of rising inequality despite repeated efforts of the Cuban authorities to control it. The fact is that the objective situation changed, and with power now concentrated in capital intensive sectors like mining and petroleum, and foreign money flowing in through tourism, the hold of the state had to diminish. The state's diminished capacity—and relevance—is surely reflected in the large layoffs announced under Raul Castro in 2010—by which time it may be argued that public sector salaries were so low in any event that they no longer could determine the future of the Cuban model.

Notes

1. This chapter is adapted from James K. Galbraith, Laura Spagnolo, and Daniel Munevar, "Inequidad salarial en Cuba durante el Período Especial," *América Latina Hoy* 48, 2008, 109–38. Domínguez, Pérez Villanueva, and Barberia (2004) provide an up-to-date survey of Cuban economic issues.
2. As a matter of disclosure, the author holds an honorary membership in the National Association of Economists and Accountants (ANEC) of the Republic of Cuba.

3. Organismo Nacional de Estadística.
4. Such an index is far from being an ideal indicator of the transformations that took place within the productive structure of the country, because it works on the assumption of the homogeneity of the goods produced and in this way ignores the performance of value-added as well as the changing productivity of work.
5. Not shown, to avoid clutter.
6. See Pérez (2000) on the characteristics and impact of FDI in Cuba throughout the 1990s.
7. For the sugarcane harvest of 2006, only forty sugar mills were officially working in the country.
8. See Cabrera (2002) for more information on the condition and achievements of the biotechnological branch in Cuba.
9. These increases occurred within the framework of "the Battle of Ideas," a group of government programs initiated in 1999 to bolster political solidarity as part of the campaign for the return of a child, Elian Gonzales, to the island.
10. The changes in each sector have two principal explanations: (1) as a direct consequence of what happened in that sector, or (2) as an indirect consequence of the changes that happen in key sectors (such as a boom in oil prices increasing employment and wages in that sector) and wind up altering the relative position of the rest of the economic sectors.
11. We could even investigate the employees of the state sector as a whole, as they have been affected by the changes in the economic structure of the country brought about by the rise of self employment. See Pérez Izquierdo, Oberto Calderón, and González Rodríguez (2004).

CHAPTER 13

Economic Inequality and the World Crisis

Cette lettre est longue, Monsieur le Président, et il est temps de conclure.
—Emile Zola, to Felix Faure, president of the French Republic

This work summarizes many years of observation and measurement. Each of its major chapters contains an element of new evidence, based on calculations not elsewhere or previously published.[1] It thus represents, taken as a whole, a large body of fresh information, even though the data sources used are commonplace and have been readily available for a long time.

What have we learned? Are there lessons to be taken from the diversely measured experiences of the United States, Europe, Latin America, and China?[2] Are there central facts or common patterns that emerge unambiguously from the evidence?

First, the evidence points clearly at the need to redefine the study of economic inequality, and to restructure, to a degree, the main lines of research in the field. In the study of global inequality, trends and common patterns emerge with great clarity and persistence. This fact alone proves that the dominant forces affecting the distribution of pay (and therefore incomes) worldwide are systematic and macroeconomic. They are the product of forces affecting the global economy in common and systematic ways, forces impinging on individual countries and perhaps modified by the institutions those countries have and the policies they apply—but nevertheless forces that originate beyond their control.

Second, these forces are largely financial in character. They have to do first and foremost with interest rates, the flow of financial investments, and the flow of payments on debts, internal and international. At the global level, the data give no support to the vast outpouring in the professional literature arguing that changes in inequality are based on so-called real factors—such as a "race between technology and education" (Goldin and Katz 2008). There is also little comfort here for the view that rising international trade and competition from low-wage countries played the dominant role—or even an important one—in the inequality statistics. On the contrary, common and financial factors explain a very large share (practically everything) that can be explained. As we saw at the end of chapter 3, if the common elements are removed then the rise in inequality that dominated the generation from 1980 to 2000 simply disappears.

Third, the superbubble in the world economy that began in 1980 and peaked in 2000 was also a supercrisis for lower-income countries and for lower-income people. Debtors lost out, relative to their creditors, at the personal and international levels. The simplest, clearest, and most compelling explanation for this phenomenon is that it was the willed consequence of policies. In particular, aggressive high-interest-rate policies transformed world finance beginning in the early 1980s; as those policies interacted with falling commodity prices and the debt burdens accumulated in Latin America, Eastern Europe, and ultimately in parts of Asia, they also transformed the balance of economic power and the structure of incomes.

Fourth, the study of national experiences substantially confirms the evidence of the global statistics. In rich countries such as the United States, we find that economic performance has become dominated since 1980 by the credit cycle; financial booms and busts drive the performance of employment, and thus prosperity is associated with rising income inequality. Further, as we examine the structure of rising inequality we find practically everywhere the same signature of a rising share of total income passing through the financial sector. The difference between the financial sector and other sources of income is—wherever we can isolate it—a large (and even the prime) source of changing inequalities. In the wake of crises, as we observe directly in the United States and in Latin America, the financial sector shrinks and inequalities tend modestly to decline.

Fifth, the ability or willingness of political systems to affect the movement of inequality is very limited in the world today. The most egalitarian regime types—communist states—have largely disappeared (though Cuba remains as a dogged exception). Islamic republics, another egalitarian type, are few and idiosyncratic. They will not be found anytime soon outside their present limited range in the world.

Apart from these, we find that in the handful of stable social democracies (most of them in Northern Europe) that remain in the world today, it is economic institutions rather than the political structure per se that explain the persistence of low inequality in spite of an unstable world climate. There is no evidence that transitions to democracy can be relied on as a general matter to reduce inequality. However, the case of Brazil under Cardoso and Lula (and now Dilma Rousseff) does demonstrate that progress toward reduction of poverty and of inequality remains possible in the modern world, given favorable external conditions, low interest rates, and a determination by government to pursue a steady policy over many years.

Sixth, there is a systematic relationship between inequality and unemployment in the workings of labor markets around the world (and especially in Europe), but it is not the one that the advocates of "labor market flexibility" have been claiming with great passion for many years. Quite the reverse: following the general insights of Harris-Todaro and Meidner-Rehn, we find that more egalitarian societies tend to have lower steady-state unemployment. They also tend to have higher rates of technical progress and productivity growth, in part by importing advanced sectors and exporting or closing down backward ones. It is therefore not an accident that over time the egalitarian social democracies of Northern Europe became rich.

The same principles apply in the United States, where wage and pay compression—which cannot be confused with income inequality—moves with and not against the rate of unemployment. It helps to explain why European integration has produced higher chronic unemployment, since integrated international labor markets are more unequal than the national labor markets were when the latter could be taken alone. And it helps to explain the relationship between the floating population (largely unemployed, much of the time) and interprovincial economic inequality in China.

Broadly, our evidence vindicates the core analysis of Simon Kuznets from more than fifty years ago: economic inequality fundamentally evolves with the changing structure of economies and the balance of power and prices across sectors. Since sectors are linked to regions (the financial sector is always headquartered in a finance capital, for instance), sectoral and regional patterns of change in inequality are closely linked.

Although Kuznets's preoccupation with the balance between agriculture and industry is now ancient economic history in most places, more recent phenomena can be understood, and quite easily, by adapting his basic insight to the contours of any particular nation or international region. And the data required to achieve this understanding are readily available for the most part. The mysteries and puzzles in the literature do owe something to the desire, often noted among economists, to cling to a point favored by prior theory, but they also owe a great deal to the efforts of researchers, operating in perfect good faith, to draw more information from inadequate records than those records are willing or able to disgorge. The panoramic views provided on these pages should serve to demystify the study of economic inequality. In point of fact, even though there are many interesting developments to study, there are very few actual puzzles in the record. Similar patterns appear again and again.

What, then, is the relationship between economic inequality and the world financial and economic crisis? Here two distinct facts require treatment.

First, the massive rise of inequality in the global economy from 1980 to 2000, with a peak in most countries—including the United States—in the millennial year, is a fundamental reflection of the concentration of income and wealth among the richest of the rich, and the corresponding financial fragility affecting everyone else. Crises, and especially debt crises, are thus not new or sudden; in global perspective we see that they have cascaded across the world for a generation, hitting Latin America and Africa in the early 1980s, the Soviet Union and its satellites in the late 1980s and through the 1990s, and much of Asia in the late 1990s.

Throughout this period inequality rose in the United States, but the prevalence of external crises also meant that the United States benefited throughout from its position as a refuge for capital. In the 1990s capital flowed in, especially to the benefit of investors in the technology sectors, whose investment euphoria produced a general nationwide prosperity right up to the initial crash of the technology sector—and its NASDAQ stock index—in March and April 2000.

The problem facing the incoming administration of George W. Bush in January 2001 was thus twofold. Externally, there was little scope remaining for extracting capital from the rest of the world. Every region that was open to crisis, with the possible exceptions of China and India, had already had one. Internally, the appeal of the major American leadership sector had worn out. What to do?

The solutions of the Bush era passed briefly via military commitments, in Afghanistan and Iraq, whose effects on internal distribution appear in the rise of the Washington metropolitan region as the leading economic winner, in geographic terms, of those years. By 2004, however, it was clear that no modern war would have a major and sustained effect on domestic economic growth and job creation at the level of the entire nation. Nor could American government effectively grow at a sufficient rate to sustain and support strong economic growth.

A remaining option was to foster the growth of demand by the world's one remaining solvent class: American households, who still had the capacity to borrow against their homes. But this, too, was limited, by the thrift of those households, by their own uncertain economic prospects, and by the general maturing of the population. Growth on the scale required demanded new markets, and these were to be found only among debtors who had not previously qualified for mortgage loans. The ground for this had been prepared over twenty years, beginning with the deregulation movements in the financial sector in the early 1980s and culminating with the repeal of Glass-Steagall in 1999 and the passage of the Commodity Futures Modernization Act in late 2000, which opened the door to unregulated financial credit default swaps on mortgage-backed securities.

Thus the Bush administration launched the "ownership society," overtly encouraging massive expansion of lending to weak credits, and relaxing the regulatory standards that had previously protected credit quality in this area. Before too long, the subprime boom was under way—a massive expansion of weakly supervised, poorly underwritten, underdocumented, and in the final analysis fraudulent loans made in vast quantities to people who, it was known, would not long be able to keep up their payments.

The financial crisis (and the world economic crisis it engendered) thus represented not so much the natural outgrowth of rising inequality as a further phase; it was the consequence of a deliberate effort to sustain a model of economic growth based on inequality that had, in the year 2000, already ended. By pressing this model past all legal and ethical limits, the United States succeeded in prolonging an "era of good feeling," and in ensuring that when the collapse came, it would utterly destroy the financial sector.

We continue to try to cope with the consequences of these extraordinary events.

Notes

1. Except in earlier journal articles from which much of this book has been adapted.
2. We could have added chapters on Russia, India, Turkey, and several smaller countries, but space, expense, and due concern for the patience of the reader suggested it would be better not to do so.

REFERENCES

Acemoglu, Daron. 1997. "Matching, Heterogeneity, and the Evolution of Income Distribution." *Journal of Economic Growth* 2(1):61–92.

———, and James A. Robinson. 2000. "Why Did the West Extend the Franchise? Democracy, Inequality, and Growth in Historical Perspective." *Quarterly Journal of Economics* 115(4):1167–99.

———. 2001. "A Theory of Political Transitions." *American Economic Review* 91(4):938–63.

———. 2002. "The Political Economy of the Kuznets Curve." *Review of Development Economics* 6(2):183–203.

———. 2006. *Economic Origins of Dictatorship and Democracy*. New York: Cambridge University Press.

Aghion, Philippe, and Peter Howitt. 1998. *Endogenous Growth Theory*. Cambridge and London: MIT Press.

Ahluwalia, Montek S. 1976. "Inequality, Poverty and Development." *Journal of Development Economics* 3(4):307–42.

Alderson, Arthur S., and François Nielsen. 2002. "Globalization and the Great U-Turn: Income Inequality Trends in 16 OECD Countries." *American Journal of Sociology* 107(5): 1244–99.

Alvarez, Mike, José Antonio Cheibub, Fernando Limongi, and Adam Przeworski. 1996. "Classifying Political Regimes." *Studies in International Comparative Development* 31:3–36.

Anand, Sudhir, and Ravi Kanbur. 1993. "Inequality and Development: A Critique." *Journal of Development Economics* 41(1):19–43.

Anuario Estadístico de Cuba. Various editions. *Oficina Nacional de Estadísticas*, La Habana, Cuba.

Arellano, Manuel, and Stephen Bond. 1991. "Some Tests of Specification for Panel Data: Monte Carlo Evidence and an Application to Employment Equations." *Review of Economic Studies* 58(2):277–97.

Arestis, Philip, and Malcolm Sawyer. 2006. *Alternative Perspectives on Economic Policies in the European Union*. London: Palgrave Macmillan.

Argentine Congress. 1991. "Convertibility Law. Act: 23.928." *Published in Boletin Oficial*, No 27.104.

———. 1993. "Creation of the Integrated System of Retirement and Pension Benefits. Act: 24.241." *Published in Boletin Oficial*, No 27.745.

Atkinson, Anthony B. 1997. "Bringing Income Distribution in from the Cold." *Economic Journal* 107(440):297–321.

———, and Andrea Brandolini. 2001. "Promise and Pitfalls in the Use of "Secondary" Data-Sets: Income Inequality in OECD Countries as a Case Study." *Journal of Economic Literature* 39(3):771–99.

Atkinson, Anthony B., Lee Rainwater, and Timothy M. Smeeding. 1995. "Income Distribution in OECD Countries: The Evidence from the Luxembourg Income Study (LIS)." Paris: Organization for Economic Cooperation and Development.

Baker, Dean, Andrew Glyn, David Howell, and John Schmitt. 2005. "Labor Market Institutions and Unemployment: A Critical Assessment of the Cross-Country Evidence." In *Fighting Unemployment: The Limits of Free Market Orthodoxy*, edited by D. R. Howell. New York: Oxford University Press.

Baker, D., and J. Schmitt. June 1998. "The Macroeconomic Roots of High European Unemployment: The Impact of Foreign Growth." Washington, DC: Economic Policy Institute. http://www.epinet.org

Baltagi, Badi H. 1995. *Econometric Analysis of Panel Data*. New York: Wiley.

———, and Ping X. Wu. 1999. "Unequally Spaced Panel Data Regressions with AR(1) Disturbances." *Econometric Theory* 15(6):814–23.

Barberia, Lorena, Xavier de Souza Briggs, and Miren Uriarte. 2004. "Commentary: The End of Egalitarianism? Economic Inequality and the Future of Social Policy in Cuba." In *The Cuban Economy at the Start of the Twenty-First Century*, edited by J. I. Domínguez, O. E. Pérez Villanueva, and L. Barberia. Cambridge: Harvard University, David Rockefeller Center for Latin American Studies.

Barro, Robert J. 2000. "Inequality and Growth in a Panel of Countries." *Journal of Economic Growth* 5(1):5–32.

———, and Jong-Wha Lee. 1994. "Data Set for a Panel Data of 138 Countries."

Bartels, Larry M. 2006. "What's the Matter with What's the Matter with Kansas?" *Quarterly Journal of Political Science* 1(2):201–26.

Beck, Thorsten, George Clarke, Alberto Groff, Philip Keefer, and Patrick Walsh. 2001. "New Tools and New Tests in Comparative Political Economy: The Database of Political Institutions." *World Bank Economic Review* 15(1):165–76.

Beijing Statistical Yearbook. 2007. Beijing: China Statistics Press.

Bénabou, Roland. 1996. "Inequality and Growth." 11–92 in *NBER Macroeconomics Annual 1996*, edited by B. S. Bernanke and J. J. Rotemberg. Cambridge, MA: MIT Press.

Berman, Eli. 2000. "Does Factor-Biased Technological Change Stifle International Convergence? Evidence from Manufacturing." *National Bureau of Economic Research (NBER) Working Paper No. 7964*.

Bernanke, Ben S. February 6, 2007. "The Level and Distribution of Economic Well-Being." Speech before Greater Omaha Chamber of Commerce, Omaha, Nebraska. Washington, DC: Federal Reserve Board.

Bernard, Andrew B., and Bradford Jensen. 1998. "Understanding Increasing and Decreasing Wage Inequality." Cambridge, MA: National Bureau of Economic Research, NBER Working Paper No. 6571.

Bernstein, Jared, Elizabeth McNichol, and Karen Lyons. 2006. "Pulling Apart: A State-by-State Analysis of Income Trends." Washington, DC: Center on Budget and Policy Priorities and the Economic Policy Institute.

Biancotti, Claudia. 2006. "A Polarization of Inequality? The Distribution of National Gini Coefficients, 1970–1996." *Journal of Economic Inequality* 4(1):1–32.

Bhalla, Surjit. 2002. *Imagine There's No Country: Poverty, Inequality, and Growth in the Era of Globalization*. Washington, DC: Institute for International Economics.

Birdsall, Nancy, David Ross, and Richard Sabot. 1995. "Inequality and Growth Reconsidered: Lessons from East Asia." *World Bank Economic Review* 9(3):477–508.

Blanchard, Olivier. 2005. "European Unemployment: The Evolution of Facts and Ideas." Cambridge, MA: National Bureau of Economic Research, NBER Working Paper No. 11750.

———, and Justin Wolfers. 1999. "The Role of Shocks and Institutions in the Rise of European Unemployment: The Aggregate Evidence." Cambridge, MA: National Bureau of Economic Research, NBER Working Paper No. 7282.

———. 2000. "The Role of Shocks and Institutions in the Rise of European Unemployment: The Aggregate Evidence." *Economic Journal* 110(462):C1–33.

Bluestone, Barry, and Bennet Harrison, 1990. *The Great U-Turn: Corporate Restructuring and the Polarizing of America*. New York: Basic Books.

Boix, Carles. 2003. *Democracy and Redistribution*. New York: Cambridge University Press.

Bollen, Kenneth A., and Burke D. Grandjean. 1981. "The Dimension(s) of Democracy: Further Issues in the Measurement and Effects of Political Democracy." *American Sociological Review* 46:232–39.

Bollen, Kenneth A., and Robert W. Jackman. 1989. "Democracy, Stability, and Dichotomies." *American Sociological Review* 54(4): 612–21.

Bound, John, and George Johnson. 1992. "Changes in the Structure of Wages in the 1980's: An Evaluation of Alternative Explanations." *American Economic Review* 82(3):371–92.

Bourguignon, François, and Thierry Verdier. 2000. "Oligarchy, Democracy, Inequality and Growth." *Journal of Development Economics* 62(2):285–313.

Bouvatier, Vincent. 2007. "Hot Money Inflows and Monetary Stability in China: How the People's Bank of China Took up the Challenge." CREM Working Paper Series. University of Rennes 1, University of Caen and CNRS.

Brady, Henry E. 2004. "An Analytical Perspective on Participatory Inequality and Income Inequality." In *Social Inequality*, edited by K. M. Neckerman. New York: Russell Sage Foundation.

Brenner, Y. S., Hartmut Kaelble, and Mark Thomas. 1991. *Income Distribution in Historical Perspective*. Cambridge: Cambridge University Press.

Breusch, Trevor, and Adrian Pagan. 1980. "The Lagrange Multiplier Test and Its Applications to Model Specifications in Econometrics." *Review of Economic Studies* 47(146):239–53.

Bruno, Michael, and Jeffrey D. Sachs. 1985. *Economics of Worldwide Stagflation*. Cambridge, MA: Harvard University Press.

Bureau of Economic Analysis (BEA). 2000. "State Personal Income, 1929–1997." Washington, DC: Regional Economic Measurement Division, U.S. Department of Commerce.

———. 2007. "Regional Economic Accounts." Washington, DC: U.S. Department of Commerce.

———. 2008. "Regional Economic Accounts: State Annual Personal Income." Washington, DC: U.S. Department of Commerce.

Bureau of Labor Statistics (BLS). 2007. "BLS Handbook of Methods." Washington, DC: U.S. Department of Labor.

Burtless, Gary. 2009. "Demographic Transformation and Economic Inequality." In *Oxford Handbook of Inequality*, edited by W. Salverda, B. Nolan, and T. M. Smeeding. Oxford and New York: Oxford University Press.

Bush, George W. January 31, 2007. "State of the Economy Address." Federal Hall, New York.

Cabrera, J. 2002. "Industria Biotecnológica y Medico Farmacéutica en Cuba." In *Estructura Económica de Cuba, Tomo I*. La Habana, Cuba: Editorial Félix Varela.

Calistri, Amy D., and James K. Galbraith. 2001. "Interindustry Wage Structure: New Evidence from the OECD." In *Inequality and Industrial Change: A Global View Cambridge*, edited by J. K. Galbraith and M. Berner. New York: Cambridge University Press.

Calmon, Paulo Du Pin, Pedro Conceição, James K. Galbraith, Vidal Garza Cantú, and Abel Hibert. 2000. "The Evolution of Industrial Earnings Inequality in Mexico and Brazil." *Review of Development Economics* 4(2):194–203.

Card, David, and John E. DiNardo. 2002. "Skill-Biased Technological Change and Rising Wage Inequality: Some Problems and Puzzles." *Journal of Labor Economics*, 20(4):733–83.

Caselli, Francesco, Gerardo Esquivel, and Fernando Lefort. 1996. "Reopening the Convergence Debate: A New Look at Cross-Country Growth Empirics." *Journal of Economic Growth* 1(3):363–89.

CEPAL. 2000. *La Economía Cubana. Reformas Estructurales y Desempeño en los Noventa.* México: Fondo de Cultura Económica.

CEPDE (Centro de Estudios de Población y Desarrollo). 2005. "Cuba: 10 años después de la Conferencia Internacional sobre la Población y el Desarrollo." Oficina Nacional de Estadísticas, La Habana, Cuba.

Chang, Jih Y., and Rati Ram. 2000. "Level of Development, Rate of Economic Growth, and Income Inequality." *Economic Development and Cultural Change* 48(4):787–99.

Chatterjee, Arnab, Sudhakar Yarlagadda, and Bikas K. Chakrabarti. 2005. "Econophysics of Wealth Distributions." Milan: Springer-Verlag Italia.

Cheibub, José Antonio, and Jennifer Gandhi. 2004. "Classifying Political Regimes: A Six-Fold Measure of Democracies and Dictatorships." Paper presented at the American Political Science Association annual meeting, Chicago, September 2–5.

Cheung, Yin-Wong, Menzie D. Chinn, and Eiji Fujii. 2006. "The Chinese Economies in Global Context: The Integration Process and Its Determinants." *Journal of the Japanese and International Economies* 20(1):128–53.

Cheung, Yin-Wong, Dickson Tam, and Matthew S. Yiu. 2006. "Does the Chinese Interest Rate Follow the U.S. Interest Rate?" Hong Kong: Hong Kong Institute for Monetary Research, Working Paper 192006.

China Statistical Yearbook. 1998–2008. Beijing: China Statistics Press.

Chong, Alberto. 2004. "Inequality, Democracy, and Persistence: Is There a Political Kuznets Curve?" *Economics & Politics* 16(2):189–212.

Ciem-Pnud. 2000. *Investigación sobre el Desarrollo Humano y Equidad en Cuba 1999.* La Habana, Cuba: Editorial Caguayo.

Cingranelli, David, and Chang-yen Tsai. 2002. "Democracy, Workers' Rights, and Income Equality: A Comparative Cross-National Analysis." Paper presented at the Annual Meeting of the American Political Science Association, Boston, August 28–September 1.

Colectivo de Autores. 2002. *Estructura Económica de Cuba, Tomo I.* La Habana, Cuba: Editorial Félix Varela.

Conceição, Pedro, and Pedro Ferreira. 2000. "The Young Person's Guide to the Theil Index: Suggesting Intuitive Interpretations and Exploring Analytical Applications." UTIP Working Paper No. 14, University of Texas at Austin.

Conceição, Pedro, and James K. Galbraith. 2000. "Constructing Long and Dense Time Series of Inequality Using the Theil Index." *Eastern Economic Journal* 26(1):61–74.

———. 2001. "Toward a New Kuznets Hypothesis: Theory and Evidence on Growth and Inequality." In *Inequality and Industrial Change: A Global View*, edited by J. K. Galbraith and M. Berner. New York: Cambridge University Press.

———. 2002. "Technological Intensity and Inter-Sectoral Dynamics of Inequality: Evidence from the OECD, 1970–1990." *International Journal of Technology, Policy and Management* 2(3):315–37.

Conceição, Pedro, James K. Galbraith, and Peter Bradford. 2001. "The Theil Index in Sequences of Nested and Hierarchic Grouping Structures: Implications for the Measurement of Inequality Through Time, with Data Aggregated at Different Levels of Industrial Classification." *Eastern Economic Journal* 27(4):491–514.

Cutright, Phillips. 1963. "National Political Development: Measurement and Analysis." *American Sociological Review* 28(2):253–64.

———. 1967. "Inequality: A Cross-National Analysis." *American Sociological Review* 32: 562–78.

Dahl, Robert A. 1971. *Polyarchy: Participation and Opposition*, New Haven: Yale University Press.

Davidson, Russell, and James G. MacKinnon. 1981. "Several Tests for Model Specification in the Presence of Alternative Hypotheses." *Econometrica* 49(3):781–93.

De la Torre, Augusto, Eduardo Levy Yeyati, and Sergio Schmukler. 2002. "Argentina's Financial Crisis: Floating Money, Sinking Banking." Mimeo. Washington, DC: World Bank.

Deininger, Klaus, and Lyn Squire. 1996. "A New Data Set Measuring Income Inequality." *World Bank Economic Review* 10(3):565–91.

———. 1998. "New Ways of Looking at Old Issues: Inequality and Growth." *Journal of Development Economics* 57(2):259–87.

DeNavas-Walt, Carmen, Bernadette D. Proctor, and Jessica C. Smith. 2008. "Income, Poverty, and Health Insurance Coverage in the United States: 2007." Washington, DC: U.S. Government Printing Office.

Desai, Raj M., Anders Olofsgard, and Tarik M. Yousef. 2003. "Democracy, Inequality, and Inflation." *American Political Science Review* 97(3): 391–406.

Dirección General de Estadística y Censos. 2003. "Informe de Resultados No. 101: Producto Bruto Geográfico de la Ciudad de Buenos Aires." Gobierno de la Ciudad de Buenos Aires, Buenos Aires.

Dollar, David, and Aart Kraay. 2002. "Growth Is Good for the Poor." *Journal of Economic Growth* 7(3):195–225.

Domínguez, Jorge I., Omar Everleny Pérez Villanueva, and Lorena Barberia. 2004. *The Cuban Economy at the Start of the Twenty-First Century*. Cambridge: Harvard University Press, David Rockefeller Center for Latin American Studies.

Duesenberry, James S. 1949. *Income, Saving, and the Theory of Consumer Behaviors*. Cambridge: Harvard University Press.

Easterly, William R., and Mirvat Sewadeh. 2001. "Global Development Network Growth Database." http://tinyurl.com/23h2fd.

Economist Intelligence Unit. 2005. *Country Profile Cuba*. London: Economist.

Edsall, Thomas B. 1984. *The New Politics of Inequality*. New York: Norton.

Elgie, Robert. 1998. "The Classification of Democratic Regime Types: Conceptual Ambiguity and Contestable Assumptions." *European Journal of Political Research* 33(2):219–38.

Elkins, Zachary. 2000. "Gradations of Democracy? Empirical Tests of Alternative Conceptualizations." *American Journal of Political Science*, 44(2):293–300.

Erikkson, Clas, and Joakim Persson. 2003. "Economic Growth, Inequality, Democratization, and the Environment." *Environmental and Resource Economics* 25(1):1–16.

Esping-Andersen, Gøsta. 1990. *The Three Worlds of Welfare Capitalism*. Princeton: Princeton University Press.

Ferguson, Thomas. 2005. "Holy Owned Subsidiary: Globalization, Religion, and Politics in the 2004 Election." In *A Defining Election: The Presidential Race of 2004*, edited by W. Crotty. Armonk, NY: Sharpe.

———, and James K. Galbraith. 1999. "The American Wage Structure: 1920–1947." *Research in Economic History* 19:205–57.

Fields, Gary S. 1980. *Poverty, Inequality, and Development*. New York: Cambridge University Press.

———. 1994. "Data for Measuring Poverty and Inequality Changes in the Developing Countries." *Journal of Development Economics* 44(1):87–102.

Fields, Gary S., and George H. Jakubson. 1994. "New Evidence on the Kuznets Curve." Cornell University, Department of Economics, Ithaca, N.Y. Cited in Deininger and Squire (1996).

Forbes, Kristin J. 2000. "A Reassessment of the Relationship Between Inequality and Growth." *American Economic Review* 90(4):869–87.

Frank, Robert H. 2007. *Falling Behind: How Rising Inequality Harms the Middle Class*. Berkeley: University of California Press.

Freedom House. 2004. "Freedom in the World 2004: The Annual Survey of Political Rights and Civil Liberties." Lanham, MD: Rowman & Littlefield.

Galbraith, James K. 1998. *Created Unequal: The Crisis in American Pay*. New York: Free Press.

———. 1999. "Globalization and Pay." *Proceedings of the American Philosophical Society* 143(2):178–86.

———. 2002a. "The Importance of Being Sufficiently Equal." *Social Philosophy & Policy* 19(1):201–24.

———. 2002b. "A Perfect Crime: Inequality in the Age of Globalization." *Daedalus* 131(1): 11–25.

———. 2006a. "Maastricht 2042 and the Fate of Europe: Toward Convergence and Full Employment." Annandale-on-Hudson, NY: Levy Economics Institute Public Policy Brief, No. 87.

———. 2006b. "The Firm, Exports, the Banks and the Real Wage in China." Note, prepared for meeting on institutional reform in China, Manchester, UK.

———. 2007a. "Global Inequality and Global Macro Economics." In *Global Inequality*, edited by D. Held and A. Kaya. Cambridge: Polity Press. Republished in Journal of Policy Modeling 29(4):587–607.

———. 2007b. "Maastricht 2042 and the Fate of Europe: Toward Convergence and Full Employment." *International Policy Analysis Unit, Friedrich-Ebert-Stiftung*.

———. 2007c. "What Is the American Model Really About? Soft Budgets and the Keynesian Devolution." *Industrial and Corporate Change* 16(1):1–18.

———. 2009. "Inequality, Unemployment and Growth: New Measures for Old Controversies." *Journal of Economic Inequality* 7(2):189–206.

———, and Maureen Berner. 2001. *Inequality and Industrial Change: A Global View*. New York: Cambridge University Press.

Galbraith, James K., Pedro Conceição, and Pedro Ferreira. 1999. "Inequality and Unemployment in Europe: The American Cure." *New Left Review* 237:28–51.

Galbraith, James K., and Enrique Garcilazo. 2004. "Unemployment, Inequality and the Policy of Europe: 1984–2000." *Banca Nazionale del Lavoro Quarterly Review* 57(228):3–28. Reprinted in Richard P. F. Holt and Steven Pressman, editors, *Empirical Post Keynesian Economics: Looking at the Real World*. Armonk, NY: Sharpe, 2007, 44–69.

———. 2005. "Pay Inequality in Europe 1995–2000: Convergence Between Countries and Stability Inside." *European Journal of Comparative Economics* 2(2):139–74.

Galbraith, James K., and Vidal Garza-Cantú. 1999. "Inequality in American Manufacturing Wages, 1920–1998: A Revised Estimate." *Journal of Economic Issues* 33(3):735–43.

Galbraith, James K., Olivier Giovannoni, and Ann J. Russo. 2007. "The Fed's Real Reaction Function: Monetary Policy, Inflation, Unemployment, Inequality—and Presidential Politics." Annandale-on-Hudson, NY: Levy Economics Institute of Bard College, Working Paper No. 511.

Galbraith, James K., and J. Travis Hale. 2006. "American Inequality: From IT Bust to Big Government Boom." *Economists' Voice* 3(8).

———. 2008. "State Income Inequality and Presidential Election Turnout and Outcomes." *Social Science Quarterly* 89(4):887–901.

Galbraith, James K., Sara Hsu, and Jianjun Li. 2007. "Is China Really Running a Trade Surplus?" UTIP Working Paper No. 45, University of Texas at Austin.

Galbraith, James K., Sara Hsu, and Wenjie Zhang, "Beijing Bubble, Beijing Bust: Inequality Trade and Capital Flow into China," *Journal of Current Chinese Affairs/China Aktuell*, 2/2009, 3–26.

Galbraith, James K., Ludmila Krytynskaia, and Qifei Wang. 2004. "The Experience of Rising Inequality in Russia and China During the Transition." *European Journal of Comparative Economics* 1(1):87–106.

Galbraith, James K., and Hyunsub Kum. 2003. "Inequality and Economic Growth: A Global View Based on Measures of Pay." *CESifo Economic Studies* 49(4):527–56.

———. 2005. "Estimating the Inequality of Household Incomes: A Statistical Approach to the Creation of a Dense and Consistent Global Data Set." *Review of Income and Wealth* (1):115–43.

Galbraith, James K., and Jiaqing Lu. 2001. "Cluster and Discriminant Analysis on Time-Series as a Research Tool." In *Inequality and Industrial Change: A Global View,* edited by J. K. Galbraith and M. Berner. New York: Cambridge University Press.

Galbraith, James K., C. Priest, and G. Purcell. 2007. "Economic Equality and Victory in War: An Empirical Investigation." *Defence and Peace Economics* 18(5).

Galbraith, James K., and Deepshikha RoyChowdhury. 2007. "The European Wage Structure, 1980–2005: How Much Flexibility Do We Have?" Austin: UTIP Working Paper No. 41, May 15.

Galbraith, James K., Deepshikha RoyChowdhury, and Sanjeev Shrivastava. 2004. "Pay Inequality in the Indian Manufacturing Sector, 1979–1998." *Economic and Political Weekly* 39(28):3139–48.

Galbraith, James K., Laura Spagnolo, and Daniel Munevar. 2008. "Inequidad Salarial en Cuba durante el Periodo Especial." *América Latina Hoy* 48:109–38.

Galbraith, James K., Laura Spagnolo, and Sergio Pinto. 2007. "Economic Inequality and Political Power: A Comparative Analysis of Argentina and Brazil." *Business and Politics* 9(1). Originally published as Galbraith, James K., Laura Spagnolo, and Sergio Pinto (February 8, 2006). "The Decline of Pay Inequality in Argentina and Brazil Following the Crises and Retreat from the Neo-liberal Model." UTIP Working Paper no. 34.

Galor, Oded, and Daniel Tsiddon. 1997a. "The Distribution of Human Capital and Economic Growth." *Journal of Economic Growth* 2(1):93–124.

———. 1997b. "Technological Progress, Mobility, and Economic Growth." *American Economic Review* 87(3):363–82.

Garcilazo, Jose Enrique. 2005. *Regional Labor Markets, Unemployment and Inequality in Europe.* Dissertation, LBJ School of Public Affairs, University of Texas at Austin.

Garcilazo-Corredera, Jose Enrique. 2007. *Regional Labor Markets: Unemployment and Inequality in Europe.* Saarbrücken: VDM Verlag Dr. Mueller e.K.

Gasparini, Leonardo. 1999. "Un Análisis de la Distribución del Ingreso en la Argentina sobre la base de Descomposiciones." In *La Distribución del Ingreso en la Argentina.* Buenos Aires: Fundación de Investigaciones Económicas Latinoamericanas.

———. 2004. "Poverty and Inequality in Argentina: Methodological Issues and Literature Review." Buenos Aires, Argentina: Centro de Estudios Distributivos, Laborales y Sociales (CEDLAS), World Bank.

Gastil, Raymond D. 1991. "The Comparative Survey of Freedom: Experiences and Suggestions." In *On Measuring Democracy: Its Consequences and Concomitants,* edited by A. Inkeles. New Brunswick, NJ: Transaction.

Gelman, Andrew, Boris Shor, Joseph Bafumi, and David Park. 2007. "Rich State, Poor State, Red State, Blue State: What's the Matter with Connecticut?" *Quarterly Journal of Political Science* 2:345–67.

Gibson, Campbell, and Kay Jung. 2002. "Historical Census Statistics on Population Totals by Race, 1790 to 1990, and by Hispanic Origin, 1970 to 1990, for the United States, Regions, Divisions, and States." Population Division Working Paper No. 56. Washington, DC: U.S. Census Bureau, U.S Department of Commerce.

Giovannoni, Olivier. 2007. "Inequality and the US Labor Force Structure." *UTIP Working Paper No. 43,* University of Texas at Austin.

Goldin, Claudia, and Lawrence F. Katz. 2008. *The Race Between Technology and Education.* Cambridge: Harvard University Press.

Gough, Ian, and Geof Wood. 2004. *Insecurity and Welfare Regimes in Asia, Africa and Latin America: Social Policy in Development Contexts.* Cambridge: Cambridge University Press.

Gradstein, Mark, and Branko Milanovic. 2004. "Does Liberté = Egalité? A Survey of the Empirical Links Between Democracy and Inequality with Some Evidence on the Transition Economies." *Journal of Economic Surveys* 18(4):515–37.

———, and Yvonne Ying. 2001. "Democracy and Income Inequality." World Bank Policy Research Working Paper No. 2561. Washington, DC: World Bank.

Green, Stephen. 2007, May 17. *On the Ground in Asia*. Shanghai: Standard Chartered Bank.

Greene, William H. 2000. *Econometric Analysis*. Upper Saddle River, NJ: Prentice Hall.

Greenspan, Alan, and Charlie Rose. 2007. "A Conversation with Alan Greenspan." *Charlie Rose Show*. PBS. WNET, Newark.

Grün, Carola, and Stephan Klasen. 2003. "Growth, Inequality, and Well-Being: Intertemporal and Global Comparisons." *CESifo Economic Studies* 49:617–59.

Gurkaynak, Refet S. 2008. "Econometric Tests of Asset Price Bubbles: Taking Stock." *Journal of Economic Surveys* 22(1):166–86.

Gurr, Ted Robert. 1974. "Persistence and Change in Political Systems, 1800–1971." *American Political Science Review* 68(4):1482–1504.

———, Keith Jaggers, and Will H. Moore. 1990. "The Transformation of the Western State: The Growth of Democracy, Autocracy, and State Power Since 1800." *Studies in Comparative International Development* 25(1):73–108.

Hadenius, Axel, and Jan Teorell. 2007. "Pathways from Authoritarianism." *Journal of Democracy* 18(1):143–56.

Harris, John R., and Michael P. Todaro. 1970. "Migration, Unemployment and Development: A Two-Sector Analysis." *American Economic Review* 60(1):126–42.

Hausman, J. A. 1978. "Specification Tests in Econometrics." *Econometrica* 46, 1251–72.

Haveman, Robert H. 1997. "Equity with Employment" *Boston Review* 22:3–13.

Heston, A., R. Summers, and B. Aten. 2002. *Penn World Table*, version 6.1. Philadelphia: Center for International Comparisons, University of Pennsylvania, http://pwt.econ.upenn.edu.

Houle, Christian. 2009. "Inequality and Democracy: Why Inequality Harms Consolidation But Does Not Affect Democratization." *World Politics* 61(4):589–622.

Howell, David R. 2005. "Fighting Unemployment: Why Labor Market 'Reforms' Are Not the Answer." New York: Bernard Schwartz Center for Economic Policy Analysis, New School for Social Research.

Hsu, Sara. 2008. "The Effect of Political Regimes on Inequality, 1963–2002." UTIP Working Paper No. 53, University of Texas at Austin.

Jackman, Robert W. 1974. "Political Democracy and Social Equality." *American Sociological Review* 39:29–45.

Jacobs, Lawrence, and Theda Skocpol. 2005. "Inequality and American Democracy: What We Know and What We Need to Learn." New York: Russell Sage Foundation.

Jones, Arthur, Jr., and Daniel H. Weinberg. 2000. "U.S. Census Bureau Current Population Reports, P60–204, The Changing Shape of the Nation's Income Distribution." Washington, DC: U.S. Government Printing Office.

Juhn, Chinhui, Kevin M. Murphy, and Brooks Pierce. 1993. "Wage Inequality and the Rise in Returns to Skill." *Journal of Political Economy* 101(3):410–42.

Katz, Lawrence F., and David H. Autor. 1998. "Changes in the Wage Structure and Earnings Inequality." In *Handbook of Labor Economics*, Vol. 3b, edited by O. Ashenfelter and D. Card. Amsterdam: North-Holland.

Keynes, John Maynard. 1936. *The General Theory of Employment Interest and Money*. London: Macmillan.

Kim, Jeongdai, and Paul A. Jargowsky. 2005. "The GINI Coefficient and Segregation on a Continuous Variable." *Research on Economic Inequality* 17:57–70.

Kim, Junmo. 2002. *The South Korean Economy: Towards a New Explanation of an Economic Miracle*. Aldershot: Ashgate.

———. 2005. *Globalization and Industrial Development*. Lincoln, NE: iUniverse.

Kitov, Ivan O. 2005. "Modelling the Average Income Dependence on Work Experience in the USA from 1967 to 2002." Society for the Study of Economic Inequality Working Paper No. 11.

———. 2007. "Modeling the Evolution of Gini Coefficient for Personal Incomes in the USA between 1947 and 2005." *MPRA Working Paper No. 2798*, University Library of Munich, Germany.

Kum, Hyunsub. 2008. "Inequality and Structural Change." UTIP Working Paper No. 54, University of Texas at Austin.

Kuznets, Simon. 1955. "Economic Growth and Income Inequality." *American Economic Review* 45(1):1–28.

La Nación. 2004, August. Buenos Aires, Argentina.

Langer, Laura. 1999. "Measuring Income Distribution Across Space and Time in the American States." *Social Science Quarterly* 80:55–67.

Lawrence, Robert Z. 2000, Spring. "Inequality in America: The Recent Evidence." *Responsive Community* 10(2):4–10.

Layard, Richard, and Stephen Nickell. 1999. "Labor Market Institutions and Economic Performance." In *Handbook of Labor Economics*, edited by O. Ashenfelte and D. Card. Amsterdam: North Holland.

———, and Richard Jackman. 2005. *Unemployment: Macroeconomic Performance and the Labour Market*. Oxford: Oxford University Press.

Lee, Cheol-Sung. 2005. "Income Inequality, Democracy, and Public Sector Size." *American Sociological Review* 70(1):158–81.

Lehmanbrown. 2002. "Foreign Exchange FAQs." http://www.lehmanbrown.com/FAQ/FAQ-Forex/2.htm.

Leip, Dave. 2007. "Dave Leip's Atlas of U.S. Presidential Elections." http://uselectionatlas.org/.

Lenski, Gerhard. 1966. *Power and Privilege: A Theory of Social Stratification*. New York: McGraw-Hill.

Levine, Ross, and David Renelt. 1992. "A Sensitivity Analysis of Cross-Country Growth Regressions." *American Economic Review* 82(4):942–63.

Levy, Frank, and Richard J. Murnane. 1992. "U.S. Earnings Levels and Earnings Inequality: A Review of Recent Trends and Proposed Explanations." *Journal of Economic Literature* 30(3):1333–81.

Li, Hongyi, Lyn Squire, and Heng-fu Zou. 1998. "Explaining International and Intertemporal Variations in Income Inequality." *Economic Journal* 108(446):26–43.

Li, Quan, and Rafael Reuveny. 2009. *Democracy and Economic Openness in an Interconnected System*. Cambridge: Cambridge University Press.

Lindert, Peter H. 1991. "Toward a Comparative History of Income and Wealth Inequality." In *Income Distribution in Historical Perspective*, edited by Y. S. Brenner, H. Kaelble, and M. Thomas. Cambridge: Cambridge University Press.

———, and Jeffrey Gale Williamson. 1985. "Growth, Equality, and History." *Explorations in Economic History* 22(4):341–77.

Lipset, Seymour Martin. 1959. "Some Social Requisites of Democracy: Economic Development and Political Legitimacy." *American Political Science Review* 53(1):69–105.

LIS. n.d. "Luxembourg Income Study." http://www.lisproject.org/.

List, John A., and Craig A. Gallet. 1999. "The Kuznets Curve: What Happens After the Inverted-U?" *Review of Development Economics* 3(2):200–206.

López-Calva, Luis Felipe, and Nora Claudia Lustig, eds. 2010. *Declining Inequality in Latin America: A Decade of Progress?* Washington, DC: Brookings Institution Press and United Nations Development Programme.

Ma, Guonan, and Robert N. McCauley. 2008. "Efficacy of China's Capital Controls: Evidence from Price and Flow Data." *Pacific Economic Review* 13(1):104–23.

Ma, Yue, and Huayu Sun. 2007. "Hot Money Inflows and Renminbi Revaluation Pressure." *Journal of Chinese Economic and Business Studies* 5(1):19–36.

Marshall, Monty G., and Keith Jaggers. 2002. *Polity IV Project: Political Regime Characteristics and Transitions, 1800–2002*. College Park, MD: Center for International Development and Conflict Management, University of Maryland. http://www.cidcm.umd.edu/inscr/polity/index.htm.

McCarty, Nolan, Keith T. Poole, and Howard Rosenthal. 2006. *Polarized America: The Dance of Ideology and Unequal Riches*, Cambridge, MA: MIT Press.

McCauley, Robert N. 2008. "Managing Recent Hot Money Inflows in Asia." ADB Institute Discussion Paper No. 99.

McDonald, Michael. 2007. "Voter Turnout Statistics." http://elections.gmu.edu/voter_turnout.htm.

McLean, Bethany, and Joseph Nocera. 2010. *All the Devils Are Here: The Hidden History of the Financial Crisis*. New York: Portfolio Hardcover.

Meidner, Rudolf, and Gosta Rehn. 1951. *Fackföreningrsrörelsen och den Fulla Sysselsättningen*, Stockholm: LO.

Milanovic, Branko. 2002a. "The Ricardian Vice: Why Sala-i-Martin's Calculations of World Income Inequality Are Wrong." New York: World Bank.

———. 2002b. "True World Income Distribution, 1988 and 1993: First Calculation Based on Household Surveys Alone." *Economic Journal* 112(476):51–92.

———. 2007. *Worlds Apart: Measuring International and Global Inequality*. Princeton: Princeton University Press.

Minc, Alain. 2011. *Un Petit Coin de Paradis*. Paris: Grasset.

Munck, Gerardo. 1996. "Disaggregating Political Regime: Conceptual Issues in the Study of Democratization." Kellogg Institute Working Paper No. 228 (reprinted in *Authoritarianism and Democracy: Soldiers and Workers in Argentina, 1976–1983*. University Park: Pennsylvania State University Press, 1998).

National Institute of Standards and Technology. 1990, August 31. Federal Information Processing Standards Publication 6–4 (FIPS 6–4). "Counties and Equivalent Entities of the United States, Its Possessions, and Associated Areas." Washington, DC: U.S. Department of Commerce. http://www.itl.nist.gov/fipspubs/fip6–4.

Neckerman, Kathryn M. 2004. "Social Inequality." New York: Russell Sage Foundation.

Nickell, Stephen. 1997. "Unemployment and Labor Market Rigidities: Europe versus North America." *Journal of Economic Perspectives* 11(3):55–74.

ONE. 2004. *Anuario Estadistico de Cuba, Version Digital*. La Habana, Cuba: Oficina Nacional Estadistica de Cuba.

Organization for Economic Cooperation and Development (OECD). 1994. *The OECD Jobs Study: Facts, Analysis, Strategies*. Paris: OECD.

Palley, Thomas I. 1998. "Restoring Prosperity: Why the U.S. Model Is Not the Answer for the United States or Europe." *Journal of Post Keynesian Economics* 20(3):337–54.

———. 1999. "The Myth of Labor Market Flexibility and the Costs of Bad Macroeconomic Policy: U.S. and European Unemployment Explained." In *Jobwunder USA—Modell für Deutschland?* (Employment Miracle USA: Model for Germany?), edited by S. Lang, M. Mayer, and C. Scherrer. Münster: Westfälisches Dampfboot.

———. 2001. "The Role of Institutions and Policies in Creating High European Unemployment: The Evidence." Annandale-on-Hudson, NY: Levy Economics Institute, Working Paper No. 336.

———. 2004. "The Causes of High Unemployment: Labor Market Sclerosis Versus Macroeconomic Policy." In *Wages, Employment, Distribution and Growth*, edited by E. Hein, A. Heise, and A. Truger. London: Palgrave/Macmillan.

Papanek, Gustav F., and Oldrich Kyn. 1986. "The Effect on Income Distribution of Development, the Growth Rate and Economic Strategy." *Journal of Development Economics* 23:55–65.

Pasinetti, Luigi L., and Michael Sattinger. 2001. "Rate of Profit and Income Distribution in Relation to the Rate of Economic Growth." In *International Library of Critical Writings in Economics,* vol. 124. *Income Distribution. Volume* 3. Income Shares and Policy: Elgar Reference Collection. Cheltenham, UK, and Northampton, MA: Elgar; distributed by American International Distribution, Williston, VT.

Paulson, Henry M. Jr. 2006. "Remarks at Columbia University." New York, August 1.

———. 2010. *On the Brink: Inside the Race to Stop the Collapse of the Global Financial System.* New York: Business Plus.

Pérez, O. 2000. "Estabilización Macroeconómica." Centro de Estudios de la Economía Cubana (CEEC), La Habana, Cuba.

Pérez Izquierdo, Victoria, Fabian Oberto Calderón, and Mayelín González Rodríguez. 2004. "Los Trabajadores por Cuenta Propia en Cuba." *Revista Cuba Siglo* 21(47).

Perotti, Roberto. 1996. "Growth, Income Distribution, and Democracy: What the Data Say." *Journal of Economic Growth* 1(2):149–87.

Phelps, Edmund. 1994. *Structural Slumps: The Modern Equilibrium Theory of Unemployment, Interest, and Assets.* Cambridge, MA: Harvard University Press.

Piketty, Thomas, and Emmanuel Saez, 2003. "Income Inequality in the United States, 1913–1998." *Quarterly Journal of Economics* 118(1):1–39.

Piven, Francis, and Richard Cloward. 1988. *Why Americans Don't Vote.* New York: Pantheon.

Porter, Michael E. 1990. *The Competitive Advantage of Nations.* New York: Free Press.

Przeworski, Adam, Michael E. Alvarez, José A. Cheibub, and Fernando Limongi. 2000. "Democracy and Development: Political Institutions and Well-Being in the World, 1950–1990." Cambridge: Cambridge University Press.

Putnam, Robert. 2000. *Bowling Alone: The Collapse and Revival of American Community.* New York: Simon and Schuster.

Pyatt, Graham. 1976. "On the Interpretation and Disaggregation of Gini Coefficients." *Economic Journal* 86(342):243–55.

Quiñones, Nancy. 2002. "El Entorno Externo de la Economía Cubana." Instituto Nacional de Investigación Económica (INIE), La Habana, Cuba.

Ram, Rati. 1997. "Level of Economic Development and Income Inequality: Evidence from the Postwar Developed World." *Southern Economic Journal* 64(2):576–83.

Randolph, Susan M., and William F. Lott. 1993. "Can the Kuznets Effect Be Relied on to Induce Equalizing Growth?" *World Development* 21(5):829–40.

Raudenbush, Stephen W., and Anthony S. Bryk. 2002. *Hierarchical Linear Models: Applications and Data Analysis Methods.* Thousand Oaks, CA: Sage.

Reuveny, Rafael, and Quan Li. 2003. "Economic Openness, Democracy, and Income Inequality: An Empirical Analysis." *Comparative Political Studies* 36(5):575–601.

Rifkin, Jeremy. 2004. *The European Dream: How Europe's Vision of the Future Is Quietly Eclipsing the American Dream.* New York: Tarcher.

Riskin, Carl, Zhao Renwei, and Shi Li. 2001. "China's Retreat from Equality: Income Distribution and Economic Transition." Armonk, NY: Sharpe.

Robinson, Sherman. 1976. "A Note on the U Hypothesis Relating Income Inequality and Economic Development." *American Economic Review* 66(3):437–40.

Rodrik, Dani. 1999. "Democracies Pay Higher Wages." *Quarterly Journal of Economics* 114(3):707–38.

Rosenstone, Steven J. 1982. "Economic Adversity and Voter Turnout." *American Journal of Political Science* 26(1):25–46.

RoyChowdhury, Deepshikha, 2008. *Flexibility in European Wage Structure and Its Implications for European Unemployment.* Ph.D. dissertation, Lyndon B. Johnson School of Public Affairs, University of Texas at Austin.

Saint-Paul, Gilles, and Thierry Verdier. 1993. "Education, Democracy, and Growth." *Journal of Development Economics* 42:399–407.

Sala-i-Martin, Xavier. 2002a. "The Disturbing 'Rise' of Global Income Inequality." Cambridge, MA: National Bureau of Economic Research, NBER Working Paper No. 8904.

———. 2002b. "The World Distribution of Income (Estimated from Individual Country Distributions)." Cambridge, MA: National Bureau of Economic Research, NBER Working Paper No. 8933.

———. 2006. "The World Distribution of Income: Falling Poverty and . . . Convergence, Period." *Quarterly Journal of Economics* 121(2):351–97.

Schor, Juliet. 2002. *The Overworked American: The Unexpected Decline of Leisure*. New York: Basic Books.

Shapiro, Robert J. 2002. "The American Economy Following the Information-Technology Bubble and Terrorist Attacks," *Fujitsu Research Institute Economic Review* 6(1):105–15.

Siebert, Horst. 1997. "Labor Market Rigidities: At the Root of Unemployment in Europe." *Journal of Economic Perspectives* 11(3):37–54.

Solow, Robert. March/April 1994. "Europe's Unnecessary Unemployment." *International Economic Insights*, 10–11.

Spagnolo, Laura. 2011. "Economic Inequality, Policy and Performance in the Formal Sectors of Argentina, Brazil and Chile: Evidence from Regional and Sectoral Data, 1994–2007." Ph.D. dissertation, Lyndon B. Johnson School of Public Affairs, University of Texas at Austin.

———, and Daniel Munevar. 2008. "After Years of (Economic) Solitude: Neoliberal Reforms and Trends in Manufacturing Sector Pay Inequality in Colombia." UTIP Working Paper No. 47, The University of Texas at Austin, Austin, Texas.

Sylwester, Kevin. 2002. "Democracy and Changes in Income Inequality." *International Journal of Business and Economics* 1(2):167–78.

Tavares, José, and Romain Wacziarg. 2001. "How Democracy Affects Growth." *European Economic Review* 45(8):1341–78.

Theil, Henry. 1972. *Statistical Decomposition Analysis: With Applications in the Social and Administrative Sciences*. Amsterdam-London: North Holland.

Thorbecke, Erik, and Chutatong Charumilind. 2002. "Economic Inequality and Its Socioeconomic Impact." *World Development* 30(9):1477–95.

Timmons, Jeffrey F. 2008. "Does Democracy Reduce Economic Inequality? If So, How?" UCLA International Institute Working Paper.

Togores, Viviana. 2002. "Cuba: Efectos Sociales de la Crisis y el Ajuste Económico de los Noventas." *Revista Cuba Siglo* 21(13). http://tinyurl.com/3btlt4a.

Tsakloglou, Panos. 1988. "Development and Inequality Revisited." *Applied Economics* 20(4):509–31.

Turvey, Ralph. 1952. *Wages Policy Under Full Employment*. London: William Hodge.

U-Echevarria Vallejo, Óscar. 2002. "Antecedentes Macroeconómicos." In *Estructura Económica de Cuba*, Tomo I. La Habana, Cuba Editorial Félix Varela. U.S. Census Bureau. 2001. "Current Population Survey, November 2000: Voting and Registration." Washington, DC: U.S. Department of Commerce.

———. 2005a. "Census 2000 Summary File 1 (SF 1) 100—Percent Data; P2.Urban and Rural-Universe: Total Population." Washington, DC: U.S. Department of Commerce.

———. 2005b. "Census 2000 Summary File 3 (SF 3) Sample Data; P52.001 Households: Total and P54.001 Households Aggregate Income." Washington, DC: U.S. Department of Commerce.

———. 2005c. "Table S4. Gini Ratios by State: 1969, 1979, 1989, 1999." Washington, DC: U.S. Department of Commerce.

———. 2006. "State Population Datasets: State by Sex, Race, and Hispanic Origin." Washington, DC: U.S. Department of Commerce.

UNIDO (United Nations Industrial Development Organization). 2001. "Industrial Statistics Database."

———. 2005. "Industrial Statistics Database."

United for a Fair Economy. 2007. "CEO Pay Charts." Boston: United for a Fair Economy.

University of Texas Inequality Project (UTIP). Complete set of working papers and datasets. http://utip.gov.utexas.edu.

Vanhanen, Tatu. 2000. "A New Dataset for Measuring Democracy, 1810–1998." *Journal of Peace Research* 37(2):251–65.

Wade, Robert H. 2002. "Globalization, Poverty and Income Distribution: Does the Liberal Argument Hold?" DESTIN Working Paper No. 33.

Wells, Jason. 2006. "Equity and Democracy: Does Income Inequality Erode Democratic Support?" Paper presented at the annual meeting of the Midwest Political Science Association, Palmer House Hilton, Chicago, Illinois, April 20.

Widestrom, Amy. 2006. "Impoverished Democracy: Economic Inequality, Residential Segregation, and the Decline of Civic Engagement." Paper presented at Sawyer Law and Politics Program Research Workshop, Syracuse, NY, January.

Wolff, Michael, 1998. *Burn Rate: How I Survived the Gold Rush Years on the Internet.* New York: Simon and Schuster.

World Institute for Development Economics Research (WIID). May, 2008. "World Income Inequality Database Version 2.0c." Helsinki: United Nations University http://www.wider.unu.edu/research/Database/en_GB/database/.

Williamson, Jeffrey G. 1982. "The Structure of Pay in Britain, 1710–1911." *Research in Economic History* 7:1–54.

———, and Peter H. Lindert. 1980. *American Inequality: A Macroeconomic History.* New York: Academic Press.

Wood, Adrian J. B. 1994. *North-South Trade, Employment and Inequality.* Oxford: Clarendon Press of Oxford University Press.

World Bank. 2007. "World Development Indicators Online (WDI)." http://www.worldbank.org/.

INDEX

THE PARTY IS OVER

THE PARTY ★★★ IS ★★★ OVER

HOW REPUBLICANS WENT CRAZY,
DEMOCRATS BECAME USELESS,
AND THE MIDDLE CLASS GOT SHAFTED

Mike Lofgren

VIKING

VIKING
Published by the Penguin Group
Penguin Group (USA) Inc., 375 Hudson Street, New York, New York 10014, U.S.A. ☆ Penguin Group (Canada), 90 Eglinton Avenue East, Suite 700, Toronto, Ontario, Canada M4P 2Y3 (a division of Pearson Penguin Canada Inc.) ☆ Penguin Books Ltd, 80 Strand, London WC2R 0RL, England ☆ Penguin Ireland, 25 St. Stephen's Green, Dublin 2, Ireland (a division of Penguin Books Ltd) ☆ Penguin Books Australia Ltd, 250 Camberwell Road, Camberwell, Victoria 3124, Australia (a division of Pearson Australia Group Pty Ltd) ☆ Penguin Books India Pvt Ltd, 11 Community Centre, Panchsheel Park, New Delhi – 110 017, India ☆ Penguin Group (NZ), 67 Apollo Drive, Rosedale, Auckland 0632, New Zealand (a division of Pearson New Zealand Ltd) ☆ Penguin Books (South Africa) (Pty) Ltd, 24 Sturdee Avenue, Rosebank, Johannesburg 2196, South Africa

Penguin Books Ltd, Registered Offices:
80 Strand, London WC2R 0RL, England

First published in 2012 by Viking Penguin,
a member of Penguin Group (USA) Inc.

3 5 7 9 10 8 6 4 2

Portions of this book appeared in different form as
"Goodbye to All That: Reflections of a GOP Operative Who Left the Cult,"
Truthout, September 3, 2011.

LIBRARY OF CONGRESS CATALOGING IN PUBLICATION DATA
Lofgren, Mike.
The party is over : how Republicans went crazy, Democrats became useless,
and the middle class got shafted / Mike Lofgren.
p. cm.
Includes bibliographical references and index.
ISBN 978-0-670-02626-5
1. Republican Party (U.S. : 1854–)—History—20th century. 2. Republican Party (U.S. : 1854–)—History—21st century. 3. Democratic Party (U.S.)—History—20th century. 4. Democratic Party (U.S.)—History—21st century. 5. Political parties—United States—History—20th century. 6. Political parties—United States—History—21st century. I. Title.

Printed in the United States of America
Set in Haarlemmer MT Std with Memphis LT Std
Designed by Daniel Lagin

This book is dedicated to the memory of

Earnest Walter Lofgren

Son of working-class Swedish immigrants, child of the Great Depression, honorable veteran of the Pacific campaign, beneficiary of the GI Bill of Rights, and holder of an advanced university degree, for patiently endeavoring to instill in his children his abiding belief in learning

CONTENTS

INTRODUCTION

This book is about America's broken political system: how it got that way, who benefits, and who loses. It is about the growing domination of the legislative process by corporate money and the corresponding decline of a broad public interest. It is about how politicians use intensely polarizing ideological issues as bait to energize their political bases—and to divert those followers away from focusing on the one overriding political issue in our society: who gets what.

As America's political dysfunction has grown worse, the economic stagnation of the middle class has deepened. This is not a result of blind economic forces, Adam Smith's invisible hand, globalization, or some other nebulous cause. Specific committees of Congress, inevitably assisted by specific K Street lobbyists, wrote legislation that achieved this result.

Why am I so sure of what I say? I worked in Congress for twenty-eight years, most of the time as a professional staff member analyzing legislation for the House and Senate budget committees. For the first twelve years I worked for John Kasich, a Republican member of the House Armed Services Committee, and my fiefdom was national security. Then I switched to the House Budget Committee when Kasich became chairman. Finally, I moved to the Senate Budget Committee under the chairmanship of Senator Judd Gregg (R-New Hampshire). My duties gave me an invaluable perspective on

government budgeting, and particularly on budgeting for national security. And they enabled me to understand that when politicians claim they will cut taxes, wage war around the planet, and balance the budget at the same time, they are spouting rank falsehoods. I was in the privileged position to see how Congress works on the inside, when the C-SPAN cameras are turned off. What I saw was not Civics 101 or *Jefferson's Manual* but an auction where political services are won by the highest bidder.

I was compelled to write this book because I became alarmed by the trends I was seeing. In particular, my own party, the Republican Party, began to scare me. After the 2008 election, Republican politicians became more and more intransigently dogmatic. They doubled down on advancing policies that transparently favored the top 1 percent of earners in this country while obstructing measures such as the extension of unemployment insurance. They seemed to want to comfort the comfortable and afflict the afflicted in the middle of the worst economic meltdown in eighty years.

And there was worse to come. Whether it was Representative Joe Wilson (R-South Carolina) boorishly yelling "You lie!"—unprecedented behavior during a joint meeting of Congress assembled to hear a presidential address—or the obscene carnival of birtherism, Obama-the-secret-Muslim, death panels, and all the rest of it, the party took on a nasty, bullying, crazy edge. From my vantage point on the budget committee I watched with a mixture of fascination and foreboding as my party was hijacked by a new crop of opportunists and true believers hell-bent on dragging the country into their jerry-built New Jerusalem: an upside-down utopia in which corporations rule; the Constitution, like science, is faith based; and war is the first, not the last, resort in foreign policy.

I suspect many of these politicians never believed what they were saying but were cynically playing to an increasingly deranged

political base that *does* believe it. Television viewers could observe the outcome of this strategy in September 2011, when the partisan audience invited to view the Republican presidential candidates' debate at the Reagan Library in California cheered and clapped at the mentions of executions and the prospect of letting the uninsured die.

Do Democrats offer a sane alternative? The explanation is more complicated, but the answer is, finally, no. They have not become an extremist party like the GOP—their politicians do not match the current crop of zanies who infest the Republican Party—but their problem lies in the opposite direction. It is not that they are fanatics or zealots; it is that most do not appear to believe in *anything* very strongly. Democrats who expect this book to be a diatribe against Republicans alone will be disappointed. The GOP has gone off the rails—it is the party I know best, and which I will describe in greater detail. But its sorry situation is a symptom of a deeper dysfunction in American politics and society for which Democrats own a considerable share of the responsibility.

The Democratic Party coasted far too long on Franklin D. Roosevelt's legacy. It became complacent and began to feel entitled to its near hegemonic position in politics, culture, and the media. When the New Right increasingly began to displace it in all three of those arenas, some liberals merely turned into ineffectual whiners and crybabies or ivory tower escapists. The bulk of Democratic politicians and operatives, however, moved in a different direction. After three straight losses in presidential elections between 1980 and 1988, they abandoned the practices of their old beliefs while continuing to espouse them in theory. These new Democrats will say anything to win an election—an objective that, in their minds, generally requires them to emulate Republicans, particularly with respect to moneygrubbing on the fund-raising circuit. Many of

them last only a term or two, because if people want a Republican, they will vote for the real thing. What has evolved in America over the last three decades is a one-and-a-half-party system, as Democrats opportunistically cleave to the "center," which, in the relativistic universe of American politics, keeps moving further to the right.

The current political dynamic is beginning to defeat the optimistic expectations of James Madison. As one of the chief architects of our federal system, Madison believed that competing factional interests would balance out one another, and that the government, like Newtonian clockwork, would keep on ticking. In times of general social harmony and tolerably shared prosperity, this theory worked well enough: Big business and big labor roughly balanced each other. But this balance has fallen terribly askew in the last thirty years. Unions ceased to be the political power and source of campaign funding they once were. Democrats increasingly turned to Wall Street and corporate America for handouts as the cost of elections kept rising. The legacy of this Faustian bargain is an ambivalent, hesitant, and split-minded party: still half-heartedly regarding itself as the party of the New Deal, the common man, the working stiff, but at the same time advancing the agenda of the corporate donors who call the shots. Money has overtaken politics so completely that factional interests are now simply competing to buy votes.

James Fallows has pointed out the shortcomings of the balance theory in the modern context: "The major parts of our political establishment are both showing operational pathologies that *each makes the other's failings worse*, rather than somehow buffering each other toward a harmonious best-of-both-worlds compromise result."[1] From what I have seen in Congress, Fallows is right: Whenever Democrats and Republicans achieve "bipartisan compromise,"

which generally happens when it comes time to restrict constitutional rights and put the next $100 billion installment for our endless wars on the national credit card, the public loses.

☆

It has been little more than a decade since a secretary of state in a Democratic administration smugly declared that the United States was "the indispensable nation." Self-satisfied pundits extolled the United States not only as the sole remaining superpower but as a *hyperpower.* A few years after that, operatives in a Republican administration pronounced the invasion of Iraq "a cakewalk" and opined that the "Greater Middle East" was yearning for the healing touch of American liberators, armed to the teeth.

In the second decade of the twenty-first century, the American establishment's bipartisan vaunting and hubris have turned to ashes. It is not by happenstance that America today looks more like a Third World country than an advanced industrial state in international comparisons of social health such as longevity, infant mortality, income distribution, social mobility, labor protection, average number of vacation days, and many other metrics. Our tax policies have ensured that the rich got richer and the rest of us got stuck with the bill. Congressional obedience to corporatized medicine ensured that Americans pay an average of 50 percent more for their health care than citizens in Western Europe. Union busting, leveraged buyouts, and the offshoring of jobs guaranteed lower wages and fewer labor protections. According to the International Monetary Fund (IMF), China—Communist China!—is on track to have a gross domestic product greater than that of the United States by 2016.

In my early youth, when tail-finned Plymouths and porthole Buicks cruised the brick-paved streets of my midwestern home-

town, we were told to clean our plates and not let the food go to waste. Had we no appreciation? There were starving children in Europe! Europe, mind you—which now has an aggregate GDP greater than that of the United States. As for China, it barely registered at the time. Chinese peasants in 1959 were eating tree bark and grass and living in little better than Bronze Age conditions courtesy of Chairman Mao and his Great Leap Forward. Now, thanks to the money men, arbitrageurs, buyout artists, and the politicians they rent, much of the former American industrial base resides in China.

Charles de Gaulle once said that the graveyards are full of indispensable men, and so it is with nations. As a historian by training, I have bad news for the political establishment in Washington: There is no divine plan guaranteeing America's global preeminence. There is also no divine plan mandating that the American middle class shall remain in existence forever. If the politicians running this country continue to pursue ideological chimeras and cater to the narrow, short-run desires of moneyed elites and extremist pressure groups while neglecting the broader national interest, we might as well resign ourselves to taking a place among the former great powers of history.

The downgrading of U.S. sovereign debt by Standard & Poor's during the summer of 2011 was an epochal event—the first credit downgrade of our nation since the ratings began in 1917. Read that credit report carefully. It was not a downgrade based on America's technical inability to redeem its debt instruments; it was primarily dictated by the political dysfunction in Washington and the expectation that things will not get better anytime soon. The rating agency turned out to be right: The ineffectuality of the so-called super committee (officially the Joint Select Committee on Deficit Reduction) a few months later, the payroll tax farce during the Christmas season, and the prospect of more government shut-

downs to come plainly show that partisan rancor is making the day-to-day process of orderly governance impossible.

This breakdown is not unique in the world. Regardless of what the apostles of American Exceptionalism may say, the United States cannot isolate itself from the tide of international events. Our malaise is part of a global governance crisis and a breakdown of laissez-faire economics. Europe, once a nearly miraculous example of stability and prosperity after its phoenixlike rise from the ashes of World War II, is experiencing an existential turning point that will decide whether peaceful and democratic integration continues or the continent regresses to a cockpit of rivalry. Political change is sweeping North Africa and the Middle East—including in some of the states that have been clients of our fading global hegemony. Even the Russian people, assumed to have been resigned to the arctic chill of authoritarian "guided" democracy, have grown restless.

A warning about decline should not be a counsel of despair. A look at basic material factors will show that the United States is not in nearly as bleak a position as our present predicament suggests. It is a continent-sized country lying mostly in the temperate zone, bounded on two sides by the largest moats in the world. It has three hundred million inhabitants who can supply a tremendous pool of human capital. It has a greater quantity of productive arable land in a suitable climate than any other country and a staggering array of natural resources—both of which a wise government would use carefully as it stewards them for the benefit of generations unborn. Compared to Greece, a rocky southern outlier of the Balkan Mountains living on foreign tourism and controlling neither its currency nor its economic policy, the substantive difficulties of the United States are trivial. America's problems are at root political problems of our own making, the result of destructive habits of mind, and these factors are amenable to solutions we can devise.

According to a CBS/New York Times poll, Congress's favorability rating stands at 9 percent, the lowest since polling began.[2] Even the prospect of "America going communist" has higher public favorability, at 11 percent, than our legislative branch. Some of this cynicism and disenchantment is the result of deliberate political engineering to make Americans lose faith in their government, as we shall see later in this book. But Americans are angry all the same, and they have cause to be angry.

Political anger can be a constructive thing. Not the blind, unthinking anger of those who have been carefully worked into a perpetual rage by the expertly trained pitchmen of political talk radio, or the anger of the single-issue zealot or culture warrior, but the steady, rational indignation of the fully informed citizen about the fact that his rights and privileges are being usurped, and that his heritage is being squandered.

This is that story as I saw it unfold—the story of the seizure of our political system by special interests—and what I believe must be done to reverse this process.

1

THE PARTY OF LINCOLN, THE PARTY OF JEFFERSON

What is the Republican Party like? What are the Democrats like? Why is there so little difference between them? And how did they get this way?

Barbara Stanwyck: "We're both rotten!"
Fred MacMurray: "Only you're a little more rotten."

—*Double Indemnity* (1944)

Those lines of dialogue from a classic film noir sum up the state of the two political parties in contemporary America. Both parties are rotten—how could they not be? The complete infestation of the political system by corporate money now requires a presidential candidate to raise upward of a billion dollars to be competitive in the general election. But the parties are not rotten in quite the same ways. Democrats have their share of machine politicians, careerists, corporate bagmen, egomaniacs, and kooks. None of them, however, quite match the members of the modern GOP.

To those millions of Americans who watched with exasperation the tragicomedy of summer 2011's debt-ceiling extension crisis, it might have come as a shock that the Republican Party is so full

of lunatics. To be sure, like any political party on Earth, the GOP has always had its share of crackpots, such as Robert K. Dornan or William E. Dannemeyer in past Congresses. But the crackpot outliers of two decades ago have become the vital core today: Eric Cantor, Steve King, Michele Bachmann, Paul Broun, Patrick McHenry, Virginia Foxx, Louie Gohmert, and Allen West. The *Congressional Directory* now reads like a casebook of lunacy. This is not to say that such specimens represent all or even most Republicans, but they have managed, through their shrillness, dogmatism, inflexibility, and belligerence, to become the center of gravity of the party. The Republican Speaker of the House, the constitutionally designated third-ranking elected official in the government, does not issue orders to them; he takes orders from them, as all of America saw during the debt-limit negotiations and the payroll tax fight.

It was this cast of characters and the pernicious ideas they represent that drove me to end a nearly thirty-year career in government: Last summer, I retired. I could see long before it happened that the Republican Party would use the debt-limit vote, an otherwise routine legislative procedure undertaken eighty-seven times since the end of World War II, to concoct an entirely artificial fiscal crisis. Then they would use that alleged fiscal crisis, literally holding the United States' and global economies hostage, to get what they wanted.

How did the Republican Party, the party of Lincoln, Theodore Roosevelt, Robert Taft, and Eisenhower, metamorphose into the intensely ideological, almost cultlike grouping of today? And how did it come to pass that the Democratic Party, the only other choice in America's ossified two-party political regime, should offer so little by way of an alternative?

☆

When I entered government in the early 1980s, the Republican Party could plausibly represent itself as a pragmatic alternative to the Democrats, who still carried a stigma from the 1960s as a party of social engineering and ideological excess. The debacle of the 1968 Democratic presidential convention in Chicago, where riots broke out, led television viewers to conclude that the Democrats could no longer govern. Back then the GOP had a moderate wing of considerable influence. People such as Senator Howard Baker, who was known as "the Great Conciliator," and Representative Bob Michel (the Republican leader in the House) had stature in the party. These were politicians of the old school, who could reach across the aisle, make a deal, and stick to it. Ronald Reagan himself, the icon and dream figure of present-day Republicans, had little reluctance to negotiate over issues of taxing and spending, declare the resulting compromise a victory, and move on.

Bipartisan coalitions were still possible back then. My first job was as a legislative assistant for Representative Kasich, who was a strongly conservative fiscal hawk from my home state of Ohio. But he was able to join forces with Ron Dellums, then one of the most liberal Democrats in Congress, to propose limits on the production of the horrendously expensive B-2 bomber to save taxpayers billions of dollars. I knew, as a staff vote counter for the project, that their coalition was well on its way to getting the majority they would need to win if a vote was called. Apparently the vote counters at the Pentagon came to the same conclusion: The Department of Defense killed further production of B-2s to avoid an embarrassing vote on the floor of the House. Congressional coalitions of this type are nearly extinct today. The only thing remotely similar since the 2008 election has been the quixotic antiwar alliance between Ron Paul and Dennis Kucinich, but both are pariahs in their own parties and rarely muster more than a handful of votes in favor of their propos-

als. And Kucinich, redistricted out of his congressional seat, will not be returning to Congress after the 2012 election.

The GOP has been gradually shedding its status as a broad coalition party and has started demanding litmus tests on fiscal, social, and foreign policy issues. There were signposts on the road ahead—the Gingrich revolution of 1995, the Clinton impeachment circus—but things got much worse after September 11, with the massive infringements of civil liberties that followed and the bluster and bravado that preceded the invasion of Iraq. By the 2010 midterm election the party had collectively lost its mind. The evidence is all around us: the debt ceiling debacle, the kamikaze politics over the payroll tax cut extension, the freak show of the Republican presidential debates. How did this happen?

Under the influence of political consultants such as Karl Rove, the GOP decided that educated and affluent (but not necessarily rich) suburban voters could be taken for granted to vote for them as the "natural governing party." The party could thus focus on gaining new adherents by sharpening its differences with the opposition. They soon discovered that they could accomplish this by promoting divisive "culture wars," and turned their focus to issues such as abortion and gay marriage. Party operatives sought to paint the Democrats as appeasers—weak on defense and uninterested in keeping the American people safe. They attacked them as faithless namby-pambys, urban elites who were out of touch with the American heartland. Their strategy reaped dividends—in 1994, Republicans captured both the House and Senate for the first time in forty years, for a twelve-year run—and it led to the party's fielding new candidates who were rabidly zealous on these issues, among others. The GOP fell increasingly under the influence of theocratic fundamentalists eager to use the resources of the state to regulate private behavior, and of neoconservative chicken hawks—some of them

ex-Democrats—who never saw a war they didn't want somebody else's kid to fight.

Republicans have traditionally been more solicitous toward the interests of the wealthy and their enterprises than their Democratic counterparts—though this did not prevent Dwight Eisenhower from seeking to maintain a high marginal tax rate on the wealthy or Ronald Reagan from saying that wages should not be taxed at a higher rate than capital. But the party has increasingly, and with single-minded focus since Barack Obama's election, devoted itself exclusively to the interests of the wealthy. Knowing that the remaining 99 percent of the population would have a hard time becoming enthusiastic over a party platform that nakedly proclaimed itself devoted to the advancement of the rich, the GOP has confected a shrewd marketing campaign: play up the culture wars and demagogue national security issues to distract voters from their real intentions. It did not take long for clever political consultants to realize that, in the absence of critical and analytical news media, the most assertive and repetitive voice will win the argument. Also, the GOP reflexively scorns so-called elites (by which it means educated, critical thinkers) to mask the way it is utterly beholden to the true American elite: the plutocracy that runs the country.

I would like to be able to contrast this characterization with a positive one of the Democrats, the supposed party of the people, to make this book a neat and simple morality tale. But the Democrats at this time offer only a weak and tepid alternative. Why? They are also in the tank with wealthy contributors.

Democrats expressed outrage, and justifiably so, at the sole-source contracts the Bush administration gave to Halliburton after the invasion of Iraq, but what do they say now about the loan guarantees the Obama administration granted to Solyndra, a now de-

funct solar power company whose campaign donations flowed to the Democratic Party?

☆

In its *Citizens United* decision in 2010, the Supreme Court ruled that corporations could spend unlimited amounts to influence elections, equating corporate money with free speech. The usual flood of money into Washington has since become an uncontrollable torrent. This further loosening of restrictions on fund-raising engendered the creation of so-called super PACs, whose donors can remain anonymous. Just one of these super PACs, Karl Rove's American Crossroads, expects to raise $250 million for the 2012 elections.

We may soon be on the verge of building the perverse utopia envisioned by the reactionary billionaire H. L. Hunt in the 1960s. Hunt, who won the deed to a huge stake in the East Texas oil fields in a poker game in 1930, attributed his wealth not just to a bit of luck and business acumen, but to his own unique moral and civic virtue. After funding the right-wing senator Joe McCarthy and the John Birch Society in the 1950s, he turned to more visionary projects. In his 1960 vanity-published book *Alpaca* he limned what he held to be an ideal society: one that grants the wealthy more votes than citizens of modest means.

The *Citizens United* decision has brought the country closer to Hunt's plutocratic utopia than we've ever been. And it has brought the Supreme Court itself back to the mental atmosphere of the 1886 Court, when a headnote—a comment not written by one of the justices—of the opinion in a case, *Santa Clara County v. Southern Pacific Railroad*, laid the foundation of "corporate personhood" and established the precedence of corporate prerogatives over citizens' rights. In those days, though, the citizenry was made of

tougher stuff. A vigorous third-party movement arose to challenge the decision. Though the People's Party ("Populists") did not achieve national power in its own right, it mobilized public opinion behind a reform movement to roll back the oligarchs' privileges. And it was at least partially successful. Its 1892 Omaha platform called out the highest court, along with the rest of the political apparatus, as rotten:

> We meet in the midst of a nation brought to the verge of moral, political, and material ruin. Corruption dominates the ballot-box, the Legislatures, the Congress, and touches even the ermine of the bench. The people are demoralized. . . . The newspapers are largely subsidized or muzzled, public opinion silenced, business prostrated, homes covered with mortgages, labor impoverished, and the land concentrating in the hands of capitalists. The urban workmen are denied the right to organize for self-protection, imported pauperized labor beats down their wages. . . . The fruits of the toil of millions are boldly stolen to build up colossal fortunes for a few, unprecedented in the history of mankind, and the possessors of these, in turn, despise the Republic and endanger liberty. From the same prolific womb of governmental injustice we breed the two great classes—tramps and millionaires.

While the Populists disappeared a few years later, much of their platform found its way into the programs of the Democratic Party and the progressive wing of the GOP under Theodore Roosevelt. Our progressive income tax system, the direct election of senators, and antitrust laws are just a few of their legacies.

Our party duopoly is one of the most locked-in and rigged systems among the nations that are commonly thought of as the West-

ern democracies. It is next to impossible now for any third party to break into this system in the way the then new third-party Republicans did in the 1850s, though many have tried. And even that example does not tell the whole story: The 1850s Republicans basically picked up the torch from the antislavery wing of the dying Whig Party. We have never had three viable parties at any one time in over two hundred years.

The Democrats and the GOP, on both the federal and state levels, are in various disguised ways written into electoral law (a practice finding no support in the Constitution), and this contrivance presents a decisive hurdle against almost all new entrants. Democrats and Republicans are almost automatically on the ballot. Third-party candidates, by contrast, must overcome onerous petition requirements, and since the state legislatures that set the qualifying regulations and draw up the voting districts are occupied exclusively by Democrats and Republicans, those who are dissatisfied with both parties are effectively disenfranchised.

As a practical matter, voters can only express dissatisfaction with the established party that happens to be in power by voting for the other established party. In 2006 and 2008, voters were angry with the Republicans, so they voted for the Democrats. Then, in 2010, they were angry with the Democrats, so they voted for the GOP. What they will do in 2012 is an open question. But we can be sure of one thing: Regardless of who wins in November 2012, the campaign for the 2014 congressional elections will begin on the day after the vote, and by January 2013 we shall start hearing about likely prospects for the 2016 presidential contest. The United States is unique in that it operates in permanent campaign mode; campaign seasons in most European countries are limited by law to a few weeks or months.

The shortcomings of the American electoral system are

thrown into ironic relief whenever the international arms of the two main parties, the National Democratic Institute (NDI) and the International Republican Institute (IRI), scold some foreign country for its political misdeeds. Yes, you read that right: The two parties have international offshoots operating abroad. Although organized as nonprofit entities legally separate from their parent parties, they carry those parties' ideological baggage much as the Comintern was the cat's-paw of the Soviet Communist Party. And they are funded by your tax dollars: Both NDI and IRI are categorized as 501(c)3 "charitable" organizations by the Internal Revenue Service, but they receive the vast bulk of their money not from private donors, who can consequently take tax deductions, but from federal funds appropriated to official government entities such as the State Department, the United States Agency for International Development, and the National Endowment for Democracy.

And what do these august bodies do, aside from supplying résumé-building slots for party operatives and board memberships for partisan officeholders burnishing their credentials as statesmen? While they are forbidden by law from providing direct funding to foreign political parties (that would be too much like the old days, when the CIA funneled subsidies through fake foundations to favored parties abroad), they accomplish nearly the same result by indirect support through get-out-the-vote strategies, "voter education," election monitoring, or favorable international publicity for the political party they prefer.

In 2011, both organizations criticized Ukraine for inhibiting new political parties' access to the ballot. How Ukraine's system differs from our own practices that restrict third-party ballot access is unclear. They also criticized Ukraine for having a system of plurality victors with no subsequent run-off vote. Again, it is not

obvious how this differs from our own system: One has only to glance back to the American presidential elections of 1992 and 1996, when the winner did not gain a majority of the popular vote, not to mention that of 2000, when the candidate with fewer votes than his major party competitor went on to become president.

Whether and how to increase access to the ballot for third parties is a complex problem, and efforts to solve it could have many unintended consequences. The same applies to rules governing how elections are decided or how electoral districts should be determined. But for the international arms of our two political parties—dependent on government funds as they are—to complain when other countries practice what has long been established here by law is a uniquely American characteristic: a blindness about the supposed perfection of our venerable democratic system of governance married to a habit of lecturing everybody under the sun. It is the same hypocrisy and arrogance that is regularly on display when the secretary of state condemns other countries for practicing torture or involvement in extrajudicial killings.

The police and petty bureaucrats in many Third World countries are openly corrupt and will take bribes in order to augment their miserable salaries. In the United States it is relatively difficult to bribe a cop to get out of a traffic ticket or to slip money to a DMV functionary to get preferential treatment. You need to go higher up the governmental food chain in order to practice corruption successfully. But you can find bribery and corruption just about anytime, year-round, in Washington. It is called a fund-raiser, when a congress member's campaign committee rents a room in a restaurant and invites a hundred or so of his or her closest friends from the lobbying shops on K Street, from industry, and from the trade

associations. I've been to a few of these over the years and often wondered whether any of the Gucci-shod participants in their two-thousand-dollar suits and monogrammed shirts imagined that they were righteously engaged in the constitutional practice of petitioning for the redress of grievances as they handed over their checks before tucking into the hors d'oeuvres.

Bill Moyers has denounced these activities as money laundering, and paints an equally unflattering portrait of each party:

> John Boehner calls on the bankers, holds out his cup, and offers them total obeisance from the House majority if only they fill it. That's now the norm, and they get away with it. GOP once again means Guardians of Privilege. Barack Obama criticizes bankers as "fat cats," and then invites them to dine at a pricey New York restaurant, where the tasting menu runs to $195 a person. That's now the norm, and they get away with it. The president has raised more money from banks, hedge funds, and private equity managers than any Republican candidate, including Mitt Romney. Inch by inch he has conceded ground to them while espousing populist rhetoric that his very actions betray.[1]

During the last thirty years, the American political system has been growing ever more dysfunctional as the cost of entry for candidates has become higher and higher. The election of 1980, when John Anderson received a respectable number of votes, may have been the last time a third-party candidate without lavish financing will have been able to do even moderately well in a presidential contest. (Ross Perot's challenge in 1992 was only feasible because he was a billionaire who could self-fund his campaign.) It is not a coincidence that as more and more money has infected the two parties,

their concern for the well-being of the vast majority of the American people has declined. The expensive political ads that pollute television after Labor Day during an election year may ooze with empathy for Joe Average, but actions speak louder than words.

It is no coincidence that as the Supreme Court has been removing the last constraints on the legalized corruption of politicians, the American standard of living has been falling at the fastest rate in decades. According to the *Christian Science Monitor*, the average individual now has $1,315 less in disposable income than he or she did three years ago, at the onset of the Great Recession at the beginning of 2008.[2] This is not only a decline when measured against our own past economic performance; it also represents a decline relative to other countries, a far cry from the post–World War II era, when the United States had by any measure the highest living standard in the world. A study by the Bertelsmann Foundation concluded that in measures of economic equality, social mobility, and poverty prevention, the United States ranks twenty-seventh out of the thirty-one advanced industrial nations belonging to the Organization for Economic Cooperation and Development. Thank God we are still ahead of Turkey, Chile, and Mexico![3]

But what does some European foundation know? The Congressional Budget Office (CBO), Congress's own budget score-keeping and economic analysis arm, which is regarded as nonpartisan and objective, reported in October 2011 that the richest 1 percent of U.S. households had doubled their share of gross income from 10 percent to 20 percent since 1979, while that of everyone else had gone down.[4] Ironically, the same day the CBO released its report, Representative Paul Ryan (R-Wisconsin), the chairman of the House Budget Committee, was reminding us yet again that even the tepid rhetoric and timid policies of President Obama amounted to "class warfare," and that Republican policies would preserve

"equality of opportunity. . . . Telling people they are stuck in their current station in life, that they are victims of circumstances beyond their control, and that the government's role is to help them cope with it—well, that's not who we are."

I should say it certainly is not. But who exactly are they, then? At the same time the CBO issued its report and Ryan made his speech, GOP presidential candidate Herman Cain was surging in popularity among the Republican base. Cain's claim to fame was a tax plan even more regressive than the current revenue system, which already taxes labor more heavily than capital; his jobs policy was a model of businesslike concision: "If you don't have a job, blame yourself!"

In the midst of the greatest and most protracted economic slump in eighty years, Cain's quip was similar in spirit to the proposal suggested by Andrew K. Mellon, President Herbert Hoover's secretary of the treasury, for dealing with the Great Depression—with the same dash of Calvinistic disdain for the destitute:

> Liquidate labor, liquidate stocks, liquidate the farmers, liquidate real estate. . . . It will purge the rottenness out of the system. High costs of living and high living will come down. People will work harder, live a more moral life. Values will be adjusted, and enterprising people will pick up the wrecks from less competent people.[5]

What America first experienced as tragedy the present generation must relive as farce.

Let us now dispose of the quaint notion that the present-day Republican Party is conservative. It has no vestige of conservatism as I once knew it, meaning prudence, caution, the tried and tested. The 1950s, when a Republican president occupied the White House, was a period of substantial real economic growth and shared

prosperity—along with a 91 percent top marginal tax rate on individual incomes, while corporate tax revenues were a markedly higher share of total federal revenue than today. President Eisenhower denounced attempts to reduce the tax rates as fiscally irresponsible. In view of the current $15 trillion national debt, perhaps Ike was right after all. Can one imagine a Republican officeholder today advocating Eisenhower's tax policies?

A seemingly trivial but telling clue that the Republican Party is no longer a conservative but rather a radical right-wing party lies in the popular choice of colors to denote the two parties. It may not have been a conscious decision, but it is in retrospect appropriate that during the 2000 election all the television networks settled on red for the GOP and blue for the Democrats. Since the French Revolution, red has consistently been the emblem of upheaval and disruption in Western nations. Blue was just as surely associated with conservatism and tradition. The traditional psychology of colors in areas of life outside politics would seem to confirm this choice. Corporate directors do not wear red pinstriped suits to connote solidity, trustworthiness, and a reliable dividend for shareholders. Only blue will do, for red is the color of instability and change. "Better dead than red!" used to be the conservatives' motto.

How is it that the media upended this social convention in 2000 with its selection of colors to designate states on studio graphics? Why do self-described conservatives now proudly proclaim themselves as "red," or "red staters"? By the 2000 election, and certainly after 9/11, the Republican Party was no longer a conservative party in the traditional sense, as that word has been understood in Western political culture. Its belief in polarizing language and tactics, a militant and militarized foreign policy, and a constant search for mortal enemies, foreign and domestic alike, qualifies the current GOP as a radical right-wing party, not a conservative one. In his

flawed but occasionally insightful book *Democracy and Populism: Fear and Hatred*, historian John Lukacs reminds us that "right wing" is not a synonym for conservative, and is not even a true variant of conservatism, although the right wing will opportunistically borrow conservative themes as the need arises. Hence, red is an appropriate color for a radical party like the present-day GOP.

But isn't that clue contradicted by Republicans' constant invocation of a "better" America that supposedly existed in the past, along with their appeal to traditional values that our ancestors allegedly kept better than we do? One branch of the American so-called conservative movement, the paleoconservatives, has honed this fetish for a lost Arcadia to an almost comic extent.* As the images of imagined pasts are sullied by some ideological defect, the paleocons keep pushing further back into the mists of time. The 1950s of *Ozzie and Harriet*, which most conventional right-wingers see in a nostalgic soft focus, was spoiled for paleoconservatives by the statist legacy of FDR. Most paleos have settled on pre–Civil War America as the golden age of their imaginations. Scratch many a paleoconservative and you will find a neo-Confederate at heart.

This romanticization of an idealized time, coupled with a ruthless leveling of traditional institutions, such as Medicare, the departments of energy and education, and the regulatory framework that has been around since the Progressive Era, has been an ever-present feature of radical right-wing movements during the twentieth century. Republican figures such as Sarah Palin, who appeal to a backward-looking "real" America in their rhetoric, somehow manage to reconcile themselves to the less romantic destruction of

---

* Some of the paleoconservatives, such as Pat Buchanan, are Republican partisans, while others profess to be alienated from electoral politics altogether, ostensibly because the Republican Party is too liberal for them.

tradition and social stability by laissez-faire capitalism. Let's face it: The Republican Party is no longer a broad-based conservative party in the historically accepted sense. It is an oligarchy with a well-developed public relations strategy designed to soothe and anesthetize its followers with appeals to tradition, security, and family even as it pursues a radical agenda that would transform the country into a Dickensian corporatocracy at home and a belligerent military empire abroad.

Against that radical Republican program the Democrats offer . . . nothing much at all. And from time to time, as we shall see, they reinforce the agenda of those who are ostensibly their opponents.

That is the Republican Party as I experienced it and the Democratic Party as I saw it at a slight distance. After the 2010 midterm election I felt the time had come for me to say good-bye to all that. There were too many logical contradictions and moral conflicts. All professional careers have their ups and downs, and on the whole, mine was a successful one that I could leave without regret or rancor. I made many good friends on the Hill, and I departed the institution on good terms with everyone. No doubt I have fewer friends now; so be it. But this book is not a confessional about personalities or relationships. It is an explanation, based on what I saw, of the dysfunction in our political system, and an assessment of what it means for our domestic prosperity, our constitutional freedoms, and our future standing in the world.

2

TACTICS: WAR MINUS THE SHOOTING

The Republican Party has used objection, obstruction, and filibustering not only to block the necessary processes of government but also in order to make ordinary Americans deeply cynical about Washington. Republicans perpetually run against government and come out on top. But, in the process, they are undermining the foundations of self-rule in a representative democracy.

All men can see these tactics whereby I conquer, but what none can see is the strategy out of which victory is evolved.

—Sun Tzu

If the American people were interested in discovering the real reasons why they are so disenchanted with government, they would do well to focus less on the campaign horse race and the personality quirks of individual candidates and more on how laws are made and the tactics used by both parties to gain parliamentary advantage. Far from being boring high school Civics 101 stuff, this is the mechanism by which governance happens—or, increasingly, does not happen.

The U.S. Senate has more complex procedural rules than any

other legislative body in the world; many of these rules are contradictory, and on any given day the Senate parliamentarian may issue a ruling that contradicts earlier rulings on analogous cases. The only thing that can keep the Senate functioning is collegiality and good faith. During periods of political consensus, such as we experienced during World War II and immediately after the war, the Senate is generally a high-functioning institution: Filibusters are rare, and the body is legislatively productive. But when there is no consensus, it is practically a miracle if any major legislation is passed. One can no more picture our current Senate producing the original Medicare act than one can imagine the Supreme Soviet passing the Bill of Rights.

Almost every bill, nominee for Senate confirmation, and routine procedural motion is nowadays subject to a Republican filibuster. It is no wonder that Washington is gridlocked: Legislating has become war minus the shooting, much as it was eighty years ago in the Weimar Republic. As Hannah Arendt observed then, a disciplined totalitarian minority can use the instruments of democratic government to undermine democracy itself. Something along these lines is at work nowadays on Capitol Hill.

During the 112th Congress obstructionism reached the level of hostage taking every few months. Everyone knows that in a hostage situation, the reckless and amoral actor has the upper hand in the negotiations, because the cautious and responsible actor is concerned about the life of the hostage, while the former does not care. The debt-ceiling extension is not the only recent example of this sort of political terrorism. Republicans were willing to lay off four thousand Federal Aviation Administration employees and seventy thousand private construction workers, and to let FAA safety inspectors work without pay—in fact, to force them to pay for their own work-related travel; how prudent is that?—in order to

strong-arm some union-busting provisions into the FAA reauthorization.

The GOP's thirst for confrontation and crisis is symptomatic of a destructive and nihilistic streak that has overtaken our political system. When one party repudiates the whole concept of compromise, it is inevitable that the government will lurch from one crisis to another. Long gone are the days of cautious and prudential conservatism. Observing the Republican obstruction during the debt-ceiling crisis of summer 2011, John B. Judis summed up the modern GOP this way:

> Over the last four decades, the Republican Party has transformed from a loyal opposition into an insurrectionary party that flouts the law when it is in the majority and threatens disorder when it is the minority. It is the party of Watergate and Iran-Contra, but also of the government shutdown in 1995 and the impeachment trial of 1999. If there is an earlier American precedent for today's Republican Party, it is the antebellum Southern Democrats of John Calhoun who threatened to nullify, or disregard, federal legislation they objected to, and who later led the fight to secede from the union over slavery.[1]

It is a truism that most people, whatever their trade or profession, want to believe that they are engaged in a useful and socially constructive endeavor, that given the option they would like to be proud of where they work and what they do. A couple of years ago a Republican committee staff director told me candidly (and proudly) that there was a method to all this obstruction and disruption. Should Republicans succeed in preventing the Senate from doing its job, it would further lower Congress's favorability rating among

the American people. In such a scenario the party that presents itself as programmatically against government—i.e., the Republican Party—will come out the relative winner. As someone who came to Washington believing that it was a privilege to do the public's business on Capitol Hill, I found this admission—or, rather, boast—troubling.

The GOP has become more open about this tactic in recent months. In January 2012, House Republican leader Eric Cantor informed the press that tax and health care legislation would be decided by the election. What he was really saying was that all legislation on taxes or health care—both central to improving the economic climate in the most severe and protracted period of economic distress since World War II—were off the table before November 2012. The media were too obtuse to notice that this was not a case of Congress not being able to get its act together. It was a case of the House Republican leader saying he would obstruct major legislation that might affect our economic recovery for an entire congressional session.

It was not always thus. In the 1980s, when I came to Washington, disposition of legislation was markedly less partisan than is the norm today. To give an example I am familiar with, let's take a quick look at the House and Senate conference to reconcile their respective defense authorization bills to establish our military policy. (During the time Representative Kasich was on the Armed Services Committee, I had a chance to watch the process up close.) In general, members of the House and the Senate defended their versions of the bill in conference regardless of their party. Thus, the division of opinion, once a bill had reached the conference committee, tended to be House versus Senate rather than Democrat versus Republican. There were significant exceptions, of course, but the usual practice was to hash out a piece of legislation

that the president would sign, rather than using the bill as a vehicle for press releases and ideological posturing. The latter is the norm today. These days the resulting piece of legislation is loaded with policy riders to rev up the parties' political bases—believe it or not, abortion amendments are often inserted in defense authorization bills—and it generally arrives on the president's desk several months late.

In those halcyon days of Reagan's America that our current crop of Republicans so love to invoke, conference committees had a markedly different feel from those of today. Select members of the respective House and Senate committees came together in an effort to produce a compromise measure that they could actually send to the president in the expectation that he would sign it. There were plenary sessions with all, or most, members in attendance during which points of difference were debated and motions that might satisfy both sides were offered. It was generally businesslike, as people concentrated on resolving substantive matters.

Thanks to the Gingrich revolution of the mid-1990s, most of today's rare conference committee meetings have all the substance and spontaneity of a North Korean party congress. Their sole purpose is to allow both sides to make statements to the press during which they hit on all the familiar talking points. The real issues are resolved informally between the committee chairs of the House and Senate committees, and those chairs themselves are usually errand boys for the positions of the Speaker of the House and the majority leader of the Senate. The whole system has become a parody of the legislative process.

Barry Goldwater, who was a senior Republican on the Senate Armed Services Committee when I started out on the Hill, and whom many regarded as an ideologue, was far less ideological than the average member of Congress today. He wouldn't have dreamed

of issuing a partisan jeremiad against his senior Democratic counterpart on the House Armed Services Committee, Bill Nichols of Alabama, let alone of campaigning against him. Barry was a crotchety old bird, but by then his principal preoccupation was reforming the Department of Defense rather than advancing an ideological agenda.

His cause in the mid-1980s was solving the systemic problems in DOD that he believed to be responsible for the catastrophic handling of the bombing of the Marine barracks in Beirut in October 1983. The hearings he called for, and parallel ones in the House, revealed a riot of military disorganization that rivaled that of the Crimean War: an unclear chain of command; almost nonexistent communications between the military services; vague rules of engagement; and poor coordination, even in the timely evacuation of the wounded. Goldwater and Nichols, both veterans with a deep understanding of the military, took the lead on investigating these debacles.

Goldwater and Nichols's subsequent determination to overhaul the military command structure took shape through legislative drafts in their respective houses of Congress. I was in many of those meetings and do not recall any partisan rancor among the members; the main opposition came from elements in DOD. Admiral James D. Watkins, the chief of naval operations, denounced the ultimate measure (much of which had been drafted by Nichols) as "un-American." Bill Nichols, a genteel and unfailingly courteous southerner who had lost a leg in the Battle of the Hürtgen Forest in World War II, was distinctly unamused. John Kasich was equally unamused, as he regarded Nichols as a friend and mentor. Can anyone imagine a mentor-protégé relationship across the aisle now? Because of these strong bipartisan loyalties, Admiral Watkins was briskly sent packing, and the legislation proceeded to passage and was signed into law by the president.

The passage of time may have smoothed some of the rougher edges off my recollections. The 1980s were not a golden era of legislation, to be sure, and military historians will judge whether the Goldwater-Nichols Department of Defense Reorganization Act of 1986 achieved any significant or lasting improvement in military performance. But what it demonstrated to a young staffer was that partisan considerations could be moderated in matters of national importance, and members of Congress were then far less overawed by the military brass than they are now. In recent years, as Vietnam has ceased to be a living memory for many new members of Congress, both parties have learned to genuflect to the judgments of "commanders in the field," even when the services presided over disasters or scandals.

An instructive contrast is offered by the legislative response almost two decades later to an even greater disaster than the Beirut bombing. After the September 11, 2001, terrorist attacks, the creation of the Department of Homeland Security was as much a legislative mess as it was an enduring monument to American gullibility and deliberately induced fearfulness. President Bush and his advisers, meaning Dick Cheney, did not want a cabinet department at first. Bush and Cheney preferred to keep homeland security functions under the executive office of the president, which would have made it free of legislative branch oversight.

When the cry from the Hill for a cabinet department became too distracting, the administration sent formal and informal legislative proposals to the Hill and bent the eventual result to its liking. In the face of all of its rhetoric about national unity (a concept that proved as fleeting as the rhetoric was mendacious and manipulative) the Bush crowd was determined to insert extraneous and divisive antiunion provisions into the legislation affecting employees of the new department. Unlike Admiral Watkins's extemporane-

ous rant in 1986, this was a coordinated ideological effort devised in tandem by the executive branch and congressional Republicans. The provisions had nothing to do with protecting the country from those whom President Bush liked to describe as "evildoers."

Some Democrats balked, including Max Cleland, a Democratic senator from Georgia. He was rewarded by Republicans on the Hill not with solidarity or understanding but with calumny. During the 2002 campaign for his Senate seat, his Republican opponent ran political ads suggesting that Cleland was aiding Osama bin Laden by opposing the antiunion provisions in the homeland security bill. Partly on the strength of those ads, his opponent, Saxby Chambliss, then a member of the House, won the election.

Like Nichols, Cleland was a war veteran, although his war was Vietnam. Like Nichols, he had lost a limb as a result of his service. He was in fact a triple amputee and had won a Silver Star and a Bronze Star for his service. His successor, the flag-waving Chambliss, avoided Vietnam thanks to five student deferments and a 1Y deferment owing to a well-timed knee injury sustained playing football. Ever the good Republican, Chambliss described his victory to his followers thus: "You have delivered tonight a strong message to the world that in conservative Georgia values matter." How did this country reach a point of such political and moral degradation that a demagogic draft evader could successfully defame a gravely wounded veteran over a red herring, when the country was supposedly united in its determination to heal the wounds of 9/11?

The answer: tactics, tactics, tactics.

To understand how hyperbolic partisanship, scorched-earth campaigns, and propaganda trumping legislation have gridlocked

Congress to the point of systemic dysfunction, it is useful to examine the meteoric career of Newton Leroy McPherson Gingrich.

Newt came to Washington in 1979, a few years before me, and by the time I arrived he was a rising star in the House Republican delegation. His bomb-throwing tactics and expert use of C-SPAN as free political advertising made him stand out from most of the other younger members of Congress. It was clear from the beginning that he was practicing a New Politics, hard-right version, but Newt really came into his own during the Clinton presidency, when he issued his "Contract with America," became the Speaker of the House, and spearheaded an aggressive showdown with the president over the budget in 1995. In 1996, after a year of legislative chaos and government shutdowns, and during which the country descended into virtual warfare between the House and the president under his speakership, I remarked to one of my colleagues that Newt would make a lousy George Washington, but he was one hell of a Robespierre.

It is often said of flawed judicial nominees that they lack a judicial temperament. But with the appropriate adjustments this critique could also be applied to other offices. People either have the temperament to legislate and govern, or they do not. George Washington is one of history's few examples of a man who could both lead a revolutionary effort and consolidate his political gains to help establish a stable and enduring governing structure. Robespierre was his polar opposite: brilliant at destroying the status quo but unable to temper his revolutionary impulses, and thus ultimately unable to rule. It wasn't long before his bold new order collapsed into military dictatorship.

Gingrich had few legislative accomplishments to point to from the sixteen years he spent in Congress prior to becoming Speaker of the House. I cannot recall any important bill that he inspired

(unlike fellow activist Dick Armey, who worked hard to get his military base closure measure adopted, or Kasich, who successfully pushed through several measures on military reform and curbing government waste), or any significant activity in his committee assignments. The committee is where members of Congress are supposed to develop issue expertise, but Gingrich, the idea man, was above such mundane toiling.

His genius lay in recognizing the demagogic potential of the House's 1979 decision to televise its proceedings gavel to gavel. While most others saw this as at best a boring civics lesson, and at worst as a TV test pattern with occasional movement, Gingrich the old history teacher recognized that it would give him a chance to broadcast his political message nationwide, free of charge, to anyone who tuned in. He was relatively uninterested in participating in debates connected with the real business of Congress: measures that authorized or appropriated funds for the operation of government. Instead, he was the first to exploit the dead time after the completion of legislative business but before the cameras went dark to make so-called special order addresses to the C-SPAN camera before an empty chamber.

Using this free megaphone Gingrich and his two cohorts, Vin Weber and Bob Walker, launched the present era of over-the-top, confrontational, media-centric politics. They lashed out at Democrats as appeasement-minded socialist fellow travelers: For starters, they were criminally negligent for failing to confront the existential threat to America from the tiny nation of Nicaragua. The House, as Gingrich saw it, was a rotten, corrupt institution largely because it was run by Democrats.

All this might have remained a minor nuisance had not the Democratic Speaker, Tip O'Neill, on one occasion directed the

C-SPAN cameras to pan the empty seats in the House chamber when Gingrich or one of his sidekicks was speaking. He sought to undermine the trio, whom he called the Three Stooges, by showing that they were addressing a deserted assembly. They instantly fought back, claiming that they were deliberately being singled out, since other members had also availed themselves of special order speeches to pontificate before an empty chamber. Most important, the resulting controversy got Gingrich and his friends the attention they craved.

The Democrats, fat and lazy after nearly three continuous decades in control of the House, didn't know how to react. Gingrich quickly seized the reins. He made hay out of the 1983 congressional sex-with-pages scandal, and in 1988 he filed an ethics complaint against the then Speaker, Jim Wright, over improper payments for a book contract (Gingrich would later be charged with similar irregularities in his own book deal). Wright stepped down, and Gingrich advanced in the ranks of the Republican leadership. Then he ranted against the unacceptable bookkeeping practices of the House bank even though he himself had kited checks. Newt was learning that relentless attack is its own Teflon.

When Republicans won control of the House in 1994, Speaker Gingrich turned the institution upside down. He ended office deliveries of buckets of ice and engaged in dozens of comparable examples of perverse and inane micromanagement, such as renaming several of the committees to suit his own visionary taste. His "reform" merely resulted in money wasted junking and reprinting stationery and committee nameplates. He slashed the funding for what was then called the General Accounting Office (now the Government Accountability Office), Congress's watchdog agency, due to his belief that it was somehow a Democrat-leaning organization,

although even arch–deficit hawk Senator Tom Coburn later said that the GAO provides ninety dollars in savings recommendations for every one dollar spent to fund the agency.

When a coup takes place in a banana republic, the new potentate renames the streets and plazas and redesigns the national flag. A similar narcissistic idiosyncrasy seemed to govern Newt's edicts. In the first year of his speakership, as I scrambled with fellow staffers on the House Budget Committee to put together the congressional budget resolution for committee consideration in the small hours of the morning, down came another edict from the Speaker: Rewrite it presenting the numbers differently. He wanted to disguise the budget cuts he had in mind, so rather than giving the committees the customary instructions telling them how much money they would have to cut, he wanted to show only the money they would have to spend.

This would have been quite a feat to achieve a few hours before committee consideration: The budget resolution consisted almost entirely of numbers, some of them thirteen digits long. "When is Newt going to ask us to do the numbers in Babylonian base sixty?" I asked a colleague, as we marveled at his impulsive ways. Nobody thought it beyond the realm of possibility for this mercurial temperament; his edicts were ever more outlandish and unpredictable. More substantively, he gutted the traditional committee system, reduced the power of committee chairmen, and centralized power in the Speaker's office. Bills reported out of a committee would mysteriously disappear and reappear rewritten. Gingrich, in his own flattering self-estimation, had become something of a prime minister, with powers comparable to those of the president.

After a year or so of Trotsky-style permanent revolution, his act began to wear thin. The government shutdown and the attempted coup against his speakership that followed weakened him.

Later, when he pushed ahead to impeach President Clinton, he ran into a buzz saw. Gingrich stepped down in the comic aftermath of the impeachment caper, and many Republicans breathed a sigh of relief.

His replacement as Speaker, Dennis Hastert, was a relatively innocuous vacuum, but Gingrich had made sweeping and irrevocable changes to the basic operation of the House. He had also effectively transformed the broader political culture. The presidential impeachment he engineered had unleashed an extraordinary, vitriolic polarization in the electorate. That the Dreyfus case of the 1990s should have been a bedroom farce was a testament to the power of culture war diversions to inflame passions and intensify divisions.

In any case, Newt's feral instinct and scorched-earth tactics lived on in the House whip and later majority leader Tom DeLay, who learned to throw his voice so that it issued from Hastert's lips. Under DeLay, also known as "the hammer," the same take-no-prisoners tactics continued until his own dethronement in late 2005 over a shady campaign finance scandal. Under DeLay, "pay for play"—the extortion of campaign funds from companies bidding for federal contracts or seeking favorable tax treatment—reached a crescendo. This was the period just before superlobbyist Jack Abramoff's arrest and imprisonment. Before his fall Abramoff made $20 million a year securing congressional favors for his clients—not least from Tom DeLay, whose staffers Abramoff hired into his lobbying firm.

The good times kept rolling through the golden years of the Bush administration, when the reflexive patriotism triggered by September 11 played to their advantage, until the Republicans hit a wall in 2006, when they lost both houses in the midterm elections. Now that the GOP was in the minority, it had little recourse in the

House, which in any case was a majoritarian body. (During their twelve years in control the Republicans had altered House rules to increase majority power beyond the already substantial level that had been the norm.)

At this point, the action shifted to the Senate. Now that the GOP was the minority party, it could avail itself of the peculiar rules and customs of the legislative chamber that vaunts itself as the world's greatest deliberate body. Despite our foreign policy elite's constant invocation of democracy as the highest ideal, America itself is not exactly a majoritarian democracy. Nowhere is that observation more in evidence than in the Senate, where the minority can prevent the majority from ruling, or even from bringing legislation to the floor.

Supreme Court justice Antonin Scalia has opined that the Senate is intentionally designed for gridlock.[2] In reality, the Constitution has relatively few provisions dealing with the Senate, and those that exist have mainly to do with member qualification, how the Senate is formed, and similar matters. The Constitution establishes vote thresholds in a few instances (ratification of treaties, for instance), but nowhere will one find the term "filibuster" or the basis for the belief that a sixty-vote threshold should be necessary for any legislative business. The Constitution merely states that the Senate, like the House (unless otherwise specified), shall make its own rules. And what rules it has made! The filibuster is a Senate rule, not a constitutional mandate. The current sixty-vote threshold is another one, which only dates back to 1975.

While it is true that founders like James Madison attempted to fashion a system to resist tyrannical accretions of power, they formulated their ideas, as did so many eighteenth-century political theorists, by analogy to the Newtonian laws that so impressed learned people of the Enlightenment. Just as the universe was a

clockwork mechanism functioning in harmony and balance, so should a system of republican governance, so far as it was practically possible to fit that template. Although the Founding Fathers had different opinions about the primacy of the central government, they certainly did not want a *liberum veto* system similar to the one that was then in place in contemporary Poland, where one delegate to the Polish Diet could prevent its functioning. The resulting gridlock that Scalia so admires contributed to Poland's inability to defend its own national existence.

But however much the Founders were influenced by Enlightenment theory, they also grappled with the exigencies of the specific conditions and interests of thirteen culturally disparate former colonies. Contrary to Scalia's picture of the Senate as an institution designed in a Platonic vacuum, the actual institution comes to us with some less savory historical baggage attached. The restrictive, minoritarian makeup and procedures of the Senate enumerated in the Constitution (most were established piecemeal at later times) did not arise solely from a disinterested desire to create a bulwark against a hypothetical future tyrant. They came into being in the first place partly as a compromise to protect slave-holding interests in the less populous southern states, by balancing the population-determined House of Representatives. The history of the Senate for the next seven decades after the founding was closely bound up with the antebellum South's defense of slavery. After the Civil War, and for the next hundred years, the Senate was often the last ditch of defense for the Jim Crow system. The current sixty-vote filibuster threshold is a reduction from the previous sixty-seven-vote requirement, and was to some extent a reaction to the bitter fights Strom Thurmond and his segregationist colleagues waged through the mid-1960s against civil rights legislation. Thus, for the first 175 years of its history, the Senate's makeup and proce-

dures assisted in the defense of slavery and segregation, with considerable success.

In recent years the Senate minority has been the ideal venue for the GOP. The Republican Party is no longer a party of governance, because it has no positive, workable agenda with which to exercise power: It has become the "anti" party par excellence. When it gains the majority in the House of Representatives, as it did in 2010, its style is so transparently primitive that it tends to alienate more voters than it attracts. But in the Senate, with its outwardly genteel procedural rigmarole, Republican politicians can hide behind institutional formalities while pursuing a strategy that consists almost entirely of negative campaigning rather than of co-governance. If one's goal is to obstruct, the Senate offers a nearly infinite variety of procedural levers with which to do so. And the result will generally be presented as "The Senate Fails to Pass . . ." rather than "The Senate GOP Obstructs . . ." by the media.

Obama had barely begun his term in office in early 2009, when Mitch McConnell, the Senate Republican leader, declared that his greatest legislative priority was . . . what? Jobs for Americans? Rescuing the financial system? Solving the housing collapse? No, none of those. His top priority was to ensure that Obama would be a one-term president. By his own admission Senator McConnell hated Obama more than he wanted to pull the country out of a deep crisis.*

The GOP's agenda is reflected in its recent embrace of the filibuster. Until 1970, filibusters were relatively rare, never exceeding single digits during the period of a two-year Congress. Their fre-

* But during the debt-ceiling negotiations the media began hailing McConnell as "the adult in the room," presumably because he was less theatrically extreme than the Tea Party freshmen.

quency steadily rose over the years, until the number in each Congress rose to the mid-to-high double digits in the early years of the Bush administration. But when the Republicans entered the minority in 2007, the number of filibusters more than doubled, to 139 during the 2007–2009 Congress. The fact that more than half of these filibusters were overcome suggests not that they were futile but that the time expended overcoming them was the whole point of the exercise.

Republicans are now operating on the Leninist principle of "the worse, the better." According to this principle, if they hold fast against every one of the administration's attempts at restarting the economy, the presidency and both houses of Congress will fall into their laps in 2012. I am not alone in ascribing nihilistic and destructive motives to the former party of Lincoln. Bruce Bartlett, who served as an economist in the Reagan administration, tried to explain our predicament in the fall of 2011.

> Basically, we're still stuck in the situation we were in three years ago, and we haven't made any progress at all, except that our problems are much worse because of political reasons, because we now have a crazy party in charge of one of the houses of our Congress, and they won't allow anything to happen, because it's in their vested interest to make things worse.[3]

Delay and gridlock have been the Republicans' principal objectives for the last three years, even as the country was fighting two wars and the economy was sliding off a cliff. They have so far been mostly successful in meeting their objectives. Undermining Americans' belief in their own institutions of self-government remains a prime GOP electoral strategy. But if delay and gridlock fall short of

producing Karl Rove's dream of thirty years of unchallengeable one-party rule, there are other, even less democratic, techniques to fall back on. Ever since Republicans won majorities in a number of state legislatures in November 2010, they have systematically attempted to make it more difficult to vote, with onerous voter ID requirements (in Wisconsin, Republicans have legislated photo IDs while shutting DMV offices in areas where Democratic constituencies live and lengthening their hours of operation in GOP-dominated ones); narrower registration periods; residency requirements that may disenfranchise university students; shutdowns of early voting; and the repeal of same-day registration.

This legislative assault is moving America in a direction diametrically opposed to the arrow of progress that has governed the last two hundred years of its history, which has been pointed toward more political participation by more citizens. At one point in 2009 the so-called Tea Party movement (which claims to be independent but overwhelmingly supports GOP candidates) even flirted briefly with the concept of repealing the Seventeenth Amendment, which provides for the popular election of senators. Republicans never tire of self-righteously lecturing other countries about the wonders of democracy; exporting democracy (at the barrel of a gun) was a signature policy of the Bush administration. But domestically they don't want *those people* voting. Those people are anyone not likely to vote Republican. As Sarah Palin would say, they are not Real Americans, and by that she means anyone who doesn't look, think, or talk like the GOP base.

Politics ain't beanbag, to be sure. But the present-day Republican Party shows less and less resemblance to one of the traditional parties in a healthy two-party system that places a premium on broad coalitions, compromise, and a nonideological worldview. When they are in power, whether in statehouses, Congress, or the

White House, Republicans are magnetically drawn to practice political overreach along with scorched-earth tactics, be it through vote suppression, the K Street Project to force lobbying firms to hire only Republicans, or outing a covert CIA agent in their own administration to settle political scores, as happened to Valerie Plame. When they are out of power they focus single-mindedly on seizing up the wheels of government to prove to the American people that government just doesn't work—at least, when the GOP is out of power. These take-no-prisoners tactics flow naturally from an embittered, Manichaean mind-set. This mentality has grave implications for the health of our constitutional system.

3

ALL WRAPPED UP IN THE CONSTITUTION

Like biblical literalists, Republicans assert that the Constitution is divinely inspired and inerrant. But also like biblical literalists, they are strangely selective about those portions of their favorite document that they care to heed, and they favor rewriting it when it stands in the way of their political agenda.

If you want total security, go to prison.
There you're fed, clothed, given medical care, and so on.
The only thing lacking . . . is freedom.

—attributed to Dwight D. Eisenhower

One may be forgiven for finding it strange that people who profess to revere the Constitution should so caustically denigrate the institution that is supposed to be the material expression of its principles. The Republican tactic of inducing public distrust of government is not only cynical, it is schizophrenic. Which is not to say that all aspects of the federal government are flawless, or that there should be no limit to its size or intrusiveness.

But while the size of the federal government has been a subject of some deliberation recently, most Republican officeholders seem oddly uninterested in government intrusiveness. Few voiced con-

cern about the effective repeal of Fourth Amendment protections against uncontrolled government surveillance, or of the weakening of habeas corpus and self-incrimination protections in the public hysteria following 9/11—or the fact that government-sanctioned torture emerged from the dark recesses of Dick Cheney's id to blot America's reputation worldwide. These unsavory developments would have horrified the Founding Fathers, but all Republicans, save for a few ineffectual dissenters, accepted them without a murmur. Should one object, they have a rote response: Boo! The terrorists will get you!

Whenever a momentary GOP hobbyhorse is *not* in the Constitution, however, Republicans of late have wanted to tinker with that supposedly perfect document. Recent years have seen constitutional amendment proposals for bans on flag burning and abortion; a federal definition of marriage (whatever happened to states' rights?); and a balanced budget (so much for countercyclical fiscal policy, or Alexander Hamilton's notions of a funded public debt). A wholesale revision of the Fourteenth Amendment definition of citizenship has also been suggested. Whatever crackpot scheme polls well with the "base," some Republican politician is bound to try to shoehorn into the Constitution.

It is said that only the Mormons believe that the Constitution is divinely inspired. But many partisan Republican voters, whether they call themselves libertarians or social conservatives, approach it with an attitude of near religious idolatry. It is an uninformed idolatry, which would seem paradoxical except that such behavior can routinely be found in all facets of life. Uncritical veneration, whether the object is a human being, an idea, or an inanimate object, leads to inaccurate judgments and doublethink. When combined with ignorance about the object in question, that veneration can lead to all manner of folly. The satirical paper *The Onion* pub-

lished a piece whose headline says it all: "Area Man Passionate Defender of What He Imagines Constitution to Be."

The Framers did an excellent job of drawing up our charter of government. In the context of the time, when almost all European states were either despotic monarchies or oligarchies like the Republic of Venice, the Constitution was well-nigh miraculous. But it was hardly perfect, because it was written by fallible human beings—however enlightened—under the stress of hard circumstances and historical legacies, not all of them exemplary.

To start with, one might think that section 2 of Article I, the line about "the whole Number of free Persons, including those bound to Service for a Term of Years, and excluding Indians not taxed, three fifths of all other Persons," might give one pause to wonder about the changeless perfection of the Constitution, let alone its divine inspiration. Indentured servitude and chattel slavery would hardly seem to be features of the harmonious earthly paradise that the people who now go to town hall meetings in tricornered hats want to project back onto American society two and a quarter centuries ago. In those days only property owners were allowed to vote in most states, and some nonindentured whites lived in conditions that looked a lot like European serfdom: For example, the patroon system in New York State's Hudson Valley, under which wealthy oligarchs such as the Rensselaer family extracted feudal rents from their tenants, lasted until the mid-1840s. And it would be entertaining to see religious fundamentalists who dream of having no wall of separation between church and state subject themselves to the religious doctrines and taxes of the then newly constituted states that had established churches, such as Connecticut and Massachusetts (the latter's state-sanctioned church was not disestablished until 1833).

Strict construction of the Constitution is a delusion, like all

forms of extreme textual interpretation, whether biblical literalism or literary deconstructionism. Old Testament verses about smiting one's foes (or exterminating whole peoples) stand in contradiction to those forbidding killing. Likewise with the Constitution: Is the constitutional right of free speech unconditional, or does it contradict the same document's promise "to ensure domestic tranquility" when that speech would levy insurrection against the government? How do we square the Tenth Amendment's grant of sovereignty to the states with the commerce clause? There are dozens of contradictions like these, and no document can be so comprehensive as to resolve them all, especially when we find ourselves having to legislate in circumstances undreamed of by the Framers.

The only way to manage them is by comity, reason, and a sense of proportion—in other words, with a sound judicial temperament. The Constitution is not a tablet hauled down from Mount Sinai but a charter of government drawn up in specific, urgent circumstances because the previous charter, the Articles of Confederation, was a failure. But for present-day Republicans, and even more for the Tea Party activists who run around in colonial garb, the Constitution is the most sacred document they have never read.

With respect to the First Amendment, almost everyone across the political spectrum is a hypocrite to some degree. We can all think of cases when we have wanted an ironclad and expansive interpretation of it to protect behavior we approve of and a narrow and exclusive reading to restrict behavior we disapprove of. But those who treat the Constitution as an inerrant text seem to have more problems than others. Money is speech, according to their view, and unlimited campaign contributions are an unfettered right for which our forefathers threw out the British tyrants. Flag burning, on the other hand, is not free expression, because they don't like it. (There is an additional irony here: The flag is a secular

symbol, so to refer to burning the flag as a "desecration," as flag amendment proponents habitually do, applies sacred language to a secular symbol, reflecting the sort of idol worship that the Bible explicitly forbids.) When opponents of a Republican administration dare to make statements critical of government policy in times of war, the faithful will accuse them of "giving aid and comfort to the enemy." But when the governor of a southern state talks about secession from the United States in response to a federal government policy he doesn't like, there is no mention of treason.

This sort of one-sidedness is rooted in a mind-set that bears resemblance, ironically enough, to Vladimir Lenin's basic precept of politics: *kto-kogo*, literally "who-whom," meaning who does what to whom. Lenin believed that revolutionary violence committed by the vanguard of the proletariat (a group conveniently defined by him alone) was perfectly legitimate. Violence committed against the vanguard of the proletariat, on the other hand, was illegitimate. We all practice in-group favoritism in everyday life, and in our ideological preferences, but most of us make a conscious effort not to let it degenerate into chronic doublethink. And as for constitutions and legal statutes, their whole purpose is to apply consistent rules and to restrain such irrational favoritism.

Perhaps the only amendment to the Constitution that people who self-identify as Republicans believe to be absolute, unfettered, and unlimited is the second one, which guarantees the right to bear arms. I, too, believe in the presumptive right of a law-abiding adult to own a firearm, and have exercised that right. But I am not persuaded that this right should extend to felons, minors, the mentally ill, or persons under a restraining order. Again, a rule of reason applies. One would also think that it might not be wise to extend the unrestricted right to purchase firearms to terrorist suspects or drug runners. But crackpot legal theorists on the right, who have no

problem when it comes to distinctly unconstitutional restrictions on rights of privacy or habeas corpus, not to mention the right to a speedy trial, to have evidence openly presented, even the right not to be tortured (all enumerated in the Bill of Rights), suddenly become unrelenting constitutional absolutists when it comes to the purchase of firearms. Why? In situations such as this, when behavior defies all rational explanation, it is generally helpful to look at the money trail.

At the same time that the Bush administration was telling us to be afraid, be very afraid, of terrorists, Attorney General John Ashcroft was fighting for the prerogative to destroy gun purchase records.[1] Had he done otherwise, he and the Bush administration would have fallen afoul of the National Rifle Association (NRA), and its political contributions might have dried up. Likewise, the straw purchases* of automatic weapons for Mexican drug cartels were protected by the "conservative" faithful in Congress who ostensibly hate illegal drugs and illegal Mexicans almost as much as they hate a disappointing haul from their latest fund-raising event. When ill-conceived sting operations set up by both the Bush and Obama administrations came to light (the Drug Enforcement Administration allowed guns to get into the hands of the cartels, ostensibly to track their movements), a House committee chaired by Republican Darrell Issa bore down on the case like Bulldog Drummond. But Issa testily forbade any mention of the flawed legal process that had permitted gunrunners for the cartels to purchase the assault rifles in question in the first place.[2] His lack of curiosity was not a sign of congenital stupidity, because most members of Congress possess a high measure of low cunning—if it were otherwise,

---

* The purchase of a firearm by one person on behalf of another person who may not have the legal right to purchase a firearm.

they would never be elected. Rather, it stemmed from an all-consuming fear of the NRA, and of how that lobby can distort facts into the corrosive charge of being "antigun." NRA propaganda is nearly as powerful an incentive as NRA contributions.

What sensitized me to this matter was less the bare facts of the case than the sheer emotional callousness of the gun lobby after the 2007 Virginia Tech shootings, when thirty-two students and faculty members were murdered. A group of belligerent activists showed up on the scene within days of the shooting, vehemently arguing that all students and faculty ought to have the right to carry a concealed firearm in the classroom. Whatever the validity of the arguments for or against this particular policy, the decision to descend on the campus to make a controversial and divisive proposal while parents were still grieving over their children amply displays the monomania and lack of empathy of gun-lobby ideologues.

When they won a majority of state legislatures in 2010, Republican politicians promptly attempted to put their idée fixe about the Second Amendment into states' statutes. Concealed carry in a bar? No problem! Concealed carry at a packed football stadium? What could possibly go wrong there? The Florida legislature passed, and Governor Rick Scott signed into law, a bill that would prohibit physicians from even *asking* patients (for example, ones exhibiting suicidal symptoms) if they owned a firearm.[3] The draft bill would have levied fines of up to $5 million and jail time for any physician who violated it, although these draconian punishments were reduced before passage. So much for the GOP's claim, loudly enunciated during the debate over the health care bill, that the government shouldn't come between patients and their doctors. The issue, of course, had nothing whatsoever to do with the legal right of a citizen to own a firearm. The Florida legislature was grandstanding on behalf of the NRA.

Is there a constitutional right for law-abiding citizens to possess firearms? Yes, there is. But it is revealing of the psychological insecurities and revenge fantasies of a large, politically active segment of the population that it should devote so much energy and passion not only to maintaining the right to possess lethal weaponry, but to expanding this prerogative in marginal or even plainly ridiculous circumstances. All this fuss over a provision that makes up less than one half of 1 percent of all of the words in the Constitution is rather puzzling. It is a pity these people do not seem to care quite so passionately about the remaining 99.5 percent.

The Third Amendment, which prevents soldiers from setting up shop in people's homes without their consent, doesn't get nearly as much attention. But with the Fourth Amendment, which protects people from warrantless search and seizure, the conservative who defends the Second Amendment to the last breath is back to Leninist who-whom thinking. For all the supposed belief in the primacy and autonomy of the individual against the state espoused by the followers of Ayn Rand, and for all the "don't tread on me" sloganeering of the Tea Party, both groups have been remarkably supine in the face of recent actions by the executive branch that have effectively rendered the Fourth Amendment null and void. The "live free or die" mantra popular among self-styled conservatives is only a self-flattering pose, effectively negated by the authoritarian national security and law and order mentality that has gripped the Republican faithful. Believing that they are the most patriotic Americans, and that they have nothing to fear, they rationalize warrantless surveillance as something the government will only use against terrorists, foreigners, criminally inclined minorities, and other evildoers.

In their indifference to the constitutional right to privacy, Republicans are, alas, on firm political if not constitutional ground.

One might think Democrats would oppose the erosion of the constitutional right to privacy, as well as all the other encroachments on civil liberties inflicted on Americans in recent years, if only on a purely opportunistic basis, even if principle alone did not incline them to do so. After all, if George Bush was *for* warrantless surveillance, Democrats must be *against* it. Accordingly, they could presumably have rallied all the voters who opposed Bush and his executive overreach by means of a polarizing issue, right? Think again. I knew the game was up in the summer of 2008 just before the Democratic convention when Candidate Obama, with all eyes upon him prior to his coronation in Denver, voted to indemnify telecommunications corporations against any claims arising from their participation in a program of unconstitutional surveillance. Since his inauguration Obama has institutionalized, and even expanded, many of the illegal measures Bush first conceived in the aftermath of the terrorist attacks.

And so it is with the Fifth, Sixth, and Eighth amendments. If George Bush took the pioneering role of engineering detentions without charge, undermining due process, forbidding the defendant to see the evidence against him, torturing, and so on, Barack Obama did nothing to reverse these measures. In so doing he made these infractions part of a corpus of secret administrative law neither accessible to nor challengeable by ordinary citizens. Our last two presidents have laid the foundation on which all police states rest.

Our present government would be less of an insulting farce if either of the two ruling parties had the honesty to propose an outright repeal of the Bill of Rights, for it is a virtual dead letter. Sad as it is to say, there would be no significant movement to prevent them from doing so. Civil liberties lawyers may cringe at that statement, but I believe the constant invocation of terrorism has so condi-

tioned the public into a state of "wholesome fear," as storm trooper leader Ernst Röhm liked to call it, that their constitutional rights mean nothing to millions of people, perhaps even a voting majority. Americans for the most part, as unattractive as the idea is, do not care very much about their rights, above all what may be the most precious right of all: what former Supreme Court justice Louis D. Brandeis called "the right to be let alone—the most comprehensive of the rights and the right most valued by civilized men." The elderly, who tend to be the most fearful and cautious age group, have in general let their exaggerated concerns about terrorism (statistically a lesser probability than a senior drowning in his bathtub) override whatever traditional concerns they might once have had about privacy. And for the young, who are growing up with Facebook and with surveillance cameras in their high schools and school buses, personal privacy, and indeed any real sense of the traditional distinction between the public and private realms, may be a meaningless abstraction.

The Republican Party has engaged in a full-scale assault on what it calls "judicial activism" (meaning judicial independence). Newt Gingrich went on a tirade about this in Iowa in December 2011, stating that if elected president he would ignore judicial decisions he didn't like—an extreme example of a widespread attitude. The party's belief that national security *as it defines it* should trump the most fundamental rights laid down by the Framers bears a heavy burden for the evisceration of the Constitution it claims to revere. Madison and the Founders were very clear on this point: that constitutional republics should not be armed camps. The GOP's version of national security—perpetual war, a bloated military budget, and diminished constitutional protections—is a far cry from anything the Founding Fathers would recognize or advocate.

Democrats—ever sensitive to the whiff of corporate money (as in their vote to indemnify the telecommunications companies for illegal surveillance), or afraid of being tarred as soft on terrorism, soft on crime, or soft in general—have closely followed the GOP's trail. None of this would have happened in the presence of a vigilant press or a resolute citizenry conscious of its rights and skeptical of distractions, scare tactics, or intimidation. Sadly, we have been dumbed down, beaten down, and conditioned into accepting the invalidation of the Constitution as the new norm with scarcely a whimper. A public that pays more attention to reality TV than its status as free citizens cannot withstand an unremitting encroachment on its liberties by calculating, unscrupulous, and power-hungry leaders. The crowning tragedy—or sick joke—is that those who have postured and preened the most ostentatiously about their devotion to the Constitution have been the most indifferent to its destruction.

For destruction it is. There are now numerous provisions in the Bill of Rights that exist on paper just as the Estates-General did during the French monarchy—it existed on paper but was moribund. If a free citizenry is too apathetic, too intimidated, too distracted, or just plain too ignorant to exercise its statutory liberties, those liberties will not last long.

4

A DEVIL'S DICTIONARY

How Republicans have mastered the art of communicating with ordinary people in their own vernacular, while Democrats remain tone-deaf and tongue-tied.

Polonius: "What do you read, my lord?"
Hamlet: "Words, words, words."

—*Hamlet*, Act 2, Scene 2

How did Republicans manage to seize control of the way Americans speak about public life? Democrats do not understand the power of language. Their initiatives are posed in impenetrable policy-speak: the Patient Protection and Affordable Care Act. The *what*? Can anyone even remember that? No wonder the pejorative "Obamacare" won out. Contrast that with the Republicans' USA PATRIOT Act (the Uniting and Strengthening America by Providing Appropriate Tools Required to Intercept and Obstruct Terrorism Act). You're a patriot, aren't you? Who would dare be against that? Most Americans do not have a college education. Do the Democrats really expect them to have a clear understanding of what a stimulus bill is supposed to do? Why didn't the White House just call it the jobs bill and keep pounding on that theme? Obama has taken a drubbing for failing to focus on jobs,

but his real mistake was not hiring more advertising types to come up with catchier names for his bills.

You know that Social Security and Medicare are in jeopardy when even Democrats refer to them as "entitlements." Entitlement has a negative sound: Somebody who says he's entitled selfishly claims something he doesn't deserve. Why not call them "earned benefits"—which is what they are, because we all contribute payroll taxes to fund them? It would never occur to a Democrat. Republicans don't make that mistake; they are relentlessly on message: There is no "estate tax"—it is the "death tax." Heaven forbid that the Walton family should have to give up one penny of its $86 billion fortune when the paterfamilias dies.

Capturing the terms of the debate through the adroit use of language has allowed the GOP to bamboozle millions of people about their own material interests. It was not always thus. You would have been hard-pressed to find an uneducated farmer during the depression of the 1890s who did not have a very accurate idea about exactly who and what was shafting him. An unemployed worker in a bread line in 1932 would have felt little gratitude to the Rockefellers or the Mellons. But that is not the case in the present economic crisis. After a riot of unbridled greed such as the world has not seen since the conquistadores' looting expeditions, after an unprecedentedly broad and rapid transfer of wealth upward by Wall Street and its corporate satellites, where has popular anger been directed? If the media are to be believed, for most of the last three and a half years the public has been incensed about "Washington spending"—which has increased mostly to provide unemployment compensation, food stamps, and Medicaid to those economically damaged by the previous decade's corporate saturnalia. Any residual anger is harmlessly diverted to pseudoissues: death panels, gay marriage, abortion, and so on.

It may seem frivolous to harp on such an abstract matter as

language at a time when we face war, a $15 trillion national debt, and a shrinking middle class. But words are the vehicles that convey political ideas, so we had better pay attention to them. There is a common misconception that language arises more or less organically, and that people use whichever word or phrase pops into their heads, much like a bird building its nest with the random twigs it sees on the ground. But in public life, political operatives have painstakingly chosen words to help shape voters' acceptance or rejection of an idea even before they have made a conscious effort to think about it.

I became aware of the overwhelming role of language in contemporary politics shortly before the 9/11 attacks. At that time, the word "homeland" was practically unused in the American vernacular. It had a slightly archaic sound to it, and was invoked generally only as a stilted translation of the German *heimat*, or as a euphemism for the bantustans created by South Africa's apartheid government in its policy to rid itself of the native population.

But strangely enough, in the summer of 2001 a newly published RAND Corporation study found its way into my congressional office in-box: *Preparing the U.S. Army for Homeland Security*. Even then it struck me as odd that someone would use that word, despite the penchant of the military-industrial complex—of which the RAND Corporation is a cog—for coining new buzzwords. Around that same time, the congressionally mandated U.S. Commission on National Security/21st Century (the so-called Hart-Rudman Commission) had issued its final report, which contained a chapter with the pretentious title "Securing the National Homeland." It is possible that the savvy bureaucrats at RAND adopted the commission's buzzword in their book's title to get in step with the evolving zeitgeist. But "homeland" was still a term no American would have used colloquially when referring to his country.

A couple of months later it was as if someone had flipped a switch: Suddenly everybody—politicians, the media, all the opinion shapers who inhabit the American landscape—was incessantly using the word "homeland" and giving no indication that it was any sort of novelty, much less that someone was conditioning them to use it. Even the normally inarticulate George W. Bush flawlessly recited his lines—lines which often included a reference to the homeland or homeland security.

Some unsung bureaucrat, or a functionary at one of the government-dependent think tanks, had clearly done his linguistic research. If the Bush administration had gone ahead and created a U.S. Department of Domestic Security it would have sounded like the interior ministry of a minor Warsaw Pact satellite state. Besides, domestic has other meanings, including the dreaded (by Republicans) "domestic partnership." The U.S. Department of Internal Defense would have been too cumbersome, and besides, what was the old Department of Defense supposed to be doing? "Homeland Security" was perfect: old-fashioned, vaguely patriotic, and unsullied by any connotation that 95 percent of Americans would be aware of. As for the remaining 5 percent, were they with us or against us?*

The linguistic offensive kicked into high gear after September 2001. Amid such cheery tidings as the self-satisfied pronouncement, by an anonymous government official, that America would be engaged in the "next Hundred Years' War,"[1] or Secretary of State Condoleezza Rice's slightly less ambitious declaration of a thirty-year "generational struggle," the Global War on Terrorism debuted to rave reviews.

---

* There is poetic justice in the fact that the new headquarters complex for the Department of Homeland Security is being constructed on the site of an abandoned mental hospital.

The war on terrorism was a propagandistic success just as surely as it was a failure both of logic and of national strategy. Nations have declared wars against other nations since time immemorial. Now, for the first time, we were declaring war on a tactic. Did this mean that the United States would be at war with the Tamil Tigers, Chechen rebels, or the Maoist guerrillas in India's West Bengal province? Presumably not, but the label was sufficiently broad that the president and his advisers could intervene anywhere militarily at will, and for an indefinite period, pursuant to the absurdly broad Authorization of Use of Military Force resolution that was rushed through a panicked and supine Congress in September 2001.

In military terms, the war on terrorism failed just as our domestic crusades symbolically styled as "wars" have failed: the war on poverty, the war on drugs. But in public relations terms, which is what the American system of governing is increasingly about—not solving problems, but shaping perceptions through the adroit use of rousing or soothing phrases—it was a smash hit. It induced courtier media personalities like Thomas Friedman to swoon over the righteousness of it all—and, more important, they swooned over the nominal author of the crusade, George W. Bush, who, as the undistinguished offspring of an elite political family, had lucked into the presidency after a disputed election.

Like an antibiotic-resistant bacterium, the war on terrorism soon mutated into something else: the war on "terror." This subtle but telling semantic shift was yet another turn of the screw. Terrorism is at least a technique of militants. Terror is an emotion. How can one make war on a subjective mental state? Yet "war on terror" has now become the shorthand label of choice of government, media, and popular speech when describing the overseas adventures that are bankrupting us.

In his 1946 essay "Politics and the English Language," George Orwell concluded that the prevailing vagueness and ambiguity of political language was a symptom of the decadence of a culture. That may be the case: a rubric like "war on terror" illustrates our national inability to make basic categorical distinctions. But Orwell underestimated the emotional power of those words and phrases, despite their imprecision and the questions they beg. He seemed to think at that time that the verbal falsity he was describing was a by-product of sloppy thinking by stupid or careless ideologues. It was only two years later, in *1984*, that he described a totalitarian society where attitudes were successfully bent and molded by the conscious efforts of political leaders to shape the language of thought. In that case, the distortion of public language was not inadvertent but deliberate.

"War on terror" is one of those phrases that conditioned us in the same manner that the proles of Orwell's Oceania were conditioned by Newspeak. Our rulers designated it as a war much as real wars like World War II. But traditional wars have a definable end and require sacrifices on the home front. So the Bush administration had to attempt to cast the war on terror as a war that demanded shared sacrifice, not as a grab for oil or a racket for defense contractors. Our sacrifices on the home front consisted of receiving a tax cut and obeying an exhortation to go shopping.

Part of the Republicans' success in this area is due to the proper use of "framing" techniques. This mainly entails using short, simple, easily understood words and phrases—positive words for what you are defending, negative words for what you are attacking. Orwell spelled it out sixty-five years ago: Use short Anglo-Saxon words with an evocative meaning and avoid fancy polysyllabic words and phrases that look as if they came from a Latin dictionary. Hence, jobs bill rather than stimulus bill.

The difference in the two parties' use of language originates in the different ways in which they generate their ideas. The source of many, if not most, Democratic policy ideas can be traced to academia: One has only to think of president of Princeton Woodrow Wilson, the New Deal's brain trust, Kennedy's best and brightest, or the Ivy League graduates who have clustered around Clinton and Obama. Their verbiage, like their thinking, has tended to be arcane, qualified, and convoluted.

Republican style can be traced back to about the same time, when Wilson was touting his political vision for a new world order, but it came from a different source. Early in the twentieth century the GOP began to borrow the techniques that their supporters in big business were developing to sell products: from the nascent trade of corporate advertising. It is no coincidence that two of the pioneers of American corporate advertising and public relations were men of decidedly reactionary impulses.

The first trailblazer was Ivy Lee. He is often considered the founder of modern public relations and the originator of corporate crisis communications.* In 1914 he went to work for the Rockefeller interests after coal miners striking at one of the mines they controlled in Ludlow, Colorado, were massacred by the National Guard. Between nineteen and twenty-five people were killed, including two women and eleven children. Lee's press releases claimed that their deaths were the result of an overturned camp stove. Ivy Lee was one of the first members of the Council on Foreign Relations when it was founded just after World War I; he was thus co-opted into America's foreign policy establishment. Shortly

* Lee is the ultimate inspiration for British Petroleum's heavy advertising of the Gulf of Mexico as an ideal vacation venue after the company despoiled it.

before he died in 1934, Congress began investigating his public relations work on behalf of the notorious German chemical monopoly I.G. Farben, which helped fund Hitler's rise to power and would later develop the poison gas used in the Nazi death camps.

The other pioneer of political public relations was Edward Bernays, a nephew of Sigmund Freud, who sharpened his skills writing prowar propaganda for the Committee on Public Information during World War I. After the war he decided that the word "propaganda" had a negative ring, due to its use by the defeated Germans; he came up with a new phrase, "public relations," which has a distinctly more Madison Avenue sound. In 1928, in his influential *Propaganda*, Bernays claimed that manipulating public opinion was a necessary part of democracy. According to his daughter, Bernays believed the common people were "not to be relied upon, [so] they had to be guided from above." She would later say that her father believed in "enlightened despotism"—a system through which intelligent men such as himself would keep the mob in line through the clever use of subliminal PR campaigns. His clients included not only such megacorporations as Procter & Gamble, the United Fruit Company, and the American Tobacco Company (through clever advertising campaigns, he sought to remove the traditional stigma against women smoking), but also Republican president Calvin Coolidge. Bernays did not feel it would be strategic to allay the public's fear of communism and urged his clients to play on popular emotions and magnify that fear. His work laid some of the foundation of the McCarthyite hysteria of the 1950s. *Life* magazine named Bernays one of the one hundred most influential Americans of the twentieth century.

It would take some time for Lee's and Bernays's pathbreaking work to percolate through the ranks of Republican discourse. But early signs can be seen in the Nixon presidency, when Vice President

Spiro Agnew appealed to the "silent majority" by sneering at an "effete corps of impudent snobs" who supposedly ruled America. Reagan, who was a natural performer, perfected the act and honed the speech patterns and disarming language that were geared to appeal to "ordinary Americans"—not so far off from Sarah Palin's real Americans. But Reagan radiated optimism, and his pose was more grandfatherly than adversarial. Despite his bedrock anticommunism, Reagan instinctively understood when it was time to negotiate with the Soviet leadership, despite the opposition of many of his advisers and movement conservatives throughout the country.

While there is a slavish cult around Reagan in the present-day Republican Party, the current GOP follows neither his basic political flexibility nor his rhetorical style. His messaging, while certainly more effective than his flat-footed opponents Carter and Mondale, was infused with cheerfulness rather than scolding, hope rather than impending doom. Reagan's rhetorical affect did not persist when he left office. A characteristic moment exemplifying the style that would succeed his occurred at the 1992 Republican convention in Houston, when Pat Buchanan fused all the elements of fear, loathing, and Manichaean ideology in his "culture wars" address. This style reached its full flower in the rhetorical techniques used by Newt Gingrich, who even sought to instruct his colleagues in the dark arts of verbal assault.

In 1990, Gingrich offered up a memo to Republican candidates titled "Language: A Key Mechanism of Control." This document was intended to be a primer on the use of language for Republicans running for office who needed to master political buzz phrases. As Gingrich modestly put it, it was for Republicans who said to themselves, "I wish I could speak like Newt." His advice was really quite straightforward. The former history teacher counseled neophytes to use optimistic or soothing words to describe their own political

program and relentlessly disparaging words to criticize their opponent's agenda. The title in itself is revealing. Note that it does not suggest that language is a key mechanism of persuasion or influence. Control is what one does to laboratory rats or prisoners of a totalitarian state, not free citizens of a democracy. If you pay close attention to Newt's own language, clues about his character always pile up.[2]

Lee, Bernays, and Gingrich have all had a lasting impact on the political use of language in America. If you seek monuments to their accomplishments, you have to look no further than your daily paper or television news program. It is to them that we owe stories about "collateral damage" rather than "dead civilians." In that spirit, allow me to offer up my own devil's dictionary of contemporary American political terms.

American Exceptionalism: a doctrine whose proponents hold that by divine dispensation America is exempt from all laws governing international norms, physics, or rationality.

authentic: used to describe a candidate who is unaware of current events and doesn't read a newspaper, and is proud of it.

class warfare: a technique by which teachers, nurses, firemen, and cashiers are believed to be oppressing derivatives traders and CEOs, which includes unreasonably complaining that their wages aren't keeping up with the cost of their health insurance.

conservative: a person profoundly respectful of heritage, tradition, and old-fashioned values while preaching the revolution and strip-mining the Grand Canyon for high-sulfur coal.

Darwin's theory of evolution: an evil doctrine that denies the teachings of the Bible. Social Darwinism, on the other hand, is

what made America great and is perfectly consistent with the Sermon on the Mount.

elites: insufferable, overeducated snobs who are not real Americans and may in fact be French. Mitt Romney (Harvard MBA and JD) and George W. Bush (Yale, Harvard) have often criticized such scoundrels.

empower: If an American worker loses his pension or Social Security, he is empowered.

free-market capitalism: the economic system by which Halliburton gets sole-source, cost-plus government contracts.

global warming: a hoax perpetrated by a worldwide conspiracy of biased scientists. Fortunately it is being combated by right-wing foundations, oil companies, televangelists, and other disinterested believers in objective fact.

job creators: the truly creative engines of economic growth in our society: real-estate flippers, mortgage-backed securities bundlers, leveraged buyout specialists, dividend drawers, and hedge-fund billionaires.

level playing field: what every lobbyist wants in the spirit of fairness. The only way to achieve it is by bribing politicians to award a sole-source contract to his client.

liberal (pronounced *librull*): a satanic ideologue who is at once a socialist leveler, an elitist defender of privilege, an atheist, and a secret Muslim determined to bring sharia law to America.

patriot: someone who loves America more than he loves the majority of the people living therein.

populist: an advocate for the interests of "real" Americans who vehemently fights for the abolition of all government regulation of Wall Street investment banks.

prolife: the unconditional support of the first nine months of a human being's existence. After that period has expired, the same human being has an unconditional right to be executed by the state, sent off to war, or die without health insurance.

real Americans: the minority of Americans who look, think, and act exactly as I do.

rogue state: a country that violates international law by committing armed aggression, torturing prisoners, assassinating opponents, and possessing weapons of mass destruction. cf: **American Exceptionalism**

sharia law: a fundamentalist religious doctrine imposed on a given political jurisdiction. Any resemblance to public statutes on abortion in the Commonwealth of Virginia is purely coincidental.

take our country back: Give us what we want right now, even if we don't know what it is.

Tea Party: people covered by Medicare who hate socialized medicine.

Washington spending: the bad sort of spending that doesn't go toward earmarks to campaign contributors, subsidies to big oil, or the military's half-trillion-dollar budget. Everyone knows the Pentagon is across the Potomac in Virginia, not in Washington.

win-win situation: see **level playing field**.

5

TAXES AND THE RICH

The GOP cares, over and above every other item on its political agenda, about the rich contributors who keep them in office. This is why tax increases on the wealthy have become an absolute Republican taboo. Caught between their own rich contributors and their voters, Democrats are conflicted and compromised.

"The very rich are different from you and me. . . ."
Yes, they have more money.

—Ernest Hemingway, taking a pot shot at F. Scott Fitzgerald in the original version of "The Snows of Kilimanjaro"

Although you won't find it in their party platform, the GOP's mission is to protect and further enrich America's plutocracy. The party's caterwauling about deficits and debt is so much eyewash to blind the public. In reality, Republicans act as bellhops for corporate America and the superrich behind those corporations. In the calculus of Washington politics as practiced by the GOP, wealthy individuals and corporations are interchangeable: Mitt Romney may have said more than he knew when he pleaded that "corporations are people!" They are indeed people, a very select group of people in executive suites and boardrooms who

draw a wildly disproportionate share of the benefits from the tax code—a tax code that the GOP has manipulated relentlessly to produce exactly that outcome.* As for the rest of us, Republicans have of late been strangely indifferent; some GOP presidential candidates have even offered proposals that would increase taxes on people of modest means. One might think Republicans would be enthusiastic about extending their tax-cut agenda to low-income earners paying regressive rates on their payroll taxes. These folks, who struggle from paycheck to paycheck just to keep their heads above water, would benefit the most from tax relief. But the GOP has been uncharacteristically hesitant when it comes to tax cuts for the ordinary Americans they claim to champion.

Whatever else President Obama has accomplished, his $4 trillion deficit reduction offer during the debt-ceiling crisis in the summer of 2011 did perform the useful service of smoking out Republican hypocrisy. The GOP refused to accept the offer because it could not abide so much as a one-tenth of 1 percent increase on the tax rates of the Walton family or the Koch brothers, much less a repeal of the carried interest rule that permits billionaire hedge fund managers to pay income tax at a lower effective rate than cops or nurses. Republicans finally settled on a deal that had far less deficit reduction—and even fewer spending cuts!—than Obama's proposal, because of their iron resolution to protect our society's overclass at all costs.

The GOP's indulgence of its campaign contributors is perhaps the single most outstanding characteristic of the party, although their rivals on the other side of the aisle are also well versed in the

* Corporations are persons? Really? Do corporations register for the draft at age eighteen? Are they called for jury duty? Legal sophistry must yield to common sense.

practice of buck raking. To give one small but illuminating example: On November 17, 2011, the House passed by a margin of 298 to 121 a measure that would define pizza as a vegetable for the purposes of the school lunch program. To quote a Reuters news article:

> "It's an important victory," said Corey Henry, spokesman for the American Frozen Food Institute (AFFI). That trade association lobbied Congress on behalf of frozen pizza sellers like ConAgra Foods Inc. and Schwan Food Co. and French fry makers McCain Foods Ltd. and J.R. Simplot Co., the latter best known as a supplier to fast-food company McDonald's Corp.[1]

During 2010, ConAgra gave $154,200 in political contributions and spent $400,000 on lobbying.[2] Granted that the average American can spare zero dollars to contribute to politicians or to lobby Congress, $154,200 divided among 535 representatives and senators comes to $288 per elected official. (In 2006, the last year that party breakouts are available, ConAgra gave 16 percent to Democrats and 84 percent to Republicans.[3]) What is noteworthy about the $288 is not how much money in aggregate washes through our political system, but how cheaply you can buy a politician.

Republicans have attempted to camouflage their solicitude for the wealthy and corporations with a fog of misleading rhetoric. John Boehner is fond of saying, "We won't raise *anyone's* taxes," as if the take-home pay of an Olive Garden waitress were inextricably bound up with whether Warren Buffett pays his capital gains as ordinary income or at a lower rate. Another chestnut is that millionaires and billionaires are "job creators." U.S. corporations have recently had their most profitable quarters in history; at the end of

2011, Apple was sitting on $97.6 billion in cash, more than the GDP of most small countries. So where are the jobs? Overwhelmingly, they went to China.[4]

Another smokescreen is the "small business" meme, since standing up for Mom and Pop's corner store is politically more attractive than shilling for a megacorporation. Raising taxes on the wealthy will kill the ability of small businesses to hire; that is the GOP lament every time some Democrat offers an amendment to increase taxes on incomes over $1 million. But the number of small businesses with an annual net taxable income over a million dollars is de minimis, if they exist at all, as they would no longer constitute small businesses. And as data from the nonpartisan Center for Economic and Policy Research have shown, small businesses account for only 7.2 percent of total employment in the United States, a significantly smaller share of total employment than in most countries of the Organization for Economic Cooperation and Development (OECD), which includes the United States, Canada, Australia, Japan, and Chile, in addition to most European countries.[5]

The GOP's inflated rhetoric about protecting small business occasionally reaches such comic levels that one is hard-pressed to distinguish it from satire. In September 2011, House Republicans issued a report condemning the supposedly job-killing regulations of the Obama administration. The administration had proposed a rule to restrict the trade in Burmese pythons, a huge, highly dangerous, and invasive species of snake that has been devastating wildlife in the Everglades and, should it prove adaptable to colder climates, could spread northward as far as coastal Delaware. The Republicans concluded that banning a reptile that can swallow an alligator or a small child might "devastate a small but thriving sector of the economy" and that the rule "has significant implications

for small businesses across the United States."[6] Now that I think about it, I wonder whether the Republicans' pro-snake position is based on their economic philosophy, or whether it is professional courtesy toward reptiles.

The GOP's ritual exalting of small business is a subset of a larger narrative in Republican messaging: the appeal to popular nostalgia for a small-town America where real Americans live. The Mom and Pop store, the local hardware emporium, the barbershop where the owner knows your name—all fit into a gauzy mental picture of a small community where the sun always seems to be shining and neighbors help one another out. Those who shape the GOP message have carefully crafted it as a counterpoint to the contrasting image of the anonymous and menacing big cities of the two coasts, where foreigners make up an increasing share of the population and alien cosmopolite ideas rule.

Yet what have Republicans done when it comes to advancing economic policies that would assure the viability of the small-town America they claim to adore? Did they support changes in the tax code to help small business fight off chain retailers? Did they oppose trade bills that would jeopardize small- and medium-size manufacturers by exposing them to competition from starvation-wage manufacturers overseas? Did they oppose tax advantages that big companies can accrue through leveraged buyouts of competitors?* I see no evidence they lifted a finger.

On the contrary, Republican ideology celebrates outsourcing, globalization, and takeovers as the glorious fruits of capitalism's "creative destruction." I saw for myself how Republican propo-

---

* Companies can write off the debt they assume to finance a takeover of another company in order to raid its pension fund, strip its assets, and liquidate the company.

nents of globalized vulture capitalism, such as Grover Norquist, Dick Armey, Phil Gramm, and Lawrence Kudlow, extolled this process as an unalloyed benefit. They were quick to denounce as socialism any attempt to mitigate its impact on society. Yet their own ideology is nothing more than an upside-down utopianism, a nineteenth-century absolutist twin of Marxism. If millions of people's interests are damaged in the process, it is a necessary and inevitable outcome of scientific laws that must never be tampered with.

I recall that in the late 1990s, some prolabor congressmen wanted to correct serious labor abuses occurring in the Northern Mariana Islands, a Pacific commonwealth of the United States. The territory was exempt from U.S. wage and workplace safety laws, but it was permitted to send garments manufactured there to the United States free of tariffs, because they were defined by law as "made in USA." There were persistent reports of near-gulag labor conditions, including barbed wire around the factories to keep workers from leaving. Forced abortions were among the abuses reportedly taking place against female workers who became pregnant, based on the idea that there shouldn't be any useless mouths to feed in a free-trade zone. To keep its privileged status, the entrepreneurs in the islands hired superlobbyist Jack Abramoff to lobby the Hill. Abramoff's friend Tom DeLay ensured that the House never considered legislation to end the abuses in the Marianas, even though one bill had a majority of House members sponsoring it. Even the sanctimonious prolife claims of the GOP receded before the dominant principle animating the party: Nothing must ever get in the way of the rich getting richer, especially when they use lobbyists to hand out cash to obliging congressmen.

When I was growing up in Ohio, both the cities and small towns had a profusion of small- to medium-size manufacturing busi-

nesses: tool-and-die works, sheet-metal fabricators, metal-casting companies, and parts suppliers for the larger industries, such as the car companies and the rubber industry. Now, thanks to this glorious creative destruction, most of them are gone—along with job security, a defined pension, and health benefits. But somebody made out pretty well in the conversion of the American economy from a diversified manufacturing colossus into a financial oligopoly. There was no one event, no single piece of legislation responsible for this transformation. But three decades of trade legislation to facilitate the offshoring of jobs, tax policies favoring looting over investment, and the deregulation of Wall Street's financial chicanery favored this transformation at every turn. And Republicans consistently favored those polices in their platform promoting free trade, tax relief, and deregulation.

Republicans have assiduously spread the myth that Americans are conspicuously overtaxed. But compared to other OECD countries, the effective rates of U.S. taxation are among the lowest. Among the thirty-three developed countries of the OECD, America's taxes are the fourth lowest; only those of Turkey, Mexico, and Chile are lower.[7] Lately the GOP has taken up the mantra that the top corporate income tax rate of 35 percent is confiscatory Bolshevism. But again, the effective rate is much lower. Did GE pay 35 percent in 2010 on its net profits of $14 billion? No. It paid zero.*

When pressed, Republicans make up misleading statistics to prove that America's fiscal burden is being borne by the rich and that the rest of us are freeloaders who don't appreciate that fact. "Half of Americans don't pay taxes" is a perennial meme. But what they leave out is that that statement refers to federal *income* taxes.

---

* The company deducted all of its losses from its GE Capital subsidiary while indefinitely deferring payment on its $10.8 billion in overseas profits.

There are millions of low-income employed people who don't pay income taxes, but they do contribute payroll taxes—among the most regressive form of taxation. According to GOP fiscal theology, however, payroll taxes don't count. Somehow Republicans have convinced themselves that since payroll taxes go into trust funds, like Social Security, they are not real taxes. Likewise, state and local sales taxes do not count, although their effect on a poor person buying necessities such as food is far more regressive than on a millionaire. This explains why Mitt Romney pays federal taxes at an effective rate of 14 percent, while a middle-income earner making sixty-four thousand dollars per year pays 13 percent.

All of these half-truths and outright lies have seeped into popular culture via the corporate-owned business press. Just listen to CNBC for a few hours and you will hear most of them in one form or another. More important politically, Republican myths about taxation have been internalized by millions of economically downscale so-called values voters, who were attracted to the GOP for other reasons (which I will explain later) but now accept this misinformation as sacred dogma. Many people believe their taxes have gone up since the 2008 election, whereas, in reality, thanks to tax provisions in the stimulus bill and Obama's initiative to temporarily reduce federal payroll taxes, they have gone *down.*

When misinformation is not enough to sustain popular support for the GOP's agenda, concealment is needed. One innocuous provision in the Dodd-Frank Wall Street Reform Act of 2010 requires public companies to make a more transparent disclosure of CEO compensation, including bonuses. The bill, which purported to fix the causes of the 2008 financial meltdown (but which had considerable input from industry lobbyists and a Wall Street–friendly Treasury Department), did not even limit the pay of chief officers of public companies but only required full disclosure of that pay. Re-

publicans are determined to repeal this provision. Of course. It would not serve Wall Street's interests if the public took an unhealthy interest in the disparities between their own incomes and those of bank CEOs. As Republican representative Spencer Bachus of Alabama told a home-state newspaper shortly after assuming the chairmanship of the House Financial Services Committee in the wake of the November 2010 election, "In Washington, the view is that the banks are to be regulated, and my view is that Washington and the regulators are there to serve the banks."[8]

On most occasions the GOP prefers to obscure its economic agenda by serving up vague platitudes about their "economic growth agenda" or "creating good jobs and getting the government off Americans' backs." Some Republican candidates are too ignorant of economic policy even to discuss it coherently: Michele Bachmann, while campaigning for the Republican presidential nomination, declared that what the country needed was to return to the tax policies of Ronald Reagan. She was obviously unaware that the tax rates under Reagan were mostly higher than at present.

Herman Cain, once the CEO of Godfather's Pizza, came up with a tax plan that was a masterpiece of marketing, with its simple "9-9-9" label that was vaguely reminiscent of a two-for-one pizza special. Cain would lower all federal income tax rates to a single 9 percent one, set the corporate rate at 9 percent, and levy a national sales tax of 9 percent. It had the sort of meretricious simplicity that would appeal both to the simple-minded and the media. And lo and behold, early on most of the press declared Cain's plan a brilliant campaign move without making any effort to evaluate its likely impact or substantive merits.

Bruce Bartlett, an economist in the Reagan and George H. W. Bush administrations, took the time to crunch the numbers.[9] His conclusion: Cain's plan decreased revenue as it drastically cut the

taxes of the wealthy and—here's the kicker—raised taxes on the least well-off. Cain did not actually propose to tax *all* income at 9 percent (so much for his plan's appealing simplicity): He actually lowered the capital gains and dividend tax rates to zero. Generally, the richer the individual is, the more likely his income is derived from capital gains and dividends, which are already taxed at less than half the top marginal income tax rate, than from his salary. This current inequity in the tax code accounts for the fact that the four hundred richest Americans have been paying an average effective federal income tax rate of 17 percent since the passage of the Bush tax cuts—little more than half of what they had paid in the early 1990s—even as their combined income quadrupled. Cain's plan would have sharply increased this disparity.

The usual Republican rationale for reducing tax rates on capital below the rates on labor is that capital gains are "double taxed."* But that is a smokescreen. The American revenue system is about taxing *individual legal entities.* Taxes on an individual, be he a wage earner or sole proprietor of a business, are only levied once; that said, all income the individual gets from whatever source (unless it is specifically exempt) is taxed. Corporations pay taxes only on their profits, a narrower category whose definition is more susceptible to creative bookkeeping. This is how GE can pay zero federal taxes in a given year. Yet that does not preclude its shareholders from realizing capital gains. Those GE shareholders are individual

* It is a fine semantic point whether corporations "pay" capital gains. They don't pay them directly insofar as an investor realizes profit by betting correctly on an investment in a company whose market valuation increases before he sells those shares. In a way, that makes the double-taxation argument even more specious, because corporate market valuation is a nontaxable event for the corporation, since it only pays taxes on its profits.

entities who are legally separate from the corporations whose shares they own. That is why they are not liable for corporate malfeasance or the company's debts. They are taxed once on the income they receive from their investments.

To argue that investors are double taxed is like saying that if Warren Buffett were to give you a billion dollars free and clear, you should pay no taxes on that sum, since Buffett was already taxed on it. Good luck with that argument when you make your not-guilty plea in federal court! The cry of "double taxation" is a perennial red herring designed to let rich speculators skate.

The Tax Policy Center did a distributional analysis of Cain's plan. The center's conclusion:

> A middle-income household making between about $64,000 and $110,000 would get hit with an average tax increase of about $4,300, lowering its after-tax income by more than 6 percent and increasing its average federal tax rate (including income, payroll, estate and its share of the corporate income tax) from 18.8 percent to 23.7 percent. By contrast, a taxpayer in the top 0.1 percent (who makes more than $2.7 million) would enjoy an average tax cut of nearly $1.4 million, increasing his after-tax income by nearly 27 percent. . . . *[A] typical household making more than $2.7 million would pay a smaller share of its income in federal taxes than one making less than $18,000.*[10] [emphasis mine]

This was the brilliant tax plan that briefly spurred Cain's meteoric rise to Republican front-runner.

At first I wondered: Did Herman Cain dream this plan up himself? If not, who whispered it in his ear, and what interests did that person represent? A little investigating uncovered the fact that

Cain's plan was the brainchild of Rich Lowrie, one of his economic advisers, who lives in Gates Mills, Ohio, a village of twenty-four hundred inhabitants east of Cleveland, and one of the wealthiest suburbs in the country.[11]

Lowrie's day job is as an investment adviser, and he has been involved with such groups as the Koch brothers–funded Club for Growth and Americans for Prosperity. His plan had substantive input from longtime Republican operatives Arthur Laffer (who, with his Laffer Curve, is a forefather of the current generation of crackpot right-wing economists) and Steve Moore, a founder of the Club for Growth and the Free Enterprise Fund, a 501(c)4 organization that promotes the political views of billionaires while remaining tax-exempt.

Still, it is a little surprising that in mid-2011, after the greatest financial meltdown in eighty years, widespread unemployment and destitution, and rising public anger over the greatest income disparity in America since the 1920s, a presidential candidate would tout a plan that would raise taxes on low- and moderate-income earners while drastically reducing them on the wealthy. Republican primary voters are notoriously tolerant of lunatic-fringe proposals, but one would think even they might grow pale at a plan that would raise taxes on the majority of them.

But in reality Cain surged in the polls after unveiling his tax plan. If the media are to be believed, he surged *because* of it. Cain's candidacy, of course, flamed out as a result of unrelated scandals. Still, his tax plan is a stunning illustration of how kamikaze tactics can advance one's political agenda. Several other GOP presidential candidates adopted similar tax proposals. Gingrich's proposal, while less draconian toward the poor and middle class, would sharply lower rates on the wealthy. According to the Tax Policy Center, filers with annual incomes above $1 million would pay tax

rates substantially less than those earning $40,000 to $50,000 a year, because in addition to the wealthy having their income tax rates drastically lowered, their investment income is not taxed at all.[12] And federal revenue would fall anywhere from $830 billion to $1.25 trillion per year when fully phased in: This would precipitate an even deeper fiscal crisis, undoubtedly leading to calls for deep cuts in Social Security and Medicare. Perhaps, given his views about those programs, that was partly his intent.

As for Mitt Romney, his initial tax plan had a similar bias: Those making more than $1 million a year would receive an average federal income tax cut of $145,000 by 2015, while those making less than $40,000 would see their federal income taxes increase. At the same time, his scheme would increase deficits by about $180 billion annually by 2015.[13] But apparently that was not enough to satisfy his contributors, so at the end of February 2012 Romney added a 20 percent cut in all income tax rates and a repeal of the alternative minimum tax. The Tax Policy Center estimated that the 20 percent rate cut would add an additional $150 billion to the deficit in 2015 alone. But even Romney looks like a tight-fisted deficit hawk compared to his late-surging rival Rick Santorum, who proposed to sharply lower income taxes and taxes on capital gains and dividends, cut corporate income taxes in half, and eliminate the inheritance tax that falls overwhelmingly on the rich. He would also triple the exemption for dependent children. According to the Committee for a Responsible Federal Budget, Santorum's tax plan would add a staggering $6 trillion to the deficit over the next ten years.[14]

The Republican presidential candidates' fiscal plans shared a common characteristic: They were all riddled with such fantastic assumptions that no neutral observer could come away with any reaction other than that Republicans are so math challenged they could not manage a lemonade stand, let alone the finances of a na-

tion of 310 million people whose government spends $3.5 trillion a year.

While lowering taxes on the wealthy is a well-known formula in the GOP's playbook, Republicans of late have become quite uncharacteristically willing to consider raising taxes. But not on the rich: They are targeting the less well-off.

My first contact with a Republican proponent of raising taxes on the poor came in 1999. Two congressional staffers and I were invited over to the Watergate offices of a campaign consultant (I hasten to stress that this was after office hours, on our own time). If elected officials stand on the bottom rung of the public's ladder of esteem, it is probably because the public is not sufficiently familiar with the work of political consultants. This gentleman, Donald Fierce, was representative of the species. His opening formalities consisted of berating us—federal employees who were subject to the Hatch Act and responsible for devoting our office hours solely to the public's business—for the fact that the presidential candidate he was advising, my boss, John Kasich, was falling far behind the George W. Bush campaign juggernaut in the race for the presidential nomination. Then he got down to business.

What policy ideas did we have to relaunch his floundering candidacy? After considerable back and forth, the consultant pitched us one of his own. What with the earned income tax credit and all, the working poor weren't paying any taxes. How about starting a national conversation on the idea that the poor should pay their fair share? I convinced him with some difficulty that a candidate whose entire public career consisted of advocating tax cuts for everybody and tax increases for nobody could hardly be expected to advocate such a policy, nor, I ventured, would it fly with the electorate (this

was the electorate of a dozen years ago). But I thought it odd that a savvy GOP fixer would suggest such a policy in the first place.

The first laying of the groundwork in public for the idea of increasing taxes on low-income earners came in a November 2002 *Wall Street Journal* editorial page comment. The working poor, less well-off retirees, and others who do not pay federal income taxes were "lucky duckies," according to the *Journal*. While the paper did not propose any specific remedy for this "problem," it worried that having so many people not paying income taxes would erode popular support for future tax cuts. The *Journal* followed up with two more editorials also using the same infantile phrase to convey its suggestion that a person earning twelve thousand dollars is somehow getting away with something if his earned income tax credit nullifies his income tax liability.

Most Republican officeholders did not come out publicly making the *Journal*'s argument, but sometime later a few, like Jim DeMint and Orin Hatch, occasionally commandeered the Senate chamber to denounce a tax policy that had allegedly allowed almost half of Americans to avoid paying federal income taxes. The whole line of argumentation strikes me as being in bad faith, as it is intended to seduce the listener into confusing people's federal income tax burden with their total tax burden. It leaves out of the equation not only federal payroll taxes, but also those also levied by state and local governments. Less wealthy individuals who are employed, including those who pay no income tax, pay federal payroll taxes that are regressive, while any income above $110,000 is not subject to the Social Security tax. Sales taxes are even more sharply regressive.

Since Obama's election in 2008, Republicans have amped up the "soak the poor" theme. They have been strangely lukewarm about maintaining a payroll tax cut, despite the fact that it would

increase the purchasing power of tens of millions of Americans who would have no choice but to recycle the money into the economy in order to buy necessities. That is strange behavior indeed from a party that claims never to have met a tax cut it didn't like; but the Tea Party–infused House Republicans have been in no mood for anything but obstruction. Their pretexts for blocking the extension of the payroll tax cut in December 2011—they wanted a one-year rather than two-month extension, and wanted to offset its cost—are not credible, because they have not insisted that any other tax cuts be offset, and have previously always been more than ready to extend expiring tax cuts for any length of time. Their real intent was to keep making extraneous demands for more concessions until negotiations collapsed. Jeff Flake, a six-term Republican from Arizona, said after the House GOP's back-down that he would "like to see [the deal] unravel completely." He went on to say that "it was a mistake," and that the payroll tax cut should not have been passed in the first place.[15]

In early 2010 the deficit-reduction advisory panel known as the Simpson-Bowles Commission got underway. As a budget committee staffer for one of the commissioners, Senator Judd Gregg of New Hampshire, I assisted the committee on an ad hoc basis. What struck me in the early stages of its deliberations was the apparent bipartisan consensus for a notional tax reform plan that involved, in the words of many of the commission members, "a broadening and flattening of the base." What could that mean? Flattening implied lowering all of the current marginal income tax rates, with the higher rates reduced more than the lower ones. The logical outcome was that wealthier taxpayers would gain more than the less well-off. To offset the loss of revenues, the tax base would have to be broadened: the logic appeared to be that hitherto exempt filers at the lower end of the income scale would have to pay income taxes.

In other words, the commission's notional scheme would largely fulfill the Republicans' tax agenda: lower rates at the top; more people paying at the bottom. But when the commission's staffers set to work to produce a written plan, they had to be conscious of the panel's overriding mandate: to reduce the deficit. So they flattened and broadened the tax base, but to offset the revenue loss they eliminated many deductions from which the wealthy benefit more, and treated capital gains and dividends as ordinary income.

As a result, their draft plan showed a net revenue increase, one which would have gone some distance in reducing future deficits. But even after getting what they said they wanted—lower rates, a broader base, and an elimination of economically inefficient tax deductions and loopholes, along with $4 trillion in outyear deficit reduction—all three House Republican members of the commission voted against the commission recommendations.

This is not the place to discuss the merits and demerits of the Simpson-Bowles deficit-reduction package. Several Democrats voted against it too, showing that the abiding concern of many of them about the deficit is—like the concern of the Republicans—more rhetorical than real. But what is significant is that it was the first serious plan to reveal what Republican priorities are, particularly among House Republicans such as Paul Ryan, whom the press has called a "serious" deficit hawk. Ryan and his two House Republican colleagues rejected a plan embodying the very tax principles—broadening and flattening income tax rates and eliminating loopholes—that they claimed to endorse.*

---

* My boss, Senator Gregg, voted for the Simpson-Bowles recommendations. He was one of the few remaining Republicans in either house of Congress more interested in deficit reduction than in saving the world by banning contraception and making gay marriage illegal. There are even fewer now: He retired at the end of 2010.

During the debt-ceiling negotiations the following summer, the administration offered several deficit-reduction proposals similar to Simpson-Bowles, and House Republicans rejected them all. By this time, with a more right-wing membership following the November 2010 elections, Senate Republicans were also taking a harder line. The result of the debt-ceiling fiasco was that no deficit-reduction deal was made. Congress simply punted the decision to the so-called super committee. When Democrats on that committee offered a plan several months later with the same level of cuts as Simpson-Bowles and only half the revenue increases, Republican committee members from both houses of Congress rejected it out of hand.

One of the reasons for all of these GOP rejections is a habit of political obstructionism that has only grown since early 2009. Most Republicans do not want to give Obama any sort of legislative accomplishment, such as a long-term deficit reduction, even if it would accord with their own political rhetoric. But another reason is that any credible deficit reduction would have to include some revenue increase. Wealthy individuals and big corporations enjoy a greater share of the national income and lower tax rates that at any time since the 1920s. Some Republicans may know that; others, like Michele Bachmann, probably have no more clue about tax policy than quantum physics. But they all know one thing: Their rich contributors must be protected at all costs, and, if possible, the rates on millionaires should be lowered even further.

Smoke and mirrors to the contrary, lowering taxes on the most favored elements of society is the sole object of Republican fiscal policy. They are not serious about deficit reduction. Their behavior has demonstrated it, and their heated rhetoric on the subject is sound and fury signifying nothing. Any serious discussion in this country about deficits and debt must proceed from that fact.

6

WORSHIPPING AT THE ALTAR OF MARS

There is no getting around the fact that the GOP loves war more than it supposedly hates deficits. But Democrats are furiously playing catch-up.

War is a racket. It always has been. It is possibly the oldest, easily the most profitable, surely the most vicious. . . . It is the only one in which the profits are reckoned in dollars and the losses in lives.

—General Smedley Butler, United States Marine Corps, twice awarded the Congressional Medal of Honor

While the me-too Democrats have set a horrible example of late of keeping up with the Joneses when it comes to waging war, they cannot hope to match the GOP in their libidinous enthusiasm for invading other countries. John McCain went so far as to propose that we mix it up with Russia—a nuclear-armed state!—during its conflict with Georgia in 2008 (remember "we are all Georgians now," a slogan that did not, fortunately, catch on), and Lindsey Graham has been relentlessly agitating for attacks on Iran and intervention in Syria. These are not fringe elements of the party, mind you; they are the leading "defense experts" tapped for the Sunday talk shows. In 2011, about a

month before House Republicans began threatening the creditworthiness of the United States in their headlong determination to cut trillions of dollars out of the budget, these same Republicans passed a defense appropriations bill that *increased* spending by $17 billion over the prior year's budget.

So much for the GOP's contention that cutting spending and reducing the deficit are their overriding, existential priorities. The Bush administration's principal contribution to sound fiscal policy was to cut taxes while waging a war—something that had never been done before in the country's history—and to leave the cost of the war out of its budget. Republicans have never been very good in math, but the Bush administration set a new low. Since then, regardless of the threat level, regardless of the size of the deficit, the dominant faction in the Republican Party can be counted on every year to seek an increase in the Pentagon's budget.

When the GOP won majorities in the House and Senate in 1994, not long after the collapse of the Warsaw Pact and the dissolution of the Soviet Union, the U.S. armed forces had recently demonstrated their crushing military superiority in the Gulf War. One would have thought this might suffice to convince any remaining skeptics that we had all the military hardware we needed. The deficit was growing seemingly intractably, and the GOP had won the 1994 election on a sweeping platform of spending cuts and the promise of a balanced budget. This was the bedrock of Newt Gingrich's "Contract with America." To balance the budget without raising taxes would have required significant cuts in almost every budgetary category. The Department of Defense (DOD) budget—which accounts for half of all discretionary spending—would have to be cut, or at least held flat. I knew the numbers because my boss was the incoming House Budget Committee chairman, John Kasich, who was charged with producing a balanced budget. Yet as

soon as the new Republican Congress was seated, the House and Senate Armed Services committees demanded that the Pentagon's six-year spending plan be increased by at least $120 billion.

I vividly recall how in January 1995 the committee chairmen hashed out their differences in the Speaker's office. Kasich told Newt and his counterparts on the Armed Services Committee that defense spending would have to be placed "under the same microscope" as all other spending if the budget was ever to be balanced. The newly minted House Armed Services Committee chairman, Floyd Spence, responded with an emotional tirade that ended with his saying that Kasich—who had spent twelve years on the Armed Services Committee—was "destroying the defense of this country." In the end, Floyd didn't get the whole loaf: He did get a modest increase of $6 billion that year, when every other department was being cut. For several years thereafter, Republicans increased every budget the Pentagon submitted by a few billion dollars, enough to poke a finger in the eye of the Clinton administration but not enough to risk a presidential veto. I occasionally found myself wondering how our political system could allow people like Floyd Spence, a man of exquisitely unsound judgment, to get into a position of significant influence on U.S. national security policy.

A cynic might conclude that this militaristic enthusiasm could be explained by the simple fact that Pentagon contractors spread a lot of bribe money around Capitol Hill. That is of course true, but there is more to it than that. Some members of Congress will claim that they are protecting constituents' jobs, but even that doesn't really explain it. The wildly uneven concentration of defense contracts and military bases means that some areas, such as Washington, D.C., and San Diego, are heavily dependent on DOD spending, but in most of the country the balance is a net negative: More is paid out in taxes to support the Pentagon than comes back in local contracts.

Economic justifications for Pentagon spending are even less persuasive when one considers that the $600 billion spent every year on the DOD generates comparatively few jobs per dollar spent. The days of Rosie the Riveter are long gone; most weapons projects now require very little touch labor. Instead, a disproportionate share is siphoned off into high-cost R&D (from which the civilian economy benefits little), exorbitant management expenditures, whopping overhead, and out-and-out padding—including, of course, the money that flows back into the coffers of political campaigns. A dollar appropriated for highway construction, health care, or education will create many more jobs than a dollar appropriated for Pentagon weapons procurement: The jobs argument is thoroughly specious.*

Take away the cash nexus and there remains a strong psychological predisposition toward war and militarism in a large part of the GOP. This tic, greatly exacerbated in the immediate aftermath of September 11 and alarmingly persistent since then, undoubtedly arises from a neurotic need to demonstrate toughness. It dovetails perfectly with the belligerent tough-guy affect one constantly hears on right-wing talk radio. Militarism springs from a psychological deficit that requires an endless series of enemies both foreign and domestic. So it is not surprising that the party that gave us Joe McCarthy and red-baiting should embrace the war on terror. To borrow the author Chris Hedges's formulation, war is a force that gives them meaning.

The results of the last decade of unbridled militarism, and of

---

* A University of Massachusetts study claims that several alternative ways of spending money would produce anywhere from 35 percent to 138 percent more jobs than spending the same amount on DOD. (http://www.peri.umass.edu/fileadmin/pdf/published_study/PERI_military_spending_2011.pdf).

the Democrats' cowardly or opportunistic refusal to oppose it, have been disastrous, both strategically and fiscally. It has damaged our respect for the Bill of Rights and severely impaired our standing in the world. Unfortunately, because of the toxic political dynamic prevailing in Washington, the militarism and the promiscuous intervention it has given rise to seem likely to abate only when the Treasury is exhausted and creditors balk at renewing loans, as happened to hubristic military empires in the past, such as Great Britain in the period between World War II and the Suez crisis or the Spanish Empire in its long slide from world power in the eighteenth century.

By a process of self-selection, acculturation, and groupthink, a majority of the members of Congress currently sitting on the defense committees of both the House and Senate have become rigid advocates of ever higher military spending, even when this position conflicts with their much advertised insistence on the need to rein in the national debt and their tiresome and hypocritical rhetorical claims that we must not leave fiscal burdens on the backs of our children. Many of these people would be similarly disposed even if there were no juicy DOD contracts producing jobs in their districts or states or helping to finance their next campaigns. The staffs of these committees have been conditioned by a similar process and often think like their bosses; many are military retirees with an emotional connection to their old services. So how did I, who worked most of my career on military issues, come to have such skeptical opinions about the defense establishment of this country?

When I arrived on the Hill during Reagan's first term, I was a conventional, mainstream Republican. I believed in the notion of peace through strength. At that time the slogan translated quite literally into spending more money on the Pentagon. The Soviet Union had invaded Afghanistan not long before, and the Warsaw

Pact seemed like a powerful and monolithic threat. I did not know then (and was probably too naïvely trusting to have believed it even if someone had tried to dispel my illusions) that the intelligence agencies were systematically inflating the Soviet threat, and that the Soviet military was far weaker than we imagined.

The senior appointees at the CIA—chief among them Robert Gates, who was then deputy director for intelligence—became so enamored of the concept of the Soviet threat that they somehow missed the fact that the collapse of the Warsaw Pact lay only a few years ahead.* The Pentagon's Defense Intelligence Agency was equally enthusiastic about inflating threats. Every year during the 1980s the Pentagon produced a lavishly illustrated publication, printed on coated paper, called *Soviet Military Power.* Many of the illustrations were color sketches of the fearsome hardware the Soviets supposedly had, or would have in the future (as with defense contractor brochures, the goal was to make the reader feel that the visual representation was real and not someone's fanciful projection). According to the cosmology of *Soviet Military Power,* the Soviets were not ten feet tall; they were twenty feet tall, with death rays projecting from their eyes.

The first crack in my credulity came in 1985, upon hearing an unclassified symposium on the Soviet Union that was held in Annapolis, Maryland. One of the experts was Murray Feshbach, then a demographer for the U.S. Census Bureau. Rather than interpreting the state of Soviet power from satellite photographs of missile fields or shipyards, he looked at available data about life expectancy at birth, fertility rates, infant mortality, nutrition, and so on, and

---

* Senators attending the hearings for Gates's confirmation as CIA director in 1991 brushed aside testimony from former CIA employees about his intelligence distortions because the fix was in, and President George H. W. Bush was not to be denied his nominee.

came to the conclusion that the USSR was a walking corpse—that it could not sustain itself as a superpower for much longer. I don't know whether he influenced any of the other congressional staffers in attendance, but it made me begin to question the prevailing wisdom critically.

My doubts as to the proper management of our military-industrial complex here at home began to grow around the same time. I worked in a congressional office representing a district in Ohio where the B-1 bomber—a project the Carter administration had canceled and the Reagan administration had revived as a cornerstone of its buildup policy—was a significant source of employment. One can generally tell which weapon system is built in a congressman's district by the contractor models on the office desks, the pictures on the walls, and the frequent presence of lobbyists from the company that builds the system. In our case, it was all B-1 all the time.

By the late 1980s, as the first production examples began to enter service, a funny thing happened—although it would not have been funny to the taxpayer who was funding the plane at a then considerable cost of $280 million each. The aircraft's defensive avionics, which were supposed to detect and neutralize enemy electronic systems seeking to find and destroy the B-1, were seriously interfering with the plane's own offensive avionics, whose goal was to help it find enemy targets and attack them. In other words, the contractors had managed to build a self-jamming bomber.

Three planes were written off in crashes shortly after the B-1 entered operational status. Two of these were caused by a poor design in the fuel or hydraulic lines. It soon became evident that needless secrecy surrounded the crash reports: The services hid the details even from Armed Services Committee members with the requisite clearances and an obvious need to know what had

happened. The B-1 was AWOL in the first Gulf war, and when it took part in operations in Kosovo in 1999, it flew only after older aircraft—like the antique B-52 it had been intended to replace—had already suppressed Serbian air defenses. There are dozens of weapons systems like the B-1 rattling around in the Pentagon's closet—cold war dinosaurs that are overpriced, underperforming, and unreliable. Every one of them has a coalition of congressional supporters who protect it from conception until decades later, when the military retires it from service; and even then, many in Congress will lobby for a reversal. Keeping these dinosaurs operating assures jobs for constituents. But at what cost to the rest of us?

What of the ethics of all this? One could take a charitable view that all the actors in a tragicomedy like the B-1 were fallible human beings who believed in the magnitude of the foreign threat and were merely optimistic about their ability to manage an important national project. The services, for their part, foster a can-do mentality among their members that does not invite naysayers. Some incidents, however, leave no doubt about an absence of good faith and honesty, because they verge upon the criminal. The official investigation into the explosion of the number-two gun turret of the USS *Iowa* on April 19, 1989, which killed forty-seven sailors, was one such incident.

The Navy's briefing on the preliminary investigation to the professional staff of the House Armed Services Committee and to the staffers of the members of the committee was a *Through the Looking Glass* event. The admiral in charge of the investigation, accompanied by the phalanx of uniformed coat holders and chart flippers who always escort the Pentagon's top brass, claimed to have it all figured out.

The explosion was an intentional act of sabotage by a Navy en-

listed man killed in the explosion who had become suicidal when his homosexual relationship with another crew member had gone bad. The perpetrator had fashioned a detonator and placed it in the firing chamber of the gun barrel. The case was all wrapped up. No defects in equipment, training, or doctrine. Up went my hand. "Uh, if the guy was suicidal, why didn't he kill himself by the usual practice of jumping off the ship's fantail at night? What's the evidence for an elaborate plan to take out his shipmates?"

The admiral had an answer for that. The FBI had assisted the Navy in carrying out the investigation and had put together a psychological profile that was, we were told, both empirical and scientific. Hartwig (Clayton Hartwig was the alleged perpetrator) was a man who would do such a thing. It just fits his profile; believe us, it's true. Other questions followed from equally skeptical staffers. There was something a little unsettling about the admiral's insistence that the tragedy was a criminal act by a man who was conveniently dead. To this day there is no definitive proof as to the cause of the *Iowa* disaster. But tests by Sandia National Laboratories and a review of the evidence by the Government Accountability Office strongly suggest the cause to have been either improper Navy training in loading the guns or defective powder. For the Navy to admit this, however, was intolerable; far better to blame a dead man.

The *Iowa* incident was a perfect counterpoint to my one previous professional experience with the Navy. For nine months in 1988 I attended courses at the Naval War College's Washington, D.C., campus. It was one of the most intellectually fulfilling experiences of my life. The students—mainly lieutenants, lieutenant commanders, and commanders, or their Marine Corps rank equivalents, were without exception bright, inquisitive, and skeptical. But something happens when officers rise into the flag ranks, and the same process occurs in the other services as well.

As the cold war drew to a close the defense establishment had evolved into a rigid, bureaucratic institution strangely emulating the defunct Soviet system it believed it had vanquished. Its real mission had become inwardly focused: to preserve the status, privileges, and prerogatives it had enjoyed. The Pentagon developed a whole vocabulary to enable this. There is no such thing in the military as a problem; there are only "issues" or "challenges." Mistakes or errors never occur. I recall watching one prototype missile test launch that blew up perhaps three seconds after liftoff. A general pronounced it "a nominal success." As the Pentagon status quo grew more entrenched, the rest of government, unfortunately, began to emulate its behavior.

This dysfunctional mutation bore evil fruit in the first decade of the twenty-first century: the Pat Tillman cover-up; Abu Ghraib; concealed atrocities; bad conditions for wounded soldiers at the Walter Reed army hospital; harassment of service personnel with post-traumatic stress disorder (PTSD). These and other cases tend to follow a set script: The incident is followed by the inevitable cover-up and denial; as the cover-up unravels, some small-fry might be thrown to the wolves; then comes absolution by means of an internally generated, phony "reform."

This procedure is now standard both in military departments and civilian agencies. If there is a procurement scandal, the solution is the Band-Aid of toothless "acquisition reform," leaving the same people to administer the programs. The failures of high-level policy judgments that played the biggest part in allowing 9/11 to occur were disguised as the much less significant failures of intelligence collection, analysis, and interagency sharing. Why? If the public were to blame policy judgments at the top, George W. Bush, Dick Cheney, Condoleezza Rice, and several cabinet secretaries might be on the hook. But if the fault could be placed on

operatives lower down the food chain, as well as on "institutional failures" of the bureaucracy, Congress and the public could be distracted by the monkey motion of "reform" and government reorganization. This is how we ended up with even more bureaucracy in the form of the Office of the Director of National Intelligence, not to mention the monstrosity of the Department of Homeland Security.

The dysfunctions of our uniformed military, our intelligence agencies (85 percent of whose funding flows through military budgets), and the rest of government did not arise overnight, and they did not form in a vacuum. They are partially the products of an odd and seldom-remarked schizophrenia that has grown up in our political culture. There are many people active in politics who claim they would man the barricades to fight to the death against socialism. But these are almost always the same people who also say they adore the U.S. military, which is probably the largest—certainly the most lavishly funded—socialist institution remaining on Earth since the collapse of the USSR and the transformation of China.

America's military bases are separate little worlds with their own law enforcement and traffic rules—not to mention their own grocery stores (commissaries), big-box stores (PXs), and so on, down to their own DOD Dependents School system, child care centers, housing, and comprehensive health care system—all of them run by the government. There are important historical reasons why these facilities arose, having to do with the low salaries of the old draft military and the frequent remoteness of military bases from retail business, schools, and essential services (on the frontier or overseas, for example). These facilities remain an important factor in the retention of military personnel, particularly those with dependents, to this day. But it is a socialist, or at least

highly welfarist state, arrangement.* Today, with the advent of the all-volunteer force, salaries are much higher; according to the Congressional Budget Office, military pay averages around the seventy-fifth percentile when compared to civilian jobs with comparable skills. Other studies by the CBO have demonstrated that in several cases, such as the commissaries (the huge retail grocery chains operated by the DOD), a cash allowance would give service members the same level of grocery benefit that they enjoy now—at substantially less cost. Yet whenever the Pentagon offers a proposal to change these arrangements—such as letting annual health care premiums for retirees rise with inflation (they have remained the same since 1995)—Congress invariably rejects it, with the free-market, fiscal hawk Republicans usually leading the opposition.

This same sort of military socialism prevails in regions of the country heavily dependent on military contracts. Loudoun County, Virginia, an outer suburb of Washington, D.C., offers a perfect example of this ethos. It is the richest county in the United States when measured by median household income.† It is very enthusiastically Republican.[1] And the number-one and number-two military contractors in the country, Lockheed Martin and Northrop Grumman, are located there. Fairfax County, the county next to Loudoun, has the second-highest median household income in the

---

* During the debate over the health care bill in 2009, a former colleague who had gone to work in the defense industry mentioned a co-worker of his—retired military—who had criticized "socialist Obamacare." As a military retiree this person would have paid an annual premium of $230 for his health insurance if he were single or $460 for himself and his family. Yes, they were earned benefits, but taxpayer subsidized nevertheless.

† Some lists count the independent city of Falls Church, Virginia, also in the Washington suburbs, as a county. If so, it would outrank Loudoun in per capita income. It, too, is heavily dependent on military spending.

country. The fifth-ranked military contractor, General Dynamics, is based there.

It is no anomaly that areas of the country heavily involved in military contracting are so wealthy. A study by the Project On Government Oversight found that in thirty-three of thirty-five job categories the government paid billions more to private companies than they would have paid government employees to do the same job.[2] On average they paid about twice as much. A source in industry has told me that DynCorp employees acting as security guards at military bases are obtained under contracts paying the company *four* dollars for every dollar the guard gets paid. Beyond the extravagant profit margins involved, this arrangement reveals that the military can no longer guard its own facilities with its own personnel.* Since the 1990s, our army can no longer even feed itself whenever it takes the field; service contractors such as Halliburton do that for the usual exorbitant markup. And the taxpayer takes a further hit, because the contractors often hire retired military personnel (or lure serving personnel to retire by offering them more pay); this means that these ostensibly private employees are frequently getting paid both a salary from the government that is washed through the contracting company, which takes its cut, *and* a government pension. To top off the bargain, this process is how the military loses some of its most experienced personnel.

The huge, uncompetitive profit margins that military contracting generates explain why the richest areas of the country are the most dependent on government. Yet the peculiar sociology of the

---

* The military would claim that they cannot have soldiers pull guard duty because they don't have enough service members to fight wars and perform domestic functions. The rebuttal is that they cannot afford to recruit more soldiers because they are locked into expensive service contracts (and useless weapons systems) that crowd out the rest of their budget.

military-industrial complex allows for a dependent population that disproportionately thinks of itself as small-government conservative. This is particularly true in outer-suburban counties like Loudoun that are rural enough to maintain the illusion of a free Jeffersonian yeomanry among the many contractor personnel whose McMansions have been sprouting up in what was once Virginia's horse country.

Republicans, in their statements on military policy, have taken to making a ritual genuflection to the notion that our elected leaders should follow the advice of military commanders—unless, of course, those commanders give advice that conflicts with what Republicans want. When in 2008 President Bush announced the scheduling of a final troop withdrawal from Iraq for the end of 2011, many Republicans breathed a sigh of relief that the albatross of an unpopular war soon would be removed from their necks. But when on October 21, 2011, Obama announced the definitive date as being December 31, 2011,* GOP presidential candidates issued harsh statements condemning the president for ceding ground to the enemy and saying that United States forces should remain in Iraq as long as the generals say we should stay.

The GOP seems to have forgotten—even more so than the Democrats, who periodically become enamored of a Wesley Clark or an Eric Shinseki—that our constitutional system of government absolutely and unconditionally requires civilian control of the military. That George Washington faced down his mutinous officers at Newburgh, New York, stands as one of the lesser-known milestones in the development of American self-government. If only it were

---

* Never mind for the moment Obama's own hypocrisy in taking political credit for the withdrawal when his own administration had been negotiating with Iraq's government for the right to keep troops there after 2011.

studied more frequently. Washington's rationale was that the army should not be allowed to overthrow or overawe the republic's properly established magistrates, else a militarized despotism would reign. This was the position of our first president, revered now in ritual as the father of his country but little remembered for his supreme accomplishment: saving the very idea of a self-governing republic.

Had Civil War policy been left in the hands of a George McClellan or an Ambrose Burnside, rather than the duly elected president, Abraham Lincoln, a disaster would have resulted that would most likely have left the country cleaved in two. Franklin Roosevelt's mostly political decision to invade North Africa in November 1942 turned out to be a good call. Harry Truman wisely fired General Douglas MacArthur and prevented a bloody and nasty Korean War from becoming a world conflagration. President Kennedy's rejection of his generals' near unanimous advice to invade Cuba may have prevented a nuclear war with the Soviet Union. But for all of Lyndon Johnson's domestic accomplishments, a second term was foreclosed to him because he listened to General William Westmoreland's fantasies of an imminently achievable victory in Vietnam. How have we forgotten all of this?

I met many generals in my career. The great majority of them thoroughly knew their jobs, were well informed, and had a broad perspective on the landscape of national security. But one thing they did not have: a certificate of election by the American people. Whatever the compelling military reasons for their advocacy of an operation, they might not fully understand the overriding diplomatic reasons a particular plan should not be pursued or the domestic fiscal complications that might make it on balance a no go. As professional executors of a given mission, they focus on that mission, and naturally, they want to complete it with 100 percent success, as they

define that. But a president must juggle a vast array of competing priorities, not least the ultimate priority of our present fiscal predicament: No mission can be sound if fulfilling it assumes resources the Treasury does not have.

As a former hired hand of government I was acutely conscious that I, too, did not hold a certificate of election. Whatever brilliant idea I might come up with, it had to be vetted by somebody who had to stand before voters. I am reasonably sure that the vast majority of our military officers understand that precept. Their commissions to lead troops in battle come from the people through their elected leaders, and their promotions must be confirmed by the Senate.

It is according to this principle that public officeholders should not sanctify the military judgment of commanders as the only criterion by which a national security policy may be formulated. Vigorous, assertive, and intelligent civilian control of the military is more important now than ever before. The United States no longer has a draft military that would be more sensitive to public sentiment, particularly in a time of war. Since September 11, 2001, the nation has been more or less continuously at war, with a volunteer military from which the general public is increasingly remote. Since 2000 the military budget has almost doubled, even after excluding the amounts spent on the wars themselves. Budgets have risen effortlessly not merely because Congress does not exercise proper oversight, but because it exacerbates the situation by throwing money at every real, claimed, or imaginary military deficiency. Even some members of Congress who are privately skeptical of the military's claims, and opposed to the announced war policy, have voted for defense spending bills, because they think that to do otherwise is politically dangerous.

This unquestioning adoration of the military, and of the mili-

tary brass in particular, can reach comic lengths. Kasich, a rare skeptic of military claims, once said in frustration about a colleague who was chairman of a subcommittee of the House Armed Services Committee: "You know, if a general came into his office and said the sky is green and the grass is blue, old ____ would look out the window and say, 'General, I believe you're right!' "

What is not so funny are the real-world consequences of this adulation. Every time General David Petraeus appeared before a congressional committee, whether to testify about Iraq or Afghanistan or to be confirmed as CIA director, the hearings were largely a waste of time. Members of Congress burned through large segments of their time-limited question periods by tossing verbal kisses to the witness and going on about what a patriot Petraeus was. There was little time to ask serious questions about the strategy of our trillion-dollar military engagement in the Muslim world and to explore alternatives. The fawning of military cheerleaders such as Joe Lieberman and Lindsey Graham reached such extravagant lengths as would have made Caesar blush. I am not advocating rudeness to generals or the kind of witness badgering one recalls from Senator Joe McCarthy's days. But if the public wants the military to perform better, give more prudent advice to its civilian leadership, and spend taxpayer money more wisely, it must elect a Congress that will dial down a few notches its habitual and childish "we support the troops!" mantra and start asking skeptical questions—and not accepting bland evasions or appeals to patriotism as a response.

Congress's worshipful attitude toward the military has come at a particularly inauspicious time and exacerbates harmful trends within the uniformed services. As military budgets have risen, the cancer of careerism, always present, has metastasized in the officer corps. Obviously, professional officers should be well compen-

sated. But a general does not retire poor: The base annual salary of a major general is $163,428, and that does not include thousands of dollars in additional spending power due to tax-free housing and subsistence allowances, subsidized grocery shopping, and free medical care. A retiring general can count on "retired pay" (as service members call their pensions) worth about two thirds of his base pay.

And unlike Douglas MacArthur, these old soldiers do not fade away. According to Bloomberg News, "The top 10 U.S. defense contractors have 30 retired senior officers or former national security officials serving on their boards. Press releases issued by those companies since 2008 announced the hiring of almost two dozen prominent flag officers or senior officials as high-ranking executives." The article also states that senior executives at the largest U.S. defense contractors are paid from $1 million to $11 million a year.*

The revolving-door nature of the military-industrial complex guarantees cost overruns, schedule slips, and poor weapon performance. Suppose an officer is a year from retirement: Is he going to blow the whistle on shoddy performance by a contractor? Both he and the contractor are conscious that a seven-figure paycheck might lie in his future (salvaging a contract potentially worth billions of dollars certainly merits the investment of a few million). Every precept in the military's code of conduct demands that he blow the whistle, but a secure, even lavish future can sorely tempt one's less noble instincts. In addition, the chances that a contractor will actually be prosecuted are vanishingly small. Federal conflict-

* Enlisted personnel separating from the service typically face a far different career future: Iraq and Afghanistan veterans have endured a substantially higher unemployment rate than the national average.

of-interest laws exist but are filled with loopholes. No word has to be spoken by either party. Neither the contractor nor the officer has to commit an overt act; the deed is accomplished instead by doing nothing.

Occasionally, someone gets caught. In 2004, a federal court sentenced Darleen Druyun, a senior Air Force procurement official, to nine months in prison for favoring Boeing in contract negotiations for a $20 billion aircraft tanker leasing deal (a procurement scandal in itself) at the same time she was speaking to Boeing about a postgovernment job. But that was the tip of the iceberg. The Commission on Wartime Contracting, created by Congress in 2008, undertook three years of investigations into contracting practices in Iraq and Afghanistan (tasks that the House and Senate Armed Services committees, as permanent committees of Congress, should have undertaken themselves). In August 2011 the commission issued a report concluding that waste, fraud, and abuse in wartime contracting resulted in losses of $31 billion to $60 billion. The estimating range is so broad because the Department of Defense, with a laughably inept system of financial management, has a hard time even detecting overpayments.

The crowning irony is that Congress often has epic fights on the floors of the two chambers over some $10 million program in a domestic agency. One could more easily accept the principle that every little bit helps, and that even a program funded at a few million annually should be rigorously scrubbed, if our national legislature did not let $600 billion defense bills pass with so little genuine scrutiny, and allow tens of billions of dollars in aggregate waste flow to contractors. Congress operates like a university faculty: The smaller the stakes, the more heated the argument.

I saw this many times in practice over the years. Congress dutifully funded, with little floor debate, the Future Combat Systems—

a family of Army combat vehicles—a program the Army estimated would cost $160 billion (independent estimates were as high as $230 billion). The funding continued year after year, until in 2009 the Pentagon finally pulled the plug on the flawed and gold-plated program. But when the issue involves a $2 million line item for a bike path or highway beautification, a vigorous floor debate ensues. The point is not to defend bike paths or highway beautification; with an annual budget deficit in excess of $1 trillion, it is hard to defend them. But if we cannot afford them, how can Congress continue to fund the F-35 Joint Strike Fighter, whose total program cost has risen to $382 billion, despite repeated Government Accountability Office warnings that it was rushed into production despite serious development flaws?

The Constitution provides for separate and independent branches of government: the separation of powers. The executive branch zealously upholds the concept of independent presidential power; its battery of lawyers doggedly fights off any perceived encroachment on its turf. The Bush administration set the gold standard for this sort of behavior, although the Obama presidency is now giving it a run for its money, particularly in the realm of war powers. The judicial branch—mostly—follows a similar policy of jealously guarding its prerogatives. Congress, however, has heaved out the window its constitutional responsibilities both to declare war and to raise and support armies, as well as to demand that the Pentagon adhere to the appropriations and accountability clauses of the Constitution.

This abdication is partly the result of emotionally immature legislators getting swept away with enthusiasm for military adventure, much as European parliaments did in the summer of 1914. It

is partly an avoidance of responsibility. But it is also, at least to some degree, due to obscure institutional arrangements that the general public has hardly heard of. The most visible and extensive executive branch liaison offices on Capitol Hill are those of the uniformed services. They provide a permanent and continual presence in the halls of Congress to lobby for their priorities. Even more submerged is the fact that many if not all members of Congress assigned to the defense committees have a "military fellow": an active-duty military officer serving a tour of duty in a Capitol Hill office. If they all wore their uniforms rather than Brooks Brothers, they would make Capitol Hill look like Fort Bragg.

So what's wrong with that? We are all part of the same government, aren't we? To be sure, the vast majority are honest people performing their assignment. A couple of them I knew more than casually, and they were good guys. But the fact that they are serving in one branch of government while being paid by an agency from another branch, and especially one with enormous institutional power and a relentless agenda, inevitably creates a conflict of interest. The sheer institutional pervasiveness of the military in the legislative branch is itself a reason for caution. There is nothing sinister about the fact that the agenda of one branch of government will conflict with the prerogatives of another branch; James Madison foresaw that possibility over two centuries ago. But it is problematic to place young military officers in an assignment that requires dual loyalty.

The matter does not end there. The congressional defense committees are loaded with people who retired from the military and are now congressional employees. Well, what of it? Isn't that where the expertise is? Most civilians don't consider how much an entire career spent in the military inspires a strong loyalty to one's service. Congress should do a better job of nurturing its own talent, as well

as better utilizing its support agencies, such as the Congressional Research Service and the Congressional Budget Office, along with the Government Accountability Office.

One of the most noisome phenomena in the Washington culture pertaining to military matters is the chicken hawk. The great majority of those serving in the military are motivated by patriotism and see the profession of arms as a job to do as well as they can. Their patriotism is usually mixed with judgments we all would feel if exposed at any length to Pentagon bureaucracy: that it is—like all bureaucracies—at its most benign like *Sergeant Bilko* and at its worst like *Catch-22*. Anyone who has had a beer at the enlisted club of a military base will know that most of the troops are not starry-eyed idealists about their trade. Having the skepticism of the realist does not keep them from doing their duty, but it does check the mindless boosterism of those who choose to avoid military service while loudly advocating war. There is nothing like the prospect of getting killed or maimed to concentrate the mind.

The chicken hawk phenomenon probably exists in other cultures and can be found throughout American history; Mark Twain addressed the same pathology over a hundred years ago when he wrote the passage about "the Loud Little Handful" in *The Mysterious Stranger,* about those who agitate for war. But the business of chicken-hawk advocacy has become a well-paid and influential vocation in modern America. Its principal venues are the neoconservative *Weekly Standard*, the supposedly liberal *New Republic*, the editorial page of the *Wall Street Journal*, and increasingly that of the *Washington Post*. It is also entrenched in think tanks such as the American Enterprise Institute and the Heritage Foundation. If you ever wondered how the United States came to be embroiled simul-

taneously in two major wars and a half dozen covert ones in the past decade, the cheerleading of Washington's laptop commandos, with their disproportionate influence in major media, has been a major factor. This is not to say that only those with military experience should have standing to discuss military policy. That would contravene the principle of civilian control of the military. But when a self-appointed group of experts almost entirely innocent of military service relentlessly advocates getting this country into one war after another, it is time to be on guard and hold on to our wallets. Besides which, their judgments are almost always wrong.

Over the last five years we have spent more money on the military—in real, inflation-adjusted dollars—than during any other five-year period since World War II. That includes the late 1960s, when the United States simultaneously faced a peer competitor with ten thousand nuclear weapons *and* sent half a million troops to Vietnam. The Pentagon is spending recklessly at a time of fiscal crisis when America's debt has been downgraded. Despite what secretaries Gates and Panetta have claimed, the DOD budget has been, next to the Bush tax cuts, the single greatest contributor to the drastic swing from surplus to deficit since 2001. When debt-service costs are included, the wars have cost about $1.7 trillion. Additionally, the Pentagon has spent about $1 trillion above inflation on its nonwar budget. Adding debt service makes that about $1.3 trillion, for a grand total of roughly $3 trillion added to the debt, courtesy of DOD. (For a quick comparison, the total Pentagon budget in the last year of the Clinton administration was $287 billion. In the last year of the Bush administration it had reached $665 billion, including the cost of the wars.)

Yet ever since the rejection of the Simpson-Bowles deficit-reduction package in December 2010, as we have been struggling to get the budget under control, every interest group inside the

Washington Beltway has been forecasting imminent doom if one cent is cut from Pentagon budgets.[3] Why? The service chiefs' doomsaying testimony to Congress has been standard for at least the three decades that I was on the Hill: Deliberate threat inflation, based in part on serious intelligence failures, has been the genesis of wasted billions. China-as-military-threat is again in vogue at the Pentagon and in Congress, though the Iranian bogeyman currently has the upper hand. There is a threat from China, but it comes not from the rust-bucket aircraft carrier it bought from Russia. China now owns about $1 trillion in U.S. Treasury securities—36 percent of all foreign holdings. According to the International Monetary Fund (IMF), China is poised to pass the United States in gross domestic product by 2016. That is the real threat we face, not death rays and stealth air fleets. If you want to gaze upon the threat China poses, not because of any inherent evil on its part but because of our own tax policy, spending priorities, "free-trade" ideology, and the general indifference of our elites, go to Youngstown, or Toledo, or some other postindustrial wasteland.[4, 5]

The United States spends about as much on its military as all other countries in the world combined. It could shave a trillion off a projected $6.1 trillion in spending over the next decade and still be miles ahead of the next power, or of any conceivable combination of powers. But what about another 9/11, ask the Cassandras? In 2001, the United States already spent as much on its military as everyone else in the world, but that did not help prevent 9/11. That disaster was an intelligence failure: That is, a failure of our intelligence agencies to some degree, but far more a failure of the cognitive intelligence and good judgment of our elected so-called leaders.

The United States is now a bloated military empire on the cusp of steady and irrevocable economic decline. Historically, the danger in such cases is that when the fiscal stability of the empire be-

gins to weaken, the governing elites double down on the very policies of military profligacy that caused the fiscal crisis in the first place. And that appears to be what the people who run America would like to do.

This doubling down on failure should come as no surprise: Powerful entrenched interests will never be tamed without a bitter and protracted struggle. The trigger for the latest round of scare tactics has been the automatic defense cuts that are supposed to ensue in 2013 if the congressional super committee could not find alternative deficit-reduction measures (it couldn't). As soon as the reality that the Pentagon might have to take budget cuts began to seep into the bureaucracy's consciousness, the drumbeat began. Secretary of Defense Leon Panetta, a supposed liberal and alleged fiscal hawk, made a preposterous statement comparing himself in his efforts to prevent defense reductions to General Anthony McAuliffe at the Battle of the Bulge saying "nuts" to the enemy. We are supposed to infer that anyone wanting to cut Pentagon extravagance for the sake of the national debt is akin to the *Wehrmacht* attacking American patriots who are holding beleaguered Bastogne.

Iran's alleged nuclear capability quickly became a feature of the increased threat mongering. For most of my three decades on Capitol Hill, threat inflators have claimed that Iran has been two years away from possessing nuclear weapons. Recycled rumors, half-truths, disinformation from foreign intelligence agencies like that of Saudi Arabia and Israel, and exaggerations have been a consistent feature of these scare tactics. By the end of 2011 these allegations were taking on an increasingly hysterical tone. The *Washington Post*, ever a bellwether of the establishment, printed an editorial demanding a sanctions regime against Iran so strict it would amount to a blockade equivalent to war, because the only other alternative was a military attack "forced on the United States."[6]

One thing that could further ratchet up the hype would be to let people who are either woefully misinformed about the world or shallow opportunists, or both, ventilate their opinions about Iran and treat their ruminations as national news. The interminable series of Republican presidential candidate debates was one more venue to make us very, very scared of Iran, and the candidates obliged. Asking a Republican candidate about Iran is almost as good as giving him a large campaign donation: It gives him a chance to show "toughness" and "seriousness" (meaning reckless belligerence) on foreign policy issues; appeal to the Israel lobby for votes and money (it is a quadrennial spectacle to watch the candidates outbid each other to the point of getting to the right even of Israel's Likud government); and devise crackbrained schemes to deal with the potentially ruinous economic consequences of an oil blockade of Iran. (Gingrich believed we could snap our fingers and quickly replace the 2.4 million barrels of oil per day that Iran exports.)

But the larger objective, beyond specific policies, is to blanket the American public with a message of fear. As long as we are fearful, as long as there is an endless list of threats, Pentagon spending can never be cut, PATRIOT Act provisions can never be repealed, and the United States will forever have the right and duty to meddle in every corner of the world. By coincidence (or not), the same day the *Post* clamored for action against Iran it ran a story that exemplifies the propaganda techniques of the national security complex.[7] The story explained that al Qaeda targets had dwindled as its leaders had been killed or captured: "We have rendered the organization that brought us 9/11 operationally ineffective," said an anonymous senior U.S. counterterrorism official. So we're on the verge of victory, right? No: "[T]he terrorist group will remain a major security threat for years." And now it looks as if the scene will shift to Yemen: The terrorist group there is a "significantly

greater threat." Moreover, we have to be concerned about lone-wolf attacks inside the United States as well. The Orwellian nature of these contradictory messages is plain: Our leaders' objective is to convince us that the sacrifice of blood and treasure has been worth it by depicting victory as within reach; nevertheless, the threat will endlessly mutate and require enormous budgets and nonstop war for the indefinite future.

Final victory is a mirage our leaders say we must chase as it recedes to the horizon. History is littered with powers that followed this ruinous path: the Spanish Empire, the Dutch Republic, the British Empire, the Soviet Union. Vaunting rhetoric to the contrary, our military policies of the last decade have left us less prosperous, less secure, and less free. A course correction is desperately needed, regardless of what our entrenched, out-of-touch, and corrupt Beltway elites think is good for us.

7

MEDIA COMPLICITY

Despite the widely believed myth of its liberalism, over the last thirty years the media landscape has become increasingly wired to favor Republicans. The press's current combination of fake objectivity and campaign fetishization has been carefully exploited by Republican strategists for political advantage.

News is what somebody somewhere wants to suppress; all the rest is advertising.

—Alfred Harmsworth, 1st Viscount Northcliffe, early-twentieth-century British press magnate

One of the most powerful metanarratives shaping Republican psychology—and Republican success—during the last several decades has been the party's unshakable belief, a belief amounting to religious faith, that a just and final victory over hated liberalism is almost within reach. According to this view, the majority of real Americans are innately conservative, and the only serious obstacle to reaching the promised land of permanent power lies in an all-powerful and diabolical liberal media conspiracy.* This conspiracy suppresses, misreports, or distorts all the

* A CBS News radio report on December 3, 2011, announcing Herman Cain's suspension of his presidential campaign was revealing. Every Cain

good things GOP candidates and officeholders are doing, and brainwashes the naturally conservative majority of the country into not seeing its own interests.

There is considerable psychological value in holding this view, because it reinforces the true believer's conviction that his ideology is sound and just, and the reason his political beliefs have not triumphed is that dark and sinister forces oppose them. This mental mechanism is an escape hatch for unwelcome facts and evidence that would otherwise undermine the faith of the follower: Should his favorite candidate or conservative hero commit a serious gaffe or become enmeshed in a scandal, he can rationalize the negative information by saying to himself that it is all a plot by the media to make conservatives look bad. Sometimes Republican candidates rise in the estimation of Republican primary voters in the wake of a scandal, as we saw with Newt in South Carolina, because being attacked by the liberal media octopus is a sure sign that you are on the right side.

And yet, at least since 1988, when Rush Limbaugh began his radio program, the Republican base has been developing its own comprehensive and interlocking media empire that operates on a separate and parallel track from the rest of the press. Except, that is, when its outpourings become sufficiently newsworthy or bizarre—think of the so-called war on Christmas—to arouse surprised comment in the wider world. For all their boo-hooing and defensiveness about the media, Republican operatives have created an impressive public relations industry in the form of talk radio, Fox News and its extended empire, the media outlets of fundamentalist churches such as Pat Robertson's *700 Club*, and other sympathetic

---

supporter the network interviewed suggested that Cain's troubles were exclusively the fault of the media.

if somewhat more outlandish affiliates such as those of Sun Myung Moon* and Richard Mellon Scaife. This media powerhouse has become an enormous cultural force, or more properly, an enormous countercultural force, with a mass following and staying power greater than the original counterculture of the 1960s.

This right-wing media powerhouse has created its own reality in order to bamboozle the gullible. On AM radio, which is totally dominated by right-wing personalities such as Limbaugh, Sean Hannity, and the rest of their tribe, insignificant issues that normal people would otherwise hardly waste their time thinking about assume the dimensions of all-encompassing conspiracies: ACORN (Association of Community Organizations for Reform Now), the New Black Panther Party, or Saul Alinsky.† This sort of thing is not unknown in our history: In the 1930s, the radio ranting of Father Coughlin had a substantial national listenership. But it is a little disconcerting that almost no one in the Republican Party will ever cross Limbaugh, even when he steps way beyond the bounds of decency—and those few who have done so have usually had to issue cringing apologies.

Should any outlet of the national media not within the orbit of reliably conservative ownership write a negative story about some aspect of the Republican agenda or Republican personalities, the media bias cry will arise. The chief demons are the *New York Times* and the *Washington Post*, and this despite their employing conserva-

* Korean billionaire Sun Myung Moon is the leader and chief deity of the Unification Church religious cult and owner of the *Washington Times*. The standing Beltway joke is that, whereas the *Washington Post* is the CIA's paper, the *Washington Times* is the KCIA's paper.

† Chicago-based political activist Saul Alinsky would have a difficult time conspiring about anything, since he has been dead for forty years. Yet it is a catechism of the lunatic right that Alinsky was a major influence on Barack Obama, who was ten years old when Alinsky passed away. "Saul Alinsky radicalism is at the heart of Obama," according to Newt Gingrich.

tive columnists such as George Will, Charles Krauthammer, Michael Gerson, Jennifer Rubin, Kathleen Parker, Ross Douthat, and David Brooks, among others. The GOP's belief in an implacably hostile anti-Republican bias persists despite both papers having enthusiastically trumpeted the false premises of the invasion of Iraq. In the last year or two, the *Post* has begun sounding like the Murdoch-subsidized *Weekly Standard* in its editorials bemoaning the possibility of even modest reductions to a Pentagon budget that has doubled in a decade, and in its strident advocacy of an Iran policy that risks all-out war.

There is a stark contrast between a vigorous, popular, and well-financed right-wing press always on the offensive about some issue or other and a diffident, sniffish, and out-of-touch mainstream press that is losing circulation and viewership despite hiring ever more explicitly ideological and controversial writers for its op-ed pages. This contrast defines the present media landscape. It is less the explicit flaws of each camp but rather the interactions between them that contribute to civic malaise and dysfunction in America. The right-wing media aggressively attempt to set the national news agenda through ever more prurient scoops—a technique pioneered by Matt Drudge in the mid-1990s—and the mainstream press, which, after ignoring the scoops for a while, reacts timidly and hesitantly, and settles on a middle-of-the-road stance that satisfies nobody and drives away readership.

Ever since the bifurcation of electronic media into a more or less respectable hard news segment and a rabidly ideological talk radio and politically propagandistic cable TV arm, the "respectable" media have been terrified of any criticism for perceived bias. Hence, they hew to the practice of false evenhandedness. Paul Krugman has skewered this tactic as a centrist cop-out. "I joked long ago," he wrote in one of his columns, "that if one party declared that the

earth was flat, the headlines would read 'Views Differ on Shape of Planet.' "[1] This sort of faux objectivity has gone so far that the *New York Times*'s current public editor, Arthur Brisbane, wrote a column naïvely asking readers whether his paper should print the truth if a public figure lied.[2]

The constant drizzle of "there the two parties go again!" stories combines with the hazy confusion of poorly informed voters to help Republicans reap electoral dividends. The United States has nearly the lowest voter participation among all the Western democracies. This is at least in part a consequence of the decline of trust in government institutions, a condition that Republicans have shrewdly exacerbated. If government is a racket, and both parties are the same, why vote? And if the uninvolved middle declines to vote, the net result is to increase the electoral clout of a more dedicated minority that is daily being whipped into a lather by three hours of Rush Limbaugh or Fox News.

Economic trends have exacerbated the prevailing drift toward ever more pervasive, and ever shallower, coverage. At one time the big metropolitan newspapers were reliable cash machines that could afford in-depth reporting. But intoxicated by the financialization of the economy, newspaper owners were not satisfied with annual profits of only 10 percent. They had to be closer to 20 percent. So they made little serious reinvestment in the core business while responding tardily and ineffectively to the digitization of media. Some owners just looted their papers, as Sam Zell did to the *Chicago Tribune*. The last five years have seen a series of failures of once venerable newspapers and magazines from coast to coast. And those who have survived have seen their newsrooms gutted and pages slashed, and foreign bureaus have been closed around the world.

Political coverage in our nation's capital suffers from its own

peculiar defects. Washington, D.C., is not a true metropolitan capital, like London or Paris. It is in reality a company town possessing little business activity other than retail, which must exist in any city, that is not directly or indirectly tied to the presence of the federal government. The expanding metropolis has crawled almost to the foothills of the Blue Ridge Mountains in the last thirty years. During my career, the Dulles corridor transformed from a rural vista between the Washington Beltway and the city's international airport into a *Futurama* landscape, where office blocks have sprouted like mushrooms. These structures house military contractors, homeland security profiteers, or information technology outfits hawking their wares to the government at a 400 percent markup. You will look in vain for a steel mill, a foundry, or an auto parts plant. Washington is a company town just as Homestead, Pennsylvania, was in the days of Andrew Carnegie, but in this case the company's product is politics (and military hardware). In a company town, everybody knows everybody else's business. The politicians and their consultants and fixers are well known to the lobbyists, contractors, and entrepreneurs.

The press fits comfortably into this incestuous ecosystem. Gone are the days of old-fashioned beat reporters who slowly worked their way up by breaking stories and ferreting out real news. Rather, more and more the establishment journalists come with journalism degrees from places like Columbia, and their "scoops" have been deliberately leaked; their outlooks evolve naturally to accommodate the attitudes of the oversized village they are reporting on.

It is probably difficult to identify with the predicament of an unemployed sheet-metal worker in Niles, Ohio, when you have reached the exalted station in your profession that results in an invitation to the annual White House Correspondents' Association Dinner. By no coincidence, the guest list includes a large number of Hollywood

personalities, whom the establishment press corps increasingly resembles. It is hard to evaluate the evening: Is the press having its fun at the politicians' expense, seeing the Leader of the Free World hamming it up on stage like a Borscht Belt comedian? Or are the politicians putting one over on reporters by co-opting them into a performance that plays on the media's vanity and social-climbing instincts as it blunts their objectivity? The vulgarity of George W. Bush's turning his Iraq policy into a parody skit, with the press corps yukking it up over his search for Saddam's purported weapons of mass destruction under his Oval Office desk, gives one pause. It is all a bit like the antics at Bohemian Grove or an initiation ceremony of Skull and Bones: the elite of our country at play. The late George Carlin's words sum up what the Washington correspondents' dinner says to the public at large: "It's a club, and you ain't in it!"

This incestuousness helps explain why the major media often break their own rules when reporting on politics. Usually, when writing about local news, human interest features, and the like, the papers fully identify the average Joe who happens to have witnessed the car crash in question or come down with the disease of the month. But the higher up one goes, and the greater the political importance of the story, the less likely the Washington media are to identify a source by name, even when (or, rather, *particularly* when) the source is putting out self-serving spin to advance the agenda of the administration, agency, or party for which he or she works.

The *Washington Post*, the hometown newsletter of the Beltway elite, is particularly egregious in this respect. From time to time its ombudsman writes a high-minded column about how the *Post* has strict internal guidelines on the use of anonymous sources. But over and over again one can pick up the paper and see front-page stories laden with phrases like "according to senior White House officials," "according to sources close to the president," "according

to a source requesting anonymity because he is not authorized to speak on the matter," and my favorite, "according to an official familiar with the president's thinking." Was that the White House psychiatrist, or maybe the first lady? In the great majority of cases these sources are blowing their organization's horn and advancing its agenda, either by praising their own policy or attacking their opponent's. Or they are launching a political trial balloon to see what the popular response will be. These people are not whistle-blowers, so why do they require the cloak of anonymity—and why does the press grant it to them?

One can understand why members of a presidential administration seek anonymity. They are still promoting their political agenda, but they are doing so by leaking classified information. Ordinarily, it is not illegal for a reporter to receive classified information (although some administrations, angered by the kind of leaks they don't like, have considered using the 1917 Espionage Act to attempt to prosecute reporters). What is clearly illegal is for a duly cleared federal employee to divulge such information.

Presidential administrations always leak like sieves. As the Beltway saying has it, "The ship of state is the only vessel that leaks from the top." But during the 2002 and 2003 run-up to the Iraq invasion, the flow of secrets became a geyser. Leaking information that could compromise sources and methods of collection is a serious matter; electronic intelligence data in particular is highly sensitive and divulging it is punished with draconian severity. Yet somehow that didn't matter when the objective was to provide a pretext for the war.

The deeper injury that the run-up to the Iraq war caused to our national security—and we shall only know the complete story in the fullness of time—lay in the flood of clues about the U.S. intelligence operations recklessly revealed by the Bush administration

during its advertising blitz. The official conclusions that justified the pretext for the war were of course nonsense. But a competent foreign intelligence service might have connected the dots among the hundreds of publicly disclosed data points to compromise the sources and methods used by our intelligence agencies.

Most people now know the disgraceful story of the selling of the Iraq invasion: how a president and his advisers spun the pretext to the public through the willing agency of the news media, and how it led to a trillion-dollar strategic disaster. Less appreciated is the more subtle long-term damage this public relations stunt may have done to U.S. national security. The successful campaign to spin the media—and most of the media rushed to set aside their own professionalism in a desire to be spun—was accompanied by unprecedented pressure on intelligence analysts to come up with something, anything, no matter how threadbare the evidence, in order to feed the media. It was a milepost in the systematic politicization of U.S. intelligence agencies. Intelligence officers got the message: Get with the program. You no longer inform the policy making; your job is to lend a veneer of plausibility to a marketing campaign for a course already determined by politicians and their campaign advisers.

And it *was* a marketing campaign. As Andrew Card, chief of staff to President Bush, disclosed in an unguarded moment when asked about the timing of the war, "From a marketing point of view, you don't introduce new products in August." The decision to go to war was a product for the administration to sell, like laundry detergent. And the media happily complied, and ran the advocacy campaign as if it were a sponsored ad. In their gullibility, however, the press failed to consider that they weren't even being paid, as they would have been if Procter & Gamble had purchased a thirty-second spot or a full-page ad.

It was about that time, in mid-2002, that I began to turn to the

online editions of the overseas press: Britain's *Guardian* or *Financial Times*, or Germany's *Der Spiegel*. It is a sad commentary on the U.S. news media—commonly believed to be operating in the freest country in the world, with explicit constitutional protections, no prior restraint on publishing, and generally much laxer libel laws—that the foreign press could write more balanced and accurate reports on a major political decision by the U.S. government than the bulk of our domestic media. The Knight-Ridder chain of newspapers (now McClatchy) was an honorable exception, as it generally showed a proper degree of skepticism about U.S. government claims.

According to a 2012 evaluation by Reporters Without Borders, the United States' press ranks as only the forty-seventh freest in the world.[3] One of the criteria the organization used to determine its ranking was whether the press in a given country practiced self-censorship, regardless of the formal legal protection it might enjoy (the United States ranked particularly poorly in the 2012 report, sliding twenty-seven places from the previous evaluation, because so many reporters had been arrested covering Occupy Wall Street protests).

The mainstream media's toxic symbiosis with our two entrenched parties and the permanent shadow government have made it difficult for the average American to assemble an accurate and coherent picture of the world, much less make informed judgments about our foreign and national security policies or understand how America is perceived abroad. Rather than strive to be objective, our media personalities have become unofficial government representatives, particularly when foreign and national security policy are concerned. And when the war drums are beating, they are more like cheerleaders than objective reporters.

Tom Friedman, the *New York Times*'s wunderkind and resident Deep Thinker on globalization, is a marquee example of this syndrome. In the run-up to the Iraq invasion, Friedman acted with all the restraint and objectivity of the World War II *Why We Fight* series, albeit with fewer facts. Here he is in an interview justifying the invasion of Iraq, using the standard tough-guy language of the coddled and comfortable who never experience combat.

> What they needed to see was American boys and girls going house to house, from Basra to Baghdad, um, and basically saying, "Which part of this sentence don't you understand?" You don't think, you know, we care about our open society, you think this bubble fantasy, we're just gonna to let it grow? Well, Suck. On. This. . . . We could have hit Saudi Arabia. It was part of that bubble. Could have hit Pakistan. We hit Iraq because we could. That's the real truth.

Likewise, here he is in another interview, justifying U.S. policy in the face of a growing insurgency:

> [A]nd sometimes it takes a two-by-four across the side of the head to get that message.

All very edifying, but when the occupation of Iraq began to stretch into years, Friedman adopted a new leitmotif: Bush had screwed up the postinvasion administration of the country. Still, Friedman flailed about for the next several years, offering one scheme after another to rescue the warmongering policy he had so recklessly promoted before finally recommending disengagement. He did not have the sense, or perhaps the intellectual honesty, to admit that all the bad consequences of the occupation, including

torture and ethnic cleansing, were the fruit of a poisoned tree. Or, in the words of former Supreme Court justice Robert Jackson, that making an unprovoked military attack is "the supreme international crime," differing from others only in that it encompasses all of the evil that follows. Yet Friedman is still pontificating from his platform at the *New York Times*, where, unchastened, he is now venting his belligerence against another Middle Eastern country: Having dispensed with Iraq, he has now turned to Iran.

Even now, almost a decade after the invasion, when the malign consequences of the military intervention have become clear—the false pretenses for the attack, the inordinate financial and human cost, the weakening of America's strategic and moral positions in the world—the establishment press is adopting a see-no-evil approach. Jon Meacham, formerly *Newsweek*'s resident intellectual, recently became a dispenser of etiquette rules for dealing with embarrassing subjects like the war. On a television talk show, he upbraided a guest for suggesting that President Bush had lied the country into war. At issue was less the facts at hand; to Meacham, sounding like Miss Manners, it was a question of civility: "To say someone lied adds a corrosive element to the public dialogue that we just don't need."[4] For self-appointed custodians of the public good, it is a lesser sin for American politicians to lie than for someone to call them out for lying.

Worse yet is Bill Kristol, who began his career as a partisan attack dog, became editor of the Murdoch-subsidized *Weekly Standard*, and graduated to a brief stint on the Platonic throne of the *New York Times* op-ed page. There are only two things that characterize his otherwise uninteresting persona: He is in favor of war in every conceivable circumstance, and he is always wrong. He is almost a reverse barometer for evaluating events. Yet he got on the payroll of the Gray Lady in 2008 for a one-year run, a dispenser of

interpretations of the news at America's prestige paper. The examples can be multiplied. The salient problem is not that they are partisan enthusiasts (the Democrats have plenty of their own people polluting the op-ed pages with their versions of the party line), but that they are so consistently wrong, and yet they are never called to account for being wrong.

Michael Gerson was George W. Bush's speechwriter at the time of the Iraq invasion. He helped fashion Bush's second inaugural address, which contained the almost apocalyptic message that America's avenging sword would liberate a Middle East in chains. The key phrase in the address, "fire in the minds of men," derived from a book of the same name about nineteenth-century revolutionaries and anarchists.[5] It is fascinating that Gerson, writing for an erstwhile proponent of a humble foreign policy, inserted words in the president's mouth proclaiming a violent revolution in the manner of Trotsky. After his heady days as the Bakunin of the Bush Doctrine, Gerson is now dispensing snack-bar opinions in the *Washington Post* on the electability of Republican candidates, and similar mundane political fodder.

Although I have mainly discussed op-ed columnists,* the same syndrome applies to a lesser extent to reporters. The case of Judith Miller and her role in drumming up the Iraq war is too well known to need recapitulation here, but fellow *Times* reporter Michael Gordon continues to act as a faithful stenographer of whichever line the government happens to be promoting on national security and foreign "threats." Bob Woodward at the *Post*, with his "just so" stories

---

* Many of these pundits are former government speechwriters and press secretaries, i.e., propagandists rather than people with any deep policy expertise. Even that is a step up from most of the rest of the pundit class, who have no discernible professional qualifications whatever other than glibness, ambition, and a natural talent for mugging at the camera.

and improbable recall of dialogue he never heard, has served as a vehicle for senior White House personnel to dispense self-aggrandizing gossip. Some of my friends used to joke that you always knew whenever Colin Powell had an official position in Washington, because Woodward would come out with a book shortly thereafter.

Some of this bad reporting may be due to the reporter's ignorance of technical subject matter having to do with budgets or weapon systems. I recall getting a phone call late in the afternoon shortly after a B-1 bomber had crashed on a training flight. I was attempting to explain to ABC News reporter Bob Zelnick that the Air Force suspected that the cause of the crash was a fire resulting from a broken fuel line in the engine nacelle. "What's a nacelle?" was the testy and impatient response from the man who had been ABC News's chief Pentagon correspondent for eight years. With that kind of subject knowledge, no wonder government spokespeople can snow the press.

Just as preadolescent boys are fascinated by secret decoder rings, the Washington media reporting on national security issues are thrilled by being in the loop about important decisions before the public hears about them. This includes being privy to classified information. Now it is true that the publication of some classified intelligence could be severely damaging to the country's security, but most of the millions of classified documents that the government generates every year are prosaic, low-level stuff whose content any reasonably well-informed person could infer. A small percentage of classified material is information of no real national security importance but whose revelation would be politically embarrassing. But who is and who is not in the loop for getting all these intelligence tidbits in Washington, the ultimate company town, is a big deal that top-level officials exploit.

More interesting than the content of classified material is how

it is used politically. The rules of declassification—there are lots of rules, but they are incoherent and contradictory—are used so arbitrarily that classified material more often becomes a means of baiting the press to advance a political agenda. Did Bradley Manning, the U.S. Army enlisted man who gave thousands of pages of sensitive government documents to the Web site WikiLeaks, damage national security? Perhaps he did, but no reasonable person with any experience in government should have taken the government at its word when it attempted to justify holding him without charge or legal counsel and in abusive conditions. Especially not when senior administration officials from both parties also leak classified information to the press to further their objectives. National security secrets have become degraded to the status of gossipy tidbits for the press. I am sure a Venn diagram of persons who want to boil Bradley Manning in oil would hardly intersect a diagram of persons who wanted similar treatment meted out to Scooter Libby for blowing the cover of a covert CIA officer—an extremely serious matter.

Just in case you think that the mainstream press learned its lesson from Iraq—about promoting the invasion of another country based on anonymous sources—we have this piece in the November 20, 2011, *Washington Post*: "Iran may have sent Libya shells for chemical weapons." And what are the documented sources for this scoop?

> U.S. officials said . . . several sources . . . [a] U.S. official with access to classified information . . . a third U.S. official said . . . [o]ne U.S. official said . . . another U.S. official said.[6]

Here we go again! Even after the complete discrediting of the pretext for the Iraq war, the mainstream media continue to follow

the shopworn Iraq template in their reporting on Iran. Three months after that anonymous revelation about Iranian machinations in Libya, the *Post* was back at it with another front-page bombshell; this time Iran was doubling down, backing Assad's regime in Syria with weapons. How do we know this?

> "The aid from Iran is increasing, and is increasingly focused on lethal assistance," said one of the officials, insisting on anonymity to discuss intelligence reports from the region. . . . U.S. officials *declined to address allegations about specific acts.* But one of the officials who spoke on the condition of anonymity said intelligence agencies have documented reports of a wide range of assistance. [7] [emphasis mine]

No intelligent person ever doubted the brutality of the Assad regime. But the eagerness of our prestige media to tie Iran to events in Syria precisely at a time when the world is already on edge about Iran's purported nuclear capabilities—a subject far more nuanced and ambiguous than you would think from reading articles in our leading papers—demonstrates the danger to our country of a credulous and uncritical press. Liberals habitually work themselves into a lather about the antics of Rush Limbaugh or Glenn Beck, but they are really just political gargoyles looking for ratings as they whip up the GOP faithful. The true danger lies in an ostensibly neutral journalism that most Americans count on to tell them what is going on in the world but which too often acts as a stenographer for powerful and self-serving factions in government operating under a cloak of anonymity. These people have misled us in the past and will mislead us in the future if they are not vigorously challenged.

8

GIVE ME THAT OLD-TIME RELIGION

The religious right provides the foot soldiers for the GOP. This fact has profound implications for the rest of the Republicans' ideological agenda.

Sin, sin, sin! You're all sinners!
You're all doomed to perdition!

—Burt Lancaster as Elmer Gantry (1960)

Having observed politics up close and personal for most of my adult lifetime, I have come to the conclusion that the rise of politicized religious fundamentalism may have been the key ingredient in the transformation of the Republican Party. Politicized religion provides a substrate of beliefs that rationalizes—at least in the minds of its followers—all three of the GOP's main tenets: wealth worship, war worship, and the permanent culture war.

Religious cranks ceased to be a minor public nuisance in this country beginning in the 1970s and grew into a major element of the Republican rank and file. Pat Robertson's strong showing in the 1988 Iowa presidential caucus signaled the gradual merger of politics and religion in the party. Unfortunately, at the time I mostly underestimated the implications of what I was seeing. It did strike

me as oddly humorous that a fundamentalist staff member in my congressional office was going to take time off to convert the heathen in Greece, a country that had been overwhelmingly Christian for almost two thousand years. I recall another point, in the early 1990s, when a different fundamentalist GOP staffer said that dinosaur fossils were a hoax. As a mere legislative mechanic toiling away in what I held to be a civil rather than ecclesiastical calling, I did not yet see that ideological impulses far different from mine were poised to capture the party of Lincoln.

The results of this takeover are all around us: If the American people poll more like Iranians or Nigerians than Europeans or Canadians on questions of evolution, scriptural inerrancy, the presence of angels and demons, and so forth, it is due to the rise of the religious right, its insertion into the public sphere by the Republican Party, and the consequent normalizing of formerly reactionary beliefs. All around us now is a prevailing anti-intellectualism and hostility to science. Politicized religion is the sheet anchor of the dreary forty-year-old culture wars.

The Constitution notwithstanding, there is now a de facto religious test for the presidency: Major candidates are encouraged (or coerced) to share their feelings about their faith in a revelatory speech, or a televangelist like Rick Warren will dragoon the candidates (as he did with Obama and McCain in 2008) to debate the finer points of Christology, offering himself as the final arbiter. Half a century after John F. Kennedy put to rest the question of whether a candidate of a minority denomination could be president, the Republican Party has reignited the kinds of seventeenth-century religious controversies that advanced democracies are supposed to have outgrown. And some in the media seem to have internalized the GOP's premise that the religion of a candidate is a matter for public debate.

Throughout the 2012 Republican presidential campaign, Mitt Romney was dogged with questions about his religion. The spark was a hitherto obscure fundamentalist preacher from Texas, Robert Jeffress, who attacked Romney's Mormonism by doubting whether he could really be considered a Christian. The media promptly set aside the issues that should have been paramount—Romney's views on economic and foreign policy—in order to spend a week giving respectful consideration to an attention-grabbing rabble-rouser. They then proceeded to pester the other candidates with the loaded question of whether they thought Romney was a Christian. CNN's Candy Crowley was particularly egregious in this respect, pressing Herman Cain and Michele Bachmann for a response and becoming indignant when they refused to answer. The question did not deserve an answer, because Crowley had set it up to legitimate a false premise: that Romney's religious belief was a legitimate issue of public debate. This is a perfect example of how the media reinforce an informal but increasingly binding religious test for public office that the Constitution formally bans. Like the British constitution, the test is no less powerful for being unwritten.

The religious right's professed insistence upon "family values"* might appear at first blush to be at odds with the anything but saintly personal behavior of many of its leading proponents. Some of this may be due to the general inability of human beings to reflect on conflicting information: I have never ceased to be amazed at how facts manage to bounce off people's consciousness like pebbles

* "Morality" in this case usually boils down to ultraconventional prudery about private sexual behavior, the standards—but not practices—of which were established in Victorian England, and which eventually caused the comic uproar that led to the Clinton impeachment. Unfortunately, morality thus defined frequently ignores other aspects of ethics.

off armor plate. But there is another, uniquely religious aspect that also comes into play: the predilection of fundamentalist denominations to believe in practice, even if not entirely in theory, in the doctrine of "cheap grace," a derisive term coined by the theologian Dietrich Bonhoeffer. By that he meant the inclination of some religious adherents to believe that once they had been "saved," not only would all past sins be wiped away, but future ones, too—so one could pretty much behave as before. Cheap grace is a divine get-out-of-jail-free card. Hence the tendency of the religious base of the Republican Party to cut some slack for the peccadilloes of candidates who claim to have been washed in the blood of the Lamb and reborn to a new and more Christian life. The religious right is willing to overlook a politician's individual foibles, no matter how poor an example he or she may make, if they publicly identify with fundamentalist values. In 2011 the Family Research Council, the fundamentalist lobbying organization, gave Representative Joe Walsh of Illinois an award for "unwavering support of the family."[1] Representative Walsh's ex-wife might beg to differ, as she claims he owes her over one hundred thousand dollars in unpaid child support, a charge he denies.

Of course, the proper rituals must be observed before an erring politician can obtain absolution. In November 2011, at a forum sponsored by religious conservatives in Iowa, all of the GOP presidential candidates struck the expected notes of contrition and humility as they laid bare their souls before the assembled congregation (the event was held in a church). Most of them, including Cain, who was then still riding high, choked up when discussing some bleak midnight of their lives (he chose not to address the fresh sexual harassment charges against him, which surely would have qualified as a trying personal experience preying on his mind). Even the old reprobate Gingrich misted up over some contrived misdeed in-

tended to distract attention from his well-known adventures in serial matrimony.

All of these gloomy obsequies of repentance having been observed, Gingrich gave a stirring example of why he is hands-down the best extemporaneous demagogue in contemporary America. Having purged his soul of all guilty transgressions, he turned his attention to the far graver sins bedeviling the American nation.

> If we look at history from the mid-1960s, we've gone from a request for toleration to an imposition of intolerance. We've gone from a request to understand others to a determination to close down those who hold traditional values. I think that we need to be very aggressive and very direct. The degree to which the left is prepared to impose intolerance and to drive out of existence traditional religion is a mortal threat to our civilization and deserves to be taken head-on and described as what it is, which is the use of government to repress the American people against their own values.

That is as good an example as any of cheap grace as practiced by seasoned statesmen like Gingrich—a bid for redemption turned on its head to provide a forum for one of the Republican Party's favorite pastimes: taking opportunistic swipes at the dreaded liberal bogeyman. How quickly one forgets one's own moral lapses when one can consider the manifold harms inflicted on our nation by godless leftists!

The GOP's growing fascination with war is connected to the fundamentalist mind-set. The Old Testament abounds in tales of slaughter—God orders the killing of Midianite male infants and

the enslavement of the balance of the population, and inspires the genocide of the Canaanites, the slaying of miscreants with the jawbone of an ass, and so on—and since American fundamentalists often seem to prefer the Old Testament to the New (particularly that portion of the New Testament known as the Sermon on the Mount), it is but a short step to approving war as a divinely inspired mission. This sort of thinking has led to such phenomena as the late televangelist Jerry Falwell once proclaiming that God was prowar.[2]

More disturbing, fundamentalist ministers have been influencing the Republican Party's Middle East policies. A fundamentalist megachurch preacher from Texas, John Hagee, has made a belief in the "rapture" (a word found nowhere in the Bible) the centerpiece of his ministry; he believes it will be triggered by an apocalyptic battle at the end of the world, in the Middle East. He contorts the Bible to predict that Russia and various Islamic countries will invade Israel and be destroyed by God. This supernatural event in turn will cause the Antichrist, whom he identifies as the head of the European Union,* to engineer a confrontation over Israel between China and the United States. Hagee heads the lobbying group Christians United for Israel, and from this perch he routinely proposes that the United States adopt the most militaristic and confrontational policies against the Islamic world, including a preemptive nuclear strike against Iran. It is not entirely by happenstance that the GOP candidates in 2012 have fallen over backward in an effort to appear ever more anti-Iran. In 2008, John McCain, not noted for public displays of piety, eagerly sought and gratefully received Hagee's endorsement of his presidential candidacy—an endorsement McCain

* The current president of the European Commission, the executive body of the European Union, is a gentleman named José Manuel Durão Barroso. Who knew?

later rejected after some bizarre remarks surfaced that Hagee had made about Hitler and the Jews.

The apocalyptic frame of reference of fundamentalists like Hagee, their belief in an imminent Armageddon, psychologically conditions them to steer the country into conflict, not only on foreign fields (some evangelicals thought Saddam was the Antichrist and therefore a suitable target for cruise missiles), but also in the realm of domestic political controversy. Compromise is a dirty word if you are doing God's bidding. It is thus perhaps hardly surprising that the most adamant proponent of the view that there was no debt-ceiling problem was Michele Bachmann, the darling of the fundamentalist right. What does it matter, anyway, if the country defaults? We shall presently abide in the bosom of the Lord.

If the world is divided between the Children of Light and the Children of Darkness, then compromise in the spirit of traditional representative government becomes difficult. As a veteran of many late-night legislative sessions, I can personally attest to the fact that achieving legislation that will pass both houses of Congress is sometimes a grubby business, like sausage making, but the practical alternatives are either anarchy or dictatorship. As deal makers like Howard Baker or Bob Dole have given way to ideological purists infused with their own sense of godly virtue, such as Rick Santorum and Bachmann, it is hardly a wonder that the GOP has become the party of no.

When those professing this kind of religious dogmatism get involved in making foreign policy, the results can be disastrous. The Israeli newspaper *Haaretz* reported that George Bush allegedly told Palestinian prime minister Mahmoud Abbas, in a meeting

about Middle East peace in 2003, "God told me to strike at al Qaeda and I struck them, and then he instructed me to strike at Saddam, which I did, and now I am determined to solve the problem in the Middle East."[3] We have come a long way from the legacy of Eisenhower and Marshall if our leaders are thinking about the intractable crises of the Middle East in that fashion.

Some liberal writers have opined that the socioeconomic gulf separating the business wing of the GOP and the religious right make it an unstable coalition that could crack. I am not so sure. There is no basic disagreement on which direction the two factions want to take the country, merely how far it should go. The plutocrats would drag us back to the Gilded Age; the theocrats to the Salem witch trials. If anything, the two groups are increasingly beginning to resemble each other. Many televangelists have espoused what has come to be known as the prosperity gospel—the health-and-wealth/name-it-and-claim-it gospel of economic entitlement. If you are wealthy, it is a sign of God's favor. If not, too bad! This rationale may explain why some poor voters will defend the prerogatives of billionaires. In any case, at the beginning of the 2012 presidential cycle, those consummate plutocrats the Koch brothers pumped money into Bachmann's campaign, so one should probably not make too much of a potential plutocrat-theocrat split.[4]

Most of the religious enthusiasts I observed during my tenure on the Hill seemed to have little reluctance to mix God and Mammon. Rick Santorum did not blink at legislative schemes to pay off his campaign contributors: In 2005 he introduced a bill to forbid the National Weather Service from providing weather forecasts for free that commercial forecasters—like AccuWeather, a Pennsylvania-

based company which had contributed to his campaign—wanted to charge for. Tom DeLay's purported concern about the dignity and sanctity of human life, touchingly on display during the controversy over whether Terri Schiavo's husband had the right to tell doctors to remove her feeding tube after seeing her comatose for fifteen years, could always be qualified by strategic infusions of campaign cash. DeLay's quashing of bills to prohibit serious labor abuses demonstrates that even religious virtue can be flexible when there are campaign donations involved.

One might imagine that the religious right's agenda would be incompatible with the concerns for privacy and individual autonomy by those who consider themselves to belong to the libertarian wing of the Republican Party—the "don't tread on me," "live free or die" crowd that Grover Norquist once called the "leave me alone" conservatives. Given their profound distaste for an oppressive and intrusive federal government, one would think they might have trepidations about a religious movement determined to impose statutory controls on private behavior that libertarians nominally hold to be nobody's business, and particularly not the government's business.

Some more libertarian-leaning Republicans have in fact pushed back against the religious right. Former House majority leader Dick Armey expressed his profound distaste for the tactics of the religious right in 2006—from the safety of the sidelines—by blasting its leadership in unequivocal terms:

> [James] Dobson and his gang of thugs are real nasty bullies. I pray devoutly every day, but being a Christian is no excuse for being stupid. There's a high demagoguery coefficient to issues like prayer in schools. Demagoguery doesn't work unless it's dumb, shallow as water on a plate. These issues are easy for the intellectually lazy and can appeal to a large de-

mographic. These issues become bigger than life, largely because they're easy. There ain't no thinking.[5]

Armey had previously been an economics professor at several cow colleges in Texas, and when he came to Congress in 1985, libertarian economics was his forte. I do not recall religious issues motivating his political ideology; instead, economics was what gripped him, particularly the flat tax, which he tirelessly promoted. I believe his departure from Congress was impelled not only by the fact that he was not on the inside track to become Speaker, but also because of his disillusionment with the culture wars, as his passionate denunciation of Dobson suggests. But later, Barack Obama's election and the rise of the Tea Party induced a miraculous change of heart in Armey, as no doubt did the need to raise money for his lobbying organization, known as FreedomWorks. By 2009, Armey had become a significant voice of the Tea Party. As such, he attempted to declare a truce between fiscal and social conservatives, who would thenceforth bury their squabbles and concentrate on dethroning the Kenyan usurper in the Oval Office. That meant soft-pedaling social issues that might alarm fiscally conservative but socially moderate voters, particularly women, who lived in the wealthier suburbs.

In September 2010 Armey took one step further in his reconciliation with the people he had called thugs and bullies when he announced that a GOP majority in Congress would again take up the abortion fight, which was only right and proper for those who held such a sincere moral conviction.[6] When the Republicans duly won the House two months later, they did precisely that. State legislatures across the country followed suit: Ohio, Texas, and Virginia enacted the most severe abortion restrictions in any legislative session in memory. Suddenly Armey didn't seem to have any problem with social issues preempting his economic agenda.

The Tea Party, which initially described itself as wholly concerned with debt, deficit, and federal overreach, gradually unmasked itself as being almost as theocratic as the activists from the religious right that Armey had denounced only a few years before. If anything, they were even slightly more disposed than the rest of the Republican Party to inject religious issues into the political realm. According to an academic study of the Tea Party, "[T]hey seek 'deeply religious' elected officials, approve of religious leaders' engaging in politics and want religion brought into political debates."[7] The Tea Party faithful are not so much libertarian as authoritarian, the furthest thing from a "live free or die" constitutionalist.

Within the GOP libertarianism is a throwaway doctrine that is rhetorically useful in certain situations but often interferes with their core, more authoritarian, beliefs. When the two precepts collide, the authoritarian reflex prevails. In 2009 it was politically useful for the GOP to present the Tea Party as independent-leaning libertarians, when in reality the group was overwhelmingly Republican, with a high quotient of GOP activists and adherents of views common among the religious right. According to a 2010 Gallup poll, eight in ten Tea Party members identify themselves as Republicans.[8] Another study found that over half identified as members of the religious right and 55 percent of Tea Partiers agree that "America has always been and is currently a Christian nation"—6 points more than even the percentage of self-described Christian conservatives who would agree to that.[9] This religious orientation should have been evident from the brouhaha that erupted in mid-2009 over the charge that the Obama administration's new health-care reform plan would set up "death panels." While there was plenty to criticize about the health-care bill, the completely bogus charge garnered disproportionate attention. Republican political consultants immediately recognized that they had found a classic

emotional issue that would resonate with the same people on the religious right who had been stirred up over the Terri Schiavo case.* The Tea Party, a supposedly independent group of fiscal conservatives outraged by Obama's profligate spending plans, fell prey to the hysteria Republican Party operatives whipped up over end-of-life counseling.[10] This self-unmasking of the Tea Party may help explain why, after three years in existence, public support for the organization has been dropping precipitously.[11]

Ayn Rand, an occasional darling of the Tea Party, has become a cult figure within the GOP in recent years. It is easy enough to see how her tough-guy, every-man-for-himself posturing would be a natural fit with the Wall Street bankers and the right-wing politicians they fund—notwithstanding the bankers' fondness for government bailouts. But Rand's philosophy found most of its adherents in the libertarian wing of the party, a group that overlaps with, but is certainly not identical to, the "business conservatives" who fund the bulk of the GOP's activities. There has always been a strong strain of rugged individualism in America, and the GOP has cleverly managed to co-opt that spirit to its advantage. The problem is that Rand proclaimed at every opportunity that she was a militant atheist who felt nothing but contempt for Christianity as a religion of weaklings possessing a slave mentality. So how do Republican candidates manage to bamboozle what is perhaps the largest single bloc in their voting base, the religious fundamentalists, about this? Certainly the ignorance of many fundamentalist values voters about the wider world and the life of the mind goes some distance toward explaining the paradox: GOP candidates

* Surveys have found a positive correlation between the fear of death and the intensity of religious motivation. See, e.g., Ya-Hui Wen, "Religiosity and Death Anxiety," *Journal of Human Resources and Adult Learning*, December 2010.

who enthuse over Rand at the same time as they thump their Bibles never have to explain this stark contradiction because most of their audience is blissfully unaware of who Ayn Rand was and what she advocated.* But voters can to some extent be forgiven their ignorance, because politicians have grown so skillful at misdirecting them about their intentions.[12]

This camouflaging of intentions is as much a strategy of the religious right and its leaders—James Dobson, Tony Perkins, Pat Robertson, and the rest—as it is of the GOP's more secular political leaders in Washington. After the debacle of the Schiavo case and the electoral loss in 2008, the religious right pulled back and regrouped. They knew that the full-bore, "theoconservative" agenda would not sell with a majority of voters. This strategy accounts for Robertson, founder of the Christian Coalition (who famously said that God sent a hurricane to New Orleans to punish the sodomites), stating the following in October 2011: "Those people in the Republican primary have got to lay off of this stuff. They're forcing their leaders, the front-runners, into positions that will mean they lose the general election." I doubt he thought the candidates held positions that were too extreme, merely that they should keep quiet about those positions until they had won the election. Max Blumenthal, author of *Republican Gomorrah*, argues that this is a "lying for Jesus" strategy that fundamentalists often adopt when dealing with the snares of a wicked and Godless world. Since Satan is the father of lies, one can be forgiven for fighting lies with lies.

Hence the policies pursued for at least two decades by the reli-

---

* Nearly two decades ago, Mark A. Noll, a professor of theology at Wheaton College and himself an evangelical, wrote *The Scandal of the Evangelical Mind* about the decline of intellectual pursuits among evangelicals.

gious right on the federal, state, and local levels. It usually starts at the school board, after some contrived uproar over sex education or liberal indoctrination. The stealthily fundamentalist school board candidates pledge to clean up the mess and "get back to basics." After a few years they capture a majority on the board, and suddenly *Catcher in the Rye* is heaved out of the curriculum and science teachers are under pressure to teach the (imaginary) controversy about evolutionary biology. This was the path to greater glory of Michele Bachmann: Her first run for public office, barely a dozen years ago, was for a seat on the school board in Stillwater, Minnesota. Up until then she had drawn a taxpayer-funded salary for five years working as an attorney for the Internal Revenue Service, not, of course, because she was one of those lazy, good-for-nothing government bureaucrats that Republican candidates routinely denounce. She was secretly studying the ways of the government beast so as to defeat it later on.

Bachmann, Rick Perry, and numerous other serving representatives and senators have all had ties to Christian Dominionism, a doctrine proclaiming that Christians are destined to dominate American politics and establish a new imperium resembling theocratic government. According to one profile of Perry, adherents of Dominionism "believe Christians—certain Christians—are destined to not just take 'dominion' over government, but stealthily climb to the commanding heights of what they term the 'Seven Mountains' of society, including the media and the arts and entertainment world."[13] Note the qualifier: "stealthily."

At the same religious forum where the GOP candidates confessed their sins, Bachmann went so far as to suggest that organized religion should keep its traditional legal privilege of tax exemption while being permitted to endorse political candidates from the pulpit.[14] The fact that government prohibits express po-

litical advocacy is in her imagination muzzling preachers rather than just being a quid pro quo for tax-exempt status equivalent to that imposed on any 501(c)3 or 501(c)4 nonprofit organization. But for Bachmann and others of like mind, this is persecution of a kind that fuels their sense of victimhood and righteous indignation.

It is not difficult to find examples in everyday life of acquaintances and associates whose ever-present sense of persecution is nothing more than a rationalization of their own anger and hostility. According to Canadian psychologist Robert Altemeyer, who has written extensively about the characteristics of the authoritarian personality, fundamentalists exhibit a high quotient of authoritarian traits:

> They are highly submissive to established authority, aggressive in the name of that authority, and conventional to the point of insisting everyone should behave as their authorities decide. They are fearful and self-righteous and have a lot of hostility in them that they readily direct toward various out-groups. They are easily incited, easily led, rather uninclined to think for themselves, largely impervious to facts and reason, and rely instead on social support to maintain their beliefs. They bring strong loyalty to their in-groups, have thick-walled, highly compartmentalized minds, use a lot of double standards in their judgments, are surprisingly unprincipled at times, and are often hypocrites.[15]

The history of Europe has largely been a history of religious wars, intolerance, and oppression: Government has been wielded countless times as the instrument and vindicator of divine truth. With the decline of formal religious belief after the senseless carnage of World War I, the aggressive and authoritarian ideologies of

the early twentieth century filled the psychological need that state-controlled religion had previously supplied. Their doctrines were often just as badly distorted as religious dogma and attracted the same sort of true believer who needed an outlet for his free-floating hostility. There will always be a large number of people who crave certainty in an uncertain world.

The United States has been fortunate to have avoided some of the worst aspects of Europe's history. Luck had something to do with it, but so did a system of governance that permitted and encouraged religious pluralism. What America did not do was mandate a religious test for office or base its foreign or domestic policies on someone's tendentious reading of the Bible. If this country ever fully uncorks the genie of politicized religion, as the Republican Party has been attempting to do, we shall long regret it.

9

NO EGGHEADS WANTED

Consistent both with its strong base of support among fundamentalists and with its authoritarian belief structure, the GOP is increasingly anti-intellectual and antiscience.

It is ironic that the United States should have been founded by intellectuals, for throughout most of our political history, the intellectual has been for the most part either an outsider, a servant or a scapegoat.

—Richard Hofstadter, *Anti-Intellectualism in American Life* (1964)

Fifty years ago, when he wrote his seminal book on the periodic waves of anti-intellectualism in America, Richard Hofstadter was highly critical of his own time. In retrospect, he was writing in a golden age of enlightenment. For it was also fifty years ago that, when a handful of kooks in the John Birch Society condemned the fluoridation of water as a communist conspiracy, the vast majority of the American people dismissed them as a fringe nuisance. The plot device of the popular movie *Dr. Strangelove* hinged on the actions of an antifluoridation fanatic, and everybody was in on the joke. But in 2011, a majority of the majority party of the United States House of Representatives voted against new consumer energy standards, arguing, among other things, that com-

pact fluorescent lightbulbs were a radical leftist conspiracy. How did we ever get here?

The problem is unfortunately not new. In 1922, not long before the Scopes Monkey Trial, Woodrow Wilson told an interviewer who asked him for his views on evolution by natural selection, "Of course, like every other man of intelligence and education I do believe in organic evolution. It surprises me that at this late date such questions should be raised." And yet, ninety years later, after the genetic engineering of crops, the Human Genome Project, the discovery of evolving antibiotic-resistant bacteria, and innumerable other evidence of the evolution of organisms, such questions are not only raised, they have become a political litmus test on the right. The wise candidate ducks the issue, while the unscrupulous one panders to the uninformed.

Whether it is Michele Bachmann announcing that the HPV vaccine causes mental retardation, or Senator James Inhofe condemning the findings of climate scientists as a "hoax," or Rick Santorum doubting the validity of evolutionary biology, there can be no question that the GOP has placed itself squarely in the camp of the flat-earthers. This is a sad legacy for a previously forward-looking party, one that established public land-grant universities under President Lincoln and created science scholarships under President Eisenhower.

In 1957, when the Soviets launched *Sputnik*, American politicians wanted to hit the panic button. What this meant in cold war terms was to throw money at the Department of Defense and initiate crash programs to develop more and better weaponry. But President Eisenhower, having already cut military spending after the Korean War (and, as a result, balanced the budget), was loath to spend that kind of money. In any case, he knew but could not reveal to the public that there were classified programs on the drawing

board that in time would redress any perceived disparity with the Soviets.

Instead, Ike proposed federal assistance to public education to improve the teaching of science and engineering, as well as scholarships to promising students. In his speeches at the time he emphasized that his science advisers had told him that the education of scientists and engineers was the highest national defense priority, *a higher priority than producing weapons.* Many of these newly minted scientists and engineers would, of course, work for the Department of Defense or NASA, but others would go on to infuse their skills into the civilian economy.

It was a shrewd argument to outflank the hawks, and a similar one to the way, a year prior to his science announcement, he had sold his idea for an interstate highway system. He knew that the nation's economic competitiveness would suffer from the antiquated roads of the 1950s, a system inferior to the autobahns he had seen in Germany at the end of World War II. To get his proposal through Congress he pitched it as the National Interstate and *Defense* Highways Act. Building a nation-spanning system of modern highways would, of course, require educating and training thousands of civil engineers.

But Eisenhower was not interested in raising up a generation of soulless technocrats. His vice president, Richard Nixon, gave an address that same year in which he emphasized the importance of teaching the humanities. Education had to be balanced: While they should establish a foundation in science, schools needed to educate the whole individual. He pledged that federal, state, and local governments would do whatever it took to make it happen, including raising teachers' salaries. Nixon's statement is an ironic counterpoint to the policies of today's Republican state governors and leg-

islators, who appear to view schoolteachers as public enemy number one. In the 1950s and 1960s both parties could claim that their platforms embraced science and learning as national priorities. President Kennedy stressed the importance of education, and his White House guest lists were notable for having a high quotient of academics and intellectuals.

The first crack in the edifice of general political support for science and learning came in about 1970—incidentally, the same time that the economy started to transform, manufacturing started trickling out of the country, and the culture wars began. It started on the far left, where dissatisfaction with the Vietnam War found an outlet in a rejection of technology. The leftist antiwar crowd did not distinguish between the ethical and proper uses of technology and napalm. Some began to show distinct aspects of Ludditism—an ironic development, given that the forces of the left had been the advocates of science and "progress" ever since the French Revolution.

Thus, some of the sillier fringe theories of the seventies: mathematics as an arbitrary construct; schools of historical revisionism so focused on history's inevitable subjectivity that they questioned the existence of facts; and so on. This tendency reached its nadir in the brief fad of deconstructionism among the European left and a few academics in America. Beneath a lot of fake erudition, proponents argued (to the extent one could make any sense of it) that there was no stable reality at all, only arbitrary linguistic systems of power and oppression.

Most of the world laughed this leftist mumbo jumbo out of existence after a few years. It was a godsend to the growing conservative movement, however, to have such an object on the left to ridicule. Its main legacy is the phrase "political correctness," a term

which has in most cases long outlived its usefulness but which right-wing talk radio continues to use incessantly as yet another weapon in its culture wars arsenal.

Anti-intellectualism as a mass phenomenon in contemporary American life arose gradually but steadily over the last thirty years, and it resides principally on the rightward end of the political spectrum. Its connection to the rise of the more extreme forms of religious fundamentalism, and their infection of the GOP's electoral base, is an obvious fact, but one which the mainstream media rarely brings up. Anti-intellectualism has been a recurring factor in American history since the country's founding; the difference between past episodes and the current situation, however, is both that it is now so closely identified with the fortunes of one of the two political parties and that it has deep institutional roots involving radio, TV, and print media as well as partisan "institutes," which generate slanted research on topics like evolution and climate change.

It is an enduring irony of history that Protestant Christianity arose as a religious reform movement among deeply learned scholars such as Luther, Calvin, and Zwingli. (By way of example, Luther's close collaborator Philipp Melanchthon studied philosophy, rhetoric, astronomy, Greek, law, mathematics, and medicine.) The reformed churches' insistence on discovering authentic religious texts, and their stress on the right and duty of all believers to be guided by their inner light on the basis of their own reading of these texts, fueled an impetus for greater popular literacy. But Protestantism's belief in scriptural inerrancy also led to offshoot denominations best characterized by doctrinal rigidity, hostility to artistic expression, and deep suspicion of intellectual activity that could undermine the accepted understanding of the revealed truth.

America has experienced periodic upwellings of evangelical

activism that have often spilled over into concrete political agendas. The Great Awakening of the early nineteenth century had variable results: It produced the Millerites, who predicted the end of the world would come on October 22, 1844, but also the movements for the abolition of slavery and women's suffrage. The anti–Wall Street populism that arose on the prairies in the late nineteenth century contained a strong element of evangelical activism. That insurgency did not quite succeed in overturning the two-party system or toppling the Wall Street barons, but it did spawn the progressive movement, which helped curb the prevailing political and economic abuses.

The evangelical insurgency of the late nineteenth and early twentieth centuries also produced the hideous excrescence of Prohibition, Comstock laws prohibiting the sale of novels by artists like Marcel Proust and James Joyce, and the all too familiar civil harassment of harmless personal behavior that seems to increase whenever zealots have the political whip hand. It was a sad capstone to a storied career that William Jennings Bryan, who stood up to the power of the money trust, championed the rights of labor, and opposed entry into the slaughter of World War I, should end his life in a Dayton, Tennessee, courtroom declaring that man is not a mammal. Perhaps he had been outraged by the Social Darwinists' perversion of Charles Darwin's scientific breakthrough. But he definitely signaled the opposition to science and intellectual life of a significant strain of American religious thought.

This strain lay mostly dormant in American political life from the 1920s until the last quarter of the twentieth century. In the meantime, a few conservatives attempted to breathe life into the notion that the movement should have a visible intellectual foundation. In the 1950s, conservatism was at a low ebb of intellectual

prestige. The liberal consensus was triumphant, and public intellectuals such as Lionel Trilling declared rather smugly:

> In the United States at this time Liberalism is not only the dominant but even the sole intellectual tradition. For it is the plain fact that nowadays there are no conservative or reactionary ideas in general circulation. This does not mean, of course, that there is no impulse to conservatism or to reaction. Such impulses are certainly very strong, perhaps even stronger than most of us know. But the conservative impulse and the reactionary impulse do not, with some isolated and some ecclesiastical exceptions, express themselves in ideas but only in action or in irritable mental gestures which seek to resemble ideas.[1]

Soon those irritable mental gestures began to cloak themselves in a fog of polysyllabic words. The mid-1950s marked the rise of a more sophisticated brand of conservative, eager to dispense with the crudities of Joe McCarthy accusing General George C. Marshall, the strategic architect of the U.S. victory in World War II, of being a Communist fellow traveler.

Foremost was William F. Buckley, Jr., who, ironically, wrote a convoluted defense of McCarthy at the time. Buckley's fondness for two-dollar words was such an affectation that it became difficult at times to know what he was saying, but he did lend a certain respectability to a conservatism still smarting from disasters stretching all the way back to the Hoover presidency. In the twilight of his life, even the reflexive cold warrior Buckley came to regret the invasion of Iraq as a disaster. Today it would be hard to picture Rush Limbaugh or Sean Hannity playing a Bach partita on the harpsichord as Buckley did.

Most of the prevailing conservative intelligentsia of the 1960s

was associated with Buckley and his *National Review*: William Rusher, who adopted a prosecutorial demeanor reprising E. G. Marshall's roles in *The Caine Mutiny* and *12 Angry Men*; James Burnham, whose single, monomaniacal message was that the Russians were coming; and Russell Kirk, headstone polisher of the memory of Burkean conservatism. As I recall, Kirk would give lectures at Washington foundations while wearing a cape. The last dull reverberation of that movement lingers on in George F. Will, who has had a thirty-year record as a public intellectual unblemished by the expression of a fresh idea.*

Whatever intellectual pretensions these gentlemen sought to inject into the conservative movement and the Republican Party has been overtaken since 1980 by the rise of the religious right. The role of religious fundamentalists in the anti-intellectual and antiscientific stands of the current Republican Party is too obvious to belabor here. Others like Max Blumenthal have commented on it, although it is a topic the major media soft-pedal. But there is another strand in the Republican base that hardly anyone mentions or even notices: the belligerent frat-boy conservative, a political lifestyle and performance art launched in the 1980s by P. J. O'Rourke. It achieved escape velocity the following decade with Rush Limbaugh, Matt Drudge, and the "Brooks Brothers riot" in 2001, when preppy GOP operatives staged fake protests of the Florida recount for the cameras. It culminated in the agent provocateur exploits of the late Andrew Breitbart and his protégé, James O'Keefe.

These men proved that it was possible not to have a single religious bone in your body and still be a Republican in good standing—by sneering at elites and intellectuals. Any nod at Christianity is the

* Correction: On March 4, 2012, Will broke his streak by saying that Republicans want to bomb Iran but are afraid of Rush Limbaugh.

tribute vice pays to virtue. Limbaugh got into minor trouble in one such transaction by suggesting that the nominally Christian Lord's Resistance Army of Uganda (LRA) was being persecuted by the crypto-Muslim Barack Obama's pledge of assistance to the Ugandan government in its fight against the LRA. Given that he is a frat-boy Republican who thinks the world terminates twelve miles off the shores of America, Limbaugh did not bother to acquaint himself with the fact that the LRA is a gang of vicious, child-murdering psychopaths. He thought he could get a two-fer by pandering to the religious right with his claim that Christians were being persecuted while feeding raw meat to the rest of his listeners by unveiling yet another one of evil Obama's manifold iniquities.

The Republicans who control the Michigan Senate took a page out of Limbaugh's book in November 2011, when they picked up a Democratic-sponsored bill to prohibit bullying in schools and eviscerated it. Their ploy hinged on creating a "reasons of conscience" loophole—claiming that it was not bullying for one schoolchild to harass another by getting in his face to express a deeply held personal belief—for instance, that the person in question would go to hell because of his assumed sexual orientation. The new bill was passed over the strenuous objections of the opposition, who said that the amendments would in effect license bullying.[2] The fundamentalist base knows how to decode the words—for "conscience" read "religion"—so it was another two-fer: The frat boys could give vent to their sociopathic bullying impulses under a fog of sanctimonious principle. Eventually the bill created so much adverse publicity that Senate Republicans dropped the provision in favor of competing language originating in the Michigan House.

Frat-boy Republicans would contest the notion that the Republican Party wishes to impose a Taliban-style theocracy in America. They display a refreshing lack of moral prudery in their

own behavior, which may help explain their sympathy for the conduct of their honorary lodge brother, the street-smart bomb-thrower Newt Gingrich. Whenever Jesus commands one of them to tread the rocky path to salvation it tends to happen, coincidentally, just prior to a run for public office. But they earn their bona fides by praising belligerence and touting ignorance of world affairs as a moral virtue, notwithstanding the fact that they have no core of fixed moral beliefs at all, religious or intellectual.*

The ultimate apogee of frat-boy conservatism came with the election, in 2000, of a frat-boy president. Some of our reflexive anti-intellectualism can be attributed to the inherent dumbing down that occurs thanks to the natural tendency of our media to focus on human-interest stories in their coverage of political candidates. Partly this is the result of the technical medium involved: The TV camera either loves a person, or it does not. A candidate who is likable, folksy, and has the common touch is far more telegenic than Adlai Stevenson delivering a position paper. And, of course, the media wise guys like to establish narratives that pigeonhole a candidate.

We didn't know much about George W. Bush in 2000, but the press filled in the gap by assuring us that he was the kind of regular guy you could have a beer with. Never mind that he was the fourth generation of an extremely wealthy political dynasty.† Al Gore, by contrast, was a stuffy, pompous bore who claimed to have invented

---

* It is no contradiction to categorize Gingrich, who fancies himself an intellectual, with the anti-intellectuals. His longtime pandering to anti-intellectual themes—i.e., through elite bashing—has been a feature of his rhetorical performance art for decades. Columnist Andrew Sullivan described him during the Republican debates as a "dumb person's idea of a smart person."

† There is also the nonsensical aspect of using the drinking buddy analogy for a recovering alcoholic. That is not a gratuitous disparagement of Bush for having had a problem in his past that he made an effort to resolve. But it was

the Internet. We all had a good laugh at that one. The media framed the narrative to suggest that anyone with intellectual pretensions was an arrogant, out-of-touch elitist with no concern for the common man. And given the fact that the budget was in balance, the nation was at peace, and the press needed a good tabloid human-interest story after the frenzy over Monica Lewinsky had abated, the media delivered prepackaged character sketches of the candidates to us on which to base our voting decisions. Enough voters pulled the lever for Bush, with a little assist from the Supreme Court, to get him over the finish line.

When the 2004 campaign rolled around, the same process repeated itself. George W. Bush, the shoot-first, ask-questions-later cowboy who didn't "do" nuance (meaning intellectual activity), versus John Kerry, the French-speaking windsurfer. That's all we needed to know. Bush, the guy who thought with his gut rather than his cerebrum; and Kerry, the dithering elitist who overanalyzed issues and coiffed his hair. Guess who won.

That is not to say that had Kerry been elected, he would have ushered in a new golden age in the American presidency. I suspect not. But the press might have given the electorate more to go on than the tiresome jock-versus-nerd cliché. They paid less attention to Kerry's 2002 vote to give Bush carte blanche for the invasion of Iraq and what that vote said about his policy judgment. The Authorization of Use of Military Force resolution was a straightforward proposition about whether to invade the wrong country. Since I was a cleared congressional staff member, I read the same thinly sourced, heavily caveated intelligence that Kerry read. It struck me

---

an embarrassing and inappropriate peg on which the media hung a shorthand character study of the man.

then as dubious and tendentious material. He voted for it. The American political system does not suffer from too much thinking and critical analysis; it is becoming crippled by their virtual absence.

An anti-intellectual base requires anti-intellectual leaders, which goes some distance toward explaining the bizarre race for the 2012 GOP presidential nomination. On occasion over the last fifty years a professional comedian such as Pat Paulsen would run for president, and we all appreciated the gag about a joke candidate making absurd statements. But the performance of the more flamboyant Republican candidates in the 2012 contest made it increasingly hard to tell the difference between reality and satire.

For a time, the more nonsensical Herman Cain's statements were, the more popular he became. "Yes, they're a military threat," Cain said about China on the *PBS NewsHour*. "They've indicated that they're trying to develop nuclear capability. . . ."[3] Well, yes, China indicated its intent very forcefully by exploding a nuclear weapon in 1964, which was big news at the time. Cain also said, "When they ask me, 'Who is the president of Ubeki-beki-beki-beki-stan-stan?' I'm going to say, 'You know, I don't know.'" The first and only president of Uzbekistan is Islam Karimov, who tortures and murders his opponents but whose country remains a vital supply route to the Afghanistan war that Cain fervently supports. A piece in *Foreign Policy* about Cain put it this way: "Rather than fake knowledge about this world, he by and large simply expresses contempt for it."[4]

Likewise, we could expect no nuance of any kind from Rick Perry, who explicitly promised as much.[5] He mooted that he might

send the U.S. military into Mexico, presumably on the "fight 'em over there so we don't have to fight 'em over here" principle. We know how well that worked out for the last Texan to occupy the Oval Office. Even Mitt Romney, educated at the best schools in the country (though his persona suggests the boss who fired you), has had to hedge his opinion about the evolution of organic life, trying to be all things to all people. He said, "I'm not exactly sure what is meant by intelligent design. But I believe God is intelligent, and I believe he designed the creation. And I believe he used the process of evolution to create the human body."

He topped that performance with his criticism of the Obama administration's foreign policy, which he said seemed to come from the "Harvard faculty lounge" rather than the battlefield. It was an odd criticism for Romney (Harvard MBA, JD) to have made, since his familiarity with Harvard's faculty lounges definitely exceeds his battlefield experience. Thus, even the educated offspring of a cosmopolitan governor has to play the man of the people who sneers at know-it-all elitists from a fancy university—the same university he happens to have attended.

Perhaps the purest expression of the anti-intellectual impulse on the campaign came from veteran culture warrior Rick Santorum. One is tempted to blink in disbelief at the thought that this man spent twelve years in the United States Senate. According to the *Des Moines Register*, here is what transpired at an Iowa university rally: "Discussing controversial classroom subjects such as evolution and global warming, Santorum said he has suggested that 'science should get out of politics.'"[6] Since I was paid to be a budget analyst rather than a theologian, I managed to retire from my career relatively unscathed by any memorable encounter with Santorum during my six years with the Senate.

Whenever the media chance to point out the ignorance (or

feigned ignorance) of a right-wing politician, it will all too often serve as a kind of vindication for the Republican faithful, who will say something along the lines of, The left-wing media (which hardly exists as a major force anymore) is once again trying to smear an honest conservative! He must be doing something right! This is the new Republican victimology: The liberal media is maliciously misrepresenting the views of a rough-hewn but sincere salt-of-the-earth conservative, even when his plain words indict him as an ignoramus or an opportunist.

By the turn of the millennium American anti-intellectualism no longer consisted of an unorganized selection of individuals holding quaint or out-of-touch views. It had become a countercultural movement that sought to influence government policy. In line with its institution building in other areas, the right wing created foundations, think tanks, and institutes in order to provide dubious "research" to lend a veneer of respectability and plausibility to its anti-intellectual positions. Many of these think tanks have set their sights on debunking supposedly bogus science.

The Seattle-based Discovery Institute, a nonprofit advocacy organization, has been the most prominent organization spearheading the effort to rebrand creationism as the pseudoscience of "intelligent design." Its principal benefactor for many years has been multimillionaire Howard Ahmanson, Jr., a proponent of theocratic government. The institute's manifesto, the so-called wedge strategy, makes it evident that disinterested scientific research is not on its agenda: It asserts that its mission is to "reverse the stifling dominance of the materialist worldview, and to replace it with a science consonant with Christian and theistic convictions."[7]

Science and religion have for a long time had a bumpy cohabita-

tion. One has only to think of Galileo and the Inquisition, or the nineteenth-century clergy's reaction to Darwin's *Origin of Species*. But up until recently, most Americans appeared to have accepted the basic principles of science taught in high school biology or chemistry class. That is unfortunately no longer the case. The influence of science skeptics is now so pervasive that in 2006 a conservative activist created a knockoff of the online encyclopedia Wikipedia called Conservapedia.[8] Its creator, an offspring of the venerable family values agitator Phyllis Schlafly, believes the earth is six thousand years old, Einstein's theory of relativity is a hoax, and evolutionary biologist Richard Dawkins shares certain characteristics with Adolf Hitler.

The far right's contempt for science and factual evidence dovetails with corporate interests in many areas—climate change; the effect of environmental toxins on health; tobacco;* junk food and obesity; conservation—and how useful that their activities should undermine the scientific evidence behind the drafting of government regulations. When in 2010 the Environmental Protection Agency proposed a rule for establishing greenhouse-gas emission limits for fossil-fuel power plants and petroleum refineries, Republicans were quick to denounce the proposal as scientific quackery. It was obvious, they said, that carbon dioxide was not a pollutant. On the contrary, it was perfectly harmless, because it was present in the very air we breathe. But that argument, while plausible to the casual TV viewer, was carefully intended to distort the real issue. The question was not whether carbon dioxide was breathable but

* A fraught if not schizophrenic issue on the religious right: Many fundamentalist churches denounce smoking in harsh moral terms, but millions of their adherents provide the Arbitron ratings for right-wing media personalities such as Limbaugh, who attack attempts to rein in smoking through ordinances and tobacco taxes.

whether adding vast quantities to the atmosphere would have a seriously adverse effect on the climate. If there is a high probability of such an effect, then carbon dioxide could be regulated as an environmental pollutant, regardless of its direct toxicity to humans.

While it is perfectly understandable that coal and oil companies would oppose legislation or regulation limiting greenhouse-gas emissions for purely business reasons, those companies can generally count on sympathetic right-wingers who do not understand the science but who react viscerally to any scientific finding that does not comport with either their gut feelings or the interests of their political contributors. Senator James Inhofe, adducing no empirical evidence, has often stated that the data suggesting humans are responsible for climate change is "a hoax." A fellow Republican in the House, John Shimkus, went further; in March 2009 he opposed the concept of climate change altogether by quoting chapter 8, verse 22, of the Book of Genesis: "[A]s long as the earth endures, seed time and harvest, cold and heat, summer and winter, day and night, will never cease." According to Shimkus, "The earth will end only when God declares its time to be over. Man will not destroy this earth. This earth will not be destroyed by a flood." This is what passes for logic and reason nowadays on Capitol Hill.

George W. Bush was too busy during his monthlong vacation in August 2001 to pay much attention to the August 6 President's Daily Brief that warned of an imminent terrorist attack ("Okay, you covered your ass," he is reported to have told his CIA briefer). What was he doing, aside from playing golf? He was working on his speech about limiting the number of stem-cell lines it was permissible for researchers to use. It was difficult to reconcile sound scientific policy with the demands of his base, but squaring that circle

was a more immediate political priority than acting on the warning that Osama bin Laden was determined to strike inside the United States.

By turning science into a malleable tool for ideological exploitation, Republicans are emulating the postmodern critics they profess to despise. For if science is merely a social construct serving the interest of whichever group happens to be ruling society, then the deconstructionists have been vindicated, and the scientific method is no more empirically meaningful than witchcraft or palm reading.

Another factor in the rise of anti-intellectualism lies in how the parties have determined which issues are on the table and which are not. Republicans have been more successful in this endeavor than Democrats. For the average American, indeed, for any American, tax policy is hard to understand; the Internal Revenue Code is contained in twenty volumes, and the interactions and unintended effects of changing the law are bewildering. There are hundreds of tax avoidance schemes that individuals and businesses may take advantage of; some are written specifically for a handful of rich persons or for a single firm. The tax write-off for corporate jets is one—how many of us get to ride in a private Gulfstream? Do taxpayers really need to subsidize their travel? Can't these corporate moguls use teleconferencing? Another criticial issue is the Greek debt crisis, which is extremely hard to understand, let alone explain. Or comprehending the national security stakes involved in tracing and decrypting electronic intercepts, or U.S. drone strikes in Pakistan and the accompanying chill they have provoked in our relations with Pakistan's government; these are momentous issues that complicate any assessment of our policy in the region.

Republicans, and many Democrats, do not want a thorough

and accurate national understanding of tax policy, bank regulation, campaign finance, drone policy, or the myriad other complex issues that lie at the heart of governing. It would alienate contributors. So, almost by mutual consent, issues like military interventionism, torture, assassination, U.S. financial support of dictators, and illegal surveillance of the American people are off the table: Too many bureaucrat and contractor toes would get stepped on.

It is a sad commentary on our society that a higher proportion of unlettered sodbusters in the 1880s had an accurate understanding of how banks, railroads, and grain wholesalers worked than the average American today has of how his pension funds are being looted, how he subsidizes corporate jets, or how he—as one individual—should come to pay more federal taxes than the entire General Electric Company. It may be more diverting to watch a televised singing contest than to learn the complex arcana of how American banks leased streetcar lines in Düsseldorf, Germany, to dodge U.S. taxes, but being a fully informed citizen requires sustained intellectual effort.[9]

Owing to the lack of serious and informed popular interest in real issues, we have the current Republican menu of pseudo-issues: abortion, gay marriage, flag burning, prayer in schools, sharia law, and so on. They are simple to grasp and well within the ambit of the average person who does not follow politics. People who wouldn't dream of venturing a thought on the European Financial Stability Fund or the London Interbank Offer Rate have a ready opinion—probably polarized in the usual fashion of American cultural politics—about whether life begins at conception. Of such things are today's American politics made. America's dysfunctional political process forces us all to take a stand on them, and so we have all been dumbed down.

Adding to the public's bamboozlement over the more complex

issues is the cottage industry of publicists, polemicists, and right-wing media personalities that has jumped into the fray. As Jonathan Chait wrote in *The New Republic*:

> Most people are not policy wonks. We rely on trusted specialists to translate these details for us. This is true as well of elected officials and their advisers. Part of the extraordinary vitriol of the health care debate stems from the fact that, on the Republican side, even the specialists believe things that are simply patently untrue. As with climate change and supply-side economics, there isn't even a common reality upon which to base the discussion.

One of the GOP's most common complaints during the health care debate was that Obama's plan would lead to "rationing." This is a scary word that is intended to conjure up visions of queuing up for meager provisions in World War II–era Britain. But if they truly believed in their own free-market dogma, Republicans would have grasped that rationing is inherent in any economic system based on price, exactly as the traditional American health care system has always been. The rich have been able to afford the best health care money can buy, while the poor cannot: That is rationing according to the ability to pay. Republicans ignore this obvious reality in their eagerness to attack Obama's plan to expand health coverage to the previously uninsured.

Paul Krugman opined in one of his columns in the *New York Times*:

> Monetary policy, fiscal policy, you name it, there's a gap. . . . [T]o meet the right's standards of political correctness now, you have to pass into another dimension, a dimension whose

boundaries are that of imagination, untrammeled by things like arithmetic or logic.[10]

Both Chait and Krugman are liberal Democrats, so their statements may sound like partisan polemics. But in explaining the voting preferences of the Republican electorate, veteran GOP pollster Ed Rogers makes the same point: "Even though Cain won't be the nominee, his candidacy tells us a lot about the psychology of GOP activists. Our team wants someone authentic, creative, fresh, bold and likeable. *And we don't have much tolerance for too many facts or too much information.*"[11] (emphasis mine)

Rigid ideology and faith-based evidence have created an alternate reality for many Republicans. A Bush administration official, during the period of national chest pounding before the invasion of Iraq, confirmed it. According to journalist Ron Suskind, a senior White House adviser told him the following:

> The aide said that guys like me were "in what we call the reality-based community," which he defined as people who "believe that solutions emerge from your judicious study of discernible reality." I nodded and murmured something about enlightenment principles and empiricism. He cut me off. "That's not the way the world really works anymore," he continued. "We're an empire now, and when we act, we create our own reality. And while you're studying that reality—judiciously, as you will—we'll act again, creating other new realities, which you can study too, and that's how things will sort out. We're history's actors . . . and you, all of you, will be left to just study what we do."[12]

People who think like that have already entered the fantasy world of *1984*, where the interrogator O'Brien reveals his philosophy to poor Winston Smith:

> We control matter because we control the mind. Reality is inside the skull. You will learn by degrees, Winston. There is nothing that we could not do. Invisibility, levitation—anything. I could float off this floor like a soap bubble if I wish to. I do not wish to, because the Party does not wish it. You must get rid of these nineteenth-century ideas about the laws of Nature. We make the laws of Nature.

More than just the passage of time separates us from the ideas of progress and education expressed by Eisenhower and his vice president, or Kennedy's New Frontier. There is now a powerful, well-financed countercultural movement that has substantial influence within the GOP. It would roll back the Enlightenment if it could.

10

A LOW DISHONEST DECADE

America's political crisis has been brewing for over thirty years. But in the first decade of the twenty-first century, the sickness threatened to become terminal.

Vanity of vanities, saith the Preacher,
vanity of vanities; all *is* vanity.

—Ecclesiastes 1:2.

The first decade of the twenty-first century opened with a farce. The Y2K doomsday scenario, which was supposed to kick in at the stroke of 12:00 A.M., January 1, 2000, turned out to be a joke. Thus began our descent into tragedy. September 11, 2001—a date that everybody knows—and September 15, 2008—when Lehman Brothers filed for bankruptcy—stand in most Americans' minds as bookends for that first decade. The period in between was marked by a strange and paradoxical cultural fusion: The hysterical fear of remorseless terrorism combined with the arrogant vaunting of a country that would redeem the whole world with a sword. These contradictory national impulses were accompanied by a bacchanalia of self-seeking and public looting that made the Teapot Dome scandal seem quaint. This was the decade of Enron, subprime mortgages, Abu Ghraib, color-coded alerts, "heck of a job, Brownie," collateralized debt obligations, the

Troubled Asset Relief Program (TARP)—all culminating in a false promise of hope and change that ran aground in the mud of corporate fund-raising.

The 9/11 attack and the Wall Street collapse resonate in memory because they were the kind of cataclysmic events that occur only a handful of times in a century. But history is not a step function that we can neatly periodize: The past always hangs on into the present, just as the future is always implied by the way we live now. Most Americans did not dance the Charleston and wear raccoon coats all through the 1920s before the crash of '29 landed them in a bread line. That depression was preceded by many signs and portents in the decade before it: a huge and growing income disparity; regressive tax policy; an inflating and collapsing real-estate market; a chronically depressed business sector; and an international banking system that would rapidly transmit the effects of depression in one country around the world. Does any of this sound familiar?

The decade of the 2000s began as it ended, with the markets in steep decline after the puncturing of a bubble. The dot-com bubble of the late 1990s was an early sign—one that everyone in power was determined to ignore or conceal, depending on their degree of ignorance—that the growing financialization of the U.S. economy, in tandem with Wall Street's seizure of policy making in Washington, had turned the country's economy into an asset-bubble machine. With the erosion of America's industrial base and the increasing stagnation of the middle class, restless capital could no longer find a lucrative return in investments producing real, tangible wealth that could be sold abroad or consumed at home. So new ways were found to pump up the value of assets—any asset, how-

ever shaky on the face of it: Create a buzz about those assets to appeal to the greed and status anxiety of investors, and then dump them before the inevitable collapse. The template was no different from that of the Dutch tulip mania of 1637.

The mounting delusion was fueled by an indulgent government and a credulous prestige press. Pundits had begun to pontificate breathlessly in the mid-1990s about a "new economy" that would overcome the business cycle and create permanent prosperity. The Internet had so revolutionized business models, they opined, that we must be on the cusp of a long period of sustained increase in productivity, low inflation, and low unemployment. Proponents enhanced the allure of their speculations by throwing around jargon like "B2B," "Kondratieff Wave cycle," and "Goldilocks economy." Economics columnists like the *Washington Post*'s James K. Glassman praised the new economy in rhapsodic terms. In 1999 Glassman and Kevin A. Hassett wrote *Dow 36,000: The New Strategy for Profiting from the Coming Rise in the Stock Market*.*

Perhaps the most fateful assistance came from the old maestro himself, Federal Reserve Board chairman Alan Greenspan. By the mid-1990s he, too, was gushing about the new economy when he wasn't too busy lobbying for repeal of the Glass-Steagall Act, which placed a legal firewall between commercial and investment banking. Under Glass-Steagall your savings account could not be put at risk by your bank's speculative ventures. But Greenspan saw Glass-Steagall and other New Deal reforms—indeed, any government regulation—as roadblocks to achieving the self-regulating

* Later others would come to appreciate Glassman's promotional talents: In 2007, President Bush nominated him to replace Karen Hughes as undersecretary of state for public diplomacy, and in 2009 he became head of the George W. Bush Institute. Hassett became an economic adviser in 2008 for Republican presidential nominee John McCain.

New Economy. One of my tasks for the House Budget Committee was to pore over Greenspan's soothsayings for statements praising the new economic paradigm. Greenspan was then at the height of his political persuasiveness, and the budget committee's staff director told me that the Fed chairman's statements about the economy could be used to justify a potential deregulatory model in the committee's reports and legislative proposals. The idea was that the report wouldn't simply consist of a bunch of hack congressmen proposing a policy, it would have the implicit endorsement of the all-knowing chairman of the independent Federal Reserve Board. I found no lack of references to suit his needs, although as I parsed through the chairman's various statements, I slowly began to wonder why the ongoing economic boom was fundamentally different from any of the other past booms that had always ended in a bust. In the late 1990s the dot-coms were the darlings of Wall Street, although their business models were absurdly precarious. Who would have thought an online pet food store would become the great hope of venture capitalists? In the period before its initial public offering, the revenues of Pets.com were only about one twentieth of what it spent on advertising, but investors were undeterred. Within a month of its IPO, the bubble burst, and Pets.com shareholders lost $300 million.

Early in 2000, the long slide began. While almost everyone remembers the stock market's panicky drop immediately after 9/11, the Dow actually fell further in the period between Bush's inauguration and 9/11 than it did in the immediate aftermath of the attack. Greenspan's low-interest-rate policy was not an emergency measure passed after the September 2001 attacks but a previously worked out plan to lift the markets after the bubble burst. So were the 2001 Bush tax cuts. During a hearing of the House Budget Committee on March 2, 2001, I listened with a growing sense of unease as Greenspan testi-

fied on the state of the economy and the rationale—his rationale, anyway—for the proposed tax cuts. At that time, the Congressional Budget Office was projecting a cumulative ten-year surplus of $5.6 trillion. Greenspan's take:

> These most recent projections, granted their tentativeness, nonetheless make clear that the highly desirable goal of paying off the federal debt is in reach and, indeed, would occur well before the end of the decade.

Pay off the federal debt? Sounds great, doesn't it? Not so, argued Greenspan:

> At zero debt, the continuing unified budget surpluses now projected under current law imply a major accumulation of private assets by the federal government. Such an accumulation would make the federal government a significant factor in our nation's capital markets and would risk significant distortion in the allocation of capital to its most productive uses. Such a distortion could be quite costly, as it is our extraordinarily effective allocation process that has enabled such impressive increases in productivity and standards of living despite a relatively low domestic saving rate.[1]

Translated from the original Greenspan-ese, this means that paying off the debt could be a *bad* thing (notwithstanding his earlier claim that it was a highly desirable goal), because the government would then be in the position of having to meddle in private markets when it invested its surplus. The notion that the United States might, as it approached zero debt, develop a sovereign wealth fund like that of Norway or China was ideological heresy for

Greenspan. From the perspective of 2012, would we rather have our current debt-to-GDP ratio of 100 percent or that of Norway, at *minus* 160 percent? Alan Greenspan thought he knew better, and he provided the keystone in his policy recommendations that helped lay the foundation of our current fiscal crisis. A decade on, instead of sitting on a $5.6 trillion ten-year surplus, as projected in 2001, we found ourselves with a record-breaking ten-year deficit of $6.2 trillion and counting.

To avert the dread consequences of actually being in a position to invest federal assets, Greenspan endorsed the Bush administration's proposed tax cuts. It is probable, in view of his later actions with regard to monetary policy, that he also privately believed the tax cuts would provide investors with extra money to help reverse the falling stock market and reinflate asset prices. Members of Congress may not have understood every word of Greenspan's Delphic mumbo jumbo, but they jumped on the fact that the chairman of the supposedly independent Federal Reserve Board had endorsed the GOP's principal ideological hobbyhorse. After all, it was the people's money. But the people who counted bore a stronger resemblance to the politicians' campaign contributors than to ordinary working stiffs. *Laissez les bons temps roulez!*

Never believe any officeholder, Republican or Democrat, who voted for these tax cuts or for their extension and claims to be concerned about deficits or debts. *The intellectual rationale for the Bush tax cuts as presented by the enormously influential Federal Reserve chairman was precisely to forestall paying off debt.* The whole complex theology about tax cuts paying for themselves or boosting the economy is mainly ex post facto rationalization. The groundwork for the present fiscal crisis was established six months before 9/11,

although the ritual squawking, mainly Republican, about debt and deficit was mysteriously shelved until after the 2008 elections. Where were the small-government Republicans during the long eight years of the Bush administration, when their revered leader, with control of both the House and Senate, practically doubled the size of the federal government? I kept waiting for one of them to speak up. But year after year I watched as ever more money was appropriated for the Pentagon, the new and impossibly wasteful Department of Homeland Security, and any number of other schemes cloaked in the ritual justification of national security without the slightest squawk of protest.

But that lay in the future. Throughout the spring and summer of 2001, the Bush administration's national security apparatus kept its eyes firmly averted from the very real possibility of a terrorist striking the United States. The watchword in early 2001 was "Military Transformation." Transformation was a Madison Avenue slogan for paying contractors billions to develop pie-in-the-sky weapon systems of marginal utility that would take two decades to field. It was a relabeling of the so-called revolution in military affairs touted by the Clinton Pentagon only the previous year (the military loves to pour old wine into new bottles). The idea was to keep on building cold war weapon systems but to load them up with even more expensive and hard-to-maintain technology; the justification for these mostly obsolete weapon systems would be backfilled by threat assessments written to order. The notion that roughly two thirds of the thousands of military casualties in the decade ahead would come from primitive homemade bombs concealed in the ground was not on the options menu.

High on the list of potential villains was China, whose forced landing of a U.S. Navy EP-3 reconnaissance aircraft on April Fools' Day 2001 seemed to goad the administration to react in predictable

fashion. While circumstances forced it to act in a diplomatically conciliatory way to get the air crew back, it leaked its own newly commissioned defense review that suggested China should now be seen as America's main probable global adversary. At the same time, the Bush administration was already gearing up to attack Iraq, as Treasury Secretary Paul O'Neill, and Richard Clarke, who was the counterterrorism coordinator on the National Security Council, later documented.

When the twin towers fell, the Bush administration's reaction was so chest thumping, scattershot, and authoritarian, its appeal to fear and blind revenge so hyperbolic, that it is not surprising in retrospect that within a year or two millions of people began to believe that 9/11 was a conspiracy orchestrated by the U.S. government.

No, it was not a conspiracy.

Bush and his advisers were unhinged by the failure of their own rigid, ideological, and self-referential thinking to prepare them for the possibility of terrorist attacks. To remedy the situation they fell back on the same patterns of circular logic that caused them to ignore al Qaeda in the first place. This tendency was fatally reinforced by a military-industrial complex that saw (and continues to see) its real mission as achieving the greatest possible throughput of dollars, while it prioritizes threats in proportion to how they might enhance contractors' cash flow. It has become a cliché to suggest that people believe in vast government conspiracies because they cannot believe a handful of private individuals acting on their own, or in loose affiliation, could pull off a hugely consequential event like 9/11. But I think a bigger reason so many people became "9/11 Truthers" is that Bush and his advisers acted in such a high-handed and dictatorial fashion in the weeks, months, and years following the attack. Citizens could be forgiven for imagining that the Bush crowd *must* have been hiding something beneath their strutting

and bluster. But the Bush administration behaved exactly as authoritarian governments behave when they are under stress. The events that followed—a needless war, a fractured alliance, the domestic paranoia and infringements of civil liberties—were the fruits of that toxic thinking.

If the actions of the president and his operatives were unworthy of their oaths of office, the behavior of tens of millions of citizens helped enable the pathology of their leaders. There is absolutely no excuse for allegedly free citizens of a democratic country to be so abysmally ignorant of the world around them when they pay taxes (about which they bellyache incessantly) to station hundreds of thousands of U.S. troops in over 150 countries, bribe dictators with billions, and fund uncountable clandestine operations whose potential to backfire is every bit as great as our funding of the Afghan mujahedin in the 1980s. People with enough sophistication to operate an iPhone should be able to locate Yemen or Afghanistan on a world map—and hold their elected officials accountable for what they do in those countries.

I can pinpoint the precise moment when I came to believe Bush and his team had gone off their rockers. The 2002 State of the Union address was the usual staged political circus into which the president's constitutionally mandated message to Congress has in recent decades degenerated. I was watching TV at home with my wife, only half paying attention to the stock political rhetoric, when a curious comment made me sit up and focus intently. After the required emotional blather, Bush got down to business: America was mortally threatened by an axis of evil: Iraq, Iran, and North Korea. Wait a minute! Iran and Iraq were mortal enemies who had fought a decade-long war against each other that left a million casualties. They hated each other like poison! North Korea, the hermit kingdom, might as well have been on the dark side of the moon as far as

the other two countries were concerned. You had to have the intellectual honesty and grasp of foreign policy of a political speechwriter to believe those three countries could form an axis of anything.*

Although during the next year the press played the "will he or won't he?" game of speculation as to whether Bush would invade Iraq, from January 2002 onward it seemed obvious to me that he was hell-bent on invading, and was grasping at any pretext to do it. By the time of the perfunctory Authorization of Use of Military Force resolution debate in October 2002, the decision was locked in. Never in U.S. history had a president asked for a declaration of war or its equivalent so long before the commencement of hostilities. It was not only an admission that there was no emergency that would justify a preemptive war, it was also cynically timed less than a month before the congressional midterm elections to apply additional political pressure on a deliberative body that was already borderline hysterical.†

That month I decided that due diligence must be done. After all, it was supposed to be my job, as the lead staffer on defense issues for the House Budget Committee, to poke holes in flawed policy positions. But few members of Congress were systematically questioning the Bush administration's evidence, and the number of skeptical Republicans among them was vanishingly small. To all appearances, their staffs were equally passive and accepting; if any

* It turned out that the author of those lines was indeed a White House speechwriter, David Frum, who went on to pen a hagiography of his former boss. It is highly indicative of the downward arc of the decade that in 2010 Frum should have been fired from his position at the American Enterprise Institute because he was insufficiently loyal to right-wing dogma.

† The 2002 midterm election was when Max Cleland was defeated with the help of scurrilous campaign spots suggesting he was aiding and abetting bin Laden.

of them were presenting alternate scenarios to their bosses, I was unaware of it. The Hill, like the rest of the country, was in the grip of a fatalistic march toward war. Being perhaps more optimistic than I am now about the persuasiveness of facts and evidence, I assembled, from unclassified or declassified sources, a one-hundred-page binder of information on Iraq's connection with al Qaeda and its putative possession of weapons of mass destruction. My conclusion was that there was no solid evidence for either assertion. I privately discussed the contents of my findings with a handful of congressmen, as well as my conclusions that the cost of an invasion and occupation of Iraq could greatly exceed the prevailing estimates.* I told those who would listen that I thought the United States might end up creating, in a U.S.-occupied Iraq, a West Bank on steroids. The congressmen did listen politely—one made a mock gesture of burying his head in his hands and said, "I wish you hadn't told me that!" But it did not change their votes. When the vote was held in the House on October 10, 2002, only 6 of 223 Republicans opposed the resolution to go to war. The following day, only 1 of 48 Senate Republicans, Lincoln Chaffee of Rhode Island, voted against it.

Less than a month before the invasion, I was the lead House Budget Committee Republican staffer for the committee's hearing on Iraq. The witness for the Department of Defense was Paul Wolfowitz, the deputy secretary of defense and one of the neoconserva-

---

* The administration's prewar estimates ranged from Deputy Secretary of Defense Paul Wolfowitz's declaration that the invasion might even be free—i.e., paid out of Iraq's oil revenues—to National Economic Council director Lawrence Lindsey's guess that it might cost $100 billion to $200 billion—an indiscretion for which he was fired. The Pentagon's own internal estimate, which it released just prior to the invasion, was $60 billion to $95 billion.

tive architects of the war. Since this was the budget committee, the question on everyone's mind was what the war would cost. While Wolfowitz did his best to dodge giving a firm answer to that question, he attempted to leave the impression that Iraq's oil revenues, plus the release of Iraqi overseas assets that had been frozen by United Nations sanctions, might cover much of the cost. He also did his best to deride the fears of the army chief of staff, General Eric Shinseki, that the occupation of Iraq could require hundreds of thousands of troops. He called such speculations "outlandish" and implied that the military's requirements in Iraq after the war might even be less than in the Balkans during the 1990s. If Congress is often woefully uninformed about national security matters, it is sometimes because the Pentagon willfully misinforms them.

A significant percentage of Americans, from the Beltway elites in their Washington sinecures to Limbaugh's know-nothing dittoheads, believe that the United States can act militarily wherever and whenever it likes with impunity. But the invasion and occupation of Iraq left a trail of evils that will haunt us for decades, not least the cost, which has exacerbated our seemingly intractable fiscal crisis. For along with that other signature Bush policy (the tax cuts), the Bush wars and their associated spending were the largest single policy contributor to the swing from surplus to deficit. I watched this happen from the vantage point of the budget committee and kept waiting for someone to cry foul. Other than one or two gadflies like Ron Paul, the so-called deficit hawks would not question one penny of military spending. At the last count, the Iraq war has cost American taxpayers $824 billion. The Afghan war cost an additional $557 billion. And because these wars were deficit financed, the Treasury had to pay about $300 billion in interest to meet the Pentagon's expenses, making the total cost about $1.7 tril-

lion. If defense were a social program, Republicans would be calling it a manifest failure, and would engage in a vigorous campaign to zero out its budget.

Let us keep in mind that the spending on Iraq and Afghanistan doesn't stop with the Pentagon budget. Congress and the administration added another trillion dollars in associated costs on such things as establishing the Homeland Security Department and increasing the budgets for the State Department and the Veterans Administration. In total, our extravagant and misguided response to 9/11—a tragedy that might have been averted altogether had a few people at the top not diverted their attention to chimerical threats—was responsible directly and indirectly for at least $4 trillion of the $12 trillion slide in the fiscal picture since 2001. Even many liberals don't get this. Paul Krugman has in the past discounted the wars as a significant factor in our vast increase in debt. By refusing to arm themselves with this argument, Democrats and liberal commentators find themselves outgunned, and they get sucked into defending a losing position when the right-wing asserts that entitlements are solely or mainly responsible for deficits. But then, many Democratic politicians already compromised themselves on the war with their votes.

The Iraq disaster revealed something else at once more indefinable and more important than money that helps explain why the last ten years have seemed so grubby and dishonest.

It is within the bounds of taste and propriety as defined by the Washington establishment to argue, as I have done, that the invasion and occupation of Iraq was a fiscal extravagance that sorely aggravated the deficit. I could on occasion persuade a Republican officeholder privately to concur with that hypothesis, even if he or

she would not say so publicly. And whether or not the Beltway cognoscenti agree, they will at least entertain as a debatable proposition the argument that the invasion was strategically unwise, and that it complicated our position in the Middle East. The frenzy of contractor looting and fraud is certainly on the table for a postmortem, although the establishment's zeal to punish the perpetrators has been lukewarm at best. One can even make the argument that Iraq was a public relations disaster that blackened the image of the United States abroad. You could argue any of those propositions on a Sunday morning talk show or publish them in an op-ed in the mainstream media—the *New York Times*, say—and no one would think too much of it.

What you must never, ever, say, however, is that the invasion of Iraq was morally indefensible and a premeditated crime for which the people responsible should be held legally accountable. To do so would result in the same averted eyes and embarrassed cough behind the hand, as if you had eaten the hostess's mashed potatoes with a soup spoon at a Georgetown dinner party. It would be more likely that you'd not be invited back to the talk show circuit than the dinner table faux pas would get you stricken from a future guest list.

I am not much of a believer in the idea that a broad sample of humanity is likely to vary significantly from another broad sample of humanity in terms of personal moral rectitude. In our private behavior we are probably no better or worse than our ancestors were, and Americans are unlikely to be innately much better or worse than Swedes, say, or Italians. But under the pressure of group norms we can be influenced to behave, particularly when acting under the shield of official duties, in ways we would never contemplate acting in our private capacity. The famous (or infamous) Milgram Experiment and dozens of other psychological

tests since then have confirmed that the pressure to conform to an authority figure or peer group can cause people to behave in shocking ways.[2]

Based on my own experience in government, I am not surprised that functionaries caught up in "the mission," and acting within a conformist and hierarchical bureaucratic culture, could behave in ways immoral and contrary to domestic statutes and international treaties. Naturally, such persons would loudly proclaim their innocence and protest that they had acted in good faith, guided by the noble motive of patriotism or the best information available at the time. What is more interesting, in a morbid way, is how people with no direct culpability in those crimes have thrown a screen of protection around the perpetrators. Others in government, the media, and so-called opinion leaders generally have been conspicuously silent about these crimes.

Only low-ranking enlisted personnel were punished for the torture at Abu Ghraib: "Different spanks for different ranks," as the military saying goes.* But what are we to think about the people higher up the food chain who sanctioned or encouraged the torture? Or those who unleashed the war in the first place? Despite the elaborate efforts of the Bush administration to disguise the Iraq war as an exercise in self-defense, it was clearly a war of aggression, a crime described by Justice Robert Jackson, the lead U.S. prosecutor at the Nuremberg war crimes tribunals after World War II, as follows:

---

* As retired Army colonel and author Andrew Bacevich has noted, the one high-ranking officer who was reprimanded and reduced in rank because of Abu Ghraib was the exception that proved the rule. Brigadier General Janis L. Karpinski, the commandant of the prison, was a female and a reserve officer to boot—not part of the favored West Point crowd. And her dereliction of duty charge had no connection with any abuses, according to the Pentagon inspector general.

> To initiate a war of aggression, therefore, is not only an international crime; it is *the supreme international crime,* differing only from other war crimes in that it contains within itself the accumulated evil of the whole.[3]

What about people like John Yoo, the deputy assistant attorney general in the Justice Department and author of the "torture memo," who defined presidential power in such a way that all constitutional protections, law, treaties, and morality itself could be set aside at will? Yoo said the following in a 2004 debate with Douglas Cassel, a Notre Dame legal scholar:

> **Cassel:** If the president deems that he's got to torture somebody, including by crushing the testicles of the person's child, there is no law that can stop him?
>
> **Yoo:** No treaty.
>
> **Cassel:** Also no law by Congress—that is what you wrote in the August 2002 memo. . . .
>
> **Yoo:** I think it depends on why the president thinks he needs to do that.

Is Yoo languishing in some federal prison for violating our statutes regarding torture, which is a crime? No, he is currently a professor of law at the University of California, Berkeley, visiting professor at the University of Chicago, and a visiting scholar at the American Enterprise Institute. President Obama and Attorney General Holder prefer to look forward, not backward. An ethical chasm separates the Great and the Good of contemporary Wash-

ington from the principle that Justice Jackson expressed at Nuremberg:

> Any resort to war is a resort to means that are inherently criminal. War inevitably is a course of killings, assaults, deprivations of liberty, and destruction of property. An honestly defensive war is, of course, legal and saves those lawfully conducting it from criminality. But inherently criminal acts cannot be defended by showing that those who committed them were engaged in a war, when war itself is illegal. The very minimum legal consequence of the treaties making aggressive wars illegal is to strip those who incite or wage them of every defense the law ever gave, and to leave war-makers subject to judgment by the usually accepted principles of the law.[4]

And here is Jackson's reproof against the notion of American Exceptionalism, the idea that "if America does it, it's OK."

> If certain acts of violation of treaties are crimes, they are crimes whether the United States does them or whether Germany does them, and we are not prepared to lay down a rule of criminal conduct against others which we would not be willing to have invoked against us.[5]

The decision to initiate an unprovoked war of aggression was, as Justice Jackson stressed, inseparable from the crimes that followed. It would hardly do to limit the focus of our attention to a miserable creature like Yoo, because all who voted for the Authorization of Use of Military Force resolution bear at least some re-

sponsibility for the atrocities that followed. Whether they let war hysteria override their collective judgment, or were too intellectually lazy to check the evidence, or cravenly feared that a no vote would be politically harmful, these officials failed in their duty to the country and to those who sent them to Washington.

But it is not enough to say that Abu Ghraib, or the renditions of prisoners to countries (including Syria) that enthusiastically tortured them, or the contractor corruption, or the decline in American prestige abroad both among foreign governments and their publics, or the fiscal damage caused by the war were all predictable consequences of the decision to go to war in the first place. I believe the toxic dynamic that led to all of these ills is one, the same, and inseparable from the belligerent and avaricious mind-set that deregulated the markets, pushed the tax cuts, encouraged subprime borrowing, and botched the handling of Hurricane Katrina. The bedrock of this mind-set is a lack of intellectual seriousness combined with ideological rigidity, sound-bite glibness, and ethical corner cutting. And power worship, whether the object of worship is money, high office, or military might. The cultural witch's brew of the last thirty years produced Ken Lay and Bernie Madoff just as surely as it produced John Yoo and Dick Cheney.

In 2006, former Watergate figure John Dean wrote a book called *Conservatives Without Conscience*. It drew heavily on Robert Altemeyer's psychological studies.* Dean wrote at length about such well-known political figures as Gingrich and DeLay, describing their ruthlessness, ethical corner cutting, and superhuman ability to constantly change their stories and keep a straight face. He

* Also in 2006, Altemeyer wrote a more popularly accessible condensation of his and other researchers' clinical studies titled *The Authoritarians* (http://members.shaw.ca/jeanaltemeyer/drbob/TheAuthoritarians.pdf).

also profiled Bush administration figures such as Cheney, Yoo, David Addington,* and Bush himself. His conclusion: These people's obsessive drive for personal power, their ruthlessness in exercising it, their recklessness and heedlessness of the consequences, and their blind faith in their own righteousness makes them authoritarian personalities, to be sure, but also exactly the wrong people to be holding power in a representative government.

This type of persona is hardly exclusive to the world of politics. In 2011 the German magazine *Der Spiegel* published a report on research at the University of St. Gallen in Switzerland that found traders at financial firms took risks greater even than those a clinical psychopath would take.[6] And this was not only to get rich on their own accounts: "It was most important to the traders to get more than their opponents," an official familiar with the research said. "And they spent a lot of energy trying to damage their opponents." That would seem to corroborate what I have seen over the many years I had a chance to observe this personality type strutting the halls of Congress. Whatever his—for this type is mostly, although not exclusively, male—announced policy goal may be, that objective is both mutable and unimportant in the larger scheme of things. What is crucial is that his own power be vindicated, and his real or perceived enemies crushed. Newt Gingrich is a museum-piece example of this type of authoritarian personality: He has vacillated between the view that health care mandates are a panacea and the work of the devil; he engineered the impeach-

* David Addington was an adviser to Cheney and the principal advocate of the theory of the "unitary executive." Stripping away the legalistic weasel words, the theory held that anything the president does is by definition legal. It is the equivalent of Richard Nixon's view of executive power as expressed to David Frost: "Well, when the president does it, that means that it is not illegal."

ment of President Clinton while entangled in his own extramarital affair; in 1995, during his epic struggle against Clinton over the government shutdown, he praised the Congressional Budget Office as an impeccably neutral arbiter of budgetary legislation, only to denounce it in late 2011 as a reactionary socialist cabal that he would abolish. The positions change, but the vitriolic denunciations and relentless desire for personal power remain. In 1978, at the beginning of his career, Gingrich told a group of College Republicans: "[O]ne of the great problems we have in the Republican Party is that we don't encourage you to be nasty." An alleged political virtue of Democrats at the time, according to Gingrich, was that the party produced "nasty people who had no respect for their elders."[7]

The first decade of the twenty-first century was a period stamped with the imprint of this type of authoritarian personality, whether in government or on Wall Street. And there were tens of millions of Americans who, although lacking the personal gumption, ambition, and leadership qualities of a Gingrich or a DeLay, nevertheless empowered them to achieve their goals. Altemeyer describes these types as "authoritarian followers." They are socially rigid, highly conventional, and strongly intolerant personalities who, absent any self-directed goals, seek achievement and satisfaction by losing themselves in a movement greater than themselves. One finds them overrepresented in reactionary political movements, fundamentalist sects, and leader cults like Scientology. They are the folks tailor-made to respond as intended when told, for example, as Bush's press secretary Ari Fleischer said after 9/11, that they had better "watch what they say"; or who nod approvingly at illegal surveillance because, if you have nothing to hide, you have nothing to fear; or who, after months of news stories saying that no weapons of mass destruction had been found in

Iraq, nevertheless insist on believing that they *were* found. Altemeyer:

> Probably about 20 to 25 percent of the adult American population is so right-wing authoritarian, so scared, so self-righteous, so ill-informed, and so dogmatic that nothing you can say or do will change their minds. They would march America into a dictatorship and probably feel that things had improved as a result. . . . And they are so submissive to their leaders that they will believe and do virtually anything they are told. They are not going to let up and they are not going away.

Twenty to 25 percent is not a majority, but it is enough to swing an election, especially when you consider that the authoritarian follower is more easily organized and mobilized than the rest of the population. Altemeyer closed with the admonition that such personality types "are not going away." The rise of the Tea Party after 2008 showed that he was a far better prognosticator than Sidney Blumenthal, who thought that the radical takeover of the GOP had "shattered the party."

Democrats appear to be somewhat less subject to this authoritarian leader-follower syndrome. As Will Rogers remarked, "I don't belong to any organized party; I'm a Democrat." By contrast, if there is anything the GOP has mastered, it is falling into line behind the dogma of the moment.* That said, the pathology is not

* Between 1994 and 2008, an individual health-care mandate was a standard GOP nostrum, promoted not only by Mitt Romney, but by Newt Gingrich when he was the highest elected Republican official in the country, and it was endorsed by the conservative Heritage Foundation. Now the mandate is the work of the devil, and authoritarian followers of the GOP, like faithful

unknown in the party of Jefferson: Scratch a Rahm Emanuel or a John Edwards and one finds the same sort of imperious authoritarian one sees on the other side of the ideological divide. And former New Jersey senator and governor Jon Corzine offers up the same sort of hypocritical moralizing and ethical corner cutting that we find in Republicans like Gingrich. Although to a lesser extent than Republicans on Iraq, Democrats have shown a disturbing tendency to buy into the Obama administration's questionable premises on Afghanistan, Pakistan, and the escalating drone campaign.

The tribal behaviors of the leaders and followers of both parties have been similar enough that remarkably little has changed since the supposedly epochal election of 2008. For all the talk of hope and change, our national security landscape is substantially the same. It is less ostentatiously theatrical than it was under the Bush administration, but it is roughly equivalent in substance, if not style.

And what about the handling of the financial crisis? Has Tim Geithner acted differently in any significant way than Hank Paulson would have? Have any of the top tier of Wall Street malefactors done jail time? On the contrary, efforts at legal redress have been so skimpy that some courts have been rejecting the Securities and Exchange Commission's proposed settlements with the big banks on the grounds that they are derisory in view of the damage the banks have done. The Obama administration has to a great extent punted the country's economic policy, for good or ill, to the unelected Federal Reserve Board.

In 2003, when the Bush administration engineered the Medi-

---

party members in Orwell's *1984*, believe "we've always been at war" against mandates.

care Prescription Drug Act, it was overtly planned as a payday for Big Pharma. The statute was rigged to prohibit the negotiation of drug prices and to prevent the reimportation of prescription medicines from Canada. Like magic, the money rained down on the vultures of K Street, including Gingrich and his corporate-funded Center for Health Transformation. In 2009, when Obama proposed the Affordable Care Act, one of the first things he did was obtain a buy-in from Big Pharma that effectively protected its profitable market rigging. Similar deals protected the insurers. Was it because he knew these interests were too strong to fight? Was it because he was conflict averse by nature and too readily sought a bad compromise? Or was it a calculation that the Democratic Party would need the contributions when the next election cycle came around? It makes no difference; the practical effect is exactly the same.

The great irony, camouflaged by the Republicans' moronic "Obama, the Kenyan socialist" rhetoric and the uproar over the Tea Party, is that the major thrust of policy in the United States remained much the same after 2008 as it was before. The outward form of Bush corporate Republicanism had pretty much played itself out politically, and everybody, even the GOP, was tired of it. Obama and the Democrats essentially stepped into the shoes of the Republicans and followed the same basic policy line, rebranded under the rubric of hope and change. There were of course modifications of emphasis, and some of the more egregious aspects of the previous administration were downplayed, but there was far more continuity than change.

And rather than engage in soul-searching about the more destructive policies of the Bush administration—the war in Iraq, the tax cuts, the negative results of outsourcing and so-called free trade—the GOP leadership decided the only necessary policy was

to be the *anti-Obama party.* With that as the sole plank in their platform—the rest could be filled in later—Republicans rushed out to Astroturf the ostensibly independent Tea Party, which, as we have seen, was in reality the activist core of the Republican base. It was easy enough to take all the inchoate venom that had built up over the previous decade thanks to 9/11, the culture wars, and the economic collapse of 2008 and focus it against Obama. Anti-Obamaism became the signature Republican political philosophy of the second decade of the century. The Tea Party's supposedly spontaneous origin in 2009 was in reality anything but accidental. The previous twenty years of well-funded networking, assisted by propaganda bullhorns like Rush Limbaugh, Fox News, and all the rest, had laid the groundwork for the emergence of an angry and rigidly inflexible new movement.

The crowning irony is that the preposterous attacks against Obama actually did the president a favor by masking his true political makeup: that of a corporate centrist who basically followed (with minor variations) the main policy line of his predecessor. After the greatest economic collapse in eighty years, a collapse predominately (although not exclusively) caused by the irresponsibility of corporate finance, the net result was a parallel shift by both established parties *to the right*: the Democrats to a vaguely center-right corporate-friendly status quo party that preserves vestiges of the social safety net for appearance's sake, and the Republicans to a fend-for-yourself leader-follower cult of conspiracies and Armageddons, of endless enemies and religious crusades.

As W. H. Auden said of an earlier period of world crisis, all the clever hopes expire of a low dishonest decade.

11

ARE THE DEMOCRATS ANY BETTER?

As Republicans have grown ideologically more rigid, Democrats have almost entirely ceased to have any core beliefs at all—and their grab for corporate money is as egregious as that of the GOP.

They've got a set of Republican waiters on one side and a set of Democratic waiters on the other side, but no matter which set of waiters brings you the dish, the legislative grub is all prepared in the same Wall Street kitchen.

—Huey Pierce Long, in a speech for the reelection of Senator Hattie Caraway (D-Arkansas), 1932

If you seek a poster child for the corporatization of the Democratic Party, you need look no farther than Jon Corzine, the now disgraced former senator and governor from New Jersey. Like Chuck Schumer, Max Baucus, and Chris Dodd, Corzine is the very model of a Wall Street Democrat. In 2000, when he decided the time had come to step down from his position as the CEO of Goldman Sachs, he bought a seat in the Senate representing New Jersey with $62 million of the compensation he had extracted from Goldman. (This hardly made a dent in his personal wealth, for he had made $400 million when the company went public.[1]) Both par-

ties love self-financing candidates, as it means they can concentrate their vast but finite party war chests on other races. In 2005, after less than a full term in the Senate, Corzine went on to run for governor of New Jersey; when his personal expenditure for that race is added to the amount he spent for his Senate seat, the combined total comes to over $100 million.*

When the New Jersey citizenry bounced him from office in November 2009, Corzine landed on his feet as CEO and chairman of MF Global, an offshoot of a British investment company dating to 1783. He deployed his considerable business acumen to tank MF Global within eighteen months. His major project was to generate increased financial returns for the firm (and himself) by investing $6 billion in the debt instruments of Portugal, Italy, Ireland, and Spain at the precise point when Europe was sliding into financial crisis. It was a business strategy about as shrewd as buying Confederate bonds after the fall of Atlanta, and Corzine forced out a company executive who objected. When the company collapsed and Congress inquired about the $1.2 billion of clients' money that had been commingled with the bad investment, Corzine was profusely apologetic. But when asked whether he would make restitution to investors out of his own wealth, he said no.

One wonders why the Democrats, the supposed party of the common folk, were so accommodating to an amoral predator like Jon Corzine. Was he an anomaly, a bad apple? Only if Robert Rubin or Timothy Geithner could also be considered anomalies: The first helped engineer the deregulation of financial markets to his own

* Excluding the gold-plated Senate campaigns of Corzine and Hillary Clinton, in 2000 the average cost of a Senate seat was $4.7 million. Corzine spent $38 million in the 2005 governor's race; his opponent, Doug Forrester, $19 million.

benefit and that of his former colleagues at Goldman Sachs;* the second was asleep at the switch at the New York Federal Reserve Bank during the prelude to the Wall Street meltdown. (After becoming Treasury secretary, Geithner successfully lobbied Congress not to pass legislation that would prevent AIG from paying out $218 million in bonuses to employees after the insurance giant had received $170 billion in bailout funds from the taxpayers.) The two men are not so different from Republican counterparts like former senator Phil Gramm of Texas, who assisted Rubin in deregulating Wall Street before jumping to a lucrative sinecure as vice chairman of the Swiss bank UBS, or Rick Scott, the current governor of Florida, who was implicated in 1997 in the largest Medicare fraud case in history; he resigned as CEO of Columbia/HCA after the company was fined $1.7 billion and found guilty of defrauding the government.[2]

As I watched the health-care debacle unfold in the Senate in 2009, the nexus between big corporate money and Democratic behavior became manifest. For reasons that may become clear only when we read Obama's White House memoir, the president punted operational control of the legislation to Congress. That meant it ended up in the lap of Democrat Max Baucus of Montana, the chairman of the Senate Finance Committee. His fund-raising prowess is legendary: Baucus received $4 million between 2003 and 2008 from the health-care industry that his committee has jurisdiction over. As soon as the committee's deliberations began, Baucus declared a single-payer solution "off the table." Whether or not single-payer had a realistic chance of becoming law, by exclud-

---

* President Clinton called Rubin, who made $126 million in cash and stock options at Citigroup, "the greatest Treasury Secretary since Alexander Hamilton."

ing it as leverage at the outset, Baucus unilaterally disarmed any possibility of extracting concessions from the health-care industry. The resulting bill mollified all the major health-care interests, including the insurance industry and Big Pharma. While the Patient Protection and Affordable Care Act may have accomplished some praiseworthy goals, such as expanding coverage to more Americans, it flunked miserably on correcting the principal flaw in U.S. health care: Our system is 50 percent more expensive than that of the thirty-four countries of the OECD while providing no better patient outcomes. And by providing for an individual mandate requiring citizens to purchase privately supplied health insurance, Baucus, with Obama's acquiescence, placed the law in constitutional jeopardy

Baucus is also noteworthy in that an extraordinary number of his former staffers—about two dozen—have gone on to become K Street lobbyists. In the case of the health-care debate, one of them, a health-care lobbyist, parachuted back into a finance committee position to help write the Affordable Care Act. If the current revolving door between K Street and the Hill sounds similar to that of the relationship between Tom DeLay and superlobbyist Jack Abramoff, the similarities don't end there: In the early 2000s, Baucus received at least nineteen thousand dollars in contributions from Abramoff, and also availed himself of Abramoff's skybox at the Verizon Center in Washington.

But isn't there a pragmatic "lesser of two evils" argument to be made for the Democrats? For sure, they are tainted by money, but aren't they simply playing by the rules of the game that is rigged by money? Aren't they generally better than the Republicans, who are Neanderthals on social issues and seemingly crazy for war? Unfortunately, while there is much to be said for pragmatism, our campaign finance and conflict of interest laws did

not fall out of the heavens; Democrats were heavily involved in shaping them.*

As for their greater trustworthiness on national security, that is not self-evident, however much Democrats may think they are saner and sounder than Republicans on issues of war and peace. In 2008, rank-and-file Democrats who had opposed the Bush administration's constant warmongering saw what they wished to see in candidate Obama. He campaigned against the Iraq war but pointedly said Afghanistan was the "good war." Nevertheless, those who voted for him assumed that his opposition to Iraq meant that he would be disposed to end, as rapidly as was feasible, even a war he supported.

Those hopes turned out to be illusory. If he was going to oppose one war, he wanted to protect himself by supporting another, more popular war. Perhaps he wanted to inoculate himself against the perennial Republican campaign charges that any Democratic candidate for the presidency is "weak on national security," or an appeaser. While many pundits have asserted that Obama was not being dishonest in his campaign speeches, as he only criticized the invasion and occupation of Iraq and not of Afghanistan, his subsequent actions were deceptive even with respect to Iraq. Obama's planned date to withdraw from Iraq was the same as that of the outgoing Bush administration: December 31, 2011. Given that this date was three years into Obama's term in office, it would hardly have been a precipitous withdrawal. Yet throughout the entire time leading up to the deadline, the Obama administration attempted to undo the timetable and conditions of the withdrawal

---

* Democrats are on somewhat firmer ground with the *Citizens United* case, as the Supreme Court appointees of Democratic presidents dissented from that decision.

plan. The December 4, 2008, Status of Forces Agreement that the Bush administration achieved with the Maliki government in Baghdad provided that, along with the withdrawal of U.S. military forces by the end of 2011, the legal immunity from Iraqi prosecution that U.S. troops had enjoyed would end. That may have been the key feature of the whole agreement: After years of suffering civilian deaths, the Iraqis were in no mood to continue to provide immunity to U.S. combat forces. But there was no way the Pentagon was going to operate in Iraq without that immunity. Throughout the Obama presidency, Defense secretaries Robert Gates and Leon Panetta shuttled back and forth between Washington and Baghdad pleading with the Maliki government to give U.S. forces the immunity they would need to stay past the deadline.

It might seem strange that the president would allow a subordinate, a cabinet secretary, particularly a Republican like Gates, to undermine an achievement that he could point to as a sign that he had kept his political promise to the millions of Americans who had elected him. Three theories could explain this. One explanation is that President-elect Obama, as an inexperienced new chief executive eager to appear a centrist, allowed Gates to dictate the terms under which he would serve in a Democratic administration.* According to that theory, Obama abdicated national security policy to an unelected permanent government of defense technocrats. Another explanation is that underneath his hope-and-change rhetoric Obama was a centrist, if not a center-rightist, in his true foreign policy inclinations; he let subordinates do the dirty work while he remained above the fray and collected his Nobel Peace

---

* I have one defense industry source (albeit only one) who says that this is what happened. If true, it could explain why DOD budget requests under Obama were *higher* than those projected by the outgoing Bush administration for the period after 2009.

Prize. A third possibility is that his fear of appearing weak on defense was such that he would make no move on foreign policy that would give an opening for Republican attacks. In any case, all these theories lead to the same result: The Obama administration's national security policies are, nuances aside, substantially the same as those of the Bush administration.

In the end, the Maliki government held firm to its demand, and Obama made a virtue of necessity, trumpeting the troop withdrawal as a promise kept. But two further developments with regard to Iraq make one doubtful both as to the president and his loyal Democratic followers in Congress. On November 29, 2011, Senator Rand Paul offered an amendment to the defense authorization bill that would declare the 2002 Authorization of Use of Military Force resolution in Iraq to have expired. Notwithstanding Senator Paul's reputation as a right-winger, like his father he bucks the trend in the GOP when it comes to military intervention. As might be expected, he only garnered three other GOP votes for his amendment. But what about the Democrats? They nominally controlled the chamber and had made such a fuss about Bush's Iraq policy in the 2006 election campaign. Only twenty-five of the fifty-three senators who caucus with the Democrats voted for Rand Paul's amendment. Whether the opponents voted from conviction or as obedient water carriers for an administration that opposed the amendment is irrelevant. The Democratic chairman of the Armed Services Committee, Carl Levin, who was among the high-profile opponents, resorted to the tiresome cliché that it would tie U.S. commanders' hands. How, exactly, if the troops they commanded had already been withdrawn and America was out of the war?

The other sign that even now we haven't quite reached "mission accomplished" in Iraq is implicit in the administration's plan for its civilian presence in that country. The total number of State De-

partment and other foreign affairs agencies' employees, plus support and security contractors, is expected to reach approximately seventeen thousand during the year after the troop withdrawal. That is roughly the size of an army division. State will, incidentally, be buying up to 110 Sikorsky S-61 helicopters over the next five years, supposedly for its day-to-day role worldwide (which hitherto was satisfied by renting or leasing helicopters as needed, suggesting that a disproportionate share of these new helicopters will find service in Iraq). Quite apart from the expense, the 110 S-61s would give State almost as big a fleet as the 137 helicopters operated by the U.S. Coast Guard, which patrols a coastline over twelve thousand miles long, in addition to the Great Lakes and inland waterways. The Obama administration's solution to a hypertrophied and disproportionately influential Pentagon is not to cut back on the DOD but to militarize other agencies.

One can barely catalogue the Democrats' many objections, over the course of George W. Bush's presidency, to his extraordinary grab for unconstitutional executive powers and his law breaking (think of illegal surveillance, torture, and the detention of prisoners without charge). But when January 20, 2009, dawned, all those objections miraculously disappeared. If Bush's policies were a dangerous excursion from constitutional practices, what are we to say now that Barack Obama has consolidated, institutionalized, and expanded those practices? Even Bush did not claim the unilateral executive right to kill U.S. citizens based on evidence only he could see, as Obama has done with his greatly expanded campaign of targeted assassinations using unmanned aerial vehicles in Pakistan, a state with 180 million people, one hundred nuclear weapons, and the potential to make our debacle in Iraq look like a sideshow. (President Ford issued an executive order explicitly banning assassinations after the CIA excesses of the 1970s, but no one

seems terribly concerned about that now.)[3] The majority of rank-and-file Democrats are quiescent, particularly members of Congress. In their eagerness to rubber-stamp these power grabs, the Democrats who control the Senate passed legislation to extend and expand presidential powers granted by the 2001 Authorization of Use of Military Force resolution. In addition, the majority of Senate Democrats ratified the Bush administration's claim that it should have the power to arrest U.S. citizens on U.S. soil and detain them indefinitely without charge. That outrageous breach of due process is now the law of the land.

On March 5, 2012, Attorney General Eric Holder finally provided a public justification for the administration's unprecedented claim that it could kill U.S. citizens at will. His perfunctory rationale amounted to saying that the persons so targeted were not denied due process, because the Constitution's guarantee of due process does not necessarily grant judicial process. In short, we don't need a judge to declare you guilty and execute you. This legal theory might have surprised the Framers of the Constitution.

Many left-leaning think tanks, like the Center for American Progress, handle the same executive branch usurpations that they criticized when Bush was in office less by explicitly praising them (for that would be too blatantly hypocritical) as by adopting a see-no-evil approach. A pervasive mentality appears to have taken over among establishment Democrats that we live under a government of men (and women) rather than laws. Illegal surveillance, indefinite detention, unlimited executive war powers, and the whole menu of executive branch encroachments were a grave breach of the Constitution, decency, and common sense when practiced by a Republican president. But now that a Democrat is in office, it is different. He is one of our people and can be trusted to wield power responsibly. He won't spy on us. He won't detain us without charge.

There's no way he will assassinate us (a power Bush never explicitly claimed). With this attitude, establishment Democrats only mirror the right-wing Republicans who cheered the PATRIOT Act, denounced criticism of illegal wiretapping, and favored all manner of illegality. They believed that they, too, were immune from having their rights violated by the government so long as "their guy" was in power.

Given that Democratic administrations are more inclined than Republican ones to espouse domestic reform policies that cost a lot of public money, it is telling that Obama has squandered hundreds of billions of dollars on Afghanistan during his first term, while having to fight protracted battles with Republicans merely to get unemployment insurance extended. Likewise, his modest public infrastructure plan (which has gone nowhere) is "paid for" by offsetting revenue increases, while he never attempted to pay for the war (which entails vastly larger sums), either with tax increases or spending cuts elsewhere in the budget. Obama has increased our expenditures in Afghanistan from $59.5 billion in the last year of the Bush administration to $115.1 billion for 2012. By the end of his first term in office his administration will have spent $413 billion on Afghanistan. Perhaps it has never occurred to Obama or his advisers that domestic reform agendas can run aground because of divisive and expensive foreign wars, as Lyndon Johnson discovered to his peril.

The DOD budget grew more under Obama than it had been projected to grow by the Bush administration. Various illegal or unconstitutional regimes involving surveillance, detention, and trial instituted by Bush have been retained, consolidated, and strengthened under Obama. On the domestic front, Timothy Geithner, Obama's Wall Street messenger boy, saw to it that there would be no

CEO compensation limits in the Dodd-Frank bill, and that the bill as a whole would be more façade than substance.

Now that Obama has stabilized the plutocracy he promised to reform, the owners of this country may look upon him as potentially dispensable as a two-term presidential aspirant. In a deep and intractable recession one can never discount the possibility that a Republican could win the presidency against an incumbent Democrat. But if the GOP nominates a candidate too deeply flawed or too right wing to be plausible, it won't really matter. The main thrust of the establishment's policies will be implemented regardless of who wins. That is the genius of our two-party system.

Birth certificates, death panels, sharia law, and all the other so-called issues that have roiled us for the past few years are the kabuki theater of American politics, like the May Day parades in the old Soviet Union. Far away from the political stage of make-believe, and behind the closed doors of corporate America, is where the real show goes on, and where the real decisions are made.

12

A WAY OUT?

What changes are necessary to right the ship of state?

We have now sunk to a depth at which re-statement of the obvious is the first duty of intelligent men.

—George Orwell, review of *Power: A New Social Analysis* by Bertrand Russell in the magazine *Adelphi*, January 1939

As we embark on the second decade of the twenty-first century, the commanding heights of corporate America—the banks, the military-industrial complex, corporate interests benefiting from huge subsidies like Big Pharma and Big Oil—largely have the government they want. They have the tax structure they desire. Under Bush appointee Chris Cox, the SEC's regulatory function was wrecked. The military has been so outsourced that the Army can no longer feed itself, while a policy of permanent war assures a perpetual cash flow to contractors. Federal law guarantees pharmaceutical companies the kind of collusive and monopolistic profiteering that antitrust laws were intended to prevent. Corporate America has posted record profits even amid the most protracted period of joblessness in post–World War II history. It is corporate nirvana.

Under these circumstances, who needs an activist government?*

---

* Apart from the Medicare Prescription Drug Act and the lucrative war and homeland security cash flows, the Bush administration engineered the No

Now that the commanding heights have achieved their objectives, a gridlocked government will work just fine, regardless of who is in charge. In any case, both parties are so dependent on corporate money for their existence that it is hard to tell them apart. When the usual cultural wars distraction ran its course—in 2011 the new Republican House initially concentrated on abortion rather than the economy—the next order of business was strident calls for immediate spending cuts in the middle of the worst recession since World War II—an action that most economists believe would contract the economy further. What they would not do is rein in the banks that were largely responsible for the recession in the first place, as a necessary precondition for a program of economic reconstruction that would also include long-term and sustainable deficit reduction.

The calculation from the top may be that the public has already forgotten how the trillion-dollar annual deficits were created in the first place: by the Bush fiscal policies, of course, but also by the transfer of trillions of dollars in illiquid (and largely useless) bank assets onto the public balance sheet thanks to the Treasury Department and the Federal Reserve. The scam was this: The banks unloaded their debts onto the taxpayer, and then the fiscal hawks dutifully began screaming about how we were drowning in debt and how Social Security and Medicare were responsible. Cuts in your earned benefits will pay for the banks' bad loans. Beautiful!

Congress played along with the game. The banksters could count on gonzo Republicans to thwart even the baby steps that some Democrats took to confront the economic crisis—when the large number of business Democrats in the Senate or the Obama

---

Child Left Behind Act, largely as a sop to the school privatization industry and the educational testing racket, and the 2005 bankruptcy revisions making it harder for consumers to discharge debt.

administration itself did not beat them to the punch. Congress sank so low in public esteem that it barely ranked above Fidel Castro in popularity. The Senate has come to resemble Kevin Phillips's description of that chamber in an earlier time:

> The U.S. Senate through the convulsive 1890s remained a citadel of millionaire industrialists, an aptly arrogant metaphor for the late Gilded Age. The Senators were, in the words of historians Samuel Eliot Morison and Henry Steele Commager, "Standard Oil Senators, sugar trust Senators, iron and steel Senators and railroad Senators, men known for their business affiliations rather than for their states." The problem no longer lay with grafters like the Tweed Machine or the Whiskey Ring; lawmaking had been institutionally captured at its source, crippling the constitutional balances set up by the framers.[1]

After Congress authorized bailing out the banks with no accountability and no attention to the too-big-to-fail syndrome that caused the crisis in the first place, it became commonplace for people to say that Wall Street had captured Congress, just as we saw in the 1890s. Even one of the Senate's own members, Dick Durbin of Illinois, went so far as to say that the banks, "frankly, own the place."[2] Then came the Supreme Court's *Citizens United* decision, which showed beyond a reasonable doubt that all three branches of the government had been captured by corporate interests.

It would be easy, under the circumstances, to declare the situation hopeless and retreat into apathy. But this is not a counsel of despair. Man-made problems must yield to man-made solutions. The place to start is the flow of money going into elections.

We can no longer afford to nibble around the edges with an-

other McCain-Feingold act to limit contributions or close loopholes or make other marginal changes that could easily be bypassed. The only rational response after decades of ever-more arcane laws and regulations, and ever-more creative evasions, is to scrap the whole system and start from square one. Get money out of elections—get *all* private money out of our public elections. Federally funded campaigns will undoubtedly create new problems, but can they be remotely as bad as the auctioning of candidates that occurs today? George Will has claimed that the amount of personal and corporate money that flows into U.S. elections is relatively insignificant compared to the national economy; if that is the case, the public can finance a much smaller sum of money to ensure that bribery and extortion do not corrupt the democratic process.

With a small, guaranteed sum to campaign with during a limited campaigning season (perhaps Labor Day until the election, which is generous compared to election campaigns in the United Kingdom, which last less than a month, or Australia, where they last about six weeks) against an opponent who would get the same amount, but no more, we could call an end to the endless campaign season (which in the House begins the day a new member is sworn in) and incumbents could at last spend time governing rather than going to fund-raisers and dialing for dollars outside their congressional offices. The public funding would be a cost-effective investment in the long run. Let us bear in mind that a few hundred thousand dollars in bundled contributions led to a $550 million loss to taxpayers in the Solyndra case; a few million dollars in Halliburton contributions led to billions in waste, fraud, and abuse in Iraq; and a few tens of millions in Wall Street contributions helped cause the loss of trillions to the economy. A politician is a hog that is grateful to whoever is rattling the stick inside the swill bucket. It

is time to take that swill bucket away from corporations and plutocrats.

In lieu of expensive paid advertising, the law should oblige television broadcasters to offer a reasonable but limited amount of free political advertising during the statutory campaign period. The broadcasters' permission from the Federal Communications Commission to use publicly owned airwaves gives them a virtual license to print money—should they not give something back to the public for that lucrative privilege? I doubt the general public would miss the blizzard of paid political spots, nor would people regret not receiving robo-calls on the eve of an election. If corporations were to try to evade the contribution ban by running their own "independent" issue ads on television, there would be no need to litigate the free speech issues involved. One could require the broadcasters, if they chose to run such ads, to provide time to a significant opposing viewpoint, given that the corporate ads would be political advocacy touching on the public interest. In the waning days of cigarette advertising on TV, the tobacco companies faced no outright advertising prohibition; rather, for every block of time they bought, tobacco opponents were permitted time to air a public service announcement opposing smoking. The antismoking spots were so devastating that, in the end, the tobacco companies asked the FCC to take all cigarette ads off the air. If the oil and gas industry wants to extol "drill, baby, drill" in an issue ad, and believes its cause is self-evident, it should have no objection to the TV audience's viewing a public service announcement about the effects of fracking on groundwater.

Public financing of elections would not be instituted in order to maintain the existing parties' duopoly of privilege. Uniform state requirements would permit third-party or independent candidates the same rights to ballot access and public financing as would ac-

crue to Democrats or Republicans. Petition requirements could be set high enough to eliminate nuisance candidates but not so high as to prevent legitimate alternatives to the two parties from participating. Open, nonpartisan primaries with the top two finishers contesting the general election could help prevent the current spectacle of hyperpartisan primaries whose winners represent the most extreme faction of the party base.

It would also help solve our present democracy deficit if we joined most of the developed world and had our congressional districts drawn by nonpartisan commissions to represent recognizable geographic areas. The current system of gerrymandering by state legislatures is a corrupt disgrace and would be instantly recognizable to a visitor from the eighteenth century as identical to the system of rotten boroughs in oligarchical Whig England. Adopting rational districts would limit the electoral appeal of extremists, members of family dynasties, and political deadwood in general.

There are other electoral and process reforms that could be instituted, but these are more than enough to begin. Many people would no doubt find utopian, if not otherworldly, what I have just advocated; K Street and the party operatives would certainly be horrified even at the thought of adopting them. But the inescapable point is that without these reforms, or reforms that are substantially similar, all the good-government legislative ideas that anyone has ever had are impossible to enact—the current status quo is wired and locked in to prevent that from happening. It is a telling commentary on what Americans really think about their so-called democracy that changing such a relatively simple and straightforward thing as the financing mechanism for elections is perceived as an unachievable fantasy. Opponents of these ideas must subcon-

sciously believe the Soviet Union of the 1980s was more amenable to reform from below than is the United States of the present day.

On the day when the first Congress meets that is beholden to the public at large rather than to big contributors, its order of business will naturally include changing the tax code, cleaning up Wall Street, and winding down the wars that are impoverishing us financially and morally. But there are other barnacles encrusting the ship of state that need attention.

Antitrust statutes have barely been enforced for thirty years. This circumstance is one of the factors involved in Big Pharma's ability to jack up health-care costs to levels far above those in other developed countries. The government has long banned the reimportation of U.S.-manufactured drugs from foreign countries on the grounds that it is difficult for the Food and Drug Administration to assure the safety of drugs that may have been repackaged, adulterated, or counterfeited. Yet millions of Americans, particularly the elderly, take their chances anyway, ordering medicines from foreign-based Internet pharmacies. Why? Among other reasons, because the Medicare Prescription Drug Act of 2003 prevents the Department of Health and Human Services from negotiating prices for drugs purchased by Medicare beneficiaries. Under this law, Big Pharma gets to sell any particular medicine at full retail price, even if the insurance plan is responsible for millions of orders of it. That is why people may pay from 20 percent, all the way up to 80 percent, less by ordering drugs from abroad. It is also why the ten-year net cost of this law is $550 billion.

The statutory ban on price negotiation with the government amounts to a conspiracy in restraint of trade—as is "pay for delay," whereby pharmaceutical companies pay their competitors not to bring comparable generic drugs to the market. So is the big corporations' "evergreening" of their pharmaceutical patents to artifi-

cially extend patent protection: This entails making minor changes to the formula of a prescription drug so that it qualifies as a "new" product subject to patent. Big Pharma will inevitably wail that it needs outsized profits so that it can reinvest that money in the research and development of lifesaving drugs. But Big Pharma spends less on R&D than on the annoying and expensive marketing campaigns for the treatment of questionable medical conditions such as Restless Leg Syndrome, Low T, or ED.

Other than through direct political contributions to candidates, one of the most effective instruments by which corporate America and the plutocratic class maintain disproportionate influence over civic life is the tax-exempt foundation. It is no coincidence that as soon as the income tax came into force in 1913, the Rockefellers, Carnegies, and other tycoons established tax-exempt foundations, ostensibly for charitable and educational purposes. While the executors of such foundations have always stressed their public purpose and burnished their philanthropic images, at their inception the foundations were a tax dodge. Their objective was to create an inextinguishable inheritance that the American Founders abhorred as the basis of the British oligarchy's control over almost all the wealth of Britain.

The reductio ad absurdum of the foundation principle is an outfit like the Heritage Foundation or Grover Norquist's Americans for Tax Reform. The billionaires who make donations to these organizations are engaging in no recognizable form of charity or philanthropy; they are involved in a form of express political advocacy that happens to be tax-exempt. The same applies to defense contractors' contributions to so-called national defense think tanks: It is just a tax-exempt form of advertising or political advocacy. Even much of the charitable support that Goldman Sachs and other corporations give to various projects is in reality an advertis-

ing expenditure or a business development investment designed to co-opt, or at least neutralize, any competing centers of influence before they can emerge. And for that they get a tax deduction as a charitable contribution and a bronze plaque thanking them for being such good corporate citizens.

It is time to scrutinize the entire nonprofit sector, particularly the charitable foundations, to see if they meet the letter and spirit of their authorizing statutes. According to the Congressional Research Service, charitable organizations alone had $1.4 trillion in revenue and $2.6 trillion in assets in 2009—a significant percentage of national income to be exempted from taxation.[3] Those that are covert lobbying arms of profit-making contributors should either be obliged to reorganize as nonexempt political advocacy organizations or dissolve. And charitable or otherwise nonprofit organizations should no longer be allowed to compensate their executives at almost the Wall Street level. Does it make sense that an organization should not pay taxes if it can funnel $5.1 million a year into the pocket of its CEO?[4]

Government process reforms to clean up corruption, improve citizen representation, and tame corporate overreach are only first steps, and over time they will become diluted and lose force and effect if the public itself does not perform the hard work of being critically informed and thinking citizens. During the decades since World War II, all manner of illusions and misconceptions have been planted in the national consciousness, and politicians have reinforced them by pandering to the people's flattering self-image of superiority over the rest of the world. According to this narrative, you can cut taxes and increase spending, because tax cuts pay for themselves; we can triumph militarily everywhere if only we have the will to win; and it is solely our superior virtue that could ever make us disliked abroad.

The people of this country must make an effort to clean out their cultural baggage of these and other fondly held illusions: illusions that make it easier for ambitious and manipulative politicians to bamboozle them and build bureaucratic empires that only sap the country's true potential. The foremost of these illusions is the complex of myths that goes by the name American Exceptionalism. No great power or empire is immune to contracting the disease of hubris that gives it an overweening sense of invincibility. Each one of those powers deemed itself as somehow special, uniquely talented, and self-evidently virtuous, and whose founding was inspired by a God who would forever ensure victory on the field of battle. I know of no scientific law or historical precedent that suggests such an immunity for any nation-state. As J. William Fulbright wrote in his book *The Arrogance of Power*:

> The causes of the malady are not entirely clear but its recurrence is one of the uniformities of history: power tends to confuse itself with virtue and a great nation is peculiarly susceptible to the idea that its power is a sign of God's favor, conferring upon it a special responsibility for other nations—to make them richer and happier and wiser, to remake them, that is, in its own shining image.

During my lifetime, one of the most harmful consequences of American Exceptionalism has been the myth of World War II. Americans still lap up the Tom Brokaw fable that Americans somehow won that war single-handedly and as a result of their uniquely virtuous characters. Few Americans know, or care, that Americans suffered less than 1 percent of the global casualties of that war, or that close to 90 percent of all German casualties were sustained fighting the Soviet Union. This is not to say the U.S. contribution

was insignificant—it was probably decisive—but it amounted to placing our thumb on the scale rather late in a titanic global struggle. And its principal element was the intelligent exploitation of America's then unparalleled industrial base: The fact that so many Russian boys rode to their deaths in combat in lend-lease trucks from the United States meant that far fewer American boys had to do the same.

That imagined act of winning World War II single-handedly gave us leave to intervene militarily in other countries whenever and wherever we liked, subvert governments we disapproved of, and carry on costly international crusades for the next sixty-five years. But how did our supposed martial virtuosity work out in practice? Was Korea a smashing, unambiguous military triumph? Was Vietnam? Or the 1982 intervention in Lebanon? How about Iraq or Afghanistan, both of which bedevil us still? At least we can notch Panama and Grenada into our rifle butts!

The United States forgot—if it ever knew—the supreme virtue of an enlightened realpolitik, which is to keep one's powder dry, intervene militarily as a last resort (rather than a first), and maintain industrial and fiscal strength at home. Those measures are the surest way of keeping power over the long run. The commentariat, mostly Republicans but also many Democrats, will ritualistically denounce this prescription as simultaneously an ostrichlike ignorance of "threats," based on a naïvely idealistic underestimating of just how dangerous the world is, and a hard-hearted betrayal of "who we are as a nation," given our unbroken record of allegedly altruistic service to mankind. If the reader thinks it takes some effort to be naïvely gullible and narrowly selfish at once, that is because the self-styled internationalists who dominate both parties grasp at any arguments, however contradictory, to rationalize a policy giving them financial and psychic rewards, even as they drive

the rest of the country toward bankruptcy. It is long past time for average Americans to switch off *Entertainment Tonight* and become well-informed citizens on foreign and national security policy issues. The professional chicken hawks, whether they are neoconservative empire builders or Democrats desperately trying not to sound weak on defense, trade in myth and mystification that require an apathetic or befuddled audience. If you want politicians to treat you as a citizen rather than as a subject, don't give them reasons to regard you with contempt.

Once we cease squandering trillions on a dead-end military adventurism that creates more enemies than it kills, we will have the resources and the policy focus to concentrate on rejoining the top tier of industrialized nations in public infrastructure, education, and health. The American Society of Civil Engineers (ASCE) estimates that repairing America's surface transportation infrastructure would require an investment of $1.7 trillion by 2020.[5] That's a lot of money; why should we spend enormous sums like that, and where will the money come from? Coincidentally, ASCE's estimate exactly matches what DOD has spent on only the direct cost of its overseas interventions since 2001, including debt service. And ASCE says that our current failing infrastructure raises annual national economic costs, due to increased vehicle operating expenses and travel delays, by $129 billion. That is roughly the average of what the government has spent annually over the last several years on our wars abroad.

There are countless DOD boondoggles beyond the war itself that if ceased could provide potential resources. Does anyone think we are going to improve public schools to the level of those in Finland by laying off teachers and going to four-day weeks? Would investing $35 billion in training teachers and paying them more be at least a start? That is the amount we spent to close unneeded mili-

tary bases in the past half decade. Base closure is one of those ideas that has great appeal to people who style themselves fiscal conservatives or smart hawks. In theory, the idea is unimpeachable: Why hang on to expensive facilities you don't need? This is why: The Pentagon will use it as an excuse to fold as much cost into the process as possible and gold-plate its remaining bases. First, the base-closing criteria are flawed: While allegedly grounded in the military value of the installation, in practice the process often amounts to closing bases in cold climates in order to shift those functions to existing bases in more southerly climes, where golf can be played all year. The receiving bases generally bulk up with the addition of expensive facilities that have little connection to military readiness: the ubiquitous golf course;* upgraded commissaries for cut-price shopping (an unnecessary facility in all but remote or overseas places; most populated areas near bases have a Sam's Club or Costco just as cheap when the commissary's subsidy is figured into the cost); and new hospital facilities, when the majority of recipients of the military's free health care are retirees, not soldiers or their dependents. The cost-estimating models the military uses overestimate savings from closing a base and underestimate the cost entailed by closing it. Congress exercises next to no scrutiny of the base-closing budget once it approves the list of bases to be closed. As fiscal pressures finally necessitate military downsizing in the next few years, it is a safe bet that the Pentagon will propose another round of base closures that would vitiate much of the savings that are supposed to come from the downsizing. Close excess bases by all means, but base closing cannot be done the way the

---

* Andrews Air Force Base's Web site reads: "Andrews boasts three 18-hole championship courses that are created from an extraordinary design and provides an enjoyable challenge for golfers at all skill levels."

Pentagon set it up to be done in 2005, when the whole process cost taxpayers $35 billion.

There are other aspects of our national security leviathan that need to be scrubbed, if not completely rethought. It is the peculiar conceit of the people who presume to rule us in our name that the American people cannot afford to run *themselves*, but that we can somehow afford to run the rest of the world. The only legitimate expenditures in the foreign affairs budget are the following: sufficient funds to conduct ordinary diplomatic and consular operations (but please, no more Baghdad embassies or similar billion-dollar sinkholes); a revolving fund to pay for disaster and humanitarian relief contingencies; funding for the monitoring and eradication of communicable diseases abroad (which has a clear benefit to everyone in an age of air travel, including the U.S. population); monitoring of nuclear proliferation; and support for international organizations, if they provide a worthwhile function and our contribution is cheaper than if we did it ourselves. That's it.

What we do not need, except under the most extraordinary circumstances, is so-called security assistance, meaning bribes to pliable dictators or otherwise corrupt countries' officials wishing to ingratiate themselves to us, all underwritten by the U.S. taxpayer. Dumping free or subsidized weapons on every area of potential conflict around the globe has had a nasty habit of boomeranging, as regimes change or weapons leak into the wrong hands (and they were probably never in the right hands to begin with). Arming the shah of Iran to the teeth did not work out very well, nor did supplying cluster bombs to Saddam Hussein in the 1980s. Arming the Afghan mujahedin during that same decade, and particularly the manner in which we did it (using Saudi and Pakistani intelligence agencies as cutouts) may have been the single most consequential policy blunder since Vietnam. And the Made in USA label probably

does not make a good impression on the local population when it is printed on the canister of a particularly potent teargas employed in Cairo's Tahrir Square, or on a cattle prod used in a Moroccan interrogation cell.

By the same token, we do not need to provide the kind of development assistance that do-gooders claim is virtuous but ends up granting a free lunch to Halliburton, Bechtel, Parsons, and other vultures. This assistance also showers payola on the kleptocrats running the countries involved. We have seen too many abandoned steel mills in the Congo, ice cream plants in Egypt, and white-elephant power plants in India (the last with loans guaranteed by the taxpayer and built by Enron, GE, and Bechtel). Other cultures stubbornly remain what they are, and no amount of missionary zeal, do-gooding, or bribery is likely to change that. This futile activity has been going on for decades: The United States spent then astronomical sums to irrigate the Helmand Valley and create the American-style town of Lashkar Gah in 1950s' Afghanistan. The development lobby, the security assistance lobby, and the corporations behind them are politically strong and will make superficially plausible national interest arguments to keep the money flowing. They will always argue that such spending is such a tiny percentage of the federal budget, or of U.S. GDP, that it is not worth cutting it. It is true that it is a relatively small amount of money in those terms, but would not $15 billion a year at least help construct water-filtration plants, smart electric grids, or advanced fuel-efficient transportation in this country—especially as the money would otherwise largely be wasted or spent in ways we might ultimately regret?

The key factor is that there is spending and there is spending. A carpenter who spends all he can spare to buy an excellent set of tools is investing; if he spends the same amount on a down payment

for a luxury car, he is squandering. "Realistic" politicians and their media echo chamber are constantly telling us we can't afford to retire, drive on decent roads, or even live as long as people in the rest of the developed world. They are usually the same people who insist that to remain the leader of the free world, we must keep pouring money down rat holes. With a $15 trillion debt, a global empire is a luxury we can no more afford than a paycheck-to-paycheck laborer can afford a Bentley.

Adjusted for inflation, the United States during the Great Depression had less than one tenth of our country's current gross domestic product. Unemployment then was more than double ours now. There were national security threats on the horizon. The hit song of 1932 was "Brother, Can You Spare a Dime?" Yet that generation constructed the Hoover Dam, the Grand Coulee Dam, the Tennessee Valley Authority, and the Golden Gate Bridge. It built or refurbished sewer and water systems and other public infrastructure, brought electricity to rural America, established places of recreation, from city parks to national parks, so that citizens could glimpse a more spacious and abundant life, and forged an industrial machine that was the wonder and envy of the world. A few years later that economic dynamo could build a Liberty ship a day and nearly a hundred thousand military aircraft a year. A couple of years after that the United States flooded the world with its new industrial goods, sparking a rising and optimistic middle-class economy—not only in America but in other parts of the globe.

With our vastly greater material base, it would seem we could achieve a national reconstruction every bit as impressive as that achieved between 1933 and 1945. But what of the human factors? Despite everything I have said about the current sad state of government, I know from three decades' personal experience that there are countless honest, dedicated, and patriotic Americans

working in all three branches and at all levels of government. They want to do a good job but are blocked, hamstrung, and demoralized by what can only be described as a corrupt and ossified political system.

Although I have severely criticized Congress as a dysfunctional institution, it will not repair itself if bright, idealistic young people stay away from it. I left it because I was old, worn out, and conscious of the fact that there is a point in life when it is simply time to go. But having had a minor hand in halting some extravagant government programs like the B-2 and a few others, I believe my time on Capitol Hill was well spent. If we are to mend our broken government, perhaps the cream of our universities' graduating classes might think twice about Wall Street or corporate law, and try public service instead.

Beyond government, among the American people at large, there is reason for tentative optimism. Despite the politicians' attempts at infecting them with the cynical belief that they won't get their Social Security, and that politics and governance are just a con game for fat cats, the generation born after about 1982 may yet give us cause for hope. Authors William Strauss and Neil Howe called this generation the Millennials in a book of the same name.[6] As with any generalization about complex social phenomena, one can criticize some of their more breathless deductions about the generation that began to reach adulthood during the decade of the 2000s. But I conclude from my own observation that the Millennials are generally optimistic and socially conscious while at the same time they shun the baby boomers' signature traits of self-righteous cant and narcissistic sense of entitlement. It is the baby boomers right now for the most part who are running the show. Over the next decade the boomers' grip on power will begin to loosen, and along with that welcome development, their tiresome and sterile

obsessions about the culture wars of the 1960s may at last reside in the dustbin of history. It is just possible that the rising generation of adults will approach the problems they face not with cookie-cutter formulas based on what is politically correct, scripturally correct, or what conforms to the dogma of some long-dead crackpot "thinker," but on what works.

If our grandparents and great-grandparents operating with the slenderest resources could accomplish the transformation of the worst economic circumstances in American history into the heyday of the more abundant life, so can the present generation work its way out of our current troubles. Distraction, mystification, fear-mongering, and the stoking of hatred are the tools that keep the American people in an apathetic and childish state. Creative and constructive work is always harder than demagoguery or fear-mongering; we have had too little of the former and too much of the latter during recent decades. At many other times Americans have overcome comparable or greater difficulties, even if the specific issues they confronted were different from our current ones. On December 1, 1862, as insurrectionist armies were encamped barely fifty miles from the national capital, Abraham Lincoln had this to say to a restive Congress:

> The dogmas of the quiet past are inadequate to the stormy present. The occasion is piled high with difficulty, and we must rise with the occasion. As our case is new, so we must think anew and act anew.

ACKNOWLEDGMENTS

I owe a debt of gratitude to Franklin C. "Chuck" Spinney for laboring through a rough draft of this work and making valuable suggestions to improve it. He detected errors of fact and interpretation that only a seasoned scholar of the national security establishment such as Chuck could have found. He also provided the unwavering encouragement necessary for me to carry through with writing this book. Eric Lofgren provided a millennial's fresh perspective on the dreary political battles we baby boomers have been fighting for so many decades. Most of all, I would like to acknowledge the unstinting loyalty and boundless patience of my wife, Alisa, for enduring the Sturm und Drang of the writing process.

NOTES

INTRODUCTION

1. "A Harsh Case Against Obama and His Opponents," *The Atlantic*, September 3, 2011; www.theatlantic.com/politics/archive/2011/09/a-harsh-case-against-obama-and-his-opponents/244512/.
2. "Congress' Approval Problem in One Chart," *Washington Post*, November 15, 2011; www.washingtonpost.com/blogs/the-fix/post/congress-approval-problem-in-one-chart/2011/11/15/gIQAkHmtON_blog.html#excerpt.

CHAPTER 1 THE PARTY OF LINCOLN, THE PARTY OF JEFFERSON

1. Bill Moyers, "Our Politicians Are Money Launderers in the Trafficking of Power and Policy," Thruthout.com, November 3, 2011; www.truth-out.org/how-did-happen/1320278111.
2. "A Long, Steep Drop for Americans' Standard of Living," *Christian Science Monitor*, October 19, 2011; www.csmonitor.com/Business/2011/1019/A-long-steep-drop-for-Americans-standard-of-living.
3. "Social Justice in the OECD—How Do the Member States Compare?" Bertelsmann Foundation; www.sgi-network.org/pdf/SGI11_Social_Justice_OECD.pdf.
4. "Trends in the Distribution of Household Income Between 1979 and 2007," Congressional Budget Office, October 2011; www.cbo.gov/doc.cfm?index=12485.
5. http://econ161.berkeley.edu/economists/keynes.html.

CHAPTER 2 TACTICS: WAR MINUS THE SHOOTING

1. "If Obama Likes Lincoln So Much, He Should Start Acting Like Him," *The New Republic*, July 30, 2011; www.tnr.com/article/john-judis/92958/obama-lincoln-debt-ceiling.
2. "Scalia: Our Political System Is 'Designed for' Gridlock," *The Atlantic*, October 6, 2011; www.theatlantic.com/national/archive/2011/10/scalia-our-political-system-is-designed-for-gridlock/246257/.
3. "Economic Experts Gather in DC to Explain Why Politics Has Doomed Us,"

Talkingpointsmemo.com, December 9, 2011; http://tpmdc.talkingpoints memo.com/2011/12/economic-experts-gather-in-dc-to-explain-why-politics-has-doomed-us.php.

CHAPTER 3 ALL WRAPPED UP IN THE CONSTITUTION

1. "Ashcroft Defends Proposal to Toss Gun Records," Associated Press, July 25, 2002; www.foxnews.com/story/0,2933,58728,00.html.
2. "At Hearing About ATF Program, Issa Mutes Witness for Promoting Gun Law Reforms," *The Hill*, June 15, 2011; http://thehill.com/blogs/blog-briefing-room/news/166715-at-hearing-about-atf-program-issa-mutes-witness-for-promoting-gun-law-reforms.
3. "Doctors Sue Rick Scott over Law Banning Them from Asking Patients About Guns," *Orlando Sentinel*, June 6, 2011; http://articles.orlandosentinel .com/2011-06-06/health/os-docs-sue-rick-scott-20110606_1_national-gun-control-group-gun-ownership-rick-scott.

CHAPTER 4 A DEVIL'S DICTIONARY

1. "Iraq 'Behind US Anthrax Outbreaks,'" *The Observer* (UK), October 14, 2001; www.guardian.co.uk/world/2001/oct/14/terrorism.afghanistan6.
2. www.informationclearinghouse.info/article4443.htm.

CHAPTER 5 TAXES AND THE RICH

1. "House Protects Pizza as a Vegetable," Reuters, November 18, 2011; www .reuters.com/article/2011/11/18/us-usa-lunch-idUSTRE7AH00020111118.
2. "Top 3 Domestic Food Manufacturers," *Corporations and Health*; www.cor porationsandhealth.org/resources/food-industry.
3. "ConAgra," Sourcewatch.com; www.sourcewatch.org/index.php?title=Con Agra.
4. "In China, Human Costs Are Built Into an iPad," *New York Times*, January 25, 2012; www.nytimes.com/2012/01/26/business/ieconomy-apples-ipad-and-the-human-costs-for-workers-in-china.html?pagewanted=all.
5. "U.S. Small Business Sector One of the Smallest Amongst Comparable Countries," Center for Economic and Policy Research, August 3, 2009; www .cepr.net/index.php/press-releases/press-releases/us-small-business-sector-among-the-smallest-in-the-world/.
6. "GOP: Python Ban Squeezes Economy," *Politico*, September 14, 2011; http:// dyn.politico.com/printstory.cfm?uuid=04F59EC8-DDB8-49C8-93A1-8F09E3F40EC5; "Broken Government: How the Administrative State Has Broken President Obama's Promise of Regulatory Reform," Committee on Oversight and Government Reform, September 14, 2011; http://oversight .house.gov/images/stories/Reports/9.13.11_Broken_Government_Report .pdf.
7. "The Numbers: How Do U.S. Taxes Compare Internationally?" Tax Policy

Center; www.taxpolicycenter.org/briefing-book/background/numbers/international.cfm.

8. "Rep. Bachus Tells Local Paper That Washington Should 'Serve' Banks," *The Hill*, December 13, 2010; http://thehill.com/blogs/on-the-money/banking-financial-institutions/133379-bachus-tells-local-paper-that-washington-should-qserveq-banks.
9. "Inside the Cain Tax Plan," *New York Times*, October 11, 2011; http://economix.blogs.nytimes.com/2011/10/11/inside-the-cain-tax-plan/.
10. Howard Gleckman, "Cain's 9-9-9 Plan Would Cut Taxes for the Rich, Raise Taxes for Almost Everyone Else," Tax Policy Center, October 18, 2011; http://taxvox.taxpolicycenter.org/2011/10/18/cain%E2%80%99s-9-9-9-plan-would-cut-taxes-for-the-rich-raise-taxes-for-almost-everyone-else/.
11. "Cain Adviser Says 9-9-9 Plan Didn't Take an Economist to Create," *Bloomberg Businessweek*, October 14, 2011; www.businessweek.com/news/2011-10-14/cain-adviser-says-9-9-9-plan-didn-t-take-an-economist-to-create.html; http://en.wikipedia.org/wiki/Gates_Mills,_Ohio.
12. "Gingrich's Tax Plan: Big Tax Cuts, Big Deficits," Tax Policy Center, December 12, 2011; http://taxvox.taxpolicycenter.org/2011/12/12/gingrich%e2%80%99s-tax-plan-big-tax-cuts-big-deficits/.
13. "The Romney Tax Plan," Tax Policy Center, January 5, 2012; http://taxpolicycenter.org/taxtopics/upload/description-Romney-plan.pdf.
14. "Primary Numbers: The GOP Candidates and the National Debt," A Committee for a Responsible Federal Budget Project; http://crfb.org/sites/default/files/primary_numbers.pdf.
15. "GOP Walks Away from Payroll Tax Debacle Bruised," National Public Radio, December 24, 2011; www.npr.org/2011/12/24/144219480/gop-walks-away-from-payroll-tax-debacle-bruised.

CHAPTER 6 WORSHIPPING AT THE ALTAR OF MARS

1. "Republican Group Under Fire for Email Featuring Obama Shot in Head," ABC News, October 31, 2011; http://abcnews.go.com/blogs/politics/2011/10/republican-group-under-fire-for-email-featuring-obama-shot-in-head/.
2. "Government Pays More in Contracts, Study Finds," *New York Times*, September 12, 2011; www.nytimes.com/2011/09/13/us/13contractor.html?_r=2.
3. "U.S. Defense on the Defensive," *Washington Post*, November 6, 2011; www.washingtonpost.com/opinions/defense-on-the-rocks/2011/11/04/gIQAKQDctM_story.html.
4. "Study: Youngstown Has Highest Poverty Rate in U.S.," WKBN News, November 3, 2011; www.wkbn.com/content/news/local/story/Study-Youngstown-Has-Highest-Poverty-Rate-in-U-S/qljniy5c9keJpSz3p2ArmA.cspx.
5. "Toledo Area Poverty Rates Named Worst in the Nation," Northwestohio.com, November 4, 2011; www.northwestohio.com/news/story.aspx?id=682599.

6. "More Half-Measures from Obama Administration on Iran," *Washington Post*, November 22, 2011; www.washingtonpost.com/opinions/more-half-measures-from-obama-administration-on-iran/2011/11/22/gIQADXxLmN_story.html.
7. "Al-Qaeda Targets Dwindle as Group Shrinks," *Washington Post*, November 22, 2011; www.washingtonpost.com/world/national-security/al-qaeda-targets-dwindle-as-group-shrinks/2011/11/22/gIQAbXJNmN_story.html.

CHAPTER 7 MEDIA COMPLICITY

1. "The Centrist Cop-Out," *New York Times*, July 28, 2011; www.nytimes.com/2011/07/29/opinion/krugman-the-centrist-cop-out.html?_r=3&hp.
2. "Should the Times Be a Truth Vigilante?," *New York Times*, January 12, 2012; http://publiceditor.blogs.nytimes.com/2012/01/12/should-the-times-be-a-truth-vigilante/.
3. "World Press Freedom Index 2011–2012," *Reporters without Borders*, January 25, 2012; http://en.rsf.org/IMG/CLASSEMENT_2012/C_GENERAL_ANG.pdf.
4. "Tavis Smiley on Morning Joe: Bush 'Lied' Us into Iraq," TheRawStory.com, September 12, 2011; www.rawstory.com/rawreplay/2011/09/tavis-smiley-on-morning-joe-bush-lied-us-into-iraq/.
5. "Radical Son: Bush May Not Have Read Dostoyevsky—But His Speechwriters Have," YuricaReport.com, February 28, 2005; www.yuricareport.com/BushSecondTerm/MoreOnBushSecondInaugural.html.
6. "Iran May Have Sent Libya Shells for Chemical Weapons," *Washington Post*, November 20, 2011; www.washingtonpost.com/world/national-security/iran-may-have-sent-libya-shells-for-chemical-weapons/2011/11/18/gIQA7RPifN_story.html.
7. "U.S. Officials: Iran Is Stepping Up Lethal Aid to Syria," *Washington Post*, March 3, 2012; www.washingtonpost.com/world/national-security/us-officials-iran-is-stepping-up-lethal-aid-to-syria/2012/03/02/gIQAGR9XpR_story.html?hpid=z1.

CHAPTER 8 GIVE ME THAT OLD-TIME RELIGION

1. "Rep. Walsh Lauded by Group for Being Pro-Family, Though Accused of Owing Child Support," *Chicago Sun-Times*, November 6, 2011; www.suntimes.com/news/politics/8598963-418/rep-walsh-lauded-by-group-for-being-pro-family-though-accused-of-owing-child-support.html.
2. "God Is Pro-war," WND.com, January 31, 2004; www.wnd.com/news/article.asp?ARTICLE_ID=36859.
3. "'Road Map Is a Life Saver for Us,' PM Abbas Tells Hamas," *Haaretz*, June 24, 2003; www.haaretz.com/print-edition/news/road-map-is-a-life-saver-for-us-pm-abbas-tells-hamas-1.92200.
4. "Michele Bachmann: The First 2012er to Get Koch Cash," *Mother Jones*, July

15, 2011; http://motherjones.com/mojo/2011/07/michele-Bachmann-koch-brothers-201.

5. "Being a Christian Is No Excuse for Being Stupid," RightWingWatch.org, September 18, 2006; www.rightwingwatch.org/2006/09/being_a_christian_is_no_excuse_for_being_stupid.html.
6. "Tea Party's Dick Armey: A GOP Majority Would Take Up Abortion Fight," *The Christian Science Monitor*, September 13, 2010; www.csmonitor.com/USA/Politics/monitor_breakfast/2010/0913/Tea-party-s-Dick-Armey-A-GOP-majority-would-take-up-abortion-fight.
7. "Crashing the Tea Party," *New York Times*, August 17, 2011; http://mobile.nytimes.com/article?a=829691&single=1&f=126.
8. "Tea Party Supporters Overlap Republican Base," Gallup, July 2, 2010; www.gallup.com/poll/141098/Tea-Party-Supporters-Overlap-Republican-Base.aspx?version=print.
9. "Religion and the Tea Party in the 2010 Election," Public Religion Research Institute, October 2010; http://publicreligion.org/site/wp-content/uploads/2010/05/Religion-and-the-Tea-Party-in-the-2010-Election-American-Values-Survey.pdf.
10. "Death Panels Begin as Reform Takes Shape," www.teaparty.org/article.php?id=186 (reprinted from *Investor's Business Daily* by the Tea Party).
11. "More Now Disagree with Tea Party—Even in Tea Party Districts," Pew Research Center, November 29, 2011; www.people-press.org/2011/11/29/more-now-disagree-with-tea-party-%E2%80%93-even-in-tea-party-districts/.
12. "Did the American Pope Really Bless Ryan's Budget?" *Time*, May 24, 2011; http://swampland.time.com/2011/05/24/did-the-american-pope-bless-ryans-budget/#ixzz1h1W5m9cI.
13. "Rick Perry's Army of God," *Texas Observer*, August 3, 2011; www.texasobserver.org/cover-story/rick-perrys-army-of-god.
14. "Candidates (Except Romney) Gather in Iowa for Doomiest and Gloomiest Debate of All," TalkingPointsMemo.com, November 19, 2011; http://2012.talkingpointsmemo.com/2011/11/candiates-except-romney-gather-in-iowa-for-doomiest-and-gloomiest-debate-of-all.php?ref=fpnewsfeed_beta.
15. Robert Altemeyer, *The Authoritarians*, 2006; http://members.shaw.ca/jeanaltemeyer/drbob/TheAuthoritarians.pdf.

CHAPTER 9 NO EGGHEADS WANTED

1. Lionel Trilling, *The Liberal Imagination*, 1950.
2. "Michigan Senate OKs Anti-Bullying Bill Despite Protests," *The Detroit News*, November 3, 2011; www.detnews.com/article/20111103/POLITICS02/111030376/1022/Michigan-Senate-OKs-anti-bullying-bill-despite-protests.
3. "Herman Cain Incorrectly Suggests China Doesn't Have Nuclear Capability," CBS News, November 2, 2011; www.cbsnews.com/8301-503544_162-201

28920-503544/herman-cain-incorrectly-suggests-china-doesnt-have-nuclear-capability/.

4. "Nobody's Gonna Make Herman Cain Talk About Foreign Policy If He Doesn't Want To," *Foreign Policy*, October 11, 2011; http://blog.foreignpolicy.com/posts/2011/10/11/nobodys_gonna_make_herman_cain_talk_about_foreign_policy_if_he_doesnt_want_to.
5. "Rick Perry to Announce Flat Tax as Part of Economic Plan," *Washington Post*, October 19, 2011; www.washingtonpost.com/politics/rick-perry-to-announce-flat-tax-as-part-of-economic-plan/2011/10/19/gIQAuWn1xL_story.html.
6. "Santorum: Parents, Not Obama, Know What Is Best for Their Child's Education," *Des Moines Register*, December 9, 2011; http://caucuses.desmoinesregister.com/2011/12/09/santorum-parents-not-obama-know-what-is-best-for-their-childs-education/.
7. "'The Wedge Document:' 'So What?'" The Discovery Institute (undated); www.discovery.org/scripts/viewDB/filesDB-download.php?id=349.
8. *Conservapedia*, www.conservapedia.com/Main_Page.
9. "Latest German Fad: Leasing Out the Subway," *New York Times*, July 10, 2003; www.nytimes.com/2003/07/10/business/latest-german-fad-leasing-out-the-subway.html?pagewanted=all&src=pm.
10. "Upton Sinclair and the Wonk Gap," *New York Times*, January 18, 2011; http://krugman.blogs.nytimes.com/2011/01/18/upton-sinclair-and-the-wonk-gap/.
11. "Two Contests for the GOP Nomination," *Washington Post*, October 24, 2011; www.washingtonpost.com/blogs/the-insiders/post/two-contests-for-the-gop-nomination/2011/10/20/gIQAPfGEAM_blog.html.
12. "Faith, Certainty and the Presidency of George W. Bush," *New York Times*, October 17, 2004; www.nytimes.com/2004/10/17/magazine/17BUSH.html?_r=3.

CHAPTER 10 A LOW DISHONEST DECADE

1. Testimony of Alan Greenspan before the House Committee on the Budget, March 2, 2001; www.gpo.gov/fdsys/pkg/CHRG-107hhrg70749/pdf/CHRG-107hhrg70749.pdf.
2. Stanley Milgram, *Obedience to Authority: An Experimental View*, 1974.
3. " Tribute to Nuremberg Prosecutor Jackson," speech by Benjamin B. Ferencz; www.roberthjackson.org/the-man/speeches-articles/speeches/speeches-related-to-robert-h-jackson/tribute-to-nuremberg-prosecutor-jackson/
4. Robert H. Jackson, " Summation for the Prosecution," July 26, 1946; http://law2.umkc.edu/faculty/projects/ftrials/nuremberg/Jackson.html.
5. *International Conference on Military Trials*, Department of State publication, 1949; http://en.wikiquote.org/wiki/Robert_H._Jackson.
6. "Share Traders More Reckless Than Psychopaths, Study Shows," *Der Spiegel*, September 26, 2011; www.spiegel.de/international/zeitgeist/0,1518,788462,00.html.

7. "1978 Speech by Gingrich," www.pbs.org/wgbh/pages/frontline/newt/newt 78speech.html.

CHAPTER 11 ARE THE DEMOCRATS ANY BETTER?

1. "Who Wants to Vote for a Multimillionaire?" *Time*, June 7, 2000; www.time .com/time/nation/article/0,8599,46866,00.html.
2. "Rick Scott: Florida's Drug Fraud Enabler?" *Mother Jones*, March 8, 2011; http://motherjones.com/mojo/2011/03/rick-scott-floridas-drug-fraud-enabler.
3. "Pakistan Doubles Its Nuclear Arsenal," *Washington Post*, January 31, 2011; www.washingtonpost.com/wp-dyn/content/article/2011/01/30/AR2011013004682.html.

CHAPTER 12 A WAY OUT?

1. Kevin Phillips, *Wealth and Democracy: A Political History of the American Rich*, 2003.
2. "Dick Durbin: Banks 'Frankly Own the Place,'" HuffingtonPost.com, May 30, 2009.
3. "An Overview of the Nonprofit and Charitable Sector," Congressional Research Service, November 17, 2009; www.fas.org/sgp/crs/misc/R40919.pdf.
4. "Slideshow: Who Are the Highest-Paid Nonprofit Executives?" *Dallas Business Journal*, September 16, 2011; www.bizjournals.com/dallas/blog/2011/09/slideshow-who-are-the-highest-paid.html.
5. "Decaying Infrastructure Costs U.S. Billions Each Year, Report Says," *Washington Post*, July 27, 2011; www.washingtonpost.com/local/decaying-infrastructure-costing-us-billions-report-says/2011/07/27/gIQAAI0zcI_story.html.
6. Neil Howe and William Strauss, *Millennials Rising: The Next Great Generation*, 2000.

INDEX

Norfolk Public Library
0 1186 11843152